D1526091

Dante's *Inferno*: Difficulty and Dead Poetry

This book represents a major re-assessment of Dante's *Inferno*, and of the place which the *Inferno* occupies in the plan of the whole *Commedia*. On evidence drawn also from the *Paradiso* and *Purgatorio*, Dr Kirkpatrick argues that Dante's thinking and poetry are subject to far greater internal tension than is commonly supposed. He then proceeds to analyse each of the thirty-four cantos of the *Inferno*, and to relate each canto in turn to its thematic and narrative context. Throughout, Dr Kirkpatrick is particularly concerned with features of language and structure which scholars have tended to overlook in emphasising the philosophical character of Dante's poetry. And while he chooses, for the sake of clarity, to write in the accessible language of interpretative criticism, he continually stresses the extent to which advances in modern critical practice may usefully be brought to bear upon Dante's writing.

The 'difficulty' of Dr Kirkpatrick's subtitle refers to the complex tensions within the poem and points up the dangers of reading it as too confident, systematic and complete an assertion of absolute truths. 'Dead poetry' is a phrase of Dante's own which suggests that writing itself is a moral process involving self-questioning, self-criticism, self-improvement – and the potential for destruction as well as renewal.

This study provides a more detailed and comprehensive guide to the poetry of the *Inferno* than any which is presently available. It will be a valuable source of reference for all readers of the *Commedia*. But the author has always kept in mind the requirements of the general reader and the student of comparative literature. Literal translations are provided for all passages which are discussed, and the argument is organised so that it can be followed as a progressive commentary on Dante's text.

CAMBRIDGE STUDIES IN MEDIEVAL LITERATURE

General Editor: Professor Alastair Minnis, Professor of Medieval
Literature, University of York

Editorial Board
Professor Piero Boitani (Professor of English, Rome)
Professor Patrick Boyde (Serena Professor of Italian, Cambridge)
Professor John Burrow, FBA (Winterstoke Professor of English, Bristol)
Peter Dronke, FBA (Reader in Medieval Latin Literature, Cambridge)
Professor John Freccero (Rosina Pierotti Professor of Italian, Stanford)
Tony Hunt (Reader in French, St Andrews)
Dr Nigel Palmer (Lecturer in Medieval German, Oxford)
Professor Winthrop Wetherbee (Professor of English, Cornell)

This new series of critical books seeks to cover the whole area of literature
written in the major medieval languages – the main European vernaculars,
and Medieval Latin and Greek – during the period *c.* 1100–*c.* 1500. Its chief
aim is to publish and stimulate fresh scholarship and criticism on medieval
literature, special emphasis being placed on understanding major works of
poetry, prose and drama in relation to the contemporary cultures and
learning which fostered them. It will accommodate studies which bring a
special expertise or neglected body of knowledge to bear on the interpretative
problems of important texts. Texts, genres and literary conventions which,
while significant in their own times and places and of considerable value to
the medievalist, have been undervalued or misrepresented in modern times,
fall within its range; and it will give space to innovative critical approaches to
medieval texts of all types.

Titles published
Dante's Inferno: *Difficulty and Dead Poetry,* by
Robin Kirkpatrick

Other titles in preparation
The Medieval Greek Romance, by Roderick Beaton
The Genesis of Piers Plowman, by Charlotte Brewer
Troubadours and Irony, by Simon Gaunt
Literary Theory in the German Middle Ages, by Walter Haug
(translation from the German)
Reformist Apocalypticism and Piers Plowman, by Kathryn Kerby-Fulton
Dante and Difference: Writing in the Commedia, by Jeremy Tambling

Dante's *Inferno*:
Difficulty and Dead Poetry

ROBIN KIRKPATRICK

University Lecturer in Italian
and Fellow of Robinson College, Cambridge

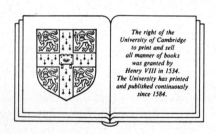

The right of the
University of Cambridge
to print and sell
all manner of books
was granted by
Henry VIII in 1534.
The University has printed
and published continuously
since 1584.

CAMBRIDGE UNIVERSITY PRESS

Cambridge
New York   New Rochelle   Melbourne   Sydney

Published by the Press Syndicate of the University of Cambridge
The Pitt Building, Trumpington Street, Cambridge CB2 1RP
32 East 57th Street, New York, NY 10022, USA
10 Stamford Road, Oakleigh, Melbourne 3166, Australia

First published 1987

Printed in Great Britain by
Woolnough Bookbinding, Irthlingborough

British Library cataloguing in publication data
Kirkpatrick, Robin
Dante's Inferno: difficulty and dead
poetry. – (Cambridge studies in medieval literature).
1. Dante Alighieri.   Divine commedia. Inferno
I. Title
851′.1   PQ4443

Library of Congress cataloguing in publication data
Kirkpatrick, Robin, 1943–
Dante's Inferno.
(Cambridge studies in medieval literature)
Bibliography.
1. Dante Alighieri, 1265–1321.   Inferno.
I. Title.   II. Series.
PQ4443.K57   1987   851′.1   87–6419

ISBN 0 521 30757 0

VN/WH

To my colleagues
in the Italian Department
at Cambridge University
and to all those students
with whom I have studied the *Commedia*
here since 1978

Contents

Acknowledgements

My thanks are above all due to my wife Wai Heung, for her work throughout, but especially in setting the camera-ready copy of this book. We acknowledge most gratefully the invaluable assistance we have received from Dr John Dawson of the Literary and Linguistic Computing Centre. I also thank the Warden and Fellows of Robinson College very warmly for a grant towards the preparation of early drafts.

A note on texts, translations and abbreviations

Throughout, I have followed what is now the standard text of the *Commedia: La Commedia secondo l'antica vulgata*, ed. G. Petrocchi, 4 vols. (Milan, 1966–7). For the minor works I have in the main followed with some adjustments the texts contained in the *testo critico* of the Società dantesca italiana (Florence, 1969). Translations throughout are my own; I emphasise – what will soon enough be obvious – that these translations do not pretend to elegance; their sole purpose is to allow the reader as far as possible to identify the structure and lexical outline of the Italian. For that reason, in all chapters where the linguistic form of the text is significant to my argument, I have also attempted to indicate line-endings. This is sometimes impossible, and I have used square brackets in these cases to show where a word in English occupies a markedly different place from its position in the original. Abbreviations are as follows:

CNV	*Convivio*
DVE	*De Vulgari Eloquentia*
Inf.	*Inferno*
Mon	*De Monarchia*
Par.	*Paradiso*
Purg.	*Purgatorio*
VN	*Vita nuova*

Preface

This book began as a series of lectures on the *Inferno* given to under-graduates at Cambridge between 1978 and 1983; and throughout the present version I have attempted to retain as far as possible the plan and style which developed as that series went on. Looking back, however, I am now inclined to believe that a proper understanding of the *Commedia* is to be sought nei-ther in the foolhardy pronouncements of the lecture-theatre nor in the pages of a book such as this has proved to be but rather in the debate that follows when authorities are silent and readers return to the text of the poem itself.

There is reason to emphasise this. In the world as Dante portrays it, espe-cially in the *Inferno*, intelligence, imagination and sensitivity are constantly under threat. The threat will not be unfamiliar to Dante's modern audience. Yet to read and discuss the *Inferno* in company with others is to realise, as Dante does himself, how hard it is to extinguish these qualities entirely. Such a reading – in which ignorance may honestly be admitted and collaboration constantly sought – will also reveal a little, at least, of what we need to do if emotion and intellect are to be trained in a worthwhile direction: words, images and stories – along with the feelings and arguments they stimulate – need to be examined and re-examined unceasingly in the hope that, slowly, we can establish between ourselves some common understanding of their im-plications.

In the *Inferno*, as we shall see, Dante's own dependence upon some such exercise is illustrated most movingly in the relationship he traces between himself, as protagonist of the poem, and his guide in Hell, the poet Virgil.

At the same time, the writing of the *Inferno* must have represented for its historical author a lonely and profoundly courageous act of self-investigation. While always alert to the dangers of stupidity and violence in the public realm, Dante is equally aware of the inward dangers of misapprehension, wil-fulness, delusion and deceit. His story suggests how easily in his own view he himself might fall victim to such confusion; yet his purpose as poet – from as early as line 4 of the *Inferno* – is 'to treat of the good' that he dis-cerned through the darkness of sin.

In this aspect, the work makes a correspondingly inward claim upon each of its readers. I doubt whether anyone who has read the *Inferno* to its end could ever again speak with absolute confidence in his or her own motives and rational arguments. (We shall see that even Virgil is not allowed that immunity.) Yet Dante's example requires that one should make the attempt, and should offer – failing an *Inferno* of one's own – some account of the response one has given to the questions that are raised both *in* and *by* the poem that Dante has left us. And that must stand as the justification for a study such as this is.

There are many ways in which this account may be settled. Dante's own response to the waste-land – public and private – in which he found himself not only led him to investigate the remedies provided by religious belief but also to assert the values embodied in science, rational ethics and literary culture. Though rarely enjoying any such comprehensiveness of view, students of the *Commedia* have tended subsequently to choose one out of three lines of inquiry suggested to them by Dante's example. There are some who will respond directly to the subtlety and force of Dante's religious teaching, and these will probably be closest in spirit to Dante himself. Others will recognise that the *Commedia* is a work with a cultural mission which – standing at a turning-point in the history of Western thought – sets out to summarise the most important developments in classical and scholastic philosophy, while also foreshadowing many of the issues which in later days have come to dominate European thinking. Readers such as these will rightly attempt to estimate the debt and contribution of Dante's work to the traditions we still inhabit. Then, finally, there are those who, like T. S. Eliot, see in the *Commedia* the unsurpassable illustration of what a poem should be like – of how words can be used and stories told; and these will claim that, whatever other demands Dante may make on our attention, his originality lies in the *way* that he writes and can only be appreciated through an undivided attention to the details of his text.

It is to this third school that the present author belongs; and a glance at the dates during which he was at work will reveal the extent to which fashion may have determined his affiliation. This book was written at the end of a decade in which, particularly in France and the United States, attention to the text of literary works had bred a more general interest in the activities of reading and writing – an interest which, in turn, was nourished by theoretical reflection upon the various systems we employ in acts of communication. In responding to these developments, which insist on both analytical detail and theoretical discussion, this book has become much longer than it was at first intended to be. But the age also requires its literary critics to state their programme or preconceptions as succinctly as possible. And on that score my own response must be a plea for a certain eclecticism. I shall in fact have failed in at least one of my aims if it is not apparent from my arguments how well the *Commedia* might respond to the critical practices which have been brought to bear recently on the twentieth-century novel and the nineteenth-century lyric. However, if I had pursued my theoretical preoccupations to a conclusion – as I once considered doing – this book would, for one thing, have been still longer than it already is. For another, it would have prevented one from seeing how far Dante himself – unaided – anticipates our present concerns. This is not to pretend that there is any exact fit. Yet Dante is (almost) as much a theorist as he is a practitioner; even discounting the discussions of language in the *De Vulgari Eloquentia* and the *Convivio*, an acute awareness of what language is or should be penetrates every canto of the *Commedia*. And just as so many practising poets have learned from Dante in the last two hundred years, there seems to be little reason why critics should not as well.

The main lines of the reading I mean to offer will be presented in the introductory chapter. But many readers may well prefer to turn without ado to the discussion of the *Inferno* itself which begins in Chapter 1; and my title – falling short of Dante's own simplicity – has been contrived to concentrate attention already on a number of my principal arguments.

When I speak of *difficulty*, here and throughout, my purpose is to strike a somewhat polemical note, and to call in question a prevailing view of the character of Dante's poem. We speak of the *Commedia* as a highly system-atic reflection of medieval Christian thinking, relying at every point upon a view of the Universe in which it was supposed that all aspects of spiritual and physical experience could be comprehensively explained. This – while true enough in its way – has, as we shall see, led some readers to suggest that Dante might well have had no difficulty at all in conceiving the world of his poem. But that, I maintain, would be a serious simplification, in regard both to the philosophy of the *Commedia* and to its working as a literary text.

In Chapter 1 – and also, to some degree, in Chapters 2 and 3 – I shall argue that the philosophical positions which Dante develops in the *Commedia* involve a far greater measure of internal tension than is commonly supposed. I shall then proceed to suggest that in any case – and regardless of the philosophy which Dante inherited from his scholastic forebears – the form in which Dante has chosen to 'do' philosophy ensures that he should contin-ually be faced with the difficulties of his own enterprise. It is surely a risky venture to present the absolute truths of religion and science in the guise of a narrative fiction; and by the way he treats his narrative Dante, as poet, not only embraces that danger but also identifies and exposes to view certain radical problems which are likely to undermine any act of argument, state-ment or judgement.

Up to a point, my concern with difficulty will lead me to treat the *Inferno* as if it were an 'open' text, in which the primary point of interest for its reader lay, not in definable meaning, but in the play of linguistic and narra-tive features. And this tendency will be pursued quite deliberately in Chap-ters 4 and 5. The subject of these chapters is the Malebolge; and this part of the *Inferno* – which receives far too little attention and may even be thought uncharacteristic of the *Inferno* at large – offers, on analysis, some of the most startling effects of poetic play in the whole *Commedia*.

Yet I cannot be wholly convinced that the *Inferno* is best read as a free invention. This is where I part company with the main body of recent criti-cism, and this, too, is where I am compelled to speak of Dante's 'dead

poetry'. The phrase is Dante's own: in the opening lines of the *Purgatorio*
the poet declares that, at last, dead poetry rises again to new life – 'e qui la
morta poesì risurga' – with the implication that the poetry he has *hitherto*
been writing in the *Inferno* has now been left behind, as if it were a sloughed
skin. At this point, the self-awareness which we have said is characteristic of
Dante is transformed into poetic self-judgement, or even condemnation, to
the extent that, in the end, the *Inferno* is a work of which Dante seems to be
ashamed. There is no reason to baulk at this suggestion. Many poets have
written retractions or palinodes; and while the notion may elude the modern
critic, a modern poet such as Geoffrey Hill can still apparently allow it to be
valid. As for Dante himself, we shall see when we turn, in the conclusion, to
the *Vita nuova* that in the earliest phase of his poetic career he was prepared
to put on public display not only the poems of which he was proud but also
those which were defective or in some way deviant. Thus poetry, however
apt to play, can also be the subject of searching moral assessment; and to
speak of 'dead poetry' is to recall that possibility in its most extreme form.

I have tried to show in an earlier book on the *Paradiso* the extent to which
speech and writing are for Dante moral acts (and, thinking ahead to work on
the *Purgatorio*, my sense is that the issue is at its subtlest there). I shall not
press exclusively upon that argument in the present work; but it does have a
number of implications for the *Inferno*. For one thing, the last cantos of the
cantica derive a great deal of their force from an impression that their author
– already writing against the grain – is fast approaching a dead-end from
which he can see no imaginative escape. For another, it will be found
throughout the *Inferno* that the speeches Dante attributes to the damned rep-
resent a pathological display of the many ways in which words can die or
become, quite literally, immoral.

But probably the most important effect of the notion of 'dead poetry' –
especially in conjunction with the notion of difficulty – is to reveal how hard
it is, in the case of the *Commedia*, to speak (as modern critics tend to do) of
an impersonal construct, where the historical author is absent or irrelevant.
The fact is – as will be seen particularly in Chapters 3 and 4 – that there are
three Dantes, all with an equal stake in the text we are reading. The historical
Dante, the Florentine exile, urgently needs to demonstrate his virtues, and the
truths in which he believes, to a hostile world. In response, Dante as poet
creates a text which is no mere celebration of a distant ideal but rather a field
of moral action: the protagonist – as Dante's own representation of himself –
certainly can waver or prove obtuse; but since the difficulties he faces are all
pitched on the plane of moral and intellectual purpose, we are bound to sup-
pose that these vicissitudes identify the actual possibilities of error or success
which the poet and exile are also likely to encounter in their own moral
determination to save and be saved.

We shall see that this view of Dante's authorial position (along with the
poet's depiction of his guide, the poet Virgil) leads one to re-interpret the
moral and philosophical purposes of the *Commedia*. It will equally allow one

to see with new emphasis how varied and complex the structure of Dante's text can be as it measures one mode of authority against another or attempts to assert (and assail) the unity of the authorial presence.

For the moment, though, my purpose must chiefly be to indicate how, in the light of these considerations, the text of the *Inferno* should be read, so that the reader – whether or not he agrees with Dante's ideology – can enter most fully into the moral and linguistic action of the *cantica*. I must also say a little more, by way of justification, about the critical procedures I have adopted in this study.

In the first place, I have decided to avoid reference to any philosophical or historical material which is not actually displayed in the text of the *Commedia* – or, at the most, in Dante's minor works. This may seem an artificial procedure, considering that Dante himself – as we have already suggested – plainly wished his poem to have a practical impact on what, now, we should call his own intellectual environment. The decision can also be seen, however, as an experimental control or prophylactic: we know from numerous studies what the *Commedia* looks like when read as an example of medieval literature; we know far less of how it looks when its internal structure is subjected to close inspection; and we may indeed have missed much – in the way of emphasis or effect – under the influence of preconception as to what a medieval Dante is likely to have said or done. Nor will the reader enter fully into the work which the poem requires (and rewards) if an external explanation – consoling as that might be – is too readily available.

In consequence, my subject is, simply, the *Inferno*, with as much reference as space allows to the *Purgatorio* and *Paradiso*. I am concerned, as far as possible, to see the *Inferno* whole.

But that simple project in turn represents a further, mildly experimental move. For six hundred years – since Boccaccio began the tradition – Dante criticism has been dominated by close reading of single cantos in the form of the Lectura Dantis. This form has many virtues; and, discussing each canto of the *Inferno* in sequence, I have attempted to retain some of these virtues. Yet there are many things in the *cantica* which will *not* be seen unless one is prepared to consider it in terms of canto-groups. For instance, narrative technique – which is often most clearly exemplified in Dante's handling of canto-breaks – can only be estimated in terms of such units. Similarly, the patterns of imagery and tonal exchange – which in Dante, as in any other poet are often more significant than explicit statement – can frequently take several cantos to develop. Nor will a concern with the grouping of cantos lead only to a deeper appreciation of coherence and architectonic in the *Commedia*. On the contrary – as we shall see in Chapters 4 and 5 – a study of canto-groups also makes clear that the structure of the poem is riven with effects of violence, incongruity and disjunction. I should finally point out that the groupings I have adopted in deciding the topic of each chapter do not correspond to the groupings which Dante himself suggests by the geographical articulation of his narrative. The divisions I have made already imply an

interpretation of underlying, and otherwise invisible, themes and issues. I am
aware that other groupings would produce or reflect quite different interpreta-
tions, and I welcome this as yet another indication of the inexhaustible
polysemy of the *Commedia*.

On a number of counts I am already aware of some of the reasons why
both scholars and critics will find the consequences of such an approach un-
acceptable. For instance, the student of cultural history may quite reasonably
object that the terminology I employ is often very far from the terminology
which Dante has developed in his own philosophical writings; this could
represent a serious breach of faith, considering how hard Dante labours, even
in the *Commedia*, at the fine art of distinguishing and defining terms. For
example, to speak, as I do in Chapters 2, 3 and 4, of 'selfhood' and 'identity'
will offend those who know (and have taught me to know) what Dante
means by *integritas*. On the other hand, the modern critic – particularly if he
has been influenced by developments in psychology – will often have reason
to complain of a comparable imprecision (and, in this case, ignorance, too).

The answer to each of these objections is the same. Drawing as I do as
much upon St Peter Damian as Derrida, as much upon Lacan as Aquinas –
and seeing no special reason to give any one of these priority of any other –
my use of terms is in part merely a consequence of the eclecticism to which I
have confessed before. More importantly, to speak in relatively neutral terms
is to allow the notions under consideration to be defined in the only way and
in the only place where the definition can be of any account – which is to say
in the process of reading the text itself. The critic may alert the reader to a
broad area of interest; but the space which his words opens up must then be
filled by an attention on the reader's part which falls not only upon passages
of explicit definition but also upon those features of texture and tone which
give colour to that definition. Jargon of any kind inhibits the exercise of this
attention, leading one to assume that the utterance of an authoritative – or
magical – word can absolve one from a duty to work at the text. These dan-
gers are particularly acute in regard to an issue as central as that of identity.
In the human images of his poem and in the situations he invents, Dante
regularly stimulates questions which are larger or more prophetic than his
scholastic philosophy is competent to deal with; at such points a reference to
a successor such as Shakespeare may be just as appropriate as a reference to
Aristotle. On the other hand, an apparent modernity of phrase may easily im-
prison a reader in the confines of new orthodoxy at precisely the point where
the reading of a text was about to demand a particular – and therefore truly
new – response to the questions it had posed. A crucial characteristic of
Dante's literary text is that it requires us to question, as we read, the status
and nature of the very faculties we exercise in our reading. Dante's own ori-
ginality in large part derives from this. But a good reader of the *Commedia*
must also be original in reassessing continually his or her own responses to
the text. The words of the critic should at best simply initiate this process.

If the literary texts we read are to be considered in any sense as 'open', then critical texts, too, must admit their own openness, and willingly abdicate authority. And this, to conclude, may explain why I have made no use of footnotes or endnotes in this volume. I hasten to say that I imply no disrespect for the many critics whom I have enjoyed reading, or for those whose work – whether I know it or not – has affected my own; some of the studies to which I owe an especial debt are, of course, listed in the select bibliography. Yet the present work is not a scholarly volume; it does not pretend to challenge or advance any particular school of thought, but seeks rather to serve as one reading among many that are possible, as an actor might perform *Othello* or a pianist the Wanderer Fantasy. The apparatus of scholarship could have suggested a desire for greater permanence in the field of academic discussion than any critic, in the nature of the profession, can reasonably hope to enjoy. On that score, I might point out that the Cambridge University Press is shortly to produce a volume by Jeremy Tambling which manages – with great brilliance – to re-define a number of the issues I have dealt with here, making sustained reference to French literary theory of the last thirty years.

The ideal format for a book such as the present would allow ample margins for comments, corrections and collaborative suggestions. And this brings me back to my starting-point. For, if the outline of this work lay in a lecture series, much of its substance is the communal product of hours of supervision with Cambridge students of Dante. There is no sign that the enthusiasm shown by an earlier generation is waning among its successors; in that sense, collaboration and correction are already under way.

It follows that in dedicating the book I have in mind very distinctly the many students who, whether they realise it or not, have contributed to it. I am equally indebted to my colleagues in the Italian Department at Cambridge, as much for their incidental comments on unconnected topics as for their formal criticism. These include Professor Uberto Limentani, Joseph Cremona, Judith Davies, Peter Dronke, Maurice Slawinski, Andrea Cane, Jon Hunt, Frank Woodhouse, Niccolò Caderni, Ann Caesar and Steven Botterill. I would also include here David Wallace – now of the University of Texas – who proved to be a most tactful and encouraging reader of early drafts. None of these will object, I think, if I extend my especial thanks to Patrick Boyde for his unfailing generosity and incisive insight. Nor will Professor Boyde object if I record the debt which I, like all other students of the *Commedia*, owe to the late Father Kenelm Foster, who died while I was preparing this volume for the press. The arguments I have presented would have been inconceivable without his *The Two Dantes*; and it is a sign of the great example and influence we have lost that his work should have made possible another which is entirely different from his in kind. My long-standing gratitude for the encouragement and interest he showed to this work can never be sufficiently repaid.

Introduction: Dante and his difficulties

I

The title of this chapter was at one time intended to be the title of the book itself. The fact that, in the event, it is not, suggests how unnatural it sounds in certain ears to ascribe 'difficulties' to the author of the *Commedia*. Of course, no one is likely to underestimate the ambitiousness or daring of Dante's project: his theme is the whole system of the Universe – as understood in his own time – and the sum of all the truths he had discovered in philosophy, science and religion. We tend, however, to assume that he could attack his subject with complete confidence, being both a competent and a committed practitioner of the sophisticated faith to which scholastic philosophers such as Aquinas had already given utterance. T. S. Eliot, for instance, can speak of the advantage that Dante possessed in being able to draw upon a dogmatic tradition which 'stood apart for understanding and assent, even without belief, from the single individual who propounds it' (*Dante* (1929), p. 37); C. S. Lewis, similarly, experiences 'the curious feeling that the great poem is writing itself, or, at most, that the tiny figure of the poet is merely giving the gentlest guiding touch ... to energies which for the most part spontaneously group themselves' ('Dante's Similes', *Studies in Medieval and Renaissance Literature* (1966), pp. 75–7).

Such comments as these point to those qualities of intellectual and artistic coherence which indisputably are a part of Dante's achievement; and not unnaturally these are the qualities which – in the uncertain climate of twentieth-century literature – have most generally attracted attention. The philosophical principles and historical reference of the *Commedia* might seem to represent an increasingly severe impediment to appreciation, but in the main the latter-day reader has been prepared to regard any such difficulty as incidental and has willingly taken instruction from the scholar and medievalist, in the knowledge that an understanding of detail will serve to reveal all the more fully the remarkable – even enviable – clarity of Dante's purpose and the symmetry of his design.

Not every reader, however, has been so persuaded. Consider, for instance, the impassioned perplexity of I. A. Richards in the face of a work which he admits to be a masterpiece:

Minds that accept, totally or in part, the concepts of the cosmos set forth in the *Commedia* and minds that reject them totally, how can they sufficiently read alike a poem so unified and precise? ... How can a poem so dependent on such principles be

1

justly read by those who think them among the most pernicious aberrations that men
have suffered?   (*Beyond* (1973), pp. 107–8)

To Richards, the *Commedia* plainly is a difficult poem, and the case admits
of no apparent remedy; for in Richards's view the difficulties of the work are
located in the intellectual and artistic principles upon which it is constructed.
Faced with the 'pernicious' implications of Dante's Christianity, Richards is
unwilling to suspend his disbelief – in the way that many have done – out of
admiration for the harmony of the structure. He is, in fact, unimpressed by
that harmony. On his account, the very qualities of coherence, clarity and
good order which hitherto have been regarded as the characteristic virtues of
the *Commedia* are themselves suspect. For Richards, it seems, the unity and
precision of the work could only have been achieved by the suppression or
distortion of issues which a reader has the right to see declared.

Now, it would be easy to suppose that Richards was here deliberately
withholding from the *Commedia* the imaginative sympathy which we are
always required to exert in dealing with works from cultures and historical
periods other than our own. Yet on two counts this would, I suggest, be a
hasty judgement, and prejudicial not only to Richards but also to an accurate
reading of the *Commedia* itself.

For one thing, Richards's approach is by no means a destructive one. On
the contrary, the fascination which mingles with his repugnance for the
Commedia is so great that he can eventually express it only by writing a
poem of his own – 'Whose Endless Jar' – which stands in the volume
Beyond as the final embodiment of his criticisms. In a word, the difficulties
which Richards discerns in Dante's scheme have occasioned an urgent re-
assessment of his own philosophical principles; he recognises that he has an
obligation to answer the questions that the *Commedia* raises, and realises
that, however different his answers may be from Dante's, he must nonethe-
less attempt to summon up as much force of phrase and argument as Dante
himself has done in arriving at *his* conclusions. This is clearly an extreme
response. Yet I shall argue that only an active – even 'creative' – reading of
the *Commedia* can do justice to the work as Dante has written it. The work is
'difficult' not because it is remote but rather because it insists upon coming
very close. Whatever our view of Dante's philosophy might be, the *Com-
media* – and in particular the *Inferno* – is designed to formulate an exception-
ally wide range of questions concerning our emotional, social and intellectual
behaviour; and we shall see that while the medieval Dante would, of course,
have required our assent to his Christian beliefs, the especial characteristic of
the *Inferno* is to reveal the pressures upon language, argument and emotional
tolerance which arise – at whatever period – in attempting to construct a
coherent solution to problems such as the work itself here raises.

In the second place, it would be wrong – on the view I have just suggested
– to suppose that Dante was unaware of the difficulties intrinsic to what
Richards calls his 'pernicious' scheme. I shall argue that the distinctive
contribution of the *Inferno* to the plan of the *Commedia* as a whole is to

demonstrate what our minds – and words – must suffer in developing any such plan; and if, in the end, we are obliged to describe the *Inferno* – as Dante himself does in *Purgatorio* I – as 'dead poetry', it is because the difficulties of constructing that plan will come to seem as destructive as they are inevitable. Certainly, in his view of the damned, Dante adduces ample evidence to suggest that the selfsame capacities we employ in pursuing our highest aspirations can also be devoted to deception, manipulation and treachery. It is equally important to see that this understanding stimulates in Dante, as author of the *Commedia*, a constant inspection of his own intellectual motives and achievements. In this light, the *Inferno* will emerge as a work which – so far from concealing or suppressing issues in the interests of order – is profoundly self-critical. Yet *that* is true of the *Commedia* at large; and before proceeding to analyse the particular difficulties which the *Inferno* confronts, we need to look more broadly at Dante's thought and poetic procedure in the *Commedia*, to see how inaccurate it would be to suppose that harmony and resolution were the only characteristics of the work.

II

A central feature of the *Commedia* is Dante's representation of himself as a pilgrim travelling from time to eternity, from Hell to Paradise; and the difficulties of the *Commedia* first begin to reveal themselves in the picture that Dante gives of this journey. The pilgrimage is shown to be arduous or perplexing at every stage. And that is the case even in Paradise. For although in the third realm the pilgrim's ascent is wholly effortless, the notions of eternity and human perfection themselves prove to be a source of constant, if fertile, perplexity. So, paradoxically enough, the first difficulty which the pilgrim faces in Heaven is that of understanding why his ascent should not, now, be difficult at all (*Par.* I 103–41). It is, he quickly learns, a fact that in a state of perfect nature, once we are free from the weight of sin, our ascent will suffer no impediment. But that fact itself strikes the uninitiated mind with the force of a miracle.

In Purgatory and Hell, the difficulties of the journey are more immediate and more comprehensible. In Purgatory, Dante is obliged to make a strenuous climb up the Mountain of Purgation; and his efforts associate him directly with the penitent spirits who accept the labours of their penance as a condition of salvation. Thus the *Purgatorio* enunciates, so to speak, an ethic of difficulty: the certainty of salvation obliges each penitent to embrace, quite willingly, the penitential task which divine justice has imposed upon him. In Hell, on the other hand, the pilgrim is never as sure as he will be in Purgatory of his own moral purposes; nor does he enjoy that companionship of kindred spirits which will mitigate his sufferings in the second realm. The particular difficulties of the first stage of the journey arise not only from the darkness and harshness of the terrain, but equally from the loneliness and spiritual danger which beset the traveller as he faces 'the battle of both the journey and the pity' (*Inf.* II 4). Where penance, by its nature, is purposeful, the pains of the damned hold – for the damned themselves – no ultimate sense or goal; and the pilgrim is frequently in danger of failing to distinguish between the turmoil of his own feelings and the fruitless passions which display themselves in the sinners he sees. Dante must strive to maintain the momentum of his passage through the underworld. Yet the circumstances of Hell are hardly propitious for clear thought, and the possibility of confusion, even of defeat, rarely seems absent from the pilgrim's mind. For instance, in the circle of the lustful, the pilgrim meets Francesca – who was murdered by her husband for adultery with his brother Paolo, and condemned to Hell for the same offence. Overcome with emotion, Dante, at the end of the encounter, falls physically into a dead faint: 'and I fell as a dead body falls' (*Inf.* v 142). This line concludes the fifth canto; and for a moment it appears that the siren-song of Francesca's sentiments might have deprived the Dante character of his power to make any further progress.

The pilgrimage, then, is a tissue of difficulties – physical, emotional and intellectual. The question is, however, whether such difficulties as these go any deeper than the level of the narrative fiction. Nothing I have said so far would suggest that they do. On the contrary, it may well be thought that the poet's ability to represent the problems of the spiritual life in vivid but fictional form is itself strong evidence of authorial control and detachment. This has certainly become the prevailing view of modern Dante critics, in their concern to avoid any naive suggestion that the passions of the protagonist can simply be identified with those of the author. It is, consequently, usual to argue that, if the Dante character does encounter difficulties on his road, the reason is that Dante, as poet, means here to portray a gradual process of spiritual education, and wishes to dramatise the conflicts which the mind experiences on its way to the truth: so when, in Canto v, the protagonist faints, this is because he is still on the foot-hills of his journey and therefore still prone to the errors of spiritual immaturity. In this reading, the protagonist will himself be subject no less than the damned to the scrutiny of the reader and to the considered judgements of the author; the representation of the protagonist will thus be seen as one of the devices which the author employs to enforce his overall programme of belief and judgement.

Yet such an interpretation suffers from serious shortcomings. On logical grounds a distinction certainly needs to be drawn between the fictional protagonist and the historical poet. Yet strikingly the distinction is one which the *Commedia* seems determined rather to blur than to insist upon. It is, for instance, quite evident that these two Dantes – poet and protagonist – have many of the same acquaintances, fear the same political disasters, and nourish the same intellectual ambitions. The poet enlists, in the defence of his own political and personal cause, the passions aroused in the protagonist by his experiences in the otherworld. Conversely, the protagonist acquires by his endeavours a high degree of prestige, which clearly the poet would wish us to credit to his own account: the favour which God is shown to have granted to the protagonist makes nonsense of the disgrace that the poet has suffered at the hands of his fellow-men.

The correspondences* between protagonist and poet are most acutely realised in the satirical and polemical passages of the poem. They are, however, nonetheless significant for that; and there can be little doubt that Dante did regard poetry as a moral instrument to serve political or apologetic purpose and engage directly with the difficulties and confusions of day-to-day existence. So in the *Convivio* Dante's express aim (*CNV* I i) is to remedy certain misapprehensions which have arisen about the meanings of his earlier poems, and to show how valuable these poems might be to any of his compatriots who love the truth. Likewise, in the *De Vulgari Eloquentia*, he speaks of how his renown as a poet made it possible for him to shrug off the indignities of exile and associate, on equal terms, with kings and princes in the secular world (*DVE* I xvii 5–6).

Against this background, the *Commedia* may rightly be seen as a work of passionate and embattled self-justification; and the implications of this, as far as they concern Dante's procedure as author of the *Commedia*, are spelled out with particular clarity in Canto XVII of the *Paradiso*. The canto belongs to a sequence in which Dante is warned by his ancestor, the crusader Cacciaguida, of the miseries which await him in his life of exile. The whole episode is cast on the pattern of Anchises's legendary meeting with Aeneas in Book VI of the *Aeneid*. Yet the evocation of the experiences of exile itself could scarcely be more realistic. And Canto XVII, concentrating no less realistically upon the conditions under which the *Commedia* will be written, reveals how conscious Dante was of the pain that the writing of his poem would cause him. The crusader Cacciaguida tells Dante, in effect, that *his* crusade will be to write the *Commedia*: when he returns to earth, he must dare to make known the sum of what he has seen in his vision (128); he must resolve, at whatever cost, to be a bold friend to truth, sparing no one the news that their kinsmen are in Hell – even if this means offending the very men on whom his livelihood, as an exile, still depends. 'Let the reader scratch wherever the itch is' (129).

There are two senses at least in which the Cacciaguida episode requires us, even now, to regard the *Commedia* as a difficult poem. For the 'itching' reader, the experience of reading will plainly – in Dante's view – be harsh and disturbing. This is one reason why Richards's angry response to the work sounds more convincing than any suggestion that – for the sake of merely literary satisfaction – we should suspend our disbelief in the course of our reading; it is hard to imagine that the Dante of the Cacciaguida episode would have been contented with admiration or (in Eliot's phrase) assent without the fervour which can produce a conversion and turn the bitter-tasting work into 'vital nourishment' (*Par.* XVII 131–2).

But the episode also alerts one to a range of difficulties which arise, first, because of the privilege that Dante claims he was granted in his vision and then subsequently from the responsibility of recording that vision. One might suppose that the visionary journey which Dante said he undertook could be understood simply as an affirmation of his own poetic authority – as a warrant for adopting a magisterial position, in the strictest sense, of omniscience. Yet, so far from justifying any such simple confidence, Dante constructs a myth of authorship in the Cacciaguida episode which associates the pursuit of truth with the miseries of exile and the sufferings of the crusader. In this regard, it is especially significant that the episode should be modelled upon the meeting between Anchises and Aeneas in Virgil's underworld. As the vision of Heaven fades, so – Cacciaguida suggests – the work of writing will begin. And this work will begin as far from Heaven as possible, with the contemplation of sin – with the writing of the *Inferno*. Like Aeneas, Dante is an exile, in the most literal sense, from his earthly homeland. But also, returning from the vision of divine order which he has momentarily enjoyed in the *patria* of Paradise, Dante is an exile from truth. The poet may still dimly know what it is like to possess a knowledge of certain truth, carrying with him his memory of Heaven as Aeneas carried his household gods from Troy to Rome. However, this awareness will serve only to magnify the arduous responsibility of arriving, in the face of opposition and distraction, at a successful conclusion.

This already suggests, then, why Dante, in his own way, may have found the systematic clarity of the *Commedia* no less hard to realise than it was for Richards to appreciate. Richards, perceiving the orderliness of the *Commedia*, was constrained to write 'Whose Endless Jar'; Dante, on his own account, 'reads' order for a first time in the *magno volume* of Paradise, and then, writing the *Inferno*, is constrained to reflect and recreate that order in a text which admits all the incoherence and absurdity of human endeavour.

The first emotion that Dante registers in the *Commedia* is one which arises not from the experiences of the Dark Wood – for the protagonist is dazed and numb in the opening moments of his journey – but rather from his awareness, as poet, of how difficult his authorial task will be:

> Tant' è amara che poco è più morte;
> ma per trattar del ben ch'i' vi trovai ...   (*Inf.* I 7–8)

(So bitter it is that death is hardly more so. / To treat, however, of the good I found there).

From the outset, it seems, Dante admits an opposition – intrinsic to his own poetic enterprise – between confusion and order. On the one hand, his narrative demands that he should evoke in imagination the experiences of the 'selva oscura', bitter as it is to do so. On the other hand, his poem has a moral aim; and the poet must thread a steady line of moral and intellectual purpose through the bitterness of his own imaginings.

The tensions that follow from this opposition run throughout the *Inferno*; and my concern, in analysing the text of the *cantica*, will be to examine the manifold forms in which these tensions display themselves. For the moment, I wish to emphasise in a more general way how the difficulties of Dante as protagonist are assimilated, throughout the *Commedia*, to those of Dante as poet. And here it is useful to anticipate a little and consider two further instances from the opening movement of the first *cantica*: the intense meeting between the protagonist and Francesca in *Inferno* v and the far-reaching decision – revealed in the opening canto – to make Virgil the guide of the protagonist. In both these cantos, the protagonist is portrayed at a point of crisis, but in both the poet also makes clear the extent to which he will submit his own literary designs to self-criticism; he also begins to show the complexity of his thinking on issues which will occupy him until the final cantos of the *Paradiso*.

At the end of his meeting with Francesca, the protagonist is overcome with pity for the sinner; and there can be no clearer indication of the distractions to which the traveller will be subject in the course of his journey. But for the poet Dante to show himself as a prey to such distraction is already, on the moral plane, a piece of self-criticism; the intellectual difficulty of the canto derives from the fact that the poet has chosen, as a representative of *luxuria*, a figure who could reveal such weaknesses in the protagonist. After all, there are many standard *exempla* that Dante could have cited if he had meant his protagonist to receive a clinical account of the effects of ungoverned appetite. Cleopatra and Semiramis appear briefly in the first half of Canto v, and so, too, does Dido: Francesca and Paolo emerge from the 'flock where Dido is' (v 85). For Dante, it seems, Dido's sins of passion had been so well authenticated by Virgil that her name could be used to designate a whole category of the damned. Yet despite the availability of such cases, Dante goes out of his way to present a contemporary instance who carries none of the self-evident notoriety of legendary examples. Moreover (if Boccaccio is to be credited) the case of Francesca was, historically, an equivocal one in which – had Dante so intended – extenuating circumstances would have been easy to find: for in Boccaccio's anecdotal account (contained in his *Esposizioni* on the *Commedia*) Francesca was induced to marry her unattractive husband by proxy in the belief that she was in fact marrying his brother Paolo. Be that as it may, Dante does allow Francesca to complicate the moral issue by claiming (109) that a husband who murders both wife and brother is guilty of a graver crime than lust, and is thus doomed to the lowest circles of Hell.

Nor are these the only complications. The force of Francesca's presence in the *Commedia* derives entirely from the speeches that Dante allocates to her. Yet these speeches seem fashioned so as to echo, quite deliberately, some of the main features of the language and thought that characterise Dante's own early poetry in the *Vita nuova*. When Francesca declares that Love takes rapid possession of any noble heart – 'Amor, ch'al cor gentil ratto s'apprende …' (100) – her words differ only very subtly from those which Dante himself had used in the *Vita nuova* when he wrote that love and the noble heart are 'one thing': 'Amore e 'l cor gentil sono una cosa' (*VN* xx).

The fifth canto, then, is difficult on two counts: in the first place, the scheme of judgements which the poet has adopted – and which he might easily have supported by reference to standard moral types – is here challenged, or even obscured, by the complexity and historical particularity he ascribes to Francesca; in the second place, the poet seems also to challenge his own historical self in allowing a sinner in Hell to use or abuse a set of words which, earlier in his career, he had uttered with the utmost sincerity.

As to the first of these points, a familiar – if by now unfashionable – response to the canto is, of course, that here, as in many subsequent cases, the imaginative sympathy which Dante feels for the character he has created threatens to discompose the dictates of moral judgement. Over-simple as this interpretation may be, no reading of the canto which failed to allow it some weight would accurately represent the force of Dante's poetic achievement. It needs to be stressed, however – as will be seen when we consider the Francesca episode in its context – that the ambiguities of the case are not accidental but, characteristically, a part of Dante's moral and narrative strategy in the canto. On the simplest level, difficulties of this kind – which also appear in the cases of Pier della Vigna, Brunetto Latini and Ulysses – clearly contribute to the dramatic effect of the episode. But the same feature points both to the way in which the canto asks to be read and also, I suggest, to the way in which Dante constructed it. And on either count the episode stands as the focus for distinctly 'creative' attention. Faced with Dante's judgements on sins such as lust, suicide and sodomy, it will never be enough for a reader simply to *understand* the conceptual principles of those judgements. That is a relatively easy task, performed on the level of philosophical generalisation. But Dante's art deals mainly in particular cases; and the ambiguities which are generated by this procedure demand of the reader a constant exercise in discrimination and analysis. We shall see in Chapter 1 the extent to which order, as Dante represents it, resides in actions rather than principles. But there can, already, be little doubt that Dante, as poet, demands no less of himself in pursuing order than he does of his reader. As in the Francesca episode, so at almost every point in the *Inferno*, Dante offers not a simple assertion of categorical judgement, but rather a demonstration of what it must mean to act out the office of judge. As judge Dante requires himself to voice, simultaneously, the principles on which his assessment rests and equally the claims that are made, in specific cases, through the mouths of the damned. A poet more concerned with his own intellectual safety or with the comforts that his vision of order had promised would, presumably, have written only the *Paradiso*.

In one respect, then, the 'difficulties' of which we are speaking are the difficulties that justice in action must always stimulate. But they are also the difficulties of *self*-judgement. Plainly, the representation of the protagonist is in some measure confessional; if Dante as protagonist swoons in misguided sympathy for Francesca's plight, it is, plausibly, because Dante as poet recognises in *himself* a propensity to do so. Then, again, as we have suggested, the Francesca episode focuses attention as much upon Dante's poetic conduct as upon his moral character; and the area of trial here, as throughout the *Inferno*, is language. The acts of analysis which Dante invites his reader to perform can only be directed upon the language of the sinners. That is all we have of them; and it is always an indication of why a sinner has been damned that his words are, in some definable way, meretricious or delusive. It is, however, Dante the poet who has allowed himself to write these words. And the implications of this are particularly clear in the Francesca episode.

For the word *amore* is one that Dante has been at great pains to define in the *Vita nuova*; and the great achievement of that early work is to establish that *amore* possesses an ethical and spiritual value transcending mere passion. That is the point of insisting 'Amore e 'l cor gentil sono una cosa'; love is identical with those qualities and virtues that bestow nobility or ethical dignity. But in *Inferno* v Dante demonstrates how that finely poised meaning can easily (to adapt Eliot's phrase) 'slip, slide, perish, decay with imprecision'. The rhetoric of Francesca's speech, with its thrice-repeated 'Amor', is highly sophisticated; the rhythms are melodious; even lulling, in their effect. Yet the danger lies precisely in that: the word itself bids fair to become seductive and to distract analysis; it invites misuse, and the poet – though writing for a dramatic character – inevitably mimes that misuse.

In this light, there is an unmistakable element of retrospective self-criticism in Canto v as Dante comes to recognise the inadequacies or positive perils of an earlier style. The canto is not, however, a palinode or retraction. On the contrary – as will be seen in *Inferno* II, and even in the last two cantos of the first *cantica* – the *Vita nuova* provides an unfailing measure of what 'living' poetry might be as opposed to the 'dead' poetry of Hell. Rather, it is the function of Canto v to indicate a need for unremitting linguistic vigilance. After all, the word *amore* is one which, later, the poet will need to employ in a technical and philosophic sense (as for instance at *Purg.* XVII 92); he will also need it for the triumphant last line of the *Commedia*, where he speaks of how the protagonist is finally moved by 'l'amor' that moves the sun and the other stars. But in *Inferno* v, the poet realises – on the page he himself is writing – that even the most crucial word in the lexicon of the *Commedia* can sometimes turn traitor. It certainly does in Francesca's mouth, when, at the climax of her lyrical outpouring (107), the word *amore* is suddenly obliterated by hatred as Francesca speaks with some venom of how the lowest circle of Hell awaits her murderer.

At all points, the text of the *Inferno* is punctuated by comparable instances of linguistic risk or rescue – often associated with the use of major conceptual terms such as *fede* (Canto XIII) or *virtute* and *canoscenza* (Canto XXVI). There will be a particular opportunity in the second half of the book to study these features more closely.

Yet none of this may go far enough to satisfy a critic, such as Richards, who objects to the monumental solidity of Dante's conceptual system. The difficulties of the poet may well be displayed in certain moments of linguistic self-examination. But *is* Dante ever radical enough to call into question the unity and precision of the intellectual or doctrinal scheme in which he has chosen to operate? I shall argue – on a number of counts – that he is, and seek to show, especially in the first three chapters of the book, how the very fact that Dante's philosophy is cast here in the form of a poetic narrative must lead one to expect a degree of tension, ambiguity and discomposure in the structure of his thought. But there is one figure who stands at the centre of all these discussions, and that is the figure of Virgil, the standard-bearer of reason and ethical purpose.

It will be evident as soon as one turns to the first canto of the *Inferno* that, in choosing Virgil to guide the protagonist through the first two regions of the afterlife, Dante has almost wilfully intertwined both solution and problem. Clearly the choice of Virgil is an artistic and intellectual decision of the utmost importance. But why should he have chosen Virgil rather than a Christian philosopher, poet or mystic? Why, so emphatically, elect a Roman and a pagan?

There are, of course, clear answers to these questions. In one respect, the decision reflects Dante's characteristic desire to affirm the value of classical thought and culture. Though the historical Virgil is no philosopher, Dante continually attributes to the Virgil of the *Commedia* a competence to deal with philosophical arguments; and the *Aeneid* provides him with an important source of ethical as well as literary examples. (We have already seen how Dante compares himself with Aeneas in the *Paradiso*.) Dante – as a late medieval thinker – is not unique in his respect for classical philosophy, nor in his concern to investigate the extent to which reason, even without revelation, might lead to truth. It is still a bold move to allot so prominent a position to a pagan; and Virgil in the *Commedia* indisputably is a pagan. Dante might easily have softened or blurred that designation. He does so in *Purgatorio* XXII, where he tampers with historical probability in order to claim that Statius was a covert Christian. But the complications surrounding Virgil arise from Dante's rejection of any such casuistry in his case; and there is a hard irony in the fact that, while Virgil becomes a mouthpiece for pure rationality, the logic of Dante's own scheme obliges him to insist that Virgil, as a pagan, must be confined to Limbo.

From the first canto to the last, the *Inferno* represents, at one and the same time, a celebration and a progressive critique of Virgil's authority. But this critique also bears upon Dante's own choice of Virgil as guide, and upon his own rationality in constructing the essentially rational plan on which the *Inferno* rests. As in the Francesca episode, so in the representation of Virgil, a major part of Dante's self-criticism is concerned with linguistic issues. Indeed, above all else Virgil embodies a principle of linguistic procedure: so, as we shall see, in Canto I, Dante – through the mouth of the protagonist – acknowledges Virgil as the master of his style (86–7); and in context it will be found that Dante wishes us to see in *his* Virgil (if not in the Virgil of the

Aeneid) a model for clear and rationally measured utterance. But having identified these qualities with Virgil – and also certain qualities of narrative organisation – Dante will proceed to question their adequacy to his own ultimate purposes. Virgil becomes, so to speak, a sub-author in the *Inferno*, whose utterances seem frequently to contrast with the framing words of the Dantean text. The portrayal of Virgil will demonstrate a continual awareness on Dante's part that the virtues of clarity and measure are essential to his enterprise in the *Inferno* yet wholly deficient as instruments for its completion.

Similar considerations will arise when we examine, not only the procedures which Virgil exemplifies, but also the substantial meaning of his presence in the *Commedia*. For Virgil incorporates the idea of justice. In a particular sense he is the representative of the Roman Empire, proclaiming the possibility and value of a society devoted to justice – as he does in his initial account of the history of Rome (*Inf.* i 70–5). In a broader sense, he displays a rational appetite for righteousness which is subtly translated into those acts of friendship and concern with which he defends and promotes the journey of the protagonist. In the relationship between Virgil and the protagonist, Dante envisages, in a most concrete way, what peace and harmony might be like under the reign of human justice. Yet by the standards of *divine* justice Virgil stands condemned to Hell. And this unforgettable fact reveals both an insufficiency in human justice and an apparent divergence between the rational conception of right conduct and the demands of the eternal law.

Of Dante's own devotion to justice – on both the human level and the divine – there cannot be the slightest doubt. As Etienne Gilson says, it is this that distinguished his thinking from that of other philosophers in his period and led him to write – while engaged upon the *Commedia* itself – his controversial work of political philosophy, the *Monarchia*. The exiled Dante knew at first hand what the consequences of human injustice could be; and in one aspect the *Inferno* is itself the representation of a corrupt and disordered society. In the *Inferno*, too, Dante asserts the remedy for such corruption: the *cantica* is an expression of his faith in (and his longing to see) the absolute authority of a God who can ultimately judge and restrain human waywardness. At the same time, the first *cantica* also shows an extraordinary awareness that certitude itself, so far from being a simple comfort, places the mind under intolerable pressures – as if (to cite Eliot yet again) 'human kind cannot bear very much reality'. The essential difficulty that Dante confronts in the *Inferno* is to realise that divine justice is an unalterable fact. So the words on the Gate of Hell in Canto iii proclaim the dreadful truth that Hell is an expression not only of divine justice but also of divine love and wisdom; it was created before humanity was created (to receive the rebel angels) and will endure eternally as the destination of sin (1–9). For the protagonist, the absolute clarity and authority of this utterance is itself a source of confusion; turning to Virgil he declares:

Maestro, il senso lor m'è duro.   (*Inf.* III 12)

(Master, the meaning of these words is hard for me.)

Now, it may well be said that this reaction belongs to the protagonist and not to the poet: the Dante character is here at the very earliest stage of his educative journey and is bound to be troubled by the evidence of divine power. There is some truth in this; and certainly in the second half of the *Inferno*, the protagonist will have 'developed' sufficiently to voice the hardest possible line, calling down divine vengeance upon sinners both dead and living.

Yet it is necessary – at least for the purposes of my present argument – to insist that Dante, as poet, shares in the intellectual perplexity he attributes to the protagonist. And at this point one needs, again, to look more broadly at the *Commedia*, particularly at the poet's treatment of justice in the *Paradiso*.

In the *Paradiso*, as we should expect, Dante provides a fully theological account – absent from the *Inferno* – of the relationship between divine justice and our human conceptions of justice; as is usually the case, the last *cantica* provides more apposite material for an understanding of earlier *cantiche* than any other commentary on the poet's thinking could do. However, what we certainly might *not* expect is that, even at the height of the *Paradiso*, Dante should raise, in the most urgent manner, the same sort of question as dismayed the protagonist in *Inferno* III. He will ask quite explicitly whether it is just that the noble pagan should be condemned to Limbo through no fault of his own, and in dealing with this specific question, the poet will touch (though less obviously) upon a number of the other difficulties which I have so far attributed to him. For instance he returns to the question, first raised by the Francesca episode, of the difficulties involved in conceiving particular instances of divine judgement. And from this it will become apparent that the divergences between divine decisions and human comprehension are not accidental but a logical feature of the relationship between Creator and creature. But this in turn reveals that, on two counts, certainty itself will be problematical in the *Inferno*: on the one hand, the absolute certainties of divine justice will prove irresistibly taxing to the human mind; and while, on the other, there is a responsibility laid upon all who approach these certainties to express them as clearly as possible, the schemes of rational certainty that human beings naturally employ in such attempts will come to seem intrinsically inadequate and prone to discomposure.

III

In a sequence extending from Canto XVIII to Canto XX of the *Paradiso*, the protagonist reaches the Heaven of Jupiter, where he meets the souls of the just. It is here that the poet finally offers his account of divine justice. Yet at the centre of the discussion, in Canto XIX, there arises the stark question of the fate of the noble pagan. Virgil's predicament is not directly mentioned –

even though, as we shall see, his presence is felt throughout the episode. Nonetheless, Dante allows the questions which bear upon his case to be put in the most controversial way.

Suppose, he argues, that, through no fault of his own, a man had lived his life in ignorance of the Christian faith – being born, in Dante's example, on the banks of the River Indus. And suppose that, although a pagan, he had attained in the course of his life to perfect virtue. Does it follow that this man must be condemned to Hell? His lack of faith and baptism may be grounds for that condemnation. Yet where is the justice in it:

> ov' è questa giustizia che 'l condanna?
> ov' è la colpa sua, se ei non crede?   (*Par.* xix 77–8)

(where is the justice which condemns him; where is his fault if he does not believe?)

Now these questions do receive an answer. In fact they receive two: one of these is explicitly offered in Canto xix; the other is implicit, and arises as much from the consideration of divine love in Cantos xxi and xxii as from the discussion of divine justice in the preceding cantos.

However, before looking at the answers, it is important to recognise how disconcerting, on Dante's own understanding, the question itself must be. If the condemnation of the virtuous pagan is allowed to stand, God will be seen to reject the achievements of which human beings are undoubtedly capable in their own unaided aspiration towards justice. Moreover, an incongruity will be revealed between the human conception of justice and the divine conception. Yet the whole plan of the *Commedia* presupposes that Dante *can* comprehend and record the judgements that God has passed on human beings; and one might well suppose that, by the time he reached the *Paradiso*, the poet had long since reconciled himself to the implications of divine law. After all, the first strict category of sinners whom Dante meets in Hell are the pagans; and notably he raises no direct question in the *Inferno* itself about their fate. Indeed if Limbo, at the very threshold of Hell, had represented a misconception, then the whole penal system which Dante develops in the first *cantica* would seem to rest on shaky ground.

Suddenly, however, in the *Paradiso* of all places, Dante urges the possibility that there *has* been a mistake, and insists that he has never been satisfied by the answers he has received. The question, he says, is one which has assailed him with extreme frequency (*Par.* xix 69). and this is surely an accurate claim. On at least three occasions in the *Commedia*, Virgil's case has been reopened, each time with considerable pathos: for instance in *Purgatorio* vi and xxii. Even more importantly, looking beyond the *Commedia* to the *Monarchia*, the same (or at least a closely related) issue has been argued, in a purely philosophical context, with comparable force. In the *Monarchia* – condemned in its own day, and beyond, by many orthodox Christian thinkers – Dante maintains that humankind, though destined for beatitude in the afterlife, is also capable of complete happiness in the temporal life under the guidance of the perfect Emperor. The Emperor derives his authority directly from God; he is divinely appointed to secure 'peace on earth for men of goodwill', and to make justice available for those, like the exile Dante, who are the victims of factional politics and divisive appetites. In the *Commedia* Virgil is, in one of his aspects, the representation of such an Emperor.

With this startling claim for the value of the temporal world and its rational sovereign, we arrive at a contradiction in Dante's thinking so acute that it led the most eminent of English Dante scholars, Father Kenelm Foster, to speak of *two* Dantes. One of these Dantes is an orthodox believer – so much so that he refuses to accept the possibilities of salvation for the noble pagan which were available in certain scholastic notions of implicit grace. The other Dante is a proto-humanist who, in Foster's phrase, is prepared 'to reduce to a minimum the conceivable contacts between human nature and divine grace' (*The Two Dantes* (1977), pp. 252–3). But in the light of Foster's comment, it is surely permissible to characterise Dante's thinking by pointing to neither one nor the other of its two aspects but rather to the power it displays in conceiving and sustaining the contradiction itself. On such a view, we need not expect the scholar or critic to decide conclusively whether Dante is or is not orthodox in his attitudes; the task of the reader will rather be to sharpen – and not to annul with explanations – the discomfort one feels at the sight of such oppositions running so deep into Dante's thought. And that, certainly, is what Dante himself does in the Justice sequence. For the two answers he proceeds to offer are either so distressing or so surprising as to disconcert any further reliance upon rational inquiry. Yet both answers reassert – albeit on unfamiliar ground – the value which Dante unfailingly attributes to the human being.

The first answer is offered in *Paradiso* xix and not surprisingly Richards finds it intolerable (*Beyond* (1973) pp. 139–42). For Dante is told that his inquiries are beside the point, and, properly, ought not to have been made at all. The crucial step in this argument is an insistence upon the direct relationship between the justice of God and his actions as Creator of the Universe. If we know God at all, we know him first and foremost as our Creator, as the power who planned and delimited the created world with his compass: 'Colui che volse il sesto / a lo stremo del mondo' (xix 40–1). This knowledge has been brought to us by revelation, through Christ and by the prophets; and for that reason alone a distinction would be possible between Christian and pagan – between those who, in possessing this revelation, know the true nature of God and those who do not. It is this line of argument that seems to inspire the Limbo canto in the *Inferno*; for, as we shall see, Dante expresses there a strong sense that Christianity is a 'historical' religion, emphasising that Christ's entry into time was a historical event, which established a clear differentiation between those who lived before and those who lived after his Incarnation.

In Canto xix itself, Dante's concern is to show that the justice of the Creator must necessarily resist any human questioning. For God, as Creator, infinitely transcends the understanding of his creature; and it is a logical condition of the knowledge which our Creator does allow us of himself that we recognise his transcendence in respect of his creation. The Word of God, in creating the world must, as Dante says at line 43, remain infinitely in excess of the world. A creature is always less than its divine Creator; and it is both an absurdity and the very origin of sin for the creature to seek to evade this condition. So Lucifer fell from the height of creation precisely because of his impatient desire to know more than he already did know; God had bestowed upon him the greatest degree of illumination, and (to follow the implications of Dante's phrasing) would have granted more; but Lucifer was unwilling to 'wait for light':

> E ciò fa certo che 'l primo superbo,
> che fu la somma d'ogne creatura,
> per non aspettar lume, cadde acerbo.   (*Par.* XIX 46–8)

(And this is attested by that first proud being who was the highest of all creatures and through not waiting for light, fell unripe.)

It remains true that God does mean to reveal his nature to his creatures. The Scriptures are one expression of this intention. Another indication is the fact that God, being himself just, should allow human beings to share in his justice. But if, while enjoying the revelation and results of divine justice (as Dante does, in travelling through Paradise), we then seek to criticise God on a matter of justice, we fall into contradiction as gross as Satan's; as Dante puts it elsewhere, the creature, in this case, will work against its Creator: 'contra il fattore adopra sua fattura' (*Purg.* XVII 102). (It is worth noting that these words are spoken by Virgil.) For if we are just at all, or have any conception of justice, the reason is that God has allowed and willed this to be so. God authorises us, as Dante puts it, to see into the shallows of his justice and consequently to conceive questions about the nature of justice. Yet the changeless depths of that ocean must remain unseen; for this is also the 'great sea of being', the reality of God:

> Però ne la giustizia sempiterna
> la vista che riceve il vostro mondo,
> com' occhio per lo mare, entro s'interna;
>   che, ben che da la proda veggia il fondo,
> in pelago nol vede ...   (*Par.* XIX 58–62)

(Therefore the justice that your world receives is absorbed into eternal justice like an eye gazing into the sea, which, although it can see the bottom close to the shore, cannot see into the depths of the ocean).

Thus, if we refuse to accept the particular evidence of God's justice – such as the condemnation of the pagan – we offend not simply an edict written, as it might be, on the Tables of the Law, but also the Creative Will on which our own existence depends.

Dante, then, provides an answer for himself which is at least clear and coherent. It amounts, of course, to an affirmation of the absolute authority of God, and on this scòre it is bound to be unacceptable to Richards. One should not, however, underestimate its importance to Dante's own thought, or indeed ignore the imaginative vigour with which it is presented. The question of justice here resolves itself into a test of belief in the Creator. And were we to say – in a word – what the subject of the whole *Commedia* is, it would be this: the relationship of Creator to creature. We shall see later how Dante introduces this essential theme in *Inferno* III at the Gate of Hell.

It is also entirely characteristic of Dante's thought in the *Commedia* that he should emphasise, as he does in *Paradiso* XIX, the specific limitations under which the mind must work, suggesting that it can *only* work efficiently when it acknowledges these limits. Elsewhere in the *Commedia* this lesson is associated not only with such Christian thinkers as Aquinas but also with Virgil and the pagan. So at *Purgatorio* III 37 it is Virgil who declares: 'State contenti, umana gente, al *quia*', insisting that the human mind should limit itself to asking what the world is actually like, rather than attempting to speculate on unanswerable questions.

Yet *is* Dante prepared to rest contented with this answer? In a sense he is not, or at least – as Canto XX will show – he does not allow his notion of limit to become simply a restrictive one. Before proceeding to that point, however, it is of the utmost importance to stress that Canto XX will also insist upon the limits of rational competence in a way which is, in fact, particularly restrictive for Dante himself. So much so, indeed, that it threatens, retrospectively, to undermine the whole project he has undertaken in the *Inferno* – which is that of writing his own account of divine judgement and, effectively, of standing in judgement upon his fellow-humans. For at the conclusion of the Justice sequence Dante makes the Eagle declare:

> E voi, mortali, tenetevi stretti
> a giudicar: ché noi, che Dio vedemo,
> non conosciamo ancor tutti li eletti.   (*Par.* XX 133–5)

(And you, O mortals, be strictly restrained in your judgements: for we who see God, do not as yet know all the elect.)

If, in Dante's view, even the blessed do not yet possess complete knowledge of those who are chosen, then what view can the living Dante suppose *he* possesses? The last thing that the poet appears to have been in the *Inferno* is 'restrained' in judgement; and to make a recommendation to restraint the final word of justice seems to threaten the whole system on which Dante has built his poem. At Canto XIX, 83, Dante insisted upon the importance of Scripture as a guide on the question of the noble pagan. What possible validity can any *other* word have concerning the ultimate questions which Dante has set himself to face in the *Commedia*?

As we proceed through Cantos XX – XXII, the second answer to Dante's initial question emerges. This, in turn, will provide an answer to the problem of how Dante should himself write under the self-imposed restriction of the lines I have just quoted. It will also lead us, ultimately, to reassess the nature of the judgemental structure which Dante has created in the *Inferno*.

However, to arrive at these conclusions we must, first, pass through a sequence which represents not so much a difficulty or controversy as an utter reversal of the expectations that Canto XIX has just engendered. For, having insisted upon a scheme of justice which – as we must suppose – explains the damnation of the pagan, the protagonist is called upon at Canto XX 68 to witness the presence in Heaven of two souls, Trajan and Rhipeus, both of whom, as far as the world could tell, were pagan at the time of their death. We have said that throughout the *Inferno* Dante in his judgements makes a deliberate choice of difficult cases – such as Francesca or Piero or Ulysses. Here a similar difficulty mingles with the complete astonishment and surprise of the Dante character as he exclaims: 'What things are these?' (XX 82). Indeed, surprise here would seem to be a calculated effect; for it involves, especially in the case of Rhipeus, a deliberately challenging use of literary sources. *Trajan*'s redemption had been spoken of by other medieval writers – and Dante himself has alluded to it already in *Purgatorio* Canto X. But the only possible source for the figure of Rhipeus is Virgil's *Aeneid*; and Virgil is concerned not with the miraculous salvation of Rhipeus but rather with his tragic death. In the five or six lines of *Aeneid* II which refer to him, Rhipeus appears as a companion of Aeneas who died on the night of the Fall of Troy. He was the most just of men, yet in spite of his justice he died. And in a fatalistic aside Virgil comments upon the mysterious will of the gods:

> cadit et Rhipeus, iustissimus unus
> qui fuit in Teucris et servantissimus aequi
> (dis aliter visum).   (*Aeneid* II 426–8)

(Rhipeus fell, too, foremost in justice among the Trojans, and most zealous for the right. The will of the gods was otherwise.)

In itself, then, the case of Rhipeus is difficult enough. But in raising it, Dante also seems determined to re-open the case of Virgil himself. Rhipeus only exists because of the *Aeneid*; no other classical text refers to him. And since Virgil's opinion of Rhipeus is now shown to have coincided with God's own judgement, the authority of the pagan poet would seem to be vindicated in the highest degree.

If Virgil can identify a just man as accurately as God can, why is he not in Paradise too? The sequence goes out of its way to arouse that question. Yet it is equally firm in disallowing any suggestion that the salvation of Rhipeus entails the salvation of his Roman originator.

For the manner in which Rhipeus and Trajan are redeemed is uncompromisingly located beyond the scope of any such rational prediction. God's action in each case is shown to have involved not simply a just recognition of deserts, but rather a particular and providential miracle. The salvation of Trajan is in the most obvious sense a miracle: for he was allowed, momentarily, to return from the dead in bodily form, so that he could confess the Christian faith in the circumstances of time and history. (Dante's phrasing twice emphasises the physical reality of this resurrection – at line 107 Trajan returns to the body; at line 115 the glorious soul returns to the flesh.) In the instance of Rhipeus, God adopts a different course, as if in his dealing with the soul of each of his creatures, the practices of the Creator follow no single or predictable scheme. Strictly, God is said to reveal himself in grace to Rhipeus so that he can enjoy explicit faith in his Creator; even in his own pagan era, the eye of the Trojan is able to perceive the depths of the 'sea' which, in Canto XIX, we are told no human eye can fathom. And the metaphors of water and cleansing which Dante uses here suggest that he viewed this revelation as an act of baptism, accomplished centuries before the rite was established: by grace, stemming from the deepest 'wellspring' (114), the eye of Rhipeus penetrates the 'primal wave' (120); thus, inspired by an unparalleled love of righteousness, he is made aware of the redemption still to come, and cleansed from 'the stench of paganism' (125).

In essence, the miracles which redeem Trajan and Rhipeus are as simple and yet unfathomable as the miracles of the Gospels: the dead are raised and the blind are allowed to see. It should, however, be emphasised that these miracles do not represent simply a violation of the laws of Nature. Nor does God simply repeal the ordinances he has previously established. In fact, he simultaneously defeats and affirms the Law. For if the salvation of Trajan and Rhipeus is contrary to rational expectation, it is nonetheless plain that the miracle of their salvation requires them to fulfil the same conditions and submit to the same laws as *deny* redemption to their pagan fellows: Trajan witnesses to the truth of Christ in the fullness of temporal and physical existence, while the vision which redeems Rhipeus is portrayed as being a sacrament – figuratively at least, a rite of baptism. The religious paradox at which we arrive is certainly beyond the scope of reason to resolve, and clearly it does not sanction any hope or prediction we may conceive for the salvation of other pagans such as Virgil: each miraculous action seems intended, specifically, to save a particular person. Yet rationality is not denied but rather redefined here: to be rational in these circumstances is to appreciate the laws which – miraculous as they may be in origin – are the laws on which God's creation depends.

In sum, the twentieth canto, conjoined with the nineteenth, offers an understanding of God and his mysteries which is essentially and specifically Christian, in its recognition both of the authority of God as Creator and of the particularity of his concern for his creatures. The laws of creation are, in this light, not intended to repress humanity but to sustain and save particular beings such as Rhipeus and Trajan: the God of the Law is also the God who, against all expectations, eternally wills the existence of all his creatures. The Law, one might say, is made for man, not man for the Law. But another way of putting this is to say that, behind divine justice, there is divine love, and these, too, are terms which Canto XX would support. Justice is certainly a 'name' for God – as the Old Testament makes clear – and remains an indispensable concept for an understanding of the divine nature. But the direct experience of God as Love is more essential still. So, in a crucial passage of Canto xx, Dante speaks of how God can mysteriously, even violently, overthrow his own dispensations, while remaining true to himself as Love. Citing the Gospel of St Matthew xi 12, Dante writes:

> Regnum celorum vïolenza pate
> da caldo amore e da viva speranza,
> che vince la divina volontate:
>   non a guisa che l'omo e l'om sobranza,
> ma vince lei perché vuole esser vinta,
> e, vinta, vince con sua beninanza.   (Par. xx 94–9)

(The kingdom of heaven suffers violence from ardent love and living hope which overcomes divine will, not in the way that a man has victory over a man; it conquers because it wishes to be conquered; and conquered, it conquers with its own goodwill.)

In speaking of the relationship between Justice and Love, one arrives at the central principle of Dante's Christian thinking in the *Commedia*, and also at the point to which I shall constantly refer whenever – and in whatever way – I subsequently allude to the *difficulties* of the poet Dante. For while it is possible and right to say, with Gilson, that a concern with Justice characterises Dante's professional interests as a philosopher, the essential concern of the *Commedia* is rather with the tension between the claims of Justice and the claims of Love.

This tension will reveal itself as much in the intellectual procedures on which the *Commedia* rests as in explicit statements such as those of *Paradiso* xx. And we shall see this as soon as we turn to the *Inferno*. Immediately, in Cantos i and ii, the rational competence of Virgil which leads the protagonist to Justice is contrasted with the miraculous intervention of Beatrice, which she makes in response to the love between herself and her devotee. We shall also see in the Limbo episode of Canto iv the close connection between Dante's treatment of Virgil in the *Inferno* and the discussion of the fate of the pagan in the *Paradiso*. For the quality which Virgil is there shown to lack is any appreciation of the mysterious 'violence' with which God acts to preserve the souls of men such as Trajan, Rhipeus or, finally, Dante himself. And something of this already emerges, in a subdued but deeply ironic form, from *Paradiso* xx. For, while Dante contentiously allows that Virgil has indeed understood the justice of Rhipeus, the very passage in the *Aeneid* which expresses this understanding also demonstrates a tragic misapprehension on Virgil's part about the nature of divinity: to human eyes, Rhipeus may have been the 'most just' of men, yet in a fatalistic aside Virgil allows that the gods saw it otherwise: 'dis aliter visum'. But this fatalism must itself disqualify him from any insight into the God of miracles with his power to redeem; and in the *Inferno* we shall see that Virgil *personaggio* is unable to respond to any evidence of redeeming power – at least when it is displayed *as* power.

As yet, however, we have said too little about the view of love which
emerges from the *Paradiso*. And only by considering this matter further shall
we answer two questions which have been held in abeyance since the
beginning of the present discussion.

First, one is bound to ask – as Dante certainly would – what dignity is left
to the human being whose salvation depends so completely on the
incalculable concern of the Christian God. Secondly, Dante must also ask
how he can conceivably act or write his poem at all when the law he wishes
to assert is ultimately enshrined in the mysterious will of the Creator.

On the first of these questions, one needs to examine more closely how a
shift of emphasis occurs in *Paradiso* xx; here – while still speaking
ostensibly of justice – Dante slowly prepares for the consideration of love
which will begin in Cantos xxi and xxii, where his subject is the ardour
shown by contemplative spirits in their ascetic devotion to God. For along
with this shift of theme Dante also effects a fundamental change in – so to
speak – the angle from which he views human nature. In the Heaven of
Jupiter, he has primarily been concerned with those aspects of human
purpose which can best be expressed or satisfied in the communal institution
of justice. It is not too much to say that his emphasis has fallen upon
humanity in its *generic* aspect: for (as the *Monarchia* shows) Dante
considered the realm of justice to be one in which *all* human beings, as
members of the human race, would, ideally, combine in the rational pursuit
of order and peace. Under the jurisdiction of the Imperial Eagle, mankind
would be united; and that is one reason why it is so painful – and so
contradictory – for Dante to contemplate, in the same sequence, the division
of mankind into pagan and Christian groups.

But in discussing the case of the noble pagan Dante also admits a change
of perspective which itself proves to be the solution to the problem. For, as
we have seen, his treatment of the two pagans Rhipeus and Trajan demands
that we should see them precisely *as* particular cases. There can be no
question at all of drawing general conclusions from their salvation or
proposing that, because two pagans have been saved, all may be; it is also
evident that Dante rigorously excludes any such form of rational argumen-
tation from his considerations. If we ask, then, where the dignity of the
human creature eventually lies, the episode already suggests that, finally, it is
located not in any product of its own rationality but rather in the relationship
which each creature can enjoy, as individual, with the person of its Creator.
And if we then ask what the writer – supposing he is Dante – must do in
examining the relationship between God and the human being, the answer
must be that, somehow, he has to make the individual case the focus of his
own most serious attentions. This will not be the *only* way of proceeding; for
everything we have said implies that rational discussion, within its sphere, is
competent and necessary. Nonetheless, we have also begun to see that the
contemplation of particular cases is a superior and more arduous intellectual
task.

In discussing the case of Francesca, one saw that, in the *Inferno*, the judgement of particular instances was always likely to be difficult; and it would have been easy to suggest that this difficulty was emotional in origin. Yet the twentieth canto of the *Paradiso* allows one to see that there is a hard intellectual issue at stake here, as if, for Dante, a broad and general overview were ultimately a comfort which the mind had to abandon in its concentration upon the particular. And certainly in the *Paradiso* it is apparent that to ask questions of a general nature about the fate of the pagan is in no way to advance intellectually, but rather to fall into a futile retreat: the truth of God is spelled out, at the last, in particular acts of love and will not yield to any general interpretation; consequently, if we repress our rational questions, we do so not in defeat but rather from a desire to appreciate ever more accurately the single instances of God's love for the individual.

Within the Justice sequence, two main features point to this alteration in intellectual stance – both of them related to the treatment of the Eagle, which is the dominant image of the canto.

One notes, first, that, in this Heaven of Paradise alone, the souls emphatically do *not* present themselves as individuals to the protagonist; they appear throughout Cantos XVIII and XIX as a community which acts in self-effacing concert, spelling out across the sky the words 'Love Justice' – *Diligite Iustitiam* – and finally forming themselves into the single shape of the Eagle (*Par.* XVIII 73–108). The most obvious implication of this is that justice requires the individual to devote himself wholly to the common interest and collaborate willingly in the enterprises of social existence. This demand is of course one which Dante will never fail to emphasise: in the *Monarchia* it is seen as the corner-stone of Roman morality, while in the *Purgatorio* a similar spirit of self-sacrifice – modelled on Christ's own acceptance of crucifixion – is shown to be equally essential in the establishment of a Christian community; in the *Inferno*, on the other hand, the damned are shown to have rejected any such demand in the course of their lives, so that Hell represents no more than a mockery of communal life. Yet it is also true that the individual himself, in Dante's view, can only be complete – paradoxically enough – when he does devote himself to the general interest; and in this light, devotion to justice finally implies not an effacement but a true affirmation of selfhood. So in Canto XIX Dante notes the remarkable fact that, when the Eagle speaks, it does not use the plural *Noi* – as one might expect a community of 'more than a thousand souls' to do – but insists throughout on the singular *Io*. In short, the just soul is certainly required to conform to a communal measure; but in doing this, each soul will in effect be speaking 'io' and magnifying that 'io' through the mouth of the community.

In Canto XX, the stress upon individuality becomes yet more evident, as Dante for a first time names six of the souls who compose the Eagle. These include, of course, Trajan and Rhipeus. But the significant feature here is that these six spirits form the *eye* of the Eagle – with King David, who is described as the 'singer of the Holy Spirit' (38) – at the pupil of the eye. For the eye of the Eagle has a special function; as Dante recalls at line 31 the eye of a mortal eagle is able to see directly into the light of the sun, and it is precisely because of this property that the Eagle can be seen not only as an emblem of justice but also as an emblem of visionary love. So in *Paradiso* XXVI 53, St John – the supreme example of mystic love – is described as the 'aguglia di Cristo'. And here lies the point of the change in Dante's imaginative emphasis: justice reveals one aspect of the order which God has created, but finally God himself will be known as Love, in mystic communion, when the visionary eye of each individual responds – as David, the 'cantor dello Spirito Santo', does – to the promptings of the Holy Spirit.

The modulation in the meaning of the Eagle marks a profound change in the direction of the *Paradiso*, which, in preparation for Dante's final meeting – 'face to face' – with God will henceforth stress the theological virtues and the mystic disciplines which the individual must cultivate in the last stages of his spiritual advance. For my present purposes, however, the last sequence I need to consider here is that which Dante devotes to the ascetics and contemplatives in Cantos XXI and XXII.

Here certainly Dante is concerned with individuals: the imagery of the sequence presents the souls as distinct wheels of light (XXI 79–81); and, of course, the contemplative life which the souls exemplify is one in which each being makes its own inward ascent to God. In fact, even here, Dante does not diminish the importance of community. By his celebration of St Benedict in Canto XXII he acknowledges, as did the historical St Benedict, that the mystic life can most satisfactorily be pursued within a monastic community, where each member is able to support the particular aspirations of each. We may indeed go further than that. For the Heaven of the Contemplatives is here the Heaven of Saturn, and one cannot forget that, mythologically, the Golden Age of Justice occured in the era of Saturn. So at Canto XXI 26, Dante recalls that in the Saturnian Age 'all evil-doing lay dead'. For all that, in the monastic community 'justice' is no longer a social rule but rather an obedience of heart which each member of the community will willingly display. The word 'heart' is one that Dante uses increasingly in this sequence of the *Paradiso*; and he has already prepared for this move from, so to speak, public to private law by speaking in Canto XX 30 of how the words of the Eagle were written upon his own heart – in the 'core ov' io le scrissi'.

This much may confirm that – without detraction from the rational dignity of the human being – the *ground* of our dignity lies in the love and obedience we display towards our Creator. It may also suggest – to follow Dante's own metaphor – that the Law must ultimately be written not on tablets of stone but upon the heart and person of the creature itself. One advances this suggestion in the confidence that it will prove applicable in the *Inferno* – where, for instance, the sinner Vanni Fucci is seen in Canto XXIV 100–2 as the passive page on which punishment inscribes the law of divine retribution. But a final example from the *Paradiso* will suggest how deeply rooted this metaphor is in Dante's thinking about the relation between God and creature.

I refer to Dante's meeting with the soul of St Peter Damian in *Paradiso* XXI – an episode which rarely receives the attention it deserves. St Peter Damian is the first spirit to approach Dante in the Heaven of Saturn; and the first question which Dante asks him is one which – one might suppose – is of the utmost importance; for it touches on the question of predestination which has been implicitly present throughout the discussion of the noble pagan: Dante wishes to know why it is that St Peter Damian has been singled out by God to speak to him:

> Perché predestinata fosti sola
> a questo officio tra le tue consorte.   (XXI 77–8)

(Why were you alone, of all your company, predestined to this task.)

Yet important as this question must seem to a knowledge of how God's choices operate, Dante is strictly not allowed to pursue it: he is told he must not move his feet towards that target (97–9). Swiftly complying, he abandons the ultimate question, and restricts himself to asking humbly 'what is your name?':

> Sì mi prescrisser le parole sue,
> ch'io lasciai la quistione e mi ritrassi
> a dimandarla umilmente chi fue.   (103–5)

(His words so set a limit upon me that I let the question be, and restricted myself to asking humbly who he was.)

Is this, then, yet another defeat for the intellectual aspirations of the protagonist? Certainly, he has been told in the Justice sequence that the 'roots' of predestination are remote from human view (XX 130-l); and his initial impatience might well display something of the impatience of the 'unripe' Lucifer. Yet his retraction is also clearly an act of obedience; and while the protagonist might easily have been driven by St Peter Damian's reproof to the confusion he suffered at the sight of Trajan and Rhipeus, there is nothing banal or trivial about the simple question he actually utters. Time and again in the *Inferno* (as in the *Purgatorio*, too), Dante will show a vivid interest in the names of his interlocutors; and there is every reason why he should: names, finally, are the baptismal signs of the recognition which God bestows upon the individual. So, in the present case, the name identifies St Peter Damian as an object of contemplative love. St Peter Damian himself stresses – appropriately enough for a contemplative – how the divine light 'points' upon him (83); and the eye of the protagonist is focused upon exactly that same point. The human presence itself marks the intersection of God's will and the inquiring mind of the protagonist. (One thinks of how in the Earthly Paradise the eyes of Beatrice reflect the image of the Gryphon – symbol of Christ – into the eyes of the protagonist (*Purg.* XXX 121-3).)

In refusing, then, to ask the speculative question, the protagonist is able to concentrate far more accurately upon God's will than any consideration of law or general principle would have allowed him to do. The human figure itself is the supreme sign and answer; and this conclusion is certainly consistent with subsequent developments in the *Paradiso*. So, in Canto XXII, Dante – having learned the lesson from St Peter Damian – asks no speculative question at all but wishes only to know the identity of the new speaker. The 'point of desire' – the 'punta del disio' (26) – is now to see St Benedict not as a radiant wheel of light but 'con imagine scoverta' (60), in his distinct human lineaments. In fact the protagonist is told that even this desire is premature; but it *will* be fulfilled, in the highest circles of Heaven (61–3). In effect, the *Paradiso* represents not an increasing evanescence of human form, but a return to a clear perception of the *imagine scoverta*. Nor is it hard to see why this should be so. For when Dante does see St Benedict – along with all the other saints – in Canto XXXII, it is clearly a moment of final preparation for the vision of God himself, where he will see God face to face and also witness the ultimate truth of the Universe in the features of Christ. So the circulation which first reveals God to Dante finally displays the human image itself:

> dentro da sé, del suo colore stesso,
> mi parve pinta de la nostra effige ...   (*Par.* XXXIII 130–1)

(within itself, of its own colour, it seemed to me painted with our human image).

This vision defeats Dante's rational comprehension; he compares himself to a mathematician baffled by the question of how to measure a circle (133–5). Yet the mystery itself is one which, so far from humiliating the human being, asserts that God, as Christ, saw fit to take on human form.

But what are the implications of this for a reading of the *Inferno*? In the first place, one has come to see that there are for Dante two distinct modes of thought, associated with, respectively, the two principles of Love and Justice. One of these is, in the most obvious sense, a rational mode, concerned with schemes, categories, questions and clear answers; and no one would dispute the validity of that mode either for the protagonist – as he pursues his journey under Virgil's guidance – or for the poet – as he diagnoses the disorder into which sin will lead human nature. Yet this, in the end, must be seen as an instrumental or provisional way in which to approach the truth. And from the first – even in dealing with the sinners of Hell – the mind of the reader, as of the poet, must shape itself to read the truth incorporated in the lives of individual beings. It will readily be agreed that Dante's art in the *Commedia* draws its strength from the vividness with which the poet has depicted individual character and circumstance. But, considering the end of the *Paradiso*, it is plain that this concern, disruptive though it may be, is not, as Romantic criticism would lead one to suppose, a sign of Dante's resistance to his own system. It is rather a product of his prevailing sense that love reveals the incarnate truth. It needs to be stressed – on the evidence of

Dante's final vision – that this mode of seeing is disruptive. Thus we shall see that, while many figures in the *Inferno* – such as Francesca, Piero and Ulysses – make claims for their own individuality, these claims inevitably fail because they have not understood how the self, as a creature of God, must be founded upon the disruptive 'violence' of divine love.

If the poetry of the *Inferno* becomes eventually 'dead', then one reason is that Dante records his failure to find here any figure who can sustain the sort of attention that he will finally be able to pay to figures such as Trajan, Rhipeus, St Peter Damian (and constantly, of course, to Beatrice). But it is also perennially difficult to attend – as Dante obliges himself to do – to the particular case. And this, one repeats, is a logical rather than an emotional difficulty. For while the human presence might be recognised as the repository of truth, the poet can only evoke these presences in the rational but provisional medium of words. And it is the *Paradiso* that affords the clearest view of how deeply this difficulty is rooted in the nature not only of argument but also of language and writing.

Note, in the Justice sequence, how strongly Dante associates the theme of justice with images of writing. So, as Dante describes how the souls of the just write *Diligite Iustitiam* across the sky, he goes out of his way to stress the composition of vowels and consonants in the sentence:

> Mostrarsi dunque in cinque volte sette
> vocali e consonanti; e io notai
> le parti sì, come mi parver dette.
>   '*DILIGITE IUSTITIAM*', primai
> fur verbo e nome di tutto 'l dipinto;
> '*QUI IUDICATIS TERRAM*', fur sezzai.   (*Par.* xviii 88–93)

(They displayed themselves in five times seven vowels and consonants; and I took note of the parts as they seemed to be uttered to me. 'Diligite Iustitiam' were the first verb and noun of all that picturing; 'Qui iudicatis terram' were the last.)

This connection is easy enough to understand: the Law, after all, has to to be written out clearly if it is to be understood and obeyed. (It is Richards – in *Beyond*, p. 111 – who points to the etymological connection between *lex*, *legend* and *legere*.) But, retrospectively, this sequence throws much light on the presentation of Virgil in the *Commedia*; for in Virgil too a devotion to the principles of justice – and Empire – is associated with the utmost care and clarity of speech.

Is there, however, any other mode of communication than this? There is: it is the language, so to say, of miracles, which Dante learns to read in contemplating the salvation of Rhipeus and Trajan. The notion of a 'miracle' held particular interest for Dante in his earliest writings: the word *miracolo* is one which he first associates metaphorically with Beatrice in the *Vita nuova*. But it does not remain a metaphor: for one thing, Dante is fully aware of the etymological relationship between *miracolo* and words which denote 'wonder' or the aiming and directing of the eye; for another, he is never wholly unaware – even in his most humanistic phases – that God as Creator continually and miraculously intervenes in his own creation. In short, there are certain truths which, while being inexpressible in words, may nonetheless be *seen*. The truths of Rhipeus and Trajan are of that order. But Beatrice is the supreme instance; and, as we shall shortly see, the image of Beatrice can only be grasped by those who are prepared to relinquish their hold on the rational and discursive constructions which seem most essential for their own well-being. The recourse, at this point, must be to the language of miracles, where sight, love and the human image are all conjoined. The damned, we may add, are not miraculous: time and again in the *Inferno* an initial moment of wonder or admiration dissolves into disappointment as the emptiness of the sinner emerges, or as the sinner himself – in unwitting denial of his own particularity – resorts to the delusive rhetoric of some commonplace type of heroism. One thinks immediately of Capaneus; but whatever is true of him will also be true of, say, Farinata, Brunetto, Ulysses and even Francesca.

IV

We have come to a point at which Dante's thinking is so closely connected with questions of linguistic form and procedure that it is bound to have influenced the way in which he wrote. Throughout the *Inferno*, the primacy which Dante grants to the image – usually, but not exclusively, the human image – will reveal the inadequacies of discursive or argumentative procedures; and these inadequacies will be most apparent in the way that Virgil is shown to speak and to solve the problems of the journey. Virgil, as we have said, can be seen as the sub-author of the *Inferno*. This, in part, means denying that the modes of discourse Virgil exemplifies are absolutely necessary for Dante's own authorial success. At the same time, the criticisms which, by implication, attach to Virgil must also be seen as criticisms of the language that Dante himself adopted in constructing his own poem.

All that we have so far suggested about the limitations of rational language could also be said of the narrative schemes that Dante develops in the first *cantica*. This point has not yet been fully developed. But as soon as we turn to Canto I of the *Inferno* we shall realise the extent to which Dante values Virgil as an epic poet, whose narrative reflects the history of Rome. History itself will there be seen as a form of providential discourse; and Virgil's task in the *Commedia* is largely to ensure that, in the case of the protagonist, the providential tale is told to its coherent conclusion. In that sense, the steady and clear-headed conduct of the journey will be entirely at one with the systematic unrolling of Dante's philosophical scheme. But again (as will appear especially in Cantos VIII and IX) the narrative patterns of the *Inferno* are far more complex than this simple model of linear progress would suggest. For one thing, the images that the narrative produces – as, for instance, images of light and darkness, speed and immobility, distortion and harmony – will themselves come to constitute a network of significant relationships, requiring of the reader a continual activity of imaginative cross-reference which modifies any simple attention to the advancing narrative. In large part, this scheme of imagery will contribute directly to a precise understanding of Dante's conceptual scheme, giving it depth and resonance. Yet such images can also be disruptive. Shock is a major feature of Dante's narrative technique. And this is not merely to emphasise the inherently dramatic nature of Dante's storytelling. On the contrary, it is precisely in the succession, throughout the *Inferno*, of moments of surprise that one finds a narrative equivalent to the difficulties which continually arise in regard to linguistic and argumentative adequacy. Dante certainly develops a coherent scheme on both a conceptual and an imaginative plane. But the form of narrative he writes leads him at all points to subvert the line of simple progress; the construction of his poem, while in one respect measured and gradual, submits, in another respect, to constant modification and redirection.

We have already seen something of this narrative procedure in the surprises that punctuate the Trajan and Rhipeus episode. But to indicate how deeply rooted this narrative pattern is in every part of the *Commedia*, one may, in conclusion, turn to what is probably the most important single episode in the whole work – the meeting between Dante and Beatrice in *Purgatorio* xxx. With the appearance of Beatrice comes the *dis*appearance of Virgil; and this suggests, on the level of theme, how deeply concerned the sequence is with the same questions of love and justice as we have already encountered in the *Paradiso*, since Beatrice can easily be seen to correspond to the former principle, and Virgil to the latter. However, the especial value of the Earthly Paradise sequence is that it indicates the extent to which, throughout Dante's text, the principles of love and justice are expressed in the play of discourse and image, and also in effects of narrative surprise.

The whole of Dante's journey through Hell and Purgatory can be seen as a preparation for his meeting with Beatrice. In Canto II of the *Inferno* the Dante character learns that it is Beatrice who has inspired his journey to salvation and she who commissions Virgil to be his guide. Virgil himself acknowledges this initiative and – particularly in the ascent of Mount Purgatory – willingly admits the superior competence of Beatrice. So, while Virgil is able to teach Dante a good deal about the philosophy of love – in the discourses of Cantos XVII and XVIII – he also confesses at *Purgatorio* XVIII 46–8 that only Beatrice will be able to give the protagonist a full account of this matter. So, too, Virgil repeatedly encourages Dante with the thought that he will eventually see Beatrice in the Earthly Paradise: at line 46 of Canto VI, he speaks of how Beatrice will appear to the protagonist 'happy and smiling on the mountain-top'; and likewise, as the travellers pass through the circle of fire that guards the summit, Virgil attempts to strengthen the resolve of his pupil by speaking of Beatrice and emphasising that, although he may *speak* of Beatrice, Dante will eventually *see* into her eyes:

> Lo dolce padre mio, per confortarmi,
> pur di Beatrice ragionando andava,
> dicendo: 'Li occhi suoi già veder parmi'.   (*Purg.* xxvii 52–4)

(My sweet father – to comfort me – went on speaking of Beatrice, saying: 'Already, it seems, I can see her eyes.')

The stress in this passage (carried largely by the continuative gerunds) falls upon the steady, persistent processes of speech and advance. Yet when the eyes of Beatrice are at last unveiled, the impact of that sight is totally at variance with anything that Virgil – or Dante's own narrative – has prepared us for. In a word, Beatrice does not smile; her first devastating response to Dante's arrival in the Earthly Paradise is to berate him as a sinner for daring to enter a region where humankind is happy (xxx 73–5). Only two cantos earlier, Virgil has declared that Dante is 'free, upright and whole', and the accolade is bestowed in a scene of, so to speak, spiritual coronation. This is what we *should* expect: Dante believes that penance is a remedy for sin; and he has participated, imaginatively, in every penance on the Mountain. Now, against the whole logic of his endeavours, he is accused yet again of vice; for all his proven devotion, he is charged with treachery to his Lady (xxx 126). In response, the protagonist has no word or argument to put forward; he is reduced to a state of incoherent tears, sighs and sobs, and cannot even utter the word 'yes' without breaking down:

> Confusione e paura insieme miste
> mi pinsero un tal 'sì' fuor de la bocca,
> al quale intender fuor mestier le viste.
> Come balestro frange, quando scocca
> da troppa tesa, la sua corda e l'arco,
> e con men foga l'asta il segno tocca,
> sì scoppia' io sottesso grave carco,
> fuori sgorgando lagrime e sospiri,
> e la voce allentò per lo suo varco.   (*Purg.* xxxi 13–21)

(Confusion and fear, mingling together, drove out of my mouth such a yes so faint that sight was needed to understand what it was. As a crossbow breaks, when unloosed with too much tension, both its string and bow, and the bolt hits the target with diminished force, so did I burst beneath this heavy burden, pouring forth tears and sighs; and the voice failed in its passage.)

The crucial elements of the narrative here are expectation and interruption. Until Beatrice appears, the scene has been one of solemn and stately triumph, entirely compatible with Virgil's predictions. The procession is a liturgical representation of the providential plan which God has spelled out in history through the prophets and the Scriptures; it is a sign that God intends his creatures to discern, in the fabric of human history, a confident declaration of his eternal purpose. So, too, Virgil, the epic poet of Rome, has expressed an understanding of history which, although pagan, attributes to human beings an ethical capacity to plan and pursue a steady course through the vicissitudes of temporal existence.

But all of this is overthrown when Beatrice appears. She is certainly the culmination of the procession; and, on an allegorical interpretation of her place in that procession, it would be easy to see her as a figure for Christ, who himself represents the summation of history. It is, however, a part of the shock of her entry that she is no more an allegorical figure than Christ himself is. On the sudden, the mind of protagonist, and of reader, is required to change its very manner of thinking (as it will be required to do again in witnessing Trajan and Rhipeus). It must now see truth incarnate in a particular human presence – as it would certainly have to do in witnessing Christ; and no expectation, however well-founded, can detract from the shock of that demand.

It follows that the scene proves 'difficult' on all the levels we have so far discussed. In the first place, it is a racking piece of confessional writing on the poet's part. In the *Inferno*, as we have said, Dante will bring the eye of judgement to bear as often – almost – upon himself as protagonist as he does upon the damned. Now, in what is undoubtedly a scene of judgement, he returns to many of the linguistic and imaginative tonalities of the first *cantica* (as, for example, at xxx 85 in describing his own frozen terror, which dissipates only very slowly). But it is almost impossible in this episode to speak of a fictional protagonist. The obvious distinction between poet and *personaggio* here collapses: the protagonist is the historical lover of Beatrice who is himself supremely a poet; and the task of the poet is here to write a scathing criticism of his own moral failings and even – considering the broken words of the protagonist – of his own literary and linguistic pretensions.

In a similar way, the episode represents the final moment in Dante's prolonged critique of Virgil. So, as the veiled Beatrice approaches, Dante turns to Virgil – as he has at every point on the journey so far – expecting his master to give him guidance, and seeking to share or moderate his experience by discussing it with a well-informed listener. But Virgil is not there:

> Ma Virgilio n'avea lasciati scemi
> di sé, Virgilio dolcissimo patre,
> Virgilio a cui per mia salute die'mi.   (*Purg.* xxx 49–51)

(But Virgil had left us bereft of himself, Virgil sweetest father, Virgil to whom I gave myself to be saved.)

There is no greater moment of discomposure in the *Commedia* than this. And the point, of course, is that, in the face of Beatrice, composure would be out of place: from the first pages of the *Vita nuova* Dante has understood the 'terror' of love; and while he gradually comes to recognise the vital distinction between the violence of passion and the violence of contemplative charity, he admits – as we have seen – the defeat of rational comprehension when he finally fixes his eye upon the human face of God. But the function of Virgil *personaggio* throughout the first two *cantiche* has been to offer the protagonist a shield of rational comfort against whatever experience assails him – discoursing, as he does even on the last cornice of Purgatory, 'per confortare' the protagonist. That shield has undoubtedly been a necessary defence in the regions of sin; it becomes a mere obstruction when the soul is confronted with the divine violence of contemplative love.

Nor is it only Virgil *personaggio* who is called into question here. For, at perhaps the most remarkable moment in the whole episode, Dante finds a way simultaneously to celebrate and to incriminate the text of the *Aeneid* itself. Thus the words on Dante's lips as he turns to find that Virgil has gone are an exact translation of a verse which Virgil himself has written. Dante – recognising that at the sight of Beatrice he 'knows again the signs of his old feeling' – writes 'conosco i segni de l'antica fiamma' (xxx 48); but Dido, in *Aeneid* IV 23, has already said 'agnosco veteris vestigia flammae', as she senses the stirrings of her love for Aeneas.

Lest the positive virtues of this allusion be overlooked, one should emphasise that such a quotation at any earlier point would have served to assert in a characteristically Dantean way the solidarity that human beings can enjoy in sharing a common culture and tradition. This appreciation of the value of classical literature has an especially strong influence upon the text of the *Purgatorio*, where the poet draws freely upon the myths, images and sentences of the classics in expressing his Christian theme. The most notable instance of this is, indeed, Dante's use of the myth of the Golden Age, which – as he allows at *Purgatorio* xxvIII 139–41 – inspired his own image of the Earthly Paradise. So, too, in *Purgatorio* IX Dante describes how the protagonist is raised to the Gate of Purgatory in terms of the myth of Ganymede – who was carried to the heavens by the eagle of Jupiter. This complex episode corresponds exactly in thought and imagery to the Justice sequence of the *Paradiso*. For in fact Dante only *dreams* of being borne up by the Eagle; as Virgil subsequently explains (*Purg.* IX 55–7), the truth is that he was carried to the Gate in the arms of his patron saint, St Lucy. In a word, the truly effective action here has been the particular and, rationally, ungraspable impact of visionary love; yet the realm of the Eagle – which includes the resources of just action, common culture, myth and discourse – retains its validity, providing, so to speak, a vocabulary in which the actions of Love can be comprehensibly spelled out. Thus in the *Commedia* Virgil acts as the spokesman for Beatrice; he is chosen as a guide initially because of his 'parole ornate' (*Inf.* II 67). We may add that in a similar way Dante relies heavily upon the picture of the underworld offered in Book VI of the *Aeneid* in constructing his own account of Hell.

Yet having said all this, the resources, so to speak, of the 'Eagle' remain no more than a repertoire of conventions, to be abandoned in the presence of truth itself. And the utterance – or writing – of the line 'conosco i segni' dramatises Dante's realisation of this. For the protagonist, in addressing himself to the absent Virgil, falls momentarily into the vacancy that lies behind the text of the *Aeneid*; in the circumstances of his meeting with Beatrice, the words of Virgil's poem stand revealed as 'dead poetry', insufficient to grasp the new moment. Thus in the *Aeneid* Virgil's line expresses unrelieved guilt and confusion over the manifestations of love; even Dido is stricken with shame at the renewal of long-dead passion. Yet there is no place for guilt in Dante's feelings for Beatrice. The protagonist may indeed be confused, but – as Beatrice will quickly make clear (*Purg.* xxx 126–32) – that confusion arises because he has failed to love with sufficient clarity or firmness of purpose. Any guilt which Dante experiences must arise from his *not* having loved Beatrice. And for that reason it is entirely inappropriate that he should group himself – by his allusion – with a figure whom, after all, he has himself condemned to Hell. To suppose that there is any common denominator between *his* love and Dido's is to distort and betray the particularity of contemplative devotion. Likewise, for the poet to make so calculated an allusion to Virgil must be taken to represent both an imitative challenge to the Latin original and, equally, a form of poetic self-betrayal. At the first appearance of Beatrice (*Purg.* xxx 22–33), Dante, understandably, and quite deliberately, began to resuscitate the lyric modes of writing that he had first developed in the *Vita nuova*. To be sure, his style here is richer than it was in the *Vita nuova*: its images are stronger, and it possesses a gravity of rhythm which must surely reflect Dante's devotion to the epic poetry of the *Aeneid*. And yet that the poet should adopt the very words of Virgil's epic at the sight of Beatrice is evidently a false step – a misapprehension of the experience he now has to deal with. In reaching Beatrice, Dante has returned to his origins; and Beatrice now proceeds to insist that the language Dante adopts – at least as protagonist – should also return in the deepest sense, to what it once had been.

So, as we have seen, the first effect of Beatrice's presence upon the protagonist is to reduce him to a mode of utterance so rudimentary that it scarcely admits (to quote *Paradiso* xviii) distinction of 'vowels and consonants'. Beatrice demands that the protagonist weep; he must suffer, in short, a humiliating return to the language of infancy. But precisely in this the protagonist is preparing to return to full *maturity* – where he will need no protection or aid from his master Virgil (xxxi 64–75). And it is significant in this regard that the first word which Beatrice speaks is the name of Dante himself, recorded here for the only time in the *Commedia*. The effect of this, in context, is immensely powerful: four times in the lines immediately preceding it, we have read the name of Virgil, as Dante expresses his irrepressible sorrow at losing him; then into the sequence comes the voice of Beatrice saying:

> Dante, perché Virgilio se ne vada,
> non pianger anco, non piangere ancora;
> ché pianger ti conven per altra spada.   (xxx 55–7)

(Dante, do not weep yet, do not weep yet, because Virgil has gone away; for you have to weep for another sword.)

Once again, surprise is the key to Dante's narrative procedure; and once again, as in *Paradiso* XX, surprise reveals the difficulty associated with contemplating the particularity of the human being. But here the particular being whom both poet and reader have to contemplate is Dante himself. Beatrice – displaying what is called at Canto XXX 81 'pietade acerba' – bitter pity – demands that Dante should now truly be himself. For her part, she 'truly is Beatrice', as she insists at line 73: 'Ben son, ben son Beatrice'. Yet for Dante to emerge from under the tutelage of Virgil is no easier than it will be for him to see Rhipeus at the eye of the Justice-Eagle, or to prefer the name of Peter Damian to a satisfying disquisition on the problem of predestination. In spite of his sins, Dante has arrived at the threshold of Paradise; and to grasp the full meaning of this is to overthrow all the rational apparatus which has so far been employed to expound the general possibility of salvation. So the text of Canto XXX itself – which is more sophisticated in its language and more complex in its fictional and allegorical schemes than any other in the *Commedia* – is on the instant broken by the elemental but irreducible name of its historical author. For Dante, the true sophistication of the canto lies in the way that it frames and affirms the penitential value of the humblest forms of utterance – names, cries and broken words. For the reader, too, the canto calls us to abandon the comforts of fiction and philosophy; we are required to envisage and respond to the moral origins of the work we are reading – and these are located in the historical *fact* of its author's existence. No merely imaginative assent to the cultural artefact will suffice; we must read 'Dante' as Dante 'reads' St Peter Damian.

In 'Whose Endless Jar', Richards describes Dante as the 'great hater'; seeing the *Commedia* as a systematic justification for hatred, he proposes that we should liberate ourselves from any desire to become 'Aquinas-wise', and be ready to respond to the 'inexhaustible surprise' of the world. If I were concerned in this book with the *Paradiso*, it would be a simple matter to show how far from 'hatred' Dante is, as a thinker and poet. And few phrases apply better to the *Purgatorio* than Richards's 'inexhaustible surprise': for the penitents seek, in Purgatory, not only a moral liberation but also the freedom to express, in their response to the created world, the full range of their natural capacities, whether physical, imaginative or emotional. But Dante's return to 'living poetry' in the second *cantica* would amount to little had he not experienced to the full the difficulties of writing the first *cantica*; where he does indeed recognise how the human mind can construct for itself intolerable confines. Yet even in the *Inferno* the underlying patterns of thought and literary procedure are, I contend, essentially the same as those I have traced in the last two *cantiche*. We have now to see in detail how they operate.

So, in Chapter 1, I shall try to show that while Dante does, of course, aspire to create order in the confusion of Hell, his conception of order is one that demands of him continual activity. The eventful journey of the protagonist is one indication that this must be so. But the intellectual activities of the poet will be seen to run parallel to those of the protagonist: the text of the opening sequence (as of every other in the *Inferno*) will submit to continual dislocation as it embraces narrative events; and beyond even that there will be the constant awareness of how images and presences must tax the competence of words.

In Chapter 2, I shall consider two of the major philosophical statements of the *Inferno* to show how Dante's philosophy in the *Commedia* – particularly in contrast to that of the *Convivio* – is both shaped and modified by the narrative requirements of the poem.

In Chapter 3, I shall look at the way in which narrative – or storytelling – becomes a moral agent in the *Inferno*, and go on to consider the ways in which Dante makes the telling of a story a test of moral competence – a test which the damned invariably fail but in which Dante, as he writes, knows that he must succeed.

These opening chapters will largely emphasise Dante's intellectual practice in the *Inferno*; the concluding chapters will rather take as their point of departure particular features of poetic and narrative procedure.

Thus in Chapter 4, concentrating upon the linguistic features of the Malebolge sequence, I shall examine what it means for Dante to write a poem in which his own moral standing is at stake in a language which according to his own definition is 'comic', and to anyone else's, harsh, violent and often obscene.

Chapter 5 will consider the management of transitional sequences in the concluding cantos of the *Inferno* – particularly those transitions which anticipate the *Purgatorio*. I shall argue that this part of the *Inferno* shows a particular interest in ambiguities of signification, and that Dante here fully admits the pathos which surrounds any pursuit of order.

In Chapter 6 I shall examine the ways in which Dante manages the end of the *Inferno* in relation to the moral theme of 'ends'; again, comparisons will be drawn between the way in which Dante approaches this problem and the way in which the damned – exemplifying possible modes of procedure – attack the same difficulty.

Finally, having seen throughout the correspondence between technical and moral difficulty, I shall try to show why Dante might have regarded the work he had produced as a travesty – though a necessary travesty – of what his true course could have been. This conclusion will compare the dead poetry of the *Inferno* with the poetry which had once 'lived' in the *Vita nuova*.

1

Action and order: Cantos I–V

I

The opening of the *Inferno* is oblique and gradual; Dante does not describe his entry into Hell until Canto III of the *Inferno*, nor does he introduce any sinner who can be recognised easily *as* a sinner – at least from the standpoint of the Seven Capital Vices – until the lustful appear in Canto V. Until Canto XI no explicit account is given either of the nature of sin or of the laws by which the damned are distributed among the various regions of Hell; in fact there is no sustained discussion of doctrine at all until the seventh canto, and even then it concerns Fortuna – the condition of temporal change rather than the principle of divine judgement.

We are accustomed to think of the *Commedia* as a work planned with great rigour; and in one respect the slow unfolding of the plan over the first eleven cantos is an indication of how systematic Dante was and wished to be in his diagnosis of sin. The *Inferno* is no wild cry of desperation; it is an analysis which recommends analysis itself as an essential part of salvation. Yet in the course of this lengthy prelude, Dante also introduces a good deal of material which complicates or strains the order he is erecting and eludes the analysis he means to offer. Certainly the sequence *is* introductory insofar as it offers an increasingly coherent account of the grades and categories of sin; it is equally an introduction in that Dante reveals here a whole range of problems that will be intrinsic to his enterprise in writing the *cantica*.

Consider Cantos I and II, which depict the first faltering attempts of the protagonist to escape from the confusions of the Dark Wood. These cantos provide little information about the eternal order of Hell; but the poet's purpose here is to speak of the very desire for order as an essential motive in the human will. At the same time, in portraying the vacillations of the protagonist, Dante also demonstrates the tragic ease with which the human mind can frustrate its own aspirations. Such confusion in consciousness is itself a symptom of sin, but the protagonist is protected from the worst consequences of that malaise by the intervention of the calm – though deeply ambiguous – figure of Virgil. As we shall see, the first two cantos are a portrayal of mental action in its most elemental phase, where the eye is dominated by the apprehension of light and dark, and leads the protagonist to respond with unregulated impulses of hope or fear to the shapes that congregate around him. And as Dante depicts the sufferings of the protagonist in his uncertain pursuit of order, so too he identifies the problems which he as a poet must likewise face when seeking to establish a pattern in his own consciousness.

Until Virgil appears at Canto I line 62, the narrative of the *Inferno* concerns a retreat rather than an advance. The opening sequence of the canto represents the initial moments in the conception of a right-minded purpose and a fledgling desire for action. But the Dante-character, to begin with, lacks any sense of the methods or discipline he will need to bring his purpose to fruition; indeed, while he is dimly conscious of what his goal must be, his mind is increasingly confused by the perception of its own divided state.

The opening *terzina* of the canto describes a return to conscious thought and the first stirrings of self-knowledge; Dante finds himself again – 'mi ritrovai' (2) – at the mid-point of his life in a dark wood, and the moment of awakening reveals that all bearings and directions have been lost: 'la diritta via era smarrita' (3). The Dante-character here recognises the value of order precisely because he knows it to be lost. But this order is already shown to be inherent in the mind's activities. For the protagonist is 'half-way' along the path of his life: the journey of human life has its own natural measure to which (as we shall see in Chapter 2) the mind may refer even before it approaches God directly. In the light of that design, the confusion which the protagonist suffers is emphatically as much an offence against nature as against God.

Arriving at the end of the wooded valley in which he has awakened, the first act of the protagonist, in his search for stability, is to raise his eyes to a hill ahead of him and fix them upon the rays of light that mould the contours of its 'shoulders':

> Ma poi ch'i' fui al piè d'un colle giunto,
> là dove terminava quella valle
> che m'avea di paura il cor compunto,
>   guardai in alto e vidi le sue spalle
> vestite già de' raggi del pianeta
> che mena dritto altrui per ogne calle.   (13–18)

(But when I had reached the foot of the hill / where the valley that had pierced my heart with fear / [came to an end], I lifted up my eyes and saw that the shoulders of the hill / were clothed already in the rays of the planet / that lead us aright whatever our road.)

In itself, this action cannot be faulted. The Hill communicates everything that the Dark Wood obscures, presenting a well-defined object both for the eye and for the light which mantles its outline to rest upon. The natural world has begun to assert itself with a promise of direction and support, and for a moment, the harmony between the human being and his environment –

which had been lost in the Dark Wood – seems to have returned. Correspondingly, the protagonist, enjoying a first moment of vision, finds that his fear is somewhat quieted: 'un poco queta' (19). For all that, the divisions in his mind remain unresolved: one part of him feels safer now, but another part is still in a state of panic: 'ancor fuggiva' (24). In the following sequence, which leads to the meeting with Virgil, it quickly emerges that, despite the virtue of his first actions, the protagonist has succeeded only in covering over or evading these divisions.

This evasion is dramatised in the sequence from line 31 to line 62, where, as Dante begins to climb the Hill, he encounters three wild beasts: in turn, a *lonza* (or she-leopard), a lion and a wolf. These three beasts are commonly seen as allegorical figures, to be interpreted, for instance, as Pleasure, Pride and Avarice. Such identifications are not unimportant – every one of the major images in the first part of the canto might be given an allegorical significance. However, there are dangers in attempting a premature or single-minded interpretation. To do this would be to view the episode from the first in the light of a settled conceptual plan. Yet the sequence – as it registers the shifts and fluctuations of consciousness – is designed to display precisely the difficulties that the protagonist experiences in arriving at such a plan.

In the first encounter of the three, the eye – which at the outset had drawn the protagonist towards the safety of the Hill – now proves to be a delusive guide. The image of the *lonza* is an immediate focus for the eye of the protagonist and is perceived with the same accuracy which characterised the earlier description of the Hill, particularly through its attention (in the word 'spalle') to outline and volume:

> Ed ecco, quasi al cominciar de l'erta,
> una lonza leggiera e presta molto,
> che di pel macolato era coverta.   (31–3)

(And there, almost at the start of the slope, / was a she-leopard, svelte and agile, / covered with a mottled pelt.)

However, for the protagonist the power of vision proves to be a mixed blessing. His eye is trained no longer upon the steady and simple object of the Hill, but upon the double-coloured and rapidly moving form of the *lonza*; and the image of the beast quickly becomes an irritation and an impediment to progress:

> e non mi si partia dinanzi al volto,
> anzi 'mpediva tanto il mio cammino,
> ch'i' fui per ritornar più volte vòlto.   (34–6)

(and it would not pass from before my face, / but rather impeded my forward path, / so that I turned many times to return.)

Even so, the protagonist is not wholly discouraged. The events take place on a spring morning, and the rising dawn encourages him to suppose that even the *lonza* must augur well for his success; the scene is irradiated with an intuition of the primal innocence known only at the creation of the world:

Temp' era dal principio del mattino,
e 'l sol montava 'n sù con quelle stelle
ch'eran con lui quando l'amor divino
   mosse di prima quelle cose belle;
sì ch'a bene sperar m'era cagione
di quella fiera a la gaetta pelle
   l'ora del tempo e la dolce stagione.   (37–43)

(The time was the beginning of the morning / and the sun was rising along with those stars / which were with him when divine love / moved for the first time these beautiful things, / so that the time of day and the sweet season gave me reason to hope well / of that beast with its charming hide.)

But innocence itself now proves dangerous. In spite of his enthusiasm, the protagonist is still a prey to anxiety; and as the second and third beasts present themselves, his view of them shimmers and clouds in new bewilderment: the air appears to tremble around the head of the lion: 'sì che parea che l'aere ne tremesse' (48). Finally, with the entry of the she-wolf, Dante's eyes are so weighed down with terror that all hope of reaching the height seems to disappear:

questa mi porse tanto di gravezza
con la paura ch'uscia di sua vista,
ch'io perdei la speranza de l'altezza.   (52–4)

(She caused me such sick heaviness / with the fear that arose from her features / that I lost all hope of reaching the height.)

The protagonist is close now to his nadir; and his encounter with the she-wolf cruelly discloses how contradictory his original aspirations were. For where, in the *lonza* sequence, distraction of the eye had deluded him, in the meeting with the *lupa* it is the very impulse to move (so far expressed, however hesitatingly, in definite advance) that turns against itself, losing 'the name of action'. The *lupa* is the embodiment of restless and futile activity; at line 58 she is characterised as the 'bestia sanza pace'. And though the protagonist remains in motion, he now suffers the loss of any capacity for calm or concerted progress as, slowly, the she-wolf drives him back to a condition – even more extreme than the bewilderment he suffered at the outset – in which light and guidance of any kind are absent:

che, venendomi 'ncontro, a poco a poco
mi ripigneva là dove 'l sol tace.   (59–60)

(which, coming towards me, little by little / was driving me back again to the place where the sun is silent.)

At this point Dante, as protagonist, discovers Virgil; and at the same point Dante, as poet – introducing into his narrative a moment of surprise unequalled till the *disappearance* of Virgil in the Earthly Paradise – brings to light a range of difficulties which will exercise his thinking and art for the whole of the subsequent *cantica*.

Already Canto I has raised a question which, in moral terms, is of the utmost importance: when the mind in its best endeavours can be afflicted, as is the protagonist, by doubt and self-division, how is it ever to be healthy and whole? This is a problem which Dante had never so directly faced before. In his earlier works, he had been concerned above all to assert the *perfection* of which human beings are capable: Beatrice in the *Vita nuova* reveals to him the beauty which God, as Creator, intended his creatures to possess, while in the *Convivio* Dante explores – with the enthusiasm of a humanist – the 'nobility' which is expressed in the rational pursuit of science and justice. In the *Inferno* Dante's confidence in human nature is abruptly challenged; and while, as we shall see, it is never wholly overthrown even here, the difficulties which are represented in Canto I reverberate throughout the *Commedia*. For instance, in the central cantos of the *Purgatorio* Dante re-states the issue philosophically in a general diagnosis of the human condition which could well be taken as a paraphrase of the action we have so far described. Through the mouth of Marco Lombardo, the protagonist is told that the fundamental movement in human consciousness is an appetite and impulse towards pleasure: at the moment of its creation, the innocent soul knows nothing save that its Creator is a '*glad* maker' and that the proper object of its pleasure is the God who created it.

> Esce di mano a lui che la vagheggia
> prima che sia, a guisa di fanciulla
> che piangendo e ridendo pargoleggia,
>   l'anima semplicetta che sa nulla,
> salvo che, mossa da lieto fattore,
> volontier torna a ciò che la trastulla.   (*Purg.* XVI 85–90)

(There issues from the hand of Him Who holds it dear / before it exists – like a child / playing its childish games in tears and laughter – / the little simple soul knowing / nothing save that, moved into being by a happy maker, / it willingly turns towards that which delights it.)

But here too lies the origin of human tragedy. For, impelled by desire, the soul willingly 'turns to that which delights it', and, unless it is checked by law and reason (*Purg.* XVI 91–6), quickly abandons the pursuit of legitimate delight – in devotion to God – for the confusion of false and trivial pleasures.

It is that confusion which Dante in *Inferno* I begins to experience as soon as the *lonza* intervenes between his eye and the holy light of the Hill; and in the light of the account later offered by Marco we should expect in Canto I that some principle of law and regulation would now appear, to restore the protagonist to the road he has lost. Yet why, when this principle does appear, should it be the poet Virgil? Why not a Christian thinker or saint, who enjoys – as the penitent Marco does – the light of God's revelation to aid him in the pursuit of Law; or at least why not a Moses or a Solomon?

To the Dante scholar these questions will seem naive (and could indeed be answered by a closer reading of *Purgatorio* XVI). But this should not be allowed to diminish the narrative impact of Virgil's first appearance in the poem. For the meeting between Dante and Virgil dramatises a moment of conversion; and the surprising thing is that the conversion arises less from a

direct realisation of Christian truth than from a sudden perception, on Dante's
part, of how the historical Virgil and the culture he represents might aid him
in his spiritual advance. In the first half of the canto, Dante realises as never
before the extent to which human beings can fall into self-contradiction. Yet
almost simultaneously, by his choice of Virgil as a guide, the poet appears to
express a renewed, and even controversial, trust in the competence of
unaided reason.

Is it, however, sufficient to speak of Virgil in Canto i as 'unaided reason'?
In later chapters, we shall see that the philosophical action which Virgil
embodies is somewhat different from that which Dante had examined in his
own early treatise on reason and wisdom, the *Convivio*. And in Canto i the
narrative details of the encounter already reveal a view of Virgil as complex
as it is surprising in its treatment of his rational virtues.

On the one hand, there can be no doubt about the moderating influence
that Virgil has upon the protagonist: by the end of the canto the latter has
acquired a steady purpose and direction in complete contrast to the wild rout
of the first half. In this respect, Virgil brings about a calculated reversal, with
results which are perfectly expressed in the balance and austerity of the final
line: 'Allor si mosse, e io li tenni dietro' – so he moved forward and I came
close behind. It is, however, also true that Virgil's task is to lead Dante into
the darkness and disorder of Hell, insisting that, if he is to escape the beasts,
he must take a course other than the direct course to the Hill. In *this* respect,
Virgil rather sharpens than resolves the difficulties of the protagonist, guiding
him into a realm where health and sanity are bound to appear increasingly
distant. As for the poet, his emphasis upon Virgil initiates a concern, which
will continue throughout the *cantica*, about the powers and limitations of the
rational machinery he himself is using to produce his text.

Returning to that text, we need first to consider how the answers and
remedies that Virgil provides are developed. At the moment of Virgil's
appearance, the actions of the protagonist, as we have seen, are suspended as
if he were fleeing in a dream before the face of the she-wolf:

> che, venendomi 'ncontro, a poco a poco
> mi ripigneva là dove '1 sol tace.   (59–60)

(which, coming towards me, little by little / was driving me back again to the place
where the sun is silent.)

The verbs which Dante chooses here seem to enact the protagonist's
condition: the inconclusive and undirected nature of his flight is underlined
by the gerund 'venendomi' – along with the phrase 'a poco a poco' and the
imperfect 'ripigneva' – while the enjambed line expresses both urgency and
imbalance. The scene is eerily silent. But here Virgil enters:

> Mentre ch'i' rovinava in basso loco,
> dinanzi a li occhi mi si fu offerto
> chi per lungo silenzio parea fioco.
> Quando vidi costui nel gran diserto,

> '*Miserere* di me', gridai a lui,
> 'qual che tu sii, od ombra od omo certo!'   (61–6)

(Rushing down as I was towards the low place, / a figure offered himself to my eyes / who seemed to be hoarse from long silence. / When I saw him in the midst of the great waste, / I cried out to him 'Have pity on me, / whether you be a man or indeed a shade!')

At first, Virgil seems no more definite or well defined than the background from which he emerges; the protagonist cries out for help, not knowing whether Virgil is 'man or shade', and Virgil's first words seem curiously inappropriate in response to a cry of sheer distress:

> Non omo, omo già fui.   (67)

(Not a man, a man I once was.)

So far from answering the plight of the protagonist, this answer focuses, almost pedantically, upon the condition of the speaker himself. Yet these fine words will resonate throughout the *Inferno*, and the fact that they have been spoken at all is the first point of importance. The self-divided protagonist, rushing headlong into the sun's silence, is made to attend to a call from beyond the limits of his own fluctuating consciousness; the melancholic introspection of, say, line 57 – 'like one who in all his thoughts weeps and grows sad' – yields before a lively curiosity about the figure before his eyes: 'can you be Virgil, the well-spring that produced so great a stream of speech?' (78–9).

The figure of Virgil at last presents an object for the attention of the protagonist to rest upon. This object is certainly not as stable and unambiguous as the sunlit Hill. Yet the very uncertainties that surround it are, in some respects, a recommendation; they provoke questions in the protagonist and also correspond to the insecurities of the protagonist: Virgil, who 'is not a man but once was a man', confesses to an existential division more severe than any of Dante's doubts have been.

Principally, however, Virgil's statement has all the intellectual clarity which the protagonist has so far failed to display. And his words are not only efficient but also rhetorically polished: the balanced phrase 'non omo, omo già fui' is built around a central chiasmus, and at once characterises Virgil as the master of style whom Dante is shortly to describe as 'colui da cu' io tolsi / lo bello stilo che m'ha fatto onore' (86–7) – the one from whom I took the fine style which has brought me honour.

With five words, then, Virgil offers a remedy against confusion. He does so, firstly, by introducing the protagonist to the possibility of companionship, and, secondly, by providing him with a model for careful speech and thought. The foundation is already laid for a relationship that will persist between guide and follower throughout the *Inferno*, in which presence and physical gesture prove no less important than clear speech. And, as we shall see, this relationship itself provides a constant standard by which to judge the violence of word and act which characterises the damned.

In Canto i, Virgil's subsequent speeches confirm and expand the implications of his opening line. Here as elsewhere, Virgil refuses to speak his own name. Instead, continuing his first address, he offers a periphrastic and rhetorically elaborate account of himself – which the protagonist cannot fail to interpret correctly – and, in doing so, begins to construct a brief but epic oration on the history of Rome:

> Nacqui *sub Iulio*, ancor che fosse tardi,
> e vissi a Roma sotto 'l buono Augusto
> nel tempo de li dèi falsi e bugiardi.
>   Poeta fui, e cantai di quel giusto
> figliuol d'Anchise che venne di Troia,
> poi che 'l superbo Ilïón fu combusto.   (70–5)

(I was born in the time of Julius, although it was late, / and lived in Rome under good Augustus / in the time of the false and lying gods. / I was a poet, and sang of that upright / son of Anchises who came from Troy / after proud Ilion was burned.)

These lines recall how Rome was conceived in the chaos and defeat of Troy; and this knowledge alone will be of value to the protagonist, who is himself now experiencing the bitterness and humiliation of defeated hope, and will consequently see that his condition is part of the general fate of humanity. At the same time, Virgil again foreshadows an answer to such disorder: there is *justice*. Aeneas is 'quel giusto' who left the ruins of Troy to found the city of Rome; and we are reminded of the nature of Aeneas's justice in the periphrasis that introduces his name: 'figliuol' (74). It is the justice of the pious man (who carried his father from Troy), exercised in defence of kinship, companionship and community. The Virgil of the *Inferno* will, in the same way, be both just and 'pious' as he seeks to foster the bond between himself and the protagonist.

Virgil begins by speaking of the origins of Rome; he ends by extending his epic prophetically into the future, continuing to recognise the disorder of history but offering at the same time a promise that history itself is governed by providential order. When the protagonist first explained his predicament to Virgil he spoke only of the she-wolf, not of the other two beasts which had stood in his path; his concern is to be rescued from the futile activity and misdirection of appetite which the 'bestia sanza pace' represents (88–90). Virgil finally gives him an assurance that the time is near when the disorders which stem from the *lupa* will cease. A saviour – the *Veltro* – will come, Virgil enigmatically declares, and with the coming of the *Veltro* – who in direct contrast to the *lupa*, seeks only 'wisdom, love, and virtue' (104) – the history of Italy, which began in the defeat of Troy, will be fulfilled; the many deaths and wounds and the sacrifices of many heroes will prove to have been worthwhile. In a word, the *Veltro* will bring peace:

> Di quella umile Italia fia salute
> per cui morì la vergine Cammilla,
> Eurialo e Turno e Niso di ferute.   (106–8)

(He will be the salvation of lowly Italy / for whom the virgin Camilla died, / and the wounded Euryalus and Turnus and Nisus.)

The canto opened in the savagery and loneliness of the Dark Wood; it ends with the promised victory of humanity and civilisation. In the midst of the protagonist's confusions, Virgil has laid before him a perspective of historical and cultural continuity; and the fact that the protagonist can respond so readily and intelligently to the presence of the Roman poet is an indication of how the links in this continuity may still be forged: the bonds of a shared civilisation can be reasserted across the divisions of time – and the poet's own choice of Virgil as his guide is as much an indication of this as are the responses of the protagonist in the narrative. But the appetite for order and the discernment shown in that response still need to be trained. And here again by the end of Canto I the protagonist has been provided with the means of ordering his own experience and consciousness. In the first place, he has been invited to see his own confusions as neither more nor less than the reflection of a universal condition; this knowledge carries with it a certain philosophical gravity which is reflected in Dante's measured and steady progress behind his master at the end of the canto. More specifically, however, Virgil has shown that precise and accurate speech can be a means to control experience. *Language* now stands like a prism between the eye and the full impact of experience, grading and analysing its nature. When Virgil first appeared to Dante, the distractions of the protagonist had arisen because he could not initially distinguish between the encouraging light of the sun on the Hill and the delusive charm of the leopard. But Virgil, by his speech and presence, has laid before Dante a world of discourse in which perception and appetite are understood at one remove from their actual impact. Indeed, if the sun falls silent, then Virgil stands as a substitute for the sun, ready to irradiate Dante with his words – and he is so described in Canto XI 91, when Dante receives from him the plan of Hell: 'O sol che sani ogni vista turbata' – O Sun who heals all troubled sight. From this point on, until his disappearance in Purgatory before the true light of Beatrice, Virgil and his words will provide a continual point of reference which – if less stable than the sunlit Hill – is more responsive than any inanimate object could ever be.

To say this, however, is to emphasise that Virgil is *not* the light. He is as he himself confesses, a shade who leads Dante into a realm of ever-increasing darkness; and towards the end of the canto, the ambiguities which flow from this initial contradiction are felt especially strongly. It is at line 91 that the protagonist learns – without yet fully understanding the consequences – that his journey to salvation involves a detour and deviation through the depths of Hell; moreover, at line 125, Virgil – acknowledging himself to be one of the damned – defines his sin as rebellion against the order of the Universe which finally resides in God as literally the Universal Emperor.

So, as the protagonist moves forward with apparent firmness of purpose at the end of Canto I, there are – whether he knows it or not – questions still to be answered. Many of these *will* be answered; for it is in Canto II that Beatrice makes her first appearance – and in this regard the second canto represents a natural development from the first. Yet it may also be said that it represents no development at all, but serves rather as a second beginning superimposed upon the first. For on the sudden, as the canto opens, the protagonist is shown to be as lonely as he was in the early phases of Canto I; indeed the uncertainty and self-doubt which he suffers now are more severe than they were initially, in being now all the more conscious:

> e io sol uno
> m'apparecchiava a sostener la guerra ...   (II 3–4)

(and I alone was the one / preparing myself to undergo the battle).

Already one is so accustomed to the presence of Virgil that it comes as a surprise to hear Dante speak of himself so emphatically as 'alone'. Yet he is alone: Virgil, after all, is no more than a shade; the battle of his life has long been concluded.

At line 10 further complications arise; we become, indeed, acutely aware that the intervention of Virgil has created as many difficulties as it has solved. For the lessons in language and thought which Virgil taught in Canto I are now shown not only to be limited in their application but also to contribute actively to the distresses of the protagonist. The protagonist has become highly articulate; and just as Virgil's first words – 'non omo, omo già fui' – represented a tragic but exact insistence upon his own true position, so here the protagonist subjects himself to a process of searching self-examination. But in this case self-criticism promotes only a sense of his own unfitness for the journey ahead; at lines 31–3 Dante, conscious that he is *not* St Paul or Aeneas, asks why he should go on a journey which neither he nor anyone else believes that he is suited for. The source of the confusion that the protagonist suffers at this point is no longer the numb ignorance of Canto I but the very sophistication of mind which he has just begun to develop. He is like one 'who unwishes that which he wished and changes his purpose through thinking anew' (37–8): to any man of intellect it will seem reasonable that Aeneas as founder of Rome, or Saint Paul as a pillar of Christian civilisation, should be granted a vision of the afterlife; but that consideration alone discloses the presumption of the protagonist, and makes him fear lest his coming should be madness. In Canto I, the protagonist drew strength from his association with the heroes of his own tradition and history; now the same awareness of history leads to invidious comparisions and a sharp sense of his own unworthiness.

What, then, is Virgil to do, when his own merits and achievements have themselves precipitated the crisis? The answer is twofold. In the first place, Virgil firmly reasserts the validity of the rational and heroic principles which seem momentarily to be endangered:

'S'i' ho ben la parola tua intesa',
rispuose del magnanimo quell' ombra,
'l'anima tua è da viltade offesa;
la qual molte fïate l'omo ingombra
sì che d'onrata impresa lo rivolve ...'   (43–7)

('If I have properly understood your words', / replied the shade of that great man, / 'your soul is infected with ignoble cowardliness – / a vice which often encumbers men, / turning them back from honourable enterprise').

Calmly and cautiously, Virgil identifies the source of Dante's distress as 'viltà'; his words display both sensitivity to Dante's predicament and an understanding of how human beings in general, thinking 'too precisely on the event', are prone to undermine their own ambitions. He himself is presented as an *exemplum* of great-heartedness; he is 'magnanimo' – and the adjective is rarely applied to him elsewhere in the *Inferno*. All in all, the passage reads as the attempt of a subtle and considerate leader to summon up in his follower a Roman spirit of clear-headed courage and determination.

As we shall see in Canto III, 'courage' – in the ethical sense which emerges from Virgil's words – will continue in Dante's thinking to be contrasted with *viltà* or baseness of spirit. Indeed, the notion contributes significantly in that canto to the scheme by which Dante initially judges the damned. For the first sinners whom Dante meets are the *ignavi* who have either lived their lives in a spirit of ignobility and *viltà* or else failed at some critically testing moment to be as 'courageous' as Virgil in Canto II insists the protagonist should be. Nor are the implications of this inconsistent with the view of virtue which emerged from the *Paradiso* and from the Earthly Paradise sequence of the *Purgatorio*. The rational virtues – and the rational procedures by which virtue is cultivated – provide a plan of moral action which is not only useful but positively necessary if the mind is to proceed in an orderly way. So, in the light of Virgil's first answer, the protagonist will regain confidence in the model of heroic and rational behaviour which was made known to him at the outset through the epic history of Canto I. The poet, likewise, will rarely hesitate, from this point on, to employ in his diagnosis of sin the language of virtue which was formed and exemplified in the ancient world.

Yet this language, as we have said, is only provisional; and if that is demonstrated in the Earthly Paradise by the wholly unpredictable disappearance of Virgil, the same point is made in Canto II by the equally unpredictable leap which Virgil has to make in arriving at the second phase of his response to Dante's doubt. To reach a solution Virgil sets out upon a rationally consequential narrative of how he was appointed Dante's guide. But on the instant the narrative line is broken. In Canto I, Virgil, insisting upon the scheme of destiny which his own *Aeneid* celebrates, had spoken consistently in epic terms. Now, his language suddenly becomes the language of lyric poetry, as he evokes the name and presence of Beatrice, saying how she came from Heaven to ask his help in the cause of her servant – her 'fedele' (98):

Lucevan li occhi suoi più che la stella;
e cominciommi a dir soave e piana,
con angelica voce, in sua favella ...   (55–7)

(Her eyes shone more than a star; / and she began to speak to me in soft and gentle tones, / in an angelic voice in her own tongue).

For the first time in the *Commedia*, the actions of love are referred to; and as in the Earthly Paradise or *Paradiso* xx, so here the answers which proceed from the actions of love are beyond the power of reason to produce, and may even be obscured by such insistent rationality as the protagonist displays at the opening of Canto II. Since the problem to be solved is one which Dante's own self-questioning has aroused, the answer will lie not in argument but in the realisation that Beatrice beyond all rational expectation was concerned for his salvation. It was Beatrice, in the *Vita nuova*, who allowed Dante to see the worth that a human being could possess; and through her, as Lucia says, Dante himself departed from the common herd – 'uscì ... de la volgare schiera' (106), proving his worth by his devotion to her. The same Beatrice enters now – as God himself does in the case of Rhipeus – to ensure Dante's moral survival. These actions are as mysterious and – to human reason – as apparently arbitrary as the act of creation itself; but they reveal the vital impetus to which the individual must respond if he is to fulfil his destiny not only as a member of the human commonwealth but also as a creature of God.

It follows that in the central sequence of the canto the crucial notion is not *viltà* or any term drawn directly from the ancient world, but a notion which had come to have especial significance in the love literature of Dante's own time. This is the notion of *pietà*, implying a concern – directed or stirred by sentiment – for the needs of a particular human being. It is true that *pietà* can be related etymologically to *pietas*, the virtue which Virgil associated with Aeneas; and, as we shall see in Canto v of the *Inferno*, Dante applies this derivation very strongly in his assessment of Francesca. But in Canto II, the word is used to express not a principle of community, but a perception of the individual in his distress at the unworthiness of his own self. So Beatrice is urged by her companion in Heaven, Lucia, to hear the piteous complaint of her lover: 'Non odi tu la pieta del suo pianto?' (106) – Do you not hear how pitiable is his weeping? And it is for the pity she has shown him that the protagonist gives thanks at line 133: 'Oh pietosa colei che mi soccorse!' – O, she who came to my aid is full of pity! Indeed, pity is so great a part of Beatrice's reaction that it extends beyond her concern for Dante to include even Virgil. For, recognising Virgil's especial merits, Beatrice promises to speak to God in praise of his efforts on Dante's behalf (73–4). This may seem inconsistent with her cursory treatment of Virgil in the Earthly Paradise. But consistency would reduce love to a law. And in the context of Canto II, Beatrice's praise for Virgil momentarily liberates him from the shackles of the judgement which he has passed upon himself in Canto I line 125, as a rebel against the Emperor of creation. Speaking of God's authority in the only terms a Roman could comprehend, Virgil was driven by the logic of the case to condemn himself in the same terms; and in the *Inferno*, judgement of that sort will come to seem increasingly suspect.

The power of Beatrice, on the other hand, lies in an ability to free human beings from the consequences of their own most accurate judgements. It may not be logical that the 'damned' Virgil should be praised to the God who has condemned him. It is, however, no *more* logical that the humble protagonist – who, on rational grounds, seems even less worthy of salvation than the great 'maestro' Virgil – should be destined for salvation. That, indeed, was the very consideration which paralysed the protagonist at the outset. But it need do so no longer, provided he remembers that the ground of his worth as a creature of God must always lie beyond even the best of his powers.

The second canto offers, we have said, a second beginning to the *Commedia*, and also reveals a second principle of order on which the subsequent work will depend. Under the guidance of Virgil, the protagonist has begun to interpret his experiences and purposes in the light of reason; this order will remain, and will provide a constant vocabulary of philosophical and ethical discussion. Now, however, another order and another vocabulary have presented themselves. *Pietà* is its central term; and, just as rationality is fulfilled in the virtue of justice, *pietà* will reach its consummation in the courtesy which Dante – as the courtly lover of Beatrice – will discover in the court of Heaven. Throughout the *Commedia* Dante systematically distinguishes between the realm of justice – where law ensures social order – and the realm of courtesy – where 'law' is generated by the inward propriety of the individual, in terms of fidelity, open-heartedness, fineness of feeling and love. Consequently, the whole scene at the centre of Canto II is set in the court of Heaven, where three courtly ladies – Rachel, Lucia and Beatrice – plead the case for recognition of one who is characterised as the courtly lover – the 'fedele' (98) – of Beatrice. Notably, at the conclusion of the canto when the protagonist again takes up his journey, the language in which this new advance is expressed reflects the sources of this new beginning. In Canto I Dante represented his progress in the bare and restrained line 'Allor si mosse, e io li tenni dietro' (136). He now speaks of his wholehearted eagerness for the journey ahead: 'Tu m'hai con disiderio il cor disposto' (136) – You have made my heart ready with desire. Similarly, the canto concludes with a line which focuses attention (as does the canto at large) upon the single figure of the protagonist as he sets out on the path: 'intrai per lo cammino alto e silvestro' (142) – I entered on that steep and wooded path. The verb here is a singular, and, more remarkably, the qualifying adjectives 'alto e silvestro' render the forthcoming journey both dangerous and exhilarating. The protagonist – in keeping with the strong chivalric and courtly colour of the canto – prepares himself to face the unknown in a spirit of vigorous adventure.

II

So far, our concern has been with the aspirations and actions of Dante as the protagonist of the *Commedia*. But what of Dante the poet? One must suppose that he, like the protagonist, is also, in his poem, pursuing order and truth; and since the issues raised in the first two cantos bear directly upon Dante's conception of intellectual and linguistic procedure, one is bound to ask how the text responds – on the level of language and form – to the problems which the narrative has brought to light. In this regard, Canto II offers a particularly clear illustration of Dante's technique; for, as we shall see, its central section is formulated so as to subject Dante to a scrutiny as searching in respect of his specifically poetic activities as that which the protagonist undergoes in respect of his spiritual ambitions. As I have already suggested, the canto revolves linguistically around two distinct registers – one associated with the rational ethic of justice, the other with the courtly ethic of love. And initially it is from the interplay of these two registers that the imaginative force of the canto derives.

The second canto opens with a description of the onset of night, repeating a familiar motif from the *Aeneid*. Dante writes:

> Lo giorno se n'andava, e l'aere bruno
> toglieva li animai che sono in terra
> da le fatiche loro ...   (1–3)

(The day was departing, and the dark air / was drawing the creatures who are on earth / from their labours).

Virgil in, for instance, *Aeneid* VIII 26–7 has:

> Nox erat et terras animalia fessa per omnia
> alituum pecudumque genus sopor altus habebat.

(It was night, and over all lands deep sleep held wearied creatures, both bird and beast.)

The Virgilian qualities of Dante's lines reflect, on a textual level, the consequences of the first encounter between the protagonist and Virgil in the narrative. Compared to the opening of Canto I – which described the dazed condition of the protagonist in a subdued mode of *sermo humilis* – this passage brings into relief the heroic character of the journey which the protagonist has undertaken. Likewise, where the protagonist draws strength from the memory of Rome, so the poet draws upon the epic idiom of Virgil's Latin with a new consciousness of the dignity of his enterprise. As will be seen, this epic elevation is qualified and questioned in the course of the canto. But in the opening verses it grows only the stronger when at line 7 Dante writes an invocation to the muses – 'O muse, o alto ingegno, or m'aiutate' – which might more obviously have been expected in Canto I. Similarly, in the speeches which Dante now gives to the protagonist, he raises his style to meet the needs of the dramatic situation. The protagonist, following Virgil's example in Canto I, reviews the history of the Roman Empire and the Roman Church, attempting to determine his own place in that history. The poet, for

his part, produces a highly wrought piece of rhetoric, unlike anything the
protagonist has so far been given to speak (and too complex in structure to
allow any clear marking of line-end in the translation):

> Io cominciai: 'Poeta che mi guidi,
> guarda la mia virtù s'ell' è possente,
> prima ch'a l'alto passo tu mi fidi.
>   Tu dici che di Silvïo il parente,
> corruttibile ancora, ad immortale
> secolo andò, e fu sensibilmente.
>   Però, se l'avversario d'ogne male
> cortese i fu, pensando l'alto effetto
> ch'uscir dovea di lui, e 'l chi e 'l quale
>   non pare indegno ad omo d'intelletto;
> ch'e' fu de l'alma Roma e di suo impero
> ne l'empireo ciel per padre eletto'.   (10–21)

(I began: 'O poet guiding me, look hard at my worth and strength, before you trust me
in this arduous course. You say that the father of Sylvius while still in his corruptible
form went to the immortal realms and was in his body. But if the enemy of all things
evil did show favour to him, this does not seem unfitting to a man of understanding,
thinking of the noble consequence which was to follow from him and who and what he
was; for he was chosen in the highest heaven as father of bountiful Rome and of her
Empire'.)

It is worth recalling at this point that Dante has much to say in his
theoretical works, the *Convivio* and the *De Vulgari Eloquentia*, about the
relationship between Latin and vernacular poetry. He regards it as essential
that the vernacular poet should learn from Latin – whether in its classical or
its scholastic form; for only Latin can provide an adequate model of
rhetorical embellishment and syntactical construction. So, here, the main
features of style are rhetorical circumlocution and sustained syntactical
articulation. Thus we read 'di Silvïo il parente' for Aeneas, 'l'avversario
d'ogne male' for God; and later 'lo Vas d'elezione' for Saint Paul; so, too, at
lines 16–18 the syntax produces both the argumentative 'però' and
'pensando' and the scholastic 'e 'l chi e 'l quale'. It is, however, no part of
Dante's poetic theory to recommend an exact imitation of the Latin model;
the vernacular poet will learn the principles of art and technique from Latin
but then apply them in a way which suits his own talent and his own chosen
themes. So, in Canto II, there are pressures beneath the surface of Dante's
imitation which lead, in the course of the canto, to a thorough modification of
the Latin example.

The first of these pressures derives from Dante's insistent treatment of
first-person pronouns. In the *Aeneid* Virgil's own epic style, though often
deeply emotive, only admits an authorial presence on very rare occasions;
and certainly the Virgil who appears in Dante's poem is notably self-effacing
– we have seen how reluctant he is in Canto I to mention his own name. Yet
in the opening *terzina* of Canto II, the steady, grave and beautifully modu-
lated movement of the Virgilian night *topos* is disrupted by the self-obsessed

emphasis of 'e io sol uno'. The syntax demands an enjambement here; but that movement would be at odds with the pauses and affective stressing of the earlier phrase, and even when the transition is accomplished, the line reveals yet another first-person pronoun '*m*'apparecchiava' followed by a disturbed even abrasive repetition of 'sì':

> da le fatiche loro; e io sol uno
>   m'apparecchiava a sostener la guerra
> sì del cammino e sì de la pietate.   (3–5)

(from their labours: and I, alone was the only one / preparing myself to bear the conflict / both of the journey and of the pity.)

Likewise, when the protagonist reaches the climax of his self-doubt, Dante writes, with a fivefold repetition of first-person pronouns:

> Ma io, perché venirvi? o chi 'l concede?
> Io non Enëa, io non Paulo sono;
> me degno a ciò né io né altri 'l crede.   (31–3)

(But I, why do I come? and who grants this to me. / I am not Aeneas; I am not Paul; / that I am worthy of this neither I nor anyone else believes.)

Here, line 32 – introducing the names of Aeneas and St Paul – is especially significant. So far, the strongest similarity between Dante's diction and the diction he attributes to Virgil has been a use of circumlocution. This is consistent with all that we have said about Virgil: in Virgil's ethic, individualities are identical with historical functions, and the self is both dignified and hidden – as Virgil himself is in his opening speech – by the cloak of its historical destiny. Thus Aeneas has not, until Canto II, been designated by his own name alone; he has appeared as either the son of Anchises or the father of Sylvius. These phrases aptly define his essential role in safeguarding the continuity of the Romano-Trojan race and point to the 'pious' devotion to family which is his supreme virtue. But this cannot be sufficient: it will certainly not be sufficient in the Earthly Paradise, where the protagonist is torn from his devotion to Virgil by the sound of his own name on Beatrice's lips; and, already in Canto I, the protagonist has been heard to utter the name 'Virgil' which Virgil himself had concealed. Now, as Dante exposes the 'io' to question, he also prepares for a comparison between himself and the heroes of the past, to be drawn not in terms of historical function (in which terms he would inevitably be defeated) but in terms of existential worth, where – in the face of God's love – one name will be as good as another.

Associated with the emphasis upon 'io', there is an increasing directness and urgency of diction which, in the lines quoted above, leads to a fragmentation of phrase, and finally to the choking convolutions of 'me degno a ciò né io né altri 'l crede'. In the phrase 'io sol uno' Dante had expressed a certain heroic pride in his own solitary endeavours; but that emotion is linked, ambiguously, with feelings of fear and loneliness, and while Dante does attempt to control these emotions – by adopting the rhetorical and argumentative dignities of Virgil's speech – he fails to do so. A direct personal voice is seeking to free itself from the constrictions of rhetoric; the moment prefigures the mute self-contempt of the protagonist in the Earthly Paradise, when – unable to respond to Beatrice – he is reduced to broken sighs and sobs.

A point has been reached at which, linguistically as well as thematically, Dante must discover how to proceed. As we shall see in the final section of the canto, the upshot will be a reconciliation between the language of Virgil and the courtly language of Beatrice – a language adapted, as Virgil's language is not, to express the subtleties and shades of individual feeling. We shall find too that the third element of diction which has now emerged – the 'speaking voice' – is also allowed a place in the synthesis.

But in the central section of the canto Dante arrives at a moment of conspicuously literary self-consciousness, where the ironies and shortcomings of the procedures he adopts in the *Inferno* are exposed to examination. It is notable, in the first place, that, in seeking to reassure the protagonist, Virgil adopts a voice which the historical Dante in the *Vita nuova* has insisted is especially his own. Virgil's first response to the distress of the protagonist had been to adopt the stance of the orator, exhorting his follower to renew his devotion to the 'onrata impresa' (II 47); but now his diction is drawn from the lexicon of the *dolce stil novo*, and his attitude, like Dante's own towards Beatrice in the *stile della loda*, is one of contemplation and praise:

> Lucevan li occhi suoi più che la stella;
> e cominciommi a dir soave e piana,
> con angelica voce, in sua favella.   (55–7)

Suddenly, the master is speaking with his disciple's voice; and it is ironic that the language Virgil employs here should be, specifically, the language of a convert – of one who has discovered in Beatrice his own 'new life'. On the instant, Virgil is exposed to view, drawn from his self-effacing shadow. Like any convert, witnessing to truth, his speech begins with an 'io' as uncharacteristic of Virgil *personaggio* as it is characteristic of Canto II at large. Yet this emphasis upon selfhood can only reveal, in Virgil's case, the emptiness of a spirit condemned to Limbo: 'Io era tra color che son sospesi' (52) – I was among those who are in suspense.

It is an early indication of the freedom with which Dante will treat his own imaginative constructions in the *Inferno* that – having just asserted, by choosing Virgil as a guide, the literary and moral value of the Roman tradition – he should now suggest the primacy of a mode of writing which antedates by twenty years all the efforts he has just expended. The irony in this case is a happy one, consistent with the lesson that the protagonist here receives: the protagonist learns that the source of the confidence he seeks is the very figure of Beatrice which Dante had already identified in the *Vita nuova* as his *beatitudo*. In the same vein, Virgil's speech is, as it were, an accolade given by the master of style to the style in which Dante had originally expressed that discovery.

This interpretation points to what, at first, must appear a vertiginous suggestion: that the complications and sophistications which Dante has now begun to countenance in writing the *Commedia* might all be unnecessary, since in his early poems to Beatrice he had already grasped the simple truth he is now seeking to recover. This is to state the question more forcefully than the evidence of Canto II will bear. Yet, as we have said, it is the poet himself who, as he begins the *Purgatorio*, speaks of the *Inferno* as 'dead poetry'; and there is a sense – justifying the title of this book – in which the poetry which Dante undertakes to write in the *Inferno* is a distraction from the lines of style he has established in his earliest work and will later resume in the *Purgatorio* and *Paradiso*. The poetry of the *cantica* is 'dead' in that it disallows the simplicity, and sweetness, of a voice speaking naturally on a theme it takes to be its natural theme. Beatrice is that theme; but after Canto II she will be recalled only rarely – and sometimes in the form of parody. From now on, Dante will be constrained to perceive her, at best, indirectly through the veil of illusion that his own imagination elaborates.

The central sequence of Canto II contains, then, a celebration of past achievements on Dante's part. But it also begins a critique of his current practice in the *Inferno* (and this will strengthen as the poet advances further in his project). And in this regard two features of the sequence deserve particular attention – the treatment of dialogue and that of the 'visual image'.

From the first canto onwards, practically every canto in the *Inferno* revolves around a dialogue between Dante and Virgil or the travellers and the damned. This is evidently a principal source of drama in the *Inferno* (though there is also a drama of events); and if we can rightly speak of characterisation in Dante's work, it is clearly because of his ability to individuate voice, tone and attitude in the responses of speaker to speaker. At the same time, dialogue in the *Commedia* has a moral function: it has already proved part of the remedy which Virgil applies to the spiritual distresses of the protagonist; and the standard of considerate and responsive speech which is set in the relationship between Dante and Virgil will reveal the shortcomings of many subsequent conversations between Dante and the sinners, as increasingly these conversations resolve into quarrels and slanging-matches.

For all that, the status of dialogue is no less ambivalent, as an instrument of moral therapy, than the other resources in Virgil's rational repertoire. In Canto II, after all, the protagonist's power of debate – with himself as well as with Virgil – brings his advance to a premature halt. And shortly, in Canto v, the protagonist will be drawn into an exchange of sympathetic words with Francesca which leaves him, 'come corpo morto', apparently unable to make any further progress.

But, if words are to be used at all, is there any alternative to dialogue? There is; and it emerges as soon as Virgil begins to speak of Beatrice. For here the single voice is, first, raised in praise rather than debate, and then proceeds to conjure up not a dialogue but a choric polyphony of voices. As

Virgil records the conversation of the Ladies in Heaven, no voice is identifiable for any particular characteristic, but each is necessary if the communal aim is to be achieved.

Virgil began his speech by adopting a posture of authorial control: 'dirotti perch' io venni' (50) – I will tell you why I came. But by now his voice has shifted, initially into Dante's idiom, and then – maintaining that idiom – into a direct quotation of the words which Beatrice spoke to him: 'O anima cortese mantoana' (58). Likewise, in reporting his own reply, the words he employs are so exactly tuned to the unfamiliar tones of courtly love that he uses the Provençalism 'aggrada' to express his obedience to Beatrice's command: 'tanto m'aggrada il tuo comandamento' (79) – your command so pleases me. He also includes in his address an apostrophe drawn precisely on the pattern of Dante's own addresses to Beatrice in the *Vita nuova* and the *Paradiso*:

> O donna di virtù sola per cui
> l'umana spezie eccede ogne contento
> di quel ciel c'ha minor li cerchi sui ...   (76–8)

(O Lady of virtue, through whom alone / human nature rises beyond all that is contained / within the heaven that encircles the least).

Nor is that all. Virgil – momentarily returning to his own linguistic sphere – asks Beatrice to give *reason* – 'la cagion' (83) – why she is unconcerned at having to descend into Hell. But as Beatrice begins her explanation, her voice too – instead of maintaining a single narrative line – divides into a multiplicity of lyric voices, describing how the Blessed Virgin, out of pity for Dante, invoked the aid of Saint Lucy, who in turn pleaded his cause with Beatrice:

> Questa chiese Lucia in suo dimando
> e disse: – Or ha bisogno il tuo fedele
> di te, e io a te lo raccomando –.
>   Lucia, nimica di ciascun crudele,
> si mosse, e venne al loco dov' i' era,
> che mi sedea con l'antica Rachele.
>   Disse: – Beatrice, loda di Dio vera,
> ché non soccorri quei che t'amò tanto.   (97–104)

(She called in request upon Lucia / and said: Your servant now has need of you; / and I commend him to you. / Lucia, enemy of all cruel hearts, / responded and came to the place where I was / sitting with the Rachel of old. / She said: Beatrice, true praise of God, / why do you not help this man who loves you so.)

These lines display an orderliness quite different from that which arises in the balanced oppositions of debate. It is an order of courtliness – of single spirits responding readily one to another – expressing and serving the peculiar needs of the individual. One notes in particular the unembarrassed play of praise around the proper names – Lucia, Beatrice, Rachel. Not until the *Purgatorio* and *Paradiso* will Dante return to any comparable organisation of speech, and when he does its importance will at once be clear. The hymns and rituals of Purgatory are appropriate forms of utterance for those who know that their own distinct identities will only be established when they lose themselves in the communal endeavour of penance. Similarly in the *Paradiso* it is a natural expression of beatitude that the souls of the blessed – for all their diversity – should join together in a polyphonic singleness of purpose. But the peculiar pain of the *Inferno* – and a symptom of 'morta poesì' – is that Dante, after prefiguring this more harmonious mode, should oblige himself to reflect in his text the dangerous, harsh and importunate voices of the sinners whom he meets. And while the voice of Virgil will, of course, provide a standard of moderation and a means of authoritative control, his competence will now be questioned on two fronts: not only by the harsh voices of the sinners but also by the knowledge that there *is* a linguistic order which admits the diversity that Virgil usually resists, and transforms it into polyphony.

So the Virgilian mode of discourse is under examination here; but discourse in a still more general sense is put to the test by the second main feature of Canto II – its visual imagery. The poetry of the *Commedia* depends no less upon visual imagery for its impact than upon conceptual clarity and linguistic measure; in T. S. Eliot's phrase, Dante is a 'visual' poet, and there is already evidence of what this means in the significant contrasts drawn in Canto I between, say, the rounded Hill and the rapid *lonza*.

Nonetheless, Eliot's description is logically dubious, for, of course, a verbal construct can at best be only a substitute for things we see; and in Canto II, Dante, displaying a heightened awareness of this tension, begins to attribute to the action of the eye a spiritual and moral force superior to the force that language can command.

His concern here is not only with the lucidity of the scene in Heaven, but also with the ways in which eyes receive light, reflect light, or express concern by weeping; and the salvation of the protagonist depends directly upon the play of light and perception. Lucia is not only the patron saint of light but Dante's own patron who (he says) once answered his prayers when his eyes were failing. It is she who initiates the rescue of Dante, urging Beatrice to fix her *eyes* upon her 'fedele'; and where Virgil's words alone fail to move him, the protagonist must draw encouragement from what those words make him see. As we shall see, the narrative of the *Inferno* continually underlines the tension between the claims of the eye and the claims of speech.

For our present purposes, however, we need to emphasise that the issue concerns not only the fictional events and psychology of the work, but also the literary organisation of the text. Dante himself seems to be peculiarly aware of the 'visual properties' of his own poetry. For if his treatment of Virgil *personaggio* can be seen as a critique of the *Aeneid* itself, a property which Dante apparently considered distinctive to his own work when compared with the *Aeneid* is its greater reliance upon the evocation of graphic detail. To this I shall return in discussing Canto III; here I would

rather stress the way in which patterns of connected and contrasting images
are formed as Dante develops his story. Underlying the narrative progress of
the *Inferno*, and beneath the level of rational discourse, there is a shifting but
coherent pattern of images which asserts the grip the poet retains over his
own material. Order of an imaginative kind is constantly maintained, and the
action of the poet is located in the silent pattern of visual details which
forms, so to speak, a ground-base in the polyphony of his own text. We have
seen already how subtly Dante plays upon the primal images of light and
darkness in the opening cantos – distinguishing the light of the sun from the
'light' of discourse and the splendour of Beatrice's eyes, while also revealing
that darkness constitutes both a distraction and a protection for the immature
mind. But in Canto ii, a conclusion to the 'second beginning' of the *Inferno*
is likewise reached through a new arrangement of images, in conjunction
with a renewed stress upon the tonal characteristics and linguistic features
which have emerged in the course of the canto.

Thus in the first place both Dante *personaggio* and Virgil *personaggio*
register the language of Beatrice in their own diction. Virgil now speaks in
tones quite different from those with which he began:

> Dunque: che è? perché, perché restai,
> perché tanta viltà nel core allette,
> perché ardire e franchezza non hai.   (121–3)

(What is it, then? Why, why do you delay? / Why do you so cleave in your heart to
cowardice? / Why are you not bold and brave?)

Here, the 'perché' which so troubled the protagonist as he weighed the pros
and cons of his earlier position has been transformed into an exhortation –
and one that depends less upon rhetorical gravity than upon the exhilarating
and surprisingly personal enthusiasm of Virgil's voice. The 'viltà' is now set
against 'ardire' and 'franchezza' – words drawn from the vocabulary of
courtly and chivalric adventure: the journey of the protagonist can now be
seen not simply as an epic but as a trial undertaken beneath the eye of the
courtly 'donna'. The protagonist responds in kind. Speaking 'come persona
franca' his words possess a fullness of rhythm, where before they were
constrained by the logical and syntactical demands of the question they
posed; and every line of the speech contains a courtly reminiscence – of pity,
faithful obedience, or courtesy itself:

> O pietosa colei che mi soccorse!
> e te cortese ch'ubidisti tosto
> a le vere parole che ti porse!   (133–5)

(O what compassion she shows, she who came to aid me; / and how courteous are you
who obeyed so rapidly / the true words she spoke to you!)

Important as these alterations are, in pointing to the development of the
protagonist, they are also registered, on the level of the text, in the poet's
own activity. An illustration of this is Dante's handling of the simile at line

127:

> Quali fioretti dal notturno gelo
> chinati e chiusi, poi che 'l sol li 'mbianca,
> si drizzan tutti aperti in loro stelo,
> tal mi fec' io di mia virtude stanca.   (127–30)

(As the little flowers [bent down and closed] by the chill of night, / when the sun whitens on them, / straighten themselves all open on the stalk, / so did I in my slackened courage.)

In keeping with the stylistic elevation that marked the opening of the second canto, this simile is built upon an epic model, and may be compared directly with an image in the *Aeneid* describing the death of Euryalus:

> volvitur Euryalus leto, pulchrosque per artus
> it cruor inque umeros cervix conlapsa recumbit:
> purpureus veluti cum flos succisus aratro
> languescit moriens, lassove papavera collo
> demisere caput pluvia cum forte gravantur.   (*Aeneid* IX 433–7)

(Euryalus rolls over in death; athwart his lovely limbs runs the blood, and his drooping neck sinks on his shoulder: as when a purple flower, severed by the plough, droops in death; or as poppies, with weary neck, bow the head, when weighted by some chance shower.)

But even in the opening lines of the canto, Dante has begun to modify the epic idiom of the *Aeneid*; and in the present case there are further modifications, reflecting the stylistic advances that have been made in the course of the canto.

So in the first place, the simile directly reflects the poet's excursus into the world of courtesy. The flower image itself – associated as it is, in the present context, with the image of morning and the return of life – recalls the imagery of lyrics from the courtly tradition, where (as, for instance, in Jaufre Rudel's 'Belhes m'es l'estius e 'l temps floritz') the lover celebrates the harmony that love inspires between his own sentiments and the promptings of the natural world. In tone, likewise, the passage is quite different from the Latin model. The elegiac pathos of Virgil's lines here gives way to a delicacy and clarity of perception. Indeed, it is almost a demonstration that Dante did have the Euryalus passage in mind that he should use the flower image to portray not a death but a moment in which life is assured and regeneration begins. Behind the simile lies the faith – necessary to Dante's advance, even though Virgil cannot command it – in a miraculous power which creates and safeguards life.

At the same time, the image expresses not only sentiment and wonder but also a scientific interest, absent from Virgil's lines, in the processes of cause and effect that lead to the straightening and opening of the flower. A comparison of this description with passages from the *Purgatorio* and *Paradiso* would show how essential such precision, in the tracing of detail, is to Dante's style. It is, however, already an indication of how intelligence must act in Dante's view that the scientific sharpness of these lines should be contrasted with the obsessive questioning that hampered the progress of the protagonist in the earlier part of the canto.

Finally, where Virgil's simile, moving as it is, remains ornamental, or at least incidental, in Virgil's overall design, Dante's image has a precise function in the imaginative pattern of the opening cantos. The evocations of light and dark which the simile contains point back to the dominant motifs of the spring morning described in Canto i 37–42. And in this progressive revelation of order, even the diminutive element in 'fior*etti*', so far from being a gratuitous moment of sentiment, points exactly to the stage of recovery at which the protagonist has now arrived. Thus Dante has certainly moved on from the Dark Wood; the sterility of that wood has begun to yield evidence of life. But the diminutive refuses to allow any exaggeration. Dante is still very far from the blooming of the great white Rose of the saints in *Paradiso* xxxi. The present moment of growth is, of course, consistent with that final flowering; for the Rose is the place in which the individual is finally celebrated – in a moment of absolute courtesy – in his relation with his Creator. And it is the ultimate possibility of such a relationship that the courtliness of the second canto has revealed to Dante. Yet this revelation can, as yet, only be fragile and fleeting. Indeed, with the first words of the following canto it will at once be brought to the test.

III

In Canto iii, the protagonist and Virgil arrive at Hell; and with the words of Hell-Gate – starkly recorded, without any narrative introduction, in the first three *terzine* of the canto – one might suppose that preliminaries were at an end. Certainly, the announcement on the Gate is as conclusive as any could be, and stresses the finality of divine opposition to sin: 'Lasciate ogne speranza, voi ch'intrate'.

Yet all is not what it seems. For, in spite of these words, there is still a story to be told: the protagonist has indeed to enter the Gate; but he does so in the course of a journey to salvation which will disprove the apparently absolute implications of the inscription. The narrative embodies surprises which overthrow the binding authority of the word. And, for the protagonist, a major element in the difficulty of the episode is that – in his exceptional case – an end must be converted into a new beginning. It is that 'story' that the experiences of the previous canto have imposed upon him; and at line 14 Virgil urges him to press forward, abandoning not hope, but rather all doubt and suspicion: 'Qui si convien lasciare ogne sospetto'.

For the poet, too, the third canto is a new beginning. In the first three *terzine*, he has, on the sudden, written lines which define the central themes of the whole *Commedia* – the justice, power, wisdom and love of God in relation to the human creature:

> Giustizia mosse il mio alto fattore;
> fecemi la divina podestate,
> la somma sapïenza e 'l primo amore.   (4–6)

(Justice moved my high maker; / divine power made me, / the highest wisdom and the primal love.)

Dante must now develop a practice to deal with the implications of these words, and there has been little in the opening two cantos to suggest what this will be. As we have seen, these two cantos were introspective, even confessional, in character. To be sure, the drama of the Dark Wood has offered an outline, so to speak, of the psychology of sin, and has suggested some of the remedies that are available for human confusion. This outline will stand as a point of reference whenever the poet subsequently depicts the words, actions or thoughts of the damned: the pattern of *their* failures will always in some measure resemble the faltering confusions of the protagonist, or in some way contrast with the standards that Virgil has here established. Yet the 'hard sense' of Hell-Gate is that the *Inferno* must concern itself not only with the psychology of sin but also with the absolute and absolutely 'external' fact of divine judgement. Hell for Dante is not simply 'within us'. That would be a comparatively comforting view (one which is adopted by many modern readers and was indeed encouraged by poets of Dante's own time, notably Cavalcanti, who knew very well how self-lacerating the psyche could be). Dante, however, reserves any such comfort for the *Purgatorio*, where penitence is seen as an infallible therapy for spiritual disorder. In the *Inferno*, as the poet now realises, his concern must be to show what it means for the human mind to meet the terrible resistance of eternal certainty. Hell-Gate declares:

> Dinanzi a me non fuor cose create
> se non etterne, e io etterno duro.   (7–8)

(Before me, nothing was created, / save eternal things, and I shall endure eternally.)

In the introductory chapter, I suggested that the words of Hell-Gate were to be taken – like the problem of the noble pagan – as a test of belief in God as Creator. One might, however, express the intellectual difficulty which this represents in secular terms by saying that Dante here tests the capacity of the human mind to conceive an absolute 'otherness'. There is, as will be seen, some warrant for that in the word 'altrui' which ends *Inferno* XXVI. And there is certainly every justification for attempting to paraphrase the problems of the *Inferno* in secular terms – or terms referring to intellectual action. For that is what Dante in this *cantica* will himself constantly do. The great difference between the problem of the noble pagan as stated in the *Paradiso* and the hard sense of Hell-Gate is that Dante emphatically does not proceed here to expound the solutions – part rational, part mystic – which eventually appear in the *Paradiso*. One notes that Virgil makes no attempt to explain the meaning of Hell-Gate to the terror-stricken protagonist; and in one sense there is no need for him to do so: the 'hardness' of the inscription lies in its unambiguous clarity. Yet Virgil might well have taken his cue from this clarity, and delivered some such lucid account of sin as he offers in *Inferno* XI, or at least stressed the redemptive purposes of the plan to which Dante's own journey conforms. Instead, he urges the protagonist to put aside intellectual cowardice and plunge still deeper into the secret things – the 'segrete cose' (21).

It will shortly be seen that Virgil's insistence upon an almost agnostic – and certainly humanistic – strength of mind has a prevailing importance in Canto III. However, while Dante does not rely here upon any systematic statement of doctrine, he does respond to the implications of Hell-Gate in another way; and that response involves him attempting, for the first time in the *Commedia*, to reflect the imperatives of divine judgement in judgements of his own, passed upon other human beings and expressed in terms of his own devising. Having so far concentrated upon the sinfulness of the protagonist and upon Virgil (whose damnation is not fullly recognised until Canto IV), the poet presents the first group of damned souls that are to be found in the *Inferno* – the *ignavi*, the trimmers or apathetic time-servers, here mixed indiscriminately with the angels who, when Lucifer rebelled, could decide neither for God nor against him (38–9). Faced with the 'otherness' of God, Dante also begins in Canto III to recognise the otherness of his fellow-men; and, by the time he reaches Francesca in Canto V, he will have realised – as the introductory chapter has led one to expect – how difficult a task it is to grasp the unique identity of another human being in a scheme of general judgement. Throughout the *Inferno*, however, cantos expressing the need to judge alternate with cantos expressing the difficulty of doing so. And certainly it is important at this point that the poet should distinguish himself from the *ignavi* and repel the example of human behaviour that their lives have offered. For, as we shall see, the essential failing of the *ignavi* lies in the utter *inactivity* of their existence in time. Yet Cantos I and II have already shown how vital it is for Dante – as poet and protagonist – to act out with the utmost vigour the role which God, through Beatrice, has revealed to him.

If Dante here distinguishes himself from the *ignavi*, it is because they themselves have done nothing in their lives to show how human beings may indeed distinguish themselves, making some mark on the world – as Virgil does – by virtue of which others may know how to live. Consequently, there is a strain of contemptuous satire in the canto (justifying Eliot's allusion to line 57 in the opening section of *The Waste Land*); and this tonality will recur at various points in the *Inferno*, notably in Canto VI, and consistently in the sequence from Canto XVIII to Canto XXX. Nor is it irrelevant to emphasise here that the canto is characterised by a high degree of literary virtuosity. In constructing the first moral judgements in the *Inferno*, Dante also displays an acute consciousness of his own prowess as a poet, alluding confidently to classical texts, and creating in his own text a far more complicated play of linguistic and narrative levels than he has hitherto attempted in the *Inferno* – or elsewhere. There can be no doubt that Dante expected to make his own

mark on the world through the force of literary achievement; and it is a
further indication of how far he felt himself to be, morally, from the apathetic
ignavi that his literary activities in Canto III should be so singularly intense.

At line 22, the reality of damnation strikes the protagonist as brutally as did
the sentences on the Gate of Hell.

But what has Virgil done to prepare the protagonist for this second shock?
He has attempted, at least, to fix the distressing scene within a frame of calm
– though not informative – discourse. Taking charge of the narrative, he has
counselled a certain moral attitude: 'put aside *viltà*' (15); and he has offered
a broad definition of the state of sin: these are the 'genti dolorose' (17) who
have lost 'the good of intellect' (18). Finally – to reaffirm the value of
physical tenderness and ordinary human companionship – he has placed his
hand in Dante's own and put on a cheerful face (20).

Yet such actions as these – valuable as they are – represent nothing but a
façade. Though line 13 declares that Virgil is one who knows the full nature
of Hell 'come persona accorta', his disciplined words disguise and mask the
depth of that experience. But Dante's own words at line 22 now respond to
the impact of the scene, and in doing so they reveal a view of human nature
and of human suffering which goes far beyond the picture that Virgil offered,
even to the extent of challenging the virtues of clarity and composure that
Virgil has sought to instil in the protagonist:

> Quivi sospiri, pianti e alti guai
> risonavan per l'aere sanza stelle,
> per ch'io al cominciar ne lagrimai.
> Diverse lingue, orribili favelle,
> parole di dolore, accenti d'ira,
> voci alte e fioche, e suon di man con elle
> facevano un tumulto, il qual s'aggira
> sempre in quell' aura sanza tempo tinta,
> come la rena quando turbo spira.   (22–30)

(Here sighs, weeping, and loud cries of sorrow, / echoed through the starless air, / so
that, as soon as I heard it, I began to weep. / Strange and diverse tongues, dreadful
utterances, / words of grief, accents of anger, / voices loud and hoarse, and with them
the sound of hands / created a tumult, that circled / for ever in that air endlessly dark, /
like sand that spirals in a whirlwind.)

By Virgil's standard these lines portray complete disorder. At the same
time, they also represent a radical reversal of the image patterns that Dante
himself has been creating in the first two cantos.

First, the central feature of the chaos depicted here is *absence*. Where the
protagonist has come to depend upon the *presence* of Virgil, he now
envisages a condition which is, emphatically, *without* time or stars. And the
mention of 'time' and 'stars' points to a further dislocation. Time – under the
aspect of providential history – has been seen as an essential measure of

fruitful activity; likewise, when Dante, in Canto II, compares Beatrice's eyes to the stars, the image depends upon the power of a star to guide and give bearings to a lost traveller. Now the foundations of order in the temporal and spatial scheme are denied, and the result of that denial is sterility. In Canto I Dante's first image of sterility was the Dark Wood itself, 'savage and harsh'; here he expresses a similar notion in the image of the vortex of sand-particles, where the earth is barren dust and process is dead circularity. In this respect – as in their passivity under the hand of divine power – the damned represent a negation of the independent growth and activity which Dante had ascribed to himself in the *fioretti* image of Canto II.

Important as these contrasts are, the particular emphasis of the passage falls upon disorder in the realm of sound and language. Every line of the second *terzina* contains a reference to speech – 'lingue', 'favelle', 'parole', 'accenti' and 'voci'; on each count, coherent utterance is reduced to sheer noise. Similarly, at the end of the canto, the voices of the sinners – which might have been devoted to praise, prayer or teaching – are raised in curses against God and every lesser agent of generation or procreation:

> Bestemmiavano Dio e lor parenti,
> l'umana spezie e 'l loco e 'l tempo e 'l seme
> di lor semenza e di lor nascimenti.   (103–5)

(They cursed God and their parents, / the human race, and the time and place and seed / of their conception and birth.)

These lines identify the extent of the challenge to which Dante must now respond: the orderliness of his advance has depended upon the confidence instilled in him by the measured dignity of Virgil's discourse and the sweetness of Beatrice's words. Now the sufficiency of these resources must be in question. Language, it seems, can be at the root of sin; the battle to re-establish order must be fought on the field of language.

Dante's first move is to reassert in a strong form the value of Virgil, along with those patterns of Virgilian language and judgement that he has just shown to be insufficient. Rising to the occasion, Virgil offers a further series of categorical judgements – supported, however, by a surprising vigour of polemical tone and vocal gesture – in which he seeks to explain why the lukewarm angels should appear in the same company as the human *ignavi*: the *ignavi* are the souls who lived in the earthly life without praise or blame, and those angels who were unable to decide either for God or against him – being unworthy of glory – mingle with this 'cattivo coro' (37). The blind life – 'cieca vita' – of such sinners is so base that they envy every other kind of sinner in Hell (47–8).

One notes that, in passing these judgements, Virgil adopts a position of authorial omniscience which derives from his (retrospective) knowledge of providential history; he now knows all about the fall of the angels. But the terms of his analysis are distinctly *not* Christian in tone. On the contrary, where the Christian spirit might have spoken of humility and withdrawal from the world, Virgil's emphasis falls upon the value of fame and glory. It is true that this involves no element of *self*-glorification; indeed, his point is that the *ignavi* acted essentially 'per sé' and not for the common good, while the lukewarm angels likewise offended against an order which depends upon a shared appreciation of divine beauty by their ignominious lack of zeal. Still, the standard he erects depends upon a recognisably 'Roman' call to heroic endeavour in the common interest.

We have said that Dante is not only idiosyncratic in the judgements he passes in this canto but also, throughout the *Commedia* – and elsewhere – concerned to assert the value of classical humanism. We shall see more of this in Chapter 2. But the first step in this project is to show that, in Canto III, there are certain moral demands so immediate and so obvious to the human eye that to evade them disqualifies the sinner from any serious moral attention: those who cannot even impress themselves on the minds of their fellows fail as human beings and deserve no favour from the God who created humanity. Nor is this inconsistent with the demands that Beatrice made upon the protagonist in Canto II: her love distinguishes him from the 'volgare schiera' (II 105); and the condition of the *ignavi* is an indication of what Dante's fate *would* have been if – failing to respond to that privilege – he had succumbed to self-doubt.

Still, from all we have said, it is not to be supposed that Dante will depend only upon the Virgilian standard of morality, or of speech, or, indeed, of narrative procedure. The limitations of Virgil's position are revealed in the very lines which seem to represent the triumphant conclusion of his opening discourse. With utter disdain he declares:

> Fama di loro il mondo esser non lassa;
> misericordia e giustizia li sdegna:
> non ragioniam di lor, ma guarda e passa.   (49–51)

(The world will not allow their fame to endure; / pity and justice alike disdain them: / let us not speak of them, but look and pass on.)

The strengths of this conclusion will at once be apparent: the lucid speaker rejects the sinners as being beneath the dignity of discourse; the Roman guardian of God's historical plan – and the guide for Dante's providential journey – determines that the sinners have no place in human history and nothing to contribute to the discursive progress of the present journey. The journey must continue without any further waste of words. But, of course Dante, as author of Canto III, does anything but simply 'look and pass on'. Two-thirds of the canto are still to come, involving further description of the *ignavi* as a group (64–8) – during which, for the first time in the *Inferno*, a single sinner is subjected to scrutiny (58–60) – and finally moving into the dramatic encounter with Charon (82–128). In the course of this, Dante will indeed 'speak', and with a vehemence that is quite at odds with Virgil's restrained contempt. He will also engage the eye in a way which Virgil's cool invitation to 'look' would hardly anticipate (we shall see, in Cantos XI and xxx, that Virgil always takes a rather disparaging view of 'looking' as an activity). And finally we shall see that the narrative, so far from pretending to omniscience, depends upon effects of shock, not only in the portrayal of Charon but also in countenancing the damnation of an unnamed sinner at line 59 whose identity cannot fail to surprise the reader. The whole purpose of Dante's procedure is, it seems, to collide with the scene from which Virgil wishes to detach him, and also – ironically enough – to meet directly the solid presence or 'otherness' of sinners who have themselves done nothing to establish any claim to attention.

So, the second sequence in the canto begins with the first sight of sinners who have hitherto only been heard as they 'facevano un tumulto':

> E io, che riguardai, vidi una 'nsegna
> che girando correva tanto ratta,
> che d'ogne posa mi parea indegna;
>   e dietro le venìa sì lunga tratta
> di gente, ch'i' non averei creduto
> che morte tanta n'avesse disfatta.   (52–7)

(And I, still staring, saw a flag / which ran swirling so fast / that it seemed to hold any pause in disdain; / and behind there came so long a train / of people that I would not have thought / that death had undone so many.)

Here, for the first time in the *Inferno* there occurs an image which is so dense and vigorous as positively to resist any allegorical or conventional interpretation. The Dark Wood, the Hill, Beatrice's eyes, even Virgil, all hold the promise of some ulterior significance – even if we should avoid any premature identification. But the image of the 'insegna' is alive with its own descriptive and fictional vigour: concentrating upon a single point of attention, Dante in one line evokes a highly complex action in which rapid forward movement – 'correva tanto ratta' – is combined with a process of encirclement – 'girando'. In a small way, this description illustrates the risks that Dante has taken in writing his fiction: words may be distracted from their moral task by the fascination of the images they evoke. Yet even here, the eye – or the imagination – possesses a moral capacity of its own; for it is the eye, perceiving the parallel between the movement of the 'insegna' and the 'lunga tratta' of the damned, that will recognise in the swirling of the flag a psychological correlative for sinners who have been dragged along in futile indecision.

The eye, then, has judgements of its own; and these combine with vehemence of voice in a second more extended passage of description:

> Questi sciaurati, che mai non fur vivi,
> erano ignudi e stimolati molto
> da mosconi e da vespe ch'eran ivi.
>   Elle rigavan lor di sangue il volto,
> che, mischiato di lagrime, a' lor piedi
> da fastidiosi vermi era ricolto.   (64–9)

(These wretches, who were never alive, / were naked and terribly stung / by the gad-flies and wasps that were there in that place, / making the faces of the sinners stream with blood / which – mixing with their tears – / was gathered up [at their feet] by loathsome worms.)

This passage opens with a direct and explicit judgement upon the souls who were never truly alive. But the style of the judgement – with its tonalities of sweeping sarcasm – is very different from that of Virgil's earlier and steadier pronouncements: there is a vehemence, amounting almost to imprecision, in the description of the damned as 'dead souls'.

In the *Inferno* at large Dante will rarely, if ever, be so comprehensive in his condemnations; the moral geography of Hell, once established, will ensure a much tighter conceptual grip on the particular manifestations of sin. Yet it should be emphasised that Dante is speaking here, not as protagonist, but in his own authorial voice (the tone is one that he adopts occasionally in the more scathing passages of the *Convivio*). And, though there is little evidence of conceptual clarity in his words, there is nonetheless an imaginative precision in the passage – of a kind which will subsequently accompany his clearer judgements throughout the *cantica*. For the images of the passage – concentrating upon the notion of a 'stimulus' – mirror and distort the central images of Canto II. There, Dante spoke of how the protagonist was impelled to act by the urgent and mysterious concern of Beatrice. To Virgil, Beatrice declares: 'I' son Beatrice che ti faccio andare' (70) – I am Beatrice who causes you to go. Virgil himself is able to make a coherent response to this stimulus, while, for the protagonist, it is not too much to say that its effect is like the light of divine love 'pointing', as we saw in the introduction, upon St Peter Damian: the urgent impulse to action is the condition of Dante's election to favour in God's eyes. In the *ignavi*, however, it is merely an indication of their *viltà* that this stimulus should strike as meaninglessly as the sting of a wasp or mosquito. They, too, have been offered divine love, but like all the damned they are unready to receive it. The *ignavi* certainly fall beneath the consideration of common justice; but their condition also enacts the 'hard sense' of Hell-Gate in which, in eternity, Love is seen to be as much the maker of Hell as Justice is. The stimulus to act and – to adopt Dante's broad formula – to live life to the full, is one which falls as confusingly and painfully upon the unprepared spirit as light upon an unhealthy eye.

Here, then, judgement is supported both by a cruel aggressiveness of voice and by coherent reference to the context of images which Dante is gradually developing. And, as one comes to the climax of this central sequence, voice and eye combine with an effect of narrative surprise as Dante adduces the first 'difficult' case in the *Inferno* of a particular sinner. For between the two images I have so far considered Dante fixes his eye upon one single member of the group:

> vidi e conobbi l'ombra di colui
> che fece per viltade il gran rifiuto.   (59–60)

(I saw and knew the shade of that one / who through base cowardice made the great refusal.)

Now, it is plainly significant that this figure is not named. We have seen in the introduction how important names are as tokens of identity, and we are shortly to see this again, particularly when Dante names Francesca. In this case, the sinner – as one of the *ignavi* – has clearly done nothing to deserve a name in the mouths of his fellows; here, as Virgil certainly would understand, not even that word is fit to be wasted on the sinner. But Dante, so far from passing on, stares into the shadowy and indeterminate vacancy – 'l'ombra di colui' – where the firm outline of the 'altrui' should have been, and this act precipitates a moment both of vicious satire and of surprise, in which the reader, too, is required actively to collaborate. For the anonymity of the sinner is so emphasised as to demand that the reader break the code of Dante's fictional text and fix upon some historical figure who might plausibly deserve the contemptuous periphrasis that Dante here formulates. So far from pretending to the omniscience which he ascribes to Virgil, Dante makes a narrative virtue, if not exactly of ignorance, then of silence, offering no overview but creating by his tactics an urgent demand for a particular point of information.

It would perhaps do no injustice to the complexity of this moment to say that the reader is free to supply any name at all for this emptiness, provided that the name arouses in him as much real venom and condemnation as Dante feels for the figure at whom he is aiming. But readers are reliably informed by their commentaries that Dante has Pope Celestine V in mind. That he should attack a Pope is, of course, itself no surprise at all: Cacciaguida in *Paradiso* XVII will urge Dante to make the highest tree-tops shake with his cries of indignation; and, as will be seen in *Inferno* XIX, it is a particular aim of the *Commedia* to demand a return to those simple and pure forms of Christian behaviour that Christ himself in the Gospels appointed his Church to pursue. But the especial difficulty of the present episode is that, by any contemporary estimate, Celestine himself was a perfect exemplar of Gospel Christianity. The Church of his day was showing itself to be increasingly interested in the advancement of its temporal and territorial power as a political institution. Until his election as Pope, however, Celestine had lived as a hermit in Umbria, exemplifying the spirit of poverty which had been an inspiration to many groups on the margins of the official Church. Not unnaturally, therefore, the unexpected election of Celestine to the Papacy raised acute hopes for reform.

Why, then, should Dante condemn Celestine before all other sinners in Hell? What is the 'hard sense' of his appearance here? Historically, the answer must lie in the fact that, within months of his election, Celestine chose to abdicate. This is the 'gran rifiuto' of which Dante speaks; and Dante certainly had good reason to regret this abdication, even apart from the disappointment of any hopes he might have had for a reform of the Church.

For the Pope who succeeded Celestine – presumably having had a hand in his abdication – was Boniface VIII, who not only represented, in Dante's view all the worst ambitions of the Church but also supported the *coup d'état* in Florence which led to the poet's exile. Dante will settle his scores with Boniface himself in *Inferno* XIX and XXVII. However, as to the present – apparently eccentric – judgement against Celestine, this is not only a striking indication of how independent Dante could be in his assessment of his fellows but also an essential move in setting up the moral system of the *Commedia*. Here, as throughout the third canto, Dante unremittingly insists upon action and energy as essential features of the moral life. The fact that the abdication of Celestine led to the election of Boniface is itself a demonstration of the untold consequences that may flow from even the most understandable evasion of moral responsibility. At the point of crisis – when he himself is faced with the 'hard sense' of what Providence demands of him – Celestine appears, in Dante's view, to have yielded to *viltà*; and, in this light, the judgement that the poet constructs is borne up on all the major currents of cross-reference in the opening sequence of the *Inferno*.

Thus in particular there is a direct parallel drawn between Celestine and Dante himself. For both, it may be said, have been 'elected' to perform a certain role in the providential plan. But where Dante (in Canto II) has overcome the doubts which this election stimulates, Celestine gives way to his own doubts; and the result of his *viltà* is not only that he forgoes the opportunity to reform the Church but also that he erases – at least from Dante's memory – the example of holy living which until that point his life had offered. Thus Dante has already begun to make heroic demands upon the courage of the individual – as he will continue to do in, for instance, the episode of Pier della Vigna; and his point is clearly to insist that the dignity and ultimate well-being of humanity depend upon the willingness of individuals to display such heroism.

It follows from these conclusions that Dante himself will be left to carry on the unfinished crusade against such figures as Boniface VIII; and we shall see that this task comes to seem, in the lower circles of Hell, not only inreasinglyly lonely but also increasingly absurd in the demands it makes upon poet and protagonist. (The next Pope that Dante meets will be visible only as a pair of writhing feet.) But in the concluding episode of Canto III some foretaste of that absurdity combines with the most forceful display of dramatic and linguistic virtuosity we have so far encountered.

In the Charon episode (82–128), Dante apparently moves away from the harsh questions of moral judgement which had been raised by Hell-Gate, and also away from the historical realities which lay behind his reference to Celestine, into an area where the imagination seems free to play upon the possibilities of literary fiction or myth. As will be seen in Chapter 3, there is a continual oscillation in the *Inferno* between, so to speak, historic and mythic modes of narrative; Canto III is the first instance of that. But our concern here must mainly be to see how Dante distinguishes his own poetic

activities in Canto III from those of Virgil in the Charon episode of *Aeneid* VI.
In outline, Dante stays close enough to Virgil to illustrate how dependent he
is in his poetic as well as his fictional *persona* upon the example that Virgil
offers. Yet the passage is also a virtuoso piece of adaptation; and the details
of Dante's text which differentiate it in style from Virgil's are here consistent
with aspects of a moral and intellectual habit which distinguish the Christian
pupil from his pagan guide.

Consider firstly Virgil's text:

> Hinc via Tartarei quae fert Acherontis ad undas.
> turbidus hic caeno vastaque voragine gurges
> aestuat atque omnem Cocyto eructat harenam.
> portitor has horrendus aquas et flumina servat
> terribili squalore Charon, cui plurima mento
> canities inculta iacet, stant lumina flamma,
> sordidus ex umeris nodo dependet amictus.   (*Aeneid* VI 295–301)

(Hence a road leads to the waters of Tartarean Acheron. Here, thick with mire and of
fathomless flood, a whirlpool seethes and belches into Cocytus all its sand. A grim
warden guards these waters and streams, terrible in his squalor – Charon, on whose chin
lies a mass of unkempt, hoary hair; his eyes are staring orbs of flame; his squalid garb
hangs by a knot from his shoulders.)

Powerful as the details of this description are, they are contained and
controlled by the steady, if responsive, progress of the narrative: Charon is
observed against the background of the waves and whirlpools of Hell, and
the details of his appearance are neither more nor less impressive than any
other in the general scene of sublime gloom.

But in Canto III of the *Inferno* any such sublimity or crescendo of
descriptive detail is absent; Dante has contrived an effect which is so
violently disruptive as to be almost comic. For with the dramatic appearance
of Charon at line 82, the journey of the protagonist is thrown out of narrative
balance; and so is the narrative itself.

Hitherto, the tenor of the canto has been dictated by three factors: the
passivity of the sinners, the controlled violence of Dante himself and the
measured words of Virgil. Moreover, immediately before the appearance of
Charon, Virgil has returned to a prominence which he had momentarily lost
while Dante concentrated his eye upon the *ignavi*: in reply to Dante's
curiosity over why the spirits are so eager to cross the first river of Hell,
Virgil counsels patience. It is not the least of his virtues as a guide that he
should teach the protagonist the value of waiting – as will appear especially
clearly in Canto IX. But here the effect of his words in the orchestration of
the canto is to introduce a pause or diminution of urgency. As a consequence,
at line 79, the journey has resumed the disciplined course which has been its
essential characteristic since Canto I:

> Allor con li occhi vergognosi e bassi,
> temendo no 'l mio dir li fosse grave,
> infino al fiume del parlar mi trassi.   (79–81)

(Then, eyes lowered and full of shame, / fearing my words had offended him, / I held back from speech till we reached the river.)

Now Charon appears. The visual impact of the appearance is stressed by the introductory 'ecco':

> Ed ecco verso venir per nave
> un vecchio...   (82–3)

(And behold, there came towards us in a boat / an old man).

But Charon also makes an impression with his words; he is the first inhabitant of Hell to speak except Virgil, and his speech is at once confusing and challenging. On the one hand, he speaks with all the violence and wild frenzy that, initially, were heard in the clamour of the damned; yet in content, and in the authority of his tone, Charon seems to be an animation of the sentence on Hell-Gate, translating the imperative of the inscription into his own vocal gesticulations:

> Guai a voi, anime prave!
> Non isperate mai veder lo cielo ...   (84–5)

(Woe to you, wicked souls! / Do not hope to see the sky again).

The attack which Charon launches here is answered, first of all, on the level of language by Virgil. But Virgil is not allowed to speak in his normal tone of aristocratic detachment. His words are clear; yet clarity itself becomes aggressively 'vocal' (he is here no speaking book), so that, in declaring how God has willed Dante's passage through Hell, his speech acquires not only a vigour corresponding to Charon's own but a formulaic and almost magical resonance; he will in fact repeat the same phrase, almost as a charm, when he faces the second guardian of Hell, Minos, in Canto v:

> E 'l duca lui: 'Caron, non ti crucciare:
> vuolsi così colà dove si puote
> ciò che si vuole, e più non dimandare'.   (94–6)

(And my master to him: 'Charon, do not cause yourself such agony: / it is willed that this should be in a place / where whatever is willed can be done: so ask no more'.)

Now, one would be unlikely to find in the *Aeneid* itself either the dislocation of the narrative line which initiates this episode or the cut-and-thrust of the dialogue with which it continues. Nor, beneath the descriptive surface of Virgil's own text, are there any of the silent suggestions and currents of meaning which run through Dante's treatment. For it is by no means insignificant that Charon's words echo the words of Hell-Gate. To note this is to realise that, in one sense, he *is* a face of judgement: to those who, like the *ignavi*, have disregarded the claims of divine love in their own life-times, the energy of that Love will present itself as grotesquely and unrelentingly as Charon presents himself to Virgil and the protagonist. Conversely, Virgil's words do tacitly point to the truth which even the Gate of Hell did not openly declare: God can, after all, break his own ordinances and – when he wishes – allow a sinner to leave as well as to enter Hell. Hell is *not* under the rule of such functionaries and petty despots as Charon.

The dialogue is alive, then, with ironies and pressures, and the same is true to an even greater extent in the second phase of the episode, where Dante focuses upon the visual image of Charon. As Charon's 'lanose gote' fall silent before the force of Virgil's words, the text shifts, following the pattern which has governed the canto at large, from a concentration upon language to a concentration upon images:

> Caron dimonio, con occhi di bragia
> loro accennando, tutte le raccoglie;
> batte col remo qualunque s'adagia.   (109–11)

(Charon the demon with eyes of glowing coal / beckoning to them collects them all together: / he beats with his oar whoever is slow.)

But within the image – as within the picture of the 'sciaurati che mai non fur vivi' – the energies of the poet's moral sense meet and balance the disruptive energies of his own imagination. Charon is now unambiguously designated 'dimonio'. But more importantly, in speaking of Charon's 'occhi di bragia', Dante resuscitates the line of light imagery – with all its moral associations – which began with the first vision of the Hill, reaching its climax in Canto II with the contemplation of Beatrice's eyes. Charon, indeed, can be seen as a parody of Beatrice and all she stands for: he enters the narrative as surprisingly as she does; he is as much a revelation of infernal energy as she is of celestial activity; and, where Beatrice's eyes shine like stars, Charon's 'occhi di bragia' are from the first no less the focus of attention, as they burn wildly through his woolly cheeks against the dull background of the swamp:

> Quinci fuor quete le lanose gote
> al nocchier de la livida palude,
> che 'ntorno a li occhi avea di fiamme rote.   (97–9)

(Then the woolly cheeks were quiet / of the helmsman of the liver-coloured marsh / who had wheels of fire around his eyes.)

It is unimaginable that Virgil, either as author of the *Aeneid* or as *personaggio*, could countenance such a play upon the essential principles of his text. Yet it is here that Dante's characteristic virtuosity resides. This virtuosity is no less moral than it is artistic; and that same coherence of structure which makes the parody possible is an indication of a control which may, indeed, be unlike the control that Virgil *personaggio* exerts, but which has the resilience to meet such unpredictable displays of energy as Charon represents. In a similar way in the final moments of the canto, Dante again modifies the great image of the autumn leaves which he has drawn from Virgil's work (where it resonates with pathos and the 'tears of things'):

> Come d'autunno si levan le foglie
> l'una appresso de l'altra, fin che 'l ramo
> vede a la terra tutte le sue spoglie,

> similemente il mal seme d'Adamo
> gittansi di quel lito ad una ad una.   (112–16)

(As autumn leaves are lifted off, / one after the other, till the branch / sees all its spoils on the ground, / likewise the evil seed of Adam flung itself one by one from that shore.)

Yet Dante's simile is no more simply pathetic than was his treatment of the *fioretti* image in the previous canto; and one reason why it is not is that it stands in significant correspondence with the *fioretti* passage, a correspondence which introduces a moral charge wholly absent from Virgil's passage. In Canto II, the protagonist may appropriately be compared to the 'fioretti', as he begins spiritually to grow and move of his own accord. But the 'leaves' of the damned souls are unnatural products of the 'mal seme d'Adamo'. They will take no further part in the processes which govern the cycle of the natural leaf; they are beyond order, life and activity – and that is precisely the condition of sin which Dante has sought to define from the first lines of the canto.

As if this were not enough, the canto ends with a wholly un-Virgilian 'terribilità': as the 'courteous' Virgil – ''l maestro cortese' (121) – quietly speaks of the 'ira di Dio', the poet Dante produces a terrifying *coup*:

> Finito questo, la buia campagna
> tremò sì forte, che de lo spavento
> la mente di sudore ancor mi bagna.
> La terra lagrimosa diede vento,
> che balenò una luce vermiglia
> la qual mi vinse ciascun sentimento;
> e caddi com l'uom cui sonno piglia.   (130–6)

(When he had finished, the dark terrain / shook so violently that [the memory] of how fearful it was / still bathes me in sweat. / The tear-soaked ground exhaled a great wind, / flashing forth a crimson light / that overcame all feeling in me; / and I fell like a man who is seized by sleep.)

The virtuosity here lies in the violence. But the violence of the conclusion exactly balances that of the opening *terzine*, establishing an order and pattern in its own energies; and if that is paradoxical, it is no more paradoxical than that Virgil should speak as calmly and composedly as he does here of the 'ira di Dio'.

Violence – focused in judgement upon the image of sin, and expressing the response of the individual to that image – will continue throughout the *Inferno* to be as much a part of Dante's procedure as the clear analysis of sin represented in the moral plan and geography of Hell. Such violence is inseparably linked with the view that Dante takes of the relationship between the Creator and the rational constructions of his creatures; and by now it will be apparent that there can be no order in the created world – at least no order which is not the product of pride – that fails to admit or respond to its impact. It is for this reason that, whenever one speaks of order in the *Commedia*, one must also speak of action.

By the end of the *Inferno*, it will be apparent that Dante is prepared to allow
a certain violation even of the rational scheme of judgements which he
himself has been constructing in the course of the *cantica*. Thus the pattern
of surprises that has already begun to reveal itself in the movement from
Canto II to Canto III will be extended to cover the transition from the first
cantica to the second, as Dante issues into the wholly unexpected world of
Purgatory. One sees already, however, in the treatment of Charon – as later
in the treatment of Minos – how ridiculous the face of judgement can be: in
Charon, Dante envisages a reduction to absurdity both of the words of Hell-
Gate and of his own zeal in driving his fellow-men to judgement.

But turning now to Canto IV, one finds that Dante is far less concerned – at
least on the surface – with the harsh judgements and vicious distinctions that
the words of Hell-Gate required him to pursue. In a complete (and in its own
way surprising) change of tone, Dante moves from a mode of satire and
vehement decision to one of muted and contemplative celebration. The
protagonist, entering Limbo, encounters the souls of the noble pagans, in
particular the souls of those poets and philosophers who founded the culture
of the classical world. These are associated in Limbo with the souls of
unbaptised children, as if to assert that, even without the benefit of revelation,
human achievement can be wholly pure. And Dante, so far from attempting
to translate into direct action the sentences of divine power, now concentrates
upon the human word. Words – and the intellectual constructions they
embody – are here taken to be a source of honour; and Dante is concerned
quite explicitly to demonstrate that classical literature is one source at least of
his own poetic prestige. Even more than the Charon episode, the poetry of
this canto draws upon classical models; and there is little sense that Dante is
seeking to 'outdo' his models as he had begun to in the previous canto.

Community, and not discrimination, is apparently the theme of Canto IV.
Yet in the end this *is* a canto of appearances. Judgement and violence may
not be as evident as they were in Canto III and will be again in Canto V. But
– secretly – stress, difficulty and judgement are still present. For one thing,
this is the first canto in which the protagonist enters a geographically defined
area of the moral plan (24). It is characteristic of the canto that this
confinement should be made to seem less like imprisonment than like
protective custody against the surrounding confusions of damnation. But the
problems that the canto faces are located precisely here. For, finally, it will
be seen that the weakness as well as the strength of the culture and
community that Dante here celebrates is to introduce a shield or mask
between the individual and the violent realities both of God and of human
wickedness.

Of the intellectual difficulties represented in Canto IV, enough has been
said in the introductory chapter. On that score, one need only emphasise how
consistently the thematic pattern of Cantos III to V anticipates the pattern

which, in the *Paradiso*, is revealed by Dante's treatment of the noble pagan: moving from the problem of the relation between the human mind and the reality of God, Dante now looks at the implications of that ultimate relationship for one's understanding of the relationships that human beings may create among themselves, in the institutions of justice and culture. He will then proceed in Canto V to deal with the claims of love in the relation of individual to individual. But in Canto IV these patterns are almost wiped away by the lyrical pause which is here introduced into the otherwise urgent progress of the narrative. The task of the poet and the protagonist will be to grasp the difficulties which lie beneath this lull. The reader, likewise, will have to see that, within a canto which seems so different from those in its immediate context, the inexorable logic of that context – expressed in images and thematic cross-references – continues to operate.

The fourth canto is dominated by two great episodes: the meeting between the two travellers, Dante and Virgil, and the 'bella scola' of classical poets (79 *et seq.*); and the approach of the travellers to the dome of light (67 *et seq.*) which serves as sanctum and stronghold for a group of pagan spirits who have distinguished themselves in many fields of action. Both episodes provide powerful images of community, and both affirm that, in intellectual terms, the human community need acknowledge no boundaries of space or time. Literature and culture annihilate such limits, and this is particularly clear in the 'bella scola' sequence.

As Virgil and Dante are proceeding through Limbo, discoursing on the theological nature of the place, their eyes are arrested by a dome of light in the distance, and then from the direction of the dome they hear a great cry that penetrates the intervening murk of Hell:

> Onorate l'altissimo poeta;
> l'ombra sua torna, ch'era dipartita.   (80–1)

(Honour to the exalted poet; / his shade, having left us, has now returned.)

This cry is uttered in unison by four great poets of antiquity – Homer, Horace, Ovid and Lucan – and it celebrates Virgil's arrival at the place he left in order to guide the protagonist on his journey, and to which he will return when the task is done.

Now, there could be no more powerful image of the unanimity that Dante thought was possible in human culture; and it is an indication of the spirit that produces such a culture that Dante should, at one and the same time, take pride in being accepted as a sixth member in the company of the ancients (102) while allowing, humbly enough, that it is Virgil to whom the company defers. Nor need one emphasise how completely the greeting here contrasts with the clamour that met the travellers in the previous circle of Hell: order is momentarily restored in the firmness and harmony of the classical voice.

Yet already there are tensions at work. Compare, firstly, the implications of the cry with those of the words on Hell-Gate: the two are different to the extent that one is an immovable inscription, the other a voice responsive to human need and impulse, but they are similar in their relation to Dante's journey. For where Dante has had to understand that the all-inclusive words of Hell-Gate do *not*, strictly, apply to him, so now he must realise that, by virtue of his destined journey, he both is and is not a member of the 'sesta compagnia'. So, at the conclusion of the canto, the company will diminish as Dante and Virgil leave it. But the opening words of the episode no more allow for such a passage than the words of Hell-Gate; they emphasise only the happiness of 'return'. It is this charmed circularity that Dante must go on to violate.

Consider, too, the contrast between the ceremonial cry and the elegiac sighs, at lines 25–7, that tell the protagonist he has arrived in Limbo. These sighs are surely the truer expression of the state of Limbo, which, throughout, is represented as a condition of lack and regret; in that vacancy, the pomp of the cry echoes as no more than a brave illusion, concealing the hard reality that inarticulate lamentation more accurately expresses.

Of the dome of light, much the same might be said. But it is of course the voice of Virgil *personaggio* that principally channels these tensions throughout the canto.

At first, there may seem to be no element of concealment in Virgil's procedure. It is he, after all, who prompts the protagonist (31) to ask who the sighing spirits of Limbo actually are; and implicit in that prompting is the great question of why the noble pagan should be damned. One has only to compare, however, Virgil's delicate treatment of the issue with the overwhelming directness that Dante musters in *Paradiso* xix – 'ov' è questa giustizia che 'l condanna' – to recognise Virgil's limitations. For where the *Paradiso* dares to pose the question in its sharpest possible form, Virgil produces an exemplary piece of exposition. Adopting the same attitude of authorial omniscience as he first assumed at Hell-Gate, Virgil proceeds logically from the accepted fact of the Incarnation to the assertion that in the light of that fact there must be a distinction between those who lived before and those who lived after Christ:

> e s'e' furon dinanzi al cristianesmo,
> non adorar debitamente a Dio:
> e di questi cotai son io medesmo.   (37–9)

(and given that they were alive before Christianity, / they did not worship God in the way that they rightly should; / and I am myself one of these.)

But this is to evade completely the tragedy of the individual case. Though his stress on 'io' – unusual in Virgil's speech – draws attention to himself, Virgil can do no more than locate himself in the pale category of the innocent; it is left to the protagonist to raise a more searching question. The protagonist has not spoken until now; Virgil has answered his own propaedeutic question.

Nonetheless, his tight-lipped teaching inspires in the protagonist the emotional response which he himself represses:

> Gran duol mi prese al cor quando lo 'ntesi,
> però che gente di molto valore
> conobbi che 'n quel limbo eran sospesi.   (43–5)

(Great sorrow gripped my heart when I heard what he said, / for I knew that many people of great worth / were kept there adrift in Limbo.)

Here, as later in the Francesca episode, the eye of pity brings to light questions that the explanatory word only glosses over; and now the protagonist demands a more precise answer:

> Dimmi, maestro mio, dimmi, segnore ...
> uscicci mai alcuno ...   (46, 49)

(Tell me, master, tell me, my lord ... / did any one ever escape from here).

In response Virgil begins his account of how at the Harrowing of Hell, Christ – or, in Virgil's words, 'un possente' – did rescue the patriarchs of Israel from perdition, consequently demonstrating that the words on Hell-Gate are not, for all their apparent authority, as accurate an expression of the reality of God's action in eternity as they might appear. But this clarification, though it answers to the letter of the protagonist's question – in that it allows that 'someone' did escape from Hell – leaves wholly unanswered the tacit demand, contained in the use of the terms 'maestro' and 'segnore', for an assurance that the noble and pagan might be saved. Indeed, Virgil's words have, in a sense, only served to indicate on this score why he has *not* been saved. For his account of the Harrowing of Hell is characteristically cast in the language of history, beginning with 'Io era nuovo in questo stato ...', and ending with 'E vo' che sappi che, dinanzi ad essi, / spiriti umani non eran salvati' (52–63). But this is the language of simple sequence, and it both shields and excludes Virgil from any view of the mysterious relation between history and the creative power of Providence. For the Christian, the sequences of temporal history are initiated, governed and finally brought to an end in judgement by a divinity capable of interrupting his own designs. One has seen this in the Rhipeus and Trajan episodes of *Paradiso* XX, and one will see its implications for Dante's own narrative procedures in the ninth canto of the *Inferno*. But Virgil is allowed to make no response at all to the surprise of the event; nor do his words register the violence of Christ's action. Significantly enough, Virgil identifies Christ only as a 'powerful one' – 'un possente' – though Virgil is attuned to the claims of honour and fame, the power of Christ is wholly beyond his competence to define.

From this point on, the question of the noble pagan is put aside as Dante begins to construct the superbly rich and mythic scene of his encounter with the great spirits of Limbo. There are few moments of greater solemnity in the *Commedia* than Dante's portrayal of the spirits with their steady and grave eyes – 'occhi tardi e gravi' – speaking little, in subdued and gentle tones: 'parlavan rado, con voci soavi' (114).

But still there are disconcerting reverberations beneath the monumental dignity of these lines. And the most troubling of these arise from the proximity of the canto to the canto of the *ignavi*. For while, on the one hand, the noble pagans stand in direct contrast to the *ignavi* – by virtue of their devotion to the common cause of learning and culture – there *is* nonetheless a similarity between the two groups, in that neither is capable of responding to the extreme claims that divine power makes upon the soul. In the light of the triumphal and liberating action of the 'possente', it is as much a limitation as a virtue on the part of the noble pagans that they should maintain measure, and that their countenances should be so composed as to display neither happiness nor sadness: 'sembianz' avevan né trista né lieta' (84). Lyrical as this line may be, its lyrical attraction begins to wither when one hears behind it an echo, at least, of the moral condemnation which described the lukewarm angels as those who 'non furon ribelli / né fur fedeli a Dio …'.

Nor is that all; for as the grip of, so to speak, Dante's moral lyric begins to tighten and emphasise the pattern of cross-reference, so other echoes are heard which recall the earliest phases of Dante's journey. Indeed, for a moment it seems that Dante's journey is leading him back to nothing but a subtler form of the Dark Wood:

> Non lasciavam l'andar perch' ei dicessi,
> ma passavam la selva tuttavia,
> la selva, dico, di spiriti spessi.   (64–6)

(We did not cease to travel forward because he was speaking, / but still passed through the wood – / the wood, I say, of thronging spirits.)

One notes the attention that Dante draws to the phrase 'la selva, dico …', and the meaning of this 'wood' is tragically clear in the paraphrase: the heavy presence of innocent but unenlightened humanity is itself as much an encumbrance to the spirit as the evident and bitter disorder that he himself experienced in his own initial, unenlightened state. Then, here, just as in Canto I, the protagonist sees ahead of him a manifestation of light:

> Non era lunga ancor la nostra via
> di qua dal sonno, quand' io vidi un foco
> ch'emisperio di tenebre vincia.   (67–9)

(We were not far advanced from the place / of my slumber, when I saw a fire / defeating a hemisphere of darkness.)

Like the Hill of Canto I, the hemisphere of light – won against the resistance of the darkness – is an image of order, inspiring the traveller with a sense of direction and hope; for it is, of course, within this hemisphere that Dante discovers the great spirits of antiquity. Yet the differences between the two images are no less acute than the similarities; where the Hill receives and reflects a play of light from beyond its own contours, the fire in the dome seems to be self-generated, and is free only within its own containment and confinement.

Then finally there is the catalogue of names that ends the canto. This epic feature firmly emphasises the difference between the pagans and the *ignavi*; it is indeed through the honour of their names in history (76–8) that the noble pagans are given a dispensation to dwell in the court-like 'castello' (106) of the dome. By the same token, however, neither their names nor the manner of their life in the 'castello' can bear comparison with the picture of true courtliness that Dante has already provided in Canto II, where the names and voices of Lucia, Beatrice and Rachel interweave in a demonstration of concern over Dante's fate. Here, the scene is almost entirely static, and names – so far from locating an object or capacity for concern – fix their owners in statuesque but immobile dignity. On this score, too, the pagans are directly contrasted with the figures, named earlier in the catalogue, of Hebrew patriarchs who were torn from Hell by the 'possente'. For in that group, too, Dante has emphasised activity – in the form of growth and generation; the dominant feature of the series was its stress upon the bond of family, beginning with Adam, 'il primo parente' (55), and moving to 'Israèl con lo padre e co' suoi nati' (59). In the list of noble pagans, however, Dante is concerned not with action or growth but with singular characteristics and separate talents. So Dante passes in silence through this gallery of – often seated – heroes; for once he does 'look and pass on', and his poetry enacts the same procedure, producing name after name until finally one name is no more distinct from any another than one voice was distinct from another in the cry that welcomed Virgil:

> I' vidi Eletra con molti compagni,
> tra ' quai conobbi Ettòr ed Enea,
> Cesare armato con li occhi grifagni.
>   Vidi Cammilla e la Pantasilea;
> da l'altra parte vidi 'l re Latino
> che con Lavina sua figlia sedea.   (121–6)

(I saw Electra with many companions, / among whom I recognised Hector and Aeneas, / Caesar armed, with eyes of a falcon. / I saw Camilla and Penthesilea; / on the other side, I saw the King Latinus / sitting with Lavinia his daughter.)

But the narrative demands that Dante, at least, should be distinguished from this group:

> La sesta compagnia in due si scema:
> per altra via mi mena il savio duca,
> fuor de la queta, ne l'aura che trema.
>   E vegno in parte ove non è che luca.   (148–51)

(The company of six diminishes to two: / my wise leader takes me by another way, / out of the calmness into the trembling air; / and I came to a place where there is nothing that shines.)

Here, forcing himself out of the protective 'hemisphere', Dante enacts not the role of the communal voice, but the violence of the 'possente'. Distinctions, after all, need to be made (and by the time he reaches the twenty-fifth canto of the *Inferno* Dante will openly claim to outdo in poetic skill at least two of the poets – Ovid and Lucan – who here accepted him into the 'sesta compagnia').

So the way is clear for another change of poetic direction; and after this mythic interlude, where moral issues were present only in the secret undertow of the imagery, Dante will shortly return to the sphere of history and moral responsibility, setting before himself one of the most difficult cases of all – that of his contemporary, Francesca da Rimini.

V

In Canto v, Dante's explicit theme is the sin of lust; as he writes at line 39, the sinners here are those who have subjected reason to the inclinations of the appetite: 'che la ragion sommettono al talento'. This is the first time in the *Inferno* – or elsewhere – that the poet has set himself to deal with a failing which has a recognisable and central place in the Christian diagnosis of sin. And there can be no doubt that, in one aspect, the canto is intended as a contribution to the Christian analysis of sexuality and appetite. With a subtle orthodoxy that only slowly reveals itself, Dante's emphasis falls firmly upon the freedom we enjoy and the responsibilities we should exercise in directing our human lives to their proper or distinctively rational end. In this respect, the canto develops themes which were first introduced in the portrayal of the protagonist in Canto i. It also provides a dramatic preparation for discussion later in the *Commedia*, where – for instance, in *Purgatorio* XVI – Dante, as we have seen, will show how individuality resides in acts of responsible free will, and require that this responsibility should extend so far as to govern the subtlest shifts of instinct and nature. So, in Canto v, Francesca, who dominates the second half of the canto, is shown to be subject to judgement in the light of the gifts of reason and free will which God has given her; and no mitigating circumstances – such as the possibility that she was beguiled into an unwanted marriage or that her husband's crime, in murdering her at the discovery of her adultery was greater than her own – is allowed to detract from her sentence. Francesca, like all the lustful, appears to assert her own selfhood. She is the first figure in the *Inferno* to do so. But she is confidently condemned by a standard which ascribes to selfhood a richer meaning and a fuller value than she is able to comprehend.

Though the sins of the flesh have provoked many a strident reaction, in Dante's time and since, the fifth canto, even in its moral aspect, is far from joining unreservedly in that chorus. For one thing, Dante, as we shall see, does not regard instinct and appetite as corrupt in themselves. Moreover, it is clear from the position of the lustful in the hierarchy of Hell that, while lust may be the most obvious target of all for the Christian moralist, it was for Dante himself among the *least* serious rather than the gravest of offences. Much worse is to follow.

Yet none of this will appease the many readers who have been disturbed to find Francesca condemned here for her love of Paolo. And while it is necessary to see that Dante has reasons for his judgement of Francesca, it is, I think, equally necessary, if one is to understand the themes and the poetic character of Canto v, to recognise that Francesca is, in the fullest sense, a difficult case.

For instance, on the level of theme, the difficulties of the episode may well lead one to consider whether lust itself is a sufficient reason for Francesca's damnation. In fact, in the perspective of the whole *Commedia*, that cannot be the case. The sin of lust does not disqualify Arnaut Daniel from a place in Purgatory (*Purg.* XXVI), while the courtesan Cunizza and the whore Rahab both find their way to Paradise (*Par.* IX). At the very least, we should allow that Dante's subject in Canto v is not merely sexual appetite but rather the far more complex question of love. As we have suggested in the introduction, Francesca in the course of the canto employs for her own purposes the word 'amore' which Dante will himself need to use in the final *terzina* of his poem; and in that light, Francesca may stand condemned on intellectual grounds for distorting a notion which is central to Dante's enterprise.

But even that may not take us far enough. Rather, we must say, I suggest, that the underlying subject of the canto is the *individual* in its relationship both with God and with its fellow-creatures. This would explain in part why the canto is so commonly – and so rightly – felt to be a disturbing one. The question of sexuality in itself inevitably stimulates a consideration of the relationships between one person and another, and represents, furthermore, the most familiar and pressing cause of moral crisis. But Dante has here recognised and sharpened the impact of these considerations. Not only is he concerned with the triangle of passion between Francesca, Paolo and the murderous husband Gianciotto; he is also concerned with the relationships that are established between one person and another by virtue of and in terms of rational judgement. For Dante, of course, God himself must be regarded as one such 'other' being; judgement, in this canto, may be seen as a reassertion of the relationship between God and the individuals he has created. In that regard, Canto v builds directly upon the thematic foundations of Canto III. But the canto is also clearly designed to display and investigate the reactions of Dante himself – in passion and in judgement, in common humanity and in heightened poetic excitement – to the 'otherness' of Francesca.

With this we come to the place of the canto in the scheme of the *Inferno* and in Dante's understanding of his own moral position and his responsibilities as a poet. Yet this does nothing at all to diminish the difficulties of the case. On the contrary, they are nowhere more acute.

Here, as throughout the preceding cantos, the protagonist is attempting to act in an orderly way; and we might suppose that the principles on which his advance depended were by now firmly established. Yet at the end of the canto he is left in a condition of apparently total disorder and inactivity, falling 'like a dead body' under the influence of Francesca. The first phase of

the *Inferno* ends not with a climax, but, seemingly, with the defeat and even
extinction of the protagonist. The work of Virgil and Beatrice appears to
have come to nothing, and even that rediscovery of his own self which began
when the protagonist 'found himself again' within the Dark Wood has, one
might think, at this point been reversed.

As for the action of the poet, we saw, when we first looked at this episode
in the Introduction how intense the task is which he has set himself here.
Taking love as his subject, he has to deal with the motive and impulse which
initiates all action – and which in the last canto of the *Commedia* will also be
revealed as the principle of all order in the created universe: 'l'amor che
move 'l sol e l'altre stelle'. He has to find words in which to order and
enforce this understanding; but these words cannot be Francesca's. Nor can
he safely rely, it appears, upon the language characteristic of his own earliest
activities as a poet, successful as those activities may have been; the
language of the *stil novo* is vitiated by the use which he allows Francesca to
make of it.

So much we have said already. But the linguistic and intellectual critique
which is conducted in the fifth canto is not simply retrospective; for if Dante
here realises that a crucial part of his present enterprise is to judge the case
of individuals, he also realises that this must involve an unprecedented
artistic interest in the evocation and construction of what we now call
'character'. Neither Dante nor, for that matter, any of his exemplars – in
classical or in vernacular poetry – had ever concerned themselves with the
representation of the individual as such. Yet in the moment of making this
departure, Canto v raises the question of whether Dante can simultaneously
evoke and judge a figure such as Francesca. He has attempted something
similar in his handling of the disruptive images of Canto III; the present case
is only the more complex.

There are, then, as every reader knows, ambiguities and tensions
particularly in the second half of Canto v. These are not accidental; they are
central to Dante's thought and procedure. They are also of crucial importance
in the design of Canto v itself. And to see how Dante realises these tensions
in his text, we need to look just as closely at the first half of the canto as at
the Francesca episode. For in the first half Dante not only summarises the
themes and achievements of the previous four cantos, but also prepares the
ground, in imaginative as well as ethical terms, for his judgement of
Francesca. Yet by the conclusion of the canto even these careful preparations
have been shown to be inadequate.

The canto opens with a strong stress upon the orderliness of Hell, upon its
geography and disposition:

> Così discesi del cerchio primaio
> giù nel secondo, che men loco cinghia
> e tanto più dolor, che punge a guaio.   (1–3)

(So I descended from the first circle / down into the second, which encircles both a lesser space / and so much greater suffering that it provokes a wail of lamentation.)

This is the first time that Dante has produced any clear indication of the plan of Hell: at the opening of Canto III, he registered the confused impact that the region made upon him; he now adopts a neutral, even mathematical, stance, tracing an inverse relation between diminishing space and increasing pain.

The geography of Hell corresponds to the broad categories of sin which Dante explains in Canto XI, and which, in each circle, he employs in his initial – categorical – judgements upon the sinners. But at line 14 a further, and rather disturbing, image of judgement emerges in the figure of Minos. He is pictured as the guardian or charge-hand of the machinery of Hell, commissioned to activate its function: his particular role is to allocate each sinner to an appropriate circle; where, hitherto, the damned have been presented more or less indiscriminately in crowds or groups, now each in turn – 'a vicenda' (14) – must come before Minos for sentencing.

Minos, then, identifies the central theme of Canto v: the judgement of *particular* cases. But already certain tensions have begun to show. For the scrutiny which Minos brings to bear upon the individual conscience is directed not by love but by a judicial concern to place the individual being in the class for which his sins have crudely qualified him. This is an inevitable aspect of judgement, but it is also potentially absurd and cruel; and this absurdity is expressed in the pantomime with which the judgements of Minos are pronounced – his tail, winding round him, indicates the number of the circle to which the sinner must go. Like Charon, Minos is drawn from Virgil's underworld, and like Charon, he represents a violent, comic vision of how judgement will appear to those who, in their lives, have not loved justice. But the comedy is not directed only at the sinners, nor at the solemn inadequacies of Virgil's scheme: Dante himself is mocked, for the actions which Minos performs are themselves a representation of the kind of judgements which Dante has performed – as illustrated by the opening of Canto v – in planning the moral geography of *Inferno*.

The representation of Minos here contrasts directly in style with the eventual treatment of Francesca. This itself is an indication of how the canto will develop: the delicate realism with which the voice of Francesca is evoked, as compared to the comic portrayal of Minos, clearly points to a resistance between the complexities of her case and the principles by which she has to be judged. There are, however, more subtle modes of judgement to be considered than Minos represents, and these too are developed in the first half of the canto.

First – as in his judgement on the *ignavi* – the poet, while offering a clear view of the sin in question, embodies his interpretation of it in a context where its implications are enriched and its connection with the imaginative development of the sequence emphasised. In line 39, Dante may speak of the sinners as 'i peccator carnali che la ragion sommettono al talento' – the carnal sinners who subject reason to inclination; but he locates this definition between two contrasted schemes of, so to speak, diagnostic imagery.

The first of these describes the especial punishment of these sinners:

> La bufera infernal, che mai non resta,
> mena li spirti con la sua rapina;
> voltando e percotendo li molesta.   (31–3)

(The tempest of Hell, which never abates, / sweeps the spirits along in its grip, / fretting them sorely as it rolls and beats upon them.)

Here, nature itself – seen in wind and weather – is a force to be feared; and so it is, too, when, in the human being, 'ragione' is subject to 'talento': like the Dark Wood of Canto I, the 'bufera infernal' is an image of wild and self-contradictory forces threatening the refinement of which – as Francesca herself will soon show – human nature is certainly capable.

In the second set of images, Dante advances a more complex view of natural instinct. These comprise the four *terzine* which compare the sinners, in a pair of virtuoso similes, to starlings and cranes:

> E come li stornei ne portan l'ali
> nel freddo tempo, a schiera larga e piena,
> così quel fiato li spiriti mali
>   di qua, di là, di giù, di sù li mena;
> nulla speranza li conforta mai,
> non che di posa, ma di minor pena.
>   E come i gru van cantando lor lai,
> faccendo in aere di sé lunga riga,
> così vid' io venir, traendo guai,
>   ombre portate da la detta briga.   (40–9)

(As starlings are borne up on their wings / in the cold season in wide-spread, thronging flocks, / so were the spirits of the damned borne on the blast / that drew them one way then another, up and down. / They have no hope, to strengthen them, of any pause or lesser pain. / As cranes go singing their lamentations, / forming of themselves a long line in the air, / so I saw them come, with their long-drawn cries of misery, / the shades borne on that toiling torment.)

Dante here allows to the birds themselves a freedom to pursue their instincts which cannot be allowed to the sinners he is actually describing. There is a discrepancy between the two terms of the simile; the birds, moved only by 'talento', possess an orderliness and innate purpose which human beings might also possess, provided they make the distinctions between themselves and the birds of the air. 'Talento' as such is not condemned here, but rather the misapprehension of the role of 'talento' in human nature.

Nature, then, offers one standard of judgement. But civilisation provides another. The fifth canto at large is much concerned to investigate the value of civilised or refined conduct – particularly in the area of linguistic refinement – while at the same time displaying the peculiar dangers that such refinement may involve. The poet himself has begun to shift into the realm of linguistic virtuosity in the sequences of similes we have just discussed: one notes the skilful mimesis of line 43, the sharply drawn contrast between *broad* throngs of starlings and *lines* of cranes, and also the elevated rhetoric of pathos in the recurrent gerund (46–7). As for Francesca, it will be a central irony of the episode that (to judge from the phrases Dante gives her) the forces of her nature should be channelled into formulaic phrases and the rituals of literary fashion – as if she herself were capable of no freer action than the birds in their instinctive capacity for patterned flight. Civilised she may be; but in her, civilisation collapses once more into conditioned reflex.

In preparation for Francesca's appearance, Dante, at lines 51–64, begins to reconcile the implications of the two preceding cantos, where the value of classical civilisation has been strongly stressed, and where the failure of the *ignavi* to contribute to the common culture has been roundly condemned. Now Dante presents a roll-call of 'more than a thousand figures' – of whom some eight are named – which parallels the muster of 'spiriti magni' in Canto iv: the exploits of lovers are, it appears, as much a part of our history as the achievements of philosophers and heroes. And certainly the lover will not be absolved from leaving a mark on the world merely because of some absorption in private sentiment. Thus the emphasis of the passage falls upon three women who were themselves rulers as well as lovers; and in every other case mentioned here the lover is one who has in some way precipitated disruption in society – be it Achilles, Tristan or Paris. The issue is clearest in the instance of Semiramis:

> fu imperadrice di molte favelle.
>   A vizio di lussuria fu sì rotta,
> che libito fé licito in sua legge,
> per tòrre il biasmo in che era condotta.   (54–7)

(She was an Empress over many tongues. / By the vice of lust she was so flawed / that she made her licentiousness legitimate / to take away the blame into which she had been led.)

Here an Empress has so far forgotten her public responsibilities as to make the law depend upon her own vices. Dante here clearly insists – as also in the cases of Dido (61–2) and Cleopatra (63) – upon the notion of rational responsibility. And it is the same insistence that emerged in the judgement of Celestine; lust is a form of abdication, with untold consequences in the social ambience. For Dante, sin, it appears, is never a private matter; and even in dealing with the most private of sins, he would hardly have understood if one concluded, as we tend to now, 'Well, that's their affair'.

Lust, then, is viewed against a demand that human beings should, in all their dealings, assume and protect their rightful natures, pursuing courses which do not detract from their dignity and value as social beings. And while Francesca is certainly not a ruler – the scene she recounts is, distinctly, a domestic interior – it is plain nonetheless that Dante applies to her the same strict requirements he applies to Dido or Semiramis.

Two features of the second half of the canto demonstrate this: the first is the use of the word 'pietà' – which is, apparently, the key to the emotional tonality of the canto; the second is the effect which Francesca has both on her lover Paolo and on Dante as protagonist.

Throughout the canto *pietà* or one of its cognates is applied to the reactions of the protagonist at Francesca's plight. And it is plain from Francesca's own use of the word that she envisages – and receives – a response of unrestrained sympathy, as when the protagonist cries: 'O anime affannate, / venite a noi parlar, s'altri nol niega' (80–1) – O weary souls, / come now to speak to us, if no other forbids. Yet in the broad context of this and preceding cantos, *pietà* must also suggest a quite different sense. From the first, Dante has been constructing a view of heroic action built on the model of Virgil's *Aeneid*; and considering not only that he refers to Dido in line 61 of Canto v but also that Francesca herself belongs to the 'schiera ov' è Dido', it is impossible to ignore the connection between the Italian *pietà* and the Latin *pietas*. In the Virgilian sense, *pietas* is the cardinal virtue of the hero Aeneas – a virtue challenged in his encounter with Dido and signifying a selfless devotion to the interests of others in family and society. Yet Francesca is allowed to weaken this word – as she will, later, the word *amore* – by a use which, on her own confession, is out of keeping with the wishes of the 're de l'universo' (91), the *King* of the Universe. Moreover, her whole story of adultery is one in which sentiment and soft feeling – *pietà* in her sense – so far from defending kin actually precipitate fratricide.

The *pietà* of Francesca also fails against a definition of the term which emerges from *Inferno* II. There *pietà* was that concern over the fate of the individual which Beatrice shows towards Dante. The word in that canto retains its emotional colouring, and does not deny the sentiment which may animate such concern. Yet, in the end, Beatrice's own *pietà* will be displayed in the fiercely critical attitude she adopts towards Dante in the Earthly Paradise; and there it becomes clear that her 'pietade acerba' (*Purg.* xxx 81) – bitter pity – is aimed, as it was more gently in Canto II, at ensuring the integrity, salvation and survival of her devotee. Where Roman *pietas* protects the unity and endurance of the state, Beatrice's *pietà* protects the unity and endurance of the individual in his inner being: so that, even though Dante is struck dumb in the Earthly Paradise and brought to the point of swooning, Beatrice's purpose is to make him 'raise his beard' and demonstrate his mature strength. This is precisely what the *pietà* of Francesca – acting alike upon the protagonist and Paolo – does not do. Both are reduced to a condition of utter inactivity by Francesca – or the *pietà* she arouses. Paolo indeed is not even named; he is simply a marginal figure, weeping while Francesca speaks and indicating, by his very insignificance, that selfhood cannot be assured in the terms that Francesca expresses.

Francesca, then, is measured against the most essential principles of Dante's thought, in regard both to responsibility and sentiment; and, in large part, it is the first half of the canto which provides that measure.

For all that, the full force of the episode, in a literary as well as a moral sense, will only be apparent if, turning now to the second half, one considers how Francesca is herself allowed to test the principles on which Dante has so far proceeded. We have seen how Dante constructs his judgement; we must now examine how, from point to point, he cuts himself adrift from the moral moorings he has established in the first half, actively creating the ambiguity or difficulty which surrounds the figure of Francesca.

The first sign of an altered direction occurs when the protagonist, at line 71, speaks of the sinners as 'donne antiche e ' cavalieri', and is moved to pity at the thought of their damnation: 'pietà mi giunse'. These phrases at once establish a distance between Virgil and the protagonist; for they are drawn directly from the culture of courtly and chivalric love which was shown, in Canto ii, to represent a moral as well as a historical advance over the culture that Virgil exemplifies. To see the lovers of antiquity as 'donne e cavalieri' is to suggest already that some aspects of their lives would be invisible from the viewpoint of Roman principle – and that Dante, as the lover of Beatrice, will be especially sensitive to these aspects. The *terzina* signals a moment of peculiar danger. Dante is distanced from Virgil, and that is inevitable: on matters of sensibility he must proceed alone, without direct assistance from Virgil (in the Earthly Paradise the author of *Aeneid* iv will prove a wholly inadequate guide to the demands of love). Yet the confusions to which Dante – now as in the Earthly Paradise – will be subject are powerfully displayed in the fact that the language of courtly love is not only the language of Beatrice in Canto ii, but also the language natural to Francesca: the book that Francesca and Paolo are reading as they kiss – the book which Francesca describes as a 'pandar' (137) – is itself a tale of the *Lady* Guinevere and the *Knight* Lancelot.

Already, then, by line 72, with its evocation of *pietà*, one is alert to a tension in the terminology of the canto. And similarly at line 82 the imagery of the sequence – employed so far to maintain a moral balance – becomes disturbingly equivocal. Dante here introduces a third in the sequence of bird similes; and, responding to the protagonist's invitation, Paolo and Francesca approach:

> Quali colombe dal disio chiamate
> con l'ali alzate e ferme al dolce nido
> vegnon per l'aere, dal voler portate;
>   cotali uscir de la schiera ov' è Dido,
> a noi venendo per l'aere maligno,
> sì forte fu l'affettüoso grido.   (82–7)

(As doves called by desire – / with wings raised and steady – [come] to the sweet nest / carried by their will through the air / so did these leave the flock where Dido is, / coming to us through the malignant air, / so strong was the feeling cry.)

In the previous images of this sequence, the 'stornei' and the 'gru' had been emblematic of the order which nature can maintain – when proportion is kept – even in the realm of 'talento'. But the *colombe* image defeats the expectations aroused by the series. It is true that when, with hind-sight, we compare this passage to others describing doves from the *Purgatorio* and *Paradiso* there are, even here, moral discriminations at work. But if, in its immediate context, we expect the image to yield an emblematic sense, we shall not only be disappointed but further confused: the emblematic associations of the dove point to peace and hope against the swirling flood of the 'bufera infernal'. And if we allow that these associations indicate the highest truths of Christian grace, then – so far from establishing any moral stability – we raise the question with which Dante and his culture were characteristically most concerned: that of how to distinguish between the manifestations of divine love and those of human love.

Thus two profoundly ambiguous passages frame the first words of Francesca (88), and these words themselves are unlike any others that Dante has so far heard – or written – in the *Inferno*, precisely because they too are ambiguous:

> O animal grazïoso e benigno
> che visitando vai per l'aere perso
> noi che tignemmo il mondo di sanguigno.   (88–90)

(O living creature, gracious and kindly, / who comes through the black air / visiting us who stained the world with the taint of blood.)

There is nothing here of the challenging clarity attributed to the words of Charon and Minos, nor any of the carefulness and epic solemnity of Virgil's opening speeches. (The comparison with Virgil will weigh increasingly against Francesca.) The only available model for the exchange between the protagonist and Francesca is the dialogue in Heaven between Beatrice and Lucia. Not only is the language of these two conversations drawn from the same courtly register, but in both cases the suggestions of voice – rich with shared emotion and drawing upon a fund of common understanding – are as significant as any statement of meaning. Here, as in Canto II, a choric play of vocal gestures is instituted – as when Dante's opening words, 'O anime affannate ...' are echoed in Francesca's opening (and only very subtly different) 'O animal grazïoso e benigno'. By the time Dante utters Francesca's name, at line 116, this mode is fully established. The name itself is unlike any other we have heard. Dido, Semiramis and Cleopatra were names surrounded by an aura of legend; Beatrice and Lucia possessed an allegorical resonance. But Francesca is the name of a historical contemporary – so much so that it may be said to express an interest in the fashions and culture of thirteenth-century France. As when 'Dante' is named in the Earthly Paradise, so here 'Francesca' evokes an immediate and particular presence, dense with as yet unanalysed possibilities.

The function, then, of the central sequence of the canto is to generate the ambiguities that run throughout its second half. And it is important at this point to pause in our examination of the text, and to consider why, in attempting a general interpretation of Canto V, one should not prematurely undo the work that its central sequence has achieved.

In the first place, to do so would be to ignore that the order which Dante seeks in his analysis of Francesca's case is *active* in nature, and equally to underestimate the activity required of the reader in Canto v. The application of the criteria which the poet has by now developed is as subtly shifting as the personality which his imagination attributes to Francesca. Intelligence can be as delicate in its responses as emotion or sense, and Dante's text is constructed so as to insist that it should be. Indeed, the reading it requires may be contrasted directly with the way in which Francesca and Paolo read the romance of Lancelot and Guinevere, allowing themselves to be drawn, by an increasingly urgent bond of shared suggestions and gesture, into obliviousness:

> Per più fïate li occhi ci sospinse
> quella lettura, e scolorocci il viso.   (130–1)

(And many times [that reading] held and brought our eyes together, / taking the colour from our faces.)

On these grounds, Francesca will be judged by her inability to conduct an accurate analysis of her moral condition. Certainly the words that Dante ascribes to her reveal a mentality with no grasp at all of its own complexities. In short, she lacks self-knowledge. And this represents a failure of activity on her part exactly comparable to the failure displayed by the *ignavi*: like them, she is unable to offer an intelligent defence or affirmation of the identity she possesses. Not only does she reduce the protagonist and Paolo to a condition of *viltà*, she herself is the fullest representation of what *viltà* has come to mean in the opening cantos.

In one respect, then, to diminish the ambiguity of the Francesca episode is to diminish the exercise of the very activity that the canto is designed to illustrate. In another respect, it is also to mistake the *subject* of the canto; for, as we have suggested, Canto v is not simply concerned with the rights and wrongs of Francesca's fate. In confronting the question of love and lust – and attempting to distinguish between them – the canto at large sets out to examine the ways in which we rule our own selfhoods and deal with the identities of our fellow-creatures. So lust is seen not simply as a submission of reason to intellect but as a desire to possess or even extinguish the identity of another being. Love, on the other hand, begins to be seen here as an acceptance of the ambiguity and opacity which must surround any creature, outside its simple relation with the Creator. To be sure, the principle of love is not explicitly declared in the canto; we must wait for the Earthly Paradise for that. But, in effect, the attitude of imaginative attention that the poet displays in his creation of Francesca – and correspondingly the imaginative excitement which most readers of the canto rightly experience – is itself a manifestation of the love which Francesca herself does not display. In this light, it is Francesca who seeks to simplify both herself and her relation to Paolo, defining it, as we shall see, solely in terms of the possession or mastery that an impersonal power of *Amor* exerts upon them both.

Against the tempting simplicity of the view embodied in Francesca's words, Dante's narrative continues to represent a subtly active response to the ambiguities of identity. Canto v is a point of intersection in a network of comparisons between Francesca and all the figures who have so far appeared in the *Inferno* – Virgil, Beatrice, the *ignavi* and, pre-eminently, the protagonist. These comparisons certainly assist in the moral analysis of Francesca's case, but the converse is also true: seeing the similarity between Francesca and Beatrice or Francesca and Virgil, one is bound to acknowledge that a penumbra of uncertainty always surrounds the assessment one person makes of another.

If the relationship of person to person is seen here to be uncertain, then so too is the relation of the self to its own self. Francesca has a way of putting this, in the pathetic words

> Nessun maggior dolore
> che ricordarsi del tempo felice
> ne la miseria; e ciò sa 'l tuo dottore.   (121–3)

(There is no greater pain / than to recall a time of happiness / in a time of misery; and that your teacher knows.)

In life, the very passage of time is likely to render the human being discordant with itself; and this discord will be magnified when the field of human action embraces the eternal as well as the temporal. Nor is this a problem which Francesca alone has to face. The canto, as we have said, represents an attempt on Dante's part to re-examine the achievements of his own earlier poetry in the light of his present enterprise. Recognising, in his picture of the defeated protagonist, the possibility of his own incoherence, the poet challenges himself to arrive at a conception of love – and a language appropriate to it – in which his earliest understanding of the emotion in the *Vita nuova* can be reconciled with a systematic appreciation of truth.

In Canto v, then, identity itself looks uncertain and ambiguous. But Dante's consideration of the question extends to an examination of the intellectual and linguistic means by which we formulate conceptions of ourselves; and here too he recognises the fallibility or delusiveness of the resources available to us. After all, to speak of 'lust' is to speak of how untrustworthy emotion and sense can be as expressions of selfhood, and of how they may disfigure the human object on which they are trained.

Dante seems to have understood the role that imagination and imaginative literature play in establishing selfhood. The modern reader will know that identity is a cultural as well as a moral phenomenon; and Francesca herself – portrayed as a reader of Romance literature – gives voice to a closely comparable understanding, allowing her kiss of love to be a fashionable reflection of the longed-for kiss between Lancelot and Guinevere.

What, then, of Dante's own narrative which frames and contains Francesca's? By now, he too has moved far away from the authoritative mode of epic history, which underpinned his opening cantos, into the more equivocal realm of private fiction. The question which runs through the canto is whether the language of fiction, invention and imagination can be reconciled with the language of morality. So alongside the line of Francesca's story there is another story to follow, which is Dante's own account of himself as protagonist. One finds here the self-critical analysis which Francesca does *not* perform. And the very indirectness of the analysis – cast in the form of a fictional encounter – proves to be a strength: Dante's own narrative allows the potential distortions that Francesca's voice introduces, and thus admits the inherent complexity of the relation of self to self. It is precisely this that neither Francesca nor any of the damned is ever shown to do.

Consider the two speeches that Dante allots to Francesca. In the second of these two – where Francesca describes the events leading to the 'sol punto' that defeats her – the narrative procedures exemplified by Francesca's account are subject to particular scrutiny. But in the first speech, comparable attention is paid to the limitations of the language in which Francesca makes her first approaches to the protagonist. Let us return now to the text, and examine these words.

The speech from line 88 to line 107 divides into three parts: an initial address to the protagonist (88–96), a *terzina* describing Francesca's place of birth (97–9) and a discourse on 'Amor' (100–7). In each of these phases, the tonal characteristics of Francesca's voice are defined with progressive subtlety; but, beneath the claims upon attention that her voice exerts, analysis reveals other voices expressing a moral claim that the speaker either ignores or seeks to repress.

The first phase of Francesca's speech establishes a speaking voice which is delicate, fluent and also capable of considerable sophistication in sustaining a long and complex periodic sentence:

> O animal grazïoso e benigno
> che visitando vai per l'aere perso
> noi che tignemmo il mondo di sanguigno,
>   se fosse amico il re de l'universo,
>   noi pregheremmo lui de la tua pace,
>   poi c'hai pietà del nostro mal perverso.   (88–93)

(O living creature, gracious and kindly, / who comes through the black air, / visiting us who stained the world with blood, / if the King of the Universe were our friend, / we should pray to him for your peace, / since you have pity on our perverse ill.)

We have already seen that the word *pietà* can yield meanings counter to Francesca's intentions. But the very fluency of her words conceals and erodes these implications. And the same may be said of her treatment of the ideas of God and prayer. The phrase 'il re de l'universo', elsewhere, could have been the starting-point for a discussion of our human relation to the source of being and truth; here the dexterity with which Francesca manages the conditional clause relegates such considerations to the margins of her own consciousness: it is left to the reader – with a knowledge, gained in Canto III, of how the Love and Justice of God created Hell – actively to realise what it means for the King of the Universe *not* to be 'friendly' to his creature.

In the case of the word 'prayer', the logical impossibility of prayer in the circumstances which Francesca describes is admitted; but the word is still used for its affective force, as part of a courtly gesture towards the protagonist. We need not say that Francesca knows what she is doing; after all, *not* to know in this case is itself incriminating. But – as part of the analysis which Francesca fails to perform – we need to recognise that personal voice and logic are here at odds.

In the *Purgatorio*, true prayer will reconcile logic with the voice of the individual; the human creature declares its needs to the only power which can, in reason, satisfy these needs. Equally, prayer in the *Purgatorio* is seen as a communal activity, in which the voices of the penitents conjoin, as do the voices of the living and the dead. In Canto II we have seen a premonition of this; and in spite of all the surface similarities between Francesca's discourse and Beatrice's, it will already be apparent that she fails on one count because, in misapprehending the nature of prayer, she cannot carry to a conclusion the rich polyphonies of speech which her voice appears to promise.

But the most immediate cause of her failure is that she is incapable of the sort of speech which Virgil has shown to lie within the competence of any rational creature. When Francesca invites sympathy for what she admits to be her 'mal perverso', her words betray (and threaten to propagate) a confusion over her present condition in Hell – as if that could admit of any sympathy. Yet it was an exactly similar confusion that Virgil avoided in the clear distinction: 'Non omo, omo già fui'. He may speak with a certain pride; but this is pride in the place he occupies in the scheme of Roman history, demonstrated through a clear account of the facts and circumstances of his birth. Even fact, however, is not safe from the single-minded mastery of Francesca's sentiment; the river Po – designating her birthplace – is presented as a mirror for her own predicament and feelings; she describes it descending to the sea in an image which is at once sexual – with its connotation of urgency and subsequent peace – and also bitterly ironic in the restless environment of the 'bufera infernal':

> Siede la terra dove nata fui
> su la marina dove 'l Po discende
> per aver pace co' seguaci sui.   (97–9)

(The land where I was born sits / by the sea where the Po goes down / to have rest with the streams that follow it.)

The differences between Francesca and Virgil, as speakers and story-tellers, will come to prominence again in the second of the speeches. But in the final phase of the first speech, the voice which plays against Francesca's own is that of the historical Dante:

Amor, ch'al cor gentil ratto s'apprende,
prese costui de la bella persona
che mi fu tolta; e 'l modo ancor m'offende.
　Amor, ch'a nullo amato amar perdona,
mi prese del costui piacer sì forte,
che, come vedi, ancor non m'abbandona.　　　　　(100–5)

(Love, which is quickly taken to the noble heart, / took him with the beauty of this bodily form / which now has been taken from me (it still grieves me how). / Love who allows no loved-one not to love, took me with so strong a pleasure in him / that, as you see, even now it does not abandon me.)

By now, the sophistication of Francesca's voice is a recognisable characteristic, and it is sustained here in a repetition of the word 'Amor' which is at once highly mannered and charm-like. Yet at the conclusion of the speech another voice breaks through; and this voice is Francesca's own, expressing a direct hatred for her murderer which cannot be controlled or shaped by any literary protestations of love. Suddenly, where the first two *terzine* have gracefully run their three-line course, the last verse splits at its second line into a broken and harsh expression of detestation:

Amor condusse noi ad una morte.
Caina attende chi a vita ci spense.　　　　　(106–7)

(Love led us both to a single death. / Caina waits for the one who put out our lives.)

As Francesca breaks off, one realises how far her words have been from the paradigm of Dante's own *stil novo*. For the sweetness of that style resides not only in melody but in the satisfaction which any writer knows on discovering his own natural voice in the written word. Thus the *Vita nuova* is, in part, an account of how Dante learns to deal with his own initial incomprehension at the impact of love, and of how he finds a language in which to express the full range of his early experience.

But if Francesca's voice loses rather than gains in sweetness, this also points to the difference in terms of moral content between Dante's pronouncements and hers. For when Dante declares in the *Vita nuova* that 'Amore e 'l cor gentil sono una cosa', his words are not only lyrical but also assert an intellectual position from which the poet will seek to defend the integrity or the 'holiness' of the human being. In the *Vita nuova*, love and the noble heart are indeed 'one thing'; which is to say that love is not – as Francesca conceives it – an overmastering or suprahuman power; it is, rather, absolutely identical with those motives of rational and honourable behaviour which render the human being 'gentil' or noble. In this light, love is the core of our moral personality. And thus it is scarcely facetious to say that Francesca is condemned for the comma she places after the word 'Amor'; for it is there that she begins to detach love from its hard-won location in the 'cor gentil', explicitly treating this apparently independent force as an excuse for irresponsible action rather than as the ground of dignity and sensitivity. This certainly is evident in what follows. For nothing is less like the Dante of the *Vita nuova* than the repetition in Francesca's speech of *prendere* and its cognates, surreptitiously paralleling the repetition of 'Amor'; love is seen violently to 'take' the heart, and 'take' the lover. Love here has ceased to be a 'mover' or an action and become an invitation to passivity.

By now, Francesca has shown herself to be deeply contradictory. She claims attention for the plight of an individual apparently caught in the machinery of Hell. Yet the love of which she speaks allows no place to the individual being in what, for Dante, would be the fullest sense of that phrase. Nor does it allow one human being to enter into any significant relationship with another. The silence of Paolo, distancing him from the talkative Francesca, is one reflection of this. But there is another, which points to a final difference between Francesca's words and the the words of the *stil novo*. For the *stil novo* is, in the *Vita nuova*, the product not only of individual talent but also of tradition, a style in which, at each new manifestation, many voices – past and present – converge and intersect. Thus, throughout the *Vita nuova* Dante admits the influence of his 'primo amico', Cavalcanti, while in 'Amore e 'l cor gentil', he alludes directly to the opening lines of the poem 'Al cor gentil repara sempre amore' by his near-contemporary, Guido Guinizelli.

But Francesca (though drawing upon the tradition in her own words) gives no new expression to the possibilities of that tradition, but rather reveals how easily these possibilities may be reversed and mortified. Her drama, so far from revealing or admitting other presences, seeks only to absorb them into her own monologue – and then, finally, is broken by the unmanageable voice of her own hatred.

Where the voices that resonate in Francesca's opening speech are the voices of lyric poets and philosophers, those which sound in the second are the voices of storytellers.

We shall see more in Chapter 3 of what it means for a character in the *Inferno* to tell a story. But here, as in many subsequent encounters, Dante treats the procedures of narrative which the sinner exemplifies as measure of their moral competence. And the standard he employs in this estimate is the standard of his present procedure; for he too, 'nel mezzo del cammin', is writing an account of his own moral endeavours, and, as we shall see, he progressively recognises the narrative of the *Commedia* to be a mode of moral organisation in which he can show an understanding of the origins and direction of his own experience. In Canto v, however, the inadequacies of Francesca's account are revealed principally by a comparison between her procedures and those adopted by Virgil, the only other storyteller who has so far appeared in the *Inferno*.

The opening *terzina* of the speech makes direct reference to Virgil, as *personaggio* and also – probably – as poet. The 'dottore' is clearly the Virgil who guides Dante through Hell and who in Limbo may well mourn the irrecoverable happiness of the temporal life; and the sentiment which Francesca expresses may itself be drawn from the *Aeneid* – or if not the

Aeneid then from classical or scholastic sources. But in both aspects of the *terzina*, the strategy of Francesca is already clear; and, so far, it is identical to that which she adopted in the first of her speeches. She seeks to associate Virgil with herself – to appropriate his voice, and to conceal whatever wisdom the apophthegm may contain beneath the pathos of her own characteristic tones. Just as the realities which surrounded her at her birth are transformed in the light of her later experiences, so, throughout her narrative, she will be one who 'speaks and weeps', offering to her audience not the neutral and authoritative words which characterise Virgil's narrative but the fluctuations of 'dubbiosi disiri'.

But the same *terzina* also indicates a radical incoherence in the scheme of her narrative. At the outset she confesses that she is not now as once she was; and in her case the statement has a particular force. Not only is the division of which she speaks irreparable – being underlined by the division between time and eternity – but the pathos that the story generates actually depends upon a sharp, though passive, realisation of this division. The story of Aeneas, on the other hand, is a story of how divisions can be overcome. Virgil's theme is the unity which human beings may establish in and through the historical scheme; and the author as well as the hero of the *Aeneid* demonstrates, in his narrative, the ethical and intellectual means by which that unity can be realised anew. So, beginning with the defeat of Troy, and ending with the promise of the *Veltro*, Virgil's narrative demonstrates a confidence in the ability of human beings to comprehend past, present and future, in thought as well as in historical action.

But the pathetic narrative of Francesca challenges this position as effectively as Dido challenges Aeneas himself. From the first, the characteristic of her narrative – beneath the plausible tonalities of her linguistic personality – is a decided dislocation of rhythm. On Francesca's own confession, this tale proclaims a fatal ignorance of the forces that intersect in her life and finally deny its continuity. So the first scene she describes shows Paolo and herself sitting alone without 'any suspicion' of what is subsequently to occur between them. Moreover, the very activity in which they are at first engaged – the reading of the romance of Lancelot and Guinevere – is acknowledged to be an evasion rather than any engagement with the scheme of time: they are reading as a pastime, 'per diletto'.

But the book has rhythms of its own which slowly possess the lovers; nor can they deny the disturbing, unspoken demands of their own natural bodies. The forces of word and nature act across the space between them – space empty of moral measure or control; and Francesca's narrative registers precisely this. Even the tonalities of her voice are less important now than the syncopated rhythm in which the steady attention of the lovers to the book is interrupted by the intermittent meeting of eyes:

> Per più fïate li occhi ci sospinse
> quella lettura, e scolorocci il viso;
> ma solo un punto fu quel che ci vinse.   (130–2)

(And many times it held and brought our eyes together, / that reading, and took from our faces the colour. / But it was one single point that overcame us.)

In this passage, even the eyes and shifts of countenance are accorded a life of their own, as if, detached from the whole person, they could act independently of the whole. So, too, Francesca interrupts the natural progression in the last line of the passage to offer an anticipation of the climax – which comes when the 'sol punto' overcomes the two lovers. In one respect, the 'sol punto' is nothing but the simple consequence of the actions which have preceded it. But, so far from tracing that consequence, Francesca represents the 'punto' itself as the agent. And now the inadequacy of her narrative reveals itself most significantly. Attempting to focus upon the elusive force of that critical moment, Francesca makes a new beginning:

> Quando leggemmo il disïato riso
> esser basciato da cotanto amante,
> questi, che mai da me non fia diviso,
>   la bocca mi basciò tutto tremante.
> Galeotto fu 'l libro e chi lo scrisse:
> quel giorno più non vi leggemmo avante.   (133–8)

(When we read that the long-desired smile / was kissed by such a lover, / this man, who will never be divided from me, / kissed my mouth, all trembling; / the book was a Galeotto and so was he who wrote it: / that day we read no further in that book.)

Here, at one and the same time, there is coherence and incoherence. Francesca's words tend to emphasise the fragments of the body – in the sophisticated but revealing phrase 'il disïato riso', and in the climactic emphasis upon the 'bocca tutto tremante'. At the same time, in the *terzina* which precedes this violent conclusion, the rhythm is that of irresistibly erotic excitement. And the conclusion to which that rhythm leads – the 'sol punto' – is one that Francesca cannot control or analyse. For her, the 'sol punto' is the point of annihilation. Yet in the perspective of the whole canto, this can also be seen as the point at which all the forces which Francesca either cannot or does not wish to understand finally converge. Natural instinct and literary suggestion combine here with the murderous passions that inspired the actions of her husband and, equally, with the divine decision that seals her eternal fate in the critical moment of passing from time to eternity. So, too, the final *terzina* of Francesca's speech is characterised by the same violence of tone which first disrupted the surface of her words in the phrase 'Caina attende chi a vita ci spense'. The last three lines are each decisively isolated one from the other; 'Galeotto fu 'l libro ...' is a gesture of almost comically evasive fretfulness; her phrase 'quel giorno ...' sounds suggestive, charged with unrealised significance.

As Francesca's narrative fails, Dante, as author, is left to provide a conclusion which is sufficient to acknowledge and control the complexities that the canto has aroused. And the narrative procedures exemplified in the last four lines illustrate a pattern which, as we shall see, underlies many of the most powerful cantos in the first *cantica*.

The conclusion reads:

> Mentre che l'uno spirto questo disse,
> l'altro piangëa; sì che di pietade
> io venni men così com' io morisse.
> E caddi come corpo morto cade.   (139–42)

(While the one spirit was saying this, / the other wept, so that out of pity / I fainted as though I had died / and fell as a dead body falls.)

Tonally, these words are in keeping with the sequence they conclude; certainly there is no question of Dante's returning to the harsh diction and imagery of the opening lines. Nor does the poet enforce the categorical judgement which he had prepared in the first half of the canto. On the contrary, he emphasises the similarity and reciprocity of the three protagonists, Francesca, Paolo and himself as character. The opening word of the *terzina* – 'mentre' – is crucial in this respect; there is no distance or division between the three figures; the stress falls on simultaneity of action and response.

It is here that the difference between Dante's action as poet and Francesca's action as narrator begins to reveal itself. For, first, the 'mentre' *does* register the poet's attempt to give a coherent account of the 'punto' which he has reached; the *terzina* admits – as Francesca's phrases do not – the complexity of the moment, envisaging how, in the moment of crisis, one scheme of events may impinge on another, just as the actions of one human being may impinge on those of another. Against the fragmentation which always threatened in Francesca's speech, Dante here prepares an active but orderly conclusion. It is equally important that Dante should promise – in the phrase 'sì che' – to trace a line of cause and effect in his account. Francesca, too, has offered to speak of the 'prima radice / del nostro amor' (124–5); but she then proceeds to cloud the line of analysis by insisting that the discussion of that 'radice' will be undertaken so as to satisfy Dante's 'affetto' (125).

In short, the conclusion of the canto enforces a tonal synthesis while at the same time introducing the language of self-critical analysis. And in this respect the function of the last four lines is consistent with that of the canto as a whole. For, as we have seen, the canto is a piece of thorough self-criticism on Dante's part – as well as representing the point of connection between his earlier treatment of *amore* and that which he will pursue in the *Commedia*. And nowhere is this more evident than in Dante's account of his own emotional defeat. Francesca, too, has told of a defeat, but the superficial glamour and the intrinsic incoherence of her words have obscured its impact. As for Dante himself, however, the canto presents him finally in the worst possible light, defeated, dead and waste. Not only are the achievements of the opening sequences of the journey challenged in this moment of disorder, but, with the emphasis upon the word 'death' in the concluding lines, Dante allows the canto to undo – or threaten to undo – the work of devotion to Beatrice which began with the title of his earliest work, the *Vita nuova*.

Yet in conclusion it needs to be emphasised that the effect of dislocation in

the narrative and in the mind of the protagonist is itself entirely consistent
with Dante's treatment of the theme of love – and the experience of love –
throughout the *Commedia* and the *Vita nuova*. The words and companionship
of Virgil can offer a steady scheme in which human action may be organised.
But beyond that, in the meeting which love allows between one being and
another, Dante admits an experience which is disruptive, inasmuch as it goes
far beyond words and rational explication. So in the opening pages of the
Vita nuova, love already appears as the 'Lord of Terrible Aspect', stirring
Dante in his 'menimi polsi', and weighing him down with its power to the
point of extinction. But the same is true in *Paradiso* xxi, where, as Dante
considers the theme of contemplative love and charity, he is deafened by a
great cry which he cannot comprehend (*Par.* xxi 139–42). Likewise, even
when the protagonist is preparing to speak of *holy* love – or charity – with St
John, he is blinded, and only recovers his sight when the examination is
concluded:

> Ahi quanto ne la mente mi commossi,
> quando mi volsi per veder Beatrice,
> per non poter veder, benché io fossi
> presso di lei, e nel mondo felice!   (*Par.* xxv 136–9)

(Ah, how troubled I was in mind, / turning to see Beatrice, / not to be able to see,
although I was / near her and in the happy world.)

In the light of these passages, the true conclusion of *Inferno* v is the
silence that supervenes as the canto ends. This is not the trembling, distressed
silence of Paolo, but a silence, dictated by the narrative proportions of the
canto, which sanely acknowledges the limits of discourse and reason. In
Francesca's own case, the dangers of speech – and of literature, too – have
been fully explored. Indeed, there is a case for saying that her fault lies not in
simple sensuality but rather in allowing literary experience to dominate her
thoughts – disguising the raw reality of passion, and shielding her from the
questions that the physical face of Paolo would have led her to ask, had she
looked steadily upon it. And all this serves to confirm the place of the canto
at large in the order of the *Inferno*. It is a canto which reveals the limit that
must lie around any linguistic project. But the difficulty which recognition of
this limit engenders is itself a stimulus to the enactment of order. Henceforth,
the underlying condition of Dante's narrative *will* be that it should admit
surprise – that it should continually acknowledge the ambiguity which
surrounds the judgement of a particular case, and that the poise and
coherence which it displays should represent not the avoidance of self-critical
introspection, but rather its product. And this remains true even though, in
the next chapter, I shall concentrate less upon the stimulus to order in
Dante's thought than upon the terms in which he expresses the order he is
now building.

2

History, nature and philosophy:
Cantos VI–XI

I

As the protagonist recovers from the stupor into which he fell at the end of Canto v, his eyes are greeted by a scene of unrelieved monotony: on every side, wherever he looks, he sees 'novi tormenti e novi tormentati' (4) – new torments and new tormented souls; tedium and unchanging squalor are dominant features in the punishment here:

> Io sono al terzo cerchio, de la piova
> etterna, maladetta, fredda e greve;
> regola e qualità mai non l'è nova ...   (VI 7–9)

(I am in the third circle, of the rain / eternal accursed, cold and heavy; / its rate and nature are never new.)

The sinners in this circle are the gluttons; they lie submerged in mud – the earth 'stinks' (12) beneath the rain – and howl like dogs in tune with the barking of Cerberus, who is the guardian of this region of Hell.

Gluttony, like lust, is a sin of disordered appetite, falling in Dante's view within the general category of incontinence. In this respect, though the sixth canto is markedly different in tone from the fifth, it does represent, in theme, a natural development. Dante now strips away the ambiguities and concealments which characterised the previous canto and, drawing the conclusion which was absent there, pictures the confusion to which human nature can be brought by an irrational and obsessive pursuit of appetite. The strength and distinctiveness of the human being reside in its devotion to truth and moral purpose; and when this devotion is obscured or distorted, the consequence is that undifferentiated – or ultimately tedious – grossness of sensibility and mind that the poet now depicts in the punishment of the gluttons. Paolo had been shown as a cipher; and appetite had made him so. Likewise – if less pathetically – the sinners throughout the sixth canto are mere vacuities, mingling with the slime of the circle as the protagonist and Virgil tread over them:

> Noi passavam su per l'ombre che adona
> la greve pioggia, e ponavam le piante
> sovra lor vanità che par persona.   (34–6)

(We passed over the shades who [are] weighed down / by the heavy rain, and set our feet / upon their emptiness which seemed to have a bodily shape.)

Canto VI, then, is connected in theme and imaginative logic to the preced-
ing canto. Yet it also marks the opening of a new phase of the *Inferno*, in
which a number of issues are introduced for the first time, and where many
of the features that marked the opening sequence are either abandoned or
modified.

Consider, for instance, the form of punishment which the sinners suffer.
From his first words, Dante portrays the punishment in this circle as being, so
to say, far more predictable than any he has so far encountered. Hitherto, the
effect of each new manifestation of Hell has been to overwhelm the pro-
tagonist; now he enters the circle almost unchallenged by its guardian
Cerberus, locating himself, with mechanical assurance, in the 'terzo cerchio',
and even implying weariness at the sight. The punishments display neither
the 'terribilità' of Canto III, nor the classical melancholy of Canto IV, nor, for
that matter, the sublimity of Canto V, where the 'bufera infernal' – although
it portrays the same violence of natural appetite as the foul weather of
Canto VI – suggests, to the post-Romantic eye, the wuthering heights of
passion. Here, the tortures which Dante has devised are those which one
expects from the most primitive depictions of Hell; an unambiguous
contempt for the grossness of human appetite is expressed in images as
disgusting in their materiality as the sin itself. Though, as we shall see, such
obvious and calculated examples of retribution become more frequent in the
lower reaches of Hell, they remain largely untypical of the *Inferno*, and they
require in Canto VI – as they will later – a special explanation.

For some reason, Dante has, it seems, subtracted an imaginative dimension
from the punishment he depicts in Canto VI, and similarly from the one
sinner whom he encounters here. The very name of this sinner – Ciacco or
the Porker – represents, as any cruel nickname must, a disparagement of
personality; but this disparagement is allowed to persist into eternity as if it
reflected an adequate characterisation of the sinner and his vices:

> Voi cittadini mi chiamaste Ciacco:
> per la dannosa colpa de la gola,
> come tu vedi, a la pioggia mi fiacco.   (52–4)

(You and my other fellow-citizens called me Ciacco: / as you see, for the baleful fault
of gluttony, / I bend destroyed beneath the rain.)

There is nothing here of the complexity that accompanied the naming of
Francesca: Ciacco himself employs the demeaning nickname as a plain indi-
cation of his own sins; and the indignity or reduction of identity which this
distortion involves is felt all the more keenly because Ciacco is shown to
desire, as if this were his natural due, the kind of recognition which
Francesca has just received from the protagonist. Rising violently from the
mud he recognises Dante – the two men were Florentine contemporaries –
and pleads that Dante, in his turn, should recognise him:

> riconoscimi, se sai:
> tu fosti, prima ch'io disfatto, fatto.   (41–2)

(Recognise me if you can: / you were made before I was unmade.)

Likewise, at the end of the conversation, collapsing with equal suddenness, Ciacco begs:

> Ma quando tu sarai nel dolce mondo,
> priegoti ch'a la mente altrui mi rechi.   (88–9)

(But when you are again in the sweet world, / I beseech you, bring me back to the minds of others.)

In reply, the protagonist is courteous. Yet he does not acknowledge any acquaintance, and quickly diverts Ciacco into a discussion of the state of Florence. Dante's main concern is to elicit from the sinner – for the first time in the *Inferno* – an account of those divisions in his native city which finally led to his own exile.

With the discussion of Florentine politics, a distinctly new element enters the *Inferno*; and this goes some way towards explaining the other alterations we have so far noted, in characterisation and the representation of punishment. From the first canto, Dante has concerned himself, in a general way, with history – largely in his portrayal of Virgil; and, in portraying Francesca, he has already represented a figure drawn from contemporary culture. However, he has not yet spoken directly of Florence or of his own historical circumstances as a Florentine exile. He will do so now in at least four of the following six cantos. Until Farinata appears in the circle of the heretics, the protagonist encounters no sinner as vivid or complete as Francesca. But the importance of this sequence lies elsewhere, in a consideration – which is sometimes aggressively controversial, sometimes philosophical – of the social and political world to which Dante belongs. Here, Dante himself – not as protagonist, or even exclusively as poet, but as a thinker and historical being – tends to replace the damned as the focus of attention. Likewise, if the punishments here cease to be as resonant or imaginatively significant as hitherto they have been (and shortly will become again), the reason is that the poet's judgements are now directed less upon the existential reality of Hell than upon his own time and circumstances. The poet here identifies the corrosive effect that sins such as greed, avarice and even heresy can have upon the fabric of temporal existence. At the same time, he now attempts to demonstrate how his vision of the afterlife can enable him to withstand the sufferings he himself is destined to undergo, as an exile, in the temporal life, and how also it can provide a practicable remedy against both his personal misfortunes and the misfortunes of the world in which, after his vision, he must return to live.

The harsh immediacy which characterises Dante's approach to the damned in these cantos reflects the satirical and polemical stance which he adopts – say, in his political epistles – in the face of actual problems. However, this shift also corresponds to a pattern so deeply rooted in Dante's mentality that there is evidence of it in every part of the *Commedia*, whether it be the *Paradiso*, the *Purgatorio* or the opening phases of the *Inferno* itself. The pattern is one which requires the mind, when it meets the limits of its proper capacities, to agree to work within these limits, and achieve whatever it can by the means which are natural to it. We have stressed that a point must always be reached where Virgil will cede to Beatrice; it is equally true that Beatrice commissions Virgil to guide the protagonist on his road to her. That commission is silently repeated now, and incorporated in Dante's change of approach. Having engaged with the essential yet almost unanswerable questions on which the *Inferno* rests, Dante now descends to issues of temporal reality which he *can* command, and begins to construct a series of solutions.

It is indicative of this that two major instances of doctrinal exposition should occur during the present sequence. The first is the account of Fortuna in Canto vii; the second is the discussion of the categories of sin occupying the whole of Canto xi. Conversely, in Canto x, which concerns the sin of heresy, Dante displays a clear understanding of how the pursuit of truth may itself result in confusion, and of how dangerous the errors of philosophers might be to their fellow-men. This must lead one to ask how Dante himself, pursuing his own historical and philosophical purposes, manages – in his own view – to avoid the errors which brought about the damnation of men such as Farinata and Cavalcante. The question concerns the practical procedures of argument and exposition which Dante, as poet, adopts in building his philosophical remedies; and in the course of this chapter there will be the opportunity to consider at some length the principles of Dante's thinking and philosophical method in the *Inferno*. But, in terms of Dante's narrative, the questions raised by the sequence are reflected most directly in the treatment of Virgil. And it is here that the complications of these six cantos reveal themselves.

For, as we have seen, the role which philosophical reason plays in the *Inferno* is ambiguous; and the difficulties which surround Virgil, as a figure for reason, are sharpened rather than diminished in the cantos we are now considering.

On the one hand, Virgil is the speaker in both of the major philosophical discussions of the sequence. In each case, his exposition is lucid and efficient; and one can safely say that Dante wished to celebrate, in his dramatic portrayal of Virgil, his own ability to pursue philosophical conclusions through the application of rational method. This is particularly clear in the eleventh canto, where his diagnosis of sin draws far more upon the principles of classical philosophy than upon the teachings of Christian morality: the account itself, which is both eclectic and philosophically fresh, carries the clear implication that reason can identify human failings, and also play a significant part in providing a remedy. On the other hand, in Cantos viii and ix, the limitations of Virgil are revealed more acutely than at any other point in the *Inferno*. Dante's guide is brought to a standstill in front of the City of Dis and is wholly unable to secure an entry without the intervention of the *Messo da Ciel*. There is a problem here which will persist in less dramatic form throughout the rest of the *Inferno*. For within the walls of Dis – enclosing all the circles of Hell which Dante has still to visit – the poet considers those sins which are the product of wilful violence and deceit; and in such a region it is surely surprising that Virgil is allowed any scope at all, since the source of deliberate violence and calculated deceit is a misapplication of that same rationality which Virgil himself proposes as a remedy.

Though Dante's difficulties are largely expressed through his portrayal of Virgil *personaggio*, we are bound to ask whether Dante, as a philosopher, would have thought that his own enterprise in the *Commedia* was in any way subject to the same ambiguities which arise in Virgil's case.

A similar question occurs when we consider that Dante has chosen as his guide not a professional philosopher but a narrative poet. This choice indicates a notable development in Dante's view of philosophical procedure. For in his earlier work, the *Convivio*, Dante had developed an ambitiously technical if not always efficient method of dealing with his own intellectual experiences. He was to do so again in the *Monarchia* with greater acumen. But in each of these two cases the model he follows is Aristotle. Why, then, when he sought a guide to philosophical procedure in the *Commedia*, should he have preferred Virgil to the 'maestro di color che sanno'?

The answer must be that in Virgil he had discovered a technique which, while not incompatible with the technique of professional philosophy, revealed, in the form of narrative, a way of dealing with experience which could not be encompassed by such philosophy alone; or else that there was some kinship in Dante's mind between the *kind* of philosophy he wished to write now and the art of poetic narrative.

We have already seen how each of these suggestions might hold good. For in the opening cantos the truth, for Dante, resides not simply in the rational propositions that our minds may produce but also in the *enactment* of our proper, rational nature. In the course of the *Commedia*, the Dante character is subject not merely to instruction but also to training; and narrative, in a simple sense, allows the poet to depict that training. But Virgil's *Aeneid* also demonstrates, quite specifically, that the pursuit of truth is an ethical function, to be carried through in the practical circumstances of history: Aeneas may be no professional philosopher, but he *does* seek peace and order; and for Dante the exile there could be no fuller expression of truth than that condition of practical harmony. Indeed the poet will eventually use the image of Rome to express the ultimate (and for him utterly practical) condition of truth which the saints enjoy in Heaven. Similarly, while the Virgil of the *Aeneid* is no more of a philosopher than Aeneas, his account of the trials of Aeneas itself represents – precisely in being a narrative – a direct imaginative engagement with moral truth.

In the sequence from Canto VI to Canto XI, Dante makes his own attempt to reconcile truth and history. It is notable that this sequence not only contains, as we have said, two important passages of doctrine, but also – in describing the entry into the City of Dis – revolves around one of the most consciously elaborate pieces of narrative in the whole *Commedia*. Thus my

argument will be throughout that the full force of Dante's philosophical posi-
tion is only comprehensible if – alongside the clear exposition of the
doctrinal passages – one allows due weight to the imaginative or more espe-
cially narrative components of the sequence. To say that the philosophy of
the *Commedia* is inseparable from its narrative and dramatic force is, of
course, to say nothing new. Yet the importance of this connection cannot be
overestimated. It is this connection that, in terms of Dante's own literary
career, marks the great advance upon the *Convivio*; and it is this same con-
junction of narrative art and philosophical discussion that allows Dante to
register the manner in which the pursuit of truth must proceed. We have seen
from the outset – and particularly in Cantos II and III – that Dante requires the
mind to be constantly open to the impact of newness and difficulty. That is
what we meant by speaking of 'action' and 'order' in his poem. Now, in a
sequence which includes the entry into the City of Dis, the unceasing play of
predictability and surprise which the narrative here engenders plainly
becomes more than a literary felicity: it expresses the conditions under which
truth must always be sought. And in such a procedure the advancement of
truth may be said to depend upon an acknowledgement of those very reverses
and ambiguities which to the professional philosopher might seem to consti-
tute a defeat.

To see the extent of this development in philosophical style, it will be
useful at the outset to look in more detail at the differences between the
Commedia, with its strong historical sense, and the relatively a-historical
Convivio. But there is another reason for attempting this comparison. For the
Convivio is Dante's earliest discussion of the theme which occupies him in
the opening cantos of the sequence – the theme of greed. As we shall see, the
discussion of gluttony occupies a central place in Dante's understanding both
of history and of philosophy.

II

The theme of *cupiditas* – considered in Canto VI under the aspect of gluttony
and in Canto VII under the aspect of avarice – is probably the most sustained
topic of moral and political discussion in Dante's mature writing: it stands at
the centre of both the *Convivio* and the *Monarchia*, and recurs with in-
creasing intensity throughout the *Commedia*. So in Canto I of the *Inferno* it
was the she-wolf of avarice – the 'bestia sanza pace' – that epitomised the
dangers which beset the protagonist; and it was against her relentless advance
that Dante evoked the assistance of Virgil. This scene is recalled in Canto VII
where the guardian of the avaricious, Pluto, is described as 'maladetto lupo'
(8) – accursed wolf; and in the course of the first *cantica* Dante goes on to
consider the many particular forms which cupidity can assume – such as
usury, robbery with violence, simony and theft. Nor does his detestation of
the vice slacken in the *Purgatorio* and *Paradiso*. In *Purgatorio* XX, the wolf
of avarice makes a further appearance, and Dante blames her insatiable

appetite for the corruption it has wrought in the Europe of his own day:

> Maladetta sie tu, antica lupa,
> che più che tutte l'altre bestie hai preda
> per la tua fame sanza fine cupa!   (*Purg.* XX 10–12)

(Be accursed, thou ancient she-wolf, / who has more prey than all the other beasts / through your hunger, unendingly deep.)

Likewise, in *Paradiso* XXVII Beatrice sees cupidity as the prime impediment to the appreciation of heavenly truth:

> Oh cupidigia, che i mortali affonde
> sì sotto te, che nessuno ha podere
> di trarre li occhi fuor de le tue onde!   (*Par.* XXVII 121–3)

(O greed who so plunges mortals / below you that no one has the power / to draw his eyes from your waves.)

The lust for possessions is seen, then, as a universal evil with dire consequences for our temporal and eternal happiness. But Dante also sees it as an evil which he himself has a particular responsibility to resist. In Canto VI, the protagonist is made to declare that, while there are circles of Hell far worse than the third, none is more disgusting: 'Nulla è sì spiacente' (48). In the overall plan of the *Inferno* greed is far from being, logically, the most serious of sins, being merely a disorder in appetite. But, against the logic of that scheme, Dante here introduces an emphasis which expresses an especial (one might almost say disordinate) hatred of the vice.

It is not difficult to appreciate why Dante should have spoken out so vigorously on this score. In the first place, he considered cupidity, as Canto VI begins to show, a direct cause of his own disgrace and exile. Here – as more explicitly in Canto XV – Dante sees greed as the origin of division in his native city, perceiving accurately, if not sympathetically, the growth of a new economic order in Florence built upon commerce and banking. Dante's fate, on his own reckoning, was largely decided by the tensions arising in this moment of social transition; and so in Canto VI he speaks in veiled terms of the opposition between those few who – like himself – seek justice and the vicious representatives of the coming age:

> Giusti son due, e non vi sono intesi;
> superbia, invidia e avarizia sono
> le tre faville c'hanno i cuori accesi.   (73–5)

(There are two just men; but they are not listened to there; / pride, envy and avarice are / the three sparks which have set all hearts alight.)

When he speaks of greed, the thought of his own unjust exile is never far from Dante's mind. But in the *Monarchia*, where Dante provides a theoretical account of his position, greed is defined, more analytically, as the logical contrary of justice. So, citing Aristotle, Dante writes in the eleventh chapter of the *Monarchia* I that 'iustitie maxime contrariatur cupiditas', and connects this point with a repeated insistence that the slightest manifestation of greed will vitiate justice: 'for where the will is not entirely untouched by cupidity, even if there is justice in it, justice will nevertheless not be there in the full brilliance of its purity'.

This *is* logical. For justice, in the course of *Monarchia* I, is defined as a virtue which preserves measure, proportion and disciplined rule in all things: 'est quedam rectitudo sive regula'. But greed is disproportionate in that it seeks to appropriate to itself things which are not properly its own. Consequently, any single act of greed will have repercussions throughout the order which justice has established, and destroy the integrity of the whole: 'cupiditas namque perseitate hominum spreta'.

From this position Dante proceeds to argue, in political terms, the necessity of Empire. For the Emperor is appointed directly by God as the embodiment of *rectitudo sive regula* – of rectitude and right rule; he is the administrator of all that exists in the temporal sphere, whether it be land or goods. Having, by right, dominion over all things, the Emperor is incapable of being greedy; he is thus free to be entirely just, and the distribution of goods which he makes among his subjects will itself be an expression of his justice. It is consistent with this argument that Virgil – as the representative of the just Empire of Rome – should be called upon in Canto I to defend the protagonist from the disorder represented by the 'bestia sanza pace'. It is also clear that the representation of Ciacco in Canto VI embodies – and in certain respects extends – the principles enunciated in the *Monarchia*. Ciacco is the first representative of that spirit of greed in Florence which leads to internal strife and isolates the city from the ideal order of the just *imperium*. But the effects of his injustice or disproportion are so radical that in Hell he loses possession of even the personal integrity and order – or, to adopt Dante's Latin word, *perseitas* – which he might claim as his own, his bodily form. On earth he has lost the dignity of a true name; in Hell he has lost any claim to corporeal shape; like the other gluttons he is a 'vanità' who, in Dante's emphatic phrase, only 'appears' to possess a human outline – 'che par persona' – and, save for his meeting with the protagonist, he mingles eternally with the slime on the floor of the third circle. The pathos and irony of the episode derive from the sinner's own sense of how deeply he relies upon the principles of order and identity which justice would have defended: he needs to be recognised, but has done nothing which merits recognition. And in this respect, the encounter also indicates the extent to which Dante himself looked to justice – as represented, in the first instance, by the Emperor – to secure his own good name against attack from his fellow-citizens. It is justice which ensures that human beings are recognised – as both Dante and Ciacco wish to be – for what they are.

Dante, then, has both personal and philosophical reasons for his special hatred of *cupiditas*. His philosophical arguments are consistent with his treatment of appetite in the Francesca episode, and indicate how greed corrodes the ethical principles upon which both the personality and the social survival of any individual must depend. This, in turn, points to a third motive for

Dante's attitude in the *cupiditas* cantos which bears particularly upon the poet's view of philosophy and philosophical procedure. For greed, in Dante's thinking, is not only opposed to justice; it also represents a perversion of the rational appetite which the philosopher is expected to exercise in his search for truth.

It is one indication of how deeply Dante understood this perversion that the title of his first philosophical work should be the *Convivio*, or 'Banquet'. He sustains this initial metaphor throughout the work, arguing in a variety of ways that the true 'food' for the human mind to feed upon is wisdom, knowledge and rectitude. However, Book IV of the *Convivio* has an especial bearing upon the issues raised in the *cupiditas* cantos.

As a whole, Book IV examines the nature of nobility and its and possible relationship with material riches. Dante is here concerned to defeat the argument that the nobility of a human being can be defined, socially, as the long-standing possession of wealth; nobility, he contends, must be seen to reside in our capacity for rational inquiry and in the philosophical love of truth. However, Dante's purpose is not to argue that appetite itself is corrupt; on the contrary it is a characteristic of his thinking, as we saw in the last chapter, that he should stress how all things are moved by desire; and in itself, appetite is morally neutral. Nor for that matter does he suggest, at least in the *Commedia*, that the objects of the physical world are necessarily contemptible. We shall see that a willingness (with certain qualifications) to prize the 'splendours' of the physical sphere constitutes an important part of the *cupiditas* cantos, marking something of an advance upon the *Convivio*. Nonetheless, Dante remains deeply concerned to define the course which the mind should take, in its expression of appetite and in its approach to the objects of the material universe.

Nowhere is this more strikingly expressed than in *Convivio* IV xii 11. For here Dante admits, as a topic of serious discussion, the possible objection that an unending search for knowledge, such as his own work seems to recommend, might be regarded as merely another form of that unending pursuit of riches which characterises the avaricious mind:

Veramente qui surge in dubbio una questione, da non trapassare sanza farla e rispondere a quella. Potrebbe dire alcuno calunniatore de la veritade che se, per crescere desiderio acquistando, le ricchezze sono imperfette e però vili, che per questa ragione sia imperfetta e vile la scienza, ne l'acquisto de la quale sempre cresce lo desiderio di quella; onde Seneca dice: 'Se l'uno de li piedi avesse nel sepulcro, apprendere vorrei.'

(At this point there arises a doubt and a question which we cannot pass by without asking and answering. Some traducer of the truth might say that if riches are imperfect and consequently base – because in acquiring them desire increases – then for the same reason knowledge is imperfect and base, since in acquiring it, the desire for that, too, always increases; so Seneca says: 'If I had one foot in the grave, I should still want to learn.')

As a preliminary to his technical answer, Dante insists upon the Neo-

platonic principle that in all our desires we seek to return to our origins: 'lo
sommo desiderio di ciascuna cosa, e prima da la natura dato, è lo ritornare a
lo suo principio' (*CNV* IV xii 14). He then offers an analogy which movingly
anticipates the whole plan of the *Commedia* itself: having said that God is the
alpha and omega of human desires, he proceeds to represent human life as a
pilgrimage of return to God in which we fulfil the purposes for which we
were first created. The *Convivio* (IV xii) anticipates some of the most
fundamental images of the *Commedia*: the straight road, the pilgrim, the
child desiring an apple, even the image of the pyramid, all recur in the
Commedia; and in outline Dante's thought here foreshadows his sustained
discussion of free will in the central cantos of the *Purgatorio*. However, the
especial importance of the argument lies in the emphasis that Dante places
upon the notion of an 'end'. For it is this notion that in the the later chapter
provides the distinction between the philosophical pursuit of appetite, and the
behaviour of the avaricious.

Thus at the conclusion of Chapter xii Dante writes:

lo buono camminatore giugne a termine e a posa; lo erroneo mai l'aggiugne, ma con
molta fatica del suo animo sempre con li occhi gulosi si mira innanzi.

(the good traveller reaches his goal and rests; the traveller who strays never reaches it,
but with much trouble of mind, gazes constantly ahead with greedy eyes).

Here it is already plain that Dante locates the fault of the avaricious not in
appetite itself, but in a waywardness which prevents them ever reaching a
state of peace and stability – the 'end' which the philosophical mind enjoys
when it arrives 'a termine e a posa'. The defining characteristic of the
'gulosi' is that their minds should never allow them to be satisfied, even
when they attain the immediate end which they have proposed to themselves:
they are *always* 'gazing ahead'.

In the *Commedia* the notion of an 'end' is given still greater prominence
than it enjoys in the *Convivio*. Thus we have already seen that in the
Commedia Dante consistently represents the *lupa*, or avarice, as a condition
of futile activity, frustrating any steady advance towards a worthwhile con-
clusion, and opposed to peace on both a social and a psychological plane.
But, to understand fully how this activity can be distinguished from
philosophical inquiry, we need to consider the thirteenth chapter of *Convivio*
IV. For here Dante shows that, whereas the desires of the avaricious are in
effect the same desire infinitely repeated, the desires of the philosopher are
constantly *renewed*. The characteristic of the philosophical mind is that it sets
itself a goal which it knows to be attainable and, having attained that goal,
proceeds to conceive a new ambition:

lo desiderio de la scienza non è sempre uno, ma è molti, e finito l'uno, viene l'altro; sì
che, propriamente parlando, non è crescere lo suo dilatare, ma successione di picciola
cosa in grande cosa.   (*CNV* IV xiii 1)

(the desire for knowledge is not always one, but is many; when one desire is ended, there comes another, so that, properly speaking, its dilation is not an increase but a succession of small things to great).

By contrast, the desire of the avaricious

è propriamente crescere, ché è sempre pur uno, si che nulla successione quivi si vede, e per nullo termine e per nulla perfezione.

(is, properly speaking, an increase, since it is always one, so that there is no succession, no goal at all, nor any perfection).

The essence of the distinction, then, is that, in seeking to accumulate rather than to progress, the avaricious never conceive a clear understanding of an end, and thus effectively reject the possibility which the philosophical mind enjoys of peace, repose and refreshment. So in Canto VI, when the protagonist wearily prepares himself to face the sight of 'new punishments and new victims', he is in fact steeling himself to act as, in Dante's account, any philosophical mind should act, as it discovers even in the successive punishments of Hell a new manifestation of truth. It is indeed the moral duty of the mind to be philosophical, seeing truth afresh in whatever it encounters. Thus the opening of the canto points clearly to the contrast between Dante's own mentality as he writes the poem and that of gluttons whom he condemns to Hell. Certainly, for the gluttons in Hell, eternity holds neither surprise nor certainty; and in this respect the sixth canto diagnoses an essential feature of damnation: it is an endless repetition of the same action or an endless insistence upon the same condition. But that it should be so is the consequence or reflection of the intellectual activities of the sinners on earth. The rain which falls upon the gluttons is never-changing: 'regola e qualità mai non l'è nova'; to the mind which desires one thing and one thing only, nothing ever can be new.

In the course of Canto VII, the distinction between avaricious and philosophical desire is sustained and made more precise. So, as Virgil begins his exposition of the doctrine of Fortuna at line 72, he insists that the protagonist should ''m bocche' – take into his mouth – the truth of his words. The metaphor belongs to the same family as produced the title of the *Convivio*, and points to a contrast between the single-minded pursuits of the avaricious and the philosophical hunger which Virgil is about to satisfy with his account of mutability. In the light of this contrast, it is entirely appropriate that Dante should locate the first piece of doctrinal discussion he attempts in the *Commedia* within the ambience of the avaricious. At the same time, the seventh canto enforces the contrast in a polemical manner, untouched by even the modicum of sympathy which the protagonist showed to Ciacco: the avarice which contaminates Florence is set starkly alongside the achievements of the Florentine philosopher, Dante who – through the mouth of Virgil – displays his own skill in the Fortuna passage.

Canto VII opens, however, at the very opposite pole from philosophical discourse with the gibberish of Pluto, the guardian of this circle, who challenges the advance of the new-comers:

> '*Pape Satàn, pape Satàn aleppe!*',
> cominciò Pluto con la voce chioccia ...   (VII 1–2)

('Pape Satan, pape Satan aleppe!', / Pluto began, with his clucking voice).

This is a startling enough beginning to a canto of doctrine; but one consistent element in the diction of the *cupiditas* cantos is a certain crudeness which Dante would have defined, in his own terms, as comic or harsh; throughout, these cantos draw upon the lower registers of vernacular speech and employ rhyme to stress the phonetic harshness of such locutions. So, for instance, Dante writes of the descent into the fourth circle:

> Così scendemmo ne la quarta lacca,
> pigliando più de la dolente ripa
> che 'l mal de l'universo tutto insacca.   (16–18)

(Thus we descended to the fourth hollow, / taking in more of the grievous bank / which parcels up all the ill of the universe.)

The word 'insacca' is comic in Dante's sense, while its rhyming position against 'lacca' brings into relief the harshness of the -*cc* consonant; similar effects can be found at Canto VII 19, 21, 52–7, 125–29, and Canto VI 15–18, 50–2.

As we shall see in later chapters, Dante's use of comic diction is invariably a part of a calculated imaginative project, and the present case is no exception. Having chosen to emphasise the grossness of the punishments in this circle, Dante can hardly avoid a comparably gross vocabulary in describing these punishments. From Canto III onwards, sin has been reflected in, and been seen to produce, some degree of linguistic confusion; and Dante here continues to develop a pointed opposition between confusion and order in the sphere of discourse. So, the avaricious and the spendthrifts yell as they collide with one another: 'gridando: "Perché tieni?" e "Perché burli?"' (30) – crying: 'Why hold on to it?' and 'Why fling it away?'. But these insults are described as an 'ontoso metro' (33) – a shameful chant; and the ironically elevated 'metro' registers the distance of the sinners from measured speech. It is one indication of how polemical and engaged Dante's defence of philosophy will always be that he should cast it in so vehemently satirical a context; and here, as more extensively in the Malebolge, the poet displays his prowess by constructing a virtuoso 'metro' of his own out of the very harshness which seems to challenge linguistic order. So, at line 22, he dexterously combines high and low style in an epic simile which draws together both classical allusion and comic diction:

> Come fa l'onda là sovra Cariddi,
> che si frange con quella in cui s'intoppa,
> così convien che qui la gente riddi.   (22–4)

(As the wave does over Charybdis / breaking against the wave it strikes, / so here the people have to dance against each other.)

In the central sequence, these violent voices are replaced by the calm philosophical utterances which the poet ascribes to Virgil. Virgil's voice is not – here or elsewhere – a polemical one; and that, as we shall see in the Malebolge, is as much a weakness as a strength. Already, his tone contrasts with that of the Dantean voice, heard in the context that frames Virgil's oration. Still, the primary contrast which the canto offers lies between the idiocy of Pluto – who is described as 'il gran nemico' (the great enemy) at Canto VI 115 – and the composure and clarity of Virgil, whose philosophical function is emphasised at Canto VII 3: he is 'quel savio gentil, che tutto seppe' – that wise and noble man who knows all things.

In common with all preceding guardians of Hell, Pluto collapses as soon as Virgil speaks to him: he drops 'like a swollen sail when the mast breaks' (13–14); and this sudden puncturing enacts the same understanding of *cupiditas* as mere *vanità*, which appeared in Canto VI. Avarice, like greed, leaves the human being bereft of all power to pursue a determined end and, consequently, of all that is distinctively human. Like the *ignavi*, the avaricious have left no mark of their own humanity on the world: the protagonist cannot hope to recognise any of them now: 'la sconoscente vita che i fé sozzi / ad ogne conoscenza or li fa bruni' (53–4) – their ignorant lives that made them squalid, / now make them dark to all recognition. Indeed the avaricious are so utterly undistinguished that at the Day of Judgement, when all other souls return to the recognisable form of their earthly bodies, they will be condemned to inhabit an eternal caricature of themselves:

> In etterno verranno a li due cozzi:
> questi resurgeranno del sepulcro
> col pugno chiuso, e questi coi crin mozzi.   (55–7)

(They will go on to eternity with their butting: / these will rise from the grave / with fists tight-closed, the others with their hair close-shaved.)

Against this, Virgil emphasises the just authority which God exerts over his creation and over history. God is seen here as Emperor of the Universe whose angels, led by St Michael, defend creation against the disorder of Satan's rebellion (12). In this same act – and in the comparable event of the Second Coming – God is acknowledged as the beginning and the end of history; his deeds shape the temporal order on which human beings must fix their minds, and in which they must seek to live justly.

The interest which Dante here shows in the Last Judgement is, as we shall see, an important feature of the sequence: and one of the ways in which the *cupiditas* cantos modify the notion of an 'end' – which so far we have considered only in the relatively 'humanistic' perspective of the *Convivio* – is by insisting that it be understood in the light of God's creative decisions. Nonetheless, the discourse of Virgil *personaggio* is consistent with the

Convivio in subject and procedure. For the pressing and immediate question
which he attacks is the question of how we should properly manage our
material fortunes: he proposes, in short, a manageable and attainable
intellectual goal, and proceeds in his speech*with an analytical clarity which
renders even the well-worn subject of Fortuna 'new'.

In this respect, however, his first move is not, in fact, altogether
satisfactory. Faced with so squalid and obvious a denial of human dignity as
avarice, Virgil's instinct – as in the circle of the *ignavi* – is to pass by
without wasting words on the sinners or their punishment: 'qual ella sia,
parole non ci appulcro' (60). So he attempts to conclude his account almost
before it has begun with a dismissive summary both of the punishment which
the avaricious suffer and of the stupidity and restlessness of avarice which –
ignoring the moral and philosophical pursuit of true purpose – would remain
unsatisfied even if it possessed all the gold under the changing moon:

> Mal dare e mal tener lo mondo pulcro
> ha tolto loro, e posti a questa zuffa:
> qual ella sia, parole non ci appulcro.
>   Or puoi, figliuol, veder la corta buffa
> d'i ben che son commessi a la fortuna,
> per che l'umana gente si rabuffa;
>   ché tutto l'oro ch'è sotto la luna
> e che già fu, di quest' anime stanche
> non poterebbe farne posare una.   (58–66)

(Evil giving and evil keeping [have taken] the lovely world / from them and placed
them in this scuffle: / I shall not embellish what that is with words. / Now you can see,
my son, the brief mockery / of the goods given over to Fortune / for which human
beings squabble among themselves. / For all the gold there is beneath the moon / or
ever was could never give rest to a single one [of these weary souls].)

These lines possess an elegant, even humorously resigned, detachment in
their observation of how human beings are outwitted by the tricks of fortune
(and by the same token the passage displays little of the vehemence which
Dante himself has generated in his own response to avarice). But for the
protagonist they are unsatisfactory in the philosophical sense that they raise
an appetite for further questions, pointing beyond the sphere of moral precept
to which Virgil has restricted himself. The protagonist, it seems, requires a
more speculative consideration of the principles which govern human life. So
Dante (as if unaware of the part that misfortune will play in his own
existence) protests complete ignorance of what fortune is. In response, Virgil
– though he continues primarily to concern himself with the folly of
humanity – now speaks of the universal principle which is embodied in
Fortuna. His argument is that, while human beings blame Fortuna when
disaster befalls them, it is a mark of sheer foolishness to do so: the changes
of fortune are an essential feature of the plan of the created universe; and, if
worldly splendours move from hand to hand and from race to race, this
should be a reason rather for rejoicing than for complaint. For by these

changes Fortuna ensures an equitable distribution of the good things of the universe. Thus, properly understood, change in the material world is an essential principle of order; and those who *do* understand Fortuna in this way will not suppose that they have any right to complain if they are deprived of good things: they will rather rejoice to have received any good at all:

> Quest' è colei ch'è tanto posta in croce
> pur da color che le dovrien dar lode,
> dandole biasmo a torto e mala voce;
>   ma ella s'è beata e ciò non ode:
> con l'altre prime creature lieta
> volve sua spera e beata si gode.   (91–6)

(She it is who is so painfully reviled / by the very beings who ought to give her praise, / blaming her wrongly and with evil words. / But she is blessed and does not hear that: / with the other first beings of creation she is joyful; / she turns her sphere and rejoices in her blessedness.)

Having delivered this authoritative oration, Virgil allows no further question. With a decisiveness characteristic of him in this canto, he insists that the protagonist should at once descend into yet more misery (97). And it may well be asked what more there is to say. Virgil has presented his argument with great efficiency; he has displayed to the full the 'parole ornate' for which Beatrice chose him as Dante's guide, and having established command over one stage of the truth is free to advance to a further stage.

Yet there *is* more to be said, even at the expense of a lengthy digression. For the Fortuna passage – which rarely receives the attention it deserves – is a major statement of Dante's own philosophical position and an illustration of the philosophical procedures he will adopt throughout the *Commedia*.

The question of mutability itself is one which had concerned the poet from the earliest phases of his philosophical career. He had faced it first in the *Vita nuova*, where he attempted to understand the frailty, changeableness and apparent disorder of human life, as revealed to him principally by the death of Beatrice. And the *Convivio* takes up the theme on a different level, in considering the subjection of the avaricious mind to transient goods and pleasures. In both of these works Dante draws heavily upon Boethius's *Consolatio Philosophiae*, and the *Consolatio* remains, of course, a major source for Dante's figure of Fortuna in the *Inferno*. But, as we shall see, Canto VII is markedly different in tone from Boethius's work; Dante here claims the right to make radical revisions of emphasis in his treatment of sources (so much so indeed that Canto VII at once attracted charges of heresy from contemporary readers).

The revisions in Canto VII are themselves – one might say – an indication of the extent to which Dante insisted upon the moral duty of all human beings to 'digest' the truth and make it their own: to do philosophy is to see the world in a new light. Dante, however, here advances not only beyond his sources but also beyond his own original view of the question. As we shall see, the Fortuna passage mirrors a concern with the designs and decisions of God as Creator which would have been quite out of place in the *Convivio*. And – no less important – the linguistic and argumentative procedures which Dante now adopts are wholly different from those of the prose treatise: for one thing, the verse he gives to Virgil is, argumentatively, more efficient than the prose of the *Convivio*; for another the location of the passage in a narrative context emphasises the extent to which the doctrine as understood in the *Commedia* is no merely speculative exercise but a point of focus for progressive and practical commitment.

At the same time, Canto VII enunciates principles which – although subject to constant development and refinement – remain central henceforth to Dante's thinking throughout the *Commedia*. Certainly, the discussion of Fortuna is an immediate and manageable *termine* or goal for the philosopher initially to set his mind upon. But it is still the first in a succession of debates on the topic which will culminate in the central cantos of the *Paradiso*, when Dante meets his forebear Cacciaguida and is told how he must stand firm against the miseries of his exile, upholding the truth and writing his poem to defend it (*Par.* XVII 37–141). Gradually, Dante comes to terms with the role that Fortune will play in his own life, while, intellectually, he also shows how – in a form of benign mutability – the same essential truth can be seen under a constantly developing aspect. This, once more, is to indicate how in the *Commedia* philosophy is to be 'done'. For at every point, whether of the *Inferno* or of the *Paradiso*, the question of Fortune will resolve itself into a test of both intellectual and moral mettle: has the philosopher stamina enough to return afresh to the question; has the man himself courage enough to act out his understanding in the face of the day-to-day sufferings that misfortune brings?

To formulate the questions in this way is also to suggest why the discussion of Fortuna should be located at the beginning of the *Inferno*. For the question of Fortuna can be regarded as a minimal test of whether a human being is fit for salvation or else so unenlightened that Hell is the only place for him: if a mind is not sufficiently philosophical to respond to a doctrine as direct in its impact as the doctrine of Fortuna – which sees God's hand even in the shift of physical objects and temporal honours – then how can it hope to progress to the higher stages of truth? It has been said that Dante judges sin in the *Inferno* by standards of human success or failure; and the test which is implied in Dante's view of Fortuna – requiring the mind to perceive certainties of intellectual principle beneath the obvious uncertainty of temporal possessions – will enable one to identify the philosophical and 'human' failings not only of the avaricious and gluttons, but also of such apparently heroic figures as Farinata, Pier della Vigna and Brunetto Latini.

How, then, does Dante define this test? His first move is to redefine the conception of fortune which Boethius offers in the early books of the

Consolatio. It is there that we find the familiar image of Fortune as the inexorable and cruel mistress of the wheel of change, imposing a constant shift from *wele* to *wo*:

> With domineering hand she moves the turning wheel,
> Like currents in a treacherous bay swept to and fro:
> Her ruthless will has just deposed once fearful kings
> While, trustless still, from low she lifts a conquered head;
> No cries of misery she hears, no tears she heeds,
> But steely-hearted laughs at groans her deeds have wrung.
> Such is the game she plays, and so she tests her strength;
> Of mighty power she makes parade when one short hour
> Sees happiness from utter desolation grow.   (*Cons. Phil.* II m. 1)

But in two respects – which affect the whole tenor of the image and the conception it expresses – Dante radically alters this traditional depiction.

In the first place, Fortuna is shown (and it is here that Dante comes close to heresy) to be a *necessary* aspect of the universal system which God has created: creation is organised in such a way as to distribute God-created light through all possible ranks of being: 'sì, ch'ogne parte ad ogne parte splende' (75); and Fortuna, or 'change', is set as a guide over the lowest order of existence – the realm of physical objects – so that even they are directed by the providential purpose and justice that God expresses in all his creation. In this view of fortune, even earthly goods – 'splendor mondani' – share in the resplendence of God's creation and cannot consequently be regarded, as Boethius leads one to supppose, as contemptible or beneath spiritual consideration.

Similar implications arise from the second feature of Dante's picture, where Dante underlines how intelligent the action of Fortuna is. There is no mention in the *Inferno* passage of the *wheel* of change – with all that *that* might suggest of merely mechanical motion. Instead, Dante speaks twice of the 'permutations' of fortune – 'che permutasse a tempo li ben vani' (79), and 'Le sue permutazion non hanno triegue' (88). The word indicates the subtlety and intelligent calculation that Dante attributes to Fortuna and is consistent with the final note of the passage, which insists that Fortuna deserves praise, not blame, for her actions: to the eye that looks at her aright – as Virgil does in his evidently celebratory speech – Fortuna possesses a beauty of her own expressing the patterns of Providence in the things of the world.

From the standpoint of popular philosophy it will already be apparent how challenging Dante's conception of fortune is. In a word, he has taken the notion of mutability which apparently emphasises all the ills and uncontrollable accidents that bear upon human life, and presented mutability itself as a principle not of disorder but of design. The philosophical spirit is required to countenance a paradox, seeing intelligence and purpose where the 'creature sciocche' will see only danger and confusion. It is this perception of order that the avaricious and the gluttons not only fail to achieve but also obscure in their anxious attempts to outwit and replace the dispensations of fortune by their getting and spending.

It may be said that the view of fortune which Dante adopts is not so much divergent from Boethius as one which rather takes into account the full development of Boethius's thought: certainly, in the last book of the *Consolatio* Boethius too will show how fortune is to be praised as an aspect of Providence. And when Dante gives his own most fully developed view of the providential hierarchy in *Paradiso* XIII, it is clear that he values Boethius's contribution to his own thinking very highly. The main speech in this canto is given to Aquinas, but the thought owes much to Boethius who appears as a companion of Aquinas in the ranks of the Christian philosophers.

The fact remains that, in emphasis, both the Fortuna passage and the cantos of Christian Philosophy in the *Paradiso* are significantly different from the *Consolatio*. Boethius is only one of many thinkers who helped to form Dante's understanding of providential order: the Heaven of the Sun represents the pursuit of truth as a communal activity, exercised by divers thinkers in divers ways; and within that community of philosophers the particular lesson which Dante ascribes to Boethius is that he taught the *fallaciousness* of worldly things:

> che 'l mondo fallace
> fa manifesto a chi di lei ben ode.   (*Par.* x 125–6)

(who made the falsity of the world / apparent to those who truly heard it out).

This is an accurate enough assessment of the Boethius of the *Consolatio*, who constantly teaches how human beings may rise, by virtue of their rational faculties, above the shifting appearances of the world and enjoy the contemplation of eternal truths. Yet, in fine, the Fortuna passage and the Heaven of Christian Philosophy indicate a more complex position than this: here, without denying the need to remain free of binding attachments to the things of this world, Dante nevertheless allows that the temporal sphere is a proper sphere of human activity, and insists that we should not evade the responsibility of acting appropriately within that sphere.

In Dante's philosophy at large, there are many indications of how important was the notion of practical action within the conditions of time; and none is more striking than his argument that we may enjoy happiness not only in eternity but also in *this* life under the rule of perfect justice which a divinely ordained Emperor would institute. In the *Purgatorio* (where penance is done to the tune of time within the spaces of an earthly mountain), the Earthly Paradise to which Virgil leads Dante is, in one aspect, a representation of the results to which practical action might ideally lead – a foreshadowing of the Golden World of Earthly Justice. But in the *Inferno* it is the Fortuna passage that, in a much grimmer way, introduces this same possibility.

To see this, we need to consider the second authority on whom Dante draws in constructing the figure of Fortuna. This authority is Solomon – whom Dante would have considered the author of the biblical *Liber Sapientiae* or Book of Wisdom; Solomon not only represents, like Boethius, a major source of reference for Dante in the *Convivio*, but also appears at the conclusion of the Heaven of the Sun (where Boethius too appears) as the supreme example of Philosophy and the love of truth.

Throughout Dante's writing the function of Solomon is to celebrate the goodness of God's creative wisdom even in its lowest manifestation; and in the Fortuna passage those same features of Dante's image that diverge from Boethius can be traced to a passage in the *Liber Sapientiae* which celebrates the wisdom which God displayed in the dispositions of the natural and physical universe. For in four respects the figures of Fortuna and Solomon's Wisdom are exactly comparable: each is mobile, each subtle, each so bright and each so perfectly pure that no human complaint or stupidity can harm her:

For in her is the spirit of understanding: holy, one, manifold, subtile, eloquent, active, undefiled, sure, sweet, loving that which is good, quick, which nothing hindereth, beneficent, gentle, kind, steadfast, assured, secure, having all power, overseeing all things, and containing all spirits, intelligible, pure, subtile. For wisdom is more active than all active things: and reacheth everywhere by reason of her purity. For she is a vapour of the power of God: and a certain pure emanation of the glory of the almighty God: and there no defiled thing cometh into her. For she is the brightness of eternal light: and the unspotted mirror of God's majesty, and the image of his goodness.

(Book of Wisdom VII 7)

For Dante, then, fortune like wisdom, may be taken to represent divine order in the realm of physical matter; and, consequently, there can be no question of the mind attempting, as Boethius suggests, simply to rise *above* the 'fallaciousness' of the world. On the contrary, there will be every reason to accept the changes of the natural world and seek the wisdom which underlies them in a spirit of philosophical inquiry. Moreover, there are two other respects in which Dante's treatment of Solomon in the *Commedia* emphasises the need to engage rather than deny the actualities of temporal life.

Thus, in the first place, Solomon in the *Paradiso* is treated as the supreme representative of practical wisdom. He appears as the ruler who had the modesty to ask only for wisdom 'sufficient to rule his kingdom' (*Par.* XIII 96). It is remarkable, even polemical on Dante's part that he should conclude a sequence of the *Paradiso* largely devoted to the representatives of speculative philosophy with an emphasis upon the supreme value of political wisdom. But this move is consistent with an underlying characteristic of the poet's thinking. One notes that the Solomon episode immediately precedes Dante's meeting in Paradise with Cacciaguida. There, the 'wisdom of Solomon' is translated into civic and quotidian terms as Dante depicts how the golden world of ancient Florence was built upon principles of practical discipline. And it is against this background that Cacciaguida finally reveals to Dante how his destiny will be to stand 'ben tetragono' (four-square) to the blows of Fortune, and particularly how – on returning from the certitude of

Heaven to the realm of 'brief contingencies' (*Par.* XIII 63) – he must undertake to write his own philosophical poem 'in pro del mondo che mal vive' (*Purg.* XXXII 103) – for the sake of the world that lives in evil ways. The responsibility to transform apparent misfortunes into destiny, and to love the truth of one's own condition – even if that condition is one of poverty, exile or restriction – falls not only upon kings or poets but upon every human being.

In the second place, we find that Solomon appears in the *Commedia* as the main spokesman of the doctrine of the resurrection of the body. In the *Paradiso*, the one speech that Solomon makes stresses that the human being will only be complete when, at the Last Judgement, it receives again the body which it lost in death. Strikingly, the Christian philosophers greet these pronouncements as the highest instance of divine truth; indeed, so far from being content with their pure, spiritual condition in Heaven as 'sempiterne fiamme' – sempiternal flames – they look forward joyously to the time when (in Dante's unambiguous phrase) they will return to their dead bodies:

> Tanto mi parver sùbiti e accorti
> e l'uno e l'altro coro a dicer 'Amme!',
> che ben mostrar disio d'i corpi morti:
>   forse non pur per lor, ma per le mamme,
> per li padri e per li altri che fuor cari
> anzi che fosser sempiterne fiamme.   (*Par.* XIV 61–6)

(They seemed to me so quick and eager / – both of these choirs – to say 'Amen!', / that they truly showed desire for their dead bodies: / not for themselves alone perhaps but for their mothers, / their fathers and others who were dear to them / before they became eternal flames.)

Among its many functions, this speech serves to make clear that Dante's attitude to physical reality could never be one of simple contempt. The human body in its physical form is assured of eternal existence; and one will look in vain for any such emphasis upon the resurrection in Boethius's *Consolatio*.

Nor is the relevance of this passage to the *cupiditas* cantos far to seek. In Canto VII, as we have seen, Dante refers quite specifically to the physical form which the avaricious will assume on the Day of Judgement. And, preceding the discussion of Fortuna, the first word of science or philosophy spoken in the *Commedia* concerns the resurrection. Thus at the conclusion of Canto VI, Virgil – explaining that Ciacco will not rise again until the Last Day – gives a vivid account of how

> Più non si desta
> di qua dal suon de l'angelica tromba,
> quando verrà la nimica podesta:
>   ciascun rivederà la trista tomba,
> ripiglierà sua carne e sua figura,
> udirà quel ch'in etterno rimbomba.   (*Inf.* VI 94–9)

(He will rise no more / before the sound of the angel's trumpet, / when the Enemy Power will come: / each will see his sad tomb again, / will take on again his flesh and form, / and hear the sound reverberating to eternity.)

Virgil then proceeds to argue – citing Aristotle – that the pains of the damned must logically be more severe when they return to the body, because only then will they be perfect and perfectly receptive, whether to the influence of pain or of pleasure:

> Ed elli a me: 'Ritorna a tua scïenza,
> che vuol, quanto la cosa è più perfetta,
> più senta il bene, e così la doglienza'.   (VI 106–8)

(And he to me: 'Go back to your science / which affirms that the more anything is perfect / the more it feels pleasure and likewise pain.')

In the logic of Canto VI, it is not difficult to see the place of the first of these passages: the emphasis upon the phrase 'sua carne e sua figura' stands in contrast to the emphasis earlier upon the *vanità* of the sinners and reveals the irony that the gluttons, while attempting to safeguard themselves by the satisfaction of their physical appetites, have failed against the model of physical nature which the Justice of God will reveal at the end of time. It is justice itself that finally insists that we take on again the nature which was given us in the order of creation; and the only way in which human beings can satisfy that nature is by their thirst for justice, or rectitude, in the temporal as in the eternal order.

So in Canto VI a dramatic contrast arises between the two Florentines, Dante and Ciacco; they were born into the same historical and geographical circumstances, yet their responses to these circumstances were wholly different – the one a philosopher, the other a cruel parody of a philosopher. Bitterly it is Ciacco, now conscious of the value of the 'vita serena' that he has misused, who declares, with repeated emphasis upon the word for physical 'making':

> tu fosti, prima ch'io disfatto, fatto.   (42)

(you, before I was unmade, was made.)

In this regard, it is impossible to ignore the case of another Florentine, also a contemporary of Dante, whom the protagonist meets atoning for his gluttony on the slopes of Purgatory. As with Ciacco, Dante is at first unable to recognise the figure who claims acquaintance: his face is wasted by the hunger of his penance. But there the resemblances between the two episodes end. For the wasting of the flesh on the penitent's face is said to reveal the outline of the word 'omo' (man) written in the bones of his nose and sockets of his eyes:

> Parean l'occhiaie anella sanza gemme:
> chi nel viso de li uomini legge 'omo'
> ben avria quivi conosciuta l'emme.   (*Purg.* XXIII 31–3)

(The sockets of their eyes seemed rings without gem-stones: / those who read 'omo' in the face of men / would here have recognised clearly the *m*.)

So far from reducing the penitent to oblivion, suffering here reveals the true imprint of human nature as 'man'. In accepting the just sentence of God, the sinner has displayed exactly that desire for recognition – in this case, recognition of his nature in the eye of its Creator – which Ciacco too wishes to have granted to him but has done nothing to deserve. So, as soon as the penitent speaks, Dante recognises him to be his friend Forese:

> Mai non l'avrei riconosciuto al viso;
> ma ne la voce sua mi fu palese
> ciò che l'aspetto in sé avea conquiso.
>   Questa favilla tutta mi raccese
> mia conoscenza a la cangiata labbia,
> e ravvisai la faccia di Forese.   (*Purg.* XXIII 43–8)

(I would never have recognised him from his face. / But in his voice was made manifest to me / that which his countenance had in itself defeated. / That spark kindled / my knowledge again by the changed features, / and I saw again the face of Forese.)

In the strange setting of the cornice of the Penitents – planted with sprigs of trees from the Garden of Eden, bearing fruit of exquisite richness – a conversation now begins which displays all the intimacy and courtesy which Ciacco claims but cannot achieve. The scene in Purgatory foreshadows the harmony which is possible between human beings when – as in the ideal order of time – they acknowledge the truth on which their being depends. But Ciacco is left displaying not merely greed, but all the divisiveness and aggression which follow from it, as he speaks, with relish, of how the most eminent of his fellow-citizens – Farinata, Tegghiaio, Rusticucci, Arrigo and Mosca – suffer pains in Hell far worse than his own:

> Ei son tra l'anime più nere;
> diverse colpe giù li grava al fondo:
> se tanto scendi, là i potrai vedere.   (*Inf.* VI 85–7)

(They are among the blackest of spirits; / different crimes weigh them down to the bottom: / if you descend that far you will be able to see them.)

In sum, there is a sense in which Fortuna, though representing nothing but disorder to the unphilosophical mind, stands as a remote foreshadowing of the Golden World which will appear finally in the Earthly Paradise. The very lucidity of the account which Dante ascribes to Virgil is an illustration of how the mind and imagination may feed upon the laws of creation. Conversely, the punishments which Dante devises for the avaricious and the gluttons demonstrate how the laws of Fortune are so elemental that they will be enforced upon those who have not willingly appreciated them. Already in the *Convivio*, Dante has written vehemently of those who cannot rise to the contemplation of wisdom:

Per che vedere omai si puote, che per lo divino provedimento lo mondo è sì ordinato che, volta la spera del sole e tornata a un punto, questa palla dove noi siamo, in ciascuna parte di sé riceve tanto tempo di luce quanto di tenebre. O ineffabile sapienza che così ordinasti, quanto è povera la nostra mente a te comprendere! E voi a cui utilitade e diletto io scrivo, in quanta cechitade vivete, non levando li occhi suso a queste cose, tenendoli fissi nel fango de la vostra stoltezza!   (*CNV* III v)

(Now it can be seen that the world is so ordained that when the sphere of the sun has revolved and returned to any point, this globe where now we are, [has] received in every part of it as long a time of light as of darkness. O unutterable Wisdom that ordains this, how poor and restricted our minds are to comprehend you! And you, for whose good and delight I write, in what blindness do you live, never lifting up your eyes to things such as this, but keeping them fixed, in your stupidity, upon the mire!)

But the polemic of these lines is reinforced in the *Inferno* by the confidence with which Dante now speaks of God's providential purpose as expressed in particular acts of judgement. So, most strikingly, the seventh canto concludes with a description of a group of sinners who are probably the wrathful and sullen but whose especial offence is to have failed to rejoice in the sweetness of the air:

> Fitti nel limo dicon: 'Tristi fummo
> ne l'aere dolce che dal sol s'allegra,
> portando dentro accidïoso fummo:
>   or ci attristiam ne la belletta negra'.
> Quest' inno si gorgoglian ne la strozza,
> ché dir nol posson con parola integra.   (*Inf.* VII 121–6)

(Stuck in the mire they say: 'We were sad / in the sweet air that the sun makes joyful, / carrying fumes of sluggishness in ourselves: / now we are sullen in this black mud'. / They gurgle this hymn in their throats, / for they are unable to speak complete words.)

The clarity of Virgil's Fortuna speech is directly contrasted with the gurgling confusion which characterises the words of these sinners; and, likewise, the rapid and intelligent permutations of Fortuna herself are balanced, in the negative sense, by the undifferentiated and sluggish mud which encloses them. So, too, the mechanical movements that the avaricious are obliged to perform are a parody of the movements of Fortuna. But the avaricious and prodigal are constrained in circles which admit no progress or succession. The sinners in Canto VII are rolling great boulders one against the other; they continually describe a half-circle which their own mentalities have created. Indeed it is here, not in the doctrinal discussion, that one sees the mechanical and predictable action which the popular view would associate with the actions of Fortune. The rationality of the avaricious has become as much a parody of rationality as the *vanità* of the gluttons was of selfhood; and judgement now enforces upon them an enactment of the patterns which might, if they had been philosophers, have revealed the nature and true purpose of the world in which they lived:

> Così tornavan per lo cerchio tetro
> da ogne mano a l'opposito punto,
> gridandosi anche loro ontoso metro;

poi si volgea ciascun, quand' era giunto,
per lo suo mezzo cerchio a l'altra giostra.   (VII 31–5)

(And so they turned back along the gloomy circle / on either hand, to the opposite
point, / these, too, screaming their chant of shame: / then each one, when he reached the
point turned / through half a circle to the next joust.)

The doctrine of fortune provides, then, the first philosophical illustration of
the principles which underlie Dante's judgement both of the sinners in Hell
and of the vices which corrupt the society in which he lives. Equally, in the
context of the *cupiditas* cantos and of the practical problems represented
there, the same passage reveals once more the virtues and the limitations of
the philosophical procedure which Dante associates with Virgil. But Virgil,
as we have suggested, may be taken in these cantos to represent Dante's own
claim to philosophical prestige. 'Prestige' is perhaps an inaccurate word,
considering that Dante, by speaking through an acknowledged 'maestro',
contrives to deflect from himself any extravagant glory; his fiction involves a
certain tactical humility. Still, in concluding this section, we may pause to
consider how Canto VII both confirms and quite significantly modifies the
philosophical procedures that Dante first developed in the *Convivio*.

First, we need hardly emphasise the value which Dante attributes to the
rational clarity exemplified in Virgil's speech. One should, however, note
that this clarity takes a surprising form in Canto VII. For Virgil, quite
strikingly, does *not* proceed by a dialectical process of question and answer.
In this respect, as in others, the speech differs from comparable speeches in
Boethius's *Consolatio*; for there it is an essential part of Boethius's teaching
that a human being should be able to rise by dialectical steps above the
miseries imposed by fortune. Likewise in the *Convivio*, Dante shows a
profound excitement over scholastic methods of argumentation – and, as a
result, generates many an unnecessary qualification or subordinate clause.
But in Canto VII Virgil permits only one intervention from his inquisitive
student and disallows any final comment on his discourse by insisting that
Dante should now descend to 'maggior pieta' (97).

What, then, are the implications of this new emphasis?

In the first place, the decisiveness of Virgil underlines the extent to which
Dante is now concerned with purposes or ends which can be defined,
achieved and truly concluded without any restlessness or false exuberance.
We have seen already how the protagonist was frustrated by his over-
ambitious desire to climb directly from the *selva oscura* to the Hill of Hope.
Virgil's words, now as in Canto I, prevent a recurrence of any such wasted
effort.

In the second place, the firmness that Virgil displays provides the
foundation for an act of contemplation. Virgil, through the words he utters,
trains the eyes of the protagonist upon the intelligent patterns of the physical
world. As he himself insists, his purpose is to make it possible for the
protagonist to *praise* Fortuna. This explains the significance of the evident

similarities between the representations of the Lady Fortuna and Beatrice in *Inferno* II. Both – like Solomon's Wisdom – are images of light and intelligence, immune to injury or reproach, rejoicing in the primal certainty of Heaven. Thus Dante writes of Fortuna (as we have seen):

> ma ella s'è beata e ciò non ode:
> con l'altre prime creature lieta
> volve sua spera e beata si gode.   (VII 94–6)

where, of Beatrice, he had written:

> I' son fatta da Dio, sua mercé, tale,
> che la vostra miseria non mi tange,
> né fiamma d'esto 'ncendio non m'assale.   (II 91–3)

In each case the figure represents an aspect of the secure possession of existence which human beings have been granted by their Creator; and in each case the appropriate response will be not to question but to see clearly and to praise what one sees.

Finally, however, in insisting upon a descent to 'greater misery', Virgil stresses a quite different and far more terrible aspect of the intellectual life as Dante must now envisage it. The pursuit of truth, it appears, must directly engage with the shock and surprises that the journey brings. Aeneas knew this; Cacciaguida knew this. And no position could better express the condition in which Dante the philosopher found himself when he became Dante the exile. It is here, too, of course, that the Fortuna passage illustrates with the utmost clarity the importance of 'difficulty' in Dante's thinking; and its implications in this respect echo throughout the *Commedia*. So, if it is a peculiarly taxing trial of the philosophical mind to see order in the apparent disorder of Fortuna, this trial, as we have said, is itself only a preparation for the trials to which a soul such as Forese will submit in Purgatory, as he makes pain itself his solace (*Purg.* XXIII). But these trials, in turn, are also a preparation for a central principle in Dante's discussion of Christian Philosophy, in Canto XI of the *Paradiso*; for there the philosophers contemplate the example of St Francis, who not only accepted poverty but loved it to the extent of marrying the loathsome hag whom all other men since Christ had shunned. Like Fortuna, Poverty is blamed and cursed by humanity, and indeed there are verbal similarities between the two portrayals, for where Fortuna is 'tanto posta in croce / pur da color che le dovrien dar lode (*Inf.* VII 91–2), Poverty is said to leap upon the cross with Christ: 'ella con Cristo salse in su la croce' (*Par.* XI 72). But the conclusion in both the Fortuna passage and the St Francis passage must be the same: to be a philosopher is to know one's relation to the divine order; and to know that is to recognise with joy, not ignorant panic, the essential poverty of any creature in regard to its Creator.

Our reference here to St Francis carries us a good way beyond Solomon, Boethius and Virgil. We have also travelled some distance now from the Dante of the *Convivio*. Though 'poverty' is already a great theme in Book IV of the *Convivio*, Dante is not there speaking of poverty or suffering as an intellectual or existential condition. But his move towards the *Commedia* demands that he should. For much of the *Convivio* had been concerned with the 'consolations' available to the philosophical mind through a reading of authorities such as Boethius and Solomon. But the lengthening experience of exile and the realisation, underlying the *Commedia*, that God is both Creator and Judge require that Dante should abandon such a refuge and meet the tragic – and ultimately miraculous – demands of a quest for truth which will lead him through infernal wastelands of absurdity and vice.

Nor will it be possible any longer for Dante to assume the detached and aristocratic position of the professional philosopher. His poem, in effect, will not allow him either to 'look and pass on', as Virgil counsels, or to adopt the passionate disdain which characterises the polemical passages of the *Convivio*. The condition under which philosophy proceeds in the *Commedia* will be a condition of narrative – and, specifically, of a narrative which depicts a succession of critical and challenging encounters, where many voices other than his own true voice are heard. 'Fortuna' herself imposes that procedure; and Dante responds with a story, in which he requires of himself that he should continually reaffirm the principles on which his thinking rests by practical acts of judgement, and where, having achieved this, he must continually engage – in response not only to Fortuna but also to the demands of philosophy – with new trials. Neither Aristotle nor Boethius could have taught Dante the practical implications of this as effectively as the author of the *Aeneid*; but even the example of Virgil as narrator will need to be recast in response to the demands which Dante here makes upon himself.

III

The narrative procedures exemplified in Cantos VIII and IX of the *Inferno*, so far from offering simply a fictional adjunct to Dante's thinking, reflect the conditions and characteristics of the intellectual procedures he adopts throughout the *cantica*. In a simple sense, the philosophical journey which Virgil initiates in Canto I is itself a portrayal of how the philosophical mind must progress steadily from point to point, and also indicates the extent to which, for Dante, moral and intellectual endeavour are interconnected. As the *Convivio* suggests, it is proper that human beings should make this journey; and at each stage the philosophical mind is required to exert its powers of judgement and moral discrimination.

There will be more to say in Chapter 3 about the ways in which Dante, as poet and narrator, develops and modifies the notion of the journey; but it is already apparent that Dante does not depend exclusively upon a representation of uninterrupted advance. We have seen the extent to which one canto, depicting one stage of the journey, tends to differ in imaginative tone from the next – as for instance in the contrasts between the conclusion of Canto II and the opening of Canto III, or those between the sophistications of

Canto V and the harshness of Canto VI. And one need only think of the usual
length of any one book in the *Aeneid* to realise that Dante has abandoned the
narrative example which Virgil provided, substituting a much shorter narra-
tive unit of roughly 150 lines for the sustained narrative sequences of the
Latin epic. This innovation permits a play of imaginative contrast which is
central to Dante's narrative method. And here, too, narrative will correspond
with aspects of Dante's philosophical procedure, displaying in particular a
continual readiness on the part of the poet to admit the impact of the 'new'.

So it is not sufficient to think of Dante's narrative as a progressive
sequence of event and logic. The image of the journey naturally suggests
some such linear model. But Cantos VIII and IX show that, in at least three
ways, the dynamics of Dante's journey – and equally of the poet's own nar-
rative and philosophical procedures – cannot be described simply in terms of
a steady development.

To begin with, the episode describing Dante's approach to the Gates of the
City of Dis is one which depicts a period of waiting and even, potentially, of
defeat; as in the first sixty lines of Canto I so here – opposed by the
inhabitants of Dis – the protagonist is in danger of finding his advance
reversed or transformed into a rout.

Secondly, as also in Canto II, the possibility of progress is shown to
depend upon the intervention of a being who has subsequently no place in
the story of the *Inferno*. In Canto II this being was Beatrice; in Canto IX it is
the *Messo da Ciel*. So far from representing a single linear action, the story
of the *Inferno* portrays a journey which can be – and needs to be –
interrupted by agencies alien to its immediate concerns. The narrative is thus
'polyphonic', in that the primary action of the narrative is accompanied by
another – on the level of divine purpose – which for the most part is remote,
though it is heard clearly enough in moments of surprise and discomposure.

Thirdly, the imagery of these two cantos begins to emphasise that,
although the protagonist is apparently advancing in a line, his journey
through eternity will finally resolve into a circle. Only in Paradise does the
protagonist realise consciously that his progress reconciles him with the
circular movement of the heavens, so that finally he can move in 'disio' and
'velle' like a wheel 'ch'igualmente è mossa' (*Par.* XXXIII 144). But in the
Purgatorio his journey is a spiral, as he climbs around the spindle of the
tapering mountain, and the same is true of his descent through the cone of
Hell – the 'empi giri' (*Inf.* X 4). In Canto VIII, the two protagonists are
reminded that Dis is the defensive encirclement of a bottomless pit when
their boat has to travel round these walls before arriving at the threshold:

> Non sanza prima far grande aggirata,
> venimmo in parte dove il nocchier forte
> 'Usciteci', gridò: 'qui è l'intrata'.   (VIII 79–81)

(Not without making first a long circuit, / we came to the place where the helmsman, in
a loud voice, / cried: 'Now get out: here is the entrance.')

In the seventh canto, the image of the sphere that Fortuna rolls has already shown how circles may be the final expression of orderly action. But the drama of the present cantos depends upon an inversion of that image. In Dis, Dante will show how, through sin, the same capacities of will and intellect which lead human beings to truth may also prove destructive. Correspondingly, the most evident images of circularity here parody divine order: the circular walls of Dis express the defensive and ingrained divisiveness of those that inhabit the City; the mystic circle of love becomes in this sequence the equally mysterious circle of hate. Yet on the level of imagery – hidden from the consciousness of the protagonist, though present in his actions – it will be found that the circle, even in this episode, is potentially orderly as well as confusingly defensive, protective as well as exclusive. Thus in the central episode of Canto VIII, Virgil is obliged to protect the encircling gunwales of the craft in which he and the protagonist are travelling from the violent assault of Filippo Argenti by an equally violent gesture of his own: 'Via costà con li altri cani!' (42) – off with you, to the other dogs!

On the levels of event and imagery, the sequence provides significant complications to the portrayal of the journey. In considering these, we can also consider a further aspect of the episode: its concern with conversion and the representation of transition. In entering the City of Dis, the protagonist discovers a kind of sin wholly different from the sins of preceding circles. Those were sins of impulse or disordered appetite, and they could have been corrected by timely moderation and self-discipline. From now on, however, down to the lowest circles of Hell, Dante deals with sins which are the product of will and reason. In violence or fraud, the human being deliberately and maliciously directs itself to a destructive purpose. Increasingly, the protagonist must realise that the essential faculties of the moral and intellectual life may themselves be agents of destruction or self-destruction. This is a baffling notion – sufficiently so to account for the sudden arrest of action in the face of Dis. But how, then, is Dante to advance?

In common with some of the most impressive moments of the *Commedia*, this episode is an account of instability, process and change. The *Purgatorio*, for instance, is from first to last an account of transition; and in the second *cantica* the narrative exactly reflects the mentality appropriate to conversion as the penitents progress from time to eternity, from sin to beatitude. But the present episode is also a scene of conversion in which Dante is made, firstly, to recognise the ingrained obduracy of sin and then to receive, from the miraculous intervention of the *Messo*, a remedy against that apparently hopeless condition. If we insist upon regarding the *Commedia* as a 'great cathedral' of ideas we shall obscure the interest which Dante evidently takes in the human capacity to respond to the demand for spiritual renewal. (I need not stress here that the demands of the transition are themselves entirely at one with the philosophical procedures developed in response to the ever-changing impact of Fortuna.) To see, however, the full extent of Dante's thinking here, one must pay close attention to the narrative art involved in portraying that advance.

Canto VIII may be divided broadly into three movements, all of which depict a violent opposition – spelled out in recurrent references to lines, both horizontal and vertical, and to circles or turnings – between the advancing protagonist and those who inhabit and defend the citadel of deliberate sin. The first phase describes the encounter between the wrathful Phlegyas, guardian of the marsh into which the river Styx flows around Dis (1–30). The second shows the meeting between the protagonist and his compatriot Filippo Argenti (31–66). Then, finally, there is the first round of the conflict between the travellers and the demons – a conflict which will not end until Canto IX, but which, in Canto VIII, concludes with an account, initially, of how the terrified protagonist is separated, for a first time, from his guide, and subsequently with a portrayal of Virgil's apparent bewilderment about how to proceed (67–130).

The opening phase of Canto VIII announces the principal motifs of the narrative. Line 1 stresses the simple linear development of the narrative – and one notes how Dante here associates the act of writing with the progress of the journey: 'Io dico, seguitando' – I say, continuing. As the fictional journey moves – steadily, it seems – towards its conclusion, the poet insists upon his own ability to make the connection between one point in his story and another. But this movement is at once complicated by the next clause in lines 1–2: 'ch'assai prima / che noi fossimo al piè de l'alta torre' – before / we arrived at the foot of the high tower. Before they reach their immediate goal, the travellers are distracted and made to consider, in anticipation, what their arrival might unleash. They see before them a circular tower, pregnant with possibilities; and on top of this tower two lights are flashing: 'due fiammette che i vedemmo porre, / e un'altra da lungi render cenno' (4–5) – two bright flames we saw put there, / and another from a distance gave a signal back. Though these are signal-lights, the protagonist cannot tell what their signal means: 'Questo che dice?' (8) – What do they say?

As the protagonists raise their eyes to the top of the tower (3), a vertical co-ordinate is revealed in the action against the horizontal progress emphasised so far. This is the first time since Dante saw the Hill in Canto I that he has had to lift his eyes; and it is from the vertical that the *Messo*, coming 'like a wind' from Heaven, will eventually intervene. Yet the only part of his action which the protagonist witnesses is cast along the same horizontal as he himself is pursuing: the *Messo* progresses across the swamp with 'dry feet' (IX 81). The trajectory of the *Messo* is initiated by the divine, but it is also reconciled to the human. However, for most of the sequence the vertical plane is represented by the tower and will stand, in complete contrast to the Hill or the *Messo*, as a source of confusion and menace.

Virgil makes no attempt to allay the apprehension that the signal-lights have aroused in his companion. Instead, he acts as he will throughout the episode; explaining nothing, he nonetheless makes it possible for the protagonist to overcome his inclination to despair, to wait with patience and courage in the face of whatever reveals itself. Virgil makes ready, not as a guide but as a bulwark, for the advent of the *Messo*. But in the first instance his actions prepare for a quite different arrival, the unexpectedly violent and rapid opposition of Phlegyas (13–17). Hitherto, the imagery of the scene has emphasised the stagnation of the 'sucide onde' (10) and the swirling fogs and vapours (12) which rise from it. Now – precipitating a movement of clean cut-and-thrust – Phlegyas appears, his boat rushing with unnatural speed across the filthy marsh:

> Corda non pinse mai da sé saetta
> che sì corresse via per l'aere snella,
> com' io vidi una nave piccioletta
> venir per l'acqua ...   (VIII 13–16)

(No string ever drove an arrow from itself / that ran so swiftly through the air / as I saw that little craft / come across the water).

Phlegyas is a parody of purposeful action – as accurate and direct as an arrow, yet running exactly counter to Dante's advance. But this malign purpose is immediately blunted by Virgil's riposte; and if Phlegyas's appearance is the first manifestation in this episode of forces external to Dante's immediate comprehension, then the figure of Dante himself is no less unexpected in Phlegyas's view. And Phlegyas is completely dumb-founded by the impact of the unexpected, as Dante finally will *not* be:

> Qual è colui che grande inganno ascolta
> che li sia fatto, e poi se ne rammarca,
> fecesi Flegïàs ne l'ira accolta.   (22–4)

(Like someone who hears how a great trick / has been played upon him and then grows bitter because of it, / so was Phlegyas gathered up in his rage.)

The demon is seen here caught in a circle of perplexity and anger, destructive to himself but beneficial to the protagonist. This is strictly the first image of encirclement in the canto; but it stands in pointed contrast to the 'turn' at line 7, when the protagonist, perplexed by the signal-lights, was able at least to refer to Virgil: 'E io mi volsi al mar di tutto 'l senno!' – and I turned to the sea of all wisdom. Here the 'turn' demonstrates an ability on the part of the protagonist to escape from the travails of his own inner self; and the liberation that this implies is emphasised by the phrase 'the sea of all wisdom' which the poet applies to Virgil. As the 'mar di tutto 'l senno', Virgil is a source of freedom as constant but as mobile as the ocean, as natural and as receptive; it is on the broad stream – the 'largo fiume' (*Inf.* I 80) – of Virgil's words, rather than on the sluggish 'pantan', that the craft of Dante's purposes proceeds.

The first sequence ends with a *terzina* that delicately draws together the main strands of the first movement:

> Lo duca mio discese ne la barca,
> e poi mi fece intrare appresso lui;
> e sol quand' io fui dentro parve carca.   (25–7)

(My guide went down into the boat, / and then had me come in beside him, / and only when I was in it did the boat seem loaded.)

Having resisted Phlegyas, Dante and Virgil are free to move forward along the horizontal of their journey. The moment is a reassertion of normal companionship, spelled out in the gestures of concern and assistance which Virgil makes towards the hesitant protagonist. Yet even here the advance is punctuated by a vertical movement, as the boat, receiving and encircling Dante's weight, sinks beneath it. This is not a trivial emphasis: we are made to realise that the purely natural conditions of weight and gravity are *un*natural in Hell; and, by the same token, we momentarily comprehend that Dante's physical passage through Hell is the consequence of a divine decree. The 'normal' horizons of Hell – its obstinacy and its rules – can be broken at God's command; but equally the normality of bodily existence is safeguarded in Dante's case by that particular dispensation. Here, as later with the descent of the *Messo*, the settled conditions both of Hell and of temporal and physical reality are seen to depend upon actions along an axis which intersects the simple line of progress.

By now the fundamental patterns of the narrative are established; and it would be possible to trace the imagery of line and circle through all subsequent phases of the narrative. But as Dante meets Filippo Argenti other questions come into play: for it is impossible to ignore the extreme cruelty that both the protagonist and Virgil here show towards the sinner. In this episode, if anywhere, Dante would seem to deserve I. A. Richards's description as 'the great hater'; and the issue becomes still more complicated when one notes that at lines 44–5 Virgil cites the Scriptures in approbation of Dante's venomous action. It needs to be stressed that in the final phase of the canto the hatred and violence of the Argenti episode is reversed and balanced by a scene in which Dante and Virgil are deposed from their position of superiority and subjected to humiliations comparable if not identical to those they have themselves inflicted upon Filippo Argenti. Yet the violence of both the initial encounter and its subsequent reversal also need to be examined as evidence of how Dante allows the narrative line of his text to be interrupted.

Similar considerations demand that one should look in some detail at the scriptural allusion of lines 44–5. In this episode, even the linguistic text does not maintain a simple level; attention is divided between Dante's words and the words and story of the Gospel incident to which he refers. (In Canto IX a similar disturbance occurs when, at the advent of the *Messo*, Dante speaks directly to his reader and demands that he should seek the meaning of the incident 'beneath' the veil of the strange verses he himself is writing.)

As Dante and Virgil proceed over the dead waters of the Styx (one notes 'Mentre' and the continuative imperfect 'corravam'), they are suddenly confronted by a figure so besmirched with slime that he seems to be brimming over with it – 'pien' – from inside:

> Mentre noi corravam la morta gora,
> dinanzi mi si fece un pien di fango,
> e disse: 'Chi se' tu che vieni anzi ora?'.						(31–3)

(While we were running over the dead channel, / there appeared before me one who was full of mud, / who said 'Who are you who come before your hour?')

The movement of advance and arrest is similar to that which occurred in the Phlegyas episode; and, as in that sequence, so here a contrast is implied between the presence of Dante in Hell – which miraculously interrupts the 'normal' order so that he 'comes before his hour' – and the 'darkness' of Argenti. But the grounds of the meeting are complicated by the fact that Dante now deals not with a mythical figure but with a historical contemporary, known and named as an individual. The episode contrasts and balances the two great mysteries that Dante discusses in the *Commedia*: the mystery of how the humble individual – who is neither 'Aeneas nor Paul' – may be destined for salvation, and the mystery of human self-destructiveness vividly realised when Filippo Argenti, at the conclusion of the scene, turns his teeth upon himself (63). In Canto VI Dante contrasted himself, in an act of practical judgement, with the historical Ciacco, and similarly in Canto VIII a judgement arises as to the relative abilities of the protagonist and Filippo to advance and achieve an orderly expression of their own selfhood. So, the first words of the protagonist to Filippo are:

> E io a lui: 'S'i' vegno, non rimango, ...'						(34)

(And I to him: 'If I come, I do not remain').

Similarly the episode concludes with Dante, as poet, declaring:

> Quivi il lasciammo, che più non ne narro.						(64)

(Here we left him and my story tells no more of him.)

This final line echoes the words which Virgil speaks in Canto III, 'non ragionam di lor', and in Canto VII, 'parole non ci appulcro'. But Dante has now extended the implications of these phrases: the sinner is no longer simply beyond the grasp of words, but also beyond the grasp of narrative art, and unworthy to be included in the story for that reason. Stories must reflect the mind's capacity for coherent and purposeful progress; and the protagonist rightly boasts of 'not remaining'. But at Canto VIII 110, he, too, will remain in doubt – 'rimagno in forse' – when Virgil leaves him. Moreover, the Furies in Canto IX will threaten to turn him into immobile stone (55), and the intervention of the *Messo* will be required if he is to escape that fate. For the moment, however, the protagonist is competent to assert the principle of his own advance, rising – with a vigour that anticipates in outline the easy power of the *Messo* – to defend himself against distraction and impediment:

> Con piangere e con lutto,
> spirito maladetto, ti rimani;
> ch'i' ti conosco, ancor sie lordo tutto.						(37–9)

(With weeping and with misery / remain, accursed spirit; / I know you filthy as you are.)

Here the tension of the encounter precipitates recognition, and the drama is a realisation of the issues which are at stake: where Dante goes on with his journey, which – transformed into the story of the *Commedia* – will teach and lead his fellow-men, Filippo Argenti is known as the 'spirito bizzarro' (62), a headstrong, wayward or, literally, eccentric being, opposed to any pursuit of settled purpose. As a Florentine, his paths in life may have crossed with Dante's; but like Ciacco, he has done nothing to pursue the true destiny of a Florentine, or deserve recognition as such:

> Quei fu al mondo persona orgogliosa;
> bontà non è che sua memoria fregi:
> così s'è l'ombra sua qui furïosa.   (46–8)

(In the world he was an arrogant person; / there is no good that decorates his memory: / and so his shade dwells in fury here.)

As philosophy condemns Ciacco, so storytelling (or history) condemns Filippo; he is left, locked up and enclosed in his own confusion and disruptiveness:

> in sé medesmo si volvea co' denti.   (63)

(he turned himself on himself with his teeth).

The image which Dante gives of Filippo, 'turned' in upon his own viciousness but attacked by his fellow-spirits, echoes that of Phlegyas, pent up – 'accolta' – in his 'inganno', and also points forwards to the picture of Dis as a city divided against itself. But the major contrast in terms of imagery is again with the circle which the protagonist and Virgil have formed at the centre of the Argenti episode. For when Virgil witnesses Dante's zeal against Filippo, he first corroborates it with an equally vicious act, 'Via costà con li altri cani' (42) – Away, back with the other dogs; and then, turning to the protagonist, embraces him:

> Lo collo poi con le braccia mi cinse;
> basciommi 'l volto e disse: 'Alma sdegnosa,
> benedetta colei che 'n te s'incinse!'.   (43–5)

(He cast his arms in an embrace around my neck; / he kissed my face and said: / 'O indignant soul: blessed be she who enclosed thee in her womb!')

The embrace of Virgil – in view of his function as the representative of Rome – amounts to a confirmation of Dante's place in history, and is also a recognition of the contribution Dante can make in defence of that community of just men which descends, in the poet's view, from Rome to Florence. But this confirmation is carried further by the blessing which Virgil calls down upon 'the womb which encircled thee'. The circle of the womb is the source of life and growth; and the actions which the protagonist has performed are here acknowledged to be consistent with and devoted to the protection of nature and normality in its most elemental manifestation.

At this point, however, readers are likely to be less concerned about the imagery of the canto than by the peculiar vehemence of Dante's treatment of Filippo. Certainly there is a tension between the tenderness of Virgil's acclamation and the viciousness of the action it celebrates. Nor is this tension diminished when one recalls that the words Virgil applies to Dante are taken from the Gospel of St Luke II 27, where, as Christ is casting out devils, a woman in the crowd cries out: 'Blessed is the womb that bare thee, and the paps which thou hast sucked.' There is much in the scene before the Gates of Dis which corresponds to the Gospel episode. In particular, Christ is discoursing at this point in the Gospel on the internal divisions which destroy the kingdom of Evil; and Dis itself will prove to be a picture of such divisions. Nevertheless, it should be noted that Jesus rejects that praise, saying: 'Yea, rather, blessed are those that hear the word of God and keep it.' In that light Dante's wrath may well seem disproportionate, as may his identification of himself with the figure of Christ.

One argument might be that this very disproportion is itself significant, as an example of dislocation in the narrative line of the canto. I shall pursue that suggestion in a moment. However, an explanation can be found in the logic of the *Inferno* both for the wrath of the protagonist and for the scriptural allusion with which the poet expresses his self-approbation. In terms of the spiritual development of the protagonist, the meeting with Argenti concludes, for the time being, the series of judgements which began with the portrayal of Francesca and Ciacco; indeed Argenti's first words are closely comparable to Francesca's and to Ciacco's: 'Vedi che son un che piango' (36) – See, I am one who weeps. But by now, it may be said, the protagonist has advanced to a point at which he can resist an appeal to emotion of the kind which Francesca has made upon him. As Canto III suggests, violence is as much a part of Dante's scheme of judgement as the measured estimations that Virgil provides. Indeed, where the protagonist has developed to a high pitch of confidence, Virgil too has apparently advanced, to a point at which he can recognise the value of the violence his disciple here displays in his judgements; incapable as he may be of such judgements himself, he applauds their force when they are made manifest, just as in Canto IV he acknowledges the power of Christ in harrowing Hell.

This reading is certainly consistent with what follows: as Virgil says at Canto IX 32–3, it is impossible to enter the City of Dis without wrath: 'la città dolente, / u' non potemo intrare omai sanz' ira'. And all the oppositions we have so far noted in the sequence occur between various *kinds* of wrath. On the one hand, there is the divisive and confusing wrath of Phlegyas and Filippo Argenti; on the other, there is the wrath of Dante, which prefigures, as we have said, the controlled and measured anger that the *Messo da Ciel* displays on the threshold of Dis. As a *sin*, anger is consistently shown in the *Commedia* to obfuscate intelligence. Thus in the *Purgatorio*, the angry spirit of Marco Lombardo does penance in a cloud of black smoke – which is 'worse than the smoke of Hell' (*Purg.* XVI 1). But Marco, as a penitent, is

engaged in converting the passions that misled him in his temporal existence
into energies consistent with the truths now revealed to him, and it is he who
utters the most comprehensive account in the *Purgatorio* of humanity's place
in the divine order. He speaks with great clarity, but also with urgency and
indignation compatible with his innately irascible temperament.

Anger, then, may be a sin, but it may also become zeal and holy wrath;
and in that aspect, wrath not only has a place in Dante's scheme of thought,
it is also a weapon necessary in the defence of that scheme.

But could Dante have claimed scriptural authority for such a position?
That he can is clear from a passage at the conclusion of the first Justice canto
in the *Paradiso*, where the poet provides a powerful picture of Christ as the
wrathful judge, who in the Gospel story drives the money-lenders from the
Temple (one notes in the following depiction of anger the same 'fummo' or
'smoke' image as is also found in the Marco Lombardo episode and the
present scene in the swamps of the Styx):

> Per ch'io prego la mente in che s'inizia
> tuo moto e tua virtute, che rimiri
> ond' esce il fummo che 'l tuo raggio vizia;
> sì ch'un'altra fïata omai s'adiri
> del comperare e vender dentro al templo
> Che si murò di segni e di martìri.   (*Par.* XVIII 118–23)

(And so I implore the mind in which begins / your motion and your power that you cast
your eyes / upon the place where the smoke that vitiates your light-rays issues, / so that
again its wrath should be directed / against the buying and selling in the Temple /
whose walls are made with martyrdom and miracles.)

This reference is clearly relevant to Canto VIII: the City of Dis is not only a
corrupt 'temple' or citadel but also an image of the corrupt city of Florence
which has locked the poet Dante out, the city which he must re-enter – in
word if not in deed – if he is to purge it of injustice. But the allusion to St
Luke in Virgil's speech is more specific in its reference than the dramatic
evocation of Christ's action in the *Paradiso*. In context, the lines which
Dante quotes precede a discussion of the way in which justice and
righteousness will eventually make themselves known in the world. The
'wicked generations' demand a sign from God, but this sign will not appear
in the form they expected:

and there shall no sign be given it, but the sign of Jonas the prophet. For as Jonas was a
sign unto the Ninevites, so shall also the Son of man be to this generation. The queen of
the South shall rise up in judgement with this generation and shall condemn them: for
she came from the utmost parts of the earth to hear the wisdom of Solomon: and,
behold, a greater than Solomon is here.   (Gospel of St Luke XI 29–31)

If, as I have suggested the portrayal of Fortuna is influenced by the Book
of Wisdom, the explicit allusion in this passage to Solomon clearly confirms
the tendency of Dante's thinking in Canto VIII: in some form, wisdom will be
revealed to an evil generation and declare itself in acts of judgement.
However, the form in which wisdom and judgement are to be expressed – the

sign which will be given – will be neither a law nor an act of divine intervention, but rather the living witness of a just man. Christ, as he comes in judgement, is the reality prefigured by Jonah. But Dante – travelling to salvation through the depths of Hell, faced as he has been in the last three circles with evidence of how evil his own generation is – must himself be seen as another such sign, in his own way and in his own time another Jonah: his presence in Hell speaks of the providential justice which offers salvation to the righteous man. Nor is it incomprehensible in this light that Virgil should honour Dante as he does. For in Dante's conception of history, the function of Rome – and of Roman justice – is to prepare the world for the revelation of the new law in the person of Christ. In Dante, at this point, Virgil perceives a prophetic foreshadowing of Christ's Second Coming.

With this, we return both to the narrative of Canto VIII – and to the argument I have been pursuing from the first chapter of this book. I have argued that wisdom and justice are to be understood not as principles but as actions incorporated and expressed in the life of the individual. Finally, if not exclusively, it is through such individuals that the truth of God's intentions are known. So, while the wrath of Dante in Canto VIII may indeed be explained and analysed, it is not in the end appropriate to rest content with mere explanations. The form in which Dante's meaning is made will be the form which his narrative provides, where the force and complexity of the human 'sign' can be fully realised.

Nothing we have said so far will provide convincing evidence against the charge that Dante here reveals himself to be the 'great hater'. Nonetheless, as we move into the final phase of the canto, it becomes clear that Dante assumes no superiority on the grounds of the achievement for which Virgil applauds him. Just as Christ in the Gospel of St Luke rejects the acclamation of the crowd and counsels patient obedience to the Word of God, so now the protagonist enters a phase in which he is obliged to wait patiently for a sign to appear – greater than he himself – in the form of the *Messo da Ciel*. As for the poet, he shows no inclination to emphasise the prestige he has just bestowed upon himself, but rather allows the narrative to complicate the issue still further by exposing and contemplating his own humiliation. A pattern is established here – to be repeated and sustained throughout the Malebolge – in which an instant of confident mastery on Dante's part is followed not simply (as in the Francesca episode) by a sequence of self-analysis but by a scene of self-laceration, even of ridicule.

So, the long closing sequence of Canto VIII is governed by features which reverse the principles of unity, action and advance on which Dante has hitherto proceeded. The episode is in fact one of complete *in*action, depicting not the pursuit of purpose but rather its fragmentation, and its imagery is consistently dominated by references to division and separation.

These references begin at line 64 with a conflict in the mental faculties of the protagonist, as – hearing the shrieks of Filippo behind him – he tries to defeat the impressions which this cry makes upon him by gazing steadfastly forwards, opening his eyes to the horror of the scene ahead: here the protagonist himself attempts to defend the simple line of his journey from a chaotic 'polyphony' of competing interests:

> ma ne l'orecchie mi percosse un duolo,
> per ch'io avante l'occhio intento sbarro.   (*Inf.* VIII 65–6)

(but grievous pain smote upon my ears, / at which I bent my eyes intently forwards).

There follows a last moment of composure in which Virgil speaks words of affectionate comfort while their boat approaches and encircles the turrets of Dis: 'Omai, figliuolo, / s'appressa la città c'ha nome Dite' (67–8) – Now, my son, the city named Dis is drawing close. But this unity dissolves in the face of the rebel angels who stand over the threshold; for their purpose is not only to resist Dante's advance but to separate him from his guide. They are prepared to deal only with Virgil; the protagonist must return unaccompanied along the foolish road he has embarked upon:

> Vien tu solo, e quei sen vada
> che sì ardito intrò per questo regno.
> Sol si ritorni per la folle strada.   (89–91)

(You come alone, and let that one depart / who has entered this realm so boldly. / Let him return alone along his foolish path.)

Virgil now approaches the gate to speak 'secretly' with the devils (88) while the protagonist is left almost 'unmade' with dread: 'disfatto' (100). With this, a double action – cast in the narrative present tense – is instituted, in which Virgil's negotiations with the devils proceed, unheard, to their unsuccessful conclusion while the protagonist remains paralysed by suspense:

> Così sen va, e quivi m'abbandona
> lo dolce padre, e io rimagno in forse,
> che sì e no nel capo mi tenciona.
> Udir non potti quello ch'a lor porse;
> ma ei non stette là con essi guari,
> che ciascun dentro a pruova si ricorse.   (109–14)

(So he goes away, leaving me here, / my sweet father, and I remain in uncertainty, / the 'yes' and 'no' contending in my head. / I could not hear what he put to them. / But he did not stay long with them / before all of them, vying with one another, rushed back inside.)

Yet as the doors close defiantly against Virgil, there also begins a movement which – while representing, to all appearances, a defeat – arouses undertones and suggestions of an ultimate, if incomprehensible, solution.

Virgil returns to Dante stripped of all confidence, and for the first time is unable to make sense of the resistance of Hell:

> Li occhi a la terra e le ciglia avea rase
> d'ogne baldanza, e dicea ne' sospiri:
> 'Chi m'ha negate le dolenti case!'.   (118–20)

(His eyes and brows were cast upon the ground, shorn / of all bravery, and between his sighs he said: / 'Who has denied me entrance to the sorrowful dwellings!')

But the first element in the recovery will prove to be the very ordinariness to which Virgil is now reduced: it is this which enables him to re-establish solidarity with Dante – on a more equal footing than has yet prevailed between them – against the monstrous abnormality of the patrols which (one notes the image) 'circle' within the walls: 'dentro s'aggiri' (123). His words as he concludes the canto corroborate this sense of solidarity: he appeals to Dante's memory of the sights which they have already seen together on their journey, recalling the words written on Hell-Gate:

> Sovr' essa vedestù la scritta morta.   (127)

(You saw the dead inscription above it.)

Where, at the Gate of Hell, it was the protagonist alone, not Virgil, who was confused, they now share that experience of dismay. Virgil has only words, memories and suggestions with which to encourage the protagonist. These, however, constitute a 'presence' which the protagonist can still rely upon; and in fact the reference to Hell-Gate – terrible as the writing on it was – does offer another source of comfort. Above and beyond the inconclusive text of Virgil's discourse there is the divine writ; and shortly the *Messo da Ciel* will appear, to translate the authority of those 'dead' words into action – into voice and human gesture. For the moment, Dante and Virgil have to wait, which is to say they must accept their own human powerlessness in the face of the mysteries of sin and the equal mysteries of divine law and deliverance.

The ninth canto opens on exactly the same note of apprehension as concludes Canto VIII. It is already so unusual for one canto to resemble its predecessor in tone that the delay imposed upon the travellers is here paralleled in the process of reading itself: our expectations of an advance in the narrative are disappointed, and the poet seems for once to relinquish his command of novelty. (The only other case in the *Inferno* where cantos are connected in such a way occurs between Cantos XXI and XXII, which, in this and other respects, offer a parodic counterpart to Cantos VIII and IX.)

In its rhythms and imagery, too, the ninth canto is comparable to the eighth. Yet the similarities stand in an inverse relationship. The opening of Canto VIII was dominated by rhythms of suspense, its conclusion by a dislocation of narrative progress. But these features are here translated gradually and surreptitiously into rhythms of anticipation, and into a sequence of pauses dictated by the almost unspeakable expectation of the *Messo da Ciel*. Similarly, we shall see, an alteration occurs in the images of line – both vertical and horizontal – and of the circle. These images, so far, have tended to express the negatives of resistance and arrest; but the *Messo* will restore them to positive significance. His function indeed is to ensure that the purpose of Dante's journey should not be 'chopped off' by the recalcitrance of Hell; the ends and motives of divine justice cannot suffer mutilation:

> Perché recalcitrate a quella voglia
> a cui non puote il fin mai esser mozzo ...?   (IX 94–5)

(Why do you so stubbornly oppose that will / whose end and aim can never be chopped off?)

The *Messo* thus defends the completeness of God's order. But Dante in his own way serves the same order by the journey he has undertaken, and also by the story he is telling; and finally in Canto IX the drama of Dante's doubt and self-contradiction (prefiguring the dramas of divided selfhood that the violent sinners suffer in Dis) resolves into a drama of conversion, as the protagonist witnesses and responds to the arrival of the *Messo*.

These features need to be traced in the details of the text of the ninth canto. But the especial relevance of the canto to my general argument is that the poet here seems peculiarly conscious of his own narrative art. As Erich Auerbach has shown, the canto represents an exercise in the poetry of the sublime which rivals the art of classical antiquity; and, while the aesthetics of the sublime may not consciously have been in Dante's mind, there is little doubt that here (as earlier in Canto III and later in Canto XXV) he pits his own narrative procedures against the achievement of the Latin epic poets. So, at the opening of the sequence Virgil *personaggio* is seen in an unexampled moment of defeat. But in the description of the Furies (45–60), Dante puts Virgil the poet – who writes of the Furies in *Aeneid* X 761 – to a comparable test. There are, furthermore, specific references here to two other Latin authors of epic poems, Statius and Ovid. Overall, where Canto VII represented a reconciliation – and transformation – of ancient philosophical authorities, Canto IX similarly reconciles and transforms the voices of the ancient poets. Likewise, where the narrative of Canto VIII was disturbed and undermined by allusions to Scripture, the ninth canto draws together the strands of classical reference in a new and confident assertion of the coherence which Dante, as poet (and Christian), is able to impose upon his developing material.

The ninth canto divides into four major phases. The first (1–33) depicts the confusion of Virgil, and records the conversation to which he resorts in the interval; the second (34–60) describes the arrival of the Furies, and the third the intervention of the *Messo* (61–105); the final phase depicts Dante's entry into the circle of the heretics and marks the transition to Canto X, where the protagonist resumes his onward march, passing among the fiery tombs that contain the heretics.

So, the canto opens with an extraordinary moment in which Virgil is dumbstruck; the very strength for which he was chosen by Beatrice – his 'parole ornate' – fails as he breaks off in apprehensive silence:

> 'Pur a noi converrà vincer la punga',
> cominciò el, 'se non ... Tal ne s'offerse.
> Oh quanto tarda a me ch'altri qui giunga!'.   (7–9)

('Yet we must win in this conflict', / he began, 'if not ... Such help was offered us. / O how long it seems to me before another comes!')

As yet, the actions of the *Messo* remain secret, and the eyes of the protagonist are prevented from penetrating the horizons from which he will arrive: 'ché l'occhio nol potea menare a lunga / per l'aere nero e per la nebbia folta' (5–6) – for the eye could not carry far through the black air and the dense fog. But Virgil does not prove entirely helpless. Here, as at the end of Canto VIII, he resorts to speech and stories. Certainly, it is the eye which will be called in the end to witness the image of the *Messo*; but until that point Virgil restricts himself to the limited circle of words or actual events which lie within his experience and narrative competence. So, in response to Dante's anxious question as to whether anyone has descended before from Limbo 'in questo fondo de la trista conca' (16) – into the bottom of this dismal hollow – Virgil tells of his own previous journey to the depths of Hell. The outline of the narrative is drawn not from the *Aeneid* but from medieval legend, and it has the air of a fiction about it. Yet even as a fiction it serves as a pastime, and this is no insignificant thing in a situation where time itself appears to be stagnant. Virgil's words are, as they will be again in Canto XI, an alternative to action. Similarly, the story provides at least a model of progress to comfort the protagonist: even a spirit from Limbo who has all hope 'cut off'(18) can make the whole journey through Hell to a conclusion in the lowest circle, '[il] cerchio di Giuda' (27):

> Quell' è 'l più basso loco e 'l più oscuro,
> e 'l più lontan dal ciel che tutto gira:
> ben so 'l cammin; però ti fa sicuro.   (IX 28–30)

(That is the lowest place and the darkest, / and the furthest from Heaven which encircles all: / I know the way well, and so be assured.)

One notes here the interplay between the image of the circle and the image of linear direction; and in this regard the passage offers a comprehensive definition of Virgil's power – which is to translate the great circles of Hell and the encompassing sky which express divine order into the manageable shape of an advancing and purposeful line.

Yet now this account, however composed and valuable, is interrupted – and interrupted by the protagonist himself. With singular inattention, the protagonist allows his eyes to be attracted *upwards*, while Virgil continues to speak, to the fiery battlements of the tower:

> E altro disse, ma non l'ho a mente;
> però che l'occhio m'avea tutto tratto
> ver' l'alta torre a la cima rovente.   (34–6)

(And he said other things but I cannot remember them; / for my eye had drawn me wholly / to the high tower with the fiery summit.)

In the time of waiting, discourse serves as a substitute for that ultimate satisfaction which the *Messo* will bring to the eye of the protagonist. But for a moment the protagonist treats Virgil almost as he had treated Filippo, shutting his ears against a sound which might distract the total concentration of his gaze. Ear and eye pursue simultaneous but independent courses; and a polyphony is established not only between the horizontal and the vertical, but also between the aural and the visual.

Even so, the protagonist does not yet see the *Messo*; instead his eyes encounter the greatest opposition so far to his advance, in the form of the Furies. The image parodies, in its plasticity, brilliance and colour, the vision of the Heavenly Ladies in Canto ii, whose intervention allowed the protagonist to overcome his earliest self-doubt. Then suddenly the Furies appear on the battlements, girt and encircled with serpents, determined apparently to undo the work of Lucia, Beatrice and the Virgin. The eyes are drawn upwards:

> dove in un punto furon dritte ratto
> tre furie infernal di sangue tinte,
> che membra feminine avieno e atto,
>   e con idre verdissime eran cinte;
> serpentelli e ceraste avien per crine,
> onde le fiere tempie erano avvinte.   (37–42)

(to a point where suddenly there had arisen / three hellish Furies, stained with blood; / their limbs and actions were those of women, / and they were girdled with brilliant green hydras; / they had little snakes and cerastes for hair, / binding their dreadful temples).

At this point, the second phase in the narrative begins; here, too, Dante begins his engagement with the poets of antiquity. Portraying the Furies, Dante is drawing upon at least three classical sources: the *Aeneid*, Ovid's *Metamorphoses* and Statius's *Thebaid*. And, in terms of its mythic significance, the reference of the Furies is as appropriate to Dante's purposes now as was his reference to the Scriptures in Canto viii. For the myth of the Furies defines the awareness which the classical world achieved of the same tragedy that Dante, as a Christian, must now proceed to resolve in his treatment of violence and fraud: humanity *can* prey upon itself; its own best intentions and capabilities can become self-contradictory, haunting the mind with the unmanageable (and unimaginable) consequences of its own actions. In that light, the allusion to Statius's *Thebaid* takes on particular relevance (of Ovid we shall have more to say in the discussion of Canto xxv). For, in brief, Statius is consistently treated in the *Commedia* as an author who understood (as Virgil did not) the evil at the heart of human existence and who sought to portray in his poetry the seemingly endless progression of violence which could beset humanity. In Statius's epic, Thebes is shown to suffer the consequences of Oedipus's tragic fate; and in the *Commedia* Thebes increasingly appears as a type of the corrupt city to which, in Dante's own terms, Florence itself corresponds. We might, moreover, suggest that it is precisely because Statius has perceived, in Dante's estimation, the ingrained force of evil in human nature that he can be taken as a representative of conversion in *Purgatorio* xxi and xxii: Statius knows that human beings cannot, by their own powers, bring about a purification of their own hearts, and consequently he responds – as Dante will respond to the *Messo* – to the coming of Christ which saves and regenerates human society.

It follows that, as the protagonist faces the Furies, one function of the narrative is precisely *not* to advance but to dwell in fascinated contemplation upon the convolutions of sin, 'seeing' to the full, without yet attempting to solve the problem. Certainly the style of description has a vividly imagistic quality which might well have been influenced by the spectacular mannerism of Statius's own Latin style.

The fact remains, however, that, until the coming of a true object for the eye to contemplate, the actions of the protagonist are subject – like any human action – to self-contradiction. The danger here is that vitality should be extinguished, as the Furies call up the Medusa to turn Dante to stone (52). Here, too, Virgil – as *personaggio* and poet – reveals in two ways his continuing importance, though in neither case does this rest upon his momentarily discredited command of 'parole ornate'. His first contribution is more of a gesture than a word:

> Così disse 'l maestro; ed elli stessi
> mi volse, e non si tenne a le mie mani,
> che con le sue ancor non mi chiudessi.   (IX 58–60)

(So said my master: and he himself / turned me round, and – not relying on my hands alone – / closed my eyes also with his own hands.)

This is an act of simple humanity – or *pietas* – of the kind which the *Aeneid* celebrates; and, in the context of the ninth canto, the gesture strongly reaffirms the value of ordinary companionship against the extravagant monstrosity of the Furies.

The same gesture also suggests the role of Virgil as *poet* in the scheme of the episode; and it is worth pausing briefly to compare the sequence with those cantos of the *Purgatorio* in which Virgil is shown to have assisted Statius in his conversion to Christianity. For, while Statius stresses how much he has learned from Virgil as an epic poet, he is mainly concerned to celebrate the spiritual influence of Virgil's 'bucolic' poetry. At *Purgatorio* XXII 57, Virgil is referred to as the author of the *Bucolics*; and the significance of these decidedly *unheroic* poems is, of course, that the Fourth Eclogue in the collection was taken as a prophecy of the coming of Christ. Virgil is thus recognised as a prophetic poet, and prophetic poetry itself may be seen as the poetry of humility and patience, expressing the ability of those who inhabit the darkness to live in expectation of the light.

But it is the same condition of humble and patient expectation that the protagonist dramatises in Canto IX. So, as Dante draws close to Virgil, he emphasises his reliance upon his master with an exceptional use of the word 'poeta': 'mi strinsi al poeta per sospetto' (51) – I drew close to the poet out of fear. For the protagonist, as for Statius in the *Purgatorio*, Virgil demonstrates not only the heroic strength which he showed in the *Aeneid* – and which has already made its contribution to Dante's advance in the *Inferno* –

but also the apparently passive strength, to wait in ignorance of what salvation will bring but also ready to release the eyes of the protagonist at the advent of salvation.

With this, we arrive at the moment – simultaneously one of reversal and advance – in which the *Messo da Ciel*, a hero but also an angelic presence, at last appears; and it is here, too, that Dante's narrative takes on its most extreme complexity.

Consider, first, the representation of the *Messo*. He, like the Furies, will eventually be presented in terms of visual imagery, but his initial approach is registered in terms of sound. At the outset, Virgil, while unable to see through the vapours of the swamp, has been described as listening for his approach: 'com' uom ch'ascolta' (4); and the sound is presented discursively in two extended epic similes (67–72, 76–8), which compare the coming of the *Messo* to a rush of wind, causing the damned to flee like frogs before a serpent. If, in the end, the visual image proves to be paramount, Dante nonetheless casts the first phase of his narrative in terms which denote his membership of the 'bella scola' of classical epic poets. But these similes celebrate a power – unknown to the classical world – which brooks no opposition; it advances with the impetus of opposing currents of heat (68) and without any resistance – 'sanz' alcun rattento' (69). The *Messo* is as invisible as the wind but powerful enough to shatter and bend the objects which stand in his path: 'per cui tremavano amendue le sponde' (66) – at which the two shores tremble; 'li rami schianta' (70) – it shatters the branches.

Then, at line 73, the protagonist is at last told to fix his eyes through the fog, peering out over the 'schiuma antica' – the age-old scum. The phrase 'schiuma antica' suggests – as does much else in the sequence – that the scene enacted here has a typological significance: the ancient stagnation of sin is now being defeated by a divine power. But, in context, the image derives an immediate force from the contrast it presents to the image of the Furies. They are viciously self-divided: 'Con l'unghie si fendea ciascuna il petto' (49) – each was rending her breast with her claws. But the *Messo* is utterly self-composed; where the Furies act in violent concert, the *Messo* acts alone; and the composure of this single figure is emphasised by the contrast which Dante creates between the 'one' whole and heroic figure and the 'thousand' or more ruined spirits that flee chaotically before him as he makes his untroubled progress, displaying a single, elegant gesture:

> vid' io più di mille anime distrutte
> fuggir così dinanzi ad un ch'al passo
> passava Stige con le piante asciutte.
>   Dal volto rimovea quell' aere grasso,
> menando la sinistra innanzi spesso;
> e sol di quell' angoscia parea lasso.   (79–84)

(I saw more than a thousand spirits, destroyed, / fleeing before a single one who passed / over the Stygian [crossing] with feet still dry. / From his countenance he removed the thick air, / wafting his left hand before him often; / and only that effort seemed to weary him.)

Once the main contrast, in regard to image and action, is established between the *Messo* and the Furies, it becomes clear that the figure of the *Messo* focuses some of the main implications of the preceding eight cantos. We have already suggested that the *Messo*, as a 'segno', is a prefiguration of Christ: this is stressed by the line above which describes him walking over the waters 'con le piante asciutte'; and his function is precisely parallel to that of the 'possente' in Canto III who, at the Harrowing of Hell, breaks open the Gates of Limbo to release the spirits of the Hebrew fathers. So now the *Messo* opens the Gates of Dis with an ease emphasised in lines 89–90 by the use of the diminutive 'verghetta':

> Venne a la porta e con una verghetta
> l'aperse.

(He came to the gate, and with a little stick / he opened it.)

But, equally, the immunity of the *Messo* to the foulness of Hell recalls the immunity of Fortuna to the complaints of ignorant humanity – as also does his power to break the resistance of material reality and breathe into it spiritual purpose. So at line 97 the *Messo* himself alludes to Canto VI when he speaks disdainfully of how his present victory recalls the earlier defeat of Cerberus:

> Che giova ne le fata dar di cozzo?
> Cerbero vostro, se ben vi ricorda,
> ne porta ancor pelato il mento e 'l gozzo.   (97–9)

(What is the use of beating your head against your fate? / Your Cerberus – if you bring that to mind – / bears still a peeled chin and throat from doing so.)

Finally, the same immunity and power are parallel to the qualities attributed to Beatrice, who in Canto II explains to Virgil why she dares to descend from Heaven, because neither the flames nor the misery of Hell can affect her: 'la vostra miseria non mi tange, / né fiamma d'esto 'ncendio non m'assale' (II 92–3).

In all of these respects, the *Messo* represents a power of perfect justice formulated not as a principle but as an action. He also demonstrates, like Beatrice, Fortuna, and finally, like Christ, the dignity and vitality which the Creator has bestowed upon human nature as its proper end. So, the image of *Messo* is wholly anthropomorphic, down to the gesture of disdain and disgust which he performs with his left hand. The only comparable figure in this regard within the main line of the action is the 'ombra' of Virgil, who stands in the same relation to the *Messo* as a photographic negative to the image which is projected when the light shines through it. Moreover, when the *Messo* speaks, he may indeed touch upon the main features of the story which Virgil tells, but he does so with a comprehensiveness and implicit grasp of the whole course of divine providence which is closed to the pagan poet:

Perché recalcitrate a quella voglia
a cui non puote il fin mai esser mozzo,
e che più volte v'ha cresciuta doglia?   (94–6)

(Why do you kick against the will / – the ends and purposes of which can never be chopped off – / and which so many times has increased your suffering?)

The *Messo*, then, emerges as a demonstration of what God intends the human being to be and how human beings are meant, finally, to act. Thus, when we come to consider Dante's representation of such individuals as Farinata, Pier della Vigna, Capaneus and Brunetto, it will be found that their failure as individuals is measured by a standard which the *Messo*, who goes with pride – 'va superbo' (71) – has already set by his stature and vigour.

Yet the *Messo* is no *simple* human figure; he is also an angelic presence, advancing along the horizontal plane proper to human nature yet descending from Heaven to do so. There is no contradiction in this. From the *Vita nuova* onwards, Dante shows a peculiarly strong interest in the notion of the angel; and the significance of the angel – as it emerges from his treatment of the 'donna angelicata', Beatrice – is threefold.

First, the angel is a pure intelligence, set over some particular sphere of creation and demonstrating the intelligent order which Providence means to prevail in creation. Secondly – as at the Annunciation – the angel announces the possible perfection of humanity. And thirdly, since the angelic message is communicated from beyond the confines of human reason, the angelic figure insists that human beings should recognise that the ground of their perfection – and ultimately of their existence – resides in the eternal 'otherness' of God. In a word, the angel is a miracle and sign demanding an attitude of praise and contemplation from ordinary humanity. So, just as the *Messo* 'va superbo' over the swamps of the Styx, Beatrice walks untroubled, hearing herself praised, through the streets of Florence: 'Ella si va sentendosi laudare'. But, like Beatrice (and the 'angelic' principle of Fortuna), the *Messo* exerts a power to shatter the stony resistance of human vices. So, from the first, Dante's love for Beatrice causes him, as we have said, to tremble 'ne la secretissima camera de lo cuore ... ne li menimi polsi' (*VN* i ii) – in the most secret chamber of the heart ... in the smallest pulse; and, later, love is said to strike such a chill into vicious spirits that all evil thoughts must freeze and perish (*VN* xix 'Donne ch'avete' 33–4). In the same way, the foundations of Hell 'tremble' at the approach of the *Messo*.

We shall see that, while the *Messo* may render human beings confident of their end, it is an essential that the individual should 'tremble' at the vital but terrible instance of God's love. Certainly the 'convert' will display this ability. Thus at the moment of Statius's conversion, in the *Purgatorio* – from a state of penance to one of beatitude – the mountain of Purgatory itself trembles to announce his salvation (*Purg.* xx 128). Likewise, in this present scene, the natural doubts and vibrant terrors of the protagonist are themselves evidence that he will *not* be turned to stone.

But, in conclusion, it is in representing the angelic *humanity* of the *Messo* that the narrative structure of the episode most clearly illustrates the attitudes of mind which Dante requires of the philosopher.

As Auerbach has shown, the narrative derives its force and suspense from the pause in the description of the *Messo*'s approach at lines 85–7 which occurs when Virgil counsels Dante to be 'reverent'. Similar breaks and pauses are characteristic of the episode at large. Yet these interruptions occur not only in the pace of the narrative but also in the level of response which the text demands. So at line 61 Dante begins the *Messo* episode with a direct appeal to his audience, anticipating Virgil's address to the protagonist, in which he asks that the reader should sharpen his intellectual eye to perceive the meaning of the sign that is now to be given (in a similar way at Canto VIII 94–6 Dante asked the reader to imagine his discomfiture at being left alone by Virgil):

> O voi ch'avete li 'ntelletti sani,
> mirate la dottrina che s'asconde
> sotto 'l velame de li versi strani.   (IX 61–3)

(O you that have healthy intellects, / gaze upon the doctrine which is hidden / beneath the veil of these strange verses.)

This appeal proclaims that the poet possesses the meaning of the episode – in contrast to the protagonist, who is ignorant, at the outset, of the message communicated by the signal-lights. But the passage also locates that meaning on a level *beyond* the present text, and in doing so it not only disturbs the simple sequence of events but also reveals a further level in the polyphony of the canto, to be discovered by the reader's own response – or at least the response of those whose eyes are 'sani'. We need not dwell upon what this meaning might be; enough has been said to suggest that the scene prefigures the historical moment at which Christ enters the world as saviour and judge to liberate humanity from its confusions. In any case, precise meaning is less important here than the way in which the poetic structure operates. For this interruption is no more an interruption than is the intervention of the *Messo*. It is rather an attempt to translate the text – or 'convert' it – to a plane on which its whole meaning can be grasped in a single moment of sane intelligence. Just as in the *Vita nuova* Dante addresses his poems to a circle of initiates – the 'fedeli d'amore' or the 'Donne ch'avete intelletto d'amore' – so here he attempts to construct a circle of intelligence with the reader, comparable to the circle which Virgil at the outset casts around the protagonist. Unlike that embrace, however, Dante's appeal is not defensive: where in the *Vita nuova* he calls his fellows to praise the beauty of Beatrice, here his reader is called upon to praise a sign which indicates how capable of conversion the human mind can be. Dante's appeal is here to a capacity which can translate from one level of understanding to another, to sustain a polyphony of significance. The *Messo* himself provides a model in this respect, as in every other, for the proper form of human action; for although he acts in direct opposition to the devils, he finally turns and leaves like one whose thoughts have, all along, been occupied on another plane:

> Poi si rivolse per la strada lorda,
> e non fé motto a noi, ma fé sembiante
> d'omo cui altra cura stringa e morda.   (100–2)

(Then he turned back along the filthy way, / saying no word to us but giving the impression / of one impelled and gnawed by other concerns.)

As for Dante himself, the striking thing about the sequence is the way in which he intersperses narrative and lyric modes of writing. Nowhere does he show more clearly his command of his newly found narrative medium; and it is one indication of how far he has moved from the lyrics of the *Vita nuova* and the *Convivio* that truth is now sought through the discouraging and defensive *velame* of rough and strange verses. Yet it is equally true that the narrative, so far from producing its meaning by simple linear development, admits a variety of levels and connections, demanding that the reader, as in the lyrics of the early works, collaborate in the making of meaning.

In Canto ix – once having established this mode – Dante resumes, in the concluding phases, the apparently steady pursuit of his narrative. After the collisions and crises which have dominated the preceding sequence, this conclusion is an anticlimax – and one which is not greatly different from the anticlimax which began these cantos, when Dante abandoned the questions of the Francesca episode so as to enter the sphere of practical action and Florentine politics. For what the protagonist now sees is an apparently natural scene, reminiscent of earthly graveyards:

> Sì come ad Arli, ove Rodano stagna,
> sì com' a Pola, presso del Carnaro
> ch'Italia chiude e suoi termini bagna,
> fanno i sepulcri tutt' il loco varo.   (112–15)

(Just as at Arles where the Rhone grows slack, / as at Pola near to Quarnero / which closes up Italy and bathes its confines, / sepulchres make all the place uneven.)

Yet the comparison cannot be exact; it stands qualified by all that we have seen in the preceding sequences. For no scene can be *natural* which makes death its end or dominant motif. One notes the prevailing stress upon images of enclosure and stagnation ('stagna', 'chiude'), and this emphasis is magnified by the first sight of the punishment of the heretics, enclosed as they are in fiery stone tombs. This image already points to the difference between the mentality of the heretic and that of, so to speak, the philosophical narrator. The heretics are those who in their pursuit of truth have, in some way, chosen death as their end and cannot allow themselves to respond to the impact or advance of divine reality. The tombs in which they are confined represent the death of purposes such as the *Messo* defends; and it is this 'death' that, in Canto x, Dante goes on to contrast directly with his own response to the 'new life' that Beatrice has brought him.

IV

The issues of narrative and philosophical procedure examined in this chapter are all dramatically embodied in Canto x. And in portraying the two heretics, Farinata and Cavalcante de Cavalcanti, Dante returns to the consideration of cases apparently comparable in difficulty to the case of Francesca. But in Canto x Dante is not concerned, as he was in Canto v, with an analysis of his own authorial procedures; rather, he attempts to apply the principles that emerge from the preceding cantos in an act of practical judgement, emphasising very clearly the *difference* between his own position and that of the other actors in the canto.

In its own way, the tenth canto is as intense as the fifth; and in certain respects the position of the individual – as he judges and is judged – is more complex than it was in the earlier instance. For one thing, in Canto v Dante considered no more than two relationships – that between Francesca and Paolo, and that between Francesca and himself as protagonist. The tenth canto, on the other hand, is built around a set of parallels and contrasts which are not only greater in number than those of the fifth but also far more various in kind. The main figures in the canto are all Florentine, but that initial similarity only underlines the divisions which the Florentines of Dante's time have managed to make among themselves in terms of political faction, social class, intellectual allegiance and spiritual calibre. So, Farinata is a magnate of the Ghibelline party, Cavalcante a Guelph aristocrat; the two were related, historically, by marriage, yet neither is shown to be aware of the other's presence. As for the protagonist, Dante presents himself as a Guelph by birth, and enters into an animated debate with Farinata on questions of politics and rank. But with Cavalcante, his conversation concerns a different and essentially domestic issue: the fate of Cavalcante's son Guido Cavalcanti. And this question in turn arouses other considerations – unmistakably present beneath the surface of the text – on matters of intellectual and literary history. As the *Vita nuova* makes plain, Guido Cavalcanti was Dante's 'first friend' and the strongest influence upon his early poetic career. Yet in introducing a reference to Guido Cavalcanti into Canto x, Dante implies a critique of his friend's own poetry which calls into play both the absent figure of Beatrice and the relatively silent witness of this scene, Virgil. Nor is it possible – once Virgil's silent presence is realised – to exclude *him* from the web of cross-reference: throughout the canto he acts as a political and poetic standard, representing the virtues both of epic poetry and of the ancient Imperial harmony which the feuds of Guelph and Ghibelline have destroyed in Florence.

In its detailed concern with the troubled society of Florence, Canto x clearly takes its place in the series which – beginning with Canto vi – considers contemporary historical issues. (The sequence will continue in the next group of cantos from xii to xvi.) Having said that, however, one is bound to ask what connection exists between issues such as these and the sin of heresy which, ostensibly, is Dante's subject in this canto; or similarly why – having taken heresy as his theme, and thus set himself to consider the deliberate violence which a philosopher might do against the truths of revelation – Dante should apparently not concern himself at all with that sin in his portrayal of Farinata and Cavalcante.

One answer to these questions must already have suggested itself. We have seen that Dante regards the appetite for truth to be innate in human beings, and consequently the pursuit of truth to be a moral duty imposed on all of us by virtue of our rational nature. We have also seen that, in Dante's view, human beings can – and should – both pursue and enact the truth within their immediate, temporal circumstances. This is the lesson of Fortuna – which Ciacco and Filippo Argenti both ignore; and, though in Canto x the presentation of character is more complete and penetrating than it was in these earlier instances, Dante will nonetheless maintain that – since the philosophical enactment of truth is the cardinal feature of any individual's conduct – so the psyche and temperament of any human being will mirror the attitude he adopts towards the truth.

The contrasted portraits of Farinata and Cavalcante show two ways in which this might be so. The dominant characteristic of Farinata as portrayed here is his unbending devotion to a chosen position. This may look impressive, but may equally be seen as a stolid obstinacy: Farinata does not acknowledge Cavalcante's presence; and when Cavalcante has finished speaking, he is emphatically shown to be 'stiff-necked': 'non mutò aspetto / né mosse collo, né piegò sua costa' (74–5) – he did not change countenance / nor did he move his neck or bend his side. Cavalcante displays a wholly different temperament. He is both hasty and limp, quick to jump to conclusions and fainting with confusion when he supposes – wrongly – that the protagonist brings news of his son's death (70–2). As intellectual types, Farinata and Cavalcante would be as easy to find engaged in saloon-bar philosophising as at a scholarly conference. In the *Commedia*, hastiness like Cavalcante's is regularly associated with heresy – as, for instance, in *Paradiso* XIII, when Dante accuses false philosophers, from the Greek Parmenides to the Christian Arrius, of running headlong in 'falsa parte ... e non sapëan dove' (119–26) – in a false direction ... and they did not know where. Likewise Farinata displays much of that ingrained recalcitrance which is said by the *Messo da Ciel* to have opposed 'so many times' the evidence of God's authority (IX 96).

Heresy, then, may be seen as the product of certain timeless and universal propensities, in intellectual conduct, to obstinacy and confusion. However, Dante's concern here is not simply with heresy in general, but also with a particular error associated with the philosophy of Epicurus. Thus, at the outset, the protagonist is informed that he has arrived at the part of the sixth circle where Epicurus is confined together with 'tutti suoi seguaci, / l'anima col corpo morta fanno' (14–15) – all his followers who would make the soul die with the body.

To pursue the topic of Epicureanism – rather than consider, for example, the more obviously heretical Pope Anastasius whom Photinus drew from the proper way – 'lo qual trasse Fotin de la via dritta' (XI 9) – raises further questions. For on a strict understanding of heresy, as an offence against the truth of revelation, the pre-Christian Epicurus can scarcely be said to merit Dante's specific judgement. Of course, for men such as Farinata and Cavalcante, living in the Christian era, to adhere to a pagan philosophy might seem a strong indictment of their retrograde obstinacy. Yet this is not Dante's main point. (He himself has an especial admiration for the philosophers of antiquity.) In the first place, the concentration upon Epicureanism emphasises the extent to which heresy is seen here as a fault in intellectual activity rather than a mistake over principle or substance; after all, the 'activities' of Aristotle and Virgil, limited as they might be, qualify them at least for Limbo.

At this point, a passage from the *Convivio* has particular bearing upon Canto X.

In the *Convivio*, Dante has deliberately undertaken *not* to speak of Beatrice and those questions of theology which are regularly associated with her. But he does at one point digress into a discussion of the immortality of the soul:

Ma però che de la immortalità de l'anima è qui toccato, farò una digressione, ragionando di quella; perché, di quella ragionando, sarà bello terminare lo parlare di quella viva Beatrice beata, de la quale più parlare in questo libro non intendo per proponimento. Dico che intra tutte le bestialitadi quella è stoltissima, vilissima e dannosissima, chi crede dopo questa vita non essere altra vita; però che, se noi rivolgiamo tutte le scritture, sì de' filosofi come de li altri savi scrittori, tutti concordano in questo, che in noi sia parte alcuna perpetuale. E questo massimamente par volere Aristotile in quello de l'Anima ... questo par volere ciascuno poeta che secondo la fede de' Gentili hanno parlato; questo vuole ciascuna legge, Giudei, Saracini, Tartari, e qualunque altri vivono secondo alcuna ragione.   (*CNV* II viii 7)

(But since I have touched here on the question of the immortality of the soul, I will introduce a digression on that subject: for to speak of that will bring to a fine conclusion the discussion of the living and blessed Beatrice – of whom I propose to say no more in this book. I say, then, that among all mindless stupidities, the most foolish, base and damnable is that which asserts there is no other life after this life: for if we turn over writings of all kinds, whether of philosophers or other wise authorities, all agree upon this: that there is in us a part which endures for ever. This, we see, is the emphatic contention of Aristotle in his book *De Anima* ... This indeed is the contention of every poet who has spoken according to the faith of the Gentiles, and the contention of every religion, whether Jewish, Saracen or Tartar – and of all who live according to any reasonable law.)

It is clear from this passage that, while the immortality of the human soul is strictly beyond the scope of rational inquiry, reason itself – as shown by every wise man and every poet – is called to make an essential act of faith in its own eternal value. For a rational being to refuse this demand – as Epicurus and those 'who make the soul die with the body' certainly do – is to fall into an absurdity, denying the perpetual existence of the very faculty which conceives that denial.

Thus even the heresy which offends against the central truth of Christianity can be judged – as it is in the prevailingly 'humanist' *Convivio* – by standards derived from our own immediate nature and proper activity. As in the case of Fortuna, a test is imposed which may in the end qualify those who pass it to appreciate the truths of revealed religion but which, in the first instance, is a test of intelligence and intellectual consistency.

The *Commedia*, however, without contradicting the *Convivio*, advances beyond the earlier work by stressing – in Canto x as elsewhere – that the fullness of human life depends upon the commitment of each creature to the living truth of its Creator. And in this regard a passage of especial importance for Canto x occurs in *Inferno* xii, where Dante refers obliquely to the tradition of atomistic philosophy which descends from Democritus to Epicurus and Lucretius. Here, Virgil describes the earthquake which shook the foundations of Hell when Christ entered it to liberate the prophets and patriarchs; and then, in passing, he enunciates the extraordinary paradox that there are those who think love itself to be a source of chaos:

> da tutte parti l'alta valle feda
> tremò sì, ch'i' pensai che l'universo
> sentisse amor, per lo qual è chi creda
> più volte il mondo in caòsso converso.   (xii 40–3)

(on every side the deep, foul valley / trembled so that I thought the universe / felt love – by which as some believe, / the world has many times been converted to chaos).

The reasoning behind this is that since, for the atomist, creation can only come about or be sustained by the collision of atomic particles, any harmony which aims to pacify this generative conflict must be a cause of non-being and chaos.

We shall see presently that the peculiarities of this doctrine correspond exactly to the peculiarities which Dante attributes to the character of Farinata. It should, however, be emphasised that the atomist position, as represented here, runs directly counter to the truth upon which the *Commedia* essentially depends – which is that love, harmoniously moving the spheres and circles of the universal system, is itself the source of creation. It is equally true that, for Dante, love defends the harmony and coherence of the human individual; to oppose the power of love is also to oppose the principle of immortality enshrined in the figure of Beatrice.

We have seen that the whole of Dante's action depends upon his response to Beatrice – or to angelic figures analogous to her. This response entails that an understanding of the miraculous foundation of human nature should be translated into day-to-day action. And this is where both Farinata and Cavalcante fail: the one resists the 'tremor' of love, the other is driven to confusion by it.

Consider, first, the representation of Farinata – which falls into two parts, interrupted at line 52 by the appearance of Cavalcante. As Dante and Virgil are proceeding through the great graveyard of the heretics – which menacingly are open now, but will be closed once and for all on the Day of Judgement (10–12) – their conversation is cut short by an unidentified voice. Having heard the protagonist speak in the Tuscan dialect, the voice claims patriotic kinship: 'O Tosco ... / La tua loquela ti fa manifesto' (22–5) – O Tuscan ... your speech makes you known. But the suddenness of the sound, so far from attracting the protagonist, terrifies him, and he huddles closer to Virgil.

> Subitamente questo suono usciò
> d'una de l'arche; però m'accostai,
> temendo, un poco più al duca mio.   (28–30)

(This sound suddenly issues / from one of the coffers; and so I drew / in fear a little closer to my leader.)

Already a degree of political polemic is implicit in the action: the unity between Dante and Virgil, the figure of Imperial authority, is reaffirmed against a speaker who proposes allegiance on grounds which are merely provincial and factious. But there is an irony here, for as a Ghibelline, Farinata himself was a supporter of the Imperial cause. Yet, so far from evoking unity or harmony, as the Emperor himself might be expected to do, his words cause only distress and discomfort. He may not, of course, intend to dismay the protagonist, but the contradictions here reflect a radical spirit of tension: espousing the conflictive philosophy of an Epicurus, Farinata displays from first to last an appetite or instinct for division.

So his first conversation with the protagonist quickly degenerates into a dispute between opposing political and differing social classes. Farinata asks 'Chi fur li maggior tuoi?' (42) – Who were your ancestors? He is quick to remark upon the antagonism which existed between himself and Dante's forebears, and points out how, in past generations, the Guelph Alighieri had been driven into exile by the Ghibellines:

> poi disse: 'Fieramente furo avversi
> a me e a miei primi e a mia parte,
> sì che per due fïate li dispersi'.   (46–8)

(Then he said: 'They were fiercely opposed / to me, to my forebears and to my party, / so that twice I cast them out.')

The same spirit of antagonism is also discernible in Farinata's final speeches, though it has shifted now to a more inward level, and is cloaked by the sinner's own estimation of his political intentions. Here he recounts the historical occasion when, after the Ghibelline victory at Montaperti, he alone spoke out – successfully – against the proposal to sack the city of Florence.

> Ma fu' io solo, là dove sofferto
> fu per ciascuna di tòrre via Fiorenza,
> colui che la difesi a viso aperto.   (91–3)

(But it was I alone, when [all were] ready to suffer / that Florence should be destroyed, / who boldly and openly defended her.)

The words and actions of Farinata speak – as does the opening appeal to his fellow-Tuscan – of his patriotism and his concern for the security of his native place. Yet, sincere as his actual speech may have been, his report of it in the context of Hell is a manifestation of pride. Whatever virtue his sentiments might inherently possess, they are turned to the cause of self-aggrandisement as Farinata conjures up phrases which underline the lonely courage of his speech – 'Ma fu' io solo là' – and the boldness of his gesture – 'a viso aperto'. These phrases, too, reveal the prevailing divisiveness of Farinata's temperament, as he stresses the difference in point of steadfastness and patriotism between himself and the members of his own party.

Heresy, then, appears in Farinata as an offence against unity. Unlike the Dante of the (relatively Ghibelline) *Monarchia*, Farinata fails to carry through the implications of his love for Florence into a defence of the unity of mankind at large; and in that respect, he is comparable to Francesca, who also failed to make an intelligent translation of a partial love into love of the whole truth.

A similar but still more essential contradiction appears in another aspect of the representation. So far, we have considered only Farinata's words. But, unlike Francesca, Farinata is presented not only through his utterances but also through a conspicuous force of physical presence. Dante here employs in the representation of the human figure the same powers of visual imagination which he first brought to bear upon the Hill in Canto I. The result is the (almost literally) monumental figure who rises from the tomb – though visible only from the waist up – and impresses himself upon the protagonist by the massive working of his chest and disdainful raising of an eyebrow:

> ed el s'ergea col petto e con la fronte
> com' avesse l'inferno a gran dispitto.   (35–6)

(and he strove upwards with breast and brow, / as if he held Hell in great contempt).

And, at Dante's account of his own bourgeois origins,

> ... ei levò le ciglia un poco in suso.   (45)

(... he raised his eyebrow a little).

The irony of all this from Dante's standpoint could scarcely be more apparent: here, intact in eternity, is the heroic physiognomy of Farinata; yet the mind which inhabited that body believed, as an Epicurean, not only that the soul dies with the body, but that the body itself dissolves at death into atoms. Farinata's continued presence, and the very impressiveness of his appearance, demonstrate the falseness of his original philosophy.

Wherever Dante speaks of heresy elsewhere in the *Commedia* he tends to suggest that the sin arises from a misapprehension of authority or a misreading of texts. But the text which Farinata misreads is that of his own being: a just realisation of the value of his own physical energy alone would have revealed to him the falsity of his Epicureanism, and in consequence the necessity – if that value was to be affirmed – of the doctrine of immortality.

It is partly for this reason that we may say that Farinata has failed by the principle of Fortuna. The Fortuna passage – and its associated doctrines – demonstrated for all to see that physical matter *could* be organised by divine intelligence; and by that standard the monumental solidity of Farinata is not dignity at all but an unresponsiveness to the evidence of providential design.

Balanced against Farinata in this regard one finds not only the humble, travelling protagonist but also the poet. For it is, of course, the poet who, in creating the figure of Farinata, 'reads' and values the text of physical nature which Farinata himself disprizes. This opposition between the sinner and the principles of narrative and philosophy which the poet is developing becomes explicit at lines 49–51 when – as a retort to Farinata's boasted defeat of Dante's ancestors – the protagonist replies:

> 'S'ei fur cacciati, ei tornar d'ogne parte',
> rispuos' io lui, 'l'una e l'altra fïata;
> ma i vostri non appreser ben quell' arte'.   (49–51)

('If they were driven out, they returned,' / I replied to him, 'on both occasions; / but yours never truly learned that art.')

This is a highly charged passage in view of Dante's own exile (to which Virgil makes veiled reference here at lines 127–9) – an exile from which he will not, literally, return. Yet the confidence of the protagonist is justified, for the *Commedia* is the proof that Dante has the 'art' which Farinata is said to lack of responding to the turns of Fortune. Farinata 'remains' – in Hell as he did in earthly exile; he is in effect the 'stone' to which Medusa might have transformed the protagonist; he will never respond to the shattering impact or 'tremor' of truth.

Taken out of context, the ironies and contradictions of Farinata's case might justifiably be regarded as tragic. But the tragedy does not outweigh the judgement which the context of Canto x enforces; and within Canto x it would not be wrong to see irony turning away from tragedy towards comedy with the appearance of Cavalcante.

For while, in itself, the case of Cavalcante is no less painful than that of Farinata, the contrast or comparison which the canto institutes in yoking together two such dissimilar figures is itself a source of comic effect. There is a particular verbal instance of this at line 73, when, as the spineless figure of Cavalcante drops from view, Dante returns to Farinata describing him as 'quell' altro magnanimo' – that other great soul. The last thing Cavalcante shows himself to be is 'great-souled'; and to pair him, as this phrase does, with Farinata on the grounds of 'magnanimity' is to undermine the apparently sound claims which Farinata might have to that title. For once, the individual does not escape from the coarse net of categorical judgement – and with good reason. For these are individuals who have abdicated that grasp upon individuality which the philosophical pursuit of truth would have strengthened; and if the proud Farinata is grouped in judgement with Cavalcante, the latter, in his turn, is associated, by the suddenness of his arrival and collapse, with the overtly comic figure of Ciacco in Canto VI. In this perspective, even the heroic exhalations of Farinata's chest begin to look ridiculous.

To speak of a strain of comedy in Canto x is to indicate a degree of tonal and structural complexity which, while present in most cantos of the *Inferno*, is best exemplified by the cantos I shall consider in the last three chapters of this book. It remains to be said, however, that, if the balanced structure of the canto does invite us to discern or analyse the common denominator between Farinata and Cavalcante, then the local detail of the text presents a 'velame' as testing in its way as the 'strani versi' of Canto IX. Locally, Dante has brought to bear all his sensitivity towards, and concern for, individual difference in stressing the apparent *un*likeness of Farinata and Cavalcante in voice, gesture and tone.

So the solemnity (or pomposity) of address which is heard in Farinata's 'O Tosco ... ' becomes in Cavalcante's case the plaintive and syntactically disturbed question:

> piangendo disse: 'Se per questo cieco
> carcere vai per altezza d'ingegno,
> mio figlio ov' è? e perché non è teco?'.   (58–60)

(Weeping, he said: 'If you go through this blind / prison by virtue of high intellect, / where is my son? and why is he not with you?')

The same confusion is heard in Cavalcante's final words:

> Di sùbito drizzato gridò: 'Come?
> dicesti "elli ebbe"? non viv' elli ancora?
> non fiere li occhi suoi lo dolce lume?'.   (67–9)

(On the sudden he started up, erect, and cried: 'What? / Did you say "he once had"? Is he no longer alive? / Do his eyes no longer receive the sweet light?')

As to physical gesture, Cavalcante – whether peering over the rim of his sepulchre as if he had risen only to his knees (54), or starting upright as in the lines above – could not be less like the immobile Farinata.

With the burning question that Cavalcante introduces we come to those further contrasts – behind and beyond the text of Canto x – between the poet Dante and Calvalcante's son, Guido. Within the psychological drama of the father, one can see a contradiction identical to that which appeared in Farinata's patriotism: the heretic is unable to argue for the enduring or universal value of love even when his own paternal affection is so immediate and strong. But, where Farinata draws attention to the ancestry and fate of the historical Dante, Cavalcante's speech raises questions concerning Dante's relation, as a poet, with his contemporaries and with literary tradition – questions, in short, which bear upon his own philosophical acumen and poetic originality.

For why is it that Dante's 'primo amico' is *not* granted a journey through the otherworld? A simple answer might be that he, like his father, has exercised his acknowledged 'altezza d'ingegno' in the pursuit of heretical or

Epicurean philosophy. That rumour certainly had some currency in Florence. But Dante's own answer renders his criticism in more definitely literary terms:

> E io a lui: 'Da me stesso non vegno:
> colui ch'attende là, per qui mi mena
> forse cui Guido vostro ebbe a disdegno'.   (61–3)

(And I to him: 'I do not come of myself alone: / the one who waits there leads me through this place / and was held perhaps in disdain by your Guido.')

Dante's reference here to Virgil (or, as some have it, to Beatrice) is crucial: it might well be said that Guido had taught Dante the 'bello stile' of his early poetry; but this master of lyric poetry has now been replaced by a guide who is an epic poet. Thus the simple but significant characteristic which Dante here attributes to Virgil is that he is a leader – though a patient one, waiting quietly for this Florentine conversation to conclude. As a leader he makes possible a journey which will end with a vision of Beatrice – whom Guido may be thought to have held in disdain. But, if Guido is tinged with the same heresy that damns his father, then his contempt for the doctrine of immortality – or Beatrice – will at once explain why he has no right to make the journey. And it is equally important that Guido should be said not to recognise the significance of Virgil. For (while this is not the place to consider Cavalcanti's anti-Virgilianism) one fact is obvious: at no time did Guido ever attempt to write an epic or narrative poem. From all we have said in this chapter this fact itself is enough to warrant a moral distinction. 'Altezza d'ingegno' may well produce a philosophical lyric, such as Cavalcanti's 'Donna mi priega', but only Virgil can teach the form in which the day-to-day realisation of truth is to be expressed, in effort and surprise.

The incapacity of the heretical mind to receive surprise or dwell sufficiently on the truths available to it is finally demonstrated by Cavalcante's violent dismay over the (mistaken) assumption that his son is dead. And – returning to Farinata – the canto concludes with a passage which reinforces this point. For at line 100 Dante learns of a limitation of vision under which all the sinners suffer in Hell: the damned cannot see the whole perspective of truth because, in spite of their knowledge of past and future, a gap occurs in their understanding when they consider events which – in the temporal sequence – are *present*:

> Noi veggiam, come quei c'ha mala luce.

(We see like those who have faulty vision.)

Though this is clearly a piece of science fiction, it is given peculiar point and pathos by Farinata's exalted reference to the sun as 'il sommo duce' – a phrase which marks the culmination of the series of references to the beauty and peace of earthly nature which began with Ciacco's nostalgic reference to the 'vita serena'. The sun is the measure and light of the present moment; and in that function the movements of the sun will rule over the penitential life of Mount Purgatory; for the penitents – their minds concentrated by pain – are characteristically concerned to make each instant of time spiritually significant. But this the damned cannot do; they cannot grasp the 'punto' of the present, the critical moment of linkage between past and future. They cannot act towards the temporal present, nor, of course, will they have any place in the 'primavera sempiterna' of beatitude when 'all time is eternally present'.

The canto concludes with a final contrast as Virgil attempts to ensure that the protagonist's own thoughts do not fall into the same divisions which affect the heretics. (The system of contrasts around which the canto itself is built are divisions of analysis, not of self-contradiction.) Dante is troubled by hints of his coming exile; but, rather than allow himself to become bewildered – 'smarrito' (125) – by that prophecy, his memory must store the truth until he can present it to Beatrice and thus understand it in the light not of the temporal sequence but of eternal unity:

> 'La mente tua conservi quel ch'udito
> hai contra te', mi comandò quel saggio;
> 'e ora attendi qui', e drizzò 'l dito:
>   'quando sarai dinanzi al dolce raggio
> di quella il cui bell' occhio tutto vede,
> da lei saprai di tua vita il vïaggio'.   (127–32)

('Let your memory retain what you have heard / against yourself,' the wise one commanded me, / 'and now mark this' (and he raised his finger): / 'when you stand in the sweet ray / of the Lady whose lovely eyes see all, / from her you will know the journey of your life.')

It is in fact Cacciaguida, not Beatrice, who addresses this question in Paradise. But that fact only underlines the meaning of the incident: the truth is known in its wholeness when the labour of life's journey – 'di tua vita il vïaggio' – is accepted as the crusading martyr Cacciaguida accepts it. Heresy is an avoidance both of due labour and of the miraculous illumination of truth.

V

There is no need to consider the eleventh canto at any great length. In this canto Dante provides a general view of the plan of Hell; and in the course of reading the *Inferno*, one naturally becomes acquainted with the categories of sin which Dante here expounds through the mouth of Virgil. We already know that sins of intemperance are punished in the upper circles of Hell, surrounding the City of Dis, and we have begun to see that, within this City, sins of deliberate malice are avenged. Virgil now proceeds to distinguish the various sins of malice more precisely; malice may be expressed in violence, whereby one attempts to injure one's neighbour, oneself, God or God's creation, or in fraud, where the sinner deliberately deceives his fellows. The sins of *violent* malice are punished in the dreadful parody of a natural landscape, or garden, which lies immediately behind the walls of Dis; sins of *fraudulent* malice are found in the pit of Malebolge which descends almost to the centre of Hell. The lowest and most confined of the circles of Hell are reserved for traitors – the worst of sinners in Dante's scheme.

Familiar as these definitions become, there are, however, features of the eleventh canto which, even here, render Dante's doctrine 'new'. Nor is it sufficient to regard the canto simply as a point of reference. It is not, after all, self-evident that Dante *needs* a point of reference. He has done without it so far, and it is easy to imagine how Virgil might have introduced the substance of this canto into his comments upon entering each of the subsequent circles of Hell.

At first view, the eleventh canto introduces a pause in the narrative action of the *Inferno*. Yet it is precisely in doing this that the canto takes its place in the logic of the *cantica*, and in this way, too, that it provides a conclusion to the present sequence. Canto XI does not stand in a position superior to the rest of the *Inferno*; it forms a part of its overall scheme, and – for all its philosophy – is governed by the same imaginative pressures as appear in more obviously dramatic cantos.

Consider, for instance, the position of the canto, immediately following the canto of heresy. Heresy has revealed itself to be an inattention to the truth; more precisely, one may agree with the fifteenth-century commentator Landino that heresy involves a particular inattention to *words*, whereby texts are carelessly or wilfully misread. It is for this reason – Landino suggests – that Virgil advises the protagonist to be 'conte' (x 39) (precise or careful) in his address to Farinata; and much of the drama in Canto x revolves around accuracy and inaccuracy in the use of language. So when the protagonist carelessly uses a past remote – 'ebbe' – in speaking of Guido Cavalcanti, the father, in a flurry of misapprehension, falls into a swoon from which he does not recover; the protagonist is obliged to repair his mistake and apologise for it (x 110–14). As to Farinata, we have already said that he is incapable, in a metaphorical sense, of 'reading' the book of his own nature; and is not only deaf to the words of Cavalcante, but also confounds the protagonist, at the very moment of claiming patriotic kinship, by the suddenness and volume of his first speech.

Against this background, the austere lucidity of Canto XI has its own significance. At line 91 Virgil is praised as the sun who heals all troubled sight, and the point is clear: whatever else it may require, the pursuit of truth cannot proceed unless the natural faculties of speech and rational discourse are efficiently employed. We may add that in this regard the eleventh canto marks a definite stylistic advance in Dante's own literary development. For while the protagonist, throughout the *Inferno*, may praise *Virgil* for his clear procedures – 'chiara procede / la tua ragione, e assai ben distingue' (67–8) – it is, of course, Dante who has written lines like

> D'ogne malizia, ch'odio in cielo acquista,
> ingiuria è 'l fine, ed ogne fin cotale
> o con forza o con frode altrui contrista.   (xi 22–4)

(Of all forms of malice which earn the hatred of heaven / the end and purpose is harm and injustice; and every such end / either by violence or fraud brings grief to others.)

The clarity and confidence of conceptual and syntactic articulation here contrasts with the often headstrong argumentation of the *Convivio*. Equally, in a context which has introduced the figure of Guido Cavalcanti, author of the philosophical 'Donna mi priega', such lines prove that Dante need not fear to be outmatched in 'altezza d'ingegno': the eleventh canto could quite reasonably be seen as an 'out-doing' of Dante's 'primo amico'. Of course, the main differences between the *Convivio* and the *Commedia* – and between Dante's poetry and Guido's – arise because Dante is now writing, without vernacular precedent, a narrative poem. This cannot mean, however, that *argumentative* competence becomes irrelevant; efficient discourse will certainly have a part in the polyphony of action which Dante is conducting.

Having said that, one must at once add that there is an ambiguity surrounding the status of clear speech, which – in Canto xi as in Cantos viii and ix – is dramatised in the portrayal of Virgil. And this becomes apparent as soon as we examine the canto not simply as a list of categories but as the description of a stage in Dante's journey.

The whole discourse is pitched against the climb which the travellers have to make down the slopes from the cemetery of the heretics. The air is thick with the dreadful stench of decay which Dante regularly associates with untruth: 'l'orrible soperchio / del puzzo che 'l profondo abisso gitta' (4–5) – the horribly overwhelming stench which the deep chasm throws up. The protagonists have to delay until they become accustomed to the smell; and discourse is represented as a way of passing time before the two are ready to descend.

> 'Lo nostro scender conviene esser tardo,
> sì che s'ausi un poco in prima il senso
> al tristo fiato; e poi no i fia riguardo'.
> Così 'l maestro; e io 'Alcun compenso',
> dissi lui, 'trova che 'l tempo non passi
> perduto'. Ed elli: 'Vedi ch'a ciò penso'.   (10–15)

('Our descent must needs be delayed, / so that our senses should first become a little more accustomed / to the vile breath: and then we shall not notice it.' / So spoke my master. And I [said to him,] 'Find some compensation, / so that time may not pass and be / wasted.' And he said, 'You see that I am thinking of that.')

We have said that the canto represents a pause in the action; but the implication of this passage is that discourse itself represents a pause. Indeed, one may go further still and suggest that discourse is here seen, literally, as a pastime, a 'compenso'. And in this respect the passage exactly anticipates its counterpart in *Purgatorio* xvii and xviii where Virgil explains the origin of sin as a perversion of love. The whole of that discourse occurs during the second night which the travellers spend on Purgatory; and the laws of Purgatory insist that no *physical* action should be performed while the sun is down.

In both the *Purgatorio* and the *Inferno*, the pause associated with Virgil's argument points to the limitation of his function: so far from being a final authority, his words represent only a preliminary statement of issues which will be understood afresh in the light of revelation and direct experience. Virgil himself says as much in the *Purgatorio*, when he directs Dante to Beatrice for a final answer on the issues he is discussing: 'da indi in là t'aspetta / pur a Beatrice' (*Purg.* XVIII 47–8) – beyond this point [of reason] awaits, still, Beatrice. No similar direction is given in Canto XI; yet in two senses it remains true that the account of sin which Virgil proceeds to give is only provisional.

For one thing, Virgil here discusses merely the *kinds* and *types* of sin without saying anything about its origins. It is only in Purgatory that Dante considers how sin arises. That is appropriate enough; for, knowing the origins of the disease, the sinner can set about curing it; and part of the optimism of Virgil's speech in Purgatory is that it reveals sin to be merely a perversion of love – which gives good grounds for hope of a remedy. In the *Inferno*, however – in this canto as also at the Gates of Dis – Dante must wait almost without hope, in T. S. Eliot's phrase, 'not being ready for hope'.

In the second place, as Virgil here admits, the discussion of sin is only a preparation for *seeing* the sins at first hand as Dante progresses:

> ma perché poi ti basti pur la vista,
> intendi come e perché son costretti.   (20–1)

(But so that seeing after this should be enough, / attend to how and why they are confined.)

One notes how perfunctory Virgil is in his reference to 'seeing'. But by now this casualness must appear suspect; for Dante has emphasised all along the superiority of that which is seen to that which is described. And while this superiority is not yet affirmed by a vision of Beatrice, sight must still be tested against everything that Beatrice is *not*; the 'seeing' which Virgil hopes to make merely 'sufficient' by his prolegomena will involve the seeing of Harpies, Minotaurs, Centaurs and kindred monsters, as well as a contemplation of the increasing perversion of the human form under the stroke of punishment. Dante's narrative imagination will challenge the moral eye, and ensure that the truth be acted in experience. So, once more, the limitations under which Virgil operates are asserted at the very moment when his powers seem most in evidence. Conversely, the recognition of Virgil's limits serves to permit a truer and more accurate celebration of those powers. His words remain the only true 'pastime' until the action of vision can begin again; and the connection is drawn here, as in Canto I, between discursive rationality and the temporal sequences which govern human existence.

This point, indeed, is made with polemical force. For in seeking to avoid heresy and error, Dante does not turn to the doctrines of the Church or to an orthodox categorisation of the capital vices. On the contrary, the opening lines of Canto XI show that a leader of the Church can himself be subject to heresy:

> ci raccostammo, in dietro, ad un coperchio
>   d'un grand' avello, ov' io vidi una scritta
> che dicea: 'Anastasio papa guardo,
> lo qual trasse Fotin de la via dritta'.   (6–9)

(We approached, backing, to the cover / of a great sepulchre, where I saw an inscription / that said: 'I watch over Pope Anastasius, whom Photinus drew from the straight way'.)

To find a safer leader than the wayward Anastasius, the protagonist turns to Virgil. It is no small part of Dante's project in the *Commedia* to suggest that the deficiencies of the contemporary Church must be repaired by a reaffirmation of rational principle. Thus, in constructing his doctrine of infernal punishment, the poet draws upon the ethics of classical antiquity. So when Virgil refers to 'Filosofia' at line 97 he means Aristotle's work; and silent use is made of Cicero's writings throughout the canto. If the image of the stench of Hell suggests the rotting corruption of the natural body, then Dante's first recourse is to the natural and rational faculties which were all that the ancient philosophers had to rely upon. Indeed, in the latter part of the canto Dante draws not upon the *Ethics* of Aristotle but upon the *Physics*: the scientific study of the natural world is itself a way to spiritual health.

As a final word on Virgil in Canto XI, one may note that, in one respect, his words *do* point beyond the competence we should expect of him, when he speaks at line 56 of how sin 'incida / pur lo vinco d'amor che fa natura' – destroys the link of love which makes nature. In the context of the heresy canto, this insistence upon love as the foundation of the created world is particularly highly charged, with suggestions of the principle that both Farinata and Cavalcante misapprehend. But even the rational Virgil seems here able to understand the importance of such a notion; and it is consistent with his appearance at the Gate of Dis that he should: here, as more extensively in the *Purgatorio*, Virgil is qualified to speak of love by virtue of the understanding of human concord that he shows in the Fourth Eclogue. The 'pause', in that light, is a true preparation and not a distraction.

In the aspects we have just considered, the eleventh canto is as much a manifesto for rational competence as it is a critique of sin. But in the final phases an overtly polemical interest begins to display itself, demonstrating – as we have seen throughout this chapter – that no principle or concept in the *Commedia* is allowed to remain inert: the application in judgement is the proof to which Dante puts every general principle.

The polemic is introduced ironically by the deceptively timid voice of the protagonist asking – with some reason, one might suppose – why usury should be grouped as a perversion along with homosexuality:

> 'Ancora in dietro un poco ti rivolvi',
> diss' io 'là dove di' ch'usura offende
> la divina bontade, e 'l groppo solvi'.   (94–6)

('Turn back a little,' / I said to him, 'to the point where you said that usury offends / divine goodness, and unravel that difficulty.')

Innocent as this question is, it conceals the beginnings of an attack upon usury which will reach its climax in Canto xvii when Dante, looking back to Florence, sees how greed has driven the noble houses of the city to become bankers. In Hell the usurious noblemen sit in squalid misery with money bags round their necks, each stamped with the armorial bearings of his ancient house:

> E com' io riguardando tra lor vegno,
> in una borsa gialla vidi azzurro
> che d'un leone avea faccia e contegno.   (*Inf.* xvii 58–60)

(And as I came, gazing, among them, / I saw azure on a yellow purse / that had the appearance and bearing of a lion.)

Canto xi draws, in justification of this judgement, on both Aristotle and the Book of Genesis. In brief, the argument is that human intelligence and art are created for us to use directly upon the natural world, which is also God's creation. Humanity must earn its living in the sweat of its brow; and in doing so it will engage as it was meant to do – and as earlier arguments in this chapter have suggested it should – with the truths embodied in the physical world. The usurer, however, pursues another course. He devotes himself to an object not of God's creation but of man's – the coin – and alienates himself still further from the natural world by using his art and intelligence to make this 'artificial' nature yield him a living. So in *Paradiso* ix, Dante speaks of the coin on which Florentine capitalism came to depend – the florin – as the 'maladetto fiore' sown by Satan and nurtured by human beings as a corrupt substitute for true nature:

> La tua città, che di colui è pianta
> che pria volse le spalle al suo fattore
> e di cui è la 'nvidia tanto pianta,
> produce e spande il maladetto fiore.   (*Par.* ix 127–30)

(Your city, the planting of him / who first turned his back upon his Maker / and from whose envy such weeping has grown, / produces and spreads abroad the accursed flower.)

The eleventh canto thus ends a sequence which began with a polemic against greed with a similar attack, informed now – after two cantos of doctrinal discussion – with a fuller sense of God's design for the natural world and of the place of humanity in that world. The final lines of the canto – spoken by Virgil – thus prefigure the *Purgatorio* with a prophetic image of a clean and healthy world which will reconcile the protagonist to nature, time and progress:

> Ma seguimi oramai che 'l gir mi piace;
> ché i Pesci guizzan su per l'orizzonta,
> e 'l Carro tutto sovra 'l Coro giace,
> e 'l balzo via là oltra si dismonta.   (*Inf.* XI 112–15)

(But follow me now, for it pleases me to go: the Fishes are quivering on the horizon, / and the whole of the Wain lies over Caurus: / and far over there is the cliff by which we descend.)

But the recovery of that nature – and its defence – require an art as vigorous as Dante's has been in the same sequence, and a voice as direct in its judgements as his has proved to be even in a canto where clinical analysis might have seemed his best resource.

3

Narrative, myth and the individual:
Cantos XII–XVI

I

In a recent study of moral theory – which speaks with much sympathy both of Aristotelian ethics and of the scholastic system built around Aristotle's work in the late Middle Ages – Alisdair McIntyre writes:

In what does the unity of an individual life consist? The answer is that its unity is the unity of a narrative embodied in a single life. To ask 'What is the good for me?' is to ask how best I might live out that unity and bring it to completion. To ask 'What is the good for man?' is to ask what all answers to the former question must have in common … The unity of a human life is the unity of a narrative quest. Quests sometimes fail, are frustrated, abandoned or dissipated into distractions; and human lives may in all these ways also fail. But the only criteria for success or failure in a human life as a whole are the criteria of success or failure in a narrated or to-be-narrated quest …

The virtues therefore are to be understood as those dispositions which … sustain us in the relevant kind of quest for the good, by enabling us to overcome the harms, dangers, temptations and distractions which we encounter, and which will furnish us with increasing self-knowledge and increasing knowledge of the good life for man, and the virtues necessary for the seeking are those which will enable us to understand what more and what else the good life for man is.

('Virtues, unity of life and the concept of a tradition' *After Virtue*, pp. 203–4)

This long quotation could usefully have been much longer. For while McIntyre makes no mention of Dante, his understanding of Aristotelian ethics is remarkably consistent with Dante's own. So this passage, along with the chapter from which it is taken, serves both to summarise the conclusions of my last two chapters and to indicate the subject of the present chapter: here, my two concerns will be to examine the portrayal of the individual in the central cantos of the *Inferno*, and to consider the function of narrative in reflecting the ethical grounds upon which – for Dante as for McIntyre – the integrity of the individual depends.

We have already seen that the order which governs human life is shown in the *Commedia* to be the order of an action directed – as any quest or any simple story must be – by a sustained sense of the goal to which it is moving. The virtues, of course, are treated only by implication in the *Inferno*, as Dante resists the vices which he represents in this *cantica*. Even so, it is clear from the cases of Francesca and Farinata that these vices may be

158

understood as forms of distraction from that 'quest' for the good upon which the protagonist *is* engaged and the sinners *should* have been engaged in the course of their lives.

We have only to consider the genesis of the line 'Nel mezzo del cammin di nostra vita' to realise how well Dante's view of virtue as expressed in 'the story of a journey' might have contributed to McIntyre's survey. Behind the first line of the *Inferno* stands a lengthy discussion in Book IV of the *Convivio*, where we find not only a comparison – examined in the last chapter – between pilgrimage and philosophical endeavour but also an account of how the arc of human life may be divided into phases, each of these four phases being ruled by virtues appropriate to it (*CNV* IV xxiv).

Consider, for instance, the second of these phases, which runs from the ages of thirty-five to forty-five (a period of life that Dante flatteringly terms *Gioventute*, or youth, on the grounds of an etymological connection with the word 'giovare', to help or bestow perfection). In this age, human beings are at the height of their powers ('è colmo della nostra vita') (*ibid.* xxvi 2–4); and there are five virtues which ought to appear at this time: these are Temperance, Fortitude (or Magnanimity), Lovingness, Courtesy and Fidelity, all of which are necessary if a 'youth', in Dante's definition, is to maintain his powers and use them efficiently for the good of others. In the *Convivio*, the model which Dante offers for such virtuous action is – significantly enough – the hero Aeneas. It is easy to see, however, that the protagonist, 'nel mezzo del cammin', has also had the opportunity, by the time he reaches the mid-point of his journey through Hell, to cultivate and display most of the same virtues.

There is, then, a pattern stamped upon every human life, and the function of the virtues is to enable that pattern to be realised most fully and efficiently. We should note that such a realisation will be progressive, and that the virtues appropriate to one age will not be suitable to any other stage of the moral journey. Hence we need never be ashamed of any virtue, sentiment or thought which has contributed to an earlier stage of our development. Our progress is progress towards the realisation of our whole nature; one age or virtue prepares for another, and finally we should be able to look back and 'bless' the way we have taken (*ibid.* xxvii 1). So Youth prepares for Mature Age, Gioventute for Senettute (which in turn precedes Old Age or *Senio*). And while, in the middle years, we pursue virtues which maintain the perfection and efficiency of our faculties, we are also preparing to devote our energies as older men to the service of our fellows:

e però che prima conviene essere perfetto, e poi la sua perfezione comunicare ad altri, conviensi questa secondaria perfezione avere appresso questa etade, cioè ne la senettute.   (*CNV* IV xxvi 4)

(and since one needs first to be perfect and then to communicate one's perfection to others, it is right that we should possess this secondary perfection at this period, that is, in old age).

We may note that, while Dante the protagonist is shown to be at the mid-point of his earthly existence, Dante the storyteller must have reached or been approaching, as he began the *Commedia* the age at which he should properly serve others, adopting the virtues of Prudence, Justice and Generosity.

On the evidence, then, of the *Convivio*, Dante would agree that the 'unity of an individual life … is the unity of a narrative embodied in a single life'. Nor can one doubt that in the *Commedia* he continues to hold and develop some such view. The importance of the journey image itself is evidence of this; and throughout the *Commedia*, as we have already begun to see, the smallest details of Dante's progress – whether fast or slow, horizontal or vertical – are likely to express a moral significance. We have also seen that the notion of narrative colours Dante's view of nature, history and philosophy, so that the judgements he passes upon the damned can be expressed in images of motion or of travelling and even through references to storytelling itself: in Canto VIII, Filippo Argenti was repulsed on the grounds of his evident unworthiness to participate in Dante's advancing narrative.

These suggestions, however, possess a particular relevance to the cantos we are about to consider. For all the major figures in the sequence from Canto XII to Canto XVI of the *Inferno* might be said – in the terms of the *Convivio* – to have made or attempted to make some 'useful' contribution to the developing story of Italian civilisation. This sequence, which strictly begins with the Ghibelline warrior Farinata and ends with the Guelph nobles who appear in Canto XVI, is dominated by eminent representatives of the generation preceding Dante's own in twelfth-century Italy. The issues that the sequence raises have particular force in Canto XIII, where Dante deals with the Imperial minister Pier della Vigna, and Canto XV, where he presents the great Florentine diplomat and educator, Brunetto Latini. Both Piero and Brunetto in their respective spheres were cultural and political leaders. Intellectually, Dante himself, as we shall see, owed something to both these men; and both – as they are represented in the *Inferno* – are as concerned as Dante is himself to assert the usefulness and unity of their own lives through the stories that they tell.

The irony is, however, that Dante, for all the respect he may have had for such men, is obliged in the *Inferno* to mark – just as forcefully as he did in the Filippo Argenti episode – the distance between himself and the sinners in Hell. Piero and Brunetto, along with Farinata and the Guelph nobles, are shown to have failed in their attempts to be useful. They are not, despite appearances, leaders but *lost* leaders: like Francesca, they threaten to distract Dante from his quest; and we shall see that the extent of their failure is represented in the *Inferno* by their failure in the arts of language and narrative. Damnation itself, of course, is an indication of an irremediable fissure in the moral personality of these figures; and it is easy to see that one reason for the condemnation which Dante expresses is that, in the secrecy of their own consciences, such men did not coherently pursue the principles they enunciated in their public lives. But Dante uses words and stories to register this flaw; and just as Farinata fails to grasp the point of connection between past and future, so the words of Brunetto and Piero show no comprehension of the underlying patterns which, in time and now in eternity, have governed their lives. What is more, the 'unity' which they are concerned to assert proves to be unity only in a meretricious sense: both Piero and Brunetto mistake the unity of public reputation for the unity which resides in the pursuit of moral truth. Narrative is not, in their cases, finally devoted to the advancement of others; and certainly Dante, as protagonist, has nothing further to learn from them.

The central cantos of the *Inferno* involve a series of intensely tragic acts of rejection. At the same time, the journey of the protagonist is increasingly seen in the same cantos to qualify Dante himself as a spiritual leader who can now replace the predecessors whom he has to reject. So in Canto XVI at lines 64–72, the Guelph nobles demand news of Florence from the protagonist, as if Dante were now the true representative of that city. But in turn this recognition points to another feature of the sequence. For – as I shall argue – it is in these cantos that Dante realises most fully the extent to which the *Commedia* itself is the work that proves his title as a spiritual leader. In writing the poem, Dante continues the task he had first conceived in the *Convivio* of vindicating his own reputation as a lover of truth and of attempting to serve the philosophical interests of his fellow-citizens. It is not so much the protagonist but rather the author of the *Commedia* who replaces Farinata, Piero, Brunetto and the Guelph nobles.

At this point, it is important to recognise that the *Commedia* marks an advance upon the *Convivio* in its conception of 'moral unity' and, correspondingly, in its view of what constitutes the 'story of a life'. As we have said, the *Commedia* – particularly in comparison with the *Convivio* – represents a renewed realisation of the force and implication of Christian truth. In a word, where the *Convivio* is a philosophical tractate with decidedly humanist tendencies, the *Commedia* is a Christian story; and this simple fact has profound implications for Dante's intellectual and literary procedures.

In one respect, there is no incompatibility at all between the Christian sense of purpose and the notions of heroic endeavour that Dante derived from the *Aeneid*, insofar as the journey of a Christian pilgrim must proceed as steadily as that of any Roman hero towards its destined end. Yet in another sense the idea of a Christian story is at odds with the simple regularity that Dante in the *Convivio* (or McIntyre) ascribes to the story of a life. For, as the protagonist himself realises in *Inferno* II, the beginnings and ends of such a story are located beyond the natural patterns of temporal life. The protagonist began his life in the hand of God as Creator, and will end it, under the guidance of Providence, in eternal beatitude. In a similar way, the Christian storyteller is bound to recognise that, beyond any narrative fiction that he himself may construct, there lies the authoritative text of the

Scriptures, where the Christian story has been told in its purest form. So far from asserting any simple unity, a story told by a Christian author must allow its unity to be challenged or unsettled: the patterns of progress which it represents can never be comprehensive or self-sufficient. Moreover, the text of any such story will itself be brought into question when set beside the images and parables of Gospel truth.

Unity, then, is an especially difficult notion to associate with the story of a Christian life; and we have already seen in Chapter 2 how Dante responds to and accepts this difficulty, both as protagonist and as narrator. From Canto VII onwards, the protagonist – directly representing the historical Dante – has been aware of how the untroubled progress of human life is threatened by the changes of fortune; and this awareness will become more acute and specific when the protagonist hears Brunetto speak of what fate has in store for his pupil (xv 55–78). But the protagonist is able to tolerate this new revelation, knowing – as he has since the Farinata episode – that he can only advance by responding philosophically to the difficulty and 'newness' that Fortuna brings about.

As for the poet, we have seen from the outset how great a part discontinuity and surprise play in Dante's narrative method. We have also observed the polyphonic structure of the *Messo da Ciel* episode; here, the 'horizontal' line of narrative action is persistently tested against a vertical co-ordinate; and likewise Dante's text is at points superimposed upon a scriptural source which either corroborates or corrects the poet's own words.

We shall continue, in the present and subsequent chapters, to examine the structural characteristics of Dante's narrative. At no point will Dante abandon the image of linear progress or ignore its moral importance; indeed it is notable that the protagonist reasserts the value of that image when, in conversation with Brunetto, he gives a comprehensive account of the origins and ultimate goal of his present journey (xv 49–54). At the same time, the action in the central cantos of the *Inferno* is increasingly agitated in design; and we need to consider the sheer variety of narrative procedures that Dante here develops. In Cantos II and V, we have seen how ready Dante is to call into question the linguistic procedures on which his poem depends. It is appropriate now, in the middle phase of his first *cantica*, that he should similarly display for inspection the repertoire of his narrative techniques. Each canto in turn contrasts in formal terms with its predecessor, and contributes some new element to the overall structure of the sequence.

Our concern, however, cannot only be with structure. Following McIntyre and the *Convivio*, one is bound to say that any critique of narrative method must also involve in Dante's case a renewed consideration of moral issues, and in particular an investigation of the principles on which the integrity of the individual depends. Since De Sanctis's time, Dante has been recognised as one of the founders of modern individualism; and while Dante's view of what constitutes an individual is very different from the view that De Sanctis projected upon the *Commedia*, no account of Dante's thinking would be complete without some consideration of his approach to the question. In one respect, the whole *Commedia* is concerned with an examination of the grounds on which individuality rests; and by the time he reaches the *Paradiso* Dante is able to deal explicitly with the ways in which the moral and theological virtues ensure that human beings are healthy in the sight of God. But, characteristically, the issue of individuality, in Dante's presentation of it, is one which is inherently problematical, and in the *Inferno* it is the recurrent *problem* of individuality that Dante investigates. Indeed, while the *Paradiso* may offer a systematic terminology in which to define the issue, it would be a mistake to adopt this too soon or too readily: to be an individual is in part to seek a definition of one's own individuality, conducting, as Dante does in the *Inferno*, a journey of self-examination, and recognising that there are available all too many false models of what an individual might be.

To define the individual in terms of narrative art is to define the nature of heroism; and these are the terms in which Dante conducts his inquiry throughout the *Inferno*. So, while acknowledging the validity of the heroic model which Aeneas offers, Dante has already recognised in Canto II that heroism must be reconciled with humility, which is to say with an understanding of the existential relationship between Creator and creature. But the present sequence, beginning with the representation of Farinata, is Dante's most intense treatment of the question. We have seen already that heroism cannot reside in mere self-affirmation: Farinata is imprisoned in the monumental image of himself which he seeks to defend: to gain one's life one must be prepared to lose it; to be whole is also to be broken.

By the time Dante reaches the *Purgatorio*, such paradoxical conclusions will seem entirely natural. There, Dante portrays the heroism which is required if one is to submit willingly to the pains of penance. The terms of the discussion are by then, of course, increasingly Christian; and, while admitting that self-questioning and even self-laceration are a part of the penitential life, the *Purgatorio* also asserts that the ultimate possibility of unity and wholeness lies in the immortality – denied by the heretic Farinata – which the Christian God offers to the human being. It is nonetheless relevant to speak at some length of the second *cantica* in the context of the central cantos of the *Inferno*. As we shall see, the *Inferno* at this point seems consistently to anticipate the themes and images of the *Purgatorio* – particularly in its treatment of suicide in Canto XIII, where the individual *seems* willingly to have abandoned a hold upon selfhood; and an important part of Dante's narrative method in this sequence is to contemplate a *lack* of the solutions that are suggested by the images of the second *cantica*.

It remains true, however, that the positive definition of heroism in these cantos arises – as does the subtlest poetic action – from the sustained (and inherently problematical) contrast that Dante draws between himself and the lost leaders of his own culture. And to see the force of this contrast, it is necessary to insist again upon the indissoluble connection between moral and literary considerations in the sequence.

For the contrast is drawn not only in terms of the content of the stories that the respective figures have to tell but also in terms of the act of narrating or writing. To write, as we have suggested, is for Dante to confront the problem of selfhood; and while Piero and Brunetto fail in this, we are invited to inspect the success which Dante himself simultaneously achieves. And when I speak of Dante here, I should repeat that I am speaking of three Dantes – of the protagonist, of the poet and of the historical figure. Critical practice would normally suggest that these three aspects of 'Dante' should be considered separately; and it is indeed an essential part of Dante's procedure, here and throughout the *Commedia*, to establish that there is a distinction. At the same time, the *Commedia* requires that we should regard these three aspects of the 'self' as interactive. The heroic protagonist is a representation of the stresses to which the historical Dante is subject and of the ideal remedies he proposes for himself. To write is to recognise the division between the possible and the actual, but also to attempt to repair that division. The *Commedia* is at every point a field of moral engagement and a test of moral perspective.

The peculiar urgency of the sequence we have now to consider derives from the sense that Dante is here attempting to find not merely solutions for his private purposes, but also solutions for a whole civilisation in peril. We have described the main figures of the sequence as 'lost leaders'; we might equally well have described them as failed fathers. Looking particularly at Piero and Brunetto, Dante sees how the natural processes of history and generation have been thwarted or turned awry: the human originals prove only to have created present sterility.

The distinction which Dante seeks to draw between himself and his predecessors is both extremely fine and extremely painful, involving – among other things – a precise understanding of the limitations of the humanist culture to which he himself contributed in the *Convivio*. It also involves an attempt to recover more remote, and healthier, origins than those represented by his immediate forebears. Few other sequences of the *Commedia* are more strongly marked by allusion to classical myth than this is, as if – like Eliot in *The Waste Land* – Dante were here attempting to 'shore fragments against his ruin' by reanimating the most primitive sources of his culture.

With the mention of myth, we come to a final feature of Dante's narrative method in the present sequence – and one which is particularly clearly illustrated in Cantos XII and XIV, which are dominated by the mythic representations of figures such as the centaurs, Capaneus and the Old Man of Crete. By contrast, Cantos XIII and XV are – on the surface at least – concerned with the diagnosis of historical decline; and the systematic relationship which Dante draws between Ghibelline and Guelph representatives in these cantos, as in Cantos X and XVI, supports and confirms Dante's concern with the history of his day. But across this thematic line there runs a series of mythic images and suggestions, radiating from Cantos XII and XIV, which simultaneously interpret and disturb the explicit development of the story. As we shall see, many of these images represent *process*, in the form of growth or running rivers; more accurately, they picture the *perversion* or frustration of natural process. And this is appropriate enough where Dante's concern is with the ways in which sin and moral failure have produced a gap in nature. But the point to be made here concerns the formal implications of this procedure. For myth is a form in which Dante can simultaneously recognise the truth and acknowledge how distant that truth still remains. In this sense, no 'myth' is more important than the Christian myth which Dante will eventually see brought to fruition in the *Purgatorio*. The *Purgatorio* is the distant origin to which Dante's own poem is seeking to return. And the possibility of that return haunts and disturbs the simple progress of the whole sequence.

Thus the unity which Dante seeks to impose in the central cantos of the *Inferno* is one that acknowledges – in both narrative and moral terms – discontinuity and distance. This is evident simply in the oscillation between cantos which are broadly historical in character or emphasis and those which revolve around myth. But each canto, of whatever general type, engenders its own peculiar form of difficulty.

II

The sins which Dante considers in Canto XII are those that involve acts of violence against our fellow-men; and the picture which emerges is one of pointlessly cruel disruption in all ranks of society. The sinners range from legendary tyrants and marauders such as Alexander (107) and Attila (134), to petty barons, highwaymen, brigands and thugs – from those who have committed 'crimes against humanity', to those who have violated the simplest and most obvious controls that civilisation, through its laws, can place upon rapacity. All the sinners are immersed in a river of boiling blood; but the degree of their immersion – whether total or only to the neck – is determined by the magnitude of their offence.

In his own way, Dante might well have understood the phrase 'crime against humanity'. For the motive to violence in all these cases is a lust for possession; all the sinners in Canto XII display a heightened and deliberate form of greed; and greed, as we have seen, represents an offence against the principles on which universal order and both the social and personal integrity of human beings depends:

> Oh cieca cupidigia e ira folle,
> che sì ci sproni ne la vita corta,
> e ne l'etterna poi sì mal c'immolle!   (XII 49–51)

(O blind cupidity and insane anger / that so spurs us on in this short life, / and steeps us so dreadfully in eternity!)

In theme, then, the twelfth canto is clearly connected with earlier considerations of social disorder in Cantos VI and X, and provides a background to the analysis of historical chaos and decline which emerges in

Cantos XIII and XV. But the narrative here is mythic rather than historic, and the central image of the canto – going beyond the implications of any earlier canto – draws particular attention to a process of violence in which, so far from pursuing the realisation of a coherent pattern, human lives throughout time generate nothing save a proliferation of anarchy. The image of the river of blood indicates the consequences which flow when the social order becomes a prey to violence, and also points to an almost organic connection between governmental cruelty and cruelty in the streets: the rule and example of an Attila licenses the actions of a local tyrant such as Azzolino. The blood flows on. And the stream of violence which Dante here envisages is the stream which subsequently will connect Capaneus – the mythical assailant of the corrupt city of Thebes – with contemporary representatives of social disorder, on both the Imperial and the civic levels, such as Piero and Brunetto.

In proposing this theme of process, Canto XII significantly develops the 'natural' imagery which was first introduced in the circles of intemperance. In the 'bufera infernal' and foul rain of those circles, the force of nature was itself seen as a potential danger to rational measure. But now nature itself is at risk from the wilful and deliberate perversity of human actions. At its worst, the rational human being can itself produce a second nature in which process is reversed and corrupted to the point of absurdity. So in Canto XII Dante begins to construct a landscape in which nature is not merely unleashed in its elemental force against the sinner, but transformed in its elements into a world of nonsensical logic. The river of blood irrigates a forest of trees which are not trees but suicides transmuted for their sins into this unnatural form (Canto XIII); and the birds which perch on the branches here are not birds but Harpies, causing the trees to shriek as they pluck at them. Further on, the scene becomes one of utter sterility, as the protagonist sees the blasphemers (Canto XIV) and sexual perverts (Canto XV) lying on, or running across, a plain of burning sand. And over that sand, there falls a sinister shower of fireflakes, descending as slowly and plumply as large snowflakes in a windless sky:

> Sovra tutto 'l sabbion, d'un cader lento,
> piovean di foco dilatate falde,
> come di neve in alpe sanza vento.　　　　　　　　　　(XIV 28–30)

(Over all the sand, slow in falling, / there rained broad flakes of fire, / like snow falling in windless mountains.)

The theme of 'the world-turned-upside-down' is familiar enough in medieval literature. But, as we saw in the last chapter, it is characteristic of Dante that he should recognise with particular force the intrinsic value of the natural world. This world is God's creation; and its patterns, rhythms and images offer – when properly understood – support for the highest of human enterprises. Now, however, Dante is concerned with the ways in which violence obliterates the natural design which human beings could have realised in their lives. More especially, the absurdity of the punishment which the violent suffer represents their alienation from the measured and well-proportioned course of life which Dante had pictured for himself in the journey images of the *Convivio*. But in conceiving a narrative which admits such absurdities, Dante himself has clearly moved beyond the *Convivio*; and the themes and images he develops in the violence cantos – transcending any simple reliance upon the measure of nature – also anticipate the central cantos of the *Purgatorio*. So, for instance, in *Purgatorio* XIV, Dante returns to the image of the river in order to represent, with profound irony, the ways in which natural process can be translated into natural degeneration; human perversity, it seems, can transform the Arno into a stream of ever-increasing corruption:

> ché dal principio suo, ov' è sì pregno
> l'alpestro monte ond' è tronco Peloro,
> che 'n pochi luoghi passa oltra quel segno,
>   infin là 've si rende per ristoro
> di quel che 'l ciel de la marina asciuga,
> ond' hanno i fiumi ciò che va con loro,
>   vertù così per nimica si fuga
> da tutti come biscia ...
>   Vassi caggendo; e quant' ella più 'ngrossa,
> tanto più trova di can farsi lupi
> la maladetta e sventurata fossa.   (*Purg.* XIV 31–8 & 49–51)

(for from its source where it swells so high – / the Apennine mountain, from which Mount Pelorus was cut – / that it is surpassed only in a few places / – down to where it yields itself to restore / the [water] that the sky soaked up from the ocean / – because of which rivers have that which flows within them, / virtue is fled from by all as an enemy / as if it were a snake. / And so it goes on falling, and the more it increases / the more it finds dogs turning themselves into wolves, / that accursed and wretched ditch.)

This passage and the canto from which it comes have an especial bearing upon the thirteenth canto of the *Inferno*. For the particular concern of the Purgatory canto is to show how the decay of civilised existence is marked by the passing of a great age of courtesy; and in the case of Pier della Vigna the courtesy of Emperor Frederick's court has degenerated into lethal envy and gossip. For the moment, however, it is enough to stress how powerfully Dante here apprehends, and mythologises, the image of the river. The potential fertility, growth and harmony of the natural world are all expressed in the cyclical life of the river – fed by the sky and flowing to the sea, which itself feeds the sky. The damned in *Inferno* XII have been as irresponsive to any such cycle as were the gluttons to the circlings of Fortune; Dante, on the other hand, simultaneously affirms the value of such images and recognises how fragile they are in the hands of perverse humanity.

It would not have been surprising on this understanding if Dante's response to a vision of such deliberate unnaturalness had been one of religious despair, in which – abandoning any expectation that nature could repair itself – all hope of redemption was made to reside in the intervention of the God who originally created that nature. There is indeed something of this in the *Purgatorio*, when at Canto xiv 115–17 Dante – anticipating King Lear's great cry 'crack nature's moulds, all germanes spill at once that makes ingrateful man' – rejoices in the barrenness of certain once-noble families who can now not 're-child' themselves, and ends with the simple religious demand that human beings should turn their eyes to the 'bellezze etterne'. Moreover, a similar mood does come to dominate the second half of the *Inferno*, in the Malebolge of Cantos xvii to xxx.

Yet, overall, this is not an attitude that Dante characteristically adopts in the *Commedia*. And it certainly has no place in the violence cantos. On the contrary, the particular purpose of this sequence is to construct a new humanism – a new confidence in human worth and culture – on the ruins of the old. In part, as we shall see, this means that Dante draws for a first time in Canto xii upon the imagery of Christian belief to affirm the continuing and eternal value of the human being. At the same time, the 'new' humanism involves – as the old humanism of Brunetto and Piero never could – a painful admission of the sinfulness and destructiveness of human beings. The honesty and imaginative vigour of that admission themselves become a source of new dignity. And here there arises a powerful irony; for to enforce that understanding Dante goes back to the myths and images of classical literature. Such a return is itself the expression of a humanism more searching than Brunetto, say, could historically muster. Yet the myths which Dante draws upon in Canto xii are myths of corruption and tragedy: the virtue of classical literature at this point is to reveal how human beings can violate their own virtues.

So in Canto xii, the first move of the humanist is to create an image which, fantastic as it is, nonetheless defines precisely the extent to which human nature may turn against itself. This is the mythic image of the Minotaur, who acts as ineffectual guardian of the first circle of violence, and stands as the first in a procession of double-natured monstrosities who will appear throughout the sequence. The myth of the Minotaur, as Ovid tells it in *Metamorphoses* viii, is suggestive of the most profound perversions in our sexual and physical nature. The Minotaur was the offspring of Pasiphaë and the bull with which she coupled as she lay in a cow modelled of wood – 'che fu concetta ne la falsa vacca ' (13); and the legend also tells of the yearly offering of seven youths and seven girls that was made to the Minotaur in the Labyrinth. Along with these suggestions, Dante also projects a moral judgement upon the monster, speaking of – 'l'infamïa di Creti' (12), 'ira bestial' (33), and even 'falsa' in the phrase 'falsa vacca' (13). And these judgements are reinforced and extended in Dante's description of the Minotaur. He does not say much about the exact nature of the hybrid. He does, however, concentrate upon its physical movements, and this becomes particularly important in the light of his concern – to be emphasised throughout this sequence – with the steady progress of his own moral journey. Stirred to life by the arrival of the protagonist, the Minotaur is

assured by Virgil that he need not fear the approach of another Theseus –
who as the legend had it, penetrated the Labyrinth to defeat him; nevertheless
he begins to buck and bridle in keeping with his bullish nature:

> Qual è quel toro che si slaccia in quella
> c'ha ricevuto già 'l colpo mortale,
> che gir non sa, ma qua e là saltella.   (*Inf.* xii 22–4)

(As a bull that breaks loose at the moment / it has received the mortal stroke, / unable
to move, bucking here and there).

The Minotaur, then, becomes an emblem of self-contradictory action, an
untrustworthy image of confusion. But against this emblem Dante now places
another, which is the image of himself – the protagonist – taking advantage
of the Minotaur's distraction to climb down the scree-slope:

> Così prendemmo via giù per lo scarco
> di quelle pietre, che spesso moviensi
> sotto i miei piedi per lo novo carco.   (28–30)

(And so we made our way down over the rubble / of those stones which often moved /
beneath my feet, because of the strange new weight upon them.)

And now a new development begins in the presentation of the protagonist.
Once before, as the protagonist stepped into the boat of Phlegyas, the reader
was made aware of the physical presence of Dante in Hell; and this is the
feature of his journey – rather than any attention simply to direction or
dynamics – that the poet now brings into relief. At first, the emphasis is very
delicately introduced; one sees the shifting of the loose stones on the slope
beneath Dante's feet, beneath the 'new' – which is to say, wonderful or sur-
prising – burden. Yet in the second half of the canto, the same phenomenon
becomes the subject of extended comment, initiated by the solemn amaze-
ment of the centaurs:

> Quando s'ebbe scoperta la gran bocca,
> disse a' compagni: 'Siete voi accorti
> che quel di retro move ciò ch'el tocca?
> Così non soglion far li piè d'i morti'.
> E 'l mio buon duca, che già li er' al petto,
> dove le due nature son consorti,
> rispuose: 'Ben è vivo ...'.   (79–85)

(And when he had uncovered his great mouth, / he said to his companions: 'Have you
noticed / that the one behind moves what he touches? / The feet of the dead do not do
so.' / And my good leader, already up to the breast / of the centaur / where its two
natures consorted together, / replied: 'He is truly alive'.)

In the early *Purgatorio*, there are a number of occasions on which the
penitents – who are, after all, spirits – show as much astonishment as the
centaurs at seeing a living body in their domain. To them, the sight is good
news; implicitly, it reveals the true condition under which they themselves
will live, after Judgement Day, in the resurrected body. In the present canto
the significance is similar; but it is sharpened by the contrast between two

kinds of hybrid nature, the protagonist on the one hand, and on the other, the Minotaur and the centaurs: the protagonist remains whole, passing through Hell unscathed by any external violence or any internal contradiction (one recalls the *Messo da Ciel*). Yet the mystery is that this wholeness depends upon his perfect possession of a twofold nature: temporal and eternal, physical and spiritual. In a similar way, *Purgatorio* XIV opens with a strong statement of this mystery, as the penitents address Dante with the words

> O anima che fitta
> nel corpo ancora inver' lo ciel ten vai...   (*Purg.* XIV 10–11)

(O soul, fixed / still in the body making your way towards heaven).

The completeness and fertility which seem to be lost in the rivers of corruption *can* be regained; but they will be carried – and signalled – by presences such as the protagonist who admit the God-given conditions under which their beings are sustained.

We have seen how the protagonist, as traveller, is brought into contrast with sinners such as Argenti and Farinata. But now – particularly in the second half of the twelfth canto – the protagonist is beginning to become a mythic figure, or better say one in whom the mystery of Christian fact replaces the mythic inventions of the ancient world. In that sense, he *is* a Theseus, extirpating the superstitions of the old mythology of minotaurs and centaurs with the reality of what – in Dante's perspective – is the simple truth: human beings, body and soul, are eternally valuable. The reaction of the centaurs to Dante's presence amounts to a celebration of this truth.

It should, however, be said that – in literary terms – this substitution is easier to describe than to make. And there emerges in the twelfth canto, particularly in the second half, a problem of narrative representation which, recurring throughout the violence cantos, will contribute considerably to their imaginative impetus.

For having entered the realm of myth and mystery – as the poet must in the act of imaginative creation – there arises the possibility that myth and mystery will becloud analysis; and this danger becomes particularly acute in the representation of the centaurs.

On the one hand, the centaurs are perfectly designed to assist and speed the journey of the protagonist – their function being to carry Dante 'in su la groppa' (95). And in this respect it is notable that the scene resembles the meeting of the 'bella scola' in Limbo in its gravity and measured progress:

> Or ci movemmo con la scorta fida
> lungo la proda del bollor vermiglio,
> dove i bolliti facieno alte strida.   (*Inf.* XII 100–2)

(Now we moved forward with our trusty escort / along the margin of the vivid red boiling, / where those who are boiled there uttered piercing shrieks.)

But there is something of a danger here, for where the great poets of Limbo pointed out to the protagonist the spirits who had united humanity by their achievements, the centaurs draw Dante's attention to those who have divided the world by violence. And the very gravity with which they perform this task is itself perilous. For it threatens to conceal or blunt the impact that the idea of tyranny must have upon those who – like the historical Dante – are its victims.

Nor is it only pagan myth that threatens to draw such a veil, for Dante himself, precisely in his evocation of the classical past, is here in danger of setting art against morality. Thus, as a background to the didactic procession of the centaurs, Dante has already created, with marvellous freedom of design, a representation of the vigorous but essentially undirected action of the centaurs as they police the banks of the river of blood.

> e tra 'l piè de la ripa ed essa, in traccia
> corrien centauri, armati di saette ... (55–6)

(and between [the ditch] and the foot of the bank, in a line / there ran centaurs armed with arrows).

Running and the shooting of arrows are an essential part of the image that Dante is creating; and these elements bring the twelfth canto into direct contrast with the relatively static cantos preceding it, which were dominated by Farinata and by Virgil's doctrinal discussion of sin. Yet here the very richness of kinetic pattern is a distraction from moral purpose. In the case of the Minotaur, ill-directed motion quickly proved to be morally emblematic, representing the very reverse of Dante's steady advance. And none of the other guardians in Hell have so far eluded moral comment. But the fantasy of movement in this canto ensures that the centaurs *do*; and this is the more striking when one considers that a further centaur will be found in Canto XXV, and that he will be treated with as much vigorous contempt as are the sinners with whom he associates. Here, however, myth and local detail are dwelt upon, it seems, for their own sake, as in the fastidiousness and elegance of Chiron's famous gesture:

> Chirón prese uno strale, e con la cocca
> fece la barba in dietro a le mascelle. (77–8)

(Chiron took an arrow, and with the notch / he put back his beard on his jaws.)

In this way, then, the second half of the canto not only celebrates the myth of the protagonist but also points to the possibility that myth may relieve the pressure to engage, in moral encounter, with historical and factual circumstances.

But this leads us to the threshold of Canto XIII, probably the richest canto in the *Inferno*. For here in recording the story of Pier della Vigna Dante obliges himself to consider a case – attested by history – which is both a parallel to and then the inverted image of his own historical life. Myth, it appears, must constantly be translated into stories – into that ethical form which reveals how particular lives are shaped and shown forth.

III

As I have suggested, the central action in the present sequence of the *Inferno* derives from a contrast, drawn with particular force in Cantos XIII and XV, between the damned, who here, pre-eminently, are the lost leaders of thirteenth-century Italy, and the new leader, Dante himself. I have stressed that by 'Dante himself' in this context I mean not only the protagonist of the poem, but also the historical Dante and Dante as author of the *Commedia*. Correspondingly, the contrast we are to pursue in Cantos XIII and XV arises on three levels – that of the story, that of historical fact and that of, so to speak, authorial conduct. It is also, however, an indication of the variety that Dante achieves in the imaginative texture of the sequence that this threefold contrast should be formulated differently in each of its cantos.

To anticipate, the formula is at its clearest in Canto XV. There a sinner, Brunetto Latini, who, historically, was a civic leader, an orator and a philosopher, meets the protagonist and talks both of his own literary achievements in the world and of the misfortunes which his pupil, the historical Dante, will suffer at the hands of his fellow-citizens. In response, the protagonist speaks unambiguously on behalf of his historical creator: he describes how his journey to salvation began in the Dark Wood (*Inf.* XV 49–54), and shows himself – for the only time in the *Inferno* – to be confident that it will conclude successfully in a meeting with Beatrice (XV 88–90). The whole of this conversation between philosophical master and ex-pupil is cast in remarkably naturalistic terms; and, while, as we shall see, this naturalism is disturbed by strong currents of irony and imaginative suggestion, the interchange invites an analytical comparison of the positions that the two speakers respectively adopt. The protagonist does not need to be taught by Brunetto how we should meet misfortune: he has the strongest possible understanding of the beginnings and ends of his own story; and his own journey, proceeding to its providential conclusion in Heaven, offers a better notion of the remedies available to an exile than any lesson he could learn from one of the damned. But this must also be true on the levels of history and authorial conduct. By now, narrative has itself become an explicit theme in the *Inferno*: Dante, in writing the philosophical narrative of the *Commedia*, is evidently in his own judgement plotting a more effective moral course than Brunetto pursued in *his* literary works; and likewise in offering this example to his fellow-humans, he must consider that he is a better 'leader' than ever Brunetto was of the Florentines.

I stress the clarity with which Dante pursues these issues in Canto XV because in this respect, the canto is, in poetic terms, quite different from Canto XIII. In this canto, there is no exchange of philosophical courtesies: the scene is set in the shrieking wood of the suicides; and the experiences it deals with are confusion, despair and, above all, loss of direction. This means, of course, that there is a pressing need on every level for Dante to grasp and express his underlying design. Yet, as will be seen when we turn to the details of the text, the canto is conceived in such a way as to resist analysis. It is written throughout in a mode of drama, as if the plan it undoubtedly contains could only be discovered by direct experience; and it follows that no merely analytical reading such as I shall offer here can do justice to that. However, a preliminary survey of the canto – especially in the light of Canto xv – will reveal the extent of the material that Dante has compressed into these 150 lines, and may also suggest why – when most urgently requiring the breadth, perspective and control that 'narrative form' implies – Dante should here adopt so intense and concentrated a linguistic style.

On the narrative plane, the thirteenth canto depicts an encounter between two human figures – the travellers Dante and Virgil – and a gnarled thorn-tree that attempts (at least) to converse as if it were still the human being, Pier della Vigna, that once it was. Thus the primary contrast in the canto is between the unthinkable form of the Man-Tree and human form in its natural, physical lineaments.

One important function of this contrast is to emphasise the value that Dante attaches to the physical body. This emphasis is consistent with the attention that was paid to the physical presence of the protagonist in Canto XII, and it contributes to a growing interest in the dignity of the body which we shall trace in Cantos XVIII to XXX of the *Inferno*. In Canto XIII itself, some of the most moving moments of the narrative describe the concern that Virgil silently shows through the gestures of his hand for the distresses of the protagonist (as at line 130).

At the same time, the contrast helps to define Dante's view of suicide, and demonstrates in particular that the sin is as much an offence, in Dante's view, against the human body as against the will of God: the delicate humanity of the protagonist and Virgil, set against the Tree that Piero has become, shows what the suicide has thrown away. Of course, Dante no doubt did believe that suicide is an offence against the Creator, who alone has the power to give life and the prerogative to take it away. Yet neither Canto XIII nor the general references to suicide in Canto XI place any obvious emphasis upon theological considerations. Indeed, the reference which Dante does make in the canto to the Last Judgement – when the souls of the suicides will dangle from the trees into which they are now transformed – is so fantastic in its *quasi*-theology as to have caused serious misgivings among the earliest of Dante's orthodox Christian commentators: by definition a soul cannot be separated from its body. Thus, at its most serious, Dante's analysis of suicide is expressed in existential rather than religious terms: he is concerned with the way in which, through suicide, the human mind is set against the human body, and also with the illogicality which allows physical power to violate and extinguish the spiritual faculties which direct our physical power. In a similar way, when dealing with the heresy of Farinata, Dante represented the denial of immortality as an irrationality, inconsistent with the dignity of the human being. The heretic, one might say, is an intellectual suicide; the suicide is likewise 'heretical' in misconstruing the value of his own existence. Piero acted as though he were no more than a tree, to be hacked down at will – and in that sense may be said to have 'chosen' the punishment he suffers in Hell. The truth is, however – as the weeping protagonist of the canto clearly demonstrates – that human beings are *not* insentient matter.

It is an indication of how Dante acts on the authorial level that, having begun to develop the myth of physical immortality in Canto XII, he should proceed in Canto XIII to recognise how this myth might be challenged at its very roots: the fact of human self-destructiveness is now starkly contraposed against the miracle of human immortality. Simply in recognising this fact, the sequence at large would be a 'difficult' one; and we shall see that, internally, the structure of Canto XIII is itself animated by a similarly difficult interplay between myth and fact.

The especial difficulty of Canto XIII, however, derives from Dante's specific choice of Pier della Vigna as his principal example of suicide. For by virtue of this choice Dante institutes a direct comparison between himself and the sinner on the level of history. As later in the depiction of Ulysses, Dante portrays a character in Hell who mirrors many of his own most serious preoccupations. But Ulysses is a pure fiction, devised as a reflecting surface in which Dante can study the dangers of his own procedures and aspirations. Piero *did* exist and *did* kill himself. He was one of the founders of the culture in Italy from which Dante sprang; he was both a leader – and a lost leader – of the epoch in which Dante himself lived, suffered and sought to establish the value of his own example.

It is, therefore, important to recall that, historically, Piero was a man who rose from humble social origins to become a chief *aide* to the Emperor Frederick II. The court of Frederick II was one in which science, jurisprudence and literature were all actively nurtured. And Piero – whose position made him an official propagandist of the court – also represented in his own writings the cultural achievements that the court embodied: Piero's vernacular poetry was written in an idiom that Dante sought to cultivate in some of his earliest poems, and his Latin letters were a model of style to subsequent generations.

In many respects, the court of Frederick II was one which exemplified precisely those social and intellectual virtues that Dante most admired. One may add that Dante was himself always ready to look critically at Frederick's achievements. As we shall see, it is one of the characteristics of Pier della Vigna in Canto XIII that even in Hell he is not prepared to criticise his master. Dante, on the other hand, has condemned Frederick as a heretic in *Inferno* X, and may even be thought to continue his critique of the *Magna Curia* in Canto XIII itself. Nonetheless, Frederick did represent for Dante the last practical expression of political good order in Italy; and even Frederick's ability to recognise and give advancement to a social inferior such as Piero –

on the grounds of native intelligence – must have recommended him to Dante.

Dante and Piero may, then, be said broadly to have shared common aspirations and literary aptitudes. But the strongest similarity between them lies in the misfortune that they both suffered. Just as Dante was exiled, under sentence of death, from the city he had served as a politician and man of letters, so Piero was destroyed by the court he had officially represented: envy and rumour led him to disgrace in Frederick's eyes, and having been tortured and blinded, he killed himself in his prison cell.

With this, we come to the essential *difference*, on the historical level, between Piero and Dante. For Dante, in response to his own disgrace, did not kill himself; he set out instead to write the *Commedia*. One might, indeed, say that Canto xiii is an exploration of the contrast between the act of suicide and the act of writing as responses to misfortune.

But is this not trivial? Can one really compare the physical torments that Piero actually underwent with the slow pains of exile or the intellectual labours of literary composition? We shall see that the canto is by no means inclined to belittle the gravity of physical pain. At the same time, a comparison on the grounds we have suggested may well have seemed valid to Dante himself. And to understand why, it is enough to recall another historical figure, the Roman Boethius, whose experiences both as a politician and as a philosopher ran parallel to those of Dante and Piero.

The philosophical works of Boethius have been in Dante's mind since *Inferno* vii, where, in general terms, he first broached the topic of misfortune. But, in history, Boethius's position was all but identical to Piero's. Like Piero, Boethius fell from favour. Imprisoned and awaiting execution he did not, however, yield to despair or contemplate suicide; he wrote the *Consolatio Philosophiae*, the *Consolation* of Philosophy, asserting that the dignity of the human being resides in its freedom to pursue, in whatever circumstances, the goals of truth and goodness. Not only was the *Consolation* a work of great importance to Dante himself in the early years of his intellectual life, but it served throughout the Dark Ages as an example to subsequent generations of intellectual and spiritual fortitude.

In the light of this example, it becomes an urgent philosophical responsibility – particularly for those, like Dante and Piero, who possess literary and intellectual talents – to avoid despair and, so far from submitting to suicide, positively rewrite the disasters of their lives in a way which might benefit others. We are bound to suppose that Dante saw the *Commedia* itself as his own bulwark against despair; and this would certainly be consistent with the conclusions of Canto xv – which is itself a canto marked by Boethian turns of phrase and argument: Dante is by that time plainly using his poem to plot a moral course for himself and for his fellows. As for Piero, suffering as he does a classic reversal of fortune, he must clearly be judged by the standard that Boethius – who might be called the inventor of Fortuna – had set.

At this point, however, one needs to look more closely at the kind of authorial action which Dante exemplifies in the thirteenth canto. For Dante's procedure itself is not, by any means, identical to that which Boethius adopts in the *Consolation*. We have seen already how, in Canto VII, Dante modifies the philosophy of the *Consolation* in both substance and procedure, beginning at that early point to create, as it were, a 'narrative philosophy' which involves a tragic acceptance of – rather than resistance to – the impact of changing experience. And the deepest level of the action in Canto XIII concerns the contrast between this tragic attitude to experience and the attitudes that Dante attributes to the false model of Piero.

Thus, in general terms, suicide may be seen as a contradiction of all the principles that – as we saw at the opening of this chapter – Dante appears to associate with narrative writing. Like a literary narrator, the suicide attempts to control or write the story of his life; he does so, however, not by realising the natural design of origins and ends which is already inscribed in his existence, but rather by anticipating its end and interrupting his own steady course towards that end.

More specifically, we shall also see that a contrast between Dante and Piero arises in the use they make of myth. Piero's suicide is itself an attempt to maintain the myth of his own reputation; and Dante too may be said to be writing the canto to demonstrate the virtue of his own response to despair. Yet Dante, as we shall see, does not here insist upon, but rather challenges, the image of himself as the privileged traveller through eternity. In Dante's procedure, there is no danger that reputation will be confused with moral and intellectual dignity; that, however, is precisely the danger that Dante identifies in the speeches he gives to Piero.

This brings us to the most essential point of contrast. The case of Piero is an exceptionally difficult one, and the distinctions between true and false action which appear in the case and account for its particular complexity are quite especially delicate. Yet Piero himself is shown, by his suicide, rather to evade than to realise the implications of his condition. It is Dante, as author of the canto, who sharpens these implications to the point of tragedy. Yet Dante cannot do this without submitting his own moral position and poetic procedures to intense scrutiny. His very choice of Piero – a case so similar to his own – as an example of suicide itself makes such scrutiny inevitable; and in examining that case Dante tests the directions he has conceived for his own life against the image of what he himself – if he despairs – might still become.

Clearly, then, the core of Canto XIII is the intense encounter between the protagonist and Pier della Vigna in the light of the large similarities and fine-drawn differences between them. This is not, however, to say – as might once have been said – that this is 'the canto of Piero'. Here, no less than in the Brunetto episode, Dante arrives at an understanding of what it means to be writing the *Commedia*; and while he does not, as in Canto XV, explicitly reveal the perspective of his whole narrative, the canto does implicitly raise issues that reach, beyond the details of any particular case, to the furthest boundaries of the *Commedia*. This is a canto in which images (and the representation of events) have a greater importance than explicit statement; and the images that Dante here introduces resonate through many subsequent cantos of the poem. Thus, to appreciate the extent of Dante's authorial action, we need, before turning to the portrayal of Piero, to look at the internal structure of the canto; then we must pursue some of the images that Dante here introduces to their final point of resolution in the *Purgatorio* and *Paradiso*. All that Dante sees here can and must be translated into moral terms; but once we have made that translation we must again return to the canto itself. For it remains true that the crucial feature of the authorial drama in Canto XIII (as later in another drama of metamorphosis, Canto XXV) is that Dante here should release a range of images – some anarchic, some pregnant with ulterior meaning – which cannot as yet be qualified or controlled by any resort to settled or systematic theology. The question is: how can the poet sustain this vision in all its tragic force without falling into the confusion that destroys Piero?

In its internal structure, Canto XIII divides into two major sections (each containing important subdivisions), followed by a coda which connects this canto to Canto XIV. The first of these sections (lines 1–109) describes the encounter with the suicide Piero; and in the coda (lines 130–51) Dante returns to the subject of suicide, describing the anonymous Florentine who hanged himself in his own house and has now been transformed into a tiny shrub. In the intervening section (lines 110–28), Dante pictures the wild flight of wastrels and spendthrifts, who maintain their human form but are hunted through the forest in which the suicides stand, causing the suicides to scream whenever their branches or trunks are injured.

The divisions of the canto point, then, to a range of contrasts, between the static trees and the violent motion of the wastrels, between the 'great' thorn-tree and the tiny shrub into which the Florentine suicide is transformed, between human form and vegetable form; and here, as in Canto X, one function of these contrasts is to reveal the moral issues of the canto, inviting the reader to grasp the common denominator between apparently disparate categories and to apprehend the principles which underlie the poet's judgements: to associate the apparently heroic sin of suicide with the trivial and frenetic sin of prodigality is to assert that material possessions are neither more nor less subject to God's law than the body and, conversely, that the human body is as much at God's disposal as are the 'splendor mondani' which, as we have seen, Fortune administers. Similarly, these contrasts point to a social and political diagnosis which continues the theme of public violence that began in Canto XII. Between the great thorn-tree of the Imperial politician Piero and the little shrub that embodies an insignificant suicide in a strife-torn city–state a comparison is established in which violence is seen to run through all ranks of society; and the suggestion arises that even suicide – apparently the most private of sins – is never actually a private matter: it is the expression of a violent undertow in the public world, and may have re-percussions, as an example of self-destruction, which run from the highest to the lowest levels of the social order.

Important, however, as such diagnoses are, it will already be apparent that the structure of the canto is designed as much to disrupt as to facilitate clear analysis; so far from pursuing a steady narrative line, the canto is plainly built upon effects of division, disturbance and disproportion – to be found as much in the rhythms of single phrases as in the larger units of structure. And these same features allow one to see the connection between the moral questions of suicide and the intellectual or authorial questions which concern the planning and plotting of a life-story.

This is, in part, to say – as frequently has been said – that the violent disruptions of the text dramatise and mimic the ultimately disruptive act of suicide. But we need to go further than that. Suicide, like writing, represents an attempt to assess a life and shape it – by imposing an end upon it – according to a certain pattern. And while, as I have said, Dante will reassert the value of the course which he himself has adopted in his own misfortunes, he also constrains himself, in considering the sin of suicide, to see how profoundly and subtly the mind may misconceive the stewardship of its own existence. In suicide, Dante acknowledges a human capacity for disruption on the most radical plane; and this leads him to envisage in this canto the ways in which the essential instruments of his own advance may be subject to dis-location. Words and perceptions are alike a prey to confusion in Canto XIII; and, on the level of the text, discourse and narrative coherence are con-tinually under pressure from the mute impact of images or sudden events.

All these effects need to be considered in detail. But enough has been said to suggest that, for the reader as well as for Dante himself, the order which underlies the thirteenth canto will be achieved by a willingness to admit rather than resist dislocation. Piero himself cannot tolerate the disruption of the life he had led, surrounded by honours; but Dante's canto demands that one should find order even among the fragments that our own minds are likely to create.

We arrive at similar conclusions if we consider the canto in its relation to the overall plan of the *Commedia*.

Consider, above all, the way in which Dante deals in this canto and else-where with the images of the tree and the forest. In its immediate context, the transformation of the suicides into trees has, again, a diagnostic function: human life is governed, in its spiritual as well as its physical aspect, by an organic principle of growth and development which should properly continue in the human being – as in the natural tree – until the end of its appointed time. So, the implications of the tree are compatible with those of the central image of the journey, which for Dante expresses the intrinsic pattern that resides in human action. But, like the image of the river of blood in

Canto XII, the tree of the suicide also acknowledges the violence which the human being can do to this pattern.

In its mythic aspect, the image considerably expands these implications. Piero comes to be judged against a background of considerations which go far beyond the confines of any single historical moment; and in his case the crucial question is whether in his life and in the story he tells to Virgil he could have contained or realised the implications which, in Hell, are borne in upon him by his transformation into a tree. But the same questions bear upon Dante, both historically, as an exile, and as author of the *Commedia*. In admitting the mythic energies of the tree image, he challenges himself to comprehend within the circuit of a single canto the whole plan of his journey in the first two *cantiche* from the Dark Wood to the 'foresta divina' of the Earthly Paradise. Where Virgil in Canto XI is allowed to expound the categories of sin in the plan of Hell, Dante in Canto XIII sets himself to grasp the full resonance of the images which are central to his project.

So, most directly, Dante accentuates the similarities between the 'selva oscura' of *Inferno* I and the wood of the suicides. Here, as at the outset, the protagonist travels through a pathless wood:

> un bosco
> che da neun sentiero era segnato.
>   Non fronda verde, ma di color fosco;
> non rami schietti, ma nodosi e 'nvolti;
> non pomi v'eran, ma stecchi con tòsco.   (XIII 2–6)

(a wood / marked by no footpath. / No green leaves, but leaves dark in colour: / no straight clean branches, but knotted, warped; / there were no apples there, but thorns with poison.)

In both cases, the image of the tree helps to express the consequences of despair: lacking direction or hope, the mind falls into sterility and confusion. But what significance does the *repetition* of such an image itself possess? In the first place, this repetition re-animates the problems of Canto I, and, casting those problems in a more intense form, recognises that one possible conclusion for Dante's despair would have been self-annihilation. At the same time, the imaginative intensity of the moment is itself the reverse of annihilation. The differences between Piero and Dante are adumbrated in Dante's willingness to admit the poignant renewal of pain, and also by the fact that the repetition indicates the outline or ghost of an order which the poet is now in the process of constructing. In the face of absurdity and despair, the imagination traces its painful patterns of repetition; even where the paths are obscured, the half-perceived regularity in the image is itself a stay against confusion.

The poet, then, recalls in Canto XIII the origins of his own story in the Dark Wood. But equally – anticipating the barely conceivable end of his journey in the Earthly Paradise – he also points forward to a number of intervening stages through which he must pass in his itinerary of imaginative recuperation. The image of the tree is progressively clarified as an emblem for order and stability. Yet in two of the subsequent passages, Dante also insists that the perception of that meaning must be as painful as it is originally in *Inferno* XIII.

The first of these passages occurs in *Purgatorio* XIV (at the culmination of the canto I quoted in discussing *Inferno* XII) where, lamenting the decay of civilisation and courtesy, Dante describes the perverse course of the river Arno. That corrupt stream irrigates its own 'trista selva'; and Dante pictures, emerging from that wood, a figure who epitomises all the barbarity and cruelty of which he has spoken throughout the canto. Of this Macbeth-like butcher he writes:

> Vende la carne loro essendo viva,
> poscia li ancide come antica belva:
> molti di vita e sé di pregio priva.
>   Sanguinoso esce de la trista selva;
> lasciala tal, che di qui a mille anni
> ne lo stato primaio non si rinselva.   (*Purg.* XIV 61–6)

(He sells their flesh still living, / and then he slays them like an ancient beast: / many of life he deprives and himself of honour. / Blood-stained he issues from the miserable wood, / leaving it such that a thousand years from now / it will not recover or again become the wood it first was.)

The implications of this passage corroborate the significance of both the *selva oscura* and the Wood of the Suicides. All three images point beyond a private condition of despair to its source or counterpart in the public world: the 'selva oscura' and the 'trista selva' are both, in part, portrayals of the violence of Dante's Tuscany. And in the blood-stained figure there is embodied the same failure of courtesy and civilisation which led, at the Sicilian court of Frederick II, to the downfall of Piero. Like *Purgatorio* XIV the thirteenth canto of the *Inferno* is concerned with courtly culture: though Piero could have been the representative of such a culture at its best – in his urbanity and literary talent – he is also, as he himself declares, the victim of the gossip and slander which are an inescapable part of life at court:

> La meretrice che mai da l'ospizio
> di Cesare non torse li occhi putti,
> morte comune e de le corti vizio ...   (*Inf.* XIII 64–6)

(The harlot who from the dwelling / of Caesar never turns her loathsome eyes, / common bane and vice of courts).

Yet *Purgatorio* XIV also marks an advance upon the *Inferno*. Desperate as the vision of the 'trista selva' certainly is, it nonetheless represents – in the strict sense – a vision, conceived and uttered by a blind penitent, Guido del Duca, in an agony of remorse. It is a part of Guido's penance to contemplate this image, and equally a part of the penance of his companion in Purgatory to hear the vision told out:

> così vid' io l'altr' anima, che volta
> stava a udir, turbarsi e farsi trista,
> poi ch'ebbe la parola a sé raccolta.   (*Purg.* XIV 70–2)

(so I saw the other soul, who had turned / to listen intently, grow troubled and oppressed / when he had taken in these words to himself).

The implications of this are clear. Even an image as dire as that of the 'trista selva' can be and should be nourished by the contemplative mind, and made to yield – as the word 'raccolta' (to gather or harvest) suggests – a spiritual profit. In effect, the mind, in concentrating upon the desecration of the primal wood, realises fully what it has lost and receives a shadowy indication of what, in penitence, it might recover. As Dante in *Inferno* XIII looks back to his own origins in guilt and despair, so, too, do the penitents of *Purgatorio* XIV. Yet clearly – to judge from the place they occupy in Purgatory – the vision of the penitents is also a premonition of the Earthly Paradise. Where the 'trista selva' will not recover its primal state in a thousand years (*Purg.* XIV 64–5), the Eden which Adam destroyed can be recovered through the pains of purgation; and that recovery will signal a return of order to the tormented individual and to the temporal sphere at large. So, before entering the Earthly Paradise, Virgil 'crowns' the protagonist in recognition of his new moral perfection. He is free, upright and whole – everything that Piero in Hell is not, and his crowning signifies, too, that under an Emperor more perfect than Frederick II a realm of justice may be established for the benefit of all humanity:

> libero, dritto e sano è tuo arbitrio,
> e fallo fora non fare a suo senno:
>   per ch'io te sovra te corono e mitrio.   (*Purg.* XXVII 140–2)

(free, upright and whole is your will, / and now it would be a mistake not to act as you think fit: / so I crown and mitre you over yourself).

One need not now hesitate to compare the visionary penitent of *Purgatorio* XIV with the poet in *Inferno* XIII. Myth and vision are forms in which the simultaneous absence and presence of order can be grasped: indeed the painful recognition of the absence of order is a condition of its ultimate realisation. But, to see how directly the attitudes of the penitent contrast with those that Dante attributes to Piero, one may pause to consider in some detail a final instance, from *Purgatorio* XXIII. Here – where Dante describes the penance of the gluttons, to which I have already referred in Chapter 2 – there is a tree as strange in its beauty as are the trees of *Inferno* XIII in their grotesqueness. The Tree of Penance is an inverted pyramid, sprayed continually by falling water:

> e come abete in alto si digrada
> di ramo in ramo, così quello in giuso
> cred' io, perché persona sù non vada.
>   Dal lato onde 'l cammin nostro era chiuso,
> cadea de l'alta roccia un liquor chiaro
> e si spandeva per le foglie suso.   (*Purg.* XXII 133–8)

(and just as a fir-tree grows less by degrees / from branch to branch [the higher it goes] so did this tree, but downwards, / I think so that people should not climb up it. / On the side where our path was blocked off, / a clear liquor fell from the high rock / and spread itself above the foliage.)

For the penitents, the tree serves a liturgical function; and as they circle continually around it, they enact a cyclical order in which spiritual progress and fertility are already implicitly restored. Equally, in their acts of worship, the penitents re-establish among themselves the bond of community and courtesy which on earth they had helped to disrupt by their vice and injustice. Effectively, this tree prefigures the trees of the 'divina foresta'.

Yet it is plainly a condition imposed upon the penitents that the meaning of the tree should only reveal itself because they are willing to devote their minds to a sight which is both paradoxical in form and painful in its effects: the beauty of the tree cruelly sharpens their appetites; and, as the spokesman of the penitents declares, this suffering is itself a comfort and a promise of health:

> E non pur una volta, questo spazzo
> girando, si rinfresca nostra pena:
> io dico pena, e dovria dir sollazzo.   (*Purg.* xxiii 70–2)

(Nor once alone, as we go around [this open ground], / is our pain renewed; / I call it pain, but rather should say solace.)

At this point a further analogy arises. For if, as we have said, the tree here prefigures the trees of the Earthly Paradise, it is also analogous, in the suffering it causes, to the 'tree' of the Cross: the penitential tree points both to the eventual restoration of order, and also to the roots and origins of that restoration in the Crucifixion and Atonement:

> ché quella voglia a li alberi ci mena
> che menò Cristo lieto a dire '*Elì*',
> quando ne liberò con la sua vena.   (73–5)

(For that same will that leads us to the trees / led Christ to cry 'Eli' / when he freed us with the blood of his veins.)

With this one returns to Pier della Vigna. There is clearly a sense in which the suicide of Piero might itself seem to be analogous to the self-sacrifice of the penitents and even of Christ himself. It is equally clear that, in Dante's view, Piero did not draw that analogy, and that his spiritual failure resides precisely there. Everything in the historical circumstances of Piero's disgrace and suffering reveal the similarity. The story of Christ's passion is the story repeated in every subsequent instance of disgrace and suffering; and we need not emphasise that, even more directly than the tree of the penitents, the tree in which Piero is punished – a thorn-tree – recalls the 'tree' on which Christ died, crowned with thorns.

Yet, so far from embracing the Christian example in submission to the inescapable reality of human suffering, Piero's suicide is confessedly an attempt at evasion:

L'animo mio, per disdegnoso gusto,
credendo col morir fuggir disdegno,
ingiusto fece me contra me giusto.   (*Inf.* XIII 70–2)

(My heart, inclined to a haughty contempt, / thinking to flee from contempt by dying, / made me unjust against my own just self.)

The action here is clearly motivated by the sinner's desire to defend his reputation against calumny and physical torment. But precisely because of that, Piero's suicide rejects the lesson in humility which makes the penitents akin to the suffering Christ. So, where the penitents submit to the paradoxes of the tree, Piero, seeking to elude the misrepresentation that slander has projected upon him, succeeds only in precipitating a further contradiction and even in slandering himself: his suicide is an unjust act directed against his own just self. Piero, in Dante's version, is locked single-mindedly into tensions of his own tragedy. Unlike the penitents, he is quite incapable of contemplating its deeper implications.

In a similar way, the very name that Piero seeks to defend by his suicide is peculiarly rich in Christian associations. For it was, of course, Saint Peter whose faith in Christ was tested by the events of the Passion; and Dante – if not Piero – realises this allusion when he allows Piero to introduce himself as the one who held both the keys of the heart of Frederick (58–9). St Peter likewise held the keys of gold and silver, of absolution and wisdom; but Piero here boasts of his authority with a heretical Emperor. And that irony becomes especially acute when one considers that, while there is nothing to suggest that Piero *did* betray the faith of his master, St Peter was indeed guilty of bad faith, and yet could still become the rock of the Church. Such ironies become miracles on a Christian understanding, but Piero is no more aware of them than he is of the resemblance between his own passion and Christ's.

For the reader, then, the thirteenth canto is alive with questions central to the myth of the Christian faith. Indeed, as we shall see, faith itself is an important theme throughout the canto. It is, however, essential to the mentality of Piero that he responds not to this myth, but to the myth of Frederick, his 'Augustus', seeking to make his lasting fame depend upon his unswerving (and ill-founded) devotion to the man who consents to his downfall. In this respect, Piero illustrates, as we have suggested, how easily myth – which, for the penitents of Purgatory as for Dante, is a vital intellectual resource – may also lead the mind away from an engagement with the brute facts of history or the cruelty of events. And at this point one may think again of Boethius, whose misfortunes led him with the utmost clarity to contemplate the 'fallaciousness of the world' (*Par.* X 125). We may also think, however, of another, less eminent figure whom Dante nonetheless celebrates – along with the Roman Emperor, Justinian – in *Paradiso* VI: Romeo, who appears at lines 127–42.

Like Piero and Boethius, Romeo was, in his smaller sphere, a counsellor of

princes, and like them he fell from favour. But the fate which Romeo suf-
fered was not imprisonment; rather, in common with Dante, he endured the
miseries of exile. The poet, in praising this example of fortitude, describes
how Romeo went begging his life crust by crust: 'mendicando sua vita a
frusto a frusto' (*Par.* VI 141). The emphasis of this phrase – falling upon the
day-to-day process of living – exactly anticipates the fuller picture which
Dante will draw in *Paradiso* XVII of his own exile, as he eats bitter salt at
another man's table and wearily climbs the stair in another man's house. And
the relevance of this emphasis to our present discussion of narrative – and of
heroism – is not far to seek: whatever comfort one may draw from the great
myths that promise ultimate order and dignity, there is an ordinary heroism
which requires us to experience each day, each crust of bread, each step on
the stair for what it is. Mere sequence and the repetition of events must be
suffered through as the condition of history. Something of this is reflected in
the narrative pattern which we can now proceed to examine in Canto XIII
itself. Here the magisterial order of words and narrative discourse is, as we
have seen, interpenetrated and disturbed by a subtler order of images; but this
order in turn is both threatened and expressed by the violence of single
events. And with this we may return to Canto XIII, allowing, now, the rhythm
of these events to dictate our reading.

From the first moments of Canto XIII, the protagonist has been assailed by
screams. Plucking at the branches of the trees, the Harpies, in a dreadful par-
ody of the Muses, 'inspire' the trees to speak. Dante is dazed – 'smarrito' –
by the sound; and lest there should be any doubt about the incredible source
of the noise, Virgil invites the protagonist to pluck a branch from a great
thorn-tree:

> Allor porsi la mano un poco avante
> e colsi un ramicel da un gran pruno ...   (31–2)

(And then my hand went a little forward, / and plucked a little branch from a great
thorn-tree.)

The phrase 'un poco avante' and the diminutive 'ramicel' suggest the timid-
ity of the gesture, but also the disproportion between the action and its effect,
for the tree at once begins to shriek as the protagonist realises the inconceiv-
able truth that these are not men imprisoned in trees but men transformed
bodily into trees. With a politeness and reasonableness which, after such an
event, are as lurid as the event itself, Virgil then explains to the tree that it
was necessary for the protagonist to perform this act if he was to have first-
hand experience (46–54). And, responding to this courtesy, the tree begins to
tell its story, hoping that by doing so its reputation on earth can be cleared –
or, as Virgil puts it, ironically enough in this sterile context, 'refreshed': 'sì
che 'n vece / d'alcun' ammenda tua fama rinfreschi / nel mondo sù' (52–4).

Piero's response is ornate and courtly, reflecting the idiom of the letters and poems for which he was famous in Duecento Italy. But equally, Dante speaks in parallel with the sinner to emphasise the incongruities of the case: instead of sap, blood and words issue from the gash in Piero's bark, again echoing the bloody sweat of Christ's Passion; and when the first words come, the line which records them is firmly divided between the words themselves and a brutal emphasis upon their vegetable source, "l tronco':

> E 'l tronco: 'Sì col dolce dir m'adeschi,
> ch'i' non posso tacere; e voi non gravi
> perch' ïo un poco a ragionar m'inveschi'.   (55–7)

(And the trunk: 'You so bait me with your sweet words / that I cannot be silent: and let it not be wearisome to you / that I should entrap myself a little while in speech.')

Even with these words a certain flaw in the sinner's language and procedure will be apparent. It has been well said that a dominant feature of Piero's diction is circumlocution. And already Piero uses a similar device, covering over the paradox and horror of his position with the preciosity of the phrase 'm'adeschi', which rhymes with the equally precious 'm'inveschi'. Both of these locutions are potentially violent, pointing to the hooking of fish or the liming of birds. Yet Piero's chiming phrases distract attention from that violence – and from the applicability of these phrases to his own tragic case as a victim.

In a canto which ends with a description of the hunted wastrels, Piero's evasion is especially striking; and throughout the episode a contrast is sustained between the attempted 'dolcezza' of Piero's address and, in the words that frame it, a harshness which entends even to Virgil's speech, when at line 30, he declares that any doubts that the protagonist might have will be chopped off – 'monchi' – when he plucks the branch.

But as Piero begins his story, his linguistic evasiveness moves into a moral key, as the speaker, proclaiming his own merits, unwittingly reveals a personality marred by shiftiness and self-delusion. His stance is one which demonstrates both pride and self-effacement, as he identifies himself not by name – a name to which, in any case, he has lost the right – but wholly in terms of his relationship with the Emperor, whom he is shortly to dignify with the title Augustus (68). His claim to nobility resides in keeping faith, or in loyalty. And we might be tempted now to cast this in a more sinister light by saying that Piero prides himself upon obeying orders. Of course, there can be no doubt that Dante would have recognised some merit in the position. Indeed, one of the themes he derived from the love-poetry of the Sicilian school was the theme of faithful service to the Lady. Even so, Book IV of the *Convivio* begins with a criticism of the Emperor Frederick's own definition of nobility in terms of social and economic standing; and one prevailing purpose of Dante's poetry is to develop, out of the suggestions of his Sicilian forebears, a notion of fidelity as a philosophical devotion to the truth. It is one thing to be the faithful *consigliere* of a Sicilian emperor, quite another to be the *fedele* of Beatrice.

As Piero proceeds, so does the revelation of his – knowing or unknowing –
deceptiveness. Piero may be complacently satisfied over his own inwardness
with Frederick:

> serrando e diserrando, sì soavi,
>   che dal secreto suo quasi ogn' uom tolsi.   (60–1)

(locking and unlocking so gently / that from his secret counsels I excluded almost every
man).

But the line also depicts the bureaucrat at work: his 'softness' – his
'dolcezza' – resides in a sinister skill to exclude others from the secret
thoughts of his master, dividing ruler from subject. It is horribly apt, in this
light, that when the truth-seeking protagonist approaches him, Piero should
be obliged to betray the secret of his own condition in the only 'harsh' words
he speaks in the canto: 'e 'l tronco suo gridò: "Perché mi schiante?"' (35) –
and the trunk screamed: 'Why do you rend me?'

In two *terzine*, then, misplaced pride and divisiveness have begun to show
beneath the veil of Piero's words, so that even his claim to have wasted his
physical substance in the service of the Emperor now looks suspiciously like
the wanton disregard for physical nature which a profligate might display or
a premonition of his own suicidal conclusion:

> fede portai al glorïoso offizio,
>   tanto ch'i' ne perde' li sonni e ' polsi.   (62–3)

(I bore such faith to the glorious office / that, by it, I lost both sleep and life).

But if Piero is himself at least latently divisive, he is – in this regard as in
his virtues – representative of a similar spirit of division in the Sicilian court
which precipitates his downfall. Here, too, words are untrustworthy; and in
the most ornate sequence of the speech Piero describes how the envious
tittle-tattle of the court turned 'Caesar' against him:

> La meretrice che mai da l'ospizio
> di Cesare non torse li occhi putti,
> morte comune e de le corti vizio,
>   infiammò contra me li animi tutti;
> e li 'nfiammati infiammar sì Augusto,
> che ' lieti onor tornaro in tristi lutti.   (64–9)

(The harlot who from the dwelling-place of / Caesar never turns her loathsome eyes, /
common bane and vice of courts, / inflamed all minds against me, / and those, inflamed,
so inflamed Augustus / that joyous honours were turned to miserable grief.)

This brings us to the account that Piero offers of his own death – only the
second account of a death, after Francesca's, in the *Inferno*. And, just as
Francesca clouds the account of her last moments with suggestive ambigui-
ties and absurd accusations against the book she was reading, so, even more
strikingly in Piero's case, the event which ought to have marked the conclu-
sion of his narrative is deflected out of sight by a flourish of verbal effect. In

Piero's telling of the tale, the end or shape of his life is as blurred as it was by the act which he – albeit indirectly – records here:

> L'animo mio, per disdegnoso gusto,
> credendo col morir fuggir disdegno,
> ingiusto fece me contra me giusto.   (70–2)

(My mind, in its disdainful mood, / thinking to escape disdain by death, / made me unjust against my own just self.)

Taken out of context, the final line expresses an unmistakably tragic contradiction. Yet the rhyme-words 'gusto–giusto' introduce an inappropriate finesse into the austere paradox while, at the same time, attracting the mind away from its concentration upon the force of the single line to an appreciation of the (admittedly very elegant) cadence of the whole *terzina*. One has only to think of Virgil's first words, 'Non omo, omo già fui', to see how gravity might have been combined with elegance; and that early line is also a touchstone in that it displays Virgil's determination to speak true. In the context of the whole *Commedia*, the contradictions in Piero's lines are not in fact tragic at all but rather contradictions in morality and logic.

At the last, Piero seeks to keep faith not only with his Emperor but also with himself; he desires, as he does in Hell, to maintain his fame and is unable to tolerate the false image which has been projected upon him by envy and rumour. In this respect, he consciously seeks the monumental dignity – unchanging in the face of vicissitude – which Dante attributes to Farinata and attempts to make of himself such a monument by the stroke of suicide. But selfhood cannot be located in such rigidity. Boethius, Romeo and Dante himself – who in *Paradiso* XVII 61–3 complains that one of the sharpest pains of exile is to be grouped indiscriminately with a crew of refugee Guelphs and Ghibellines – all understand that human beings must tolerate not only the physical changes of life and death, but equally the shifting and even erroneous conceptions that others may form about them. So it is Forese Donati – wearing the word *omo* in *Purgatorio* XXIII, simultaneously a mask and revelation of his essence – who shows that true identity rests precisely in being known and judged by another being, God. To be just – and not unjust against one's just self – one must accept the sentence of God.

And even Piero is finally obliged to do this. His story does not end with his death as he thought it would; it continues into eternity. Attempting to assert in eternity the fidelity which constituted, in his own estimation, the core of his personality, he protests his unswerving devotion to Frederick. But at the very moment of doing so he reveals, in a dreadful return to the paradox of the speaking tree, the nature of the image that has been cast upon him in judgement. Affirming his loyalty by the most essential part of his present nature, he is obliged to swear by the roots of the tree he now is:

> Per le nove radici d'esto legno
> vi giuro che già mai non ruppi fede.   (73–4)

(By the strange new roots of this tree, / I swear to you that I never broke faith.)

And the image of the root itself asserts not fidelity, but the principles of measured growth and life which Piero has offended by his suicide.

Piero has no more to add to his life-story. But this is not the end of his speech; and we shall not exhaust the significance either of the judgement upon Piero or of the thirteenth canto at large without considering the contrast which arises in moral terms between Piero and the two travellers, and in terms of speech and storytelling between Piero and Dante as poet.

The second half of the canto is dominated by three factors: the horrified silence of the protagonist, the discourse of Virgil and the virtuosity of Dante's narrative as it moves from the static first phase into the mobility of the second. And each of these features contributes to the answer which Dante himself makes on the question that has defeated Piero.

The question is how the mind is to deal with its own capacity for untruth, fantasy, fiction and horror; and, equally, how it is to shape its own life without being distorted or betrayed by the words it must use in doing so. On earth, Piero was broken both by the lies of others and by a delusive image of his own nature, while in Hell his words betray him and are mocked by the facts of his position. How is Dante as speaker and storyteller to avoid a similar defeat?

One part of the answer is located in Virgil, who appears, here, not only as *personaggio* but also as the poet of the *Aeneid*; Dante draws his image of man transformed into tree from the Polydorus episode in *Aeneid* III 22 *et seq*. As *personaggio*, Virgil continues the courteous mode of address which marked his first approach to Piero, but he combines it now with a scientific inquiry into the present condition of Piero in Hell, asking not about the man's earthly life, but rather about his weird mode of existence in Hell. Where Piero, for his own purpose, limits his story to the temporal phase, Virgil – implicitly demanding completeness – requires that Piero should place himself in the perspective of eternity. But the conversation has something of the function of discourse in the eleventh canto, 'passing time' profitably while the protagonist is unable to speak; Dante has been urged to speak – 'non perder l'ora' (80) – but he cannot do so: 'Domandal tu ancora ... / ch'i' non potrei, tanta pietà m'accora' (82–4). In a similar way, the model of the *Aeneid* is a demonstration that poets can conceive horrors such as this metamorphosis and still pursue a moral purpose. If Virgil *personaggio* offers the cool interest of the rational mind as a remedy for the distress of Dante *personaggio*, Virgil the poet provides Dante with a myth which demonstrates the potential endurance and adaptability of his literary culture.

Even so, Virgil no less than the dumbstruck protagonist is on trial in this canto. Indeed, Virgil himself initiates the trial at line 19, when he insists that Dante should prove the nature of the trees by his own actions, since words – be they even the words of the *Aeneid* – would be insufficient to describe what the protagonist must now experience: 'sì vederai / cose che torrien fede al mio sermone' (20–1). Likewise, in the famous line 25, 'Cred' ïo ch'ei credette ch'io credesse' (I think he thought I thought) Dante acknowledges that the confusion of the scene tests his belief both in Virgil and in Virgil's understanding of the protagonist.

We have seen that the question of faith – in the sense of loyalty – is central to the moral dilemma of Piero. Now line 25 extends the question to the relationship of the two travellers. On the level of loyalty, a parallel and contrast arise, in that the protagonist can trust Virgil – as type of the philosopher king – in a way which Piero cannot or should not trust his own 'Augustus'. But equally, the authority of Virgil as a literary source is under examination. In the event, Dante's fiction (oddly) admits the reliability of Virgil's model: human beings can be transformed into trees. But in a canto where words – in the form of lies, gossip and fictions – are especially precarious, it is significant that this confirmation only arises through direct, physical experience. This experience – as in many earlier instances – involves the unmediated action of the eye. But more especially in the present case, the protagonist has to participate in an action, triggering off an *event* before he can fall back upon the comfort of Virgil's words.

At issue, then, are the status and trustworthiness of language itself; and it is not surprising – especially in view of the arguments we have pursued in earlier chapters – that the issue affects the manner in which Dante the poet here modifies the image he has taken from the *Aeneid*. Thus the canto begins with the mythic figures of the Harpies, who are significantly heightened in colour and effect (as, say, Charon and the Furies have been earlier) so that images themselves become as eloquent as discourse. But the especial shock which Dante sets himself to register here arises from the forcible conjunction in Piero of the mythic and the historical; so far from veiling the moral issue – as conceivably it did in the case of the centaurs – the interpenetration of the mythic and the historical challenges Dante to find a sense in which the myth might be factually or philosophically true. We have seen how in Canto III, similes and motifs from the *Aeneid* are modified by being associated with acts of judgement. Here, in this description of the metamorphosis, it is part of the challenge that Dante should not allow his text to become merely spectacular – after the fashion of Ovidian *grand guignol*. The surprise is that the myth and the paradox can contain a moral truth. To the eye which is determined to discover the truth, nothing is merely a fiction; any product of the human imagination, however bizarre, may contain a *ben* or moral truth.

The canto, then, in raising the general question of faith, raises very acutely the question of the faith which relatively we can place in words and in images. Faith in the fullest sense of the word is described thus in *Paradiso* XXIV (64–5):

> fede è sustanza di cose sperate
> e argomento de le non parventi.

(Faith is the substance of things that are hoped for / and the argument for things not seen.)

In this light, the silence of the protagonist in the latter part of the canto provides as much of a comment on the proceedings as does Virgil's silent presence in Canto x (and later in Canto xv), where it amounts to a comment upon the internal dissensions and verbal confusions of the Florentine participants in the scene. Dante's *pietà*, in the context of the disordered courtesy depicted in the story of Frederick's backbiting court, cannot fail to be charged with the sense it has had since Canto II, suggesting that certain conditions can only be fully realised through the eye. Virgil may suppose in Canto XI that 'seeing' will be sufficient. But 'seeing' meant seeing the man growing from his strange new roots, his 'nuove radici'; and the protagonist – silent before this same fact – is here a forerunner of the poet who in the 'ineffability *topos*' of the *Paradiso* will refuse to attempt to speak on matters which exceed the competence of language.

So the conversation between Piero and Virgil is governed and overcast from the first by the unspeaking presence of the protagonist; and, from the first, their words are poised uncomfortably on the edge of nonsense. Piero, for instance, now attempts to swear an oath to his own credibility; he in fact attempts to bring words to their highest pitch of authority – to give words a magical power, to transform discourse into deed and make language 'performative'. Yet, so far from producing any such verbal event, he gives birth only to the abortive 'per le nuove radici'. And not only does a similar criticism extend to Virgil's words, it also involves the poet Dante in an implicit critique of his own narrative constructions.

So Virgil attempts to speak courteously and scientifically to Piero; and Piero himself is now brought to a level of plain-speaking which he has not attained before: 'Brievemente sarà risposto a voi' (93). Yet the very fact that the conversation can occur in this manner hides away the implications of the phrase 'le nuove radici'; nor is this even – by Dante's standards – a scientific discourse, but rather a piece of science-fiction. Piero is obliged to speak of how, when Minos ascribes a soul to the seventh circle,

> Cade in la selva, e non l'è parte scelta;
> ma là dove fortuna la balestra,
> quivi germoglia come gran di spelta.   (97–9)

(It falls into the wood, and no definite place is chosen; / but there, wherever fortune hurls it, / it sprouts like a grain of spelt.)

One has only to compare this passage with – say – the account which Dante offers in *Purgatorio* xxv of procreation and gestation to see how far it is in style from the careful gravity of scientific expression which Dante eventually can achieve. And in part the unsatisfactoriness of the analysis, from this point of view, is precisely that it does draw upon the mythic references to Minos and the Harpies, as if the common language in which Piero, Virgil and the poet must speak is one of cultural allusion. Momentarily, the poet loses his moral grip over these allusions as he did in the canto of the centaurs; and this is confirmed by a moment which is at once the most vivid imaginative stroke in the speech and also doctrinally the crux which early commentators found especially hard to resolve.

At line 106, Piero extends his story to the limits of time, the Day of Judgement. Virgil has asked if any suicide is ever disentangled from its present enclosure: 's'alcuna mai di tai membra si spiega' (90); the story has to be carried to its natural end not simply in terms of the pattern of *this* life, but in terms of the whole eternal pattern which God has initiated. Yet the description of this end represents a powerful flight of fantasy on Piero's – and ultimately on Dante's – part:

> Come l'altre verrem per nostre spoglie,
> ma non però ch'alcuna sen rivesta,
> ché non è giusto aver ciò ch'om si toglie.
>   Qui le strascineremo, e per la mesta
> selva saranno i nostri corpi appesi,
> ciascuno al prun de l'ombra sua molesta.   (103–8)

(Like the others we shall come for our spoils, / but not so that any shall in fact reclothe himself; / for it is not just that a man have that which he takes away from himself. / Here we shall drag them and through the dismal / wood our bodies shall be hung, / each on the thorn of its dire and tormented shade.)

Now, from an orthodox point of view, it is inconceivable that the body should be separated from its soul: such a notion contradicts the very definition of a soul as the 'form' of the body which Dante derives from Aristotle – to whom he refers in Canto VI, when he first speaks of the resurrection of the dead. To be sure, there is a rough justice in the eternal separation envisaged here. But as we shall see in later cantos, Dante at times invites us to view with suspicion the mechanical neatness of the *contrappassi* which he himself has devised for the purposes of his fiction. And if the vigour of this horrific conception temporarily obscures the true science which Dante must have received from Aristotle and his Christian followers, then this only demonstrates how misleading the most powerful discourse may be. This may be Piero's last *word* on his own case; but behind the word is the image of the tree, and that image communicates – as silently as the silent protagonist – a truer understanding of doctrines which only faith can realise. Physical life is the inalienable possession of human beings; Christ affirms this in his Passion and Resurrection, and reaffirms it in judgement upon the suicides, by allotting to them a punishment which drives home both the meaning of his suffering on the Cross and the inescapable reality of growth and regeneration.

By now it will be apparent that Canto XIII is no less polyphonic in its play upon word and image than was Canto IX. This becomes especially clear in the final phase of the canto. The travellers are concentrating their attention upon the treetrunk, thinking that even now he has not properly finished his speech, when suddenly the hunt of the profligates bursts through the forest

(109–11). The scene is distinctly visual: 'ed ecco due da la sinistra costa' (115) – and behold two from the left side. But it is also a scene in which actual events are described – as violent as the event which Piero chooses to exclude from his narrative, passing so smoothly over any description of his own death. Equally, it is an action in which words take on the force of physical blows: the dignity and sophistications of Piero's speech dissolve into sheer noise, and the tragic tone is replaced by comedy, even farce:

> Quel dinanzi: 'Or accorri, accorri, morte!'.
> E l'altro, cui pareva tardar troppo,
> gridava: 'Lano, sì non furo accorte
> le gambe tue a le giostre dal Toppo!'.   (118–21)

(The foremost: 'Now make haste, make haste, death.' / And the other, who seemed to himself too slow, / yelled 'Lano, [your legs] were not so prompt / at the joust of Toppo!')

Of the many differences between the poet Dante and his recognised predecessors in the tradition of vernacular love-poetry, none is more striking than his decision to admit – along with the value of narrative – the value of all registers of language from the comic to the sublime. In this respect he is markedly different from Piero the poet as well as from Piero the political figure. The characteristic of the Sicilian school to which Piero belonged was to seek linguistic polish and to cultivate an aristocratic urbanity of diction. But Dante in Canto XIII fends off no words at all. In response to the events which the narrative records – be they shrieks or the snapping of undergrowth, or moments of intellectual bafflement – the language shifts through all appropriate forms.

So a contrast emerges – and can be traced throughout the canto – between the meretricious *dolcezza* which Piero displays and the harshness of the idiom which Dante adopts as narrator. And nowhere is this more apparent than in the opening lines of the canto:

> Non era ancor di là Nesso arrivato,
> quando noi ci mettemmo per un bosco
> che da neun sentiero era segnato.
>   Non fronda verde, ma di color fosco;
> non rami schietti, ma nodosi e 'nvolti;
> non pomi v'eran, ma stecchi con tòsco.
>   Non han sì aspri sterpi né sì folti
> quelle fiere selvagge che 'n odio hanno
> tra Cecina e Corneto i luoghi còlti.   (1–9)

(Nessus had not yet arrived on the other side / when we moved into a wood, / unmarked by any footpath. / No green leaves, but dark in colour; / no smooth clean branches but knotted and warped. / There were no apples there but poisonous twigs. / No copses so harsh and dense / have those wild beasts who hate / the cultivated places between Cecina and Corneto.)

These lines are sometimes taken to be a pastiche of Pier della Vigna's own involute style. Yet if they are, they are also governed by a rhythm and structure closer to Virgil's 'non omo, omo già fui' than to the 'ingiusto fece me contra me giusto' attributed to Piero; and in that regard they provide a touchstone for the linguistic judgements we have passed in analysing Piero's discourse.

Thus the passage proposes an absurdity and a contradiction as difficult in imaginative terms as that which Piero has faced in moral terms. These lines are at once an attempt to create and control a nonsense. However, the rhetorical repetitions are used not as they would have been by Piero simply to dignify the poet by his own virtuosity, but rather to expose him to the harshness of his own imaginings: the 'non' is a rhetorical flourish, almost a conceit; but at the same time it is an admission of how, at a certain point, the mind must cede before an unspeakable reality. Much the same could be said of the pause which arises at the centre of each of these lines. In one aspect, this distinguishes Dante from Piero in terms of control and analytical power. Yet this same feature also serves to draw attention to each imagistic fragment of the description and points to the divisions and oppositions which the poet is prepared to countenance in pursuit of the truth.

We do not say, then, that Dante's linguistic position offers merely greater control than Piero's, but rather that it admits – as the words of Piero do not – the peculiar tensions to which language will be subject throughout the canto. A similar complexity arises in Dante's formulation of the narrative as compared with the story which he gives to Piero. The wood which Dante enters here is, and yet is not, the wood of Canto I. There is, from the first, the sense that Dante's procedure depends upon the pursuit of a systematic pattern even in its underlying and half-realised cross-reference of images; alongside the myths of Polydorus and the Harpies, Dante has now his own myth to draw upon. Yet so far from attempting to assert the similarity, or insisting as Piero does that his thought and identity should assume a single unitary shape, the whole effort of imagination here is devoted to making 'new' the horror of the wood. Dante's story is moving to an end as all stories should. But the poet's technique – at least in the *Inferno* – is one which ensures that 'every end is a new beginning'. So, while the first line of the canto points to the capacity for motion which Dante has celebrated in the canto of the centaurs, he now shows himself yet again to be arrested in a directionless wood – 'da neun sentiero era segnato' – hypnotised by senseless images which interrupt his advance. Dante, representing himself as protagonist, allows the images of the absurd scene – delusive as they may be – to be projected upon himself.

The Dante of Canto XIII might well be compared to the Tiresias of T. S. Eliot's *The Waste Land*:

> (And I Tiresias have foresuffered all
> Enacted on this same divan or bed;
> I who have sat by Thebes below the wall
> And walked among the lowest of the dead.)   (243–6)

The myth of the dreadful landscape and the condition of Piero – historically Dante's predecessor and moral inferior, but his successor in the sequence of the *Commedia* – must both be allowed to play through him: only by allowing this travesty can he hope to arrive at the wood of the Earthly Paradise. For it is precisely such a 'travesty' that penance will require in Purgatory. Our end, as human beings, does not lie within our own keeping (even though the suicide supposes it does), for that end will finally be declared in the form of an event wholly beyond the domain of human mastery, the supreme event of divine judgement. Certainly the order and pattern which Dante painfully affirms in the thirteenth canto are one aspect of the control which any human being – or storyteller – must exert over his own life. Yet the conclusion and coda after the events of the hunt point to the equally necessary openness which has to be kept in readiness for the ultimate event.

The wastrels have rushed through the wood being torn limb from limb as they go (128), and Virgil leads Dante gently towards a little bush, ripped to pieces as a sinner tried to hide behind it. At the opening of Canto XIV, the protagonist will seek to make reparation to the bush, gathering its scattered leaves beneath it, and thus in spirit, reversing the injury he did to Piero's thorn-tree with an act of weird piety. He attempts to restore 'normality' to the bush – and for a moment Virgil's concern for him, as so often, seems to mark a return to a sphere of ordinary human decency and order.

Yet this normality is not allowed to bring the canto to a harmonious conclusion. Instead the conclusion is dominated by the voice of the anonymous suicide confined in his bush.

The words of introduction and identification which the bush utters bear close comparison with Piero della Vigna's opening address. This suicide is a Florentine:

> I' fui de la città che nel Batista
> mutò 'l primo padrone ...   (143–4)

(I was of that city that, for the Baptist / changed its first patron).

This is as self-effacing as Piero; and, like Piero, the Florentine defines himself in terms of the culture from which he springs. But here the culture is one which, in its history and its civic myths, overtly cultivates violent division. For where Piero defends the unity of the Empire – good in itself but built upon insecure ground in the figure of Frederick – the suicide appeals to a myth in which Mars appears as the legendary patron of Florence. Nor is that all: for the legend is that Mars was angered when Florence adopted St John the Baptist as patron in his stead, and would have led the city to utter destruction had it not been that a statue of him still remained intact somewhere in the city. The interweaving ironies of this legend are too complex to pursue here. It is nonetheless clear that the Florentine recalls in his apparently simple phrases a tradition of violence which he himself acts out in the humblest way when he makes a gibbet of his own house (151).

The story of the Florentine is the story of a man who passively voices an ambiguous and delusive legend. But why should Dante allow such a voice to end his canto? Is it in any sense a fitting conclusion? It is, I suggest, precisely because it simultaneously completes and disturbs the patterns which the canto has created.

Thus in the first place, parallels arise between the Florentine and Piero, and, of course, between the anonymous citizen and his compatriot Dante. These parallels diminish the stature of Piero, by demonstrating that, in his moral position, he is neither more nor less than the squalid domestic suicide. Yet by the same token they enhance the figure of Dante. He shares the cultural and historical origins of the other two members of the group. In him, however – for all the untruth, and strife which flow from these origins – there is also a promise, which he is translating into reality. The unity of the ideal Imperial court (embodied in Virgil) is part of the promise. The possibility of regeneration is another; and St John has shown the way to that (the reference to Baptism and to the flow of the Arno (146) has its own contribution to make to that theme).

Yet precisely by ending with the words of the Florentine, rather than with Virgil's or his own, Dante does *not* allow the implications of these images to be stated clearly. The threefold comparison – with all its ironies and tensions – is itself his point of arrival. As in Canto x, the *velame* which is hung before the reader is painted with the figures of individual men; and to penetrate that veil one must 'read' one's fellow-creatures. Piero would not allow himself to be read by others. It is the mark of Dante's actual superiority – and the true conclusion of the canto – that he permits his readers, here as elsewhere in the *Inferno*, to look at him both as he is and as he might have been or might still become, for good or ill, in the course of his imaginative and historic enterprise.

IV

We have said that the cantos in the sequence from Canto xii to Canto xvi differ markedly in their narrative structure; and the fourteenth canto is certainly quite distinct in this regard from the cantos which precede and follow it, even though in theme it sustains the prevailing discussion of violence, lost leadership and the grounds of human individuality.

Where Cantos xiii and xv concentrate for the most part upon the historical figures of Pier della Vigna and Brunetto Latini, attention is divided equally in Canto xiv between two legendary figures. The first is Capaneus – one of the 'Seven against Thebes' – who appears as the representative of the sin of blasphemy, where the sinner violates the dignity of God; the second is the Old Man of Crete – whom Virgil describes in a fable which explains the origins of the rivers of Hell while also reflecting the Latin poet's own sense of the decadence of humanity.

In itself, the portrayal of Capaneus (43–75) displays many of the characteristics which appear in Dante's depiction of such individuals as Farinata, Piero and Brunetto. As part of that series, the figure, in a moral sense, crystallises the questions concerning the relation between human identity and divine will which are tacitly posed whenever Dante allows his sinners an apparently free and dramatic expression of their personalities. So at line 46, the attention of the protagonist is drawn to a sinner who (so it seems) takes no heed of the punishment he is suffering: 'chi è quel grande che non par che curi / lo 'ncendio ...?' – Who is that great one who appears not to mind the fire? Capaneus is one of the two most overtly rebellious figures in Hell; and in Canto xxv 14–15, Dante takes him as a standard by which to judge the extent of human pride. Thus the moral issues raised by the figure of Capaneus extend beyond blasphemy to a consideration of the greatest of all sins. Dante does not deal directly with pride until *Purgatorio* x–xii. But the grounds of Dante's judgement upon the pride of Capaneus become quite clear in the course of *Inferno* xii. Despite the immediacy and impact of Capaneus's words, the function of the episode at large is to turn drama into emblem. Here, more explicitly than anywhere else in the *Inferno*, Dante shows, through images, that the human individual can pretend to no integrity or wholeness whatsoever unless it rediscovers itself in the truth of God as Creator. Correspondingly, the canto pictures the division and sterility which human beings suffer in claiming any independent dignity. The heroism of self-assertion is shown to be deeply foolish; and in place of such false heroism Dante constructs and substitutes another mode in which the value of the individual is founded upon humility, care and intellectual moderation.

These conclusions are, as we shall see, executed in a number of different ways through the details of language and narrative structure in the canto. But the principal indication of Dante's moral purpose is that Capaneus in the first half of the canto should be balanced so exactly against the Old Man of Crete – the *Veglio* – in the second. This coupling itself leads us to view Capaneus as an emblem – almost as a figure in a didactic tableau – rather than a dramatic hero; and any pretensions which Capaneus might have to heroic stature are undermined by Virgil's account of the decadence from which all humanity inevitably suffers. In the myth of the Old Man of Crete, mankind possesses a head of gold and a torso of silver. But the statue is cracked, its right foot is clay, and its tears of lamentation form the rivers of Hell (xiv 106–14).

The balances, then, in the narrative formulation of the canto contribute to an exact analysis of the themes of sin and individuality – as they do also in, say, Canto x; and there is significantly none of that intensity or disproportion of imaginative emphasis which characterises Canto xiii. The canto is not tragic (it is even at times close to comedy); and myth and legend themselves – ceasing either to distract or to stimulate – conspire with clarity of diction and narrative articulation to subserve a moral purpose.

The success of these techniques is brought into relief when one considers that the particular subject of the canto is blasphemy. For blasphemy represents a misuse of language; and here, as in dealing with heresy, Dante's concern is not simply with the offence which the sinner gives to his Creator, but also with the perverse and destructively unnatural use which he makes of his human faculties of speech. We shall see that in the case of Capaneus, language itself, so far from proving consistent with moral and narrative purpose, disturbs and contradicts the inner pattern of beginnings, middles and ends which (as the *Convivio* makes clear) provides the natural framework for the 'story of a life'. In Capaneus's mouth an epic story dissolves into nonsense. And the extent to which this represents an offence as much to human order as to divine purpose is stressed by a further balance which Dante insists upon between the pagan speaker Capaneus and Virgil – who is, of course, both a master of words and himself a pagan. In Canto xiv, an opposition arises between the model of coherent speech which Virgil represents and the corruption of speech which displays itself in Capaneus; at lines 61–6, Virgil is said to speak louder than he has ever done before in castigating Capaneus:

> Allora il duca mio parlò di forza
> tanto, ch'i' non l'avea sì forte udito:
> 'O Capaneo, in ciò che non s'ammorza
>   la tua superbia, se' tu più punito;
> nullo martiro, fuor che la tua rabbia,
> sarebbe al tuo furor dolor compito'.   (61–6)

(Then my guide spoke out with a force / so great that I had not heard him speak so forcefully before: / 'O Capaneus, in that [your pride] is undiminished, / so are you punished; / no chastisement except your rage itself / could be a pain appropriate to your fury.')

If, in a moral sense, the Old Man of Crete is balanced against Capaneus, then so too is Virgil, in regard to language and procedure, both in his initial encounter with the sinner and in his measured and sensitive account of the *Veglio*.

We need to consider, however, not only the intrinsic contrasts in the canto, but also what stage the canto represents in the progress of Dante himself as poet, and what contribution it makes to Dante's formulation of his own story.

Here no less than in the previous canto – or the next – Dante meditates upon the narrative plan and fundamental images of his own fiction: the stated purpose of the *Veglio* speech is to explain the origin of the rivers which Dante has invented as part of the narrative scene in the violence cantos. But in Dante's own case – as in the case of Capaneus – there appears to be the possibility of a tension between the linguistic and narrative aspects of his enterprise. For there is much linguistic virtuosity in this canto, amounting at times to stylistic mannerism. And we are bound to ask what distinguishes Dante's display of linguistic pride from Capaneus's. It will be no surprise if we return to the sense that the narrative plan of the canto insists upon a moderation and proportion in Dante's own case which Capaneus cannot command.

The canto opens with the curious attempt that the protagonist makes to re-
unite the scattered leaves of the anonymous Florentine suicide: 'Poi che la
carità del natio loco / mi strinse' (1–2) – For love of my native place con-
strained me. This action argues a growing habituation in the protagonist to
the grotesque conditions of Hell; he can maintain and express his normal
feelings of patriotic kinship even when to do so requires a gesture as outland-
ish as this. Correspondingly, the poet approaches the description of the new
scene with a certainty of tone and purpose in direct contrast to the opening of
Canto XIII, where his words were designed to exacerbate the contradictions in
the image of the wood, which he now describes, with an easy detachment, as
'la dolorosa selva' (10). Here, he displays a confidence in his own fiction as
an exact reproduction of divine 'art', and sets out with some deliberation and
assumed authority to particularise the scene before him. 'Newness' here no
longer precipitates tragic confusion, but invites both poet and reader to
contemplate a show of art:

> Indi venimmo al fine ove si parte
> lo secondo giron dal terzo, e dove
> si vede di giustizia orribil arte.
> A ben manifestar le cose nove,
> dico che arrivammo ad una landa ...   (4–8)

(Then we came to the boundary / where the second circle [is divided] from the third,
and where / one sees the dreadful art of Justice. / To make clear these strange new
things, / I say that we arrived at a plain).

The compatibility between the geography of Hell and divine purpose is
further emphasised in line 16 by an exclamation of horrified admiration at the
unambiguous meaning of God's law:

> O vendetta di Dio, quanto tu dei
> esser temuta da ciascun che legge
> ciò che fu manifesto a li occhi mei!   (16–18)

(O vengeance of God, how must you / be feared by all who read / that which was made
manifest to my eyes!)

As Dante has read the significance of that vengeance in his vision, so the
reader may find it exactly recorded in Dante's words.

One notes here the sureness with which Dante claims to translate the
images he has seen into words which will be morally valuable for the reader:
for once, any tension between word and image appears to have been abol-
ished. So, in bringing out the moral fruit from his description of the burning
sand where the blasphemers lie, Dante's language – so far from being defen-
sively moral – displays a freedom in the confident treatment of local detail
which, in its own way, marks a development from Canto XIII. The harshness
of style which reflected the moral test of Canto XIII is here transformed into a
play of manneristic conceits, as Dante manipulates the oxymorons of fertility
and sterility, heat and cold: the wood of the suicides is a 'garland' for the

desert of the blasphemers (10); the burning flakes which fall on the sinners
are not self-consuming but an eternal burning (37), or a fresh scorching –
'l'arsura fresca' (42). This sequence includes a virtuoso comparison (which
draws upon and possibly seeks to outdo Guido Cavalcanti) between the
'dilate falde' of fire flakes and the fall of snow in the windless Alps: 'come
di neve in alpe sanza vento' (30); and, in turn, this comparison, drawn from a
northern climate, immediately precedes an exotic and extended simile
referring to Alexander's expedition to India:

> Quali Alessandro in quelle parti calde
> d'Indïa vide sopra 'l süo stuolo
> fiamme cadere infino a terra salde ...   (31–3)

(As Alexander in the hot regions / of India saw – over his army – / flames entire fall to
the ground.)

If agony looses the tongues of the blasphemers (27), then equally Dante's
confidence and moral command appear to have loosened his.

   The play upon contradiction reaches its climax at the line in which Dante
introduces Capaneus: the sinner *seems* to disregard the pain he suffers – he is
not 'matured' by the hot rain (48) and gains nothing from the display of
divine power which surrounds him. So when Capaneus speaks, he does so
against the background of Dante's linguistic display, as well as that of the
authoritative reproof which Virgil utters at line 63. Moreover, Dante has
already pre-empted Capaneus's position by a repeated assertion that he only
'appears' to withstand his suffering (46, 48, as, later, 69 and 70). And from
first to last Capaneus's heroism and disdain of God – 'e par ch'elli abbia /
Dio in disdegno' (69–70) – are revealed as an effect of *trompe l'oeil*. Florid
and impressive though Capaneus's language may be, on analysis it proves to
be incoherent and incapable of asserting a firm identity; it possesses neither
the stability of Virgil's words nor the imaginative vitality which Dante
manifests in the text at large:

> gridò: 'Qual io fui vivo, tal son morto.
>   Se Giove stanchi 'l suo fabbro da cui
> crucciato prese la folgore aguta
> onde l'ultimo dì percosso fui;
>   o s'elli stanchi li altri a muta a muta
> in Mongibello a la focina negra,
> chiamando "Buon Vulcano, aiuta, aiuta!",
>   sì com' el fece a la pugna di Flegra,
> e me saetti con tutta sua forza:
> non ne potrebbe aver vendetta allegra'.   (51–60)

(He yelled: 'What I was living, that am I dead, / though Jove should tire out his
blacksmith, from whom / in anger he took the sharp thunderbolt, / with which I was
stricken on my last day; / and even if he wore out others, one by one, / at the black
forge in Mongibello / crying "Help, help, good Vulcan", / as he did in the strife of
Phlegra, / and launched upon me with all his might; / he would not by that achieve
joyous vengeance.')

One notes here the disproportion between the lengthy conditional construction and its lame and negative conclusion – which in fact allows that God *may* have vengeance even if it is not 'allegra'. One notes too the welter of figurative language and mythic allusion, as well as the confusion of syntax, which characterises the speech at large. The mismanagement of word and cultural forms here defeats the demands of orderly narration. And much might be said – which *will* be said in discussing Ulysses – about the failure of this legendary figure to contribute to the traditions which pagan culture, at its most fertile, can advance. Capaneus is no Roman hero, fostering the progress of providential history; he is, and remains, a warrior implicated in the history of Thebes – a city which, as we have said, represents for Dante a place of corruption where violence is endemic and proliferates through generations of strife between families and close kinsmen.

However, to appreciate the moral and linguistic implications of Capaneus's speech, it is sufficient to consider only the opening line of the speech: 'Qual io fui vivo, tal son morto'. This represents a strong claim to heroic integrity. Yet – especially against the background of Piero's 'ingiusto fece me contra me giusto' and Virgil's 'non omo, omo già fui' – the logical fissures in the assertion are at once apparent. To affirm that 'what I was living, that am I dead' is to beg the question of what in fact the sinner was when he was alive, and to invite the ironic comment that – while indeed he may have preserved his identity in Hell – it would have been better for him had he failed to do so.

In a single line, Capaneus has defined one of the essential conditions of all the sinners in Hell: that they preserve unaltered the petrified characteristics of their earthly lives and seek to make that itself a point of pride. Like Piero, Capaneus desires to maintain the myth of his own heroic self. But violence is nothing to that purpose. Certainly in the *Purgatorio* the penitents will reveal the value of abdicating any such myth, and in the *Inferno*, since the Fortuna canto, Dante has developed an early version of a similar understanding. Nature, as God's creation, must be allowed to act upon the core of selfhood. And this must even be allowed to precipitate tragedy, as an agent of truth. But Capaneus's confused 'Qual io fui vivo' does not possess the tragic force which is – potentially – present in Piero's 'ingiusto fece me …'. The only contribution to truth which Capaneus can make lies not in the telling of his own story but – ironically enough – in the place which Dante gives him as an emblem of pride and degeneration, in the story of the *Commedia*.

The issues surrounding Capaneus – as pagan and speaker – are developed in the second half of Canto xiv in the explicit comparison which Dante offers between the linguistic and intellectual techniques of Capaneus and those which Virgil – as another pagan – adopts in telling the story of the *Veglio*. However, before going on to this, the sin of blasphemy itself needs to be considered more closely. As we have said, in Dante's general view of language, blasphemy is an offence not simply against God but also against the essential nature of language. And this can be supported if we follow the arguments of the *De Vulgari Eloquentia*, where it appears that the essential function of language is to praise God in recognition of the relation between creature and Creator. Thus the first word that Adam spoke in Eden was the word 'God' itself, uttered as joyful acknowledgement of the act of creation:

rationabile est quod ante qui fuit inciperit a gaudio; et cum nullum gaudium sit extra Deum sed totum in Deo ... consequens est quod primus loquens primo et ante omnia dixisset, 'Deus'.   (*DVE* I iv 4)

(It is reasonable to suppose that before [the Fall] all speech began in joy, and since there is no joy save in God and all joy is in him, it follows that speaking for the first time man said in the first place and before all else, 'God'.)

Against this picture of linguistic innocence, Dante shortly proceeds to picture the linguistic equivalent of the Fall, when, as a punishment for the pride – like Capaneus's – which led men to build the Tower of Babel, a confusion of tongues was spread among them (*DVE* I vi-vii). But for Dante an essential task of the poet is to return to the idiom of praise which characterised Adam's first words. Thus in the *Vita nuova*, the poems in which, on Dante's own account, he first discovers his own poetic voice are in 'the style of praise' (*VN* XVIII). And even in these early phases, the style of praise – precisely because it inherently accepts the conditions under which language was first employed – already displays both technical and moral features which stand as a contrast to the features which are displayed in the Capaneus speech. Since praise is a recognition of some superior object or excellence – such as Beatrice or God – the stance of the poet in such a style will be one of humility. But this humility itself, so far from leading to abasement or distress, permits the poet to proceed in a lucid, self-possessed and even analytic manner, acknowledging the natural limits and natural competence of his speech. So – to set against the bombast of Capaneus – Dante in 'Donne ch'avete' (*VN* XIX) has already written:

> Ed io non vo' parlar sì altamente,
> ch'io divenisse per temenza vile.   (9–10)

(However, I will not attempt a style so lofty / as to make me faint-hearted through fear.)

There will be more to say about the praise-style in the final chapter of this book. It is, as we have already suggested in Chapter 1, the principle by which to measure what is or is not 'dead poetry' in Dante's view. Thus in the *Paradiso* the poet will return to this style – though, now, much modified and sharpened by experience. And the opening lines of the last *cantica* are enough to show how far, linguistically, he will by then have removed himself from the Babelic perils of Capaneus:

> La gloria di colui che tutto move
> per l'universo penetra, e risplende
> in una parte più e meno altrove.   (*Par.* I 1–3)

(The glory of him who moves all things, / penetrates the universe, and shines back / in one part more and less elsewhere.)

Here the rain of fire which falls upon Capaneus has been transfigured into the light which constitutes the very order and degree of the universe; and in praising that order Dante's own language is as efficient and syntactically clear as Capaneus's is not.

For Dante the peculiar tragedy – and difficulty – of the *Inferno*, as will be seen increasingly from the 'dead poetry' of the Malebolge, is that he cannot yet allow himself to write in the natural style of praise, but must rather mimic the confusions of a Capaneus. It is also, however, a particular beauty of the fourteenth canto that Dante should discern in Virgil's speech not only an alternative to Capaneus's but also a subtle prefiguration, or pagan equivalent, of the praise-style, developing as he writes the *Veglio* speeches – a delicate, if temporary, remedy for the linguistic distresses of the *Inferno*. In a word, Virgil's speech is a model of linguistic and narrative self-possession.

At line 91, the protagonist registers an especial degree of attention to Virgil's words, as well he might, having been told that the river of blood by which they are walking – 'li cui rossore ancor mi raccapriccia' – is the most notable feature in Hell since the Gate of Hell itself:

> Queste parole fuor del duca mio;
> per ch'io 'l pregai che mi largisse 'l pasto
> di cui largito m'avèa il disio.   (*Inf.* xiv 91–3)

(These were the words of my guide; / therefore I besought him to grant me the repast / for which he had aroused my appetite.)

We are led, then, to expect some spectacular revelation; and, insofar as Virgil's theme is the violent self-destructiveness of humanity, we are not disappointed. But the notable feature of the speaker's tone is its measure and gravity, and on the simplest level, this is enough to emphasise that blasphemy – raising vapours of unconsidered emphasis – is a crime against the true spirit of speech. But the significance of Virgil's tone extends further than that. For instance, although he is portraying the corruptions of humanity – which, as we have said, is a subject Dante particularly associates with the Statius of the *Thebaid* – Virgil adopts none of the extravagance which characterises Statius's style. Nor, for that matter, has his speech any of the qualities of conceited display which were a feature of Dante's own style in the early part of the canto. Instead, after the vigorous exchanges of the first half, this speech is elegiac and essentially undramatic; and as Dante – who is after all *writing* the speech – slowly unrolls the myth, he allows himself the relief of constructing a passage which simply records that sense of the 'tears of things' which the *Aeneid* has once and for all established:

> 'In mezzo mar siede un paese guasto',
> diss' elli allora, 'che s'appella Creta,
> sotto 'l cui rege fu già 'l mondo casto.
> Una montagna v'è che già fu lieta
> d'acqua e di fronde, che si chiamò Ida;
> or è diserta come cosa vieta.

Rëa la scelse già per cuna fida
del suo figliuolo, e per celarlo meglio,
quando piangea, vi facea far le grida...'   (94–102)

('In the midst of the ocean there lies a wasteland,' / he then said, 'which is called
Crete, / under whose king the world was once pure. / There is a mountain there which
once was glad / with its waters and leaves; it was called Mount Ida; / now it is deserted
like a thing forbidden. / Rhea chose it in times gone by as a trustworthy cradle / for her
son, and, so as to conceal him better, / had cries made over it whenever he wept'.)

There is no occasion for praise in anything that Virgil speaks of here, save
praise for things that are irremediably a part of the past – the 'mondo casto'
and the waters and leaves of the 'happy mountain'. Indeed, before even
speaking of the Old Man of Crete, Virgil has envisaged a conflict extending
back to a time yet earlier than the era of Jupiter; for Jupiter is the child
whom Rhea hides from Saturn on the island of Crete. Yet the balance of
mind that Virgil maintains at the moment of revealing these conflicts is as
great as if he were celebrating Beatrice. So the repeated past-remote,
associated with *già* – 'fu già 'l mondo casto', 'che già fu lieta' – gives due
weight to the pathos of the vision, while preserving complete command over
the rhetorical structure of the verse.

In the true praise-style, the recognition of the inevitable distance between
the lover and the object of his love is itself the source of modesty and clarity
of speech. In Virgil's case, the same qualities proceed from a similar if tragic
recognition of the distance between the present and the true and original state
of happiness which human beings once enjoyed. That recognition, so far
from justifying violence, is expressed in a tone of quiet awe, of 'religious'
deference to the mysterious, which even the pagan world knew how to
cultivate – and which Capaneus, in his defiance of Jupiter, prides himself on
rejecting. But the linguistic correlative of that deference is a diction which, in
being restrained and comprehensible, reinforces the bonds between speaker
and speaker in the face of those mysteries. So Virgil is able to 'feed the
appetite' of the protagonist, having 'enlarged his desire' (93). Indeed,
precisely in writing a pastiche of Virgil's *lacrimae rerum* and in allowing
Virgil to speak on his behalf, Dante demonstrates the solidarity and
community which can arise between human beings when they *do* recognise
the conditions under which language should properly operate.

But what is true here of language is also true on the broader level of
narrative and myth. We have said that Dante forces Capaneus to participate
willy-nilly in the moral structure which Dante as narrator is developing. Yet
in a reversal of this move, which denies any possibility of self-assertive pride
on the part of protagonist or poet, Dante, in the second half of the canto,
entrusts the whole account of human corruption – which is the theme of the
Inferno – to the voice of Virgil. Nothing could be more different from
Virgil's account of the 'paese guasto' than Dante's own prevailing polemic
against the wasteland in his own time and in his own spirit. Yet the very
fiction which Dante has constructed in Hell, with its gates and rivers, is now

given over to Virgil, for him to explain. The canto began with an especially strong assertion of the compatibility between God's judgement – his 'vendetta' – and Dante's fictional construction. It amounts almost to a retraction of such confidence that Dante should finally allow this fictional plan to be revealed now as a myth and a fiction in the humane and captivating tone of the Latin poet. The plan of judgement becomes the subject of a moving but essentially fabulous tale, as Virgil traces the course of the rivers of Hell from the weeping eyes of the *Veglio* to the terrain through which the travellers are now moving:

> Lor corso in questa valle si diroccia;
> fanno Acheronte, Stige e Flegetonta;
> poi sen van giù per questa stretta doccia. (115–17)

(Their course descends from rock to rock into this valley: / they make Acheron, Styx and Phlegethon; / then they go down by this narrow conduit.)

This is not, however, to deny but rather to redefine the function of the myth. There could after all be few more distressingly exact images for the truth of the human condition than this, where the only continuity available to us, in Dante's view, is the continuity between the present miseries of temporal corruption and the miseries of Hell. At the same time, stories and myths themselves constitute a bond between teller and audience, providing an alternative to rational or philosophical discourse. A myth is a story shared by many, as, here, the story of the rivers of Hell is shared between Dante and Virgil. It is the voice of a tribe divided from its origins, accumulating material which defines its common purposes and understanding. But, precisely *as* a fiction or construction of the mind, the myth testifies to the conditions under which the mind, exiled from truth, must always operate. In *Paradiso* xxvi, Dante makes Adam declare that no product of the mind can ever be wholly stable:

> ché nullo effetto mai razïonabile
> per lo piacere uman che rinovella
> seguendo il cielo, sempre fu durabile. (*Par.* xxvi 127–9)

(for no effect of reason at all lasted forever, /for human preferences are ever renewed / following the influence of the heavens).

Adam's particular concern is, of course, language and the changes of the vernacular. But to tell stories as Virgil and Dante do in Canto xiv, is to acknowledge that the same conditions also govern narrative structures: where the stories of Piero and Capaneus are intended to defend and enhance their own status, those of Dante and Virgil are contributions to the common pursuit of a distant truth.

In Canto xi of the *Inferno*, Dante celebrated and defined the rational competence of Virgil as the moral geographer of Hell; in the second half of Canto xiv, he represents Virgil 'Philomythes' – lover of myths – in a similar spirit, while at the same time exposing to view his own procedures as a maker of myths, which include not only the myth of Hell but also the myth of Virgil *personaggio* himself. To confirm the interpretation of Dante's position and procedure on this matter, we may finally turn to two sequences of the *Purgatorio* which are foreshadowed quite distinctly in the fourteenth canto of the *Inferno*.

The first is the Earthly Paradise, which is not only anticipated, as we have seen, throughout the violence cantos as the anti-type of the disorder which Dante here envisages, but is also referred to, at lines 130–1 of Canto XIV, as the site of another eternal river – Lethe, the river of forgetting. As soon as the protagonist arrives in the Earthly Paradise, he learns that this is the place which poets have dreamed of throughout the ages:

> Quelli ch'anticamente poetaro
> l'età de l'oro e suo stato felice,
> forse in Parnaso esto loco sognaro.
>   Qui fu innocente l'umana radice;
> qui primavera sempre e ogne frutto;
> nettare è questo di che ciascun dice.   (*Purg.* XXVIII 139–44)

(Those who in ancient times wrote verses / of the age of gold and its happy state, / perhaps dreamed in Parnassus of this place. / Here the root of humanity was innocent. / Here there was unending spring and every fruit. / This is the nectar of which each one tells.)

These lines – significantly rhyming 'poetaro' and 'sognaro', to write poetry and to dream – point directly to the value of those resources that one might describe as irrational in keeping alive our communal expectations of peace and natural order. (And indeed throughout the *Purgatorio* Dante emphasises the contribution that dreams and legends make to the advancement of the protagonist.) But note how 'forse' tempers the affirmative character of the judgement. When Dante first arrives in the Earthly Paradise, the perfect beauty of the place is said to 'temper the light of the sun' to the eye of the travellers. And if this is the function of nature, then so is it also, in one respect, the function of those myths which are drawn from nature. In Canto XIV Virgil allows Dante's mind to tolerate, through his myth, the otherwise intolerable truth of the continuing corruption of human nature.

At the same time, the *forse* which is intrinsic to all myths and fictions, may be perceived in another way, as a deterrent against taking pride in the constructions of the mind. Thus, when Dante portrays the sin of pride in Canto XII of the *Purgatorio*, he shows the protagonist travelling with head bent to read a great bas-relief which depicts how, throughout history, human beings and angels have been humbled by God, from the fall of Satan to the destruction of Babel and beyond, to the ruin of Troy and the fall of Saul, Arachne and Rehoboam. The story of human nature is expressed in the myth of its progressive defeat; and that is the myth which the penitent mind must learn to contemplate.

But the lesson goes further than in *Purgatorio* XII. For the whole sequence of some thirty-five lines is written as an acrostic in which the initial letters of

each verse spell out the word man *omo*, as they do – cumulatively – in the
final *terzina* of the sequence:

> Vedeva Troia in cenere e in caverne;
> o Ilïón, come te basso e vile
> mostrava il segno che lì si discerne!   (*Purg.* xii 61–3)

(I saw Troy in ashes and ruin. / O Ilion, how base and vile / it showed you, the image
that one sees so clearly there!)

We have suggested that Capaneus is a hero in *trompe l'oeil*. But the images
on the pavement of pride are precisely that, as they play, in a game of art,
upon the senses – and sense of reality – of all those who observe them. And
Dante emphasises the pleasure of that ambiguity when, at *Purgatorio* x lines
61–3, his eyes observing another sculpted scene tell him that there *is* the
smoke of incense where his nose tells him there is not: 'li occhi e 'l naso / e
al sì e al no discordi fensi'. But God's truth is enacted in that game: man is
made as an image which is not self-sufficient; and only those who, in
contemplating that image, respond aright to the art of God will understand
their dependency on the certainty beneath the image. But once that is under-
stood, we shall be able to spell out coherently – in the secondary medium of
language – the true story and name of our race – *omo*. This is what Dante
does when he records his primary vision in the acrostic verses of the
Purgatorio. To be whole, then, human beings must *remember* themselves, in
full knowledge of the divisions, ambiguities and confusions to which their
minds are subject. And all that we have said suggests why Capaneus, and
those whom he resembles in the *Inferno*, cannot do this. They are unable to
'piece themselves together' because they insist upon being *apart*, distinct and
separate, wholly rejecting the techniques which would have led them back
into union with the whole.

In the final lines of the fourteenth canto, Dante promises an end to that
seemingly endless telling and retelling of the human story which 'remem-
brance' requires. The river of Lethe offers oblivion:

> Letè vedrai, ma fuor di questa fossa,
> là dove vanno l'anime a lavarsi
> quando la colpa pentuta è rimossa.   (*Inf.* xiv 136–8)

(You will see Lethe, but beyond this ditch, / there where souls go to cleanse them-
selves / when guilt through repentance is removed.)

If violence divides the sinner from himself, repentance and forgetting will
finally divide him from his own divisiveness; but until this promise is
fulfilled the process – and the story – must continue. And just as, in Canto iv,
the protagonist is constrained to leave the security of the dome of light to
face again the reality of Hell, so now he must leave the security of Virgil's
words, forgetting the calm conclusions that the poet's moral emblems have
provided, to confront anew a historical instance of human perversion, with all
the difficulties involved in his meeting with Brunetto Latini.

V

The distinctive feature of *Inferno* xv is that Dante here decisively abandons mythic ornament and, concentrating on Brunetto Latini, sets the sinner – as we shall see – in an imaginative ambience which emphasises his historical importance and character. Like Pier della Vigna, Brunetto is a representative of the culture from which Dante's own philosophy and poetry derive. Similarly in political terms Brunetto balances Piero; for his position in the Guelph republic of Florence was exactly comparable to Piero's at the Imperial (and Ghibelline) court of Frederick II: Brunetto was a diplomat and leading minister in Florence; he was also a man of letters, who composed an encyclopaedic compendium of knowledge, the *Tresor* – of which, he speaks at line 119 – and a *rettorica* based largely on the rhetorical teaching of Cicero. Moreover, where the cultural influence of Piero upon Dante was at best somewhat remote, the influence of Brunetto is acknowledged in Canto xv itself to have been much more intimate and far reaching. In some sense, he was Dante's teacher. And Dante admits the strength of this relationship when the protagonist at line 83 speaks of Brunetto as the 'cara e buona imagine paterna' – the dear and good image of fatherhood. Likewise, Dante expresses the extent of Brunetto's influence in the assertion – extraordinary in the light of Dante's present journey to Paradise – that it was this damned soul who taught the protagonist how human beings may become eternal: 'm'insegnavate come l'uom s'etterna' (85).

In choosing as an example of unnatural vice a sinner who undoubtedly played a part in his own history, Dante directs his attention to the actual course of human history and to particular cultural influences, rather than to the general conditions or underlying pressures which myth elsewhere expresses in the sequence. It is equally clear that he sets out now to examine the ways in which the story of one man's life may contribute to and then finally – and very painfully – diverge from the story of another. But these considerations are immeasurably complicated by the fact that Dante in Canto xv traces the course of both Brunetto's story and his own to an ultimate conclusion in a realm beyond historical time. It is fully recognised that the end of any true story must be located in eternity. And one function of the canto is to show the tensions that arise in the story of a temporal life when this is realised: the canto is concerned with the pressures to which the details of any temporal story must submit in the perspective of eternity. Throughout, Canto xv is firmly cast on the plane of recognisably human reality – which is itself surprising against the background of distorted nature which has so far dominated the violence sequence.

So the central figure of the canto, Brunetto Latini, is not transformed as was Piero, but is so completely human in form that, despite the dreadful burns he suffers from the fiery rain, he can still be compared to a limber athlete running in the *palio* at Verona (121–2). So too the encounter between Brunetto and the protagonist follows a very natural course dictated by

rhythms of normal discourse. These rhythms range from conversational cour-
tesy to oratorical spleen. But the canto at large displays none of the violent
interruptions or divisions of action that characterised Cantos x and xiii – or
not, at least, until its final phase, where the advance of another group of
sinners hastens Brunetto forwards (115–17). Nor is the conversation between
the two Florentines directed or punctuated by Virgil (save for one uncharac-
teristically pithy interjection at line 99).

Yet, as will be seen, the silent presence of Virgil itself exerts a dislocating
and critical influence over the words of the canto; beneath the surface of
action and discourse, the themes of preceding cantos – and the questions that
these cantos raise concerning linguistic and narrative form – continue to exert
an influence, disturbing the simplicity and realism of the exchanges between
Brunetto and the protagonist.

In this respect, the opening lines deserve particular attention. These serve
to establish the differences in tone between Canto xv and its precursors. At
the same time they bring into sharp relief the connection in theme between
this canto and its context.

Dante and Virgil are walking along a dyke or bank beside the river whose
origins Virgil has just described, but are shielded from the fire flakes by a
vapour which rises from the stream of blood. In an extended simile, Dante
compares the dyke to those built by the Flemings or Paduans in the world of
time:

> Quali Fiamminghi tra Guizzante e Bruggia,
> temendo 'l fiotto che 'nver' lor s'avventa,
> fanno lo schermo perché 'l mar si fuggia;
> e quali Padoan lungo la Brenta,
> per difender lor ville e lor castelli,
> anzi che Carentana il caldo senta.   (4–9)

(As the Flemings between Wissant and Bruges, / in fear of the flood that welters
towards them, / build a screen to keep the sea at bay, / and as the Paduans do, along the
Brenta, / to defend their villages and castles, / before Carentana feels the heat.)

The particularity of these environmental details clearly detaches the canto
from the earlier spheres of fantasy and myth; but the simile also introduces a
theme central to Canto xv; that of the conflict between nature and art. In
considering the sinners in this circle – exemplified by Brunetto – Dante will
admit that human skill and intelligence can themselves violate the principles
of nature on which human life depends and alienate particular human beings
from the origins of their existence. This opening simile does not reveal the
depths of that perversion. But it does demonstrate, as simple fact, that human
beings are constrained to defend themselves by their arts against the move-
ments of nature; and notably this defence is also represented – in the word
'schermo' – as a form of veiling or screening.

From this point on, the canto prepares for the meeting with Brunetto. But
the imagery continues to emphasise the constructions of human art in the
form of the city. Thus the 'wood' – which, bizarre as it might be, is still an

oblique reminder of the principle of nature – has now fallen from view:

> Già eravam da la selva rimossi
> tanto, ch'i' non avrei visto dov' era,
> perch' io in dietro rivolto mi fossi.   (13–15)

(By now we were so distant from the wood / that I should not have seen where it was / if I had turned myself about.)

And the first sight of Brunetto is said to occur in a half-light which in a city might force one passer-by to peer at another so as to make out his features.

As a backdrop for the meeting with Brunetto, an urban panorama is exactly appropriate. The politics of Brunetto, as well as his arts of rhetoric, were designed to foster and sustain the communities of the early city-republics. In general, it should be said, the city is *not* set against nature in Dante; indeed, Paradise is conceived both as a garden (*Par.* XXIII) and as the 'Rome of which Christ is a Roman' (*Purg.* XXXII 102). Yet Canto xv persistently points to the strains that can arise within the walls of a city, and equally indicates the reason for the building of such walls – as a bulwark against the stresses of the outer world:

> quando incontrammo d'anime una schiera
> che venian lungo l'argine, e ciascuna
> ci riguardava come suol da sera
>   guardare uno altro sotto nuova luna;
> e sì ver' noi aguzzavan le ciglia
> come 'l vecchio sartor fa ne la cruna.   (16–21)

(when we met a troop of spirits / who were coming along the bank, and each of them / looked at us, in the way that at evening / one man will look at another under a new moon; / and they sharpened their brows towards us / as an old tailor does at the eye of a needle).

Here, the thin light of the crescent moon is seen to be, at the least, unhelpful to human beings as they gather in their communities, and it also carries some suggestion of menace: the sharp horns of the moon have a place in a pattern which is shortly to evoke the metallic sharpness of a tailor's needle. Then too the tailor simile itself broadens the sense that humanity – as a matter of mortal fact – must fight the realities of its natural condition. The skill of the tailor is his necessary remedy against beggarhood; and he is obliged to exercise his craft even when the natural onset of age unfits him for it. And finally what does a tailor do save *clothe* – or veil – his customers against their natural nakedness?

The simile of the tailor, since T. S. Eliot praised it, is regularly taken as an instance of Dante's precise realism and concreteness of image – which is as it should be. Yet here, again, it seems Dante's artifice conceals a wealth of further meaning, as did the earlier simile of the dyke. What is more, on the level of narrative structure the simile prepares for a moment when such meanings can no longer be held at bay behind the veil of simile but erupt in an intensely dramatic moment of surprise and naked recognition.

As Dante is progressing along the raised bank, he feels a tug at his clothing (significantly, one of the very few references to Dante's dress in the *Inferno*), as if an acquaintance among the 'famiglia' had recognised him: 'fui conosciuto da un, che mi prese ...' (23). The gesture is as everyday as could be imagined, and its ordinariness is stressed by the word 'famiglia'. Yet the oddity of the moment is revealed as soon as one proceeds, over the line-break, to find that Dante has been tugged not by the sleeve but by the *hem* of his gown – 'per lo lembo' (24) – by a spirit running at his feet. This minute instance of discomposure in the normal scheme is immediately magnified by the amazement which Brunetto registers in his first words, and multiplied still further by the shock which the protagonist correspondingly displays:

> Così adocchiato da cotal famiglia,
> fui conosciuto da un, che mi prese
> per lo lembo e gridò: 'Qual maraviglia!'
>   E io, quando 'l suo braccio a me distese,
> ficcaï li occhi per lo cotto aspetto,
> sì che 'l viso abbrusciato non difese
>   la conoscenza süa al mio 'ntelletto;
> e chinando la mano a la sua faccia,
> rispuosi: 'Siete voi qui, ser Brunetto?'   (22–30)

(Eyed so by this family, / I was recognised by one of them who took me / by the hem and cried out: 'What a wonder!'. / And I – when he stretched out his arms to me – / fixed my eyes through the baked features, / so that the scorching of his face could not defend / from my intellect the knowledge of him. / And bending down my hand to his face, / I replied: 'Are you here, Ser Brunetto?'.)

By now, one need not emphasise how the moment of narrative surprise reflects the difficulty of judging particular cases of sin: if judgement can be passed upon a man who taught others 'how to be eternal', the analysis behind that judgement is bound to be unusually stringent. And so it will prove. But in the canto sequence which we are discussing, this meeting has also a more particular significance. For it *is* a moment of recognition both of men and of the issues incarnate in their lives: the narrative event – almost an *historical* event – marks the simultaneous expression of the two great myths which Dante has been pursuing from the beginning of the *Inferno*: from this point on, the mystery of damnation is counterpoised, throughout the episode, against the mystery of Dante's salvation; corruption is balanced against redemption. Yet, as recognition of Brunetto dawns through the mask of his punishment – as defences break down – the contrast is made in terms of historical figures and demands to be considered as *more* than a myth.

So now the protagonist can no longer keep the moral message of the Old Man of Crete in the domain of legend – at once awe-inspiring and comfortingly circumscribed by words. He has now to acknowledge in Brunetto a contemporary counterpart to the *Veglio*; and having seen beneath Brunetto's 'cotto aspetto' – a phrase which recalls the 'terra cotta' on which the *Veglio* insecurely rests (xiv 110) – the 'cara e buona imagine paterna', he has also to see that the paternal image is in itself an image of damnation. The meeting

insists upon the inexplicable self-divisiveness of spirit which even a recognis-
able and hitherto familiar identity can conceal. The Old Man of Crete,
standing on desolate territory is, in Virgil's account, a manageable, even
beautiful, representation of mankind's alienation from its own nature. But the
cruellest line in Canto xv describes Brunetto as 'de l'umana natura posto in
bando' (81): precisely, *exiled* from human nature. In fact, Brunetto did, like
Dante, suffer a period of exile from Florence. But the truth which Dante has
now to accept, as he exclaims in wonderment 'Siete voi qui, ser Brunetto?',
is not only that human beings are capable of suffering and exile at the hands
of others, but that they may unaccountably divide themselves from their own
identities, proving incoherent in spite of the highest human intelligence, and
disappointing those who imagined that intelligence alone could ensure a
stable and reliable selfhood.

On the other hand, however, Brunetto has equally to acknowledge the
miracle, the *meraviglia*, which violates simple intelligence and declares that
the apparent courses of nature can be reversed: a man may travel to eternity
in the flesh; a spiritual 'son' can take precedence over an intellectual father.
It will be a part of Brunetto's tragedy that in Hell – as presumably, *mutatis
mutandis*, on earth – he is actually *less* able to recognise this living sign of
the truth than were the double-natured centaurs of Canto xii.

In another respect, too, the crisis of this meeting insists upon a connection
with the dominant themes of the sequence. We have said that Dante here
writes a series of dramas of substitution in which the lost leaders of the past
are replaced by Dante himself, as both protagonist and poet. But the grounds
for that substitution are especially clear in Canto xv; one purpose of the
canto is to make them so. Plainly enough, the qualification of the protagonist
resides at heart in that miraculous integrity, secured through the regenerative
power of God which Brunetto is now obliged to acknowledge. However,
from that fundamental position other reasons derive; and these are to be
observed in such comprehensibly human terms as the management of lan-
guage and the processes of argument. In keeping with its prevailing intimacy
of tone and naturalness of proportion, the canto proceeds to examine how the
conscious mind unearths and copes with the truths – be they miraculous or
logical – on which its identity ultimately depends; and this examination is
conducted through a sustained counterpointing of Dante's position and
Brunetto's, on both the historical plane and the plane of their fictional
meeting.

Consider, for instance, the contrasts which Dante suggests on the historical
level of literary activity. The great achievement of Brunetto – which Dante
allows him to recommend to posterity at line 119 – was the *Tresor*, a work
which, as its name suggests, was an encyclopaedic attempt to gather up the
'treasure' of knowledge which the citizens of Florence would require for
their intellectual well-being. Dante might be expected to approve this project,
for his own *Convivio* apparently represents a similar enterprise. Yet the very
titles of the two works point to differences which are carried through into the

fine detail of language and structure. The *Tresor* is essentially a compendium of knowledge; the *Convivio* is a work which demands that the reader should 'eat' or banquet upon the truth, and make it part of himself. Likewise, where the *Tresor* is essentially expository in style, the argumentative, even polemical, character of the *Convivio* reveals a mentality which is determined to grip and 'appropriate' the truth. But if this can be said of the *Convivio*, it can be said with even greater conviction of the *Commedia*, which, in aiming to offer an account of the 'whole truth', employs all the available resources of narrative as well as argument.

Correspondingly, in the conversation between Dante and Brunetto the finest nuances of speech communicate the judgement against Brunetto, and at the same time indicate Dante's view of where his own superiority lies.

Thus the first contrast arises in regard to a quality of mental balance, and to the relative ability of the two speakers to comprehend the irony of their present situation. Brunetto's first speech – in response to the courteous and familiar suggestion of the protagonist that he should sit and speak for a while – enunciates, without irony or even horror, the laws of Hell which forbid him ever to stand still. His statement of these laws is factual; he betrays no more a sense of the incongruity of his case than did Piero when he swore by the new roots of his trunk:

> Però va oltre: i' ti verrò a' panni;
> e poi rigiugnerò la mia masnada,
> che va piangendo i suoi etterni danni.   (40–2)

(And so go on: I will follow at your skirts; / and then I will rejoin my company / which goes weeping its eternal harm.)

Against this, the poise of the protagonist – in both a literal and a spiritual sense – is especially remarkable. Recalling his strange act of piety towards the Florentine suicide, Dante, while not daring to descend from the banks of the dyke, still contrives to demonstrate his reverence for Brunetto:

> Io non osava scender de la strada
> per andar par di lui; ma 'l capo chino
> tenea com' uom che reverente vada.   (43–5)

(I did not dare to descend from the road / to go on a level with him; but I held my head bent / like one who walks with respect and reverence.)

This image, in which Dante deftly reconciles his opposing impulses of admiration and recoil, prepares directly for a sequence in which the protagonist tells the story (in a way that McIntyre would have wished) of his present quest for a greater reconciliation than his meeting with Brunetto can ever represent – his reconciliation with God. Now that Brunetto has offered an account of his own present condition in Hell, the protagonist is required to account for *his*.

It is here that Brunetto proves incapable of comprehending that disruption, and at the same time demonstrates a significant ignorance of Virgil, who is literally the master of the way:

> Qual fortuna o destino
> anzi l'ultimo dì qua giù ti mena?
> e chi è questi che mostra 'l cammino?   (46–8)

(What chance or destiny / brings you here before the final day? / And who is he who shows you the way?)

In reply, Dante is at once able to give a coherent *résumé* of his story; even though that story includes events and actions which have no place in any normal sequence of events. Untroubled by the thought that he comes before his time – 'avanti che l'età mia fosse piena' (50) – he is able to maintain the tone of intimacy, and of familiarity with the special conditions of his own journey, which sounded so uncomfortable when Brunetto spoke of how he was accommodated in Hell:

> 'Là sù di sopra, in la vita serena',
> rispuos' io lui, 'mi smarri' in una valle,
> avanti che l'età mia fosse piena.
>   Pur ier mattina le volsi le spalle:
> questi m'apparve, tornand' ïo in quella,
> e reducemi a ca per questo calle'.   (49–54)

('Above, there in the tranquil life', I replied to him, / 'I lost myself in a valley / before my time was complete. / Only yesterday morning I turned my back on it: / but he appeared to me, as once again I was returning to it, / and leads me back home by this path.')

Dante here speaks easily of what happened 'yesterday morning', and brings the account to a movingly simple conclusion with a use of the dialect form of the word *casa* – truncated as in everyday speech to *ca*. On the instant, the urban imagery of the canto is translated into an image that pictures Dante's return (note 'reducemi', leading me *back*) to his true home and place of origin.

   The speech which Brunetto now utters fails, firstly, in its complete lack of any such simplicity. It is the speech of a rhetorician whose task, as Brunetto defines it in the *Rettorica*, is to strengthen the bonds of community by his persuasions and nurture a common voice among his fellow-citizens. But increasingly Brunetto's words reveal him as a propagandist, attempting – without realising how futile the attempt is, in view of the distance between himself and Dante – to repossess his former pupil and claim for himself the paternity which has just been ascribed to Virgil:

> Ed elli a me: 'Se tu segui tua stella,
> non puoi fallire a glorïoso porto,
> se ben m'accorsi ne la vita bella;
>   e s'io non fossi sì per tempo morto,
> veggendo il cielo a te così benigno,
> dato t'avrei a l'opera conforto.   (55–60)

(And he to me: 'If you follow your star, / you cannot fail to arrive at the glorious harbour, / if I knew you aright in the lovely life. / And had I not died so early, / seeing the heavens so kindly to you, / I would have given you strength in the task.')

The crucial factor in the diction here is the ornate and elevated phraseology of 'tua stella', 'vita bella' and 'glorïoso porto'. And the last of these phrases, especially when compared with the 'ca' uttered by the protagonist, prepares one to receive all that follows as a 'periphrastic study in a worn-out' rhetorical tradition. So, precisely in seeking these resonant phrases, Brunetto – whether he intends to or not – obscures the true origin and motive of Dante's journey in God's love, ascribing it to the influence of the stars and destiny. The symptoms of a linguistic disease which affected Farinata and Capaneus reappear; and it is apparent that Brunetto's art as a rhetorician is here doing violence to the very nature of the enterprise on which the salvation of his pupil depends.

This violence moves on to another plane in the lines which follow. Now, speaking of the present corruption of Florence, Brunetto adduces the myth of Florence as the 'sementa santa' (76) – the true heir – of Rome, and blames the disruptions of the present upon the influx of immigrants from the surrounding countryside. (The inhabitants of Fiesole (61–3) were thought to be descendants of the Catiline conspirators, enemies to the security of Rome.) This myth is indeed one which Dante himself seeks to revive; and he will sanction arguments very similar to those which Brunetto here employs in the Cacciaguida cantos of the *Paradiso*. But Brunetto still displays how distant he is in spirit and word from the Roman Virgil whom he ignores. There is now none of the gravity which marked, say, Virgil's account of the *Veglio*. Instead, the speech degenerates into virulent abuse, entirely incompatible with its initial pretensions to unity and civic order. The myth of Rome, so far from offering the promise of unity, becomes a weapon in Brunetto's hand, and his language itself belies any respect for the urbanity which the myth itself recommends:

> Faccian le bestie fiesolane strame
> di lor medesme, e non tocchin la pianta,
> s'alcuna surge ancora in lor letame,
>   in cui riviva la sementa santa
> di que' Roman che vi rïmaser quando
> fu fatto il nido di malizia tanta.   (73–8)

(Let the beasts of Fiesole make litter / of themselves and not touch the plant / (if there is any that still springs up in their dung-hill), / in which survives the holy seed / of those Romans who remained there when / it became the nest of so much malice.)

Here the language of the farmyard replaces the *lacrimae rerum* of Canto xiv. And in the same imagery we also hear a fear and an abuse of the natural: the fastidious distaste of the intellectual for the language he has chosen to use consorts with a certain relish at his own daring.

It may be objected that, in voicing this polemic, Brunetto stands proxy for Dante himself. There is good reason to argue thus; and in Canto xvi we shall have to consider what grounds of authority Dante himself would claim for such an attack. But here the second speech of the protagonist displays a cal-

culated reversal of Brunetto's tone and purpose. In syntactical form, how-
ever, the speech is designed as a parallel to Brunetto's, being built around an
almost identical series of conditional clauses:

> 'Se fosse tutto pieno il mio dimando',
> rispuos' io lui, 'voi non sareste ancora
> de l'umana natura posto in bando;
>   ché 'n la mente m'è fitta, e or m'accora,
> la cara e buona imagine paterna
> di voi quando nel mondo ad ora ad ora
>   m'insegnavate come l'uom s'etterna:
> e quant' io l'abbia in grado, mentr' io vivo
> convien che ne la mia lingua si scerna.
>   Ciò che narrate di mio corso scrivo,
> e serbolo a chiosar con altro testo
> a donna che saprà, s'a lei arrivo.
>   Tanto vogl' io che vi sia manifesto,
> pur che mia coscïenza non mi garra,
> ch'a la Fortuna, come vuol, son presto.
>   Non è nuova a li orecchi miei tal arra:
> però giri Fortuna la sua rota
> come le piace, e 'l villan la sua marra'.   (79–96)

('If my desires were all fulfilled,' / I replied to him, 'you would not now / be in exile
from human nature. / For fixed in my memory and piercing now to my heart / is the
dear and good image of you, as a father, / when hour after hour in the world / you
taught me how a man becomes eternal: / [it is right] while I live / that my tongue
should tell [how great my gratitude is to you]. / That which you tell me of my course, I
write, / and keep with another text / for a Lady to annotate who will, if I arrive there,
know how to do so. / This much I wish to be clear to you, / as long as conscience does
not quarrel with me, / I am ready for Fortuna, whatever she wills. / It is not new to my
ears, this pledge; / and so let Fortuna as she pleases turn her wheel, / and the peasant
his hoe.')

This speech needs to be quoted in full, since the point is that – unlike
Brunetto's speech – it maintains, throughout its length, a fluency and a poise
which are the intellectual and verbal counterpart of Dante's first gesture of
distant reverence. And that poise – beginning with the conditional clause – is
made possible by a command of irony, clarity of syntax and comprehensive-
ness of view which confidently embrace the eternal future as well as the
temporal past.

The conditional clauses with which Brunetto began – 'Se tu segui tua stella
...', 'e s'io non fossi sì per tempo morto' – conceal both the heretical
reference to astral determinism and the logical impossibility of reversing the
impact of death. Dante's phrase, on the contrary, not only acknowledges
unflinchingly the actual impossibility of fulfilling his own wishes for
Brunetto, but inaugurates a supremely clear and sustained view of Brunetto
in relation to the protagonist: praise and critical judgement, affection and
logic are all articulated here without the slightest discomposure. The sentence
structure can accommodate phrases as strong in themselves as 'la cara e

buona imagine paterna'; yet the protagonist still tacitly insists that the teaching he received from Brunetto – though helping him to arrive at his present position in eternity – was received emphatically in the scheme of time, 'nel mondo ad ora ad ora'. There is an irony in these two lines (84–5) which Brunetto could never command: but even that is not over-stressed, any more than the qualified promise to speak of his gratitude as long as he lives. It is true that, as in Canto XIII, Dante *will* tell the praises of the sinner; but in the context of the whole canto he cannot do so without telling the whole truth, which includes a record of the damnation of the sinner. So the speech ends with an emphasis upon the clarity which the protagonist has sought to achieve – 'ne la mia lingua si scerna' – and an equal stress upon the comprehensiveness of the account which he must render 'a donna che saprà', when he arrives at the end of his journey in Paradise.

This passage, then, is Dante's own present alternative to the measured style of Virgil in Canto XIV; like Virgil, he keeps alive here the essential myths of paternity and learning and admits to the intellectual conditions under which these myths are entertained. Indeed, the speech is so finely tuned to these conditions that Dante can find a place for Brunetto in the narrative of his life as he could *not* for Filippo Argenti. He can even descend to the same linguistic register as his master without detriment, as when he accepts the prophecy of misfortune – though characteristically pointing out that he has already assimilated the lesson, with a rural phrase that likens fortune to a tiller of the soil. The phrase does no violence to the notion of fortune, of nature, of the 'villan' or even for that matter of Brunetto. Its very neutrality is evidence of the balance which Dante here maintains.

Significantly enough, it is at this point that Virgil intervenes, speaking with unemphatic pithiness, and a brevity which contrasts directly with Brunetto's rhetorical amplitude. Hitherto, Virgil has been mute. Yet his silent presence has itself sent a shimmer of irony through the whole conversation between Brunetto and his one-time student. For Virgil, after all, is Dante's new teacher. The fictional Virgil has replaced the historical Brunetto; the old has re-emerged to replace the new. And, as always, Virgil represents a standard by which the thought and language of the sinners may be assessed. Thus the fact that he should be made to underline the teaching about Fortuna is itself an indication of the extent to which he has supplanted Brunetto. For, while the Virgil of both the *Aeneid* and of *Inferno* VII is clearly Dante's mentor in the ways of Fortuna, this was the subject that previously Brunetto had made his own. Indeed, all that the humanist Brunetto *had* to teach was an ethic of resistance to Fortuna. And even then, it seems he had no sense of how fortune might itself be – as it is in Canto VII – a painful but accurate messenger of nature. Nature, in the guise of Fortuna, is held at bay by Brunetto's philosophy; and therein lies the violence for which he is condemned.

The final sequence of the canto is dominated by the desire – characteristic of Dante himself – to gain an exhaustive view of the scene in this circle; and by the equally characteristic sense – on Brunetto's part, that time, as another manifestation of nature, is against him:

ché 'l tempo saria corto a tanto suono.   (105)

(for the time would be too short for such a sound).

In considering this final section, however, one cannot avoid a question which has much exercised scholars over the last few decades: the question of whether Brunetto is condemned for homosexuality. It is not difficult to see that the strange combination, in the tone of the canto, between intimacy and shock might exactly reflect a reaction, on Dante's part, to a distressing sexual advance. It is equally easy to see that intellectual violence can take many forms, and that many forms of it are indeed represented in the language and arguments of Brunetto. There is nothing absurd in suggesting, as Pézard does, that Brunetto might be condemned for writing his 'Treasure' in French: such an act would obstruct the very nature or purpose of the exercise – which was to communicate truth to the author's Florentine compatriots – and might well be interpreted as an act of violence. Nor is it absurd to argue that the politicians, lawyers and lecturers in literature who come after Brunetto in this circle have all, in one way or another, erected barriers between the mind and the truths of nature.

Yet, overall, such considerations are irrelevant, and may indeed distract one from the dominant image of the sequence, which is that of the sterility that human beings can impose upon themselves. When violence is done to truth, growth ceases; Dante cannot, finally, be the 'child' of the violent Brunetto. Only a story such as Dante's, which responds to nature in the way that Fortuna teaches one to respond, with poise and agility, can successfully regenerate the tired roots. And in that regard, Brunetto's final words, urging the virtues of the *Tresor* – significantly rendered here in a native Italian form as *Tesoro* – are themselves an unknowing self-condemnation as much as an accolade. They are a claim to fame which ignores the degree to which all fame must be founded – as Dante founds his own – upon criticism and self-criticism. Further, to base a reputation upon a *book* is itself to allow an arte-fact to replace the driving force of nature. (Virgil only once refers to the *Aeneid* in the *Inferno*, and then almost disparagingly, in Canto xx; nor need he refer to it, for his literary voice, so far from being stilled in ink and paper, has become the natural voice of Dante's intellectual guide.) So, in the end, Brunetto is compelled to respond to a natural but, to him, incomprehensible drive, running as if to complete the race from which, in life, he had with-drawn into artifice. The image of the race insists upon the potential wholeness which any life can contain as it moves towards its chosen or proper end. But the gap which Brunetto is obliged to maintain between him-self and the group that follows is also, unavoidably, an emblem of the fissures which intellect itself can open up in the community which, rightly, it ought to serve.

VI

The image which concludes Canto xv, of Brunetto as a runner who wins rather than loses his race, has been taken even by a critic as acute as T. S. Eliot to indicate the ambiguity of Dante's feelings towards the sinner he is constrained to condemn. All we have said about the portrayal of Brunetto suggests that this is a mistaken view; and indeed, within the simile itself, the associations of 'green' in the flag for which the race is run, and of fluent and purposeful action in the race itself point ironically to the principles which the violence of Brunetto's mind has offended: his punishment insists that – pointless as the exercise must be – the sinner should still move towards the goal or end which is designated by green, the colour of fertility. Even in Hell the sinner's story has to be told.

Nevertheless, it would be contrary to the argument I am pursuing to suggest that Brunetto was morally an easy case for Dante to settle. There are elements in the final image of Canto xv which point to the possible dignity, if not of Brunetto, then of the *imagine* of human nature which he still retains. And these elements are given even stronger emphasis in the image of athletic activity which introduces the sinners in Canto xvi. Three spirits suddenly detach themselves from the running crowd – three spirits who in circumstances other than those of Hell would, says Virgil, have deserved Dante's respect (18). Even now, the protagonist is required to be courteous to them (15).

Still running beneath the rain of fire – as they have to, since their punishment is the same as Brunetto's – the three spirits form themselves into a circle before Dante's eyes.

> e quando a noi fuor giunti,
> fenno una rota di sé tutti e trei,
>   qual sogliono i campion far nudi e unti,
> avvisando lor presa e lor vantaggio,
> prima che sien tra lor battuti e punti,
>   così rotando, ciascuno il visaggio
> drizzava a me, sì che 'n contraro il collo
> faceva ai piè continüo vïaggio.   (xvi 20–7)

(And when they had reached us, / they made a wheel of themselves, all three together. / As champions, naked and oiled, are accustomed to do, / looking out for a grip or an advantage / before exchanging blows and thrusts, / so, wheeling around, each kept his face / directed at me, so that the neck continually travelled / on a course contrary to the feet.)

Clearly enough, there is an element of the grotesque, and also suggestions of conflict, in the torsion of these bodies. But, for a moment, the efforts of the sinners are concentrated in the perfection of circular motion, and the image points with almost Grecian vigour and plasticity to the strength of the human physique.

The three spirits are all Florentines; they are the last – save one, Mosca – of those whom Ciacco named in Canto vi. All are Guelph noblemen of the generation preceding Dante's own; and contemporary records speak at length of their exploits, particularly in opposition to the Ghibelline cause which Farinata represents. None of these reports makes mention of homosexuality – ostensibly the sin for which they are all condemned; and there is even less reason here than in the case of Brunetto to pursue that question.

For the canto is not, in terms of poetic character, designed to raise or examine any such particular question. Rather, the episode is one in which historical figures are translated into emblems: the Florentine noblemen have many things in common with both Capaneus and the Old Man of Crete; and the especial character of this canto, in regard to theme, derives from its tendency to conflate, in a single group of figures, the implications which were presented analytically in the parallels between Capaneus and the *Veglio*. What might have been and what is – the lost ideal and the present corruption – are here inextricably linked. Thus on the one hand the noblemen *are* noble. They are representatives of what human nature – and the proto-humanist culture of Florence – might have produced if its history had pursued a healthy course. These sinners demonstrate the highest that humanity is capable of in terms of both social and political aspiration, and also – to judge from the image of the wrestlers – in terms of physical strength and stature. Yet they are still sinners, locked in a circle which is also a *fight* and only temporarily conceals the tensions which the sinners propagate and suffer. Even at its best humanity is subject to divisions, torments and contradictions.

It is vital to insist – in the perspective of the whole *Commedia* – that the image of the Florentine noblemen does indeed affirm the potential nobility and integrity of human nature. For Dante is about to present – in the long sequence of the Malebolge – a wholly different view. And this begins in Canto xvii with Dante's depiction of the usurious noblemen – of whom we have already seen something in Chapter 2. In this later canto, the other side of Florentine history is depicted – again in emblematic form; for the nobles of Canto xvii are those who have become so degenerate that their own armorial emblems are now hung around their bestial necks as trade-signs of the banking-houses to which, in life, they devoted their labours. For all that, the originality of the first half of the *Inferno* is to insist that, however contradictory and self-deluding particular human beings may be, there are resources in our nature – represented by Virgil, the protagonist and the poet Dante – which allow us to remedy our own diseases. It is equally a sign of the originality and character of the *Inferno* at large that, having established a position which, from some points of view, represents a daringly unorthodox confidence in human nature, Dante should then proceed to dismantle this edifice in the cantos that follow, calling into question not only Virgil and the protagonist – who have been put to the test before – but also the principles on which his own poem is constructed.

In some measure, then, the sixteenth canto, along with the seventeenth, is a canto of transition. It is more accurate, however, to regard it as a pause in the narrative, or even as a moment of poise: for certainly the ironic skill with which Dante celebrates his Florentine forebears while still maintaining his moral distance from them exactly corresponds to the poise which the protagonist achieved in Canto xv. At the same time, the canto both veils and reveals the tensions that its theme introduces. The pause here – unlike the philosophical pause of Canto xi – leads to polemic rather than reflection; but the polemic itself is not immune to internal stress. We are concerned here with a subtle shift of authority from the best representatives of old Florentine culture to the callow vessel of the new, represented by Dante himself. The distinction is, however, even finer than the distinction between Dante and Piero. And, as we might expect by now, Dante, in affirming his own position, also reveals the stresses that run counter to his own prestige. His authority is that of a tragic voice, a voice which, as we shall see, is hard-won from the dangers of confusion and silence.

The central action of the canto begins when the nobles approach the protagonist in search of some authoritative word about the state of Florence. And, at first view, they are so far from being sinners as to possess a heightened view both of the corruption of the culture to which they belonged and of the remedies that the protagonist himself might embody.

Thus the intention of the noblemen in approaching is to seek some definite word about the state of Florence: they acknowledge the degeneracy of their native place – 'nostra terra prava' (9). They also recognise in Dante a figure who can give them a clear and final answer; and in doing so, here as elsewhere in the canto, these Florentines – unlike Brunetto – achieve a poise of their own in speech, comparable to that which they achieve in their athletic action. In word as in gesture the irony of their position is almost consciously realised:

> cortesia e valor dì se dimora
> ne la nostra città sì come suole,
> o se del tutto se n'è gita fora. (67–9)

(say whether courtesy and valour abide / in our city as they used to, / or have they wholly gone out of it?)

This question is pitched in terms which embody the main themes of the whole sequence we have been considering in this chapter: the Florentines are concerned with civilisation at its most sophisticated – as expressed in 'cortesia' and 'valore' – and with the possibility of such civilisation enduring in a world of change. Indeed these words would not be out of place in the mouths of the penitents in *Purgatorio* xiv, whose concern, likewise, is with the passing of valour and courtesy.

But the answer which Dante gives here, as the authorised spokesman, is neither poised nor civilised. It is a disruptive howl of lamentation; recalling the sudden loudness with which Virgil reproves Capaneus, Dante cries:

'La gente nuova e i sùbiti guadagni
orgoglio e dismisura han generata,
Fiorenza, in te, sì che tu già ten piagni'.
Così gridai con la faccia levata ...   (73–6)

('The new people and the sudden gains / have engendered pride and excess in thee, / O Florence, so that you already weep for it.' / So I cried out with upturned face.)

With this, the questions specific to Canto xvi are all brought into play. These concern, firstly, the grounds of authority on which Dante as protagonist makes this violent assault. But they also concern the status of the poet. For, even more clearly than in, say, the attack on Filippo Argenti, the *terzina* represents a moment at which the interests and voice of the poet – as an embattled, historical Florentine – are exactly identified.

Now, it will prove that the ground of the authority which Dante claims is located precisely in that same identification of poet and protagonist which initially seems so disconcerting.

But to consider, first, the simple case of the protagonist, it is easy to see that the sixteenth canto brings to a conclusion the celebration of the myth of Dante which began, in Canto xii, when the centaurs admired the way in which the protagonist, by virtue of his corporeal body, 'moved that which he touched' (xii 81). So at lines 27–33, the Florentines contrast their own tortured condition with the immunity which the protagonist enjoys in Hell: 'che i vivi piedi / così sicuro per lo 'nferno freghi' (32–3); and similarly, they introduce their request for news with the words:

'Se lungamente l'anima conduca
le membra tue', rispuose quelli ancora,
'e se la fama tua dopo te luca ...'   (64–6)

('So may your soul, guide / your body [for long],' he then replied, / 'and so may your fame shine after you'.)

The sinners here come closer to recognising the ground of Dante's spiritual authority than any other sinners until the early cantos of the *Purgatorio*. But the form of the speech is almost as significant as its content; for this too reflects what might have been or should have been. Note in particular the use of conditional syntax. The same conditional was to be found in the opening speech of the nobles (as it is also at line 79 and line 46). And this is no incidental issue; both Brunetto and Capaneus in their own ways had difficulties with the conditional – as did Francesca in basing her meretricious appeal to Dante upon the unrealisable condition of God's friendship. In the case of the Florentine nobles, however, the syntax is perfectly formed and employed. Their speech is, in part, a *captatio benevolentiae*, in part an oath and prayer. And they ground this appeal on the firm recognition of the complex truth which is manifested in the protagonist, that a human being is a union of the eternal spirit and temporal body. It is, thus, a sign of their own achievement that the nobles can successfully employ a linguistic form which records the conditions – or polyphonies – of this truth. One recalls how Pier della Vigna

attempted to give the magical authority of an oath to his words, only to end
with a grotesque appeal to the new roots by which he lives in Hell.

Yet might not this elegant and controlled syntax, for once, be all *too* well
formed? And what of the construction of Dante's own polemical riposte?
Dante begins by repeating, in abbreviated form, the tale which he has told to
Brunetto, stressing both the completeness which his journey and narrative
alike display, and also the contradiction implied in having to pursue this
completeness by travelling to the centre of Hell:

> Lascio lo fele e vo per dolci pomi
> promessi a me per lo verace duca;
> ma 'nfino al centro pria convien ch'i' tomi.   (61–3)

(I leave the gall and go for the sweet apples, / promised to me by the true leader; / but
first I must fall to the very centre.)

We need not stress the extent to which this *terzina* founds the authority of
the protagonist on his moral journey. We should, however, note that it *is* an
abbreviated account; and this feature begins to reveal, both here and in the
subsequent cry of condemnation, the foundation of Dante's *poetic* authority.
For the abbreviation is made possible by the accumulation of imagery and
narrative events in the context of surrounding cantos. It is not merely coher-
ence of syntax and word that informs Dante's polemical outburst in lines
73–5, but a strength of allusion to those images, drawn from nature, which
have been seen in perverted form throughout the preceding cantos – and will
again be evoked in Canto XVII when Dante pictures the artificial nature which
usury has created for itself.

To repeat:

> La gente nuova e i sùbiti guadagni
> orgoglio e dismisura han generata,
> Fiorenza, in te ...   (73–5)

The key to the abbreviation is 'generata', a word which unlocks all that
Dante has cumulatively said in these cantos about the generative processes of
nature and their interruption. But 'orgoglio' takes similar strength from the
considerations of pride in Canto XIV, as does the word 'dismisura'; for behind
'dismisura' lies a whole field of reference to the vices which human beings
display when they forgo the courtly and civilised cultivation of good
manners. Finally – if more distantly – there is the irony of 'nuova': the sur-
prising gains of the *nouveaux riches* have produced not a 'vita nuova' but
rather a strange vacancy in nature, comparable to the 'new' roots of Pier
della Vigna's tree.

So far, then, from being disruptive, Dante's voice tears through the veil of
the narrative episode to reveal the underlying principles and trends of thought
of the *Commedia*; and the same may be said, on the level of myth and image,
about the speech beginning 'Lascio lo fele e vo per dolci pomi' (61). For the
word 'pomi', with its associations of rounded maturity, is enriched and sup-
ported by previous references to the sterile wood of Canto XIII – 'non pomi

v'eran ma stecchi con tosco' (xiii 6) – and the 'lazzi sorbi' of Brunetto's speech (xv 65), as well, of course, as containing an implicit allusion to the apple of the Fall. (Adam, in *Paradiso* xxvi 91–2, is spoken of as the only apple that was ever produced ripe.)

So, just as the protagonist dexterously handles conditional syntax in Canto xv, his *imagery* here serves to reveal the polyphonies of his narrative. And this is the more understandable because articulate speech – so far from commanding unquestioned authority – is in fact shown to be under threat in the narrative of Canto xvi. And to appreciate this we should, finally, consider how Dante brings the mythic procedures of the violence sequence to their climax in this canto.

For the dialogue between Dante and the Florentines is framed by two great mythic images of Dante's own construction. The first of these, certainly, suggests how myth and image may support articulate utterance; but the second recalls the conditions of insecurity under which all human endeavour, utterance and achievement inevitably proceed.

The narrative scene in Canto xvi is dominated, from the opening lines, by the sound of falling waters. The protagonist is close to the point where all the rivers of Hell pour down into the pit of the Malebolge. At first, these waters merely rumble and hiss, at a distance:

> Già era in loco onde s'udia 'l rimbombo
> de l'acqua che cadea ne l'altro giro,
> simile a quel che l'arnie fanno rombo.   (1–3)

(Already I was in a place where could be heard the resounding / of the water that fell into the next circle, / like the hum that bees make in their hives.)

In this relatively innocuous form, even the waters of Hell can support the suggestions of progressing life and fertility which the protagonist himself asserts both by his presence and by the images of his diatribe. The comparison of the sound to that of bees in a hive confirms this, introducing a pastoral note which records the busyness and creativeness of the natural world when – undisturbed by human depredations – it is allowed to store up for itself its own natural products. (We need not pause to contrast the bees and the usurers.)

Yet as a moment in a myth of Dante's own making – that of the moral geography of Hell – the image is shot through with ironies. These waters, originating in the tears of the *Veglio*, pour into the void of Hell; and, as the protagonist draws closer to them at the end of the canto, the full implications of the myth that Dante has written reveal themselves. For now, in the first place, the waters *do* silence comprehensible speech, as if they presented an image too complex and large for words to contain. So at lines 92–3,

> 'l suon de l'acqua n'era sì vicino,
> che per parlar saremmo a pena uditi.

(the sound of the water was so close to us / that in speaking we should hardly have been heard).

To be sure, in an extended geographical simile Dante attempts to compare this waterfall to a manageably natural waterfall which he has seen in the Apennines (94–105). The fact remains that he is comparing the swift clean waters of the river Acquacheta ('quiet water') with the sullied 'acqua tinta' (104) of Hell. And, in the silence which this infernal waterfall enforces on the human voice, there is worse to follow.

For a moment, the protagonist stands teetering on the edge of the chasm, and – in a gesture of both confidence and abandon – he strips off his belt. This action has troubled commentators from the first; but in the dramatic and thematic development of this sequence, it is easy enough to interpret. This is the belt with which Dante had thought to bind the *lonza* (107–8) in Canto I; and the *lonza* was the earliest manifestation of sin which he encountered. Now, it seems, in completing the first great phase of his infernal journey, the protagonist has reached so great an understanding of sin – and is so secure in his moral position, as the new leader of his race and culture – that the restraint of the belt, with its associations of the humility of a friar's habit, is no longer necessary. So, only in *Purgatorio* I will the protagonist be girded again with the reed of humility (*Purg.* I 133); and that girding will prove merely a preparation for the ultimate freedom of moral dominion which Dante enjoys in the Earthly Paradise.

But the same gesture is also one which summons up hitherto unknown terrors. That is its purpose in the narrative – to invoke a new manifestation of Hell; and the protagonist, in the moment before the response is given, is driven back upon his own thoughts – since Virgil can barely hear him – to wonder what will now ensue, knowing only that it must be something utterly new and unexpected.

> 'E' pur convien che novità risponda',
> dicea fra me medesmo, 'al novo cenno
> che 'l maestro con l'occhio sì seconda'.   (115–17)

('It must surely be that some new thing will follow,' / I said to myself, 'from the strange new sign / that my master follows with his eye.')

It is not until Canto XVII that Dante confronts the monster that now appears. This is Geryon, the 'sozza imagine di froda' (XVII 7) – the foul image of the fraud; and once this image does appear Dante will be able to give it a definite moral meaning. Indeed Geryon – with the face of a just man and the body of a serpent (XVII 10–12) – is the third in the sequence of delusive old men that began with the Old Man of Crete and proceeded to the 'cara e buona imagine' of Brunetto. In that series, the 'fraudulence' of Geryon will be seen, in a moral light, as the summation of all Dante's disappointment over the past generations which have defrauded him by their false examples.

But the crucial factor in the structure of Canto XVI is that, in building the myth of this monstrosity, Dante does *not* allow himself the comfort of a moral conclusion. It is indeed better to be silent, he declares, until incredible things show their true face (124–6). And in the silence of this 'unfinished' canto the myth is allowed to work its way into Dante's – and the reader's – imagination as a dislocating rather than comforting feature:

> ch'i' vidi per quell' aere grosso e scuro
> venir notando una figura in suso,
> maravigliosa ad ogne cor sicuro.   (130–2)

(that I saw through that thick, dark air / a figure coming swimming up, / amazing to any steadfast heart).

Thus Dante's heart is not 'secure' in the face of what he sees; and this is a remarkable reversal in a canto which began with a celebration of Dante's safety beneath the rain of fire. In effect, the heart is never secure from its own fantasies. The very currents of imagination which need to be revived if human beings are to be saved from the burning contradictions of their own natures can themselves become fraudulent fictions and subtle mendacities. This is the moral problem which Dante will confront throughout the Malebolge, and Virgil indicates as much when he speaks at lines 121–2. For here he does not comfort Dante with a mythic 'dream' of the Earthly Paradise, but rather sharpens the apprehension of the protagonist against the nightmare which he has already anticipated:

> El disse a me: 'Tosto verrà di sovra
> ciò ch'io attendo e che il tuo pensier sogna'.

(And he said to me: 'Soon that will emerge / which I am waiting for and your mind dreams of.')

Yet, as a conclusion to Canto XVI, it is the dreadful distress of this dreaming anticipation that sets the seal on Dante's authority. Pier della Vigna swore 'per le nove radici d'esto legno', and Dante, in the midst of describing the advent of Geryon, also swears to the truth of what he has seen:

> per le note
> di questa comedìa, lettor, ti giuro ...   (127–8)

(by the notes / of this comedy, reader, I swear).

The *Commedia* is acquiring for Dante the status of a heart or head – or Bible – which can itself be invoked in witness to the truth. Yet it has this status only because Dante can realise in himself a condition as absurd – and tragic – as the position of Piero. Piero resisted and sought to cloud that absurdity beneath his rhetoric. In Dante's case, the very myths and nightmares he is conceiving bring the absurdity into so sharp a consciousness that words cannot contain them. And so the story goes on. Geryon will indeed be an instrument or means for Dante to proceed to the next stage of his journey. But that is as much as to say that the even linear advancement of the journey depends upon an ability to admit into consciousness the lacerating experience of vacancy or discontinuity, and the sudden eruption of uncontrollable and delusive images. The moral journey must learn to encompass or accept that any authoritative word may be subject to confusion.

4

Comedy and identity: Cantos XVII–XXIII

I

In Canto XVII of the *Inferno*, Dante descends from the circles of violence to the Malebolge, the region of Hell in which sins of fraud and deliberate deceit are punished. The descent throughout is both terrifying and absurd. The canto opens with the voice of Virgil, who commands Dante to observe the monster Geryon – part man, part reptile, the embodiment of deceit:

> Ecco la fiera con la coda aguzza,
> che passa i monti e rompe i muri e l'armi!
> Ecco colei che tutto 'l mondo appuzza!   (*Inf.* XVII 1–3)

(Behold the beast with the sharp pointed tail, / who passes over mountains and breaks down city-walls and weapons. / Behold the one whose stench pollutes the whole world.)

Dante and Virgil have now to pursue their journey on the back of this beast. Elsewhere in the *Inferno* and *Purgatorio*, the two travellers proceed (save for occasional assistance) on foot, climbing upwards or downwards according to the terrain. But here, in a pre-emptive parody of the journey in Paradise, they are obliged to fly – and to fly *downwards*. The strangeness of the descent is emphasised by a description which combines fantasy with a strong imaginative grasp of the realities of hovering flight:

> rota e discende, ma non me n'accorgo
> se non che al viso e di sotto mi venta.   (116–17)

(it wheels and descends, but I notice nothing / save that the wind plays against my face and beneath me).

In full, the account of Geryon occupies almost a canto and a half; and by its length as well as its imaginative peculiarity, it marks off the Malebolge from preceding cantos, preparing for a sequence quite distinct in thought and style from the first half of the *Inferno* – and no less different from every subsequent movement of the *Commedia*.

To De Sanctis, the Malebolge is the 'realm of Dantean comedy'. This is a useful description and points to a number of the major differences between the Malebolge and earlier cantos of the *Inferno*.

The most striking difference – as De Sanctis observes – occurs in the representation of the sinners, and in the status which Dante allots to them. In the circles of violence, the poet has been largely concerned to examine the nature and extent of human heroism. However, few of the sinners in the Malebolge could be mistaken for heroes. In the main, they are petty cheats – like the flatterers and seducers of the first two bolge, or the alchemists, con-men and mountebanks of the last. Dante represents these sinners with considerable vigour. But the vigour derives from a precise and often realistic observation of the crudest forms of speech and behaviour. The poet has here set himself to examine the trivialisation, which occurs in pursuing deceitful aims, of the rational nature proper to humanity; and only in exceptional cases is there any question of the interest he takes in an inhabitant of this region outweighing the contempt he expresses for the radical perversity of deceit.

Here, as in other examples of comic writing, a restriction in the status of the individual to some more or less realistic dimension is complemented by an emphasis upon social or communal behaviour. Sins of fraud are sins that thrive upon the body of society. The various relationships of kinship, common purpose and trust which are incorporated in the social organism provide a gamut of opportunities for the deceiver to play upon; and, in anatomising these possibilities, Dante presents as complete a picture of a corrupt society as he did earlier of the corrupt individual. The setting of the Malebolge is not – as in the circles of violence – a landscape, where the perversions of physical nature can be registered, but a city-scape where rock is cut into channels to resemble the products and constructions of human design – be they castle-moats, alleys, or sewers. Correspondingly, the sinners here tend to be represented as members of a community, degraded and self-punishing; and they display the characteristics which brought them to Hell in the response they make to other members of their present group. Thus the characteristic mode of discourse in the Malebolge is not monologue or discussion but rather quarrel. And in recording these quarrels – as also in depicting the foul circumstances which beset the sinners – the poetry of the Malebolge becomes 'comic' in a sense which Dante himself would have understood. To Dante, comic writing is writing cast in the lowest linguistic register; and in the Malebolge, there is no conceivable vulgarism or obscenity which the poet will not willingly adopt in the interests of mimesis and linguistic realism. Typical of this is the passage which concludes the Malebolge, depicting the scuffle between Sinon and Adam of Brescia:

> E l'un di lor, che si recò a noia
> forse d'esser nomato sì oscuro,
> col pugno li percosse l'epa croia.
>   Quella sonò come fosse un tamburo;
> e mastro Adamo li percosse il volto
> col braccio suo, che non parve men duro,
>   dicendo a lui: 'Ancor che mi sia tolto
> lo muover per le membra che son gravi,
> ho io il braccio a tal mestiere sciolto'.
>   Ond' ei rispuose: 'Quando tu andavi

al fuoco, non l'avei tu così presto;
ma sì e più l'avei quando coniavi'.   (*Inf.* xxx 100–11)

(And one of them, offended / perhaps to be named so unillustriously, / smote the taut belly of the other with his fist. / The belly sounded, as if it had been a drum; / and Master Adam struck back with a blow to the face / with his arm which seemed just as hard, / saying: 'Even if [the weight of my limbs] deprives me of movement, / my arm is still free for a job like this.' / To which he replied: 'When you went / to the fire you weren't so quick of hand; / but you were – and more so – at your coiner's craft.')

Along with these alterations in the portrayal of the damned, the Malebolge also displays an alteration in the portrayal of punishment. Petty and wretched as the sinners may have been in life, the punishments that Dante devises for them here underline – excessively, one might suppose – the extent of their degradation. The pandars, for instance, wallow in filth which 'seems to have come from human privies' (*Inf.* xviii 114), while in the last bolgia the sinners endure a range of demeaning ailments from madness and dropsy to a leprous rash which the sinners scratch 'like cooks de-scaling fish' (*Inf.* xxix 82–4). So far from attempting in any way to mitigate the cruelty of this vision, Dante apparently welcomes the display, and, in a spirit of peculiarly vicious comedy, rejoices at the sight of the human being helplessly caught in the machinery of divine vengeance:

O somma sapïenza, quanta è l'arte
che mostri in cielo, in terra e nel mal mondo,
e quanto giusto tua virtù comparte!   (*Inf.* xix 10–12)

(O utmost wisdom, how great is the art / which you display in heaven, on earth and in the evil world, / and how just are the dispensations of your goodness!)

Few punishments in the early *Inferno* could be read as simple demonstrations of revenge; indeed, it is one of the most original achievements of the earlier cantos that, in the greater number of cases, the punishments are correlative to the spiritual and psychological condition of the sinners themselves. The images of Farinata's tomb, Piero's thorn-tree, and the fire which falls upon Brunetto all make a complex appeal to the reader's imagination; they require one to discover for oneself a connection between the sophisticated speech and attitudes which the sinners display and the underlying condition of the spirits as demonstrated by their position in Hell. In the Malebolge, however, there is rarely any similar complication of appeal. On the contrary, Dante has, it appears, suddenly chosen to draw upon a familiar lexicon of medieval images. Where many of the earlier punishments were derived from classical sources, and drew much of their complexity from that, Dante now – and only now – introduces the Hell of popular fantasy, of boiling pitch, of consuming fire and of devils who torment their victims with the lash and the knife. And these images are presented, more often than not, with a disgust that might have come from the crudest ascetic writings. So, when Dante meets the great seducer Jason, no words are exchanged between protagonist and sinner; though the sin of seduction may seem scarcely distinguishable from that of adultery, there is no conversation here of the kind which passed between Dante and Francesca. Instead, the visual image is allowed to speak; attention is focused sadistically upon the incongruity between the regal appearance that the sinner still retains and the sordidness of the punishment he suffers, as he plods silently through the excrement of the first bolgia scourged by attendant devils:

> Del vecchio ponte guardavam la traccia
> che venìa verso noi da l'altra banda,
> e che la ferza similmente scaccia.
>   E 'l buon maestro, sanza mia dimanda,
> mi disse: 'Guarda quel grande che vene;
> e per dolor non par lagrima spanda:
>   quanto aspetto reale ancor ritene!'   (*Inf*. XVIII 79–85)

(From the ancient bridge, we observed the track / of those who came towards us on the other side, / whom likewise the lash urged on. / And, without my asking, my good master / said to me: 'Look at that great man coming now / seeming to shed no tears of pain. / What a royal appearance he still has!')

It will be obvious by this time how far Dante has distanced himself in the Malebolge from the position he developed in the first half of the *Inferno*. It may also be obvious why even now this sequence does not receive the critical attention it deserves. Readers are still inclined to suppose that the moral dramas of the first part of the *cantica* represent the fullest and most characteristic expression of Dante's art. Nor would I want in any way to diminish the interest of those sixteen cantos: though Dante may now pierce the illusions of human grandeur seeking continually to redefine the grounds on which selfhood depends, it is nonetheless an aspect both of his Christian humanism and of his art in general that he should consistently defend the dignity of the human being.

Yet the very strength of that initial concern makes the retreat or reversal of the Malebolge all the more worthy of attention. On the moral level, the contempt which Dante here displays is not altogether incomprehensible. Indeed, many readers will share his detestation of lying and chicanery – while his attitude to suicide and sodomy might be harder to tolerate. Yet the issue is confused by the way in which the poet's judgement spills over into a pathological distaste for the fleshly nature and frailties of humanity (reminding the English reader of Swift or the Shakespeare of *Troilus and Cressida*). So when Dante compares the sinners in the tenth bolgia to the sick, putrefying in a crowded hospital at the height of summer (*Inf*. XXXIX 46–51), or Hecuba running mad like a dog at the loss of her children (*Inf*. XXX 16–22), his disgust apparently attaches as much to the victims of evil as to its perpetrators.

From passages such as these, it is clear that, overall, the Malebolge represents both a sustained exercise in intellectual surprise in the pattern of the *Commedia* and a searching critique of the very positions which Dante has hitherto sought to establish in his poem. Indeed this reversal amounts, in places, to a form of poetic self-betrayal; and if the *Inferno* at large may be regarded as an instance of 'dead poetry', then it is the Malebolge that provides the most acute evidence of what this phrase implies.

At the same time, the sequence also contains – inappropriately, one might think – evidence of an increasing awareness on Dante's part of the prestige of his own poetry. The principal illustration of this occurs in Canto xxv where Dante, at the height of a scene describing the hallucinatory metamorphoses of the thieves, proclaims the superiority of his art over that of Ovid and Lucan. But already in the Geryon episode, the poet gives free rein to virtuosity – at the very moment where he describes the terror of the protagonist – in a sequence which not only combines realism with bizarre fiction but also draws flamboyantly upon the repertoire of classical mythology:

> Maggior paura non credo che fosse
> quando Fetonte abbandonò li freni,
> per che 'l ciel, come pare ancor, si cosse;
>   né quando Icaro misero le reni
> sentì spennar per la scaldata cera,
> gridando il padre a lui 'Mala via tieni!'.   (*Inf.* xvii 106–11)

(I do not think there was greater fear / when Phaeton let loose the reins, / so that the sky – as it seems to be still – was burned; / nor when poor Icarus [felt] his loins / unfeather at the melting of the wax, / and his father cried to him: 'Look, you are taking the wrong path.')

It is a paradox – characteristic of the Malebolge – that the sequence at large should represent simultaneously an act of self-betrayal and an act of conscious artistry. Here we may confidently speak of an *art* of difficulty. And, as we shall see, the manifestations of this art are primarily to be observed in the minute details of the text. Indeed, if the Malebolge is comic, then it is so in the sense that Dante here writes in the full realisation of how subversive – even of his own proposed purposes – the text he is writing must be: from canto to canto he erects positions only to dismantle them in what follows.

However, before beginning the analysis of this process, it is important to stress that there *is* a logic, as well as a chain of disruption, in the developments which the Malebolge pursues. And the linguistic and narrative details of the sequence play against this logic. To emphasise this – and to avoid any loss of direction in the details of the analysis – it is as well to begin with an overview of the Malebolge in its thematic structure.

We have seen already that, thematically, the Geryon episode provides a conclusion to the Brunetto episode, indicating the way in which by the end of the circles of violence, human pretensions to dignity or justice have come to appear illusory and fraudulent. The deceit which Dante examines in the Malebolge is the condition which human beings must suffer when their own leaders betray them.

But from this initial shift of emphasis there follow a number of others, which are pursued systematically throughout the Malebolge. In the first place, many of the themes and attitudes expressed in the sequence are recognisably religious in stamp. This may seem surprising when the surface of the text is so distinctly marked with despair and disgust; but the very sense that the human intellect is helpless in the face of its own perversions prepares Dante to look directly to God as his only source of strength and stability.

In this light, the cruel simplicity of many of the punishments that the sinners suffer here emerges as evidence that in eternity, if not in time, there are after all clear principles of retribution; to the eye which looks for God's 'art' in these punishments there is the promise of an otherwise inaccessible order. Similarly, constructing the Malebolge in a satirical spirit – as a pattern of corrupt society – Dante is also looking with a distinctly religious eye to the moment when the Last Judgement will again reveal truth in the world and cleanse it of its imperfections. In the words of W. B. Yeats, it is a sign that 'the second coming is at hand' that 'the best lack all conviction and the worst are full of passionate intensity'; and Dante reveals his own authority for such a vision by a series of direct references to the Apocalypse (or Book of Revelation) of St John, where the progressive and terminal corruption of mankind is taken to mean that Judgement is near. So in Canto XIX, depicting the corrupt Church as the Whore of Babylon, Dante openly alludes to the Book of Revelation:

> Di voi pastor s'accorse il Vangelista;
> quando colei che siede sopra l'acque
> puttaneggiar coi regi a lui fu vista.   (*Inf.* XIX 106–8)

(Of shepherds such as you the Evangelist took note; / when she who sits upon the waters / was seen by him, whoring it with the rulers of the world.)

The sequence of allusions to which this belongs began as early as the Geryon episode. For the monster Geryon is portrayed, in terms drawn from Apocalypse XI, as arising from the pit with stinging tail. Likewise, the disasters and disease which dominate the last two bolge recall the images of war which the Apocalypse declares will befall humanity in the days before the end. Moreover, the narrative structure of the second half of the *Inferno* mirrors the movements of these last days: as the protagonist moves from one dreary 'pouch' to the next in the concentric rings of the Malebolge, he appears to make little progress – as though the world were stagnant with evil. Yet the closer he gets to the bottom of the pit – and to Satan who is confined there – the closer he is to the revelation and freedom he will enjoy in Purgatory. As in the Book of Revelation, so here, order is approached through seemingly absolute disorder.

The images and the plan of the Malebolge suggest, then, a distinctly religious solution to the problem of evil. Correspondingly, the portrayal of the human figure points here to a Christian diagnosis of the human condition and of sinfulness which is later developed in the *Purgatorio*. In earlier cantos even the sin of heresy was viewed as a perversion of rationality, and examined in relation to its social and domestic consequences. But in the Malebolge there is at least one sin which could only be conceived in strictly Christian terms, the sin of simony – examined in Canto XIX – which involves the sale or misapplication of those sacramental gifts that the Church was founded to protect. Likewise, in Canto XXVII, Dante returns to his attack upon the corruptions of the contemporary Church, when he exposes the treacheries of Pope Boniface VIII in his lust for temporal dominion.

So Dante now goes on to develop the conclusions he had reached in his earlier anatomy of human nature by demonstrating – with an unmistakable allusion to Christian doctrine – that human identity can only be secured through an enforcement of the relationship between the creature and the God who created him. For all the skill in rational manipulation which the deceitful display, there is at heart a vacancy or insecurity, resulting from their ignorance of this truth, which in Hell stands finally revealed. So in Canto XXIV Dante presents an all but blasphemous parody of the truth which in Christian doctrine asssures human beings of eternal selfhood – the truth of the Resurrection: when the thief Vanni Fucci is reduced to ash by the bite of a serpent, his remains are on the instant made to resume their former shape; and in describing this second transformation Dante applies to Vanni Fucci the image of the phoenix, which is regularly employed as an image for the Resurrection of Christ himself:

> e poi che fu a terra sì distrutto,
> la polver si raccolse per sé stessa
> e 'n quel medesmo ritornò di butto.
>   Così per li gran savi si confessa
> che la fenice more e poi rinasce,
> quando al cinquecentesimo anno appressa ...   (*Inf.* XXIV 103–8)

(And so lying destroyed upon the ground, / his dust of its own accord drew itself together again, / returning on the instant to its self-same shape. / Thus it is declared by the great wise men / that the phoenix dies and is then reborn / as it draws near to its five hundredth year.)

The punishment of the thieves does not reside simply in the destruction of identity, but also in the inescapable determination of the Creator to mark his creature with his own Law, and to refuse the sinner any comfort in oblivion. This theme, however, is carried through not only, in the representation of punishment, but, conversely, in the way that the poet represents the Dante-character in the Malebolge. Strengthening the suggestions which began in *Inferno* XII – and developing, from Canto XVI, the theme of the protagonist as the new leader – Dante now presents the protagonist as a living demonstration of what God's intentions for humanity truly are.

Thus in several passages the emphasis of the imagery falls upon the wholeness and completeness of identity which the protagonist is allowed to preserve in Hell: where the sinners are lacerated by their punishments, Dante's own journey through the Malebolge demonstrates the miraculous fact that, in spite of their frailties and criminality, individuals can be granted security and integrity. Most strikingly, in Canto XXVIII – where the schismatics are continually wounded by the swords of devils – the damned are brought up short with astonishment at the sight of one who is allowed to remain intact:

> Un altro, che forata avea la gola
> e tronco 'l naso infin sotto le ciglia,
> e non avea mai ch'una orecchia sola,
> ristato a riguardar per maraviglia
> con li altri ...   (*Inf.* XXVIII 64–8)

(And another, who had his throat pierced through / and his nose cut off to beneath the eyebrow, / and then had only a single ear, / stopped dead to gaze in wonder / with the others.)

Finally, in pursuing his Christian theme, Dante here begins to concern himself more with the *conscience* of at least some of his characters than he did in portraying the public and monumental heroes of the circles of violence. This is particularly evident in his lengthy treatment of Guido da Montefeltro, which occupies almost the whole of Canto XXVII – a portrayal intended to reveal a lack of any heartfelt belief in a man who had available to him all the most sophisticated resources of Christian thought and penitence. However, for more positive evidence of Dante's new concern with conscience we shall need to look again at his representation of the protagonist, and above all at the interest he now shows in the subtlety and shifts of his inner self. Canto XXIII, which concerns the 'inward' sin of hypocrisy, is particularly significant in this regard.

All that has been said so far, about the religious cast of the Malebolge, leads one to expect a corresponding reassessment of the rational Virgil. After all, reason itself is shown to be corrupt in the Malebolge – along with the social institutions which reason has created; and if Virgil represents to Dante the purposes and value of temporal history, then these purposes, too, are obscured in the apparent stagnation of the Malebolge. The Malebolge brings sharply into relief those ambiguities in Virgil's position which have been present since his first appearance in Canto I; and it follows that, within the narrative, the authority of Virgil over the protagonist should be somewhat diminished, as, for instance, in Canto XXIII, when Virgil is struck with incomprehension at the sight of the crucified Caiaphas.

Yet in these circumstances, Virgil is also shown to possess a resilience which is hardly less surprising than the competence Dante initially ascribed to him as guide to the mysteries of Hell. This resilience will eventually equip Virgil to lead Dante into Purgatory – where he might appear to have no place at all. The changes which now occur in the function and status of Dante's guide represent not a diminution of his powers but a preparation for the role he will play in the second *cantica*.

This is apparent, first of all, in the emphasis which Dante places in the Malebolge upon the prophetic powers of Virgil. Hitherto, Virgil has been seen largely as a representative of Empire – of the moral and social order which human beings can enjoy in the temporal life. But in the *Purgatorio* he will appear – explicitly at one point – as the 'cantor de' buccolici carmi' (*Purg*. XXII 57), the author of the *Eclogues*; and, as we have already seen in Chapter 3, his pastoral poems are regarded in the Earthly Paradise as prophetic 'dreams' (*Purg*. XXIX 139–41) which keep alive the hope of a Golden Age. The Malebolge is the reverse of everything a Golden Age might be. Yet even here Virgil will prove able to provide prophetic indications of what an age of perfect justice could be like. Canto XX, in particular, provides a sustained demonstration of this. For Dante is concerned here with the damnation of false prophets; and much of the canto is devoted to Virgil's own speech in which obliquely he attempts to clear himself of any taint of sorcery which might attach to him by association with his native city of Mantua – a city supposedly founded by the witch Manto.

Equally, it is one of Virgil's most important duties in the Malebolge to ensure that the protagonist himself should be, in the fullest sense, a 'seer' – one who *sees*; where earlier Virgil taught Dante discrimination in thought and word, his concern now will be that the protagonist should indeed see, and, through seeing, exhaust the significance of the vision he has been granted. In Canto XXVIII, he asserts that his task is to give Dante 'full experience' of Hell (48); and in the cantos that follow, he is repeatedly concerned to regulate Dante's vision, either by urging him to see all that there is to see in the allotted time (*Inf*. XXIX 11–12), or by repressing his desire to gaze obsessively at the sights of the final bolgia (*Inf*. XXIX 4–6; XXX 131–2). It is thus significant that Virgil explains his own presence and purpose in the Malebolge in the following terms:

> I' son un che discendo
> con questo vivo giù di balzo in balzo,
> e di mostrar lo 'nferno a lui intendo.   (*Inf*. XXIX 94–6)

(I am one who goes down / with this living man from ridge to ridge, / meaning to show him Hell.)

Rationality, insofar as it implies the capacity to observe or establish a scheme of relationships, may be in question throughout the Malebolge; but reason can also be understood as a capacity to contemplate the shattered fragments without confusion, and in that sense it remains a potent force throughout the Malebolge.

The changes in the position of Virgil point back to the alterations which occur in the position of Dante as poet in the Malebolge. Corresponding to his attention to the prophetic role of Virgil – and to the interest he takes in the protagonist as leader and exemplar – Dante as poet here assumes, in one aspect, a peculiarly authoritative stance. So, adopting the same tone he ascribed to the protagonist in Canto XVI, the poet steps forward in a number of passages to make a direct address to the reader or a direct satirical attack upon the corruption of the cities of Tuscany. He, as well as Virgil, is a prophet, and he speaks as such in, for instance, Canto XXVI – where he sarcastically praises Florence for having contributed five of her citizens to the bolgia of the thieves, and then speaks of his longing for the destruction of his native city – or, likewise, in Canto XXV, where he calls down destruction upon the city of Pistoia:

> Ahi Pistoia, Pistoia, ché non stanzi
> d'incenerarti sì che più non duri ...   (*Inf.* XXV 10–11)

(Ah! Pistoia, Pistoia, why do you not resolve / to burn yourself to ashes, and thus endure no longer?)

These two invocations are part of a sequence of judgements which culminates in the sixth canto of the *Purgatorio*, lines 76–151, where Dante, in the language of an Old Testament prophet crying woe to the cities of the plain, exclaims against the waywardness of Italy at large – 'Ahi serva Italia, di dolore ostello' – and recognises that the ill-will and recalcitrance of his fellow-Italians is so deeply ingrained as to make necessary the intervention of God's own judgement:

> O è preparazion, che ne l'abisso
> del tuo consiglio fai per alcun bene
> in tutto de l'accorger nostro scisso?   (*Purg.* VI 121–3)

(Or is it a preparation that [you are making] in the abyss / of your counsel for some good end / wholly cut off from our seeing?)

In claiming authority for his poem as a vehicle of justice, it will be seen that Dante differentiates his own prophetic act from that which he associates with Virgil. And, predictably enough, the Christian prophet – aware as he is both of God's justice and of the sanctity which divine truth bestows upon the human being – affirms that his position is superior to that of his pagan forebear.

Yet we shall not understand the grounds of the authority which Dante here claims for his poem unless we realise that they reveal as much an attitude of self-criticism as of self-praise. So, while portraying his own miraculous immunity to corruption throughout the sequence, Dante also displays an equally strong tendency to present himself, as character, in a ludicrous light – as vulnerable as are the damned themselves, and no less subject than they are to degradation. This is especially evident in the comedy of the twenty-first and twenty-second cantos, where, in presenting the sin of barratry for which Dante was himself sentenced to exile and death (falsely, one assumes), the poet makes the protagonist an object of ridicule, crouching in terror behind a rock lest the devils of this bolgia should 'touch him on the rump' with their meat-hooks (*Inf.* XXXI 58–63; 100–1).

I have entitled this chapter 'Comedy and Identity' with the intention, partly, of suggesting how crucial the comedy of the Malebolge is to the definition of Dante's theme of identity. The issue, however, is one which concerns not only the themes of the poem but also its practices and intellectual authority. From the point in Canto XVI at which Dante swears by 'the notes of this comedy', the strength and self-consciousness with which he views his own poem are apparent. Yet, as we shall see, the authority of the text is undermined in the process of writing no less than the dignity of the protagonist.

This disruption is evident in two principal features of the sequence – though, in effect, there can be no general characterisation of effects as subtle and local as Dante here produces.

In the first place, the very dependence upon the image – upon the thing *seen* – calls into question the status of Dante's written text. Throughout, Dante will make continual use of the word *vidi* – I saw. And this feature may, on the one hand, amount to an assertion of authority; Dante's *vidi* possesses much of the solemnity of the Latin phrase employed in the Book of Revelation. Yet the images which Dante sees are not only acknowledged, in some cases, to be beyond the scope of speech to render, but in many instances represent not any authorised vision, but a free, even licentious, indulgence of the imagination. Whatever the overt moral purpose of the text might be, one cannot deny the subliminal power of images such as that, in Canto XVIII, of the sinners sunk in excrement, or of human beings transformed – in a parody of copulation – into snakes in Canto XXV. Continually, in the text of the Malebolge, sacred images war with the profane, and they rarely seem assured of victory.

In the second place, even where the diction of the Malebolge does assert some command over the vision which Dante records, the *words* which the poet uses are themselves far from being, in any simple sense, authoritative, so that the question must again arise as to what the grounds are of Dante's intellectual authority. He seems, indeed, quite acutely conscious that, in dealing with the sin of fraud, the fictions of a poet may themselves be closely akin to acts of deceit.

Ranging from the heights of virtuosity to the depths of scatology, the Malebolge acknowledges an inherent lability in language which Dante had already recognised – but sought to resist – in the *De Vulgari Eloquentia*. His art now requires him to admit that lability and still achieve an authoritative poise. With which we may turn at once to the eighteenth canto; for, among many other things, this canto may well be taken as a revision of the views of linguistic authority which Dante proposed in the *De Vulgari Eloquentia*.

II

The first eighteen lines of *Inferno* XVIII provide a general, introductory plan of the Malebolge. The previous canto concludes its lengthy and dream-like account of Dante's flight on Geryon with the rapid departure of the monster: 'si dileguò come da corda cocca' (*Inf.* XVII 136) – he shot off like a bolt from a bow. The canto-break underlines the instantaneous clearing of the earlier confusing scene, and prepares for an abrupt contrast. In place of the slow descent into vacancy evoked in Canto XVII, Canto XVIII offers an image of fixity and apparently unshakeable order:

> Luogo è in inferno detto Malebolge,
> tutto di pietra di color ferrigno,
> come la cerchia che dintorno il volge.   (*Inf.* XVIII 1–3)

(There is a place in Hell called Malebolge, / all made of stone the colour of iron, / as is the circle which goes around it.)

Where the Geryon episode enacts Dante's detachment from the previous circles, the opening *terzine* of the Malebolge proclaim a distinctly new beginning. Stationed immediately after the canto-break, the declaration 'Luogo è in inferno detto Malebolge' has indeed far more the appearance of a true beginning than the oblique and hesitant opening of *Inferno* I. 'Nel mezzo del cammin di nostra vita' is hedged around with metaphor and scriptural allusion; the Malebolge, on the other hand, begins with a statement of seemingly unassailable fact.

From the first line on, the introductory sequence might easily be read as a demonstration of authorial omniscience. In previous parts of the *Inferno*, the author tends to defer the detailed consideration of any part of Hell until the Dante character arrives to explore it. Thus, as we have seen, the plan offered in Canto XI – which itself occurs at a significantly late stage in Dante's journey – reveals as much the inadequacy as the competence of any general or comprehensive survey. Now, however, little seems to be deferred or left to subsequent exploration. The whole geometrical geography of the Malebolge is contained in the first six *terzine* of Canto XVIII; and, while Dante does say that he will speak in more detail about each of the bolge, his words also affirm how clearly the whole project lies exposed before his eyes:

> Nel dritto mezzo del campo maligno
> vaneggia un pozzo assai largo e profondo,
> di cui *suo loco* dicerò l'ordigno.   (4–6)

(Right at the centre of the malignant plain, / there opened up a well both broad and deep; / I will speak of its structure in the appropriate place.)

Yet, firm as all this seems, the passage, in its linguistic texture, is as disturbing as the sequence that it introduces consistently proves to be. Consider in the first place the overtly factual nature of the opening line. In one aspect, this line prepares the reader for the 'realism' of language that characterises the Malebolge. Yet it is also a piece of conscious virtuosity, marked by Latinate diction and allusion to the *Aeneid*. The Latin phrase *suo loco* enforces the poet's mastery over his plan by a learned locution, while similarly the adjective 'ferrigno' (2) recalls the Virgilian 'ferrugineus' (*Aeneid* VI 305). In fact, even the apparently neutral phrase 'luogo è' conceals a rhetorical *topos* – that of *descriptio loci* – which appears, for instance, in

Aeneid I 529–30: 'est locus, Hesperiam Grai cognomine dicunt, / terra antiqua, potens armis atque ubere glaebae'.

In Canto xx Virgil opens his account of the founding of Mantua with an extended example of *descriptio loci*:

> Loco è nel mezzo là dove 'l trentino
> pastore e quel di Brescia e 'l veronese
> segnar poria, s'e' fesse quel cammino.   (*Inf.* xx 67–9)

(There is a place in the middle (of that region) where [the Bishops] of Trent / and of Brescia and of Verona, / could all claim authority to make the holy sign if they went that way.)

This is enough to suggest how closely Dante associated the *topos* with the Virgilian style; and, in considering Canto xx, we shall see that, for Dante, there is a sense in which Virgil's poetry could be considered as a celebration of place. After all, the *Aeneid* prophesies the return to a place of rest after years of wandering in alien lands, while the *Georgics* and *Eclogues* picture landscapes which are places of either fruitful labour or idyllic repose. At the same time, a comparison of the use that Virgil makes of the *topos* in Canto xx and the use that Dante here makes of it *in propria persona* reveals at once the peculiarity of the phrase in Canto xviii. Dante may indeed be asserting his command over the repertoire of rhetorical devices. Yet the command becomes ironic and strained when applied not to the description of a natural place but to a location which is the very site of fiction and falsity. The solemn precision of the line points to a place of unreality, in which the principles of labour and civility – embodied in Virgil's poetry – are mocked, and where the city walls imprison those sinners who, by their deceit, have sought to drain all certainty and significance from the contour of our natural human habitat.

The first line, then, by virtue of its rhetorical elevation invites close attention; yet the more attention one gives to it, the more shifting and discomforting it proves to be. Thus even the second half of the line is out of true with the first: 'Luogo è' is a formula which appears to admit of no ambiguity; yet the phrase quickly becomes ambiguous when associated with the evidently fantastic neologism 'Malebolge'. The word 'Malebolge' – the evil pouches – is comic in the Dantean sense by virtue of its linguistic vulgarity. But it is also comic in that it subverts the dignity of the opening phrase; and on such a view even the word 'inferno' begins to look less secure than it ought in a text which, overall, regards Hell as a realm of moral judgements: alongside the obviously fictitious 'Malebolge', 'inferno' itself has the appearance of a fiction.

The order and fixity of the Malebolge are, then, called into question by the very language in which Dante defines that plan. And this is important in two respects.

Most radically, one now begins to have doubts about the whole project of judgement on which the *Inferno* is based. At first view, the geometric rigour of the Malebolge strengthens and clarifies the moral geography which, while underpinning the previous cantos, had frequently enough been obscured by emotional or imaginative resonance. And in one aspect we need not doubt that this *is* the function of the Malebolge; the rings of concentric circles, each spanned by a bridge, provide a series of theatrical spaces where the deceitful are exposed to the clear and superior vision of the protagonist. It is, however, equally true that, from the first, such clarity of outline can itself be delusive. Not only does the protagonist enter the realm by a descent into a void but the architecture of the Malebolge – compared to that of a fortress with moats and ditches – guards no solid fortress at all, only a second emptiness, the 'well' into which Dante is lowered on the shoulders of the giant Nimrod in Canto XXX. Moreover, it soon becomes apparent that the structure of the Malebolge is by no means as perfect as the opening of Canto XVIII might lead one to suppose. For, as Dante discovers in Canto XXII, the bridges over the sixth bolgia have all been broken by the earthquake which accompanied the entry of Christ into Hell on Easter Saturday. As a result, Dante and Virgil have to submit to the indignity of climbing from one bolgia to another; and in the cantos which prepare for and describe this climb – Cantos XXIII and XXIV – doubts will be cast upon the very authority to judge which Dante claims at the opening of the sequence.

In a similar way, the first line of Canto XVIII is a sure indication of where the poetic interest of the Malebolge sequence will be located. At the outset, the regularity of Dante's narrative plan of the Malebolge foreshadows a sequence in which surprise and imaginative exploration will have little place. Yet the effect of exploration will here occur less on the level of narrative – which is largely dictated by the single-minded movement from one bolgia to the next – than on the linguistic level of the text. One must look to the activity of the poet, not to that of the *personaggio*, if one is to appreciate the extent to which surprise and difficulty still govern the writing of the *Commedia*.

As we move into the body of Canto XVIII, the question of linguistic texture becomes especially acute. For not only does the canto admit a confrontation between the language of the text – more scatalogical than anywhere else in the *Inferno* – and the clear outline of moral architecture, but the sins depicted in the canto are also sins with a distinctively linguistic character. The sinners are seducers and flatterers whose manipulation of language amounts to a corruption of the primary instruments of reason; and in representing this sin Dante displays a marked awareness of the dangers residing in language, and of his own responsibility to escape the perversities that the sinners here exemplify.

It is consistent with Dante's initial emphasis upon geographical order that the structural plan of Canto XVIII itself should be exceptionally clear. Unlike any other canto in the *Inferno*, the eighteenth deals with two categories of sinner – the seducers and the flatterers – disposed in two distinct bolge. This structural feature emphasises that the construction of the Malebolge allows

the Dante character an advantage over what he sees; the ease with which he
passes between the bolge is stressed at line 70: 'We climbed very easily'.
Likewise, at line 109, the two protagonists manage the apparatus with equal
facility, climbing to the summit of the bridge to secure a full view of the
scene beneath. Earlier, too, Dante's position on the bridge has allowed him to
observe very precisely the highly organised flow and counterflow of spirits
beneath the lash of the devils – a movement that Dante compares to a system
of crowd control employed in Rome in the Jubilee Year of 1300:

> come i Roman per l'essercito molto,
> l'anno del giubileo, su per lo ponte
> hanno a passar la gente modo colto,
>   che da l'un lato tutti hanno la fronte
> verso 'l castello e vanno a Santo Pietro,
> da l'altra sponda vanno verso 'l monte.   (*Inf.* XVIII 28–33)

(so, because of the great crowds of people / in the year of the Jubilee, [the Romans took
measures] on the bridge / to allow folk to pass, / ensuring that on one side all have their
faces / towards the castle and towards Saint Peter's, / and on the other side towards the
Mount).

Corresponding to the division effected by the architecture of the bolgia, the
canto is divided into four balanced episodes, focused in turn upon
Caccianemico, Jason, Alessio Interminei and Thais. On the surface, these
characters are very diverse – witness the contrast between the heroic Jason
and the squalid Alessio – but the grouping erases peculiarities or idiosyncra-
sies and encourages an analytical view of moral similarities and common
factors. Thus the canto is different from, say, the fifth canto, where –
concerned with the judgement of individual cases – Dante creates a dispro-
portion between his presentation of the exemplars of lust such as Cleopatra,
Semiramis and Dido and the particular figure of Francesca. This difference is
also seen in the ways that Cantos v and XVIII – both concerned with sexual
appetite and meretricious words – respectively conclude. For, where the fifth
canto ends with the ambiguity of 'e caddi come corpo morto cadde', the
eighteenth closes with a firm and final injunction, as Virgil insists that
enough is enough: 'E quinci sian le nostre viste sazie' (136) – and let our
eyes be satisfied with that. Here, the phases of the narrative coincide exactly
with the orderly articulation of the poet's judgement.

In one aspect, then, the canto continues to display an aspiration to control
or clarity which stands in dramatic contrast to the lies and concealments that
Dante attributes to the sinners. Thus the function of Virgil's words
throughout the canto is to direct and sharpen the gaze of the protagonist as it
falls upon the inhabitants of the bolge. So Virgil urges:

> Attienti, e fa che feggia
> lo viso in te di quest' altri mal nati.   (75–6)

(Attend, and let / the look [of these other ill-born souls] strike upon you.)

Similarly, at line 83 he commands Dante to gaze upon that great one:

'Guarda quel grande'; and at line 128 Virgil insists that he should 'drive his eyesight forward': '"fa che pinghe", / mi disse, "il viso un poco più avante"'.

The emphasis here upon the action of the eye is all the greater because the sinners seek to hide both from the protagonist and from the truth about their own condition. In earlier circles of Hell, the sinners have been eager to affirm the extent of their dignity on earth. The sinners in the Malebolge have no claim on that score. Yet they are still constrained to speak and show themselves; they become vessels for their own condemnation as the truth seeks them out and forces them to speak even to their own discredit. So Alessio Interminei, the third of the sinners, reacts violently when picked out by Dante's eye; but he is still obliged to talk unambiguously about his crime and about the sentence passed upon him in Hell:

> Quei mi sgridò: 'Perché se' tu sì gordo
> di riguardar più me che li altri brutti?'
> ...
> Ed elli allor, battendosi la zucca:
> 'Qua giù m'hanno sommerso le lusinghe
> ond' io non ebbi mai la lingua stucca'.   (118–19; 124–6)

(He yelled to me 'Why are you so greedy / to gaze on me rather than on the other foul ones?' ... / And he in reply, battering his own noddle: / 'I am submerged down here because of the flatteries / of which my tongue was never tired.')

Likewise, in the first encounter of the canto, it is the 'aggressive eye' of the protagonist that first fixes upon Caccianemico, forcing the sinner to speak with his clear tongue, with 'chiara favella':

> Mentr' io andava, li occhi miei in uno
> furo scontrati; e io sì tosto dissi:
> 'Già di veder costui non son digiuno'.
> Per ch'ïo a figurarlo i piedi affissi;
> ...
> Ed elli a me: 'Mal volontier lo dico;
> ma sforzami la tua chiara favella,
> che mi fa sovvenir del mondo antico'.   (*Inf.* XVIII 40–3; 52–4)

(And as I went on my eyes / were struck by those [of another]; and I said at once: / 'I do not lack for seeing him already.' / So I fixed my feet to figure him out / ... And he said to me: 'Unwillingly I say it; / but your clear tongue compels me, / making me remember the former world.')

In subsequent cantos, as we have said, there will be occasions when Virgil reproves the protagonist for excessive attention to the horrors of the bolge; and, in these later cantos, eye and voice, sight and word do not always co-operate as completely as they do in this case. Yet even in Canto XVIII, balance and clarity are not as easily achieved as I have so far suggested.

For, while there is no conflict in the narrative between the protagonist and his guide, there is nonetheless an implicit readjustment in Dante's view of Virgil; and this readjustment concerns in particular the status of Virgil's own

'chiara favella': for, where the *personaggio* engages in quarrelsome ex-
changes with Caccianemico and Alessio, the poet also represents Virgil in
such a way as to underline the differences between the language of his classi-
cal guide and the language that his own vision requires him to employ.

Thus at the centre of the canto Virgil tells the tale of how Jason seduced
and abandoned Hypsiphile. The tone and linguistic level of the speech mark
it off completely from its context:

> Quelli è Iasón, che per cuore e per senno
> li Colchi del monton privati féne.
>   Ello passò per l'isola di Lenno
> poi che l'ardite femmine spietate
> tutti li maschi loro a morte dienno.
>   Ivi con segni e con parole ornate
> Isifile ingannò, la giovinetta
> che prima avea tutte l'altre ingannate.
> Lasciolla quivi, gravida, soletta.   (*Inf.* XVIII 86–94)

(That is Jason, who by boldness and intelligence / deprived the men of Colchis of their
ram. / He went to the isle of Lemnos / after the bold and pitiless women / had put all
their men to death. / There, with tokens and fine phrases, / he beguiled Hypsiphile, the
young girl / who before had beguiled all the others. / He left her there, great with child,
alone.)

The filth and confinement of the first bolgia disappear beneath the epic eleva-
tion of these lines, as they evoke the cleanliness and movement of the open
sea; and the coarseness of emotion which characterises the canto at large is
replaced by an elegiac pathos over the fate of the forsaken girl.

Yet, easy as it is to find in this passage a relief from the foulness of the
bolgia, its weakness lies precisely in being a relief. Virgil here describes a
sinner, Jason, who in his new circumstances is little more than a silent
automaton, momentarily picked out from the crowds of 'sferzati'. But the
weakness of his words lies in their inability to comprehend the complexity of
the situation in which Jason is set. Here, as later, his rhetoric shields the
Dante character from the ugliness which the canto at large is determined to
reveal. There is surely no mistaking in this canto a strong undercurrent of
sadism and sexual fear; Dante constantly refers to the sinners as objects on
whom the devils practise, to the point at which they become nameless
'sferzati' or 'frustati' beneath the lash. Virgil, however, only glances at this
area of experience with a brief reference to the sexual nightmare in which the
'ardite femmine spietate' put their consorts to death; and this reference itself
would be little more than a mythological flourish were it not that the context
in which Dante has placed it reveals, psychologically, its more dangerous
edge.

This is not, of course, to suggest that Virgil's words are without value.
Thus it is Virgil who indicates, on the level of human decency, the full
nature of the offence which seduction involves. The lonely and pregnant
figure of Hypsiphile which his words portray, stands as an image of the

essential value of sexuality in creating the life of the child and in sustaining the relationship of parenthood. And the pathos of Virgil's tone is as much a reproach to those who play upon these relationships as are the violent and explicit condemnations which appear elsewhere in the canto. The fineness of feeling and common humanity that Virgil displays stand in direct contrast to the crass single-mindedness which Jason still retains in Hell.

Yet to say this is to value Virgil less for the evident dignity of his words or the correctness of his moral judgements than for the warmth and complexity of his presence. Virgil asserts his position, so to speak, by vocal gesture rather than by the diametric oppositions of judgement which Dante adopts in his approach to the sinners; and if one does derive a moral sense from Virgil's words, it is less by the application of clear-cut principle than by a responsiveness to the human voice – comparable to Virgil's own responsiveness to Hypsiphile.

The impact which Virgil makes here will be repeated in subsequent cantos of the Malebolge, as increasingly he comes to represent not so much philosophical reason as the voice of moderation and moral commonsense. The fact remains that there is a marked difference between the tenor of Virgil's words and that of the eighteenth canto at large. So for instance, the protagonist, when confronting Caccianemico, adapts his own language to the language of the Bolognese interlocutor with the phrase 'Ma che ti mena a sì pungenti salse?' (51) – what is it brings you to such a piquant stew? The word 'salse' is both 'comic' in its register and sarcastic by virtue of the local reference, in 'salse', either to the sauces of Bologna or to an unhealthy locality of that city. And the poet, in his use of comic language far outdoes the protagonist: the latter is at least distanced from the sewers of the bolgia by his position on the ditch-wall; the poet must risk descending to such virtuoso displays of foulness as

> Quindi sentimmo gente che si nicchia
> ne l'altra bolgia e che col muso scuffa;
> e sé medesma con le palme picchia.
> Le ripe eran grommate d'una muffa;
> per l'alito di giù che vi s'appasta,
> che con li occhi e col naso facea zuffa.   (103–8)

(We heard from that point people whining / in the other bolgia, snuffling in their snouts / and slapping themselves with their palms. / The banks were encrusted with a mildew / from the rising vapours – / [squabbling with the eye and nose] – that formed themselves there in solid layers.)

There is, too, a comparable difference between Virgil and Dante in regard to the structure of the stories that they tell. If Virgil's words do constitute a miniature epic, it is because they pursue and represent a single line of action, organised around the exploits of the hero. Four incidents in Jason's life are touched upon – the theft of the Golden Fleece, the episode with the Amazons, the seduction of Hypsiphile and that of Medea. But all four episodes are related to the central strand of Jason's sea-journey: 'Ello passò per l'isola di Lenno' (88) – And then he went to the island of Lemnos. Correspondingly, the authorial voice of Virgil – though shifting in tone from one episode to the next – maintains a steady command over the whole line of the narrative.

Now, Dante too claimed command over his narrative in the opening lines of the canto; but the grounds on which this claim is based are not those of a Virgilian epic. The four episodes which Dante describes in the eighteenth canto are moments *not* of progress in a journey, but rather of stasis and crisis; and if the Dante character does eventually make progress in response to the crisis of each episode it is only because he sees and *rejects* what he encounters here as morally worthless. The characteristic emphasis of this narrative falls upon recognition and rejection. So in meeting Alessio, Dante recalls that he has seen the man before in life 'coi capelli asciutti' (121) – with his head not besmirched with filth – and now takes the opportunity of this 'second' meeting to effect a final repudiation. The same is true of the encounter with Caccianemico, whom Dante recognises from earlier meetings by his 'fazion' (49) – his features. On a different plane, the Jason episode, too, when viewed in the perspective of the whole of the canto, is itself a drama of rejection. Virgil may outline the bold epic progress of Jason; but Dante parodies this progress in his portrayal of the mechanical and insentient march of the figure through the mire. Jason is one in the series of false heroes which began with Capaneus and will end with Ulysses; and in portraying him Dante here challenges himself to evoke, and simultaneously abandon, any such model.

The naive history which Virgil exemplifies in his epic insertion is replaced, then, in the canto as a whole by a history of judgements and analyses pursued in moments of intense engagement rather than authorial detachment. It follows that the narrative structure of the canto possesses none of the simple linearity that Virgil's narrative displays. The four episodes into which the canto is divided are all different in narrative stance and stylistic register. So, while in Virgil's account of Jason there may be epic pretension, the meeting with Caccianemico is built around the 'sconcia novella' – or dirty story – in which Caccianemico involved himself:

> I' fui colui che la Ghisolabella
> condussi a far la voglia del marchese,
> come che suoni la sconcia novella.					(55–7)

(I was the one who [led] Ghisolabella / to do the will of the Marchese, / as the foul tale tells.)

Caccianemico hints here at decadent passions and perverse practices against his own sister which would not have been out of place in the *Decameron*. Then, in yet another vein, the canto concludes with an episode modelled upon the comic drama of Terence's *The Eunuch*, as Virgil, in his description of the sinners, evokes the speaking voices of the whore Thais and her customer. Moreover, beneath this variety of forms, Dante's text constantly stimulates that sense of the play upon fact and fiction which began with his initial invention of the word Malebolge: for instance, personal acquaintances are here coupled more emphatically than anywhere else in the *Inferno* with figures drawn from myth and classical literature.

If the opening line of the canto proved insecure, then so now does the apparently authoritative plan of the canto in admitting simultaneously the lability of language and the variety of narrative forms. And the risk which such a procedure involves is graphically illustrated by the fact that Virgil can describe the lies of Jason, the seducer, in exactly the phrase that was first used by Beatrice in Canto II to define Virgil's own qualification as a guide for Dante: where Virgil was required to use his 'parole ornate' in aiding Dante, Jason brings the same fine words to bear upon Hypsiphile:

> Ivi con segni e con parole ornate
> Isifile ingannò ...   (91–2)

(There, with signs and well-wrought phrases / he beguiled Hypsiphile.)

Even Virgil's words – and Beatrice's – can shift perversely on the tongue.

But as well as admitting a risk, the canto also indicates a solution – and a solution not only to the question of how Dante should avoid lies and blandishments, but also to the more general question, presented first in the *De Vulgari Eloquentia*, of how he should countenance and remedy the inherent instability of human language.

The points of similarity and difference between the eighteenth canto and the *De Vulgari Eloquentia* can, of course, be illustrated, initially, by the attitude to comic vulgarisms and provincial utterance. In defining the lexicon of the 'tragic' *Volgare Illustre*, Dante disallowed precisely those forms of language which are characteristic of Canto XVIII; and he would have mentioned only so as to rectify the provincialisms he attributes here to Caccianemico and Alessio – the former, at line 61, alluding to the Bolognese *sipa*, and the latter, at line 124, employing the Lucchese *zucca* for 'head'. These colouristic moments of dialect contribute, of course, to Dante's characterisation of the sinners. But, considering the role that Virgil plays in the canto, as the standard – at least provisionally – of linguistic order, one may reasonably suppose that Dante here means to depict that same fragmentation of linguistic order – and of Empire – which, in his theoretical writings, a due attention to the rules of Latin 'grammar' is intended to remedy.

We may go further, extending these suggestions as Dante would do from the linguistic to the social sphere. For in the *De Vulgari Eloquentia*, Dante sees in the linguistic anarchy of Italy a sign that there is no court or centre of political and moral excellence in the peninsula. On the other hand, the task of the poet must be to assist in the rectification of that problem. The intellectuals of Italy, writing and speaking in a vernacular refined to express their highest intellectual aspirations, will come to constitute a true Italian court, in which just and respectful relationship would again be possible between one person and another. In such a court, the identities of human beings would shine through in the language that they speak and be recognised appropriately by every other member of that court. Dante, so he claims, has already experienced something of this in the honour which his own high style has brought him:

Quod autem honore sublimet, in promptu est. Nonne domestici sui reges, marchiones, comites et magnates quoslibet fama vincunt? Minime hoc probatione indiget. Quantum vero suos familiares gloriosos efficiat, nos ipsi novimus, qui huius dulcedine glorie nostrum exilium postergamus.   (*DVE* I xvii 5)

(That it may elevate in honour is at once apparent. For do not the servants (of the *Volgare Illustre*) exceed in repute any king, marquis, count or baron at all? It is hardly necessary to argue this. For I myself know how renowned it makes its followers, I who, because of the sweetness of that renown, make light of my exile.)

Now nothing could be further from this than the scandals to which the lies and flatteries of the sinners in Canto xviii have led. Already in Canto xiii the poet has shown how the greatest of courts can be afflicted by the 'common vice' of malicious tale-bearing; and as Dante begins to depict, in the Malebolge, the extent to which civilised relationships can be eroded by sin, he repeats this theme in a darker tonality. The decay of true courtliness which Caccianemico and Jason precipitate by their false words extends beyond the social sphere to affect the most essential relationships of sexuality and kinship.

But, precisely in extending the question thus far, Dante also points to the difference between the answers he provides in Canto xviii and those which he projected in the *De Vulgari Eloquentia*. In moral terms, corruption is now seen to run so deep that a rectification of the relationships distorted by flattery and seduction will only come about when the deepest of all possible relationships is re-established, the existential relationship between Creator and creature. And ironically, for the sinners in Hell this relationship has been re-established; the punishments they suffer, as an expression of divine justice, are the only form of that relationship that they will ever now know.

For Dante, too, their punishments are a manifestation of the underlying principles on which true order ultimately depends; and he too must assert its force. But just as the punishment represents a bond far deeper than any social or political relationship, so must the language in which Dante seeks to express the stability of that bond go deeper than any language of social decency. The punishments here are an expression of two extremes. On the one hand, they reflect the inescapable orderliness of God; on the other, they indicate that, unless humanity responds to that order, it imprisons itself in its own waste materiality. Only in the full realisation of that truth can stability be achieved and wasting matter be animated with significance or meaning. It is this realisation that the words of flatterers and seducers seek to confuse, glossing fact with convenient fiction. Dante's linguistic task in Canto XVIII is to avoid their example.

So, in describing the punishments, Dante calls a spade a spade – in a way which the sinners would have been unable to do – since only thus can the full grasp of Creator upon creature be understood, and meaning be given to what would otherwise be utterly meaningless; and so, as we shall see, Dante is concerned henceforth in the Malebolge not only with the formal niceties of language but also with the fact that words may, at one and the same time, both threaten and assert significance.

In Canto XVIII, then, Dante travels a considerable distance from the linguistic sphere of the *De Vulgari Eloquentia* – the sphere which Virgil represents in the *Commedia* itself. This departure is inevitable, given the concern of the *Commedia* with the existential and logical relationships between human beings and God. But plainly to proceed as Dante does in Canto XVIII involves a perilous alteration as to the view which he took in the *De Vulgari Eloquentia* of his own authority or dignity as a speaker. In the *De Vulgari Eloquentia*, the poet asserted that the refinement of his language assured him of honour; his identity – threatened by exile – depended upon the recognition accorded to his poetic achievements. Here, his descent from the linguistic purity of the *De Vulgari Eloquentia* implies a very different understanding of the grounds on which the dignity and identity of the speaker himself depend. In spiritual terms, the Malebolge is designed, as we have said, to acknowledge that the individual has no identity at all save that which resides in his relationship with God. That truth is the ground of Dante's divine 'comedy'. There is, however, a linguistic correlative to this under- standing. Now, so far from asserting any univocal mastery over his own words, the poet makes himself a channel through which all possible accents may run. Ultimately, he may direct these accents to the service of truth. But the pain of speaking 'where silence would be more fitting' is not, on that account, any the less acute. This pain – or comic discomposure – grows the greater as the *Inferno* proceeds. And we see already something of the lengths to which Dante will be led in the concluding moments of Canto XVIII.

The canto ends with the representation of the whore Thais. Thais herself, however, does not speak. It is Virgil who tells her story and adopts her voice. So, as Virgil directs Dante's eye to the scratching figure 'che là si graffia con l'ungie merdose' (131), we find that even Virgil's language cannot remain as lucid and elevated as it promised to be in the Jason sequence. In describing the second of the two legendary figures in the canto, Virgil's voice descends, literally, to the comic level, mimicking the voices both of the anxious cus- tomer and of the whore herself, who fakes sexual satisfaction with the words 'Anzi meravigliose' (135) – no, it was wonderful. It is, however, to the poet Dante (not to the fictional Virgil) that these words must have been the more distressing. For, contained within them, there is a gross parody of all that Dante avowedly holds most valuable. Thus the false relationship between whore and customer parodies the true or sublimated relationship between himself and Beatrice; and one cannot ignore how Thais's words – in their emphasis upon 'grazie' and 'meravigliose' – travesty the language of grace and miracles which Dante has made his own in the *Vita nuova*.

But if, in this respect, Dante here admits a subversive parody of his own poetic self, there is also in the same conclusion a countervailing pressure. We have, says Virgil, 'seen enough'. The bolgia is left behind like waste matter; but Dante has already begun to absorb and give meaning to its salient – and apparently senseless – images. As he proceeds to Canto XIX, Jason will be taken up and used rhetorically as a figure for the false pope, Boniface VIII. Likewise, the images of the whore and her *drudo* will be transmuted into a figure for the Church as Whore of Babylon, courted by the Princes of the World. Eventually, this same image will reappear at the top of Purgatory, where Dante – sitting with Beatrice – watches the Whore of Babylon dally once more with her *drudo* in the masque of the False Church. By that time the principles which Dante has risked offending in Canto XVIII will have reasserted their competence to endow all words and experience with sense.

III

The linguistic and structural variety of the Malebolge is well illustrated by the differences between the opening of Canto XVIII and the opening of Canto XIX. Where Canto XVIII began with a clear account of the geography of Hell – asserting the poet's control over his narrative, while also revealing the fictional nature of that construction – Canto XIX begins abruptly with an impassioned tirade against the corrupt clergy, or simonists. No overt connection is made with the narrative of Canto XVIII; nor is the voice identified as belonging to any character within the fiction. Moreover, the diction of the first two *terzine* has nothing of the ambiguity or comic triviality which typified the previous canto; on the contrary, the voice is elevated in its passion and its rhetoric; and though its accents are tortured, it affirms a simple moral judgement with authoritative confidence and vigour:

> O Simon mago, o miseri seguaci
> che le cose di Dio, che di bontate
> deon essere spose, e voi rapaci
> 　　per oro e per argento avolterate,
> or convien che per voi suoni la tromba,
> però che ne la terza bolgia state.　　　　　　　　(XIX 1–6)

(O Simon Magus, O you his wretched followers, / you rapacious ones, who in your lust for gold and silver prostitute the things of God which should be wedded only to goodness, now it is right that the trumpet should sound for you; for you are found in the third bolgia.)

We shall see that these lines are characteristic of the canto they introduce both in their suddenness and in their dependence upon vocal gesture. As to their content, however, it is not, of course, difficult to recognise here the vehement indignation of the poet himself, speaking out on an issue which concerned him very closely throughout his life. Here for the first time in the *Commedia*, Dante inveighs against the corruption of the Church at the hands of its contemporary leaders. And to find a philosophical account of Dante's thinking on this question, we need only turn to the *Monarchia*, where the poet traces the decadence of the Church to the confusion between the temporal and spiritual spheres of government which arose from the Donation of Constantine. So in Canto XIX, as also in the *Monarchia*, Dante laments the Donation:

> Ahi, Costantin, di quanto mal fu matre,
> non la tua conversion, ma quella dote
> che da te prese il primo ricco patre!   (115–17)

(Ah, Constantine, how great an evil did it bring to birth / not your conversion, but that dowry / which the first rich father took from you!)

But in the context of the *Inferno* the poet's attack is more intense and more comprehensive than it is in the *Monarchia*. For one thing, the cutting edge of his satire falls very sharply upon the failings of the contemporary Church. The one sinner with whom Dante speaks here is Pope Nicholas III who reigned between 1277 and 1280 – though Nicholas is also allowed to incriminate Pope Boniface VIII, Dante's exact contemporary. At the same time, the poet extends his vision of corruption to include both the origins of Church history and its ultimate perversion in the hands of the Anti-Christ. To the historian Villani, it was Nicholas III who first sold ecclesiastical offices for gain. But in Canto XIX Dante envisages a decadent succession of 'miseri seguaci', going back in mockery of the true Apostolic succession to the earliest days of the Church, when Simon Magus, who gives his name to the sin of simony, attempted to buy – from the first Apostles – the apparently magical powers of the sacraments. Nor will this corruption end until the end of time; indeed one sign of the imminence of Judgement Day is the sight of the Church reduced to the Whore of Babylon, flirting with the Princes of the World:

> Di voi pastor s'accorse il Vangelista,
> quando colei che siede sopra l'acque
> puttaneggiar coi regi a lui fu vista.   (106–8)

(It was shepherds such as you that the Evangelist knew of / when she who sits above the waters / was seen by him, whoring it with the kings.)

In both the *Monarchia* and Canto XIX the argument against the involvement of the Church in temporal concerns is essentially a simple one: the Church can only be true to its mission if it accepts totally, as the condition of its existence, the poverty which Christ enjoined upon the first disciples. Canto XIX is designed, in one aspect, as a defence of that simple proposition; but the canto is also conceived as an account of the confusions which arise when the simplicity of the Gospel truth is ignored or traduced. In this respect, Canto XIX is a contribution to the analysis of deceit and intellectual perversity which began in Canto XVIII; and though the present canto is different in style and structure from its predecessor, it nonetheless draws directly upon the imagery of the first two bolge in pursuit of its theme.

So we have already seen that the literal seductions and prostitutions which are punished in the foregoing bolge anticipate, metaphorically, the seduction which temporal possessions exert upon the 'whoring' Church. And these imaginative connections point also to a similarity between the sin of simony and the sins of flattery and seduction. For if the flatterers and seducers pervert the essential relationships between human beings by their false use of language, so the Church – which should be the true repository of God's word in the temporal world – perverts a more essential relationship still: it obscures by its avarice the path which God has established between himself and his creatures. To sell the sacraments is to pollute the source on which the health and sanity of humankind depend.

To understand how deeply Dante would have associated the sins of the first and the second bolge, we have only to recall that, in the *Paradiso*, Beatrice will come to represent for Dante the true Church in its sacramental function. As Beatrice guides and cares for her devotee, so should the ideal Church for its followers. In that light, however, the corruption of the Church is as much a travesty of its own true role as Thais is a travesty of Beatrice; and the shock of that realisation threatens the principle on which the selfhood of the poet – and the *Commedia* too – fundamentally reside.

As we shall see, the nineteenth canto registers this shock to the full. At the same time it also formulates, and answers, a peculiarly intense question of intellectual procedure. For if the corruption of the Church so thoroughly erodes the foundations upon which the identity and selfhood of its follower depend, one is bound to ask what certainty the self ever can possess, and what authority or stability it can ever claim for its utterances. Going beyond the linguistic question (and the dangers) of Canto xviii, the present canto envisages a threat to the existential relationship between creature and Creator.

Now, we have seen that Canto xix opens with an especially authoritative judgement on the part of the poet. The vigour of that sudden voice, and its provenance, were surprising until identified by reference to the *Monarchia*. Yet as the canto itself proceeds, Dante, so far from dissipating the surprise of the opening lines, rather extends the effect of it into a sustained depiction of the absurdity which ensues when the true principles of authority are obscured. Surprise of one sort or another is the central motif of the canto. So in the central episode, the Dante character delivers the longest and most solemn speech that he utters in the *Inferno*. Yet the dignity and import of this speech are wholly undermined by its being addressed to a pair of writhing feet. The punishment allotted to the simonists is that they should be inverted in wells, one on top of the other, so that, in speaking to Nicholas – the most recently dead in the line of simonist popes – Dante must communicate his just indignation to the protruding soles of the Pontiff, which, for good measure, have been oiled and set alight:

> Le piante erano a tutti accese intrambe;
> per che sì forte guizzavan le giunte,
> che spezzate averien ritorte e strambe.   (25–7)

(All of them had their soles alight; / and the joints so writhed because of that / that they would have burst through any restraint or cord.)

Before the protagonist begins his address to Nicholas, Dante admits that it may have been 'troppo folle' to raise his voice in these circumstances. The admission is sarcastic; but it must also admit of an exact application in so ludicrous a setting: it really is all mad. And in fact the authority which Dante claims for himself in this canto is inseparable from a recognition of the absurdity of that claim. Similar as this canto may be in subject to the *Monarchia*, we could scarcely be further from the realm of logical argument to which Dante, as a professional philosopher, there aspires. Nor is his authority now based upon the simple superiority which the architecture of the Malebolge *seems* earlier to grant the protagonist. On the contrary, the protagonist goes down into the bolgia to make his speech; and, instead of displaying the unalloyed confidence that marked his address to the Florentine nobles of Canto XVI, his words here are disturbed throughout by currents of embarrassment, deference and irony:

> E se non fosse ch'ancor lo mi vieta
> la reverenza de le somme chiavi
> che tu tenesti ne la vita lieta,
> io userei parole ancor più gravi.   (100–3)

(And were it not that reverence for the keys of your high office / which you held in the happy life [restrains me] / I would use still harsher words than these.)

In one sense – particularly in regard to the protagonist – the claim to authority rests on a fairly simple foundation; in a world where the true sources of authority have been vitiated by greed, it falls to the individual himself to assume what authority he can, even if in doing so he inevitably reveals his own insecurity and folly. Throughout the canto the protagonist adds the role of true priest to the role of civic leader which he assumed in Canto XVI. For instance, in a brutal image drawn from the judicial proceedings of contemporary Florence, Dante compares himself, as he stands alongside the up-turned Nicholas, with a friar administering the last rites to a murderer condemned to death by *propagginazione* (suffocation head downwards in a ditch):

> Io stava come 'l frate che confessa
> lo perfido assessin, che, poi ch'è fitto,
> richiama lui per che la morte cessa.   (49–51)

(I stood like the friar who confesses / the perfidious murderer, who, once he is fixed, / calls the friar back to put off the moment of death.)

But the complexity of the canto – as far as it bears upon the authority of the poet himself – is apparent when one recalls that, in its opening phases, the historical Dante has entered a similar claim to priestly authority on his own account. The claim is made in a strangely emphatic simile intended to explain the appearance and size of the wells in which the popes are punished. For here Dante apparently records an episode from his own past life: the wells he says (16–21) are comparable to certain baptismal fonts in the floor of the Baptistry of Florence; he then goes on to speak of how once, when he saw a man suffocating in such a font, he himself came to the rescue by breaking the covering, only to find himself blamed for damaging the property of the Church. In this case, Dante could certainly claim to have acted as the 'true priest': where the Church – making a god out of gold and silver as it does throughout Canto XIX – is concerned more with the rights of property than of life, Dante does indeed take on the redeeming function of the Church, performing – in fact if not in name – the life-giving sacrament for which the font was originally constructed. In this light, the obscure line 'e questo sia suggel ch'ogn' omo sganni' (21) is an indication of Dante's determination to use the canto as a means of cleansing the slur which had been cast upon his name.

Throughout the *Inferno* Dante employs the *personaggio* as a device for accomplishing various acts of self-examination, self-definition and self-criticism. But never before has he made so complete an identification between himself and his fictional creation. Why, then, does it occur at this particular point?

It is clear that the *Commedia* here becomes a means by which the poet justifies and celebrates his own person, on the level of quite particular historical interests. This is to admit (as Croce, say, would be unwilling to do) that Dante's 'practical' moral concerns had a direct bearing upon his poetic choices and procedures. Thus in Canto XIX the fiction – which in Canto XVIII possessed a disruptive vivacity – becomes subordinate to Dante's moral fervour, acting as a sounding-board for personal indignation. And, as a whole, the canto does seem to be conceived as an oblique act of retribution against the pope whose corruptions Dante most detested, Boniface VIII. Conversely, in identifying so closely with the priestly eloquence of the protagonist, Dante attracts to himself, by artistic sleight of hand, the authority which the protagonist is here shown to enjoy.

This procedure is entirely in keeping with the theme of Canto XIX: seeing so acutely that the Church has failed to fulfil its historical task, Dante, in an historical and distinctly practical act, proposes himself and his own poem as a remedy.

Yet we shall not realise the full force of that remedy unless we admit that, in allowing so close an identification between poet and *personaggio*, Dante has created as many problems as he has solved. For surely the poet must now share not only the kudos of the *personaggio*, but also the ridicule which surrounds him in his bizarre colloquy. This will certainly be true in the barrators sequence of Cantos XXI and XXII where the *personaggio*, in flight from the devils of the bolgia, cuts a thoroughly ludicrous figure. But here – in a canto which concerns the grounds on which identity and selfhood depend – it is an essential part of Dante's procedure that he should assert his own authority not, as in the *Monarchia*, by a masterful act of professional philosophy, but rather by the creation of a form which subtly admits the ignominies and absurdities to which the self is always subject in the temporal world. Identity is a supremely comic subject – as, in a moral sense, it always must be to the Christian who places his selfhood in the hands of God. But as a poet too Dante must realise now the comedy of his position with especial sharpness: here, as in Canto xviii, his authority rests upon the constantly shifting foundation of fictional constructs and volatile language.

The authority of the canto is inseparable, then, from its comedy; and poetically its principal characteristic is a constant movement from the affirmation of prestige to the acceptance of ridicule. Thus, while Dante twice emphasises the elevation of the speech he addresses to Nicholas – as when he refers to it at line 89 as a chant or 'metro' – it is nonetheless true that he concludes as he began, by drawing attention to its plain absurdity:

> E mentr' io li cantava cotai note,
> o ira o cosci̇enza che 'l mordesse,
> forte spingava con ambo le piote. (118–20)

(And while thus I sang these notes to him, / as if anger or conscience were biting him, / he flailed both his soles.)

Similar effects are to be observed in all the major features of the canto – from the conception of the punishment, to the progress of the narrative, and even to the activity of the poet, whose text at certain moments is made to admit, as we shall see, its own inadequacy.

Consider again the punishment allotted to the simonists. At first view, the upturning of the popes in their wells has simply an effect of anarchic farce. Yet the depth of the comedy here lies not in the anarchy but in the absolute *appropriateness* and unexpected fit of the punishment. So far from there being an absence of meaning here, there is an excess. The submersion of the sinners, one above the other in the wells, is a parodic representation of the Apostolic succession; and similarly the tongues of flame that flicker over the feet of the simonists parody the flames that descended upon the heads of the true Apostles at Whitsuntide. It is, however, the image of the foot itself that, improbably, carries the greatest weight of meaning. In Canto xviii the banal features of physical existence remained resistant to interpretation. But from the moment that Dante describes the simonists as 'miseri seguaci', the act of faithful following – involving the obedience of the foot – is a central issue in the canto. Thus at the climax of his oration the protagonist reproves Nicholas with a reminder of the words which Christ spoke to the first disciples, simply 'Come behind me': 'Viemmi retro' (93).

In this light, it fits exactly that the punishment of the simonist should be located in his feet. This, however, is not to speak simply of a calculated *contrappasso*, but also of that exhilaration at the abundance of meaning which Dante himself expresses when he cries out, in admiration at the wisdom and art of God:

> O somma sapïenza, quanta è l'arte
> che mostri in cielo, in terra e nel mal mondo.   (10–11)

(O highest Wisdom, how great is the art / that you display in heaven, on earth and in the evil world.)

One may add that a consequence of simony is to disallow any such exhilaration. Like the gluttons and avaricious of earlier cantos, the simonists – who have 'made a god of gold and silver' (112) – reduce all things to *one* thing in their single-minded pursuit of wealth, depriving objects of that possibility of significance which, in God's art – or Dante's – even the most trivial things can possess.

In contrast to the simonists, Dante, through his apostrophe to divine art, recognises how small his capacities are in comparison with the infinite possibilities of the 'art' that God can produce. And with this a further phase of the comedy begins, culminating in the first encounter with Nicholas. For while, on the one hand, it clearly is a demonstration of the prestige of the poet that he should enjoy the art of God – and be able to transcribe it into a text of his own – it is equally true that any such appreciation will lay bare his own smallness and incoherence. The narrative now proceeds to emphasise this: at the moment when Dante, urged on by Virgil, is preparing to launch his attack upon Nicholas, he is struck dumb by the greeting he receives:

> Ed el gridò: 'Se' tu già costì ritto,
> se' tu già costì ritto, Bonifazio?
> Di parecchi anni mi mentì lo scritto ...'.
>   Tal mi fec' io, quai son color che stanno,
> per non intender ciò ch'è lor risposto
> quasi scornati e risponder non sanno.   (52–4; 58–60)

(And he cried out: 'Are you already upright there, / are you already upright there, Bonifazio? / By a good few years the writings lied to me ...'. / I became like those who stand, / unable to grasp the answer they have received, / as though mocked and not knowing how to reply.)

Like many another comedy, this is a comedy of mistaken identity. Dante here allows himself to be represented, momentarily, as his own worst enemy; and if Nicholas is caught in the trammels of divine art, so, for an instant, the protagonist is caught in the insane consequences of simony. Suddenly, the primal sacrament of baptism is reversed; the corrupt Church, so far from fulfilling its sacramental function, cannot even use correctly the names that have been given at baptism; and without this God-given sanction the identity of the individual becomes arbitrary and indeterminate.

When Dante arrives at the Earthly Paradise, Beatrice, as the representative of the true Church, receives him with the one utterance of the poet's own name that occurs in the *Commedia*. In the circumstances of the third bolgia, however, the protagonist is quite unable to assert himself directly. The most he can do is follow Virgil's advice and repeat, with the utmost urgency, 'Non son colui, non son colui che credi' (62) – I am not the one, I am not the one that you think. This is a thoroughly Virgilian course to adopt, recalling the definite but modest motif with which Virgil introduced himself in Canto I: 'Non omo, omo già fui.' But it is, significantly, a negative response: '*non* son ... *non* son'. Selfhood here rests upon very insecure foundations. Lacking the sanction of God, the self is an all but insubstantial being – a screen which receives whatever constructions others may put upon it, possessing only an imperfect instrument for self-assertion in the rational but negative language that Virgil recommends. Yet there is another resource, offered by comic art itself. For it is through this art that Dante can grasp the limitations of his own identity; the comedy here is not only a comedy of errors, but also one of recognition.

With this, we come to the third and most complex aspect of the comedy in Canto XIX. Parallel to the depiction of incoherence in the protagonist, the text of the canto is so designed as to admit its own inadequacies as a vehicle for the truth. For this text, of course, is no more than a *written* account of Dante's vision; and that fact represents a limitation in two respects: the true word in this canto is shown to lie not in writing – indeed the one reference to 'lo scritto' accuses it of lying (54); instead, authority must reside either in the energy of a speaking voice or else in the absolute force of the Scriptures. In this canto Dante's text proves inferior to the scriptural text; but writing of any kind is here inferior to speech.

Thus, as we have already seen, the opening of the canto possesses much of the urgency of the speaking voice; and the main feature of the canto is the speech which Dante delivers to Pope Nicholas. However, it is also notable that the language both of the opening *terzine* and of the central speech draws very directly upon the language of the Gospels. Indeed, there is probably no other canto in the *Commedia* which makes such sustained reference to Scripture. It is one of the most surprising features of the transition from Canto XVIII to Canto XIX that Dante should exchanged the ugly triviality of the one for the scriptural simplicity of the other: 'low' language now becomes *sermo humilis*.

So, at line 91, Dante quotes – from St Matthew's Gospel – the words of Christ to the first pope, St Peter:

> quanto tesoro volle
> Nostro Segnore in prima da San Pietro
> ch'ei ponesse le chiavi in sua balìa?
> Certo non chiese se non 'Viemmi retro'.   (90–3)

(How much treasure / did Our Lord ask in the first place of Saint Peter / that he should place the keys in his safe-keeping? / Certainly he demanded no more than 'Follow me'.)

So too the name of Simon Magus in the opening lines is drawn from the Acts of the Apostles, while even where the speech rises to its satirical climax, in picturing the Whore of Babylon, Dante explicitly cites his source, the Book of Revelation: 'Di voi pastor s'accorse il Vangelista' (106). In other cases where the reference is not explicit, it is nonetheless clear that the inspiration for Dante's phrases or rhythms is the imagery or idiom of Scripture:

> ché la vostra avarizia il mondo attrista
> calcando i buoni e sollevando i pravi.   (104–5)

(for your avarice makes the whole world miserable, / stamping upon the good and raising up the bad).

or:

> Fatto v'avete dio d'oro e d'argento.   (112)

(You have made a god for yourself of gold and silver.)

Such lines as these are as impassioned as they are simple. But that too is a reason for their authority. Dante is aware, it seems, of a language of judgement, quite different from the sophisticated language of his own literary constructions, which possesses an obvious and immediate rightness. And here the comedy is that Dante should appeal, beyond the elaborate artifice of judgement which he has created in the canto, to the authority of Christian commonsense. It is self-evidently *wrong* that gold and silver should be transformed into gods; and Dante – vainly, of course – invites a simple and natural moral response from Nicholas with a series of rhetorical questions: 'quanto tesoro volle / Nostro Segnore ...?' (90–1). Likewise, the only immediate escape from the maze of mistaken identity is the unquestionable assertion 'I am not he'.

The natural voice, then, is made the custodian of truths which the written text cannot enforce. And the same conclusion is indicated by the appeal which Dante makes to the authority of the Scriptures. For while the Scriptures are indeed 'written', they are also written pre-eminently as a record of the words that Christ *spoke* to his disciples. Moreover, in these spoken words an ungraspable authority and moral rightness do conspicuously display themselves. St Peter did not need to question Christ; hearing his voice, he simply followed him.

In the effect of Christ's words upon St Peter there is a comedy of absurd – or miraculous – simplicity; and Canto XIX proves finally to offer a defence of such simplicity. In spiritual terms, the paradox is that there would be no authority at all – no rock of the Church nor secure identity – were it not for a willingness on the part of the disciple to abdicate the demands of self, in silent obedience to the voice of Christ. But, poetically, Dante's own text displays a comparable obedience, in the deference it shows to the native power of common speech and Scripture. Thus the authority which Dante now claims rests on different foundations from that which he discovered in the eighteenth canto, when the violent eye asserted its rights. But in both cases Dante arrives at a position beyond the reach of rational control, through a readiness to acknowledge the limitations and insufficiencies of the medium in which he has chosen to work.

This is not, however, to suggest that rationality – or for that matter, the everyday view of the integrity of the self – has no importance here. The final moments of Canto xix are marked by a comedy very different in tone from the farce of the central sequence in which Dante defines the continuing significance of Virgil.

Though Virgil has been silent throughout the central episode of the canto – as is understandable when the point at issue concerns the perversions and mysterious resources of the Christian Church – it is, for all that, he who first urged Dante to speak. And now the protagonist goes back to Virgil. He returns from the ridiculous and embarrassingly exposed position which he had adopted in addressing Nicholas, to be greeted with an embrace of almost extravagant vigour. The master has viewed the performance of his pupil with warmth and even complacency:

> con sì contenta labbia sempre attese
> lo suon de le parole vere espresse.   (122–3)

(He listened carefully, with satisfaction on his lips, / to the sound of the words of truth that I uttered.)

And now Virgil enfolds the protagonist in his arms to carry him onwards:

> Però con ambo le braccia mi prese;
> e poi che tutto su mi s'ebbe al petto,
> rimontò per la via onde discese.   (124–6)

(And so he took me in both his arms, / and when he had me firmly upon his breast, / he went up again by the road he had come down.)

No words are spoken here by the master of words. But the physical embrace is itself significant in a canto dominated hitherto by the image of a grotesquely inverted human form. The comedy is, in the gentlest sense, a comedy of recognition: we are asked to recognise in Virgil not a power of rational argument, but a prevailing normality, a presence which expresses itself in acts of physical concern and straightforward kindness. This normality may be open to question, for it cannot take account of the disconcerting realities which lie beneath its own surface. So in Cantos xxi and xxii Dante will return to his vision of the fragility of his own selfhood. But here the 'obviousness' of Virgil's humanity is itself acknowledged as a support and source of sanity. In Canto xx, which concentrates more closely upon Virgil than any other canto of the *Inferno*, Dante proceeds to investigate further the value and limits of such normality.

IV

The nineteenth canto closes with a contrast between distortion and normality, in regard both to the physical identity of the individual and to the pattern of human relationships; and this same contrast is explored still further in the opening phase of the twentieth canto.

First, the punishment suffered in the fourth bolgia, though deceptively simple, involves an even greater distortion of physical form than the punishment of the simonists. As Dante and Virgil enter the bolgia, they see a solemn procession, moving around the circle at the slow pace which 'a litany takes in this world' (xx 9). No other group of sinners since the pagans of Limbo have been credited with such composure; and we shall wait until the opening cantos of the *Purgatorio* for any comparable picture. But here the litany is not actually being sung as it will be in the *Purgatorio*; the sinners proceed in silence save for their weeping: 'tacendo e lagrimando' (8). Indeed none of them speaks at all in the course of the canto. Throughout, the human figure remains an object for the eye to rest upon. And as Dante concentrates his gaze upon the procession, he realises that the sinners are in fact hideously misshapen: their heads have been turned round on their shoulders as if by some preternatural paralysis (17), so that, as they march forward, with eyes to the front, their heels travel foremost and their tears 'bathe the cleft in their buttocks' (24). At this unnatural sight, the protagonist weeps tears of natural pity; and the poet invites his reader to join in that pity, at seeing our image, close to, so distorted: 'la nostra imagine di presso ... sì torta' (22–3).

It is important, as we shall see, not to underestimate the painfulness of this vision, in which, despite a semblance of normality, all integrity is denied to the human form. It is also important to recognise that, in Virgil's eyes at least, the punishment deserves no pity whatsoever; in his view it should be regarded quite dispassionately as an instance of retributive justice. The sinners here were all soothsayers or magicians; and, commenting on the case of Amphiaraus, Virgil offers a brusque rationale for the suffering that they now endure:

> Mira c'ha fatto petto de le spalle;
> perché volse veder troppo davante,
> di retro guarda e fa retroso calle.   (xx 37–9)

(Behold how he has made a breast of his shoulders; / because he desired to see too far forward, / he now looks behind and makes his way backwards.)

Virgil, then, implicitly insists that there are limits which the human mind cannot properly transgress. This notion bears directly upon the sinners in the present circle, who have all used their minds in absurd attempts to command the future. But it is also important as a preparation for later cantos of the Malebolge, where, in particular, Ulysses in Canto xxvi will be shown to disregard the natural boundaries of human inquiry. Beyond that too Virgil anticipates his own words at *Purgatorio* iii 37: human beings should content themselves with asking questions about the world as it actually *is*; and not aspire to know what, logically, they cannot know.

Virgil's judgement, then, has a relevance to the future of Dante's poem. At the same time it serves to link Canto xx in theme to earlier cantos of the Malebolge. Dante will be concerned throughout the canto with the way in which the mind is used in acts of prophecy, which is to say he is concerned with the *relationships* that the mind can establish between the present and the future, the temporal and the eternal, the natural and the supernatural. In some way, the soothsayers have perverted the course of these relationships; they are thus fit company for the seducers, who pervert the relationship between man and woman, and the simonists, who practise upon the relationship between God and humanity. But in *what* way, specifically?

In pursuing this question, Dante is led, in Canto xx, to draw a complex set of distinctions between true and false prophecy, and between the various forms that true prophecy may take. Considering that the *Commedia* itself is avowedly a prophetic work, this canto, like its two immediate predecessors, will clearly have something to say about the grounds of authority on which Dante himself must rest his case. Yet for most of the canto attention is focused upon the figure of Virgil. Virgil, too, is a prophet, the author of the fourth Eclogue and the sixth book of the *Aeneid*. However, in the Middle Ages, he also had a reputation as a magician and soothsayer; and where, in Canto xix, Dante was concerned to vindicate his own moral reputation, representing himself as a true 'priest' – 'ch'ogn' omo sganni' (xix 21) – so Virgil is allowed to speak obliquely in his own defence, and distinguish himself from such perverse figures of the classical world as Tiresias, Aruns and Manto. This canto, like the Limbo canto, represents an investigation of pagan culture. It recognises, as the Limbo canto does not, the stupidity of which even the pagan world was capable; it also gives a richer account than any other canto in the *Commedia* of why Dante chose Virgil as his guide. Since that choice represents one of the most crucial decisions that Dante took in writing the *Commedia*, it is impossible that he should reconsider Virgil's case without reflecting upon the principles of his own intellectual procedure. So, in the course of his analysis, Dante is led to a distinction, not only between false and true prophets but also between the position which Virgil, as a pagan, is obliged to adopt and that which he himself can assume by virtue of his Christianity. If, then, we return to the opening of the canto, we shall see at once that Dante displays an especially acute consciousness of his own art, and this will lead us eventually to modify our original view of Virgil's pronouncement upon the sinners.

In the opening *terzina* Dante displays an almost pedantic interest in the numerical plan of the *Commedia*:

> Di nova pena mi coven far versi
> e dar matera al ventesimo canto
> de la prima canzon, ch'è d'i sommersi.   (1–3)

(Of new pain I have now to make my verse, / and find a subject for the twentieth canto / of the first of the cantiche, which concerns those sunk to the depths.)

Dante here takes stock of his own poem in a tone of neutral calculation (rather as Virgil is made to speak so coolly of the punishment of the soothsayers). But then, in complete contrast, a second instance of poetic self-awareness occurs, expressed, however, in immediate and moving terms. For in registering the pity which the sight of the sinners inspires, Dante turns to the reader and seeks to enlist their passionate sympathy:

> Se Dio ti lasci, lettor, prender frutto
> di tua lezione, or pensa per te stesso
> com' io potea tener lo viso asciutto,
>   quando la nostra imagine di presso
> vidi sì torta ...   (19–23)

(So God may grant you, reader, that you gather fruit / from your reading, now think for yourself / whether I could have kept my countenance dry / when I saw close at hand the image of humanity / so turned askew.)

At one moment, Dante displays an overall grasp of the plan of the *Commedia*, at the next, descending to the emotions of the moment, he shows himself to be profoundly disturbed by the *details* which the execution of the plan requires him to conceive, to the extent that he interrupts the steady progress of the narrative and even suggests that the real profit or 'frutto' of the *Commedia* is available only to those who share his emotion.

It is at this point that the distinction between Dante and Virgil begins to reveal itself. For Virgil now reprimands the protagonist for the same emotion which Dante, as author, recommends to his own reader; indeed Virgil nowhere speaks more acerbically:

> Ancor se' tu de li altri sciocchi?
> Qui vive la pietà quand' è ben morta;
> chi è più scellerato che colui
> che al giudicio divin passion comporta?   (27–30)

(Are you then still like the other fools? / Here pity lives when it is truly dead. / Who is more wicked than one / who cannot tolerate the judgement of God?)

At first sight, of course, Virgil has good reason for his reprimand. By now, it might be supposed, the protagonist is sufficiently accustomed to the sights of Hell not to give way to pity. Moreover, Virgil seems simply to affirm the authority of divine judgement: the soothsayers repine at the divine dispensation – 'passion comporta' – and the protagonist will be little better than they are if he cannot tolerate the punishment decreed for such sinners. As in his cold account of the *contrappasso* allotted to the sinners, so here Virgil appears to be acting as the guardian of the plan of Hell and as spokesman for the scheme of damnation.

Yet in the end it is Virgil, not Dante, who is here the false prophet. Certainly he fails to diagnose the nature of Dante's pity, and misapprehends the position which Dante after all recommends to his reader: Dante does *not* say that he is weeping for the sinners themselves; rather he weeps to see the image of humanity in its bodily nature so tormented and turned awry.

Though the twentieth canto offers an apology for Virgil, Dante's opening move is to reveal a number of essential limitations in Virgil's authority. In the first place, Virgil fails to recognise the supreme importance of 'nostra imagine'. He could, of course, hardly be expected to recognise it. For it is a distinctive feature of Christian philosophy – and of Christian prophecy – to declare the enduring significance of the physical nature which human beings will enjoy at the Resurrection. As we have seen, the first doctrinal statement in the *Inferno* at Canto vi concerned the Resurrection; and in Canto xx, the protagonist – weeping at the offence which the punishment gives to the sanctity of the the human form – begins a series of references to the value of bodily nature which culminates, in Canto xxiv, in a horrified vision of human individuals transformed into serpents.

So, tragically, the pagan Virgil is blind to the true nature of Dante's pity and must yield to a prophet who, rightly, appeals over his head to the sympathies of the Christian reader. There is, however, a further limitation in the very clarity and firmness with which Virgil utters his reproach. For to oppose Dante's pity in such categorical terms, and to insist so rigorously upon the rightness of the *contrappasso*, is to deny a certain subtlety and responsiveness of emotion which by now have begun to occupy an important place in his own relationship with the protagonist. The cutting edge of his judgement in Canto xx grates against the more delicate and particular spirit which he has evoked, at the end of the previous canto, by his silent gesture of solidarity.

There is, then, an attempt at logical mastery in Virgil's words which, even if it were justified, might be less valuable than his earlier assertion of ordinary human decency. And precisely in making this attempt, it is Virgil, not Dante, who – momentarily – should be grouped with the false prophets and soothsayers. For their sin – expressing discontent not so much with God as with the normal disposition of the world – likewise represents an attempt at mastery in which the sinner exerts his mind against the limits imposed upon it by physical and temporal nature. We shall see, of course, as soon as Virgil begins his main speech, that he is no true associate of the soothsayers. The fact remains that, if Virgil is the custodian of law and the *contrappasso*, it is Dante, as poet, who now acts as the champion of moderation and decency; and indeed the principal indication of this is that, for most of the canto, Dante's concern is to celebrate in Virgil the very qualities of simple 'character' which Virgil would be unable to recognise in himself. So, at the conclusion of the canto there occurs a moment of humane comedy which exactly parallels the conclusion of Canto xix. Among the procession of sooth-sayers, Virgil notes the presence of one Euripilus. As Virgil says, with modest vagueness, Euripilus appears among the minor figures in the *dramatis personae* of the *Aeneid*. But the author of the *Aeneid* has forgotten exactly *where*, and must rely upon his assiduous disciple to identify the reference:

> Euripilo ebbe nome, e così 'l canta
> l'alta mia tragedìa in alcun loco:
> ben lo sai tu che la sai tutta quanta.   (112–14)

(His name was Euripilus; and so sings / in some place my high tragedy: / you certainly will know where, for you know as much of the work as there is.)

At this moment, the *Aeneid* is less important as a proof of Virgil's intellectual prowess than as an occasion for the play of respect and good humour between master and pupil. Thus the canto finally draws attention once again to the presence and voice of Virgil. Let us also note that hitherto Virgil's stance in the canto has been distinctly that of the literary man and author of a great text; his account of the prophets and mages of antiquity inevitably draws very heavily upon the authorities of classical mythology. And this would seem unexceptionable were it not that here – as in Canto XIX – Dante appears to admit the primacy of the spoken word over the written: his own address to the reader breaks the frame of the text in an approximation to speech; the natural voice, it seems, rather than the authoritative tome, is the proper medium for prophecy. (And what else would one expect from an author who chose so deliberately to write his prophetic comedy in the vernacular?)

As we turn, then, to the central speech of the canto, we should expect, certainly, to find grounds for a distinction between Virgil's procedure as a prophet and the practices of which the sinners here were guilty. At the same time, we should also expect that Dante will pursue his critique of Virgil's position. This is not to detract from the celebration of Virgil; in subjecting his maestro, if not to ridicule, then to close scrutiny, Dante behaves towards him only as he behaves towards *himself* in the cantos which precede and follow Canto XX.

Virgil begins his speech with an urgent demand that the protagonist should raise his bowed head and observe the procession of magicians as it passes before him: 'Drizza la testa, drizza e vedi ...' (31) – raise your head, raise it and see. In fact Dante has already observed the details of the punishment with appalling sharpness, in his realistic image of paralysis; and in the event Virgil does not, as he speaks, achieve any clearer focus. On the contrary, his words rather distract attention from the present case of the sinners to their mythological past; Virgil, in effect, presents to the protagonist a series of snippets from classical legend which become increasingly fascinating for their own sake. Even his earlier punctilious references to the *contrappasso* are outweighed by the fabulous attractions of the narrative.

Thus, two highly Ovidian *terzine* are devoted to a sensational change, suffered by Tiresias from man to woman – and no mention is made of his present transformation in Hell. Likewise, in the case of Aruns, where the *contrappasso* is mentioned, the punishment seems to have no more moral content than it would have if it were a piece of Ovidian perversity:

> Aronta è quel ch'al ventre il s'atterga,
> che ne' monti di Luni, dove ronca
> lo Carrarese che di sotto alberga ...   (46–8)

(Aruns is he who holds his back to the belly [of Tiresias] / [Aruns] who in the mountains of Luni, where hoes / the Carrarese who lodges beneath ...)

All in all, the list of soothsayers that Virgil offers does nothing to extract the essence of the moral condition which the image of the procession promises to display. It might have been otherwise, for, viewed in the context of Canto XIX, Dante is still as concerned as he was in that canto to picture a history of progressive decadence; parallel to the perversion of the Apostolic tradition, Dante here adumbrates a more primitive perversion, by virtue of which human beings throughout the ages have sought – ironically enough – to command history and conflate the present with the future. But Virgil's list, so far from bringing out this pessimistic view, has an epic sonority to it and makes studied, if silent, reference to three authors from the classical tradition – Lucan, Statius and Ovid – who occupied a place of particular importance in Dante's mind. Each of these authors contributes one story to the collection which Virgil here constructs; and one might well be inclined to examine how pagan magicians are held in counterpoint throughout the passage with pagan poets, as if the civilised art of poetry had the power to subsume and dominate the atavistic spirit of superstition. Virgil speaks as the voice of an urbane tradition in which the barbarities of magic have become the subject, merely, of compelling narrative. But there is a danger in this that Virgil should veil the full danger of superstition in a cloak of literary glamour. When Dante himself in Canto xxv makes direct and explicit use of Lucan and Ovid, it will be to emphasise (as he does elsewhere in his use of Statius) that he, in *his* prophetic vision, must face far greater horrors than the classical poets could ever conceive.

The weakness in Virgil's narrative approach is compatible with his earlier insistence upon divine judgement. His tendency is to distract attention away from the complexity of the particular instance to a more remote consideration of, in the one case, a general law and, in the other, a legendary exemplar; we need not stress that such a procedure is consistent with his management of myth in, say, Canto XIV of the *Inferno*.

At the same time, such a procedure displays a strength as well as a weakness. For, increasingly, the interest of his speech comes to reside in its powerful description of temporal geography. So the account of Aruns – marching grotesquely in the confinement of the bolgia – becomes an evocative piece of landscape poetry, in which Virgil finds occasion to describe the mountains where Aruns lived in his earthly existence:

> Aronta è quel ch'al ventre li s'atterga,
> che ne' monti di Luni, dove ronca
> lo Carrarese che di sotto alberga,
>   ebbe tra ' bianchi marmi la spelonca
> per sua dimora; onde a guardar le stelle
> e 'l mar non li era la veduta tronca.   (46–51)

(Aruns is he who holds his back to the belly of the other. / In the mountains of Luni – where hoes the Carrarese who lodges beneath – / he had a cave [for his dwelling] among the white marble; / [his view,] looking out from that to the stars / and the sea, was not interrupted.)

In Canto XVIII, Virgil's account of Jason and Hypsiphile introduced a similar naturalness into the squalor of the Malebolge. And now the value of such 'naturalness' is confirmed by the dominance it assumes in the central part of Virgil's present speech – which concerns the founding of Mantua.

It is in this passage – directly following the account of Aruns's habitation – that Virgil may be said to offer his defence against the charge of sorcery. For the point of his allusion to Mantua is to insist that his native city did *not* owe its foundation to the witch Manto. The city – along with its citizens – carries no such sinister taint; its origins were entirely comprehensible, an expression simply of economic – one might say 'ecological' – motives and pressures. Thus the defence begins with a lengthy picture of the landscape of Lombardy – a landscape animated not by magic, but rather by the vital waters which gather in the lakes and marshes around Mantua:

> Suso in Italia bella giace un laco,
> a piè de l'Alpe che serra Lamagna
> sovra Tiralli, c'ha nome Benaco.
> Per mille fonti, credo, e più si bagna
> tra Garda e Val Camonica e Pennino
> de l'acqua che nel detto laco stagna.
> Loco è nel mezzo là dove 'l trentino
> pastore e quel di Brescia e 'l veronese
> segnar poria, s'e' fesse quel cammino.   (61–9)

(High in lovely Italy there lies a lake, / at the foot of the mountains that lock in Germany / over the Tyrol: the name of that lake is Benaco. / [Appennino] is bathed, I suppose, by more than a thousand springs / between Garda and Val Camonica, / by the water that settles in the lake there; / and in the middle is a place where the [pastors of] Trent / and Brescia and Verona / might all give their blessing if they went that way.)

As Virgil goes on to explain, the marshes around Mantua offered an excellent natural defence, which was why Manto, fleeing from Thebes, chose to stop there. And if others joined her, they were moved by a recognition of Manto's strategic sense, not by any cult of her magical powers:

> Li uomini poi che 'ntorno erano sparti
> s'accolsero a quel loco, ch'era forte
> per lo pantan ch'avea da tutte parti.
> ...
> e per colei che 'l loco prima elesse,
> Mantüa l'appellar sanz' altra sorte.   (88-90; 92-3)

(Men who had been scattered in the region around / then gathered in that place, which was strong / because of the marsh lying all around it / ... And from her who first chose the place, / they called it Mantua without any other augury.)

The city which thus grew up is thus named after Manto, but not because of her magical powers. With characteristic modesty, then, Virgil has set himself to defend the honour of his *patria*. But in doing so he reveals – whether he intends to or not – the qualities and intellectual interests which distinguish him, as a prophet, from the false prophets of the bolgia and recommend him, as a poet, to the poet of the *Commedia*. The speech is a celebration of the natural world and of the ability which human beings possess to make a home for themselves within that world. On Virgil's showing, there is no need for magicians to seek perverse and unnatural solutions; the prophet's task is to clarify the courses which human beings can follow within their natural limits. Thus, in one aspect, the landscape which Virgil depicts here is the idyllic landscape of the *Eclogues* – the poems in which Virgil, for Dante, would have demonstrated his prophetic powers most clearly. Yet it is also a landscape in which men work and plan their lives as they do in the *Georgics*, by harnessing the opportunities that their environment presents. And, finally, it is a landscape in which refugees can defend themselves and rebuild their lives, as the Trojans of the *Aeneid* continually seek to do.

In the context of that most bizarre of landscapes, the Malebolge, there can be no doubt of the value of Virgil's position; his 'loco è' here at line 67 announces a geographical actuality where Dante's own 'Luogo è in inferno detto Malebolge' is the product of a mind which is almost dizzy with its own fictions. Moreover – in marked contrast to the sinners of the Malebolge – Virgil is able to ascribe meaning and solidity to the objects of the world. The flatterers and seducers evade the real world with their lies; the simonists deprive all objects of sacramental meaning by their blinkered pursuit of riches. As for the sorcerers, their offence is now revealed – in a way which their punishment has already suggested – as an offence against that deeply vigorous normality which Virgil here defends.

In the Earthly Paradise, as we have seen in Chapter 3, Virgil – along with other poets of antiquity – is praised by Matelda for having dreamed of a golden world and kept alive in his verses a belief in the possible perfection of nature. That belief is justified by the Earthly Paradise; and, by the same token, the classical poet is justified as a true prophet. Yet in the Earthly Paradise Virgil is also taken suddenly from Dante's side. And, in conclusion, we must stress again that in Canto xx the awareness of Virgil's value is constantly accompanied by an awareness of his limitations. For however valuable Virgil's speech may be as a relief from the distresses of the Malebolge, it is also, precisely in being a relief, a distraction. Indeed it is notable that even in his picture of the Lombard landscape, Virgil's words conceal or gloss over tensions and tragedies for which that landscape itself is a backdrop. So the Veronese fortress at Peschiera – set up against the infractions of the Brescians and Bergamaschi – is said to be a 'bello e forte arnese', as if it were more important to Virgil as a picturesque feature than as a sign of strife. Likewise, the account of Manto, daughter of the Theban seer Tiresias, makes no mention of the wild and rooted corruptions of that city which – as Virgil, in fact, does acknowledge – was the sacred city of Bacchus. Virgil's words are a shield against such considerations, and valuable in being so; but they are also a veil drawn over them.

There are, however, two poets who know how to pierce this veil. One of these is Statius, to whom Virgil tacitly alludes in the Manto sequence; and

we have already seen that Dante associates Statius with a peculiarly intense
awareness not of human potential, but of human decadence. The view of
what is 'normal' in humanity must include that perception. The second poet
at work here – Dante himself – is about to give his own account of 'Thebes'
in the trivial but anarchic farce that ensues in Cantos XXI and XXII. There
comedy, in the harshest sense, will be needed to picture the total disorder
which follows upon the corruption of good government.

As for Canto XX, it ends on a note of quiet comedy, in which Virgil does
go some way towards recognising the ingrained perversity of the human
mind, while still maintaining his own characteristic good measure and
temperateness.

At line 100, the protagonist, though thanking Virgil for his lengthy
ragionamenti, insists that they should return to the matter in hand by looking
in closer detail at the individuals who make up the procession:

> Ma dimmi, de la gente che procede,
> se tu ne vedi alcun degno di nota;
> ché solo a ciò la mia mente rifiede.   (103–5)

(But tell me – of the people passing before us / if you see any worthy of note; / for to
that alone my mind reverts.)

This stands almost as an equivalent of Virgil's earlier reproach to the
protagonist. The latter now insists that seeing must finally outweigh all
discourse, and Virgil's response is not altogether satisfactory on that score.
What he does offer, however, is a composed and mildly comic survey of how
the ambition to attain magical powers has obsessed all sorts and conditions of
human beings throughout the ages – distracting them from their natural
relationships and occupations, so that life becomes a trivial joke at the mercy
of 'magiche frode'.

So, one of the procession is the obscure and unnamed augur who assisted
Calchas in forwarding the Trojan War. But in the same rank as this heroic or
legendary figure, there is the rather Chaucerian cobbler Asdente, 'giving up
leather and string' (119) for wizardry. And, finally, there are the women –
again unnamed – who have preferred to make spells 'with herbs and images'
(122–4) rather than stay at home with needle and thread. In each case,
Virgil's comedy communicates a resigned recognition of just how normal it
is for human beings to abandon their normal courses.

V

The twentieth canto is plainly a narrative pause between the comic action of
Canto XIX and the farce of Cantos XXI and XXII. In this respect, it is compar-
able to the eleventh canto, in which also Virgil is the dominant figure. And,
like Canto XI, Canto XX stands as a point of reference, defining some of the
essential features of Dante's plan and procedure in the *Inferno*. For while the
canto does not, of course, offer a categorical account of sin in the way that

Canto xi does, Dante nonetheless draws together and charges with fresh meaning a number of themes and images which are hidden at a secondary level of the text in the Malebolge. So we shall see, in the sequence from Canto xxiv to Canto xxvii, a continuing interest in the dignity of physical nature and a continuing concern to define the proper action of the mind within the limits of that nature. Virgil's words express – on Dante's behalf – a promise not only of intellectual, but also of imaginative, coherence.

At the same time, a mind which is fully to realise such coherence must also be prepared to recognise, as the 'prophet' Dante does, that the suggestions and images on which it feeds are not in themselves final realities and may be disordered by the very reality – of a transcendent God in relation to the mystery of sin – which sanctioned their use in the first place. That, from the first, has been the sense of the relationship between Virgil and Beatrice; and it is from the same source that the difficulties of Dante himself descend. The plan which the poet has conceived – on both an intellectual and an imaginative plane – must be pursued in acts of critical analysis, and sustained in the face of the contradictions which the analysis itself produces. So in the case of the central image of Canto xx – which is Virgil himself – the full meaning and identity of Virgil is grasped only through a willingness to look beyond the obvious import of his words, granting as much significance to his tone and gesture as to his deliberate statements. Moreover, if the canto does represent an apology for Virgil, then this apology is effective only because it honestly admits to a critical awareness of Virgil's limitations.

But, of course, Dante's main purpose in the *Commedia* is to apply a similar analysis to himself in a continuing process of criticism and celebration. The culmination of this process is the meeting – both painful and triumphant – with Beatrice in the Earthly Paradise. However, on the way to Beatrice there are few more powerful instances of Dante's procedure than Cantos xxi and xxii. Here Dante brings to light the questions which have been held in abeyance during Virgil's discourse, and starkly confronts the contradictions located both in his own historical identity and in the literary identity which in the *Commedia* he has set himself to construct.

Thus, in the first place, the sin which Dante considers in these cantos is one which, historically, was of peculiar concern to him. It is the sin of barratry, or corruption in public offices. But, as Dante presents it, this sin is not only the source of all disorder in the social life, but also the offence for which he himself was exiled from Florence. One supposes that the charges against him were false; and in one respect the purpose of these cantos is clearly to represent the chaos – of which Dante himself was a victim – that ensues when the leaders of a society devote themselves to the pursuit of self-interest. Thus Dante's attention falls more upon the rulers and guardians of the fifth bolgia – as if the bolgia itself were a model of corrupt society – than upon the sinners who are confined within it. But these rulers are actually devils, a 'fiera compagnia' organised according to military rank. And what

follows reads like a premonition of totalitarian violence. The consequence of
dishonesty in public office is an abdication of humane concern; relationship –
a theme in all of the previous bolge – is utterly eroded, and ultimately the
human being becomes not merely an object, as it was to the seducer or the
flatterer, but the passive token in a heartless game. So power decays into
violence; and some of the most vivid moments of the sequence are those in
which the devils act like brutal police-guards towards their prisoners:

> E Libicocco 'Troppo avem sofferto',
> disse; e preseli 'l braccio col runciglio,
> sì che, stracciando, ne portò un lacerto.   (xxii 70–2)

(And Libicocco said 'We have endured too much'. / And he grabbed his arm with his
hook, / so that, in tearing it, he carried away a muscle.)

Overall, Dante offers in these cantos not only a picture of violence, but
also an extended account of the effect of dishonesty and downright lying in
dissolving the bonds of trust between one person and another. So the
sequence ends with the malicious misdirections that the devils give to the
two travellers; and Dante comes to a conclusion in Canto xxiii with the
realisation that the devil is the very 'father of lies' (xxiii 144). Considering
that the main effect of social disorder upon Dante himself was to make him
the subject of false accusations, this emphasis is understandable. Yet the
striking thing is that, in writing the sequence, Dante makes no explicit
attempt to clear his own name. We have seen in Canto xix how Dante could
use the *Commedia* as an instrument in his own defence. Here, however, he
makes no direct appeal to his reader. On the contrary, the picture which
Dante presents of himself is not only ludicrous but also ambiguous; the
protagonist is in constant danger of being assailed by the devils, even when
Virgil insists that God has sanctioned his journey through Hell (xxi 79–84),
and when the devils threaten to hook him in the rump (xxi 101), the position
of the protagonist is all but identical with those who are justly punished for
barratry in the bolgia.

If, in earlier cantos, Dante makes it especially difficult to see, for instance,
the guilt of Francesca, in Cantos xxi and xxii, he makes it equally difficult
for the reader to perceive his own innocence. Indeed it is, as we shall find, a
property of Dante's art in this canto that he should use it to obscure and
erode the commonsense view which might readily have absolved him. But
from this point of view the sequence calls into question not only Dante's
historical integrity, but also the literary integrity of the *Commedia* itself.
There are indeed times in these two cantos when the art of the poet seems
positively devoted to the service of untruth. The extraordinary vivacity and
imaginative force of the fiction threaten frequently to distract from the moral
issue; the techniques which Dante characteristically adopts here are designed,
it appears, rather to release than to control an anarchic energy.

The last *terzina* of Canto XX had insisted, as we should expect, upon the moderating influence of natural processes, and had drawn a connection between these processes and the plan of Dante's journey through Hell. As if to assure Dante that there is an underlying rightness to his visionary journey, Virgil points out that the protagonist must not spend another night in Hell:

> e già iernotte fu la luna tonda:
> ben ten de' ricordar, ché non ti nocque
> alcuna volta per la selva fonda.   (XX 127–9)

(And last night already the moon was round. / You must remember that well, for it was not unhelpful to you / sometimes in the deep wood.)

In a similar vein, Canto XXI opens with an emphasis upon the steady progress of the travellers:

> Così di ponte in ponte, altro parlando
> che la mia comedìa cantar non cura,
> venimmo ...   (XXI 1–3)

(So from bridge to bridge we went on, speaking of things / which do not concern my comedy; / and we came ...)

The travellers are moving calmly over the scheme of bridges provided for their journey; the apparent ease of their command is stressed by the phrase 'altro parlando': a bond of common interest exists between them which evokes from beyond the confines of the absurd journey – or the 'comic' text which describes it – the voice of ordinary humanity. But then suddenly the singularity of Hell, and the demands of Dante's infernal vision, reassert themselves. And there is a strong sense that, so far from making progress, Dante has to return here to the desperate condition of *Inferno* I, translating his distress into an even darker key than it originally had. Already at the end of Canto XX, Virgil had recalled the origins of Dante's journey in the Dark Wood; and at Canto XXI line 84 – as he parleys for Dante's safe-conduct with the devils – he will insist that it is Dante's destiny to go unscathed through the wild and *wooded* way of Hell – through 'questo cammin silvestro'. There is much else in this sequence – dominated as it is by a representation of frenetic and cruel activity – to suggest that Dante deliberately reanimates the experiences of loss and distraction which inspired the first sixty lines of *Inferno* I.

After the Virgilian excursus of Canto XX into the natural landscape of Lombardy, Dante and the reader must realise anew that they are still caught in the fantasy of the Malebolge. So the name 'Malebolge' is here repeated, displacing at once the names of actual locations which had dominated Virgil's litany:

> restammo per veder l'altra fessura
> di Malebolge e li altri pianti vani;
> e vidila mirabilmente oscura.   (4–6)

(we stopped to see into the other fissure / of Malebolge and the next pointless tears; / and wonderfully dark we saw it.)

It is the phrase 'mirabilmente oscura' that provides the first indication of how corrosive Dante will now allow his text to be. For not only does the line introduce an emphasis upon darkness which the poet will here develop with great imaginative vigour; it also admits an ironic play upon a term which is of central importance in Dante's intellectual lexicon – the word *mirabile*. The word tells emphatically of wonder and contemplative admiration; Beatrice is the true object of wonder from the *Vita nuova* onwards, while Paradise will be described as '*mirabil* primavera'. But in that case to speak of darkness and negation as 'wonderful' is to infect an adjective normally reserved for moments of utter simplicity and brilliance with a perverse complexity.

The text has already begun to prove delusive, and a detailed examination of the long simile which Dante now introduces will indicate how deep this delusiveness can go:

> Quale ne l'arzanà de' Viniziani
> bolle l'inverno la tenace pece
> a rimpalmare i legni lor non sani,
>   ché navicar non ponno – in quella vece
> chi fa suo legno novo e chi ristoppa
> le coste a quel che più vïaggi fece;
>   chi ribatte da proda e chi da poppa;
> altri fa remi e altri volge sarte;
> chi terzeruolo e artimon rintoppa –:
>   tal, non per foco ma per divin' arte,
> bollia là giuso una pegola spessa,
> che 'nviscava la ripa d'ogne parte.   (7–18)

(As in the Arsenal of the Venetians / the clinging pitch boils in winter / to caulk the timbers of unsound ships – / for they cannot at that time put to sea – so that instead / some build for themselves new ships, some repair / the ribs of a ship which has already made many voyages; / some hammer at the prow, some at the stern; / others make oars while others still twist ropes; / some patch the jib and mainsail; / so, not by fire but by the art of God, / a thick pitch boils down there, / which glued up the bank on either side.)

The first effect of this simile is to interrupt the narrative – as if to master the disruptive wonder of the darkness with a display of authorial virtuosity. The image has an evidently epic dimension to it; and in that respect it is comparable to the simile which opens Canto XXII, where Dante compares the 'fiera compagnia' of devils to a band of chivalric knights asserting their victory over a conquered countryside and engaging in triumphant tournaments 'con trombe ... con campane, / con tamburi e con cenni di castella' (XXII 7–9). But this is mock-epic; as Dante says, this is precisely what the troop of devils was *not* like, and at the end of Canto XXI, the signal for the troop to move is the trumpet-call of their leader's backside:

> ma prima avea ciascun la lingua stretta
> coi denti, verso lor duca, per cenno;
> ed elli avea del cul fatto trombetta.   (XXI 137–9)

(But each of them first grasped his tongue between / his teeth, pointing towards their leader, as a sign. / And he made a trumpet of his rear.)

In the Arsenal image the mockery is more insidious. Indeed, in some respects, the simile makes a positive contribution to the development of Dante's themes. Certainly, the mockery does not reside in the realism with which the factory-work is described. That, in itself, has a positive function: it sustains the concern with the dignity of natural activity and prepares for a number of similar 'work' images in Cantos XXIII–XXV. Moreover, the picture of purposeful labour which is given here provides a criterion by which to assess the destructive practices of the barrators and the inane malignancy of the devils in this bolgia. Where barratry amounts to a travesty of common endeavour, this image offers a picture of how productive individuals can be when each performs his appropriate task: 'chi ribatte da proda e chi da poppa ... chi terzeruolo e artimon rintoppa'. Finally, one notes that the common task is one which brings its participants into harmony with the movement of the seasons and reminds them constantly of broader horizons. There is no alienation in this factory; its craftsmen are working through the winter so that, in the spring, their ships can set out again with healthy keels on the open seas.

In itself, then, the description of the Arsenal represents a moment of thematic synthesis. Yet, as Dante attaches vehicle to tenor, all the work *he* has done in constructing the simile proves futile and disproportionate. For this whole scene of varied activity has been created to define a single detail: the blackness of the pitch in which the barrators are submerged is identical to that of the pitch used in the Venetian Arsenal. And this one detail generates suggestions wholly at odds with the prevailing implications of the simile itself; the viscosity of the pitch – 'che 'nviscava la ripa d'ogne parte' (18) – is a reversal of all the previous display of lithe skill, and the reversal is even more decisive as Dante continues:

> I' vedea lei, ma non vedëa in essa
> mai che le bolle che 'l bollor levava,
> e gonfiar tutta, e riseder compressa.   (19–21)

(This I saw, but saw nothing in it / except the bubbles which the bubbling raised, / and all swelling and falling back compressed.)

Now, Dante is not even concerned with the tactile and visual qualities of the pitch; rather – returning to the paradox of 'mirabilmente oscura' – he seeks to grasp a substantial nothingness, a black emptiness, a tautological bubbling of bubbles out of bubbles.

The effect, then, of the initial image is not to establish authorial control at all, but to cheat – through an effect of disproportion – the attention that the reader has paid to it.

The poet is here manipulating his reader. And if this sounds an unlikely practice for an author of Dante's gravity, consider the following passage from the *Paradiso*, which in this respect is similar (though different in every other respect). At the opening of *Paradiso* Canto XIII, Dante wishes to describe how he is surrounded, in the Heaven of the Sun, by a circle of dancing lights – the souls of the Christian philosophers. Eighteen lines are spent in comparing these souls to stars, gathered from every region of the natural sky so as to give some approximate indication of luminosity and vigour:

> Imagini, chi bene intender cupe
> quel ch'i' or vidi – e ritegna l'image,
> mentre ch'io dico, come ferma rupe –,
>   quindici stelle che 'n diverse plage
> lo cielo avvivan di tanto sereno
> che soperchia de l'aere ogne compage ...   (*Par.* XIII 1–6)

(Let anyone who wishes to understand aright / [what I now saw,] imagine – and retain the image / while I speak like a steady rock – / fifteen of those stars which in various parts / enliven the sky with such clarity / that it overcomes all the dense weave of the air.)

Yet at the end of this passage – which is too long to quote in full – Dante confesses that the expense of imagination has produced only a shadow of the truth – indeed it is barely even that:

> e avrà quasi l'ombra de la vera
> costellazione e de la doppia danza
> che circulava il punto dov' io era.   (19–21)

(and he will have almost the shadow of the true / constellation and the double dance / which circled around the point where I was).

Now, as I have argued elsewhere, the whole of the *Paradiso* is built upon a disproportion which Dante himself acknowledges between what he actually saw in Heaven and what he can relate in words about his experiences. It is indeed an essential part of Christian wisdom in the Heaven of the Sun to recognise how inadequate the instruments of human reason and language must ultimately be. At the same time, the vision of Paradise assures Dante that God, as Creator of the world, allows created objects, such as stars, to be employed – on the understanding that they are no more than tokens – in the representation of otherwise ineffable truths. So, the making of meaning here becomes a game, sanctioned by God and supported by rational activity, and the passage shows how this game may involve a free-ranging exercise of imagination and observational power – after which the revelation of how little one has really achieved comes not as a mockery, but rather as a delightfully comic recall to the conditions in which the human mind must always act.

At the end of *Inferno* XXII Dante will invite his reader to witness a 'nuovo ludo' – a new game (XXII 118). But there, as throughout this episode, the game is one which, unlike *Paradiso* XIII, does not enliven the imagination of the onlooker. Still less does it allow that objects can serve to point beyond themselves to the Creator. Here every object that might perform that function is dragged back, by its narrative application, into a context which emphasises only its materiality and lack of meaning.

So, at the conclusion, when Dante speaks of the falcon and the sparrowhawk (XXII 131; 140), the images are given none of the symbolic resonance which they *will* have, say, in *Purgatorio* Canto XIX where Dante can associate the peregrine falcon with the pilgrim soul (since both display a desire to return to their earthly or heavenly masters). In the present episode the two birds are merely ciphers for animal violence. The falcon is seen, in a distinctly comic passage, as the terror of any local duck:

> non altrimenti l'anitra di botto,
> quando 'l falcon s'appressa, giù s'attuffa ...   (*Inf.* XXII 130–1)

(precisely so, the duck on the sudden / dives down when the hawk draws near).

So, too, the *sparvier* displays no meaning but only menacing claws:

> Ma l'altro fu bene sparvier grifagno
> ad artigliar ben lui ...   (XXII 139–40)

(But the other was truly a sparrowhawk, / clawing him well and truly.)

In a more extended sense, the first incident in the narrative involves a daringly parodic reduction not of a natural object but of the liturgical object of a cult devotion – an object whose true function would indeed have been to point to a meaning beyond itself, as do the images of the *Paradiso*. The devils at Canto XXI 48 taunt the barrators – who are predominantly said to be men of Lucca – with the words

> Qui non ha loco il Santo Volto!   (XXI 48)

(Here the Holy Visage has no place!)

The *Santo Volto*, in this case, was a crucifix of black wood to which the Lucchesi ascribed miraculous powers; on earth, even the blackness of an object could become luminous with significance and power. But in this circle the reverse is true: all meaning is reduced, irresistibly, to negation, obscurity and cynicism.

It is, above all else, the sheer pace of Dante's narrative that allows such cynicism to propagate; its anarchic action allows no time for contemplation or the cultivation of significance.

Consider the passage which immediately follows the Arsenal image. As the Dante character stares fixedly at the nothingness of the pitch, he is thrown into confusion by a sudden apparition which translates the blackness of the pitch into menacing life:

> Mentr' io là giù fisamente mirava,
> lo duca mio, dicendo 'Guarda, guarda!',
> mi trasse a sé del loco dov' io stava.
>   Allor mi volsi come l'uom cui tarda
> di veder quel che li convien fuggire
> e cui paura sùbita sgagliarda,
>   che, per veder, non indugia 'l partire:

e vidi dietro a noi un diavol nero
correndo su per lo scoglio venire.   (xxi 22–30)

(While I gazed down fixedly there, / my guide, saying 'Look, look!', / drew me to himself from the place where I was standing. / Then I turned like one who longs / to see what he has to flee from, / who is unmanned by sudden fear, / so that he does not delay his flight for the sake of seeing; / and I saw behind us a black devil / come running over the rock.)

The interest here lies entirely in the vigour of the action – caught in the gerund of 'correndo'. 'Nothingness' itself now becomes agile; and the tensions of the image are enhanced in the next lines when Dante attributes sharp contour and strength of shoulder to this menacing vacancy:

L'omero suo, ch'era aguto e superbo,
carcava un peccator con ambo l'anche,
e quei tenea de' piè ghermito 'l nerbo.   (34–6)

(His shoulders, which were haughty and sharp, / were loaded with the thighs of two sinners; / and he held, hooked, the sinews of each.)

John Donne could speak of a 'quintessence even from nothingness', and some such phrase would be needed here to capture the force of Dante's image. But in Dante's own terms, a particular nonsense arises at this point, insofar as the obsessive image of the devil pictures a kind of motion – violent and undirected – which contrasts completely with the steady journey of the protagonist 'di ponte in ponte'. As with the *lupa* of *Inferno* i, the most sinister aspect of the devil is the unresolved activity he represents. In both the devil and the *lupa* Dante envisages the same nightmarish suspension of action without fixed goal or healthy purpose; in both cases, this is rendered by the gerund: where the *lupa* came always closer to Dante – 'venendomi incontro' – the devil is always running – 'correndo'.

A larger and quite unmistakable parallel also exists between Dante's vision of the devil and the episode in Cantos viii and ix when his advancing journey seemed most likely to be frustrated. Now as before, the progress of the protagonist has been arrested; and, as before, Virgil will shortly leave Dante, to parley with the devils. Moreover, the words which Virgil speaks, in the course of this parley, adduce the providential sanction Dante's journey in precisely the way that the *Messo da Ciel* has taught. Where the *Messo* insists that the 'destined end should never be cut short', Virgil insists:

Lascian' andar, ché nel cielo è voluto
ch'i' mostri altrui questo cammin silvestro.   (xxi 83–4)

(Let us go forward; for it is willed in Heaven / that I should show this wooded way to another.)

Yet in the Malebolge there is no *Messo* to second Virgil's appeal. On the contrary, there are even close parallels between the *Messo* and the running devil – who may thus be taken as a parodic version of the earlier figure: where the *Messo* expressed pride with his disdainful left hand, so the devil expresses it – and there is a similar plasticity here – with his sharp, raised shoulders. Certainly Dante's response to the two figures is similar: where he wrote of the *Messo* 'Ahi quanto mi parea pien di disdegno ...', he now writes of the devil:

> Ahi quant' elli era ne l'aspetto fero!
> e quanto mi parea ne l'atto acerbo ...   (31–2)

(Ah, how ferocious he was in his appearance / and how sour he seemed to me in his actions!)

Such similarities, of course, point to the essential difference between the two scenes. The *Messo* releases Dante from his paralysis by reminding him that there are powers that support his journey – beyond the journey itself – and the implications of this are reflected in the appeal which Dante makes that those who have 'intelletti sani' should seek out the doctrine behind his strange verses. There is no comparable appeal in the barratry sequence. On the contrary, the very function of the text is to resist any such inspection. Dante here remains unrelievedly obsessed – and allows himself to be so – with the images that his own imagination has created; only on two occasions does he suggest that there is any dimension other than the immediate level of his fiction. On the first of these, he does reflect upon his work, but only to emphasise the obsessiveness of the fiction itself:

> I' vidi, e anco il cor me n'accapriccia ...   (XXII 31)

(I saw, and still my heart skips within me at it).

Likewise, on the second occasion, he addresses the reader, and seeks to implicate him still further in the fascinations of the farce:

> O tu che leggi, udirai nuovo ludo ...   (XXII 118)

(O you who are reading, you will hear a new game).

Not surprisingly, then, the two protagonists are themselves caught in a game which seems to promise no conclusion or relief – either from a divine source, or from commonsense, or even from an assurance of detachment on the author's part. There is indeed a prevailing sense of authorial licence in this canto which – although it will recur in later cantos of the *Inferno* – is nonetheless deeply uncharacteristic of Dante. And if further evidence were needed, it should be sufficient to cite the profoundly anarchic moment which occurs at the end of Virgil's negotiations. These negotiations are in fact successful; and for the space of two words one supposes that Virgil is about to celebrate this success with a resonant return to the high style:

> E 'l duca mio a me. 'O tu ...   (XXI 88)

(And my leader to me: 'O thou'...)

But with the next phrase he utters – 'che siedi' (who sits) – we are on the verge of the ludicrous; seated heroes are a rarity. With the following line the descent into bathos is complete:

tra li scheggion del ponte quatto quatto.   (89)

(squatting among the great splinters of the bridge).

Not only is the Dante character – in the very moment when his dignity is vindicated – revealed to be squatting timorously behind a rock, but Virgil, in declaring as much, is obliged positively to quack the words 'quatto quatto' in a vulgarism which wholly demeans the elevation of his exordium.

We have said that the canto admits of no intervention or relief. And this is all the more remarkable considering that in the last phases of Canto xxi Dante makes pointed reference to an event which, hitherto, has always indicated God's power to intervene in history, and also his ability to break the locks of Hell itself – the occasion, that is, when Christ harrowed Hell. On this occasion, Dante is now told, the whole of Hell shook, and its roads and bridges were broken down:

> Ier, più oltre cinqu' ore che quest' otta,
> mille dugento con sessanta sei
> anni compié che qui la via fu rotta.   (112–14)

(Yesterday, five hours beyond this hour, / one thousand two hundred and sixty-six / years were completed since the way here was broken.)

All earlier references to this occurrence have proved significant, as, for instance, when Virgil spoke of 'un possente' in Canto iv, and all subsequent references will be so. Yet here the devils appear to have possessed themselves of the event and drained it of everything save its most literal force. The very precision of dating in the account they give displays the power of the devils to replace the incomprehensible truth with the force of apparently factual schemes and certainties and to substitute gross fact for animating violence. And this is the first move in another game of lies. For, having asserted their specious authority over the divine event, the devils at once proceed to the lie direct, inducing the protagonist to believe that there is still one bridge intact. As the protagonist and Virgil will painfully discover in the next canto, there are no bridges standing in this bolgia.

But is not the author of the *Commedia* involved at this point in a piece of narrative chicanery? After all, he said nothing about the breaking of the bridges in the overview he offered in Canto xviii; he is now playing fast and loose with the narrative expectations of his readers. This has never happened before; nor will it happen again. Yet the moment is one of some consequence for what follows in the *Inferno*. For, just as the earthquake in fact shakes the foundations of Hell, Dante will increasingly invite us henceforth to consider whether the scheme of judgement embodied in the geography of Hell is as stable or trustworthy as hitherto one must have supposed it to be. Dante will soon show himself struggling without the assistance of the bridges which so far he has enjoyed in the Malebolge. And that struggle – which the devils delude him into thinking will *not* be necessary – is a direct result of divine violence. It is the devils who speak as masters of certainty. To be sure, Satan, as Dante describes him in Canto XXIII, is the father of lies (144). But he is also said to be a 'logician' in Canto XXVII, and already in Canto XXI he is shown to be at least a tactician and leader, convincing others of certainties to which they possess no right. We shall eventually have to ask whether Dante may not call into question those very qualities of leadership, logic and unwavering certainty which have, until now, most signally characterised his demeanour in the Malebolge.

But these are questions for the twenty-third canto. For as we proceed through Canto XXII we find nothing save a confirmation of the farcical logic which has bound Dante upon the wheel of his own constructions in Canto XXI. The very fact that the cantos are linked is itself a part of that confirmation. At almost every other point of the poem, the conclusiveness of the canto form is itself instrumental in ensuring that the poet should constantly have to begin again, re-engaging with the issues that his subject generates. Indeed, there are only two comparable cases of coupling; in the one – Cantos VIII and IX – this coupling leads to a heightening of tension, while in the other – Cantos XXVI and XXVII – it allows a sharp distinction to be drawn between two types of false counsel. In the present case, the effect is one of sterile repetition. Under the gross and misleading *duce* Malacoda, the journey of the protagonist dissolves into a parody of his solemn exit from Limbo – under the guidance of Virgil; and the narrative action is correspondingly stagnant.

Yet Canto XXII does have one especial function. With extreme viciousness it emphasises the vision – which the Malebolge at large persistently offers – of how easily the settled state of the human being can be lacerated and torn to shreds. In this canto the barrators are in the clutches both of their guardians and of their own dissensions; in these circumstances, it is sufficient for a man to speak or even to be named, to find himself a target for false accusation and torture. So in the central episode Ciampolo is constrained – as much by Dante as by the devils – to reveal his own history and the names of his fellow-sinners; and his reward is to have his arm ripped to tatters and then to be derided for his shiftiness when he displeases the devils (70–2).

In Canto XXVIII Dante will present a more comprehensive account of bodily anguish. But there he will at least show some wariness at taking such a theme as the subject of a poem, pronouncing an emphatic judgement upon his fellow-poet Bertran de Born, whose verses were renowned for their delight in destruction. That could almost stand as a retraction for the poetry of the barrators sequence. But there is no such retraction in the present context. So, when Dante addresses his reader with the words 'O you who are reading, you shall *hear* of a new game' (118), he looks forward to a response so shrill that it will be *heard* rather than simply read; and attention is directed not beyond the canto but rather to the vicious hunt with which it concludes.

There is, in a sense, no natural end to this canto, nor any promise that, as we turn the page, we shall discover anything new. Indeed, its last line still points back over its own shoulder at the scene behind:

E noi lasciammo lor così 'mpacciati.   (XXII 151)

(And we left them thus embroiled.)

To summarise, then, let us return briefly to the end of Canto XXI – to the point at which Malacoda, as leader of the 'fiera compagnia' performs a roll-call of his squad:

'Tra'ti avante, Alichino, e Calcabrina',
cominciò elli a dire, 'e tu, Cagnazzo;
e Barbariccia guidi la decina.
    Libicocco vegn' oltre e Draghignazzo,
Ciriatto sannuto e Graffiacane
e Farfarello e Rubicante pazzo'.   (XXI 118–23)

('Draw forward, Alichino and Calcabrina', / he began to say, 'and you, Cagnazzo; / and Barbariccia, you lead the ten. / Let Libicocco come as well, and Draghignazzo, / Ciriatto, the tusked one, and Graffiacane, / and Farfarello and crazy Rubicante.')

Since Canto XIX, the giving of names has been an issue in the Malebolge. A name is a token of identity which – in the Christian view – God, no less than human beings, is bound to respect; but the gusto with which Dante constructs this mock-heroic catalogue of fictions undermines any such obligation – which is precisely the point. As in the name of Malebolge itself, Dante is momentarily allowing fiction full rein. But in Canto XXII, these fictions are interspersed with the names of historical personages; and this itself is enough to reveal how close to a fiction is the identity of anyone in a world where identities depend upon words that are 'bought and sold' (XXI 41–2) – as, in the world of barratry, they may be. It is not surprising that Pirandello could write an excellent account of this sequence.

VI

In its themes and its structural characteristics, the twenty-third canto stands as an appropriate conclusion to the first phase of the Malebolge. The canto is broadly comic in its effect; and while the tone of the comedy is different alike from the absurdities or farce of preceding cantos, in a number of respects it is far more varied. The virtuosity of the poet continues to display itself; and beneath a surface less brilliant than that of earlier cantos, Canto XXIII continues to develop the prevailing theme of identity.

From the first it is clear that the anarchy which Dante countenanced in the previous episode has, in some way, been allayed in Canto XXIII. The canto opens with the protagonist and Virgil – unembarrassed by any escort of devils – making a measured and careful advance to the next circle, where hypocrisy is punished:

Taciti, soli, sanza compagnia …

(silent, alone, without an escort now).

A new gravity of rhythm and tone are at once apparent; but a more suprising contrast, in regard to intellectual procedure, is suggested by the next *terzina*:

> Vòlt' era in su la favola d'Isopo
> lo mio pensier per la presente rissa,
> dov' el parlò de la rana e del topo;
>   ché più non si pareggia 'mo' e 'issa'
> che l'un con l'altro fa, se ben s'accoppia
> principio e fine con la mente fissa.   (XXIII 4–9)

([My thoughts] were turned by the present quarrel to the fable of Aesop, / where he speaks of the frog and the mouse; / for 'Yes' and 'Aye' are not more alike / than the one case is to the other, if one links / the beginning and the end properly with an attentive mind.)

In the previous sequence, we saw how, alive as the cantos were with animal imagery, this imagery proved empty of meaning, so that the emblematic significance which some of these images might normally have held was deliberately eroded. Here, a moment of moral reflection is informed by the simplest of analogies, communicated in an equally simple literary form, the fable – which relates in this case an incident of frustrated treachery and guile exactly comparable to an incident witnessed in the previous bolgia. The mock-epic analogies of the last two cantos have disappeared. And precisely in returning to the 'humble speech' of the fable, the poet attains a certain balance; working from this simple foundation, he finds that the natural world, even in its petty ferocity, can offer guidance in the pursuit of moral purposes.

In Canto XIX, Dante ascribed authority to a voice which spoke – from beyond the literary confines of the text – in the simple accents of Scripture. Here, in a similar way, the linguistic and narrative sophistications which had produced the perversities of Cantos XXI and XXII disappear in a move which is comic both in its reliance upon ordinary modes of language and thought and also in its admission that textual virtuosity has reached a limit.

In a similar vein, one notes how unequivocal in moral implication is the punishment which Dante here allots to the sinners. These are the hypocrites; and their punishment is to wear cloaks which outwardly are gilded and cut in the fashion of monastic habits but which beneath the surface, are crushingly constructed of lead:

> Là giù trovammo una gente dipinta
> che giva intorno assai con lenti passi,
> piangendo e nel sembiante stanca e vinta.
>   Elli avean cappe con cappucci bassi
> dinanzi a li occhi, fatte de la taglia
> che in Clugnì per li monaci fassi.
>   Di fuor dorate son, sì ch'elli abbaglia;
> ma dentro tutte piombo, e gravi tanto,
> che Federigo le mettea di paglia.
> Oh in etterno faticoso manto!   (58–67)

(Down there we found a painted people / who were going around with very slow steps, / weeping and weary and vanquished in their countenance. / They wore cloaks with deep hoods / over their eyes, cut in the style / that is made for the monks of Cluny. / Outwardly they were gilded, so that they glittered dazzlingly; / but inside they were all of lead and so heavy / that Frederick's cloak was straw beside them. / O wearisome mantle for eternity!)

Hypocrisy, then, is viewed in an immediately comprehensible way as spiritual fraud. Images of clothing – as a concealment for inward corruption – are to be found throughout the canto. Plainly, the hypocrites qualify for the circles of fraud. And Dante, in devising a punishment which so clearly identifies the nature of the sin, declares his own unadorned determination to establish a final, confident reckoning with all the problems of fraud and fiction which have occupied him since he began the Malebolge.

And so, up to a point, he does. Yet to appreciate the force of that conclusion, we need to look more closely at the nature of hypocrisy, and to realise how far the judgement that Dante asserts is still defended by effects of comedy.

In the first place, the sin of hypocrisy is one which brings into sharp focus the question of identity which has occupied Dante since the beginning of the Malebolge. In the hypocrites – the 'painted people' – a deceit is practised on the self, so that selfhood is soon no more than a dangerous fiction. Thus the monumental cloaks that the hypocrites wear are not only punishments but also indications of defensive pride. Like Farinata, Pier della Vigna, Capaneus and Brunetto, the sinners are imprisoned in their own rigid constructions of identity, unaware that selfhood can only be assured by submission to the will of the Creator. It is consequently a source of amazement to the hypocrites – as it was once to the centaurs – that Dante should move freely, and in the flesh, through the otherworld; for his 'privilege' depends precisely upon his submission to the Will that the hypocrites have hidden from:

> Costui par vivo a l'atto de la gola;
> e s'e' son morti, per qual privilegio
> vanno scoperti de la grave stola?   (88–90)

(That one seems to be alive, by the movement of his throat; / and if the two travellers are dead, by what privilege / do they go without the covering of the heavy stole?)

Notably, the hypocrites stress the relative nakedness of the protagonist; for that exposure itself demonstrates an integrity of physical form which the 'clothing' of the hypocrites cannot allow them to declare.

At the same time, to speak of hypocrisy is to raise questions which concern not only the surface and display of identity but also the inward movements of conscience. Certainly, hypocrisy is a fraud exercised upon the opinions of others. But as Dante represents it, the sin is also a fraud against the inner being, whereby the sinner misrepresents to himself his own best aspirations. Thus the cloaks of the hypocrites, in life as in Hell, inhibit all spontaneous movement; and, again, at their meeting with the protagonist, the hypocrites display a 'haste' of mind impeded by the weights they carry and by their incomprehension of the freedom that Dante enjoys in Hell:

> e vidi due mostrar gran fretta
> de l'animo, col viso, d'esser meco;
> ma tardavali 'l carco e la via stretta.   (82–4)

(And I saw two showing great haste / of mind, through their looks, to be with me; / but the weight and the narrow way held them back.)

Against this, the canto is much concerned with the inner shifts and stirrings of the mind of the protagonist. The whole of the opening section, between lines 1 and 33, is occupied by an interior monologue as the protagonist fluctuates in fear of a renewed assault from the devils. And so far from these thoughts being inhibited, the climax of this opening movement is marked by an insistence upon the perfect reciprocity between Dante's inner thoughts and those of Virgil. As Virgil declares,

> Pur mo venieno i tuo' pensier tra ' miei,
> con simile atto e con simile faccia,
> sì che d'intrambi un sol consiglio fei.   (28–30)

(Just now your thoughts were coming to mingle with mine, / with the same import and the same appearance, / so that I have made of both a single resolve.)

In the contrast, then, which he draws between the hypocrites and the protagonist, Dante restates an essentially Christian view of identity – as dependent upon devotion to God's design – and also introduces a concern with conscience which he will pursue especially in Canto XXVII where he considers the case of Guido da Montefeltro. But the judgement he passes on these grounds is still to be modified by the comedy of the cantos: indeed, nowhere more so than in the twenty-third canto. For at its climax we are brought to consider, in a form more acute than anywhere else in the *Inferno*, the whole question of Dante's right to stand in judgement upon his fellow-men; and on the instant all the simple moral equations we have emphasised so far are thrown into confusion.

At line 109, the protagonist is proceeding along the queue of hypocrites, in conversation with two of them who had belonged to the order of *Frati Godenti* – a Christian community of laymen which had gained some notoriety for the laxness of its spiritual discipline. The position of the protagonist is secure; he is in no danger from the devil; and, compared with the laboured movements of the hypocrites, his normal walking-pace appears to be a pleasing lightness of foot. Having listened to the words of one of the *frati*, the protagonist begins to speak. He does so with a confidence further justified by the absolute clarity of the *contrappasso* and the infamous reputation of his interlocutor. But then, at the moment a word of judgement begins to pass his lips, he is interrupted by a sudden incomprehensible sight; and the sentence dies on his lips:

> Io cominciai: 'O frati, i vostri mali ...':
> ma più non dissi, ch'a l'occhio mi corse
> un, crucifisso in terra con tre pali.   (109–11)

(I began: 'O brothers, your ill-doing ...'. / But I said no more for there ran to my eyes / the sight of one crucified with three stakes upon the ground.)

The crucified figure is Caiaphas, who alone among his fellow-hypocrites is naked, and who lies in the path of the leaden-cloaked procession, so that all who take this path have to trample over him.

The surprise of this moment is evident not only for the protagonist but also for the reader who is following the steady narrative line of the canto. And the surprise at once raises important questions.

In the first place, why should Caiaphas be condemned as a hypocrite? Guilty as he may be for his own condemnation of Christ, he would not seem to be guilty of hypocrisy, at least on the understanding of the sin which prevailed in the opening half of the canto. In the second place, why should the protagonist fall silent at the sight of Caiaphas. Whatever the nature of the sinner's guilt, he would seem to offer a far more obvious target for Christian indignation than the trivial *frati*.

On the first count, Caiaphas here introduces a new dimension into the interpretation of hypocrisy. Certainly, his action in condemning Christ cannot be regarded as dissimulation; on the contrary, his judgement, by his own lights, was all too highly principled and explicit. But that itself suggests another conception of hypocrisy which, so far, has only been hinted at in the tedious weight which the *contrappasso* imposes. If this is taken to indicate a certain irresponsiveness or slowness of spirit then Caiaphas too, is a hypocrite: when Christ stands in person before him – defenceless and exposed to view – he offers, if his judge could only see it, a direct encounter with the truths of revelation. But Caiaphas resists. He is, and remains, the representative of the Old Law which Christ has come to fulfil and overthrow. He asserts that Law unbendingly; it becomes for him the defence that any hypocrite will seek to make when challenged to examine his conscience anew. Caiaphas hides from the spirit of redemption and renewal expressed in the Atonement, and in Hell he is consequently naked to the action of divine justice.

From this it should be apparent why the protagonist is interrupted so violently; for he too has an 'Old Law' of his own to defend, and in the moment of passing judgement upon the *Frati Godenti* is about to become a hypocrite himself. His words and judgements – however justified by the scheme of punishment – are on the point of petrifying into sanctimony and preconception. He too is about to assert a rigidly established scheme of judgement. In itself, this scheme is no more reprehensible than the scheme of the Old Testament Law; but plainly it may become so if taken too confidently as an occasion for pride and spiritual inertia. But words fail as Dante is brought to contemplate an utterly singular and profoundly ironic image of what judgement can mean. Thus the disruption that this image causes itself saves Dante from hypocrisy; it is left in fact to the hypocrite *frate* to continue in the vein of judgement and provide an impassive comment on the sins and punishment of Caiaphas (117–23).

The implications of this moment reach far beyond the confines of Canto XXIII. For one thing, they offer immediate evidence for the argument I have been pursuing since (in the Introduction) I discussed the Earthly Paradise: Dante as poet is deeply aware of the dangers as well as the difficulties involved in the act of judgement. In this regard, it is significant that at the sight of Caiaphas, Virgil too is struck with amazement:

> Allor vid' io maravigliar Virgilio
> sovra colui ch'era disteso in croce
> tanto vilmente ne l'etterno essilio.   (124–6)

(Then I saw Virgil astonished at the sight / of the figure stretched out on the cross / so basely in the eternal exile.)

One recalls that Virgil will also be 'weighed down' with amazement at the sight of Beatrice in the Earthly Paradise. And while the two episodes are, on the surface, completely different, both insist in their way upon the mystery of Christian redemption and upon the crucial importance of things *seen* to the revelation of Christian truth. Virgil can understand neither grace nor the history – in which the high priest Caiaphas was an actor – of the Passion of Christ; he cannot see what is at stake. In both cases, there is a deep, subversive comedy in the undermining of those rational expectations that Virgil consistently represents.

The dangers of judgement – even when uttered by a Christian – will come to occupy a place of particular importance in subsequent cantos of the *Inferno*. However, I do not here wish to stress or anticipate the established lines of my general argument. (The critic too can easily become a hypocrite.) Let us, rather, look more closely now at the text of Canto XXIII. For my general arguments will have no point at all unless they lead one to a renewed awareness of the particular effects of difficulty that a canto such as the twenty-third displays. As Dante needs constantly to revise the positions he adopts in the sphere of judgement, so we need constantly to re-read the cantos we thought we had concluded. And, indeed, viewed from the standpoint of the Caiaphas incident, Canto XXIII will begin to look very different from the mere summary that at first it seemed to be.

One notes, first, that when earlier I diagnosed the nature of Caiaphas's hypocrisy, the language I used was that of the crude *contrappasso* – of the 'biter bit', of the judge brought to judgement. But now we have seen that such terms can never be used so confidently. The meaning of the episode may well prove to be 'judge not lest you yourself be judged'. And two features of the poetry in this passage will lead us to see that such a meaning entails a radical alteration in the language we use to interpret the punishment.

For one thing, note the plasticity with which Dante conceives the sudden image of Caiaphas's nakedness:

> Quando mi vide, tutto si distorse,
> soffiando ne la barba con sospiri.   (112–13)

(When he saw me, he writhed all over, / puffing into his beard with his sighs.)

The realistic detail – particularly of the puffing beard – firmly resists the easy interpretative equations one drew originally between the cloaks of the hypocrites and their sin. And an even greater resistance is offered by, in the second place, the ironic complexity of the punishment reserved for Caiaphas. Comedy here approaches blasphemy: Caiaphas like Christ is crucified, 'in croce' (125); like Christ, he is placed at a crossroad. History was wholly changed by the Atonement; but Caiaphas marks the road for those who will never change; and, finally, where Christ took upon himself the sins of the world, Caiaphas suffers from the heavy burden of the damned marching across his body. We cannot settle to the act of judgement here: the imagination is far too dazzled by the cross-lights of analogy and irony.

But if we now look back, briefly, over the canto at large it will be seen that – emanating from, and preparing for, the surprise of Caiaphas's crucifixion – there are features throughout which exactly correspond to that intense moment of ironic confusion. There is from the first an unmistakable emphasis upon visual effect, corresponding to the descriptive vigour of the Caiaphas scene and also to the prestige which Dante attributes to the actions of the eye: one will now, for instance, note the *chiaroscuro* which gives to the hypocrites glittering cloaks but deeply-shadowed eyes. At the same time, the canto is much concerned with images of motion – with progression and arrest, with fixity and poise; and these images reflect, in turn, upon the mental dynamics that allow or prohibit the intellectual sluggardliness which Dante identifies in hypocrisy.

To begin again. The canto opens with a strong emphasis upon the steady and simple progress of the two travellers, apparently free from impediment and secure in each other's company. This progress is matched in simplicity by the language that Dante employs; and the integrity of the moment of companionship is celebrated by a plain comparison of the travellers to silent, wayfaring friars:

> Taciti, soli, sanza compagnia
> n'andavam l'un dinanzi e l'altro dopo,
> come frati minor vanno per via.   (1–3)

(Silent, alone and unescorted now, / we went on the one behind the other, / as minor friars go along their way.)

But in that silence, the mind of the protagonist begins at once to shift and recoil. There is an inward journey more complicated than the journey spelled out in physical steps. Fear and imagination work together to invent and foretell an 'imagined hunt' (33) – which, even though it is only a premonition, has a palpable physical effect. The canto, as we have suggested, pays unusual attention to the inner workings of the mind. But it is also concerned with the spontaneous translation of sentiment into gesture and physical response – as, here, terror finds an exact and undisguisable expression in the bristling of the hairs on Dante's body:

E come l'un pensier de l'altro scoppia,
così nacque di quello un altro poi,
che la prima paura mi fé doppia.
    Io pensava così ...
Già mi sentia tutti arricciar li peli
de la paura e stava in dietro intento ...   (10–13; 19–20)

(And as one thought breaks out from another, / so from this a further thought was born, / which made my first fear double. My thoughts ran thus ... / Already I felt all my hairs bristle / and I was looking back with fear).

At no point does Dante here depart from the simple register of feelings, words and reactions with which the canto began: the psychology is as ordinary as any could be. Yet the narrative points to the essential distinction between the protagonist and the hypocrites. The animation itself provides one such contrast. But, beyond that, while Dante is describing the impact of varying thoughts, his account points to processes, developments and an ultimate coherence which are denied to the hypocrites. Their punishment tells of difficulty in movement and of discontinuity between the internal life and the external. But in the protagonist thought here *breeds* thought, and remains thought even though it is impelled by trepidation. Already Dante is preparing for the shock he will receive at the sight of Caiaphas. Moreover, thought also resolves into silent gesture – which, in turn, produces an uninhibited appeal to Virgil for assurance. In comparison, the only hypocrite who responds with equal directness is Caiaphas, snorting with indignation at the disgrace of his exposure to view.

The naive reactions of the protagonist lead to the first moment of poise in the canto. Later, the hypocrites will be described as balances 'creaking' under the weight they bear (101–2). But Dante by confessing his fears, discovers in his guide that perfect – un-creaking – reciprocity of thought which Virgil celebrates in words that introduce the most impressive light image in the early phases of the canto:

E quei: 'S'i' fossi di piombato vetro,
l'imagine di fuor tua non trarrei
più tosto a me, che quella dentro 'mpetro.
    Pur mo venieno i tuo' pensier tra ' miei,
con simile atto e con simile faccia,
sì che d'intrambi un sol consiglio fei'.   (25–30)

(And he: 'If I were of leaded glass, / I should not draw your outward image / to me more rapidly than I receive and fix the inward image (of your thoughts). / Just now your thoughts were coming to mingle with mine, / with the same import and the same appearance; / so that I have made of both a single resolve.')

Virgil's speech displays a continuing interest in the annihilation of the boundaries between the internal and the external. One notes too, in the reference to the clarity and responsiveness of leaded glass – in other words, the shining mirror of Virgil's mind – a pre-emptive stroke of comedy: if the leaden cloaks of the hypocrites point to deadness of mind, Virgil has already displayed how unnatural that deadness is; even *lead* can be turned to account and made animate with the human image. Moreover, there is, in this first image of light, an emphasis upon an entirely commonplace marvel – but a marvel nonetheless. Simply it is, after all, possible for one person to understand another. And that is something that the hypocrite obscures by his defensive fear.

The opening phase of the canto prepares in a number of ways for the main episode, not least in adding a further element to the diagnosis of hypocrisy. For if the mutual openness of Dante and Virgil contrasts with the self-defensiveness of the hypocrite, then so too does their readiness to match and compare their feelings and thoughts: the Pharisee is one who is unwilling to stand comparison with the publican or sinner. At the same time, the opening sequence looks back to the barrators sequence in theme as well as narrative incident. As we have seen, the barratry canto brings to a climax the discussion, which began in Canto XVIII, of the various ways in which relationship can be corroded and meaning consequently decay. Now, with the reference to Aesop's fables, a simple set of relationships is re-established which will now form the foundation for subsequent action.

The second phase of the canto also refers both backwards and ahead. The narrative link, of course, is especially clear. The fears which Dante has earlier conceived are on the instant translated into reality: the sound of the imagined chase is actually heard, and there is a rapid change of narrative pace as Virgil abruptly abandons his words of consolation and seizes Dante in a gesture of physical concern and comfort:

> Lo duca mio di sùbito mi prese,
> come la madre ch'al romore è desta
> e vede presso a sé le fiamme accese,
>   che prende il figlio e fugge e non s'arresta,
> avendo più di lui che di sé cura,
> tanto che solo una camiscia vesta;
>   e giù dal collo de la ripa dura
> supin si diede a la pendente roccia,
> che l'un de' lati a l'altra bolgia tura.
>   Non corse mai sì tosto acqua per doccia
> a volger ruota di molin terragno,
> quand' ella più verso le pale approccia,
>   come 'l maestro mio per quel vivagno.   (37–49)

(My guide snatched me up on the instant, / like a mother who is awakened by a sound / and sees fire alight close by her, / who takes up her son, and flees and does not stop, / having a greater care for him than for herself, / so much so that she wears nothing more than her shift. / And down from the ridge of the hard bank / he slid on his back, giving himself to the sloping rock-face / which closes up one side of the other bolgia. / Water never ran so swiftly through a race / to turn the wheel of a land-mill, / when it comes the closest to the spokes, / as my master did down that border.)

Here, the frenzy of the previous two cantos appears to have returned. Yet in at least three ways the action is now quite different. First, this action is distinctly projected *forward*, admitting of no hindrance or delay. In the second place, the sequence – so far from being anarchic – is alive with possible significance for the subsequent canto. In the simile, we see a mother dressed 'only in a shift', reckless of her own security; and we need not stress the difference between this and the unnatural stolidity of the over-dressed hypocrites: a naked and natural energy is released which hypocrisy seeks to repress. And the same point is enforced by the image of the mill-race. Here, against the artifice of the 'painted people', Dante evokes the primal energy of water – just as in the first simile he has spoken of fire. Elemental fluency and the brilliance of running water both render a meaning: the elements will respond to human work and purpose. Like the earlier image of the Venetian Arsenal, the image of the waterwheel is one of a series which, in the next three cantos, will trace the course of ordinary work through all its phases from frustrated enterprise to well-earned rest. And it is entirely appropriate that this series should appear in the canto of the hypocrites, where the image of punishment correspondingly indicates the sterile labours which the mind conceives in the furtherance of a fictional dignity.

It is, finally, on the level of Dante's own textual labour that this passage appears most clearly a moment both of effort and of poise. For in drawing these two comparisons, Dante has certainly striven to elevate his style; yet he has not returned to the mock-epic disproportions of the previous sequence, nor claimed any resounding dignity for his classical master, but has rather reaffirmed the plainness of the opening *terzine*. These similes do, of course, have an epic dimension. But the epic tone is here at the service of the most natural and normal impulses of self-preservation; and the comic incongruity in the comparison of Virgil to a desperate mother serves to confirm the value of Virgil as a simple human presence which Canto XX had first begun to emphasise. The narrative of the barrators sequence had demeaned both Virgil and the protagonist; here the two travellers are restored to dignity on a footing which admits, without flinching, the possibility of ridicule.

Arriving at the central sequence, one is now ready for a comedy of comparisons, played out in terms of dynamics and light. Again the pace of the narrative changes, and again the change is abrupt. Dante is still in mid-flight – the devils being seen at the top of the ridge – when his eyes are caught and held, in muted anticipation of the Caiaphas sequence, by the procession of hypocrites. As soon as the eye is trained upon these dazzlingly insignificant forms, the comparisons begin:

> Noi ci volgemmo ancor pur a man manca
> con loro insieme, intenti al tristo pianto;
>   ma per lo peso quella gente stanca
> venìa sì pian, che noi eravam nuovi
> di compagnia ad ogne mover d'anca.   (68–72)

(We turned still to the left / to keep with them, intent upon their dreary weeping; / but because of the weight those weary people / came so slowly that we were at new / company with every movement of the hip.)

The contrast plainly lies between the lumbering and monotonous gait of the hypocrites and the varied, decisive movements of the travellers. But Dante gives it emphasis, pointing to the resolution with which the protagonist and Virgil turn to the left and to the naked anatomical origins of their action: 'ad ogne mover d'anca'. By now, even the most obvious features of the scene have aquired a charge of meaning, so the travellers have only to proceed at a normal pace to find themselves, surprisingly, in new company at every step. And with this there begins a comic sequence in which Dante's purpose is not so much to deride the hypocrites as to celebrate the unexpected dignity which attaches to the simplest movements of the physical body.

The hypocrites are astonished at Dante's progress, as he himself will be later at the sight of Caiaphas; so one of the damned cries out in an ironic phrase which also combines in a stroke the colouristic and kinetic motifs of the canto:

> Tenete i piedi,
> voi correte sì per l'aura fosca!   (77–8)

(Stay your feet, / O you running so swiftly through the dark air.)

Speed and darkness – implying also slowness and light – are here drawn together in a kind of synaesthesia. And when Dante does stop, the sinners note, with the same precision with which he will note the beard of Caiaphas, the moving throat which marks the protagonist as a living man:

> Costui par vivo a l'atto de la gola.   (88)

(That one seems alive by the movement of his throat.)

This brings us to the first climax of the canto, which, unlike the Caiaphas incident, stresses the poise of the protagonist. Asked to identify himself, Dante's answer is plain enough:

> E io a loro: 'I' fui nato e cresciuto
> sovra 'l bel fiume d'Arno a la gran villa,
> e son col corpo ch'i' ho sempre avuto'.   (94–6)

(And I to them: 'I was born and grew up / by the banks of the lovely Arno in the great city, / and I am still in the body that I always had.')

Yet we have only to recall the contortions of self-defence which Dante went through in Canto XIX to realise the value of this plain-speaking. The statement of fact is itself rich in suggestion: the continuity of life is stressed in the temporal scheme – 'nato e cresciuto' – and in the astonishing projection of bodily form into eternity: 'e son col corpo ...'. Equally, the reference to the river Arno echoes the mill-race image of the central section; and the modest qualification 'bel' – in a context where light has been strongly stressed – irradiates the river with a recognition of its natural sheen.

These last suggestions are the more strongly felt as Dante pronounces his own question to the hypocrites:

> Ma voi chi siete, a cui tanto distilla
> quant' i' veggio dolor giù per le guance?
> e che pena è in voi che sì sfavilla?   (97–9)

(But who are you, for whom [I see such sorrow distilled] down your cheeks; / and what punishment is it that flashes so on you?)

Water has become the distillation of fruitless tears; and the light comes only from the glint of the gilded cloak.

Throughout, the canto has been constructed not only around a portrayal of forward movement, but also around a pattern of cross-references, balances and correspondences. And it is, of course, this pattern that is beginning to harden into a formula – along with the formula of the *contrappasso* – when Dante suddenly encounters Caiaphas. Here we need only emphasise the force of the metaphor which introduces this sequence. As words break down and the march forward halts, it is the eye that now responds to a 'run':

> ma più non dissi, ch'a l'occhio mi corse
> un, crucifisso in terra ...   (110–11)

(But I said no more, for to my eye there ran / the sight of one crucified on the ground.)

And with that 'run' – in which the eye is a passive target – the narrative movement is suddenly reversed. This is the one event in the canto which Virgil does not initiate; and suddenly the previous 'speed' of the protagonist fails. Nor can the violence of this instant be mitigated by the spontaneous reciprocation of the opening lines. Until this point, the canto has consistently emphasised the action and interaction of groups and couples. Beginning with the frog and the mouse – who, in Dante's phrase, matched the case of the devils as exactly as 'yes' matches 'aye' – proceeding through the duet of Dante and Virgil, and arriving at the *Frati Godenti* – who jointly held an office which required only one man to fill it (106): over this whole varied spectrum, the reader has been invited consistently to think in terms of categories and classes. But now the emphasis falls upon a unique case: '*un*, crucifisso in terra'. And the singularity of Caiaphas is underscored by the fact that it so exactly mirrors, and yet is so utterly distinct from, the case of that other 'one' – Christ himself – whom Caiaphas saw fit to execute for the greater good of his own religious group:

> Quel confitto che tu miri,
> consigliò i Farisei che convenia
> porre un uom per lo popolo a' martìri.   (115–17)

(That man – there transfixed – whom you gaze at, / advised the Pharisees that it was right / to put one man to torment for the sake of a whole people.)

As for the protagonist – lacking any guidance from the dumbfounded Virgil – he too must face that vision entirely alone; he must attempt to perceive, within the untellable contradictions of this comic moment, a sign of the same truth and justice as Caiaphas was unable to see in the face of Christ himself. Only in doing that will he realise what it means to judge.

In the end, of course, one does return to words, reason and Virgil. But we have rarely seen in the *Inferno* so decisive an opposition between, on the one hand, words and reason, and, on the other the singularity of the visionary moment. And the conclusion, so far from obscuring that opposition, registers on two counts Virgil's – albeit limited – acknowledgement of its implications.

As one would expect, Virgil is eager to press on with the appointed journey. He is, however, also concerned with *how* he should proceed; for the bridges which he had expected to find in this bolgia are after all not standing. And in resolving this problem he comes to an understanding which, in one respect, confirms the worst suspicions about human nature that the Malebolge has so far aroused and, in another, asserts the liberating force that resides in God's design. First, Virgil has to realise that the devils have lied in assuring him that the bridges can be crossed: the Devil is a liar and 'the father of lies' (144). And to say this is to recognise, at the least, how subject to error and distortion any construction of human intelligence can be. Even Virgil's plan – and Dante's own for the *Inferno* – can be frustrated by malign intentions. At the same time, the lies of the devils clearly demonstrate how fallible is the linguistic medium which Virgil was appointed to administer. There is, then, reason for Virgil to be 'turbato' (146).

What does remain, however, where words fail, is the human presence. So in the final lines of the canto, Virgil is as silent as he was at its beginning, and no longer confident but deeply enclosed in his own emotions:

> Appresso il duca a gran passi sen gì
> turbato un poco d'ira nel sembiante;
> ond' io da li 'ncarcati mi parti'
> dietro a le poste de le care piante.   (145–8)

(Then my guide went on with great strides, / a little disturbed by anger in his countenance; / at which I left the loaded spirits, / following the prints of his beloved feet.)

But this subtly human picture provides a final counterpart to the image of Caiaphas – as Virgil is seen pursuing 'with great strides' the road that Caiaphas had interrupted, responsive where the sinner is violent and aghast. The image reasserts every value that Dante has associated with Virgil since *Inferno* I; but its especial emphasis falls upon the affective 'care' (dear) in the final line. Even a silent Virgil can be *seen*, and loved; and the tenderness he inspires is itself sufficient to exhort the protagonist. The journey continues – as it began in this canto – under the renewed stimulus of intuitive sympathy.

5

Signs in transition and the pathos of order: Cantos XXIV–XXVII

One distinctive feature of the cantos I shall consider in the present chapter is that all four contain passages which point beyond the horizons of the *Inferno* and in some way anticipate the *Purgatorio*. An instance of this is the central action of Canto XXIV, where Virgil and the protagonist – having discovered that the bridge over the sixth bolgia is in ruins – are obliged to clamber from the bolgia of the hypocrites to the bolgia of the thieves; for in the course of this climb Virgil urges the protagonist on by reminding him of the even more laborious ascent he will shortly have to make on Mount Purgatory:

> Più lunga scala convien che si saglia;
> non basta da costoro esser partito.   (*Inf.* XXIV 55–6)

(A longer stair than this we have to climb; / it is not enough to have left these – the hypocrites – behind.)

In Cantos XXVI and XXVII, the case is more complex but no less explicit. In the first of these cantos, Ulysses speaks of how his ship was wrecked on the shores of the mountain which Dante will later identify as Mount Purgatory; and in Canto I of the *Purgatorio* – where this identification is corroborated – Dante emphasises the contrast between his own intellectual adventure and the 'folle volo' of Ulysses, applying to himself *verbatim* a phrase which first occurs at the climax of Ulysses's tale: where Ulysses is destroyed 'com' altrui piacque' (*Inf.* XXVI 141) – 'as another wished' – the protagonist on the shores of Purgatory is girded 'com' altrui piacque' with the reed of humility (*Purg.* I 133). Canto XXVII of the *Inferno* prepares for a similar, though more elaborate, parallel with the fifth canto of the *Purgatorio*; in two exactly balanced scenes, where the powers of Heaven and Hell are shown in conflict over the soul and body of the sinner, Dante firstly describes the damnation of Guido da Montefeltro, and then in the second *cantica* the salvation of his son Buonconte.

In the one remaining canto of the present group, Canto XXV, no such explicit parallel emerges. Yet on the level of implication, the connections are stronger here than at any other point in the sequence. For Canto XXV – describing the bolgia of the thieves – is the scene, as it were, of Dante's Paradise Lost: against a background of images evoking utter sterility and darkness, the protagonist witnesses the satanic transformation of human beings into serpents; and Dante as poet both foreshadows and parodies the redemption of human nature which he will finally represent through images of natural harmony in the Earthly Paradise on the summit of Purgatory.

In the light of these references, it is easy to see that in some sense the four cantos at the centre of the Malebolge are transitional in character. And that description is further justified by the fact that in at least three of these four cantos Dante gives particular prominence to the image of the journey. Here, as throughout the *Commedia*, journeying is seen emblematically as an expression of those activities of will and intellect which enable us, in our moral lives, to change or advance from point to point. This figurative significance, however, is rarely so clearly stated or strongly stressed as it is in Canto XXIV of the *Inferno*, where Dante depicts his own arduous progress, as protagonist, over the rocks of the sixth bolgia. And this emphasis, in turn, prepares for the far more complex – even ambiguous – treatment of the journey image which begins in Canto XXVI, where the journey of Ulysses, which is itself a pursuit of knowledge and experience, leads to destruction rather than to moral advance.

We shall, then, be concerned in this chapter with the ways in which Dante – in terms of his moral theme and in the organisation of his material – begins to effect an advance towards the second realm of his poem.

Yet it is evident, simply from the narrative plan of the *Inferno*, that the sequence we are now considering cannot be regarded as transitional in any simple sense. After all, Dante is still very far from the threshold of Purgatory. Indeed, he has still to complete the Malebolge. And beyond the Malebolge there lie the last four cantos of the first *cantica*, which are devoted to the ultimate sin of treachery. Here, as we shall see in the next chapter, the dominant images of the sequence are images not of progress but of ice and imprisonment; and in concentrating on these, Dante – so far from emphasising the imminence of his escape into Purgatory – draws attention, rather, to the immobility of the damned and the desperate finality of their fate. In these last cantos, the narrative impetus and imaginative expectations which gather in the central cantos of the Malebolge are brought to an abrupt and apparently total halt.

In that perspective, Cantos XXIV to XXVII of the *Inferno* might be described not as a transition but, just as accurately, as a false dawn or as a premature prophecy of escape. More accurately still, one might say that the sequence, while being traversed by suggestions and pressures from beyond its own confines, represents a pause or point of collection for some of the major issues of the *Commedia*. Certainly, in the immediate action of the Malebolge, the sequence, as we shall see, proves at one and the same time to be quite different in tone from the cantos that precede and follow it, and equally to summarise some of the main issues that we have been concerned with in the last chapter. However, in a wider context than the Malebolge itself, we should not by now be unfamiliar with sequences that stand apart from, or interrupt, the main line of narrative action. Throughout, effects of this sort constitute a principal feature of the difficulty of Dante's narrative procedure; and, to see more clearly the implications of this notion in the present case, it is useful to recall briefly the details of the episode in which the narrative pattern of advance and arrest first declared itself: which is to say, the first major transitional passage in the *Inferno*, where Dante attempts to enter the City of Dis.

Here, it will be recalled, at the very moment of transition, a pause occurred because Virgil was unable to command an entry at the Gates of Dis; and the journey of the two travellers was delayed until the *Messo da Ciel* arrived to open the gates on their behalf.

Now, there are undoubtedly significant differences between the present cantos of the Malebolge and the Dis episode. For one thing, the narrative of the protagonist, though subject to arrest and disturbance, does not now encounter any outward impediment as obvious as the Gates of Dis. We shall be concerned here with the ways in which the protagonist overcomes the *internal* impediments of physical weakness or distraction; and we shall see that he receives no assistance from any external agency such as the *Messo da Ciel*. The action of the sequence is as much concerned with the travail of conscience as with the dramas of physical travelling; and one notes that, in this respect, the sequence develops the concern with interiority which began in the bolgia of the hypocrites.

Nonetheless, there are at least three ways in which the issues raised in the Dis sequence will continue to concern us throughout the coming chapter. In respect of moral theme, we shall see – as, following the Dis episode, one saw for a first time in Dante's treatment of the heretic Farinata – the need for the individual to be open in mind to the impact of the 'new', even if this means the apparent destruction of integrity, or the humiliation of aspirations such as Vanni Fucci, Ulysses and Guido will be seen to entertain. So too on the level of narrative and textual structure we shall find dislocations of the kind which arose in the Dis episode through Dante's reference to scriptural and classical sources and in his direct addresses to the reader. But the third and most important resemblance lies in a discernible similarity between Dante's position as poet in the present sequence and the position he attributes to Virgil in the earlier episode.

Let us, on that score, again recall the details of that scene. It was, of course, precisely in this episode that Dante displayed most fully the virtues and limitations of the guide he had chosen for himself in Hell. Thus Virgil – while incapable of effecting an advance – does make it possible for Dante as protagonist to wait without confusion for the coming of the *Messo da Ciel*; in that sense his function is to instil a necessary patience into the protagonist. But, as we have seen, Dante also suggests here the prophetic role which he would have attributed to the poetry of the historical Virgil: Virgil keeps alive in the protagonist the vague but certain hope that deliverance is somehow possible; and in this regard he performs the task that Dante must have thought was performed by the prophetic author of the Fourth Eclogue. On the other hand, Virgil is able to offer no clear philosophical account of the *Messo* or of the problems dramatised in the action at the Gates of Dis. He had proved his powers of discourse only a canto earlier in his account of Fortuna; but now his words break into fragmented and truncated phrases which are so ambiguous that they increase rather than diminish the fears of his pupil (IX 7–8). Virgil here comforts Dante not by his 'parole ornate' but by his physical presence.

In outline the same pattern may explain the apparently anomalous position of Cantos XXIV to XXVII in the structure of the *Inferno*. Here Dante's imagination has dimly conceived what is eventually to come in the *Purgatorio*. (And note that we are speaking emphatically of Dante the poet: the premonitions of *Purgatorio* which we have observed in the sequence occur almost exclusively on the level of imagery and narrative plan). To this extent, the sequence is prophetic, in suggesting to the reader that there are ways of interpreting experience *other* than those which Dante is at present pursuing in the *Inferno*. At the same time, the prophecy, which is still far from being realised, emerges only in fragmentary suggestions in the implications of imagery. Thus the reader of the *Commedia* may be said to stand in the same relation to its author as, in the Dis episode, the Dante character stands to Virgil. As we shall see, there are many broken words and ambiguities in the sequence which the reader must tolerate in seeking to discern the ultimate order which Dante here seems to promise.

From this point of view, the sequence represents an intensification of issues that we discussed in the previous chapter. We have seen – for instance in Canto XIX where Dante as protagonist addresses Pope Nicholas III – how concerned Dante is in the Malebolge to assert his own prestige and authority. At the same time, his affirmation of identity is based upon the shifting sands of poetic language and narrative fiction; and the poet implicitly admits, in the comedy of the sequence, that on those grounds identity will be in constant danger of crumbling and constantly need to be rebuilt. So, too, in the present sequence Dante speaks out vigorously against the corruptions of contemporary Italy, attacking Pistoia, in Canto XXV as the nest of factional strife between Black and White Guelphs, and likewise uttering a scathing diatribe against his own native city, Florence, at the opening of Canto XXVI. Nor is Dante here speaking simply as protagonist. Both passages are the product of the authorial voice, addressing problems of immediate interest to the historical Dante; and in both cases, one recognises the tones of an Old Testament prophet vehemently measuring the disorders of the temporal world against the promise of absolute order which his vision of God has granted to him.

So Dante as poet certainly re-emphasises that position of prestige – as prophet and political leader – which he has been cultivating since the central cantos of the *Inferno*. At the same time, he also shows a renewed awareness of how easy it is even for the most exalted leaders to *mis*lead their followers and perpetrate deceit. Cantos XXVI and XXVII both deal with the sin of false counsel; and, while the linguistic level in each of these cantos is markedly different from the comic level that Dante sustains elsewhere in the Malebolge, each of the cantos in its own way suggests, as we shall see, how easily language – even at its most elevated, persuasive and clear – may prove fallacious.

As an assertion of Dante's own poetic prestige, Canto XXV occupies a position of especial importance in the present sequence. Here – at the centre of a sequence concerned with transition and the ultimate order of divinity – Dante witnesses a dreadful parody of transition and order in the transformations of thief to snake and snake to thief. But at the height of this vision Dante responds by producing – on a literary as much as a moral plane – a conscious transformation of his own. Lucan and Ovid have spoken in Latin of how the human form may be subject to metamorphosis; but now at lines 94–9, Dante, as vernacular poet, proudly declares that his own art outdoes the classical model. And here, in the interplay between classical and vernacular texts, there arises a sense in which the inherent lability of language that Dante always acknowledges can be turned to good effect. For, while Dante undoubtedly draws upon the repertoire of images and rhetorical devices which he had discovered in Lucan and Ovid, he founds his own claim to poetic merit upon his ability to alter and reapply such resources – developed, as it were, by *literary* leaders of the past – in pursuit of his own design. Linguistic changeability is here the source and condition of artistic fruitfulness.

Yet to see the reverse of this, we have only to turn from Canto XXV to Canto XXVI. Here Dante not only admits – in his portrayal of Ulysses – how misleading a classical model may be, but also, as we shall see, uses the canto to inspect and criticise some of the most essential principles of his own poetic procedure in the *Inferno*. It is here, moreover, that the reader is most likely to be a prey to the ambiguities and broken utterances of Dante's text. For Dante – so far from calling us to witness his own poetic virtuosity – formulates the issues of the canto in such a way as to make it exceptionally difficult for us to perceive where our sympathies or admiration should be directed.

In the opening pages of this book, I suggested that there were grounds for viewing the *Inferno* as an 'open' text, and that, with due qualification, we should expect to find evidence – especially in the Malebolge – of free invention in the play of linguistic signs. There are no cantos which illustrate better the value of such an approach – or, for that matter, the corresponding need for qualification – than the four we are now considering.

In this regard, it is particularly important to consider how Dante deals here with the theme of order. Running through the sequence, there is an extreme concern with the ways in which sin disorders or seeks to threaten both the natural and the divine dispensation: Ulysess challenges the limits set upon human knowledge, Guido attempts to manipulate to his own advantage the

divine plan embodied in the institutions of the Christian Church, while Vanni
Fucci is not only a thief – appropriating to himself possessions which, on any
just and orderly understanding, belonged to others – but also stands con-
demned particularly for violating the sacristy of a church in Pistoia and mak-
ing off with sacramental objects. Against this, we should surely expect that
Dante would make some decisive affirmation of divine order; in terms of the
text, we should expect, that is to say, some sort of closure or programmatic
statement of meaning. Yet strikingly this is precisely what Dante's text does
not provide. Just as Virgil at the Gates of Dis offers no philosophical remedy
against the disorder which the protagonist at that point is facing, so the poet
now intrudes no philosophical definition into the linguistic and narrative
action which he has here set in motion. (Indeed the only breath of philosophy
or diagnosis here is found in the mouth of the devils in Canto xxvii who
claim that they are logicians in their arguments over Guido's soul.)

Now we shall see – particularly in Canto xxiv – that Dante does assert the
underlying stability and dynamic force of the divine system against the
disorderliness of the sinners. But he does so as it were silently, and without
the comfort of philosophy, through the images of the sequence. And both
poet and reader, in the process of seeking some coherent meaning in these
images, are obliged to envisage to the full the anarchy and confusion which
the images initially stimulate.

In Chapter 1, we saw how, as early as the fourth line of the *Inferno*, Dante
set himself 'to treat of the good' that he was able to discern beneath the
anarchic surface of sin; and we saw too how this led him to act out the
principles of divine order in his own words and deeds. There is still some
sense of this in a canto such as *Inferno* xxiv. Yet by now it is equally
appropriate to speak of the *pathos* of order. Certainly, all the sinners in the
present sequence are made forcibly aware of the demands of divine order;
and nowhere does Dante depict more vigorously the action of God's ven-
geance. Yet – in this agitated pause – the text of these cantos itself demands
a comparable submission from its reader to an order which, at best, we only
dimly perceive through the veils of imagery and narrative distraction; and to
appreciate this fully we must allow, if only temporarily, that the human
capacity for signification is here at issue, and that the signs which Dante, on
various levels, brings into play, do have a tendency to float free from their
natural points of reference.

It follows from this that any interpretation of the moral significance of the
sequence must be accompanied by a close consideration of its textual and
structural features.

In part, this is to say that we must continue to examine, as we have since
the beginning of the Malebolge, the ways in which language itself, on the
level of diction, shifts between the two extreme poles of rhetorical elevation
and linguistic comedy. I would, however, stress that Dante shows an increas-
ing interest throughout the sequence with the linguistic categories of clarity
and ambiguity; this comes to its climax in the portrayal of Guido da

Montefeltro, where clarity of word and argument – in the absence of good conscience – prove to be dangerous and destructive.

More specifically, we must consider two other kinds of sign which are especially prominent here. One is the visual sign, which Dante renders in the images of his text; the other is the sign represented by the human figure itself. Throughout the *Inferno* – as indeed throughout the *Commedia* – the image and the human figure provide, as it were, alternatives to the signs of linguistic discourse. So, in the previous chapter we have observed how Dante's power of 'seeing' renders him superior to the malicious chatter of the sinners; we have also seen how Virgil himself becomes more important as a figure for human normality than as a fount of discourse. But now even these two forms of signification become subject to distortion.

As to the images of the sequence, we shall see that to an extent unparalleled in the rest of the *Inferno* these images perform an intensely symbolic function while releasing a disturbing range of archetypal and subliminal suggestions. Thus Canto XXVI is dominated by the fire of Ulysses's punishment and by the waters over which he travels in his final voyage. On the one hand, these images possess a gamut of positive associations, ranging from suggestions of purification to those of intellectual ardour. And so too in Canto XXVII, where fire is also the dominant image, Dante, from the first, associates the motif with those activities of human manufacture and art which take fire as their instrument. On the other hand, fire is seen also as a destructive and dangerous element, the destroyer of cities and – especially in Canto XXVII – an instrument of torture as well as craft. In a similar way, the serpent images of Canto XXIV may well recall the theological myth of Paradise Lost. Yet the scene which Dante creates here is equally rich in reference to the arts of magic and – in its depiction of perverse transformation – persistently evokes a range of primitive, sexual reference.

In Canto XXIV 140, the thief Vanni Fucci wishes to deprive Dante of the pleasure he might take in the *sight* of how the sinners in the seventh bolgia are punished, and so speaks of the defeat which Dante's political party will suffer at the hands of their enemies: 'Ma perché di tal vista tu non godi …'. This is enough to indicate the extent to which Dante's authority still depends upon his powers of vision. And in that respect, his riposte to Vanni Fucci is contained not so much in discourse as in that intensification of the vision of punishment which occurs in Canto XXV: the historical Dante may indeed suffer in the throes of factional politics; but as poet and visionary he can still see the whole truth expressed in the punishment, and mere words cannot prevent him. Yet at the end of the twenty-fifth canto, Dante acknowledges that the vision may itself have been so strange and disconcerting as to mar the page that he is writing: 'e qui mi scusi / la novità, se fior la penna abborra' (XXV 143–4). Here, seeing can be as dangerous as speech, and this becomes particularly true when the eye directs itself upon the human image.

Thus it is notable that Cantos XXIV to XXVII are distinct from the cantos that precede and follow them in the Malebolge by virtue of the magnitude of the

human presences which appear in them. In two cases – those of Ulysses and
of Guido – we cannot strictly speak of the human *figure*, since the two sin-
ners appear only in the form of the flames into which they have been trans-
mogrified. However, this annihilation will itself prove to be significant. And
the point at issue can best be illustrated initially by considering the case of
Vanni Fucci, who is at one point in the action a heap of ashes, at another an
intensely vigorous human shape. Bitten by a snake in Canto xxiv, Vanni first
dissolves into his elements and then on the instant returns to human form:

> Ne O sì tosto mai né I si scrisse,
> com' el s'accese e arse, e cener tutto
> convenne che cascando divenisse;
> e poi che fu a terra sì distrutto,
> la polver si raccolse per sé stessa,
> e 'n quel medesmo ritornò di butto.   (xxiv 100–5)

(No 'O' or 'I' was ever written as fast / as he flared up and was burned, / and had to
sink down all turned to ash. / And so lying destroyed upon the ground, / his dust of its
own accord drew itself together again, / and returned on the instant to what it was
before.)

At first view, Vanni Fucci belongs among the trivial and gross sinners who
people the majority of the bolge. But Vanni will prove to be the most
startlingly anarchic figure in the *Inferno*; and Dante confirms this when in
Canto xxv 14 he asserts that Vanni was the proudest figure that he saw in
Hell. In part, Dante's point here must certainly be that human pride is no
more than an illusory veil drawn over the triviality which Vanni, like every
other figure in the Malebolge, essentially displays. But to see the issue more
precisely one must note the terms in which Dante suggests this point, observ-
ing in particular the way in which the punishment that Vanni suffers is
compared directly to an act of writing: neither the letter *i* nor the letter *o*
could be written as fast as divine vengeance was exercised upon the sinner.

Now this image, of course, gives immediate support to the notion that the
human being in this sequence is itself to be regarded as a sign. And this in
turn suggests a conclusion in moral terms which – as we shall see when we
look in more detail at the passage – is entirely compatible with Dante's use
of the writing image in other parts of the *Commedia*: the human being has, it
appears, a duty to read aright and occupy its own position in the divine
sentence. We saw in the introductory chapter how the souls of the just –
particularly Rhipeus and Trajan – respond to this obligation. But the proud
do not; and we shall certainly see that both Ulysses and Guido in their
different ways might well be accused of misreading their own selves and
their own position in the world.

From a structural point of view, however, the remarkable thing is that
Dante – so late in the *Inferno* – should have allowed, or even invited, the
reader to misconstrue the human sign. Thus in the cases of Ulysses and
Guido the figures are so ambiguous that Dante himself may be thought to
have misread or at least been in danger of imitating the delusive example of

their actions. He too might easily be mistaken for – and might still, as he writes the *Commedia*, be in danger of becoming – an intellectual adventurer like Ulysses. As for Guido da Montefeltro, Dante, by including *him* among the false counsellors, admits all but explicitly that he himself has indeed misinterpreted the significance of the historical life of that figure. For in the *Convivio*, as we shall see, Dante expresses the utmost admiration for the historical Guido, as a model of how we should conduct and regulate our earthly lives.

In this regard, the figures of the sequence are not only equivocal as signs, but even appear chosen to stand as distorting mirrors in which Dante must contemplate his own deepest ambitions and purposes. And while this may not seem to apply to Vanni Fucci, the procedure in that case is simply more brutal than it is in the two later instances. For Vanni Fucci stands as the absolute opposite and ultimate distortion of Dante himself: both Vanni and Dante are men of pride; both in their way utter factional prophecies; and when Fucci assails the protagonist with a gleeful warning of the ills that will befall the historical Dante, the poet exerts his imagination to conceive the fitting counter-thrust that he delivers in Canto xxv.

On the level, then, of human signs as also on the level of linguistic and visual signs, the sequence displays a pathos of order. Throughout the *Commedia*, it is true, of course, that the human figure stands as the ultimate sign in which truth must be expressed. Order is never, for Dante, a matter merely of principle or design; it is rather a condition which must be embodied and shown forth in the life of the individual. So, in Paradise Beatrice and the saints are themselves living proof that the truth can become incarnate. So too in the *Inferno* and *Purgatorio*, Virgil remains an embodiment of all that can be realised in a human life through the action of reason, while the protagonist, as we have seen, also seeks to enact that order by all the means available to him. But the human figure – shifting, as it does in the present sequence, between the extremes of irrepressible pride and utter annihilation – is not only the most essential but also the least trustworthy of the forms in which we are to spell out a view of order. And Dante's imagination – as well as his Christian faith – clearly demands that he should make that attempt, however great the disorders that he must consequently tolerate.

II

Canto xxiv divides into two distinctly contrasted parts. In the second part of the canto – which is dominated by Vanni Fucci – we shall see exemplified all the ambiguities on the level of linguistic, visual and 'human' signs which are typical of the sequence at a whole. However, the first half of the canto is, on the surface, completely different in character. It is here that Dante, concentrating upon the progress of the protagonist and Virgil, resuscitates the moral image which is central not only to the present sequence, but also to the

Commedia at large: the image of the journey. He establishes here an emblem which stands as a clear point of reference for every subsequent portrayal of travelling or transition – whether fruitful or devious – that the sequence offers. Equally, the opening phase of the canto displays, in a positive aspect, many of the structural and linguistic features which elsewhere can seem dangerous or disconcerting; and in this regard, the canto prepares directly for the free and confident virtuosity of Canto xxv. At the same time, it is difficult to forget that the poise of the first half of the canto will be disrupted by the confusions of the second. The structural division of the canto is itself an illustration of transition and the pathos of transition in Dante's narrative text; and when the voice of Vanni Fucci assails the protagonist, the journey, for an instant, loses all its silent momentum in a welter of malicious words.

Between the sixth and seventh bolge – the bolgia of the hypocrites and the bolgia of the thieves – all the hitherto reliable bridges of the Malebolge have been reduced to ruins, despite the assurances of the devils in Canto xxii; and in consequence Virgil and Dante are obliged to rely upon main force in scrambling from one stage of their journey to the next.

Unlike other transitional cantos in the *Inferno*, the twenty-fourth canto marks no major division in the geography of Hell. Nor does Dante here picture the intervention of any supra-human agency in the story of his advance. It should, however, be remembered that the reason why the bridges have been broken is that the Harrowing of Hell sent irresistible shock waves through the material fabric of the region; and this already suggests a moral point of some importance. Dante may not be assisted directly by Providence here. Yet the climb would not be necessary were it not for the miraculous action of Providence; and the miracle is that God should have thrust his chosen subject back upon the essential resources of his physical nature. Thus the value of human nature at its simplest is allowed to reassert itself in the climb. But for that same reason, the episode also contributes an important strand to the theme of pride which, as we have said, will come into prominence in Cantos xxv and xxvi and has already begun to develop in the portrayal of the hypocrites in Canto xxiii.

In the canto of the hypocrites, we saw that Dante demanded – in a way that foreshadowed the ethics of the *Purgatorio* – that the mind should constantly re-engage with its essential spiritual purposes if it is to avoid the petrifaction of pride. Human beings are required to *work* if they are to assert their dignity – and, as we shall see, neither the thief Vanni Fucci, nor the ingenuous adventurer Ulysses, nor the corner-cutting Guido da Montefeltro will prove to know what work really means. Our human dignity – as Dante has asserted in one way or another since the Fortuna episode – resides in a willingness to undergo the apparent indignities of labour in the natural and temporal dispensation. This conclusion has a stylistic and imaginative

counterpart. For it implies that our pride – even where it is not derisory – is
the proper subject of comedy. We have seen how, in the early Malebolge,
comedy is a function of the theme of identity. Now Dante depicts himself in
terms which are both comic and realistic – as being utterly overwhelmed by
the climb he has to make. His breath is driven from his lungs: 'la lena m'era
del polmon sì munta' (43). (One notes, in anticipation, the irony of this:
Dante as protagonist is reduced to breathless silence where Dante as poet in
the following canto gives apparently untroubled vent to his detestation of
Pistoia, thievery and envy in a display of verbal pyrotechnics.) So, the heroic
mountaineer is constrained, in the course of his climb, to sit and receive the
reproaches of his guide, who insists that no one ever won fame by 'lolling on
a feather cushion or hiding under a blanket' (47–8). In the *Purgatorio* an
exactly comparable moment of comedy occurs on the cornices of Pride,
where the penitents, labouring under the weight of massive boulders, are
lightly mocked by the onomatopoeia which Dante introduces into their pant-
ing complaints: 'Piangendo parea dicer: "Più non posso"' (*Purg.* x 139) –
and weeping they appeared to say: 'More I cannot'.

The implications, both moral and poetic, of the opening sequence are
summarised in Virgil's speech of exhortation and reproach:

> 'Omai convien che tu così ti spoltre',
> disse 'l maestro; 'ché, seggendo in piuma,
> in fama non si vien, né sotto coltre;
>   sanza la qual chi sua vita consuma,
> cotal vestigio in terra di sé lascia,
> qual fummo in aere e in acqua la schiuma.
>   E però leva sù; vinci l'ambascia
> con l'animo che vince ogne battaglia,
> se col suo grave corpo non s'accascia'.   (XXIV 46–54)

('Now, in this way you must bestir yourself,' / my master said; 'for, sitting on feathers /
or beneath the blanket never brought anyone to fame; / without which whoever
consumes his own life / leaves of himself on earth a vestige / such as smoke in the air
and foam on the water. / And so get up: defeat your distressful breathing / with the
spirit that wins every battle / if it does not sink down with its heavy body'.)

Here Virgil enunciates an ethic of Herculean labour, while also recalling in
soberly elegiac tones the transitoriness of human existence. But note too how
varied in tone this oration is, as it moves between the high heroic rhetoric of
'vince ogne battaglia' and the pathos of 'qual fummo in aere e in acqua la
schiuma', and encompasses on the way the uncharacteristically trivial
locutions 'piuma' – feather-pillow – and 'coltre' – blanket. This is the first
instance of how shifting the linguistic surface of the sequence will be. But,
for the moment, we must emphasise the moral importance of these shifts. We
have only to compare the last *terzina* of Virgil's speech with the similar
words that Brunetto Latini speaks in Canto XV to appreciate the greater
vitality that Dante attributes to Virgil's injunctions: the heroism that Virgil
recommends is expressed not in worn-out rhetorical formulae, but with a

directness of the speaking voice – 'e però leva sù' – which moves easily over a whole gamut of verbal nuance. This is language at work, tuned to its object and morally fertile in a way that Brunetto's words could never be. One notes, moreover, the difference in comic tone between the cruel hoax which ensures that Brunetto should never win the prize he is aiming at and the self-critical humour with which Dante here envisages his own labours. Pride is defensive; work requires an openness – which is also an affirmation of wholeness – to every tremor of breath, word and tired nerve that the moral climb induces.

So Virgil here voices and illustrates the moral meaning of the climb. And his speech will prove to be no less important (particularly in considering the Ulysses episode) as a measure of clarity and linguistic vigour than his opening words – 'Non omo, omo già fui' – proved to be throughout the first half of the *Inferno*.

But behind Virgil stands the poet Dante, and his text too reflects in even subtler ways the linguistic and structural properties we have now begun to examine.

Consider the opening lines of Canto XXIV. The previous canto had concluded with an observation – realistic in pitch – of the fluctuations of feeling which Virgil *personaggio* suffered at being fooled by the lies of the devils. Similar fluctuations on the part of the protagonist form the subject of the first eighteen lines of Canto XXIV; and realism, too, is a part of the description of the scene which Dante now evokes. Yet the prevailing style of the passage is almost excessively decorative; and simply in its extraordinary length, the simile which Dante here introduces constitutes a striking example of those disproportions and dislocations that we are to discover elsewhere in the structure of the canto:

> In quella parte del giovanetto anno
> che 'l sole i crin sotto l'Aquario tempra
> e già le notti al mezzo dì sen vanno,
>   quando la brina in su la terra assempra
> l'imagine di sua sorella bianca,
> ma poco dura a la sua penna tempra,
>   lo villanello a cui la roba manca,
> si leva, e guarda, e vede la campagna
> biancheggiar tutta; ond' ei si batte l'anca,
>   ritorna in casa, e qua e là si lagna,
> come 'l tapin che non sa che si faccia;
> poi riede, e la speranza ringavagna,
>   veggendo 'l mondo aver cangiata faccia
> in poco d'ora, e prende suo vincastro
> e fuor le pecorelle a pascer caccia.
>   Così mi fece sbigottir lo mastro
> quand' io li vidi sì turbar la fronte,
> e così tosto al mal giunse lo 'mpiastro.   (1–18)

(In that part of the youthful year / when the sun moderates the locks of its rays under Aquarius / and already the nights fade towards half the day, / when the hoar-frost on the ground copies / the image of its white sister – / but the tone of its pen lasts only a short time – / the peasant, lacking for the things that sustain him, / gets up and looks out, and sees that the fields / have grown white: at which he strikes his thigh, / goes back into his house, and goes up and down grumbling, / like a miserable wretch who does not know what to do: / then he comes out again and revives his hopes, / seeing that the world has changed its countenance / in so little time; he takes his crook / and drives out his sheep to pasture. / So my master dismayed me / when I saw his brow so troubled, / and then the plaster quickly came to the hurt.)

We cannot here pause to do sufficient justice to the range of rhetorical and linguistic devices employed in this passage, save to say that the passage is more varied, and, even, more extravagant than any that Dante attributes to Virgil in the canto. It is, however, relevant to examine more closely the effects of disproportion which occur within the passage itself as well as in its relation to its context. Thus, in the first place, one notes the incongruity between the grandiloquence of the simile and the relative simplicity of the subject to which it refers. Certainly, the peasant-worker is translated – for the most part – far beyond his linguistic station. But the same could be said of the *feelings* to which Dante is actually referring here. These are the everyday sentiments of apprehension, timidity and subsequent relief. Indeed, the purpose of the passage is precisely to demonstrate that the anxieties of the protagonist are, after all, rather silly in the light of Virgil's renewed good humour. Yet in order to describe the changes in this simple *inner* landscape, Dante turns to the *outer* world of nature, evoking the most resonant images of cold, warmth, hunger, growth, brilliance and changing light.

Earlier, I spoke of how words and signs in this sequence tended to detach themselves from their obvious points of reference. Clearly, the opening lines of this canto justify that suggestion. At first, however, it may be thought that the pattern is one which has occurred before. For instance, in the Arsenal image of Canto XXI the reader will certainly be disappointed in any attempt to relate tenor to vehicle in the simile. Yet in a sense the reverse is true in Canto XXIV. For, once we can tolerate the disorderly fact that the simile has no strictly narrative application, there appears an abundance of possible meanings to which we can convert these lines. The very detachment of the simile from its immediate context invites the reader to consider what points of connection there might be, beneath the surface of the narrative sequence, which can justify the imaginative attention that Dante has exerted upon the passage. The discomposure of surface alerts our expectations to some hidden rationale; and these expectations are not disappointed.

In the first place, the passage is only the most conspicuous in a sequence of natural images which began in Canto XXII – with its references to dogs, hawks and dolphins – and has already produced, in Canto XXIII, a striking comparison between the speed with which Dante and Virgil flee from the devils and the speed of a mill-race:

> Non corse mai sì tosto acqua per doccia
> a volger ruota di molin terragno,
> quand' ella più verso le pale approccia ...   (XXIII 46–8)

(Water never ran so swiftly through a sluice, / to turn the wheel of a land-mill / when it approaches nearest to the paddles).

Like the description of the *villan*, this passage points to an association between the movements of the natural world and the purposes of human construction and labour: the mill-stream is harnessed to human design; the *villan* is frustrated until he is able to get on with the work in hand as the weather changes. In this respect, the two passages confirm that – as Dante moves away from the bolgia of barratry – he has begun to envisage a possible reconciliation between human beings, in their normal lineaments, and the natural environment of human life; and by Canto XXVI that reconciliation, portrayed in another pastoral simile, has become a part of the poet's theme. Here, describing the flames in which the counsellors of fraud are confined, Dante produces an image of harvest which exactly parallels the winter scene of Canto XXIV, depicting not the frustration of work, but the fruition to which it can come within the cycle of the seasons:

> Quante 'l villan ch'al poggio si riposa,
> nel tempo che colui che 'l mondo schiara
> la faccia sua a noi tien meno ascosa,
>   come la mosca cede a la zanzara,
> vede lucciole giù per la vallea,
> forse colà dov' e' vendemmia e ara: (XXVI 25–30)

(As many [fireflies] as the peasant [sees] – / at the time when he that illuminates the world / holds his face least hidden to us, / at the hour when the fly gives way to the mosquito – / down there along the valley / where perhaps he gathers the grape and tills.)

Against the background of the Malebolge, where humanity is wholly divided from its natural origins, these images express, as we shall see, not only a view of the physical harmony between the human and the natural, but also an understanding of how the desires and intentions of the human being may properly be trained upon the objects of the physical world: the 'work' that the *villan* of Canto XXVI performs is a work of contemplation, as he sits in a scene which embodies the fruit of the changing hours and seasons. In this sense, the series of nature-and-work images not only depicts the kind of harmony which Dante is looking to restore in the depths of the Malebolge, but also points to the habits of mind which will lead to an appreciation of that underlying compatibility between humanity and nature. Certainly, in a sequence which reaches its climax with the false counsellors Ulysses and Guido, the *villan* – even from the marginal position of the simile – will come to act as a pastoral counterpart to the heroic strivings and confusions that are depicted in the main narrative action. Along with Dante himself, the true hero of this sequence is the *villan*, whose very humility allows him to focus attention and effort upon the object most nearly to hand.

One function, then, of the opening image in Canto XXIV is to contribute to the development of that standard of judgement which will be brought to bear with particular force upon those who, for all their intelligence, have been unable or unwilling to reconcile themselves to the sphere of their proper human activity.

But what contribution does the passage make to the theme, so to say, of signification in the sequence? Above all else, the virtuosity of these lines clearly points forward to the poetic display of Canto XXV where – despite the unnatural horror which there replaces the pastoral celebrations of Canto XXIV – Dante also works on his text in the apparent confidence that signs, of whatever kind, can be so manipulated as to yield meanings where none existed before. But Canto XXIV also suggests in two ways the grounds on which Dante might base that confidence in the possibility of signification.

In the first place, Nature itself is seen in Canto XXIV as a system of signs. The *villan* reads the natural world outside his doors; and though at first the signs are so ambiguous or impenetrable as to leave him in a state of paralysed frustration, he nonetheless regulates his behaviour in conformity to the alterations of the physical environment. The *villan* at least is confident, on the level of commonsense and common experience, that the mute images of the natural world embody a secret order of things and changing states.

But the same may be said, in the second place, of the human sign. We are, after all, concerned here with the gaze that Dante nervously fixes upon Virgil's countenance. And here, as throughout the canto, Dante allows that there must be a certain element of illegibility about the inner thoughts of another person. So, likewise, at line 23 Virgil is shown to preface his response to the protagonist with private and secret meditation, and then to address himself to his follower with a delicacy and far-sightedness which both exceed immediate comprehension:

> Le braccia aperse, dopo alcun consiglio
> eletto seco riguardando prima
> ben la ruina, e diedemi di piglio.
> E come quei ch'adopera ed estima,
> che sempre par che 'nnanzi si proveggia,
> così ...   (XXIV 22–7)

(He opened his arms – after some counsel / taken within himself, looking first / well at the ruin – and then laid hold of me. / And like one who works and reckons, / always seeming to think and look ahead / thus).

Likewise, in a strangely colloquial and markedly hypothetical aside at line 36, Dante professes ignorance of how Virgil might have responded to the climb, had the topography of the Malebolge been even more severe than it actually was: 'non so di lui, ma io sarei ben vinto' – I don't know about him, but I would have been completely defeated. From the first, then, the canto shows an interest in areas of misapprehension which would seem to have little place in the relationship between Dante and Virgil. Yet to attribute, as Dante does here, such independence of thought and emotion to his leader is to enhance one's awareness of Virgil's ordinary human presence. The Virgil who pursues his own train of thought in this canto is also the Virgil who lifts and urges the protagonist onwards to safety: his presence is as valuable and normal as the presence of the *villan* in his workmanlike landscape. So too the protagonist – to please his guide – feigns a better courage than in fact he feels: 'mostrandomi fornito / meglio di lena ch'i' non mi sentia' (58–9) – showing myself better furnished with breath than I felt myself to be; and with this it becomes clear that the canto has a prevailing interest in the secrecy, frauds and shifts of thought and emotion which characterise the simple relationship of any one person and another. The actuality of both Virgil and the protagonist is established at this point by the very opacity of their responses each to each. But if, in his treatment of the *villan*, Dante progressively reveals the confidence which human beings rightly should be able to take in the world around them, so here he extends this confidence to the sphere of the human relationships into which the individual may enter. One human being may not fully grasp the thoughts or intentions of another, or appreciate entirely the motives that shape his actions. But the simple presence of the companion is itself an assurance – or may be – of a wholeness and coherence of design. Ulysses and Guido, as we shall see, are characteristically either intolerant or unaware of the presence of other beings: subtle as Ulysses's mind can be, he is concerned rather to master rather than to admit the subtleties of feelings that his companions might evince, while Guido pursues the authority of papal absolution to a point at which he blinds himself to the deviousness – evident as this is – of the Pope with whom he is treating. Against this, the relationship which Dante depicts between the protagonist and Virgil in this canto offers as much evidence of how confident the mind might be in its dealings with others as does the *villan* of the confidence that we may properly enjoy in our natural environment.

Canto XXIV, then, opens with a promise of coherence in the face of shifting weathers and of shifting thoughts. And this promise will be fully redeemed – on behalf of the reader as well as the poet and protagonist – as soon as Dante begins the *Purgatorio*. For in Purgatory not only do natural changes of time and solar change contribute directly to the salvation – or wholeness – of the penitent, but the ungraspable play of emotion between one penitent and another is shown to be as real a part of the penitential life as it is here of the relationship between Dante and Virgil. In this respect, the simile may be regarded as prophetic, announcing an order which has yet to be realised in full.

More immediately, however, we must consider the second half of the present canto. And here – even before the appearance of Vanni Fucci – the character of Dante's text changes so drastically as to undermine all the confidence and coherence that we have just seen constructed.

Consider, for instance, the two comparisons which are used to describe the seventh bolgia and the punishment which the thieves suffer within it. The bolgia is a sterile space swarming with serpents more various than could be found, says Dante, even in Libya:

> Più non si vanti Libia con sua rena;
> ché se chelidri, iaculi e faree
> produce, e cencri con anfisibena,

né tante pestilenzie né sì ree
mostrò già mai con tutta l'Etïopia
né con ciò che di sopra al Mar Rosso èe.   (85–90)

(Let Libya with all her sands boast no more! / For if she [produces] chelydri, jaculi and phareae / and chencres with amphisbaena, / pestilences so great and malignant / she never showed forth with all Ethiopia / nor with all [the land] that lies on the Red Sea.)

And within the bolgia, one of the sinners – who proves to be Vanni Fucci – having been reduced to ashes by the bite of one of these reptiles, is violently restored to his former shape, as if an essential part of his punishment were that he should *not* be allowed the comfort of extinction. His rebirth is compared to the rebirth of the phoenix:

Così per li gran savi si confessa
che la fenice more e poi rinasce,
quando al cinquecentesimo anno appressa;
    erba né biado in sua vita non pasce,
ma sol d'incenso lagrime e d'amomo,
e nardo e mirra son l'ultime fasce.   (106–11)

(Thus, so the great sages affirm, / the phoenix dies and is born again, / when it approaches its five hundredth year. / During its life it feeds not on herb or grain, / but only on the tears of incense and amomum; / and nard and myrrh are its last burial-sheet.)

These two comparisons, both exotic in character, have nothing in common with the pastoral simile which opened the canto, save in displaying a similar degree of virtuosity. In the first case, moreover, the point of the comparison is precisely that there *is* a disproportion between the scene which Dante witnessed and any that might have been seen on earth, even in Libya; the scene is ungraspable for all the strength of imagination or technicality of diction that the poet may bring to bear upon it. In the second case, too, there is an evident incongruity in the application of the phoenix image to the sinner Vanni Fucci. For the phoenix is regularly an emblem for the resurrected Christ, though here applied to a preternatural resurrection which affects the sinner as painfully as the destruction that precedes it. Unlike the Libya image, the phoenix comparison emphasises the possibility of wholeness, not pestilence and death. To that extent – at least insofar as it points to the ultimate wholeness which Christ secures for humanity – the simile is consistent with the implications of the *villan* image. But the promise it offers in adducing, obliquely, the doctrine of resurrection is a promise we can only perceive through the veil of parody; and to acknowledge that parody at all is to admit comparisons which come close to being a blasphemous perversion. Signs here, so far from being merely ambiguous, have become positively dangerous.

In both these introductory comparisons, Dante has made use of classical models; but in both cases, the model has proved, at the very least, unhelpful or delusive. There is reason here for Dante to attempt that vigorous rewriting of the classical model which he proceeds to perform in the consciously

'vernacular' idiom of Canto xxv. But first the vernacular must erupt with all
the crude vigour that Dante ascribes to Vanni Fucci, who, breaking through
the classical integument in which he is initially presented, immediately chal-
lenges all forms of coherent signification and reduces them all, unmistakably,
to blasphemy.

As Dante and Virgil progress towards the seventh bolgia, the subtle inter-
play between them of mutual comfort reaches its climax in a remarkable in-
stance of friendly feigning which shows discourse to be neither more nor less
than a means to disguise the physical reality of the climb. Dante goes on
speaking as much as he can, so as not to appear exhausted – 'parlando
andava per non parer fievole' (64); and the bravado of speech here has its
point in maintaining both companionship and the appearance, at least, of
heroic stature. But at precisely this point a dreadful voice is heard, which
throws into confusion the pretensions of the two travellers:

> Parlando andava per non parer fievole;
> onde una voce uscì de l'altro fosso,
> a parlar formar disconvenevole.   (64–6)

(I went on speaking, so as not to appear exhausted; / when a voice issued from the next
ditch, / ill-suited for forming words.)

This may not be Vanni Fucci himself; but the voice speaks as Vanni must
speak, screaming at the bite of the serpent. Words here begin to disintegrate,
and sight too is at risk. For, eager to identify the source of this inhuman cry,
Dante and Virgil – having at last reached the summit of the cliff – now
immediately begin to venture down its other face; and words are relegated to
silence as they do so:

> 'così giù veggio e neente affiguro'.
>   'Altra risposta', disse, 'non ti rendo
> se non lo far; ché la dimanda onesta
> si de' seguir con l'opera tacendo'.   (75–8)

('but I look down and see nothing.' / 'I give you', he replied, 'no other reply / save the
action; for a fit demand / should be followed in silence by the deed.')

As so often before, the question underlying Dante's procedure as poet in the
following canto will concern the relative status of perception and speech; and
certainly the figure of Vanni Fucci is designed to challenge the sanity of the
protagonist on the plane both of perception and of language.

Thus, as the protagonist sees deep into the pit of serpents – 'e vidivi entro
terribile stipa / di serpenti ...' (82–3) – he witnesses the first transformation,
performed, as we have seen, as quickly before his eyes as the writing of the
smallest letters in the alphabet:

> Ed ecco a un ch'era da nostra proda,
> s'avventò un serpente che 'l trafisse
> là dove 'l collo a le spalle s'annoda.   (97–9)

(And behold: at one who was near our bank / a serpent darted and transfixed him / there
where the neck is knotted to the shoulder.)

The human form of the sinner is instantaneously destroyed and re-established. The action indeed seems almost to envisage a new, unthinkable dimension in which the distinctions established by volume and time have no permanence at all. Within the confines of this dimension, a battle of words is now joined between Dante and his malign mirror image, in which both contend for linguistic command and control of the available imaginative space. The subtle interplay of secret thoughts and emotions which began the canto gives way to a direct 'flyting', in which Vanni on the one hand and Dante as poet and protagonist on the other each seeks to discompose the security – or wholeness – of the other.

So the very sight of the punishment which Vanni suffers is enough to challenge any simple confidence in the integrity or stability of the human person. But Vanni proves also to be a more active threat; for he is certainly more than a simple thief. As we have seen, Dante describes him as the 'proudest spirit' that he encountered in Hell, and the obscene directness of his challenge to God in Canto XXV is only the most outrageous expression of the crimes for which he is condemned to Hell. So, as he himself declares, he was the 'ladro a la sagrestia d'i belli arredi' (138) – the thief who stole the fine fittings from the sacristy. His deeds from the first have been sacrilegious, disturbing the very signs of God's presence that the church contains. So, too, his hatred of Dante is motivated by sheer envy – which is the sin of the serpent and of Satan in Eden – at the sight of the divine favour displayed in the protagonist.

Thus Fucci is shown to resent very deeply the advantage which the protagonist has over him. In response to Virgil's command that he should declare his name (121), Vanni has been forced to speak of his own character in terms of the clearest self-condemnation:

> Vita bestial mi piacque e non umana,
> sì come a mul ch'i' fui; son Vanni Fucci
> bestia, e Pistoia mi fu degna tana.   (124–6)

(The life of a beast pleased me, not human life, / mule that I was: I am Vanni Fucci, / the beast, and Pistoia was a fitting den for me.)

The protagonist in his turn has unambiguously recognised Vanni for what he was: 'omo di sangue e di crucci' (129) – a man of blood and rage. Now, however, Vanni attempts to obscure this clear, final and 'legible' definition of his moral nature by unsettling the mind of the protagonist. And Dante, as poet and prophet, allows the sinner to end the canto with his own malicious speech of prophecy:

> Ma perché di tal vista tu non godi,
> se mai sarai di fuor da' luoghi bui
> apri li orecchi al mio annunzio, e odi.   (140–2)

(But so that you may not rejoice in the sight, / if ever you escape from these dark regions, / open your ears and hear what I foretell.)

Dante's party will come to disaster, and Vanni declares it, as he concludes, to injure Dante:

E detto l'ho perché doler ti debbia.   (151)

(And I have said this so as to grieve you.)

So the canto ends with no indication of how the episode is to continue, with no hint of how a transition is to be made; the balance and clarity which characterised the opening parts of the canto have been wholly destroyed. The recalcitrant pride of the 'mule' has replaced the dignified humanity of the two travellers, and the senseless and divisive voice of the sinner echoes (with the ring of truth) in the imagination of both reader and historical author. Now, however, we turn to a canto, wholly different in structure from Canto XXIV, which expresses in fullest measure the pathos of order. For where Virgil's voice has dominated the centre of the present canto, and that of Vanni its conclusion, the one voice which is heard from first to last in the following canto is the voice of the poet himself, striving as he has from the outset in the *Inferno* to treat of the good which can be perceived even through the veil of the poet's own worst imaginings.

III

With the opening *terzina* of Canto XXV, language reaches its nadir in an act as remote from praise as any could be; and at the same time the human figure, which throughout the thieves sequence is subject to the extreme degradations that punishment imposes upon it, degrades itself morally by shaping itself to a gesture of truculent obscenity. Though God has revealed his power to him only moments ago, Vanni persists in defiance, directing heavenwards the sign of the figs with both his fists, the thumbs projecting through clenched fingers in imitation of the sexual act:

Al fine de le sue parole il ladro
le mani alzò con amendue le fiche,
gridando: 'Togli, Dio, ch'a te le squadro!'.   (*Inf.* XXV 1–3)

(His words at an end, the thief / hoisted both his hands aloft – in each of them the fig-sign – / yelling: 'God, that's for you; I'm aiming them at you!')

As the canto proceeds, Vanni's blasphemy, and more especially his obscenity, will continue to resonate in an undercurrent of sexual imagery. At the same time, Dante has already begun to exert himself to control the implications of the image he has created. So, if no sinner in Hell is prouder than Vanni Fucci (14), then nowhere in the *Inferno* does the poet envisage with such precision the moral order in eternity that renders pride ridiculous. For the sinner is immediately assailed by the snakes which populate the bolgia; and where Vanni's own gesture is vain and ineffectual, the snakes proceed with exact calculation to repress the flailing hands and the voice of the sinner. The action of the sinner is as vigorously drawn as any in the *Inferno*. Yet the vigour of the sinner is equalled by that of the response it evokes. As instruments of divine revenge, two serpents seize upon Vanni to throttle him and bind his hands down; and the protagonist is shown to approve entirely of this response:

> Da indi in qua mi fuor le serpi amiche,
> perch' una li s'avvolse allora al collo,
> come dicesse 'Non vo' che più diche';
> e un'altra a le braccia, e rilegollo,
> ribadendo sé stessa sì dinanzi,
> che non potea con esse dare un crollo. (4–9)

(From that point on the serpents were my friends. / First, one of them wound itself around his neck, / as if to say: 'I'll have you speak no more'; / and then, at his arms, a second bound him tighter still, / knotting itself about him, / so the sinner in its links could neither shake nor stir.)

From this point on, no human figure is allowed any stable presence in the canto. Indeed, the next figure to appear is hardly human at all. It is the centaur Cacus; and even in his case, as in Vanni's, the human means of expression are precisely extinguished by the snakes as they bind him from thorax to lower lip. As Vanni exits (unable any longer to speak), Cacus enters in pursuit. But he too is throttled by the snakes:

> El si fuggì che non parlò più verbo:
> e io vidi un centauro pien di rabbia
> venir chiamando: 'Ov' è, ov' è l'acerbo?'
> Maremma non cred' io che tante n'abbia,
> quante bisce elli avea su per la groppa
> infin ove comincia nostra labbia. (16–21)

(He fled; he spoke no further word. / And then I saw a centaur, all enraged, / who cried as he came: 'Where is he, then, where is the sour creature?'. / There cannot be, I think, in all the region of Maremma / as many snakes as were around that centaur, / upward from its animal haunch to the point at which the countenance of the human being begins.)

But if the sinners are silenced, the poet is not; already he has begun to replace the Dante character as the point of moral reference in the canto. For it is the poet who stands out of the frame of the narrative at line 10 to deliver a judgement upon Vanni and his native city, Pistoia:

> Ah! Pistoia, Pistoia, ché non stanzi
> d'incenerarti sì che più non duri,
> poi che 'n mal fare il seme tuo avanzi? (10–12)

(Ah Pistoia, Pistoia, why do you not resolve / to burn yourself to ashes, and thus endure no longer? / For you outdo in the wrong you do the seed you sprang from.)

This judgement – cast in prophetic tones – is Dante's answer to the prophecy which Vanni uttered in the previous canto. Clearly Dante associates his own judgements with the peculiar authority that God has given him in allowing him to envisage the whole of truth in his journey through eternity. But the poet is required to enact this order in the words he writes; and from this point on the force of the canto derives from an interplay of subliminal suggestion, in the imagery that Dante releases in the canto and the moral fervour with which he seeks to control it. For the reader, the point of reference in a canto where otherwise the human figure is absent and chaos seems very close is the action of the poet.

In terms of moral principle, the images of transformation on which Dante concentrates throughout the canto are themselves significant. Though it is here, at first view, that the evidence of anarchy principally arises, it is also true that the picture of unceasing change directly recalls the treatment of change which occurred as early as Canto VII in the depiction of Fortuna. And it is appropriate to bear in mind that earlier sequence when assessing the reasons for Dante's judgement of theft: the odium in which he holds the sin might well seem to be excessive until one recalls that theft is a form of malicious greed. As we saw in the Fortuna passage, the divine dispensation allows for the possession of goods, provided that human beings understand the condition under which these goods are possessed. Fortuna is the law that God has set over the 'ben vani' of the physical world so that things must continually change hands, in permutations (VII 79; 88) incomprehensible to human beings. Theft, in its turn, is a knowing and violent attempt to evade that condition; and in this light the punishment that the thieves endure amounts to a forcible insistence upon the law against which the sinners offended.

If Canto XXV looks back to Canto VII of the *Inferno*, it also looks forward to Canto XVIII of the *Paradiso*, where Dante celebrates the conformity that humanity may enjoy through justice with the design of God. Here too Dante depicts a scene of metamorphosis; the souls of the just move before Dante's eyes through a series of transformations, first spelling out the words *Diligite Iustitiam* before him, and finally coming to rest in the form of an eagle – the emblem of both justice and love:

> e quïetata ciascuna in suo loco,
> la testa e 'l collo d'un'aguglia vidi
> rappresentare a quel distinto foco.   (*Par.* XVIII 106–8)

(Each of them [I saw] now still within its place, / – the head and neck of an Eagle / depicted in the sharp-lined fire.)

Not only do the thieves undergo a comparable series of changes, but Vanni too was first associated, as are the just in Paradise, with the act of writing: Dante saw the sinner transformed (at XXIV 100) faster than *i* or *o* could be written. We have already suggested the significance of this parallel: where the thief, having meddled with the divine dispensation, is passive and broken before the word of God, the just move freely in the order of its creative mystery.

Canto XXV, then, occupies an important place in Dante's progressive treatment of the theme of order. But the poet, like the just of *Paradiso* XVIII, has

the responsibility of 'writing' God's justice in such a way as to affirm order
in the face of all the evidence of change and anarchy. Canto XXV does not so
much discuss the theme of order as enact it; and the question we must now
consider is how the canto is composed so as to achieve this.

The opening of the canto already gives an indication of Dante's procedure.
For while, taken out of context, Vanni's obscene gesture of defiance is an
apparent expression of anarchic energy, the very placing of the incident after
the canto-break isolates that gesture and exposes it to judgement. Vanni's
action is not allowed to appear as a coherent climax to his defiant speech; on
the contrary, by introducing an hiatus into the presentation of Vanni, Dante
allows himself the whole of the subsequent canto in which to provide his
own reply to the disconcerting prophecy that Vanni was allowed to utter in
the previous canto. On another level, the highly conscious artistry to which
Dante draws attention at the culmination of the transformation scene is
already tacitly in evidence in the Cacus sequence of the opening lines.
Although the history of Cacus is told through the mouth of Virgil
personaggio, the representation of Cacus is also an attempt to transform, or
even outdo, the description of the monstrosity which Virgil the poet offers in
Aeneid VIII. Virgil's story in the *Aeneid* certainly tells of the desecration of
the sacred territory of Rome by the marauder; and so too in the *Inferno* he
speaks of how 'beneath the rock of the Aventine Hill, Cacus time and time
over made a lake of blood' (26–7). The *Aeneid*, moreover, tells of the de-
fence of Rome and the ultimate defeat of the beast by Hercules; and again
Dante's words here accurately reflect their source, speaking of how Cacus
died beneath the club of Hercules (32). But in the present context, it is Dante
who occupies the role of Hercules as the defender of spiritual order – and a
demi-god destined for Paradise. And just as he, in the twenty-fifth canto at
large, translates the Virgilian theme of order and justice from a purely social
to a spiritual level, so in constructing his own image of Cacus he goes far
beyond the Virgilian model. In the *Aeneid*, Cacus is referred to simply as
'semihomo' (194). Yet Dante has built this suggestion into the vivid and
plastic image of a centaur writhing with snakes:

> Sovra le spalle, dietro da la coppa,
> con l'ali aperte li giacea un draco
> e quello affuoca qualunque s'intoppa.   (*Inf.* XXV 22–4)

(Over its shoulders, behind the nape, / a dragon was lying, its wings outspread; /
whatever it strikes upon it sets on fire.)

We saw as early as the Charon episode in Canto III how Dante can
deliberately challenge Virgil's art. Here the challenge produces a picture of
lurid disorder at the very root of existence in the hybrid beast. In this respect,
the representation of Cacus prepares for the main action of the canto. For it is
precisely such images – and his own power to conceive them – that Dante
must now proceed to deal with.

Thus we come to the transformations which dominate the centre of the canto. As the centaur runs by, Virgil is interrupted by the arrival of three more thieves:

> Mentre che sì parlava, ed el trascorse,
> e tre spiriti venner sotto noi,
> de' quai né io né 'l duca mio s'accorse,
>   se non quando gridar: 'Chi siete voi?';
> per che nostra novella si ristette,
> e intendemmo pur ad essi poi.   (34–9)

(The centaur as Virgil was speaking ran by, / and beneath us there came three spirits, / whom neither I nor my leader had noticed / until they shouted out: 'So who are you?' / Our talk was interrupted by this / and we turned our attention solely on them.)

At first, the action here is entirely comprehensible, even banal. Nothing could be more normal than the question that the spirits ask, or the comic impudence with which they break in upon Virgil's solemn discourse. Natural, however, as these figures appear, their demeanour echoes the truculence of Vanni Fucci, and pitted against them is a power unaccountable in design and magnitude. Thus the everyday question which they proceed to ask, inquiring of the whereabouts of an acquaintance – 'Cianfa dove fia rimaso?' (43): Cianfa, where has he got to? – is itself the act which releases the first of the transformations. For the missing Cianfa is the six-legged serpent who now leaps on the questioner:

> Com' io tenea levate in lor le ciglia,
> e un serpente con sei piè si lancia
> dinanzi a l'uno, e tutto a lui s'appiglia.   (49–51)

(As, with straining eyes, I stared upon them, / a six-footed serpent darts up / in front of one of them, and grapples itself all around him.)

From now on, the reader has to contemplate not only the humiliation of the human figure, but also an action that appears to contravene all schemes of thought that are natural to the human mind. Yet Dante acknowledges the problem that this poses. With a gesture of authority, the protagonist presumes to silence Virgil; sensing that a mystery is to reveal itself, he seems to recognise the incapacity of the rational mind to comment upon it. At the same time, the poet turns directly to the reader:

> Se tu se' or, lettore, a creder lento
> ciò ch'io dirò, non sarà maraviglia,
> ché io che 'l vidi, a pena il mi consento.   (46–8)

(If you are slow at this point, reader, to credit / what I tell you, it will not be remarkable, / for I who observed it can barely allow myself to believe.)

Here, the twenty-fifth canto touches upon an essential characteristic of the *Inferno*. We are asked to believe the unbelievable. And, though the poet excuses *disbelief*, he offers his own example as an encouragement to the reader to exert his own attentions.

Co' piè di mezzo li avvinse la pancia
e con li anterïor le braccia prese;
poi li addentò e l'una e l'altra guancia;
    li diretani a le cosce distese,
e miseli la coda tra 'mbedue
e dietro per le ren sù la ritese.
    Ellera abbarbicata mai non fue
ad alber sì, come l'orribil fiera
per l'altrui membra avviticchiò le sue.
    Poi s'appiccar, come di calda cera
fossero stati, e mischiar lor colore,
né l'un né l'altro già parea quel ch'era:
    come procede innanzi da l'ardore,
per lo papiro suso, un color bruno
che non è nero ancora e 'l bianco more.   (52–66)

(With its middle feet it clasped the paunch; / the arms were taken by those at the front. / It sank its teeth into either cheek. / Extending its hind-legs the length of each thigh, / it now stuck its tail in between them, / bending it up behind the loins. / No growth of ivy, tangled / in a tree, ever clung so tenaciously as that appalling monster, / weaving its parts around and through the other like tendrils. / And then, as if the two of them were heated wax, they stuck together; / their colourings began to mix, / and neither had the look of what, at first, he had been. / So [when a sheet of paper catches fire,] / a shadow precedes the spreading flame, / not black and yet the whiteness dies.)

Implicitly, the closing lines of this passage convey how difficult – even perilous – the description that Dante here attempts must be. At lines 143–4 Dante will suggest that the novelty of his subject may well have confused his pen. The same possibility, however, is touched upon in the image of burning paper; the subject almost has the power to destroy the page on which the poet seeks to confine it. Yet language – as Dante also implies – is capable of containing within its bounds the most extreme abnormalities. For the image of the ivy is an allusion to Ovid's *Metamorphoses* iv 365, the image of melting wax an allusion to Lucan's *Pharsalia* ix 782. And, while, later, Dante presumes to outdo both Ovid and Lucan, he relies here on his solidarity with the example of those who have preceded him in describing metamorphosis; their language itself constitutes a model and a norm. Dante now enunciates a norm of his own, expressed in three aspects of the imagery that dominates the following transformations.

The first of these is number. As created order presents itself to the mind in the permutations of Fortune, so the adumbration of a greater truth appears in an unremitting play on the factors one, two and zero. Three sinners approach, yet the perfection symbolised by this number is destroyed as the serpent fuses, with its own six legs, the arms, cheeks and thighs of the single man. Nor is any unity created by this fusion; the grotesque miscegenation produces only a negation of number:

Li altri due 'l riguardavano, e ciascuno
gridava: 'Omè, Agnel, come ti muti!
Vedi che già non se' né due né uno'.   (67–9)

(The others looked on, and each of them, / dismayed, exclaimed: 'Agnello, how you change! / Look, you are already neither two nor one.')

The sense of number, however, is not absent. For while the sinners themselves are passive in their recognition of it, the poet's own verse sustains the sense with the utmost vigour. This is especially evident in the handling of the caesura. Throughout the *Commedia* the placing of the caesura is a vital feature of Dante's technique. And something of the subtlety he can attain by it is seen from the following lines, where the Christian philosophers celebrate, as the thieves cannot, the perfection of number in the Trinity, singing of

> Quell' uno e due e tre che sempre vive
> e regna sempre in tre e 'n due e 'n uno.   *(Par.* xiv 28–9)

(That one and two and three that lives for ever / and reigns for ever in three and two and one.)

The fluency of such a passage is wholly lacking in Canto xxv. Here the pause is employed throughout to bring into relief the clash and contrast of number. Thus, not pausing to elaborate the pathetic cry of the sinners, the canto goes on, with its unremitting articulation:

> Già eran li due capi un divenuti
> quando n'apparver due figure miste
> in una faccia, ov' eran due perduti.
>   Fersi le braccia due di quattro liste;
> le cosce con le gambe e 'l ventre e 'l casso
> divenner membra che non fuor mai viste.
>   Ogne primaio aspetto ivi era casso:
> due e nessun l'imagine perversa
> parea; e tal sen gio con lento passo.   (70–8)

(The heads of the two by this time were one; / and two profiles were seen mingling / within one single face where two had vanished. / Replacing four arm-lengths, two arms had appeared. / Out of legs, out of thighs, out of stomach and chest, / members were made of a kind never seen. / Now every original feature had been erased. / [A semblance] it was of both two and none, that perverse image. / And such as it was it then moved away at a slow pace.)

Important, however, as number is, there appear simultaneously two other groups of images to enforce its significance. The first derives from the natural world in its simplest aspect. Already the tangles of the snakes have been compared to ivy. And images of this kind, in the context of the cantos that precede and follow the twenty-fifth, have especial force. For, as we have seen, both Cantos xxiv and xxvi make emphatic reference to the natural world, the former beginning with its great depiction of a peasant in a winter landscape, the latter matching this with a simile of summer and repose. The force of these passages could hardly be clearer: to an eye stricken by the sights of Hell, the natural world – the sphere of humanity's natural labour – offers evidence of health and good order. This certainly is the force of the image in the passage that follows:

Come 'l ramarro sotto la gran fersa
dei dì canicular, cangiando sepe,
folgore par se la via attraversa,
    sì pareva, venendo verso l'epe
de li altri due, un serpentello acceso,
livido e nero come gran di pepe;
    e quella parte onde prima è preso
nostro alimento, a l'un di lor trafisse;
poi cadde giuso innanzi lui disteso.
    Lo trafitto 'l mirò, ma nulla disse;
anzi, co' piè fermati, sbadigliava
pur come sonno o febbre l'assalisse.
    Elli 'l serpente e quei lui riguardava;
l'un per la piaga e l'altro per la bocca
fummavan forte, e 'l fummo si scontrava.   (79–93)

(As a lizard, beneath the great lash / of the heat of high summer, cutting from hedgerow to hedgerow, / is lightning, it seems, if it crosses your path, / so likewise [a serpent – small, keen and burning –] / as black as a grain of pepper, and livid, / now struck at the guts of the other two. / [And one it transfixed] at the point where our earliest nourishment enters. / And then it fell back and stretched all its length before him. / Transfixed, he stared down; he said nothing at all. / But stock-still he yawned / as though hit by sleep or a fever. / As he eyed the serpent, the serpent eyed him. / The wound of the one and the mouth of the other / gave out a dense smoke. The columns of smoke came together.)

Here with the utmost vigour and design the lizard is shown in its natural habitat; the heat of the summer day is evoked, the lines of the footpath are clearly defined by the movement of the lizard across them, and also by the emphasis that 'sepe' (hedgerow) gives to its lateral limit. Such detail stands precisely in contradistinction to the details of the punishment: a sinister smoke replaces the clearness of the summer day, confusion replaces clarity, and passivity the agile movements of the lizard. In such a context, the lizard – unchanged – is the rare and strange.

With this one arrives at the last and most searching appeal to normality. For the transformations are presented throughout as a parody of sexual union. It is here that Fucci's initial obscenity proves to have been no random outburst; the laws of creation that Fucci mocks in pride and blasphemy are laws that, rightly – if partially – express themselves in human sexuality. We are asked in Canto XXV to believe that, in spite of what the imagination might conjure up, these laws provide a pattern essential to our nature.

For a direct expression of Dante's own belief in this, we should have to turn to the twenty-fifth canto of the *Purgatorio*, where the poet, discussing conception and gestation, explains the union of soul and body – a union that Dante compares to that of the sun's heat and the liquor of the grape in wine (*Purg.* XXV 77–8). But, in this parallel canto of the *Inferno*, the truth must be grasped obliquely through a scene of birth, copulation and death. We have seen already the monstrous birth of the 'imagine perversa' that slouches off at line 77. We now see an act of penetration at the navel, 'the point where

our earliest nourishment enters', which leads to nothing but the magical
smoke and the sickly relaxation of the sinner's yawn.

It is at the climax of this unnatural scene that Dante expresses most acutely
his awareness of his own poetic standing:

> Taccia Lucano omai là dov' e' tocca
> del misero Sabello e di Nasidio,
> e attenda a udir quel ch'or si scocca.
>   Taccia di Cadmo e d'Aretusa Ovidio,
> ché se quello in serpente e quella in fonte
> converte poetando, io non lo 'nvidio;
>   ché due nature mai a fronte a fronte
> non trasmutò si ch'amendue le forme
> a cambiar lor matera fosser pronte.   (94–102)

(Let Lucan now fall silent when he comes to tell / of wretched Sabellus and Nasidius, /
and pause to attend to what here shall be shot forth. / Let Ovid be silent about Cadmus
and Arethusa; / for if he made a serpent of one and of one a well-spring / in writing his
verses, I feel no envy at all for that; / for [he never altered] two natures, eye to eye, / so
that each distinctive form / was quick to change its specific matter with another.)

The transformations that follow differ in a number of respects from the
earlier set. Yet the stance of the author is consistent here with that which he
has adopted from the opening of the canto. Against the disorderly sugges-
tions that his own images generate, the poet asserts the value of natural order.
This assertion, however, requires of him the utmost sophistication in the
exercise of his art. And to some degree that sophistication is drawn from the
models of Latin literature: where Fucci's blasphemy is the flowering of the
evil seed of Pistoia, so Dante's own art – at one with justice – has its roots in
the example of the authors whom he now presumes to outdo. There is thus a
conscious elevation of style not only in allusions to the Latin poets, but also
in the form of the similes that Dante here employs; and at line 16 there
occurs a conspicuous Latinism that suggests how such stylistic features may
possess for Dante a moral significance. Thus, as Vanni flees, the poet
indicates that silence was forced upon Fucci, not with a simple 'parola', but
with the Latinate 'verbo':

> El si fuggì che non parlò più verbo.

The distance between the 'bestia' and the poet himself is enforced precisely
by the elegance (not to mention the religious force) of the word that Dante
chooses.

But how, then, is the poet distinguished from the Latin authorities? Even
before lines 94–102 the art of the canto has asserted its independence. The
strength of visual imagery and of rhythmic articulation are both characteristic
of Dante. But he also draws throughout upon a harsh native lexicon. To
describe the sights of Hell the poet needs 'rime aspre e chiocce' (*Inf.*
xxxii 1), and Canto xxv is distinguished not only by elevation of diction but
also by words of such vernacular strength as 'epe' (82), 'ascelle' (112),
'muso' (123) and 'zavorra' (142).

With such locutions the canto acquires distinctness from the Latin model. Yet Dante, in his address to Lucan and Ovid, still insists upon the authority of his own text. And this insistence is compatible with an earlier feature of the canto, the silencing of Virgil himself. At line 45 Dante as protagonist silences Virgil so as to give all his attention to the unfolding of his metamorphosis, and in the silence that this creates Dante directly addresses the reader of his own poem. But, tacitly, the poet has already acted in a similar way in a sequence that at first appears to express the authority of the *Aeneid* – the description of Cacus. As we have said, the *Aeneid* speaks of Cacus only as a *semihomo* (VIII 194). Yet Dante has transformed the figure into a centaur, and doing so takes as his point of reference not Virgil's poem but his own *Commedia*. The centaurs have already appeared in Canto XII as the guardians of those who have sinned by violent greed. Virgil is made to emphasise this connection. However, the progressive vision of greed, robbery and theft reveals an understanding of these sins that only the Christian could comprehend. Virgil sees a social offence in Cacus's behaviour; the Christian observes a deformation in the greater law: the human mind is the custodian of its own natural being, and sins of the mind must resonate throughout all aspects of its proper form.

When Dante wept in *Inferno* XX at the sight of the perversion of 'nostra imagine', Virgil upbraided him. The reproof, however, demonstrates the same limitation as Lucan and Ovid also display. For much as Virgil may value the moral nature of man, he cannot, as a pagan, be thought to comprehend the truth – essential to Christian belief – that the form of a human being is itself guaranteed in the eternal plan of creation. This is the truth that the Resurrection declares. This is the truth that is borne upon Dante himself by the beauty and – for him the quite literal – immortality of Beatrice. And this, in the twenty-fifth canto, is the *ben* and *frutto* that the imagination of the reader must attempt to comprehend even if Virgil cannot. That the author of the canto can himself do so is the point of distinction between his metamorphoses and those of Lucan and Ovid.

Consider, first, how Lucan treats the death of Sabellus. Bitten by a *seps*, his body begins to dissolve, revealing, sinew by sinew, bone by bone, the whole anatomy of human kind:

> Quidquid homo est, aperit pestis natura profana.
>
> (*Pharsalia* IX 779)

(The whole frame of man is revealed by the awful nature of that disease.)

The anatomy itself is a wonderful piece of work; and Dante, scientifically, would doubtless have admired it. Once revealed, however, the wonder is, for Lucan, that the work – reduced to a pool of corruption – should melt away like snow before the warm south wind:

> calido non ocius Austro
> Nix resoluta cadit nec solem cera sequetur.   (*ibid.* 781–2)

(Snow does not melt and vanish more quickly before the warm south wind, nor will wax be affected faster by the sun.)

In Dante's transformations, on the other hand, the wonder is that nothing – or nothing proper to the human body – is ever beyond recall. The ashes of Vanni Fucci return on the instant to their proper shape. And now, in the final transformations, the punishment observes a similar, though more elaborate, economy.

Here 'man-shape' and snake-form are interchanged. But the rule that guides these changes is a rule of inverse progression: a part that is cancelled in one of the creatures is produced simultaneously in the body of the other. And at no point does the penalty allow that any excess of matter should remain unaccounted for. Thus, while each of the sinners undergoes a total change in his identity, their punishment itself insists on the value of identity or distinctive shape:

> Insieme si rispuosero a tai norme,
> che 'l serpente la coda in forca fesse,
> e 'l feruto ristrinse insieme l'orme.
>   Le gambe con le cosce seco stesse
> s'appiccar sì, che 'n poco la giuntura
> non facea segno alcun che si paresse.
>   Togliea la coda fessa la figura
> che si perdeva là, e la sua pelle
> si facea molle, e quella di là dura.
>   Io vidi intrar le braccia per l'ascelle,
> e i due piè de la fiera, ch'eran corti,
> tanto allungar quanto accorciavan quelle.
>   Poscia li piè di rietro, insieme attorti,
> diventaron lo membro che l'uom cela,
> e 'l misero del suo n'avea due porti.   (103–17)

(They answered in reciprocity to the rules of the change: / the tail of the snake split open and it formed a fork; / the footprints of the stricken man drew in upon themselves and met. / Thigh closed on thigh, the legs / adhering, so that soon, of the joint between them, / no trace at all was seen. / The riven tail took on the form / that, in one place, now disappeared and the skin / here grew soft as there it grew hard. / I saw the arms shrink up towards the armpits; / both lengthened to the same extent as these were shortened. / And then, plaited together, the two hind-legs / became the part that a man keeps hidden. / The wretch from his member put forth a corresponding pair.)

In earlier sequences the imagination of the poet has affirmed the principles of motion and number; here the *frutto* beneath the horror is the truth that, in eternity, the individuality of human beings is guaranteed (*Inf.* VI 97–8). Lucan, no less than the sinners who suffer its consequence, must be ignorant of this truth. And Ovid too will fall within the ban. For metamorphosis – to consider only the Cadmus episode – so far from being a punishment, is portrayed by Ovid as a fate that the wife of Cadmus knowingly chooses. Seeing her husband transformed into a serpent, she entreats the gods that she may become what he has become (*Metamorphoses* IV 593–5). Such a desire, for

Dante, would be not only a physical but a moral nonsense. Indeed, the human figure in Dante's thought is of such importance that the final *bolgia* contains men who have merely changed their shape by impersonating other men. The attitude, moreover, that Ovid adopts as he pictures the scene must appear no less repugnant. For the scene of change is surrounded by pathos and by a delicate, even erotic pleasure, as the two 'gentle' beasts move off, their coils intertwining:

> at illa
> lubrica permulcet cristati colla draconis,
> et subito duo sunt iunctoque volumine serpunt,
> donec in adpositi nemoris subiere latebras.   (*ibid.* 598–601)

(But she only stroked the sleek neck of the crested dragon, and suddenly there were two serpents – intertwining their folds – which crawled away soon and hid in a nearby wood.)

Where Ovid's effect is pathetic, Dante's effect is harshly scientific; where Ovid finds sensuality, Dante finds perversity – translating into a parody of healthy love the images that Ovid's text may here have suggested to him.

Rejecting, however, the myths of Ovid, the poet affirms the *frutto* of his Christian understanding by a concentration in the following lines on two particular images, which convey, throughout the *Commedia*, his sense of the value of human form – the images of the eye and of the face.

Thus the two creatures, as their muzzles change, fix upon each other the 'unholy lights' of their eyes:

> Mentre che 'l fummo l'uno e l'altro vela
> di color novo, e genera 'l pel suso
> per l'una parte e da l'altra il dipela,
>   l'un si levò e l'altro cadde giuso,
> non torcendo però le lucerne empie,
> sotto le quai ciascun cambiava muso.
>   Quel ch'era dritto, il trasse ver' le tempie,
> e di troppa matera ch'in là venne
> uscir li orecchi de le gote scempie;
>   ciò che non corse in dietro e si ritenne
> di quel soverchio, fé naso a la faccia
> e le labbra ingrossò quanto convenne.   (118–29)

(With smoke casting over the one and the other a veil / of strange new colour – causing the hair to appear / in one place that it stripped away elsewhere – / the one found his feet, the other fell prostrate. / Neither averted, however, his unholy lights, / beneath which both were changing their snouts. / He that was upright pulled his towards his temples; / from excess of matter moving there, / ears appeared upon naked cheeks. / [Of any surplus] retained that did not run back, / a nose was fashioned for that face, / and the lips grew as thick as they needed to be.)

No reader of either the *Vita nuova* or the *Paradiso* could fail to be offended by this. For the eyes and – finally – the smile of Beatrice make clear to Dante how beautiful the human person may be to God as well as to men. We shall have more to say about the importance of the smile in the next chapter.

But here we need only recall that, when in *Paradiso* XXXIII Dante himself finally approaches God, the encounter is one of face and eye. It is also an encounter that expresses the ultimate value of change. For, as Dante gazes on the being of God, his own self and the image of God are both transformed; God 'works' towards the responsive eye of Dante:

> una sola parvenza,
> mutandom' io, a me si travagliava.   (*Par.* XXXIII 113–14)

(One sole appearance / changed itself for me as I was changing.)

And the final act is that God should offer to Dante the face of His own humanity:

> mi parve pinta de la nostra effige.   (131)

(It appeared to me painted with our very image.)

The meeting of eyes in the *Paradiso* is a moment of pure activity; in *Inferno* XXV, the eyes of the sinners are empty and passive; but the eye of Dante the poet is not, endeavouring even here to discern and express a notion of order.

With this one reaches the final phase of the transformation. For the word of the poet, in counterpoint to the sufferings of the sinners, has provided in Canto XXV the only illustration of natural activity. And now the poet returns to the theme of language: as the canto began with a contrast between the poet's own virtuosity and the blasphemous obscenities of Fucci, so now it ends with a vision of the sinner's tongue, degraded and deformed. The newly made serpent goes hissing across the floor of the bolgia; the newly made man, when he opens his mouth, only spits and then utters words of sheer spite:

> Quel che giacëa, il muso innanzi caccia,
> e li orecchi ritira per la testa
> come face le corna la lumaccia;
> e la lingua, ch'avëa unita e presta
> prima a parlar, si fende, e la forcuta
> ne l'altro si richiude; e 'l fummo resta.
> L'anima ch'era fiera divenuta,
> suffolando si fugge per la valle,
> e l'altro dietro a lui parlando sputa.
> Poscia li volse le novelle spalle,
> e disse a l'altro: 'I' vo' che Buoso corra,
> com' ho fatt' io, carpon per questo calle'.   (*Inf.* XXV 130–41)

(Laid flat, the other drove its muzzle outwards, / then drew in its ears at its head / like the horns of a snail. / Its tongue had been whole once, and ready / in speaking. Now it forked, / while the fork of his counterpart healed. And then the smoke stopped. / Changed now to the form of a brute, the soul of the human / ran hissing away down the valley floor; / the other one spits, as he speaks behind him. / Turning his back – with its newly made shoulders – / 'I'll have Buoso scuttle,' he said to the other, / 'as I have, crabwise, the length of this road.')

The changes now are ended. They have been guided throughout by an apprehension of the order that resides in the power of God. Yet the point of resolution for the themes and images of Canto xxv lies in the *Purgatorio* and the *Paradiso*, and here we are not allowed to rest in contemplation of the patterns of truth. Nor does the force of the canto derive from design or pattern alone, but also from the effort that the poet, as he writes, must make to impose design upon his own imaginings. The effort is cruel, as the vision is cruel. And in that respect the final lines of the canto provide a telling conclusion.

Here for the last time we are asked to listen to the voice, which was raised first against Fucci and Pistoia, as the poet works to exhaust the evil he has seen:

> Cosi vid' io la settima zavorra
> mutare e trasmutare; e qui mi scusi
> la novità se fior la penna abborra.
>   E avvegna che li occhi miei confusi
> fossero alquanto e l'animo smagato,
> non poter quei fuggirsi tanto chiusi,
>   ch'i' non scorgessi ben Puccio Sciancato;
> ed era quel che sol, di tre compagni
> che venner prima, non era mutato;
>   l'altr' era quel che tu, Gaville, piagni.   (142–51)

(And so I beheld the ballast in the seventh keel / change and interchange. Let me be excused / by the strangeness of it if my pen has failed. / And yet, although my eyes were reeling / somewhat, and my mind astray, / these two could not make off so stealthily / that I did not discern quite clearly Puccio Sciancato. / Alone of the three in that company / who had come first, he was unchanged. / The other is he, Gaville, who has made you weep.)

Of the sinners whom Dante has encountered in the seventh bolgia, only one remains unchanged. The apparent immunity, however, of this isolated figure wins him no credit. His name is spoken to single him out for especial odium. The name itself, indeed, carries with it an unrelenting contempt – Puccio Sciancato, Puccio the Cripple – as though in this entirely marginal, yet historical, figure Dante wished his reader to see how humanity, even apart from the effects of damnation, might be turned awry in body as in spirit. It would be hard to overestimate the viciousness of these lines, and it might perhaps be comforting to suggest that the voice was that of Dante *personaggio*, still deeply involved with sin. Yet this cannot be. It is the voice of the author who has known from the opening lines of his poem that to remember evil is a labour 'so bitter that death is hardly more so'. And vicious as the voice appears for most of the canto, its purpose has been to defend the value of normality and order. In Canto xx – presenting the image of the soothsayers – Dante appeals to the reader, as we have seen, over the head of Virgil, in his distress at the distortion which the human body suffers; he seeks there to establish a community of normal emotion against the evidence of human perversity. The twenty-fifth canto pursues the same end. But built as it is, from the first appearance of Vanni Fucci, around painfully parodic references to the Resurrection, Dante here recognises to the full that the only foundation for human normality is the incalculable power of the ~~ator. His own words register the strain which any mind must suffer when it seeks to respond to that power.

IV

To anyone who reads the *Inferno* sequentially from canto to canto, it is likely that, at first appearance, a certain change will seem to have occurred between the twenty-fifth canto and the twenty-sixth. In the Malebolge, Dante has so far been concerned to picture the total subjection of the human being to divine justice. It is consistent with this concern that, in the cantos we have just examined, the poet has envisaged the massive triviality of Vanni Fucci, and traced the defeat of that sinner as he violently submits to punishment. But the central character of *Inferno* XXVI is the intellectual adventurer, Ulysses; and the canto comes to a climax – significantly, without comment from either Virgil or Dante as protagonist – with Ulysses's account of the journey he took at the end of his earthly days in search of 'virtue and knowledge' (XXVI 120). Ulysses is no trivial figure, and he has regularly been seen as an heroic defender of human ambition, whose actions and words encourage one to question the authority of any restriction imposed upon our nature by a supra-human power.

There can be few modern readers who do not feel some distress at the fate which Dante allots to Ulysses, considering that, as well as dying in the course of his quest, he is damned to Hell for attempting it. We shall see that there is good reason to be distressed by the story of Ulysses and, for that matter, by the twenty-sixth canto at large. Indeed, I shall argue that any interpretation which does not positively sharpen a reader's sense of discomfort must have failed to understand the issues that the canto raises.

This, however, is by no means to suggest that we should sympathise uncritically with the aspirations that Dante attributes to Ulysses. Nor should one allow the undoubted importance of the Ulysses episode to obscure the place which this episode occupies within the structure of the twenty-sixth canto, or the place of this canto in the context of those that precede and follow it.

For one thing, while it is, of course, Dante who devises the stirring words of Ulysses's story, it is also Dante who has placed Ulysses in the Malebolge – and arraigned him, by locating him in the eighth of these ditches – on a *prima facie* case of misleading his fellow-men. We need from the outset in this episode to remind ourselves that Ulysses is a creature of Dante's devising (and not of God's); it is Dante's imagination that has decided the circumstances in which Ulysses should be set. And on that understanding, 'context' must invite one to temper the sympathies one may reasonably feel for the central figure of the canto with a critical and, equally, reasonable analysis of his circumstances and actions in Hell.

As we shall see, this analysis proves damaging; for a close inspection of the words that Ulysses utters will certainly show that his intellectual and linguistic procedures are fallacious, and no less deceitful than those of any other sinner in the circles of fraud. Indeed, it will appear that, despite an initial effect of incongruence, there is after all a moral kinship between Ulysses and Vanni Fucci: in the end, Ulysses – resisting divine restraint – is little better than the 'mule' who descrated the sacristy; and where one sinner is annihilated in Hell by the bite of a serpent, the other, having been metamorphosed into the fire of his own punishment, is deprived of any corporeal identity.

Such a conclusion is, in some respects, familiar – as if the purpose of analysis might merely be to confirm the worst suspicions of those who see Ulysses as the Promethean victim of a tyrannical deity. Yet we cannot, I think, wholly avoid an interpretation of this sort; and, in one respect, the appeal to context can only serve to strengthen it, by disallowing the familiar escape whereby Dante's religious obligation to condemn Ulysses is taken to be at odds with his human sympathies. We have hinted already that Dante's imagination is no less involved in conceiving the punishment of the sinner than in his conception of the sinner himself. We are obliged to consider images of annihilation in the fire of Hell as well as images of human daring; and this suggestion will gather even greater weight when one examines the internal images which surround Ulysses in Canto XXVI. I would only add that when we consider these images, they will produce a subtler and more acceptable diagnosis of his case, whereby humanity is preserved even though its saviour is not Ulysses.

For all that, we have so far indicated only one of the ways in which context affects our understanding of the canto. There is another; and this – in keeping with the suggestions I made at the outset – will show that the distress we feel at any diagnosis of Ulysses's case, whether rough or subtle, is a valuable and essential part of our reading.

Three cantos ago, in his portrayal of the hypocrites, Dante as poet refused to allow himself as protagonist any opportunity of complacent comfort in the act of judgement; and in Canto XXIV the long climb that Dante and Virgil make out of the bolgia of hypocrisy can be seen as a comparable check upon complacency. But in this perspective, we should expect that, by now, Dante's strategy would require him to make some further countermove against himself. His judgement against Vanni Fucci in the interim has been decisively outspoken, to the point of stimulating an almost flamboyant display of authorial pride. But in Canto XXVI, abandoning the satirical mode which has so far tended to characterise the Malebolge, Dante adopts for one canto at least a far more problematical procedure: where Vanni was forcibly silenced, Ulysses speaks without interruption; where the action in Canto XXV portrays a single unspeakable process, the action of Canto XXVI is twofold, spanning a story of eternal punishment and a story of temporal courage – and allowing free play to the equivocal suggestions and incongruities that arise on each level of the narrative. As we shall see, the twenty-sixth canto consistently generates a certain ambiguity of viewpoint, along with corresponding effects of tragic irony. A halt is called to the simple development of moral confidence which the twenty-fifth canto might seem to have encouraged.

On such a view, Canto xxvi will display – as the title of this chapter suggests it may – a pathos of order, whereby coherence is continually in question and where the question itself always promises a new coherence. It should, however, be noted that an interpretation of this sort leads us away from any exclusive concentration upon the figure of Ulysses. Our attention must shift to the action of the poet, or rather to those mental actions that the reader repeats in reading the text that the poet offers. For now it will appear that judgement itself is a tragic act: on the one hand, the need for both conceptual clarity and imaginative coherence is surely legitimate and necessary if we are to judge at all; on the other hand, imagination and analysis will feed upon the incongruities they observe in the process of judgement, and – recognising in them the defining features of particular cases – resist the judgement we are bound to pursue.

By now, no doubt, this conclusion will seem predictable, deriving as it does from all the arguments I have been pursuing since the opening pages of this book. Certainly the twenty-sixth canto serves better than any other as evidence of the difficulties Dante creates for himself in the *Inferno*. The implication of this, however, for the present discussion, is *not* that I should rehearse my own arguments, but rather that we should return to the details of Dante's text, and – inspecting *his* words as closely as those he consigns to Ulysses – consider how the act of writing in this instance sustains the conflict of judgement. Before doing that, it is also worth asking, in a wider context than the Malebolge, whether the case of Ulysses differs from earlier cases of difficulty, or, if so, whether the canto in which he appears has any specific function in the development of the *Commedia* at large.

Thematically, for instance, there are important connections to be drawn between Dante's response to Ulysses and his response to Brunetto Latini. In both episodes, Dante is concerned with questions of intellectual leadership and example; in both, he stresses that connections are to be made between intellectual conduct and moral aim, and defines the disciplines to which the mind must be subject – if it is to produce a fruitful conclusion – by implying a contrast between the behaviour of the sinners and his own procedures as protagonist, poet and Florentine exile. Thus, where the protagonist has to restrain himself in Canto xv from showing more than a distant reverence for Brunetto, so at the beginning of the Ulysses episode, he comes close to losing his head at his first sight of the punishment visited upon false counsellors:

> Allor mi dolsi, e ora mi ridoglio
> quando drizzo la mente a ciò ch'io vidi,
> e più lo 'ngegno affreno ch'i' non soglio,
> perché non corra che virtù nol guidi.   (xxvi 19–22)

(It pained me then, and it pains me now / when I fix my mind on what I saw, / and – more than usually – I restrain my mind / so as not to run where virtue does not guide.)

Here, as in the Brunetto canto, Dante already insists that the consciousness of good and bad must censor the direction that intelligence alone might incline us to pursue.

'Perché non corra che virtù nol guidi'. This line is regularly taken as a key to the moral meaning of Canto XXVI, and with good reason. One cannot, in any case, be reminded too often of the dangers that intelligence itself can precipitate, or of the responsibilities entailed in the possession of high ability. That realisation carries its own tragic charge; and in the twenty-sixth canto Dante does much to stress such an understanding, particularly by the comparisons he implies between Ulysses's ambition and the painstaking concern that Virgil displays over the advancement of the protagonist.

One cannot, however, suppose that even this formula is an adequate expression of Dante's purpose. On the contrary, the essence of the discipline which Dante imposes upon intelligence is the discipline of a tragic awareness which eludes and challenges all types of formulation. In this respect, Canto XXVI has much in common with Canto XIII; and the deepest irony of both cantos is that the tragic hero should in each case show no awareness of the depths of his own tragedy. Ulysses makes no complaint against his fate either in Hell or upon Earth – and, on that score, stands in direct contrast to his Christian counterpart, Guido da Montefeltro, who in Canto XXVII speaks with unceasing rancour of what has befallen him.

A similar point can be made more fully – and with closer reference to Dante's own action as poet in Canto XXVI – if one turns to the differences between this canto and its predecessors in the circles of violence.

In two crucial respects, the figure whom Dante has here created is entirely unlike Pier della Vigna or Brunetto Latini. In the first place, Ulysses is a pagan; in the second place, Dante has not drawn him from the realm of contemporary history, but rather from the pages of myth, legend and fiction.

To recognise that Ulysses is a pagan, and thus condemned for an offence of the mind committed against a God whom he could not conceivably have known, is to recognise one of the fundamental reasons for the distress which the episode causes in its readers. And here the arguments we have drawn from 'context' to explain the unhappy link between Ulysses and Vanni Fucci seem far less cogent. It is true, in simple terms, that if Dante had wished to celebrate Ulysses's virtues, he could have found a place for him in Limbo; and it is equally true that the reasons why Ulysses is not in Limbo – as we shall see – are forcefully expressed by the internal images of the canto. Nonetheless, it is beyond question that Dante's response to Ulysses is very different from his response to the other figures of pagan antiquity whom he shows to be worthy of actual punishment. Jason appears as a speechless automaton in the first canto of the Malebolge; Capaneus asserts himself with a fatuous bombast which only the most ingrained Romantic could find appealing. And there need have been no difficulty at all in associating Ulysses with either of these sinners: one was an adventurous seaman, the other is taken, in Canto XXV, as a dire example of rebellious pride.

Yet, so far from stressing such connections as these, Dante goes out of his way to link Ulysses with Virgil. The Roman is shown to insist pointedly upon speaking to the Greek. Certainly, in the contrast that ensues many reasons emerge to explain why Ulysses fails to qualify for Limbo. However, as we shall see, it is also true that the canto gives Ulysses the chance to subvert the authority of Virgil; we might even say that Ulysses is intended to articulate many of the extreme questions, concerning the fate of the pagan, which Virgil is too moderate and self-effacing to pose. This is not to say that Ulysses consciously states these questions in the canto: his tragedy, like Virgil's, will still reside in his inability to formulate the tragic question; the question of the pagan is rather one which emerges from Dante's own formulation of the scene. Nonetheless, it does at times appear that Virgil and Ulysses – while representing alternative forms of paganism – are brothers under the skin, and, together, resuscitate the general problem of paganism itself.

This is confirmed by two other features of the sequence. For instance, one should note that in Canto XXVII Dante goes on to consider another case of false counsel, that of Guido da Montefeltro; and we shall see that – without relaxing his condemnation of Ulysses for the particular sins he has committed – Dante does draw a powerful distinction between the ways in which pagan and Christian may misapprehend or betray the pursuit of knowledge. More important still, Dante, as we have said, has begun in the central cantos of the Malebolge to cultivate the notion of Purgatory. To Dante, as a Christian, Purgatory would have represented the promise of ultimate order, for it is here that the reconcilation of human beings and God is worked out, through penitence and the gospel of redemption. But in Canto XXVI Dante emphasises the pathos, not the promise of order: when Ulysses is wrecked on the shores of Purgatory (and Dante could have located the wreck wherever he wished), the event underlines the insuperable distinction which makes it possible for the Christian – but not the pagan – to atone for his sins in the light of grace and revelation. For a moment at least, the orderliness which gives purpose to Dante's Christian journey is perceived as a piece of moral good luck.

I need hardly emphasise that in this light the twenty-six canto raises most of the issues which I originally discussed in dealing with the Justice cantos of the *Paradiso*. However, it is worth stressing the extent to which the problem raised by the pagan is, for Dante, a problem of *writing* as well as of judgement. To conceive of a pagan at all is to perform an act of imaginative recuperation, stimulated by the reading of classical texts. But, to that extent, any question concerning the pagan involves not only a question of moral or doctrinal principle but a potential conflict between the activity of judgement – which aims to 'close' issues – and the activity of the imagination which aims to open them up.

This, of course, is close to saying, with the Romantics, that a discrepancy exists between Dante's Christian principles and his human sympathies; and that position still forms as good a starting-point as any for a discussion of the *Commedia*. I would, however, insist, firstly, that there are internal reasons for admitting the conflict, and secondly that the issues it raises are more complex than the Romantics allowed. In acknowledging the merits of a pre-Christian culture, Dante already goes some way towards allowing that moral standards may be culturally determined. But, since it is his own literary imagination which reveals this to him, the conflict of value which follows is one which occurs essentially within the poet who has undertaken both to imagine and to judge.

I would add that it is this conflict of value that distinguishes the Ulysses canto from the circles of violence, and this too that – on a higher plane than that of judgement – makes the writing of Canto XXVI a moral act. In the wasteland which Dante depicts throughout the circles of violence, the poet's concern is to present himself as arbiter and prop of the values which underlay the Christian culture of thirteenth-century Italy; and, so far from perceiving a problem in the revival of pagan culture, he saw that revival as one of the means which he might employ to reveal the shortcomings of figures such as Brunetto and Pier della Vigna. Now, however, his story brings him to a moment of reflection upon that procedure; and once again it becomes clear that the moral act is one which admits, on the level of introspection, that judgement is not an assertive but a tragic procedure. (As we shall see, Canto XXVI opens with a judgement against Florence which is bitterly ironic in its tone.)

These considerations bring us directly to the second respect in which the canto differs from earlier instances of difficulty: the fact that Ulysses is not an historical figure, but rather a mythic or fictive invention.

In outline, there are in fact certain important resemblances between the narrative use which Dante makes of myth here and his use of it in the circles of violence. Just as the Old Man of Crete is translated into, and challenged by, Brunetto Latini, so Ulysses becomes eventually the Guido da Montefeltro of Canto XXVII, where, returning to history, Dante produces a distinctly realistic account of psychological manoeuvres in the field of thirteenth-century Italian politics. Moreover, the myth of Ulysses is closely comparable in meaning to the myth of the Old Man of Crete: both allow that the 'head' of humanity may be 'golden'; both acknowledge that there is a fissure or flaw in human nature which invalidates our highest aspirations, and which, as human beings – unless aided by grace – we can never aspire to remedy.

When the waters close over Ulysses (whose next incarnation will be as a tongue of fire in Hell), the canto expresses a grave elegiac dignity which harks back to Virgil's tale of the Old Man of Crete. But the same passage also recalls, in imagery and tone, the moment in Canto XXIV where Virgil himself allows that human endeavour may, in the end, be nothing more than smoke in the air or foam upon the water. The question is: what follows from this? The answer cannot be mere resignation or fatalism. For, while the sad perception of transience or fault may well be taken as the ultimate check upon complacency, it is notable that, in Virgil's mouth, this perception is uttered in the course of a call for renewed action on the part of the protagonist. Nor does this call sound very different from Ulysses's great exhortation to his men that they should not waste the little time remaining to them in the 'picciola vigilia / d'i nostri sensi' (114–15).

Unlike the myth of the Old Man of Crete, the myth of Ulysses admits a concern with the spirit of quest. This observation is predictable enough. But in the light of the similarity between Virgil's words and those of Ulysses, it is, I think, important to insist once more that the moral issue here is very finely poised. To do anything at all requires the will to do *something*. Indeed, it is Dante himself who chose the apathetic *ignavi* as the first category of sinner in the *Inferno*. But it is also true that the will to do anything (regardless of what it is that we do) can amount to an evasion of the work required to discover what in fact is good for us to do. That evasion may, in some measure, be Ulysses's false step. And it certainly follows from much that we have said so far that the twenty-sixth canto should be seen as Dante's own attempt to admit but also to regulate the intellectual ambition which rescues us from a passive fatalism.

In saying this, our attention moves, as it has done before, from the figure of Ulysses to the figure of the poet; and it now becomes especially important to recognise that Ulysses is not only a myth but also a fiction. Dante did not know Homer; and, while Latin authors would have supplied him with the outline of the Homeric story, critics have sought in vain to discover a source for Dante's account of Ulysses's last voyage and death. We may safely assume that the last thirty lines of the canto are – as reading them would alone tell us – an exceptional flight of narrative invention.

But what does this mean for our reading of the canto overall? It means that yet another turn has been given to the skein of its irony. For in any account of intellectual ambition the capacity of the human mind for fiction must itself be an issue: if our aspirations are doomed to failure, then any aspiration at all must be a fiction. At the same time, if our aspirations are admissible, then fiction – as a sort of rhetoric – may serve to encourage or sharpen our appetites; then again, it may equally well foster false dreams and illusions. Whatever the case may be, Dante has, by composing a philosophical inquiry in fictional form, put himself in danger. Seeking an historical example of the Ulysses myth, we do not need to turn to Guido da Montefeltro; Dante himself stands as Brunetto to Ulysses's Old Man of Crete.

Since the beginning of the Malebolge, Dante has played upon the fine line which has to be drawn between the deceptions he condemns in the sinners and the linguistic and narrative practices which he must adopt in constructing his own fiction. In a well-worn phrase of recent criticism, the sequence is 'about writing'. And so is Canto xxvi. But this canto is also about the morality of writing. And in creating Ulysses Dante has created, as we have suggested, a mirror image of himself, so that fiction – performing a moral analysis – may reflect upon its own powers and limitations.

Thus Dante himself, at the opening of the canto, suggests that the act of conceiving the subject and scene of the canto reopens an otherwise dormant pain: 'Allor mi dolsi, e ora mi ridoglio' (19) – it pained me then, and it pains me now. On the one hand, as Dante's immediate attempt at restraint suggests, this feeling might easily lead to a dangerously distracting sympathy. On the other hand, enough has been said about the value of distress in this canto to recognise that its origin – and justification – are to be found here. Certainly, when Dante as poet writes his fictional account of Ulysses's journey, he is true to the spirit of this early line. For it is in the *fiction* that we observe the closest and most perplexing similarities between Dante and Ulysses – which is not to say that Dante feels sympathy for some independent or pre-existent being, but rather that he has knowingly formed the figure as a focus for difficulty. Thus when Ulysses demands that his followers should not willingly

> negar l'esperïenza,
> di retro al sol, del mondo sanza gente.   (116–17)

(refuse / experience, behind the sun, of the world without people).

his words seem to anticipate exactly the words in which, two cantos later, Virgil will explain the purpose of Dante's journey through Hell:

> ma per dar lui esperïenza piena
> a me, che morto son, convien menarlo
> per lo 'nferno qua giù di giro in giro.   (XXVIII 48–50)

(but to give him full experience / I, who am dead, must lead him / down in Hell from circle to circle).

So, too, Ulysses speaks of his burning desire to know 'the vices and virtues of men'. In both cases, it is clear that the comparison which these phrases stimulate must bear upon Dante as poet as well as upon the protagonist: the journey which Dante's poem describes is itself a pursuit of knowledge and an investigation into the vices and virtues of men. Moreover, like Ulysses, the poet Dante is also conspicuously a storyteller and rhetorician who speaks for the purpose of encouraging others to acquire similar knowledge.

In Canto XXV, we have just seen, Dante asserts the energy and prestige of his own art in contest with the writings of Lucan and Ovid. Although in Canto XXVI there is no comparable affirmation, a similar confidence must have inspired Dante's attempts to rewrite and recast the various Latin sources that speak of Ulysses. Moreover, it is clear from the way in which Dante subsequently refers to Ulysses in the *Commedia* that he knew himself to have constructed here a cardinal point of reference in the overall scheme of his poem. No other episode in the *Inferno* is so frequently or so openly alluded to; and we shall see later, from two of these four allusions, how significant the Ulysses episode must have been to him. Here, it is enough to cite the other two allusions, in both of which Dante offers a clear diagnosis of the difference he saw between Ulysses's case and his own actual case. In Canto XIX of the *Purgatorio* the Siren appears and identifies herself as one who turned Ulysses from the course he intended to take (*Purg.* XIX 22). The Siren here, appearing in a dream to Dante, represents that perversity in the human mind which leads it to mistake its own contructions – or fictions – for an ultimate good; but the dream occurs at exactly the moment in Purgatory where the protagonist has recognised and freed himself from the dangers of such confusion. Somewhat similarly, in *Paradiso* XXVII, as Dante looks down from the *primum mobile*, he sees traced on the globe of the earth 'the mad course that Ulysses took': 'il folle varco d'Ulisse' (*Par.* XXVII 79–87). But, in arriving at the *primum mobile*, which is the heavenly sphere that initiates all movement in space and time, the protagonist actually does bring to fruition the knowledge that can be gained by the pursuit of experience: the experience of the senses which Ulysses says he seeks may indeed be the starting-point for the operations of the mind; but knowledge, to be truly such, must be knowledge of certainties, established by analysing the causes of things back to their elements and to the very source of cause and effect in the *primum mobile*.

This much suggests, then, that Canto XXVI occupies a crucial position in the orderly plan of the *Commedia* on which the poet had every reason to pride himself. But just as in Canto XXV the order that the poet affirms is pitched against an apprehension of primal and disruptive power, so even more extensively here the canto calls into question the essential principles on which the *Commedia* rests. Indeed, in the very act of transforming the ancients, Dante introduces the major ironies of the canto. Journeys may have a purpose and goal, as Dante must clearly have believed when he set out to write 'nel mezzo del cammin'. But, in creating Ulysses, Dante recognises that journeys can also be perverse, moving consciously away from any goal, resting-place or home. And language too may fail when words with the highest intellectual dignity such as 'virtue' and 'knowledge' can degenerate into the oratorical slogans with which Ulysses deceives both himself, his companions – and many generations of readers.

How, then, to connect? How are plans and projects to be realised, when time and sin undermine our legitimate ambitions, and when the instruments with which we pursue these ambitions are liable constantly to be confused with fiction and false rhetoric?

There are questions here which make *Inferno* XXVI as worthy of serious philosophical attention as the *Oresteia* or *King Lear*. But our purpose now in reading the canto cannot be to seek any final answer; it must rather be to observe in detail how the text stimulates and sustains the question itself.

The canto opens with an ironic voice raised in hatred against the corruption of Florence:

> Godi, Fiorenza, poi che se' sì grande
> che per mare e per terra batti l'ali,
> e per lo 'nferno tuo nome si spande!
> Tra li ladron trovai cinque cotali

tuoi cittadini onde mi ven vergogna,
e tu in grande orranza non ne sali.   (XXVI 1–6)

(Florence rejoice, for you are so great / that you beat your wings over land and sea, /
and even through Hell you spread your name. / Among the thieves I found five such /
who were your citizens; at that, shame comes over me, / and you do not rise to great
honour by it.)

At first view, this diatribe has more of a place in the twenty-fifth canto
than in the twenty-sixth; it is a deferred judgement upon the last five of the
thieves whom Dante has seen transformed in the previous bolgia. Nonethe-
less, as part of Canto XXVI, it deserves attention in the context of this canto
on three counts. In the first place, the passage already betrays a particular
attitude to the act of judgement: above the categorical judgements expressed
in the geographical divisions of Hell, a direct and impassioned voice is heard,
enforcing its position with almost idiosyncratic vigour. Secondly, it is this
voice that will contrast, throughout the second half of the canto, with the
speaking voice of Ulysses himself. And, finally, the very disturbance of the
canto structure which the voice introduces – and the apparent distortion of
the thematic unity – need to be noted, since a similar disturbance will be a
feature of Dante's procedure throughout the first half of the canto.

We need not delay long over the first count. We have seen often enough
how the moral categories which Dante employs need to be enacted in partic-
ular acts of judgement. Since Canto VI, this has been especially true at
moments where Dante is dealing with the corruptions of his native Florence.
But we have also seen in Canto XIX that the direct voice can command an
authority in support of its judgements greater than that which resides in the
formulae on which the text essentially depends. In the present case, the
immediacy of the voice contrasts with the highly literary stance of the pre-
vious canto, in its attention to the words of Lucan and Ovid, and with the
frame of legend from which Ulysses is drawn. And the dominant character-
istic of this voice is its irony.

Once Ulysses begins to speak, with his vigorous 'quando' at line 90, he
does not glance aside from his single-minded account of the 'folle volo'; he
can thus speak of his 'ardore' (97) – his burning desire for knowledge –
without once acknowledging that he now burns in Hell; and at no point is he
conscious of how his search to be at one with his human origins – his
'semenza' (118) – leads him away from his natural home.

But in Dante's case the sharpness of the irony in the opening terzine is
determined by the fact that he directs his voice at his own homeland. In this
moment of judgement, Dante adopts simultaneously the positions of a Greek
and of a Trojan, of a Ulysses and of an Aeneas. The corruptions of Florence
have left him as homeless as Aeneas was; but like Ulysses he now wills the
destruction of the Florentine Troy:

Ma se presso al mattin del ver si sogna,
tu sentirai, di qua da picciol tempo,

di quel che Prato, non ch'altri, t'agogna.
E se già fosse, non saria per tempo.
Così foss' ei, da che pur esser dee!
ché più mi graverà, com' più m'attempo.   (7–12)

(But if close to morning we dream of the truth, / you will feel, before very long, / that which Prato, as well as others, aches to see befall you. / And if that already had come to pass, it would not be too soon. / Would that it were now as it must be; / for it will weigh the more on me, the more my time goes by.)

Notably, the complexity of levels which Dante spans in his judgement is seen not only in his irony but also by an elaborate play of tense sequences and a corresponding dislocation of rhythm. The dream which Dante has is no comforting myth or enthusiastic response to distant horizons; it is a demand, rather, that he should bestride the past and the future, seeing corruption, hoping for justice and allowing, throughout, the tragic tension of that vision to weigh ever more heavily upon him. There is no simple effect of sequence here, and the energetic contortion of rhythm which characterises the voice in these terzine is in keeping with the third feature of the opening passage – its connection, across the canto-break, with the previous canto. There too there was, at one and the same time, juncture and interruption; and this in turn points to a feature which dominates Dante's narrative procedure in the opening phase of the canto. Before Ulysses begins his speech, the construction of the canto is characterised in a number of ways by disproportion and disturbance. This is seen particularly in the ill-assorted pair of similes which introduces the figure of Ulysses in his flame – the pastoral image of the *villan* and the fireflies (25–30), and the scriptural reference to Elijah's ascent. We have noted at the opening of Canto XXIV the apparently gratuitous attention that Dante gives to the first image of the *villan*. As in that earlier case, so here such disproportions will be evidence of the coherence which Dante, as poet, seeks to maintain in submitting to the disturbances of a transitional phase – where the realisation both of his origins and of his end impinges upon him.

However, the first move that the poet makes – after the intervention of his own voice in the opening *terzine* – is to reassert the simple notion of coherent progress regularly expressed by the image of the journey, and at the same time to enunciate a simple moral comment upon *curiositas*. So, after witnessing the transformation of the thieves, the travellers again pick up their steady, if laborious, journey:

Noi ci partimmo, su per le scalee
che n'avea fatto iborni a scender pria,
rimontò 'l duca mio e trasse mee;
e proseguendo la solinga via,
tra le schegge e tra ' rocchi de lo scoglio
lo piè sanza la man non si spedia.   (13–18)

(And so we left, and up the stairs / which, when we descended them earlier, had made us pale, / my leader remounted, drawing me behind him; / and going along our solitary way / among the sharp rocks and buttresses of the cliff, / the foot made no progress without the hand.)

One need not emphasise that this picture of step-by-step progress recalls the gradualness which Virgil instilled in the protagonist in the midst of his own 'mad flight' in *Inferno* I, and prepares for a direct contrast between the dynamics of Dante's journey and those of Ulysses's adventure. Yet, on inspection, even this simple and essential image is itself subject to dislocation. For one thing, the poet is quick to intervene again at line 19, expressing the horror which he feels, now as then, at the sight that greeted him in the eighth bolgia. The unity of feeling which he claims – although a painful unity – expresses a command over past and present which Ulysses will be unable to claim, because he cannot know the mechanism which effected his transition from his past condition on earth to his present condition in Hell. But the synthesis which the poet achieves in resuscitating the pain also contrasts with the slow advance over ignorance which the protagonist here accomplishes, and it rather foreshadows the mode of vision which the spirits in Purgatory will adopt as they remember – while sure of their salvation – the sins and disorders of the past.

Stylistically too this passage is more varied than a plain emphasis upon the journey of the protagonist seems to require. An elevation of tone begins with the much-discussed use of the arcane word 'iborni' at line 14, while, in stating his moral position, Dante also shifts into a distinctly Latinate tonality which comes close to the dead idiom of Brunetto's rhetoric. So, referring obliquely to God's grace and to providence, Dante speaks of 'stella bona o miglior cosa' and ends with the striking Latinism of 'm'invidi' – to 'waste' or 'make vain':

> sì che, se stella bona o miglior cosa
> m'ha dato 'l ben ch'io stessi nol m'invidi.   (23–4)

(so that, if a good star or a better thing / has given me the good, I should not myself make it waste).

Disturbing as this elevation is, it is in effect a stylistic preparation for the next section of the canto, where Dante shifts into the mode of simile. The use of simile itself suggests a raising of rhetorical level; and within the frame of simile Dante develops two descriptions which are so detailed as to be almost independent of the main narrative. Here, the complexity of narrative level becomes especially apparent when one realises that it is within the 'sub-plot' of these two similes that Dante has expressed most subtly the moral principle by which he judges Ulysses. We might indeed say – as we have suggested before – that the true hero of the canto is neither Ulysses nor the protagonist, but the *villan* to whom Dante here devotes two *terzine*:

> Quante 'l villan ch'al poggio si riposa,
> nel tempo che colui che 'l mondo schiara
> la faccia sua a noi tien meno ascosa,
> come la mosca cede a la zanzara,

vede lucciole giù per la vallea,
forse colà dov' e' vendemmia e ara.   (25–30)

(As many [fireflies] as the peasant [sees], resting on the hill-side, / at the season that he
who lights the world / least hides his face from us, / when the fly yields to the gnat, /
looking down into the valley, / there perhaps where he gathers grapes and ploughs.)

Let us pause, then, to consider why this humble figure deserves to be des-
cribed as the hero of the canto. In the first place, the simile associates the
villan directly with the humble Dante *personaggio* who witnesses his own
'firefly' scene; and we have seen, since at least Canto xx, how great a value
Dante places upon the normality that Virgil celebrates in his account of Man-
tua and in his own pastoral poetry. But the essential surprise of Canto xxvi is
that the imagination is invited to play across the incongruity between the
villan and Ulysses, and, in contradistinguishing the two figures, come to see
the moral force that resides in the former.

So where Ulysses, transgressing established limits, goes out over the level
surface of the seas, until finally the seas level over *him*, the *villan* is at rest,
contained by the hill-side, looking down into a scene which is both enclosed
and warm with the heat of the summer evening. In Ulysses's case, the trajec-
tory of his 'folle volo' leads practically to a collision with the Hill of Purga-
tory, which seems dark to him: 'bruna / per la distanza' (133–4); the valley
of the *villan* is dark only with the natural darkness of night, and even that
darkness is enlivened by the light of the fireflies. Then – most significantly –
where Ulysses is wrecked in a moment of crisis and incomprehension, the
villan is wholly at one with the cycles of time and nature: the scheme which
he inhabits is one that allows legitimate rest to follow honest work. The
smallest creatures of the world – the 'mosca' and the 'zanzara' – move with
that cycle; and the cycle itself is one which spans the large movements of the
seasons from ploughing to harvest, the shift from day to night and the precise
moment of change in which the 'fly yields to the gnat'. As the *villan* contem-
plates the scene, all these movements come to fruition before him. But for
Ulysses the search to see and know leads only to a moment of disintegration.
From the first, his journey is heading for a sterile world; he exhorts his crew
to come with him into a 'world without people' (117), while the phrase 'di
retro al sol' in the same line may well suggest some inconceivable goal
beyond and behind the sun. Certainly, his journey leads to no illumination.
He presses on beneath the cycles and patterns of the moon and stars (126–9);
but as the dark mountain of Purgatory looms up before him, there is no
happiness or sense of recognition. Joy is cut short by the whirlwind which
breaks from the unknown land, the 'nova terra':

> Cinque volte racceso e tante casso
> lo lume era di sotto la luna,
> poi che 'ntrati eravam ne l'alto passo,
>   quando n'apparve una montagna, bruna
> per la distanza, e parvemi alta tanto

quanto veduta non avĕa alcuna.
   Noi ci allegrammo, e tosto tornò in pianto;
ché de la nova terra un turbo nacque
e percosse del legno il primo canto.   (130–8)

Five times had been lit up and five times quenched / the light which the moon sends down / since we had entered on that high endeavour, / when a mountain appeared to us, dark / in the distance, and higher, it seemed to me, / than any I had ever seen. / We rejoiced at that, but it soon turned to grief; / for a whirlwind rose up from that new land, / and struck the forward part of our ship.)

As Ulysses's ship is mastered by the circling of the storm, one inevitably recalls the revenge which order and process take upon the thieves in Canto xxv. Ulysses's action has set him at odds with the natural world and, even in terms of human knowledge, perception and achievement, he is less than the *villan*, whose whole course has been consistent with the intrinsic movements of natural life. In this light, indeed, Ulysses contradicts not a divine edict but a law of his own natural being: for those same requirements and boundaries which, from Ulysses's point of view, might seem to be limitations and restrictions, are revealed by the image of the *villan* to be the patterns and ends that ensure our characteristic existence. As the *villan* rests in the confines of the valley, his own labours and the movements of day and seasons are simultaneously brought to fruition. It is the *villan* who asserts the possibilities that reside in the human being, not Ulysses.

The *villan* image, then, draws together a number of themes that have been gathering since the early cantos of the Malebolge. The same, however, could *not* be said of the second simile, which is quite out of keeping with the larger context of the Malebolge, and equally incongruous in its immediate location. The *villan* image – clearly owing much to pastoral models in classical poetry – asserts the value of moderation and order; the second simile alludes to a bizarre and violent episode in the fourth Book of Kings ii 11–12 which describes how the prophet Elijah ascends to Heaven. Where the *villan* enjoys the consummation of a natural process, the Elijah simile pictures an interruption of the natural order as violent as Ulysses's shipwreck and subsequent descent into the fires of Hell. Thus, Elijah is transported bodily to Heaven in a chariot of fire; and, in a further surreal circumstance – to which Dante refers in the opening lines of the passage – a group of children is set upon at the same moment and torn limb from limb by a pack of bears (for having mocked the prophet Elisha, who was observing the scene):

E qual colui che si vengiò con li orsi
vide 'l carro d'Elia al dipartire,
quando i cavalli al cielo erti levorsi,
   che nol pòtea sì con li occhi seguire,
ch'el vedesse altro che la fiamma sola,
sì come nuvoletta, in sù salire ...   (34–9)

(And as he who was avenged by bears / saw the chariot of Elijah at the moment of its ascent, / when the horses rose erect to Heaven / – and could not follow them further with his eyes / than to see merely the flame / rising up, as if it were a little cloud).

Yet incongruous as this passage is, it still has a bearing upon important aspects of Ulysses's case; and while, in theme, it introduces material which is new to the Malebolge, it also reminds one of the relevance to this great narrative canto of a narrative pattern we saw first in the entry to the City of Dis.

Thus, in the moral scheme, the simile – while stressing the notion of deference to the unknowable power of divinity – also recognises that the God of the Scriptures allows to human beings a power, in prophecy, to see beyond our natural limits, and declares that God will even break the laws of the natural order to receive the prophet. The insolence of the children is thus punished as an act of irreligion; and when Virgil shortly speaks of how Ulysses stole the Palladium, he identifies in Ulysses a similar spirit of irreligion, which offends even the pagan conception of what is due to the gods. At the same time, the simile admits that limit *can* be broken – though only for those who have a place in the prophetic history of revelation. It also insists that the proper end of a human being is located beyond the natural, in the eternity to which Elijah is carried. But these considerations are a further indication of why Ulysses must fail – and they point to the irreducibly tragic element in his case, the accident of his paganism. Ulysses is no prophet; and, so far from directing his intellect to an end beyond the natural, his whole purpose is to defend himself – in what he calls the 'little vigil of the senses still remaining' (114–15) – from a future which holds nothing save death. But the same lines also confirm the status of Dante himself as he appears in the opening *terzine*. For his position there is clearly that of the prophet who, in calling down vengeance on his native city, invokes the judgement of a power beyond time.

While authorising the prophetic stance which Dante here adopts, the Elijah passage also exemplifies, on the level of narrative, a pattern which reflects the underlying strategy of the *Inferno*. In the *Messo da Ciel* episode, we have seen the degree to which the narrative of the *cantica* depends upon the intersection of, so to say, horizontal and vertical co-ordinates, or, to put it another way, upon the tension between progress and intervention. This pattern is exactly repeated in the present canto. For, of course, Ulysses's headlong – and linear – pursuit of 'esperïenza' is interrupted by the sudden steep rise of Mount Purgatory; and this parallels the movement which has been established, in a positive sense, by the Elijah simile, where revelation is consummated along the same vertical axis. On the horizontal (or *historical*) plane, the Elijah passage is also concerned with the ways in which knowledge is sought and transmitted, in this case not by speech-makers and adventurers but by prophets; for the prophetic mantle of Elijah falls upon the shoulders of Elisha, who is here seen to witness the ascent of his predecessor. Yet in this case, as in the *Messo da Ciel* episode, the advance in prophetic understanding is secured by a raising of the eyes to the transcendent; and so the vertical emphasis is peculiarly strong, as Elisha watches the chariot disappear, drawn by horses 'raised steeply to heaven' – 'i cavalli al cielo erti' (36) – to a point at which it seems no more than a little cloud: 'come nuvoletta' (39).

Having said that, one can easily see that the whole rhythm of the section before Ulysses's speech, with its interruptions and sudden distortions, is a function of the same structural rhythm. Thus in a real sense the two similes represent an interruption to the text, in which Dante admits the authority of the two cardinal texts of prophecy – the Scriptures themselves and the pastoral poetry of Virgil, which included, of course, the Fourth Eclogue. Moreover, in their immediate application, it is notable that the purpose of these two similes is to stress a certain disproportion in Dante's perception of the bolgia: great as the flames will prove to be at closer quarters, they are at first sight as small as and no more menacing than fireflies or little clouds.

The first sixty lines of the canto have, then, defined its essential character, displaying a high degree of subtlety in their pursuit of moral coherence, but equally proving open, in terms of textual procedure, to effects of surprise, dislocation and irony. The greatest surprise of all, of course, will be the appearance of Ulysses, who is allowed to subvert or render dubious all the charges that have been laid against him. But in the meanwhile the central phase of the canto is dominated by the voice of Virgil, who, before addressing Ulysses, articulates a series of specific allegations against him, based particularly upon a Roman estimate of the Greek enemy.

As the narrative continues – having already emphasised the laborious steadiness of Dante's advance – it now shows Virgil attempting, as in Canto IX, to shield Dante from the full complexity and violence of the scene before him. So looking into the bolgia, he offers a somewhat anodyne statement of the obvious, informing Dante that the flames he sees are in fact the souls of a new group of sinners. But the protagonist is politely unimpressed by this:

> 'Maestro mio', rispuos' io, 'per udirti
> son io più certo; ma già m'era avviso
> che così fosse ...'.   (49–51)

('Master,' I replied, 'having heard this, / I am the more certain; but I was already aware / of that'.)

Characteristically, Dante wishes to focus upon a particular case, a great two-horned flame that he sees, burning as if on the funeral pyre of Eteocles and his brother. Even then Virgil, if not prevaricating, nonetheless attempts to mediate between Dante and the flame, relating a second-hand account of the legendary wrong-doings of Ulysses. It is in the course of this account that

Virgil enunciates the Roman judgement against Ulysses. Thus Ulysses burns
in Hell for having devised the stratagem of the Wooden Horse which led to
the downfall of Troy:

> si geme
> l'agguato del caval che fé la porta
> onde uscì de' Romani il gentil seme.   (58–60)

(He groans / for the ambush of the horse, opening the gate / from which the seed of the
Romans issued.)

It was Ulysses, moreover, who led Achilles to desert his lady Deidamia (62)
and who stole the tutelary statue of Pallas Athene from Troy (63).

Virgil, then, impugns the destructive guile of Ulysses, his impiety, his
irreligion and his heartlessness; and Dante must, of course, have understood
these judgements. Yet they are all plainly too easy: the protagonist is not
satisfied, for he wishes not only to contemplate the historical tableau of
judgement that Virgil provides, but to *speak* with the sinner. The danger of
this desire is emphasised by the fact that, while Virgil consents, he insists
that he himself must be the speaker.

The protagonist allows Ulysses to speak uninterruptedly from this point
forward. But at the same point the poet now produces the narrative *coup* that
releases all the tension that has gathered in the foregoing sequence and all the
ambiguities that are inherent in his own version of the Ulysses legend.

The Ulysses speech begins in a mode of primitive magic, the two-tongued
flame shifting and flickering like an omen or oracle before Dante's eye:

> Lo maggior corno de la fiamma antica
> cominciò a crollarsi mormorando ...   (85–6)

(The greater horn of the ancient flame / began murmuringly to shake.)

Then – fire struggling with wind (87), as if the elements were at war – the
tongue of fire speaks:

> indi la cima qua e là menando,
> come fosse la lingua che parlasse,
> gittò voce di fuori ...   (88–90)

(Then dragging its tip to and fro, / as if it were a tongue that spoke, / it flung forth its
voice.)

The force and impetus of Ulysses's utterance stands in contrast to the
moderation which has been characteristic of Virgil throughout this canto; and
in the first phase of his speech, Ulysses is allowed to engage still more
directly with the principles and standards which Virgil embodies. For not
only do these lines locate him as a contemporary of Aeneas – travelling the
Mediterranean as victor while Aeneas travels as a refugee; they also issue a
direct challenge to the essential virtues of Aeneas that Virgil celebrated in his
own epic poem:

> Quando
> mi diparti' da Circe, che sottrasse

me più d'un anno là presso a Gaeta,
prima che sì Enëa la nomasse,
    né dolcezza di figlio, né la pieta
del vecchio padre, né 'l debito amore
lo qual dovea Penelopè far lieta,
    vincer potero dentro a me l'ardore
ch'i' ebbi a divenir del mondo esperto ...   (90–8)

(When / I got myself away from Circe, who detained / me for more than a year near Gaeta, / before Aeneas had given it that name, / neither sweetness of child, nor reverence / for my old father, nor the due love / that should have made Penelope glad, / could overcome within me the ardour / I had to gain experience of the world.)

With the mention at line 94 of *pieta*, Ulysses places himself in open opposition to 'pius' Aeneas. And this opposition goes deep. For in the first place Ulysses, with his repeated and exhilarating negative, rejects precisely that concern for family and kin which led Aeneas – on the night when Troy was destroyed – to carry his ageing father on his shoulders from the flames, and then return to the burning city in search of his wife Creusa. In Aeneas's case, this delicate and active concern for others becomes the motive of his whole journey; he is determined to found a city, built upon *pietas*, that will harbour and protect his fellows. His journey has a distinct aim; and that aim – though sanctioned and directed by the gods – is defined above all by its profound humanity. But Ulysses's voyage has no such purpose or sanction. He does not know where it will lead him; all he does know is that, so far from protecting his companions, his plans will expose them to a further round of the perils which, already, have so greatly diminished their number:

ma misi me per l'alto mare aperto
sol con un legno e con quella compagna
picciola da la qual non fui diserto.   (100–2)

(But I put out upon the open sea / with a single keel, along with that company, / small as it was, which had not yet deserted me.)

Now it may well be said that the contrast between Ulysses and Aeneas itself supplies a sufficient judgement against the Greek – and that, in introducing it, Ulysses is made to condemn himself as, in some way, all of his great predecessors in the *Inferno* have done. Certainly, this contrast explains why Ulysses should be consigned to the lower circles of Hell rather than to Limbo. Ulysses's search for knowledge makes no contribution to the well-being of others. Ulysses builds no history or tradition of thought. Nor does he intend to. His aims, such as they are, remain ill-defined, save that they point decisively away from any stable community such as Rome represents. For Dante, it is clear that the pagan at his best – as pictured in Limbo – could instruct others how to *live* with others within the acknowledged boundaries of human nature. And by that standard, Ulysses is no hero of humanity but an archetypal example of the lost leaders that Dante first considered in the circles of violence.

Yet all this may seem as nothing compared with the energy that Ulysses displays. (The spirits of Limbo are static; and, after all, so is the *villan*, seated on his hill-side.) Here, however, we must begin to consider more closely the contrast that Dante suggests between himself and Ulysses. For what Dante has created in the concluding phase of the canto is a vision of intellectual innocence, entirely at odds with his own ironic and tragic insight. We may long for the vigour, clarity and even coherence that Ulysses displays in his narrative. But – taken on Ulysses's terms – these qualities are themselves shown to be a veil of illusion, concealing from view the tensions and contradictions that lie beneath. For the reader as for the poet, the true expression of intellectual energy must be to analyse – without any easy resort to preconception or judgement – the way these cross-currents flow.

We have noted already the irony of the word 'ardore' in Ulysses's mouth; but it would be easy to extend the range of its ironic reference. For beyond any purpose that Ulysses could conceive, the image of fire evokes, simultaneously, notions of destruction and refinement, of process and of grace. If the flame of Ulysses's punishment points to an ardour of thought – which, in life, might easily devise the burning of Troy – then it also anticipates the fires which purify the last group of sinners whom Dante ever meets (in *Purgatorio* XXVI) or, beyond that, the burning virtues of love which underlie the *Paradiso*. Penitence and grace are found both within and beyond the conflict of the elements.

Similarly, on the level of language rather than image, one should note how easily Ulysses effaces the moral terms by which he might have been judged; it is he himself who speaks of the love which is 'due' to Penelope (96), and he who recognises that the pillars of Hercules are a sign that 'man should not pass beyond' (109). But the rhythmic energy of the speech rejects the condemnation as soon as it is made; and the reader is left to gather and enforce the moral suggestions for himself, referring, across the grain of Ulysses's speech, to those features of the context which might corroborate the judgement.

In this regard, some of the subtlest pressures of the canto are exerted upon the word 'picciola', which Ulysses repeats three times, speaking of the 'picciola vigilia / d'i nostri sensi' (114–15), of the 'orazion picciola' with which he sways his companions (123) and of his crew as 'quella compagna / picciola' (101–2). In all of these cases, there is a pretence – whether deliberate or not – of modesty and humility which argues, in the context of the canto at large, a recognition of limit; the *villan* too is 'small'. Yet Ulysses, so far from conducting these terms to a moral conclusion, releases suggestions in the word which are at once elegiac and proud. The brevity of human life and its fragility are expressed in two of these cases. Yet when Ulysses indicates how small an instrument he needed to persuade his followers, weakness, limit and vulnerability become an occasion for glory.

The ironies which run unnoticed through Ulysses's speech are all the more striking when one considers that the whole purpose of the 'picciola orazion' is to expound a commanding intellectual plan, and to exert a mastery of language over the audience. With unshakeable confidence, Ulysses urges his followers to consider the origins and purposes of their own existence, and prides himself precisely on the wholehearted and immediate response which his words evoke:

> 'Considerate la vostra semenza:
> fatti non foste a viver come bruti,
> ma per seguir virtute e canoscenza'.
>   Li miei compagni fec' io sì aguti,
> con questa orazion picciola, al cammino,
> che a pena poscia li avrei ritenuti.   (118–23)

('Consider your seed and origins; / you were not made to live like brutes, / but to pursue virtue and knowledge.' / I made my companions so keen / with this little speech to set out on the road, / that I could hardly have restrained them then.)

This speech, then, is the core of Ulysses's claim to intellectual dignity and rhetorical skill. But what does it conceal?

In the first place, note that, while Ulysses insists his crewmen should consider their origins, it is precisely this that the impetus of his speech allows neither them nor the speaker himself to do. At first view, Ulysses is indeed attempting – as is Dante himself 'nel mezzo del cammin' – to project a coherent story upon an existence threatened by darkness and death. In effect, however, his words deny the very considerations which are needful if the story is to be told successfully. Ignoring any question of achievable end or ultimate object, Ulysses is content with the exhilaration of the response he unleashes; his one aim is vehemence, and he admits neither a reasonable investigation of horizons nor any space for disciplined introspection. Above all, his words are in no way words of guidance; the terms he employs remain resonant but undefined. What sense does he communicate of the meaning of virtue and knowledge? What *technique* for arriving at the truth do his words propose?

In all of these respects, Ulysses mirrors only to distort the whole procedure of Dante himself as poet and protagonist in the *Commedia*. From the moment that the protagonist saw the Hill in Canto I he knew what his end and goal should be: Virgil's careful discipline has given him the technical means to arrive at that end; and a canto such as the twenty-sixth represents an even more intense method of self-scrutiny than any that Virgil teaches. But nowhere are such differences more important than in the attitude which Ulysses and Dante, respectively, adopt to their audiences and to the figures who people the stories they tell. And Dante seems to recognise this. For as late as the *Paradiso* there occurs an implicit but unmistakable reference to *Inferno* XXVI: when, on the threshold of his final labour, in *Paradiso* II, Dante – recognising the daring of his new enterprise – turns to the reader and says, in words which echo precisely the imagery and the imperative tonality of Ulysses's speech:

> O voi che siete in piccioletta barca,
> desiderosi d'ascoltar, sequiti

> dietro al mio legno che cantando varca,
> tornate a riveder li vostri liti:
> non vi mettete in pelago, ché forse,
> perdendo me, rimarreste smarriti.   (*Par.* II 1–6)

(O you who in a little boat, / eager to hear, have followed on / behind my craft which as it makes its way is singing, / turn back to look again upon your shores; / do not put out upon the open sea, for perhaps / in losing me, you would be left bewildered.)

But there is in this speech precisely no attempt such as Ulysses makes to master or compel the 'picciola compagna' to any mad flight. On the contrary, Dante's concern is that the 'piccioletta barca' among his fleet of readers should be so honestly aware of its limitations that it would turn back at the realisation of its own incompetence. Nor is Dante's speech uttered in accents of disparagement; his demand for caution, self-examination or – in a word – consideration, is one which allows even the ill-equipped reader the dignity of decision.

By now, it will be clear that the overriding characteristic of Ulysses is a disregard for the independence and existence of others, whether the Trojans or Penelope, or his companions and crewmen. And the significance of this is realised at the climax of Ulysses's story. For, as Ulysses recounts the circlings of his ship in its final throes, he now recognises, behind his destruction, the power of 'another' who, so far from yielding to his influence, remains even now unknown and unnamed:

> Tre volte il fé girar con tutte l'acque;
> a la quarta levar la poppa in suso
> e la prora ire in giù, com' altrui piacque,
> infin che 'l mar fu sovra noi richiuso.   (*Inf.* XXVI 139–42)

(Three times it made the ship whirl around with all the waters, / at the fourth making the stern rise up / and the prow go down as it pleased another, / until the sea closed over us again.)

Here – for all his unconcern with 'ends' – Ulysses does arrive at the inescapable end of natural life, his own death. As we have already seen, the orderliness of that end – in the perspective of divinity – is emphasised by the stress upon circularity, and also – as in Canto XXV – by a play upon notions of number. Equally, the intervention of the divine is signalled by the abrupt descent of Ulysses's ship, plunging prow foremost through the waters on a course which will lead the sinner to re-emerge as a fire in Hell. At the same time, the nature of the principle he has offended is hardly one which insists upon limit as a restriction or inhibition. The agent of that principle is the moving ocean, which draws the traveller into its circuit, while still continuing to work and shift above him. And beyond that, as Ulysses dimly recognises, there is the will of the *Altrui*. Finally, the truth resides not in a pattern or scheme of lines and boundaries, but in the will of another being, more subtle and more powerful than the most guileful and impressive of human intelligences. So Dante in the last *terzine* of the *Paradiso* will eventually see – beyond the circulations and geometric patterns in which God first presents himself – a final miraculous vision of God in the form of humanity itself, 'nostra effige'. But this is a form of knowledge to which Ulysses – even if he were a Christian – is from the first ill-adapted, precisely by the disregard he shows towards the immediate manifestations of the *Altrui* in wife, family and dependants. The final irony is that true knowledge is not only beyond the reach of Ulysses's mind but also too close at hand, too finely intertwined with the nature of humanity, for Ulysses – with his fear of mortality and his eye for distant horizions – ever to recognise. Nor is it necessary to wait for the *Paradiso* to see what for Dante it might mean, in a positive sense, to be reconciled with the *Altrui*. For it is this reconciliation that Dante dramatises in the first canto of the *Purgatorio* – at the end of which he makes a direct allusion to the Ulysses episode.

Having arrived at the deserted beach of Purgatory, the protagonist submits to a ritual of purification; Virgil washes the grime of Hell from his face, and then proceeds to bind his waist with a reed plucked from the shallows of the shore:

> Venimmo poi in sul lito diserto,
> che mai non vide navicar sue acque
> omo, che di tornar sia poscia esperto.
>   Quivi mi cinse sì com' altrui piacque:
> oh maraviglia! ché qual elli scelse
> l'umile pianta, cotal si rinacque
> subitamente là onde l'avelse.   (*Purg.* I 130–6)

(We came then to the deserted beach, / which never saw sailing across its waters / any man who after knew how to return. / There I girded myself as another wished. / O wonder; for just as he plucked / the humble plant, its like was at once reborn / from whence he had wrenched it.)

Here, the phrase 'com' altrui piacque' is an unprecedented repetition of the penultimate line of *Inferno* XXVI. There can be no doubt that a parallel with *Inferno* XXVI is deliberately being drawn; for the allusion to *Inferno* XXVI is equally strong in lines 131–2, with the recognition that the seas around Purgatory have never been sailed save by those who – in the key word of *Inferno* XXVI – were not sufficiently 'esperto' to return. From this initial point of similarity, however, there radiates a wide range of contrasts between the intellectual positions of Dante and of Ulysses, and between the imagery and action of the two episodes.

Most obviously, the humility which Dante here displays stands in direct contrast to the *hubris* of Ulysses. Yet nothing could be clearer than that the scene in Purgatory defines humility not merely as deference to a greater power, but as the essential condition of any fruitful activity. In deferring to the *Altrui* of God – here expressing his design through the *altrui* of Cato, who has just commanded this girding – Dante is indeed accepting the conditions that God has placed upon his existence. But his submission is also a submission to the hand of Virgil as he performs the rite of initiation; and if there were any doubt that this ceremony represents as much an entry into the

fullness of human life as a preparation for the approach to God, we need only
consider the extreme delicacy and tenderness which Virgil displayed earlier
as he cleansed the tear-stained cheeks of the protagonist with dew:

> ambo le mani in su l'erbetta sparte
> soavemente 'l mio maestro pose:
> ond'io che fui accorto di sua arte,
>   porsi ver' lui le guance lagrimose.   (*Purg.* I 124–7)

(Both hands spread out on the grass / my master gently placed; / at which understanding
his design, / I leant my tear-stained cheeks towards him.)

In effect, the function which Virgil performs here is one which not only
distinguishes him from Ulysses but also reveals a new aspect of his impor-
tance to Dante. Hitherto, while Virgil's human presence has always been
important, he has represented, above all, a reliable source of authority in
word and thought. But now his rationality puts on a different face, and one
which will dominate the representation of Virgil throughout the *Purgatorio*.
For now he becomes the custodian of the myths – and of the rituals which
enact those myths – on which the sanity and cohesion of the human commu-
nity depend. Human reason is expressed not only in the explicit statements of
philosophy, but also in that perception of pattern and order which is
embodied in the silent language of image and ceremonial gestures; and
Virgil's 'art' – of which Dante is here 'aware' – resides in his ability to
apply this language. But rationality in such a sense is wholly unknown to
Ulysses. The community that he attempts to inspire is one which responds to
the impact of the spoken word and commanding purpose. Moreover, while
Ulysses is himself one of the great myths of European culture – and serves as
such in Dante's poem – his whole course in the *Inferno* Canto XXVI is one
which destroys and opposes the mythic origins of humanity. Just as he des-
troyed the home of the Romans, so he ignores the essential call of his own
origins in Ithaca and brings his companions, not to a silent consummation of
comradeship, but to frenetic destruction. At that moment of destruction, the
patterns of nature, which Virgil draws upon in enlisting the fading dew and
bending reed to his liturgical purposes, reassert themselves with the utmost
violence. It is significant that this violence should proceed from Purgatory,
for on the top of that mountain is located the original home of humanity –
the Earthly Paradise, which even pagan poets have celebrated in their myths.

Religio – a deference to the numinous and unknown – is a virtue which
even the pagan mind could appreciate; and Virgil, throughout the *Inferno* and
Purgatorio, displays it as distinctly as Ulysses does not. But *religio* is an
aspect of reason, not an abdication. And in *Purgatorio* I it is triumphantly
clear that the mind can only function at its best – avoiding false counsel and
rejoicing in true 'esperienza' – when it does acknowledge the limits that are
proper to it. Indeed it is precisely here in the first canto of the *Purgatorio*,
that both the *villan* and the prophet come into their own as intellectual
heroes. For, in looking at the reed on the 'molle limo' of the shore, the

protagonist fixes his eye on a detail as apparently insignificant as the fireflies in the valley; and seeing it so precisely, he effectively sees more than Ulysses ever did on his tempestuous voyage. Moreover, this same reed also bears miraculous meaning, revealing to the eye which contemplates it 'prophetically' the marvel that ensures growth and rebirth even to the most trivial feature of the created world. Nor is this an isolated feature of the text. For the mentality which speaks through Dante's own style from the first canto onward in the *Purgatorio* is one which combines an almost scientific precision in its observation of detail with an awareness that any detail of the world can yield a meaning beyond itself. So, earlier, as Dante describes his first view of the island, he writes:

> Questa isoletta intorno ad imo ad imo,
> là giù colà dove la batte l'onda,
> porta di giunchi sovra 'l molle limo.   (*Purg.* I 100–2)

(This little island all around its base – / there where the waves beat – / bore reeds upon its soft mud.)

and likewise continues to chart the interaction of vital energies in the process of the dawn:

> L'alba vinceva l'ora mattutina
> che fuggia innanzi, sì che di lontano
> conobbi il tremolar de la marina.   (*Purg.* I 115–17)

(The dawn was winning over the morning hour / which fled before it, so that at a distance / I could see the trembling of the sea.)

Here perception and intelligence are entirely at home and able to observe both the orderliness that acts beneath the movement of waves and light, and also an emblematic victory of light over darkness. This is the same mountain which for Ulysses was 'higher than any he had ever seen' and 'dark in the distance'. For Dante, strikingly, it is an 'isoletta', a *little* island; and light of all kinds – from the stars, the sun and, eventually, the faces of angels – plays upon it.

It will surely be clear by now why Ulysses is a false counsellor. His fault lies not merely in particular acts of guile but in a radical perversion of intelligence which disallows any concentration on those external objects – whether human or physical – which the mind should naturally feed upon. The *altrui*, in whatever aspect, is endangered by a single-mindedness which, in Ulysses as in Farinata, Pier and Brunetto, aims at a self-enclosing dignity. Indeed, Ulysses does not even acknowledge the other sinner – his comrade Diomedes – who is burning in the same twin-fire as he. The *villan*, observing the 'otherness' of the fireflies in his attitude of comic normality, remains a far more reliable guide to moral and intellectual action.

As for Dante, the fiction of the twenty-sixth canto must itself be taken as an indication of how deeply concerned his writing invariably is with the *altrui* in all its manifestations. Certainly, Dante's story allows 'Ulysses' a freedom to speak which Ulysses in his own story does not allow to his followers. More importantly, his writing here envisages with exceptional force the opacity which must lie at the centre of any other being. As a pagan, Ulysses, like all other pagans, is irreducibly 'other' to the Christian Dante; and, like Trajan and Rhipeus, he serves to reveal the inadequacy of any order which does not submit to the questions raised by the otherness of the individual being. The choice of a pagan as subject helps to state this understanding in a negative sense. But when Dante sees God in Paradise or Beatrice in Purgatory, they are not what he expected; they are entirely other. And what is more, Dante too in the course of these meetings must see himself as another, reflected in the streams of the Earthly Paradise or the human visage of the Deity. Only thus will he see that he is, after all, the creation – or new creation – of God and Beatrice. But even his own creation, Ulysses, is a mirror image, his *alter ego*; and though this may be the *best* image that Dante can produce of himself, he must finally detach himself from it, leaving Ulysses behind in a region of Hell where fiction is condemned as falsehood. Morally and poetically, *order* for Dante involves not comfort, but risk and a recognition that the core of any being must always lie beyond the limits of its own dead self.

V

There have been critics who – refusing to be overawed by the Ulysses episode – have seen in the portrayal of Guido Dante's most complete analysis of the psychology of sin. Certainly Guido is allowed more space than any other sinner in the *Inferno*; his conversation with the protagonist, beginning at line 7, does not conclude until the penultimate *terzina* of the canto; and throughout, Dante's concern is to investigate a mind which has deliberately and knowingly chosen to follow a sinful course. It is this that distinguishes Guido from Ulysses, who cannot, at least, be thought *consciously* to aim at self-destruction. Of course, there are similarities between the two cases – emphasised by the fact that Dante allots two cantos to the depiction of the same sin; and in part – as will be seen – these similarities allow Dante to pronounce a final judgement upon the inherently ambiguous case of Ulysses. At the same time, the coupling emphasises the especial perversity of Guido: in his case, the misuse of intellect has reduced a Christian to the same level as the pagan Ulysses. Guido enjoys all the benefits of Christian revelation: not only is he living in the Christian era but – as history confirms – demonstrate at the end of his life a notional understanding of the truths of revelation when he entered the order of St Francis. Moreover – though this proves to be a doubtful privilege – Guido is shown to be on intimate terms with the successor of St Peter, Pope Boniface VIII. Yet at the moment of transition, at the critical meeting-point, in death, of time and eternity, Guido fails as completely as Ulysses did on his approach to Purgatory.

In Ulysses, Dante depicted the 'profound surface' of pagan culture. In

Canto XXVII his subject is the mentality and language of Christianity, as displayed in the workings or failures of conscience. Christianity, it appears, opens up inner vistas which are closed to the pagan mind; but these same vistas can prove to be a labyrinth in which self-consciousness itself becomes destructive. In this light, it is not surprising that T. S. Eliot should have cited lines 61–3 of Canto XXVII as an epigraph to *The Love Song of J. Alfred Prufrock* – and thus have associated Guido with Hamlet, who also appears in Eliot's poem. Guido, Hamlet and Prufrock are the sterile products of Christian civilisation, ruined by their own capacity for introspection and by an over-sophisticated manipulation of the intentions and motives which Christianity requires the intellect to cultivate.

In the canto of the hypocrites, Dante had already begun to explore the inner life of the conscience; and, thematically, the portrayal of Guido provides a connection between the discussion of hypocrisy and the discussion of treachery in the last cantos – where plausibility of surface is seen, in the traitor, to conceal an utter erosion of inner truth. But the especial importance of the canto lies in the urgency of the questions it raises for the Christian author of the *Commedia*. As we have seen, the Ulysses episode is an exercise in self-examination and, as such, remains a point of reference throughout the subsequent *Commedia*. The same could said, in an even stronger sense, of Canto XXVII. In Ulysses, Dante creates a fictional figure to mirror the fundamental issues of his present enterprise; but in portraying Guido, he returns from myth to history and reconsiders a case which he himself first raised in the *Convivio* and (implicitly) will raise again in *Purgatorio* v. As a false counsellor, Guido in Hell will demonstrate how the Christian mind may, so to speak, re-convert itself to sin, misreading and perverting all the signs of truth that the Christian is privileged to witness. Faced with that example, Dante recognises errors of judgement that he himself has made in the past and, by rectifying that judgement in Canto XXVII, reasserts his grip over his own literary and historical design. For Dante no less than for Guido, Canto XXVII is a canto of crisis and change in which the coherence of an intellectual life-story is brought to the test.

In the *Convivio* Guido appears as a reliable example of how the story of a life is to be told; so far from being a false counsellor, it is he who shows how the Christian may bring the arc of his natural existence to its proper conclusion. The historical Guido has indeed been taken, by the historical Dante, as a human sign of how each human should end his life. So in the *Convivio*, Dante has argued that in the fourth and last age of life, as death approaches, the mind should devote itself entirely to the contemplation of God:

Rendesi dunque a Dio la nobile anima in questa etade, e attende lo fine di questa vita con molto desiderio ...   (*CNV* IV xxviii 7)

(So in this age the noble soul offers itself to God and waits with great longing for the end of this life.)

In becoming a friar, Guido, it appeared, did precisely this; and in the *Convivio* he is praised on that account as 'lo nobilissimo Guido montefel-trano' (*ibid.* 8). Now, as he reverses that judgement, Dante uses words and images which exactly recall the *Convivio*: in the paragraphs preceding the example of Guido, Dante had spoken of human life in terms of a ship travelling to its port:

la naturale morte è quasi a noi porto di lunga navigazione e riposo. Ed è così come il buono marinaro: come esso appropinqua al porto cala le sue vele ... così noi dovemo calare le vele de le nostre mondane operazioni ...   (*ibid.* 3)

(Our natural death is for us like the port and the rest we reach after long sailing. In this sense: as the good sailor, drawing near to the port, lowers the sail ... so should we lower the sails of our worldly activities.)

In Canto XXVII, the same emblems recur in the mouth of Guido, at the very point in his story where he begins to recount how he has ignored their implications:

> Quando mi vidi giunto in quella parte
> di mia etade, ove ciascun dovrebbe
> calar le vele e raccoglier le sarte ...   (*Inf.* XXVII 79–81)

(When I saw that I had come to that part / of my life where each of us should / lower the sail and draw in the rigging.)

Like Aeneas, the historical Guido had, in the *Convivio*, demonstrated an understanding of the 'shape' of life which – as we saw in Chapter 3 – proved to be essential for Dante's conception of narrative in the *Commedia*: to tell the story of a life is to tell, as in the story of a journey, the beginnings, ends and stages that constitute its intrinsic design. But now the true understanding of that design has been entrusted to such humble figures as, for example, the *villan* of Canto XXVI. Moreover, in Ulysses we have seen how journeys can be retrograde and lead to nothing but extinction. Now, in Canto XXVII, the words of praise which Guido has once appeared to deserve are put in the sinner's mouth as part of an ironic self-judgement, indicating ignorance and confusion. Equally, the references to 'sailing' and the 'port' serve to transform the excitements of Ulysses's story into a moral *exemplum*. Guido has still a function in Dante's design; but, so far from providing a positive example, he is employed as a vessel for the poet's final analysis and judgement of false counsel.

While the image of the journey is, of course, essential to Dante's narrative and moral conceptions in the *Commedia*, it is also a mark of how far the poet has travelled from the view which he himself proposed in the humanistic and philosophical *Convivio* that his treatment of the conception in the twenty-seventh canto should be coloured by urgent considerations of judgement and the ironies of dramatic voice. We have seen throughout how, in response to the new thematic demands of the *Commedia*, Dante modifies the simple model of linear narrative, allowing in particular for moments of synthesis or for the revelatory impact of the image. In Cantos XXVI and XXVII, Dante is concerned in a literal sense with the moment of revelation – the moment of absolute certainty which the pagan Ulysses cannot enjoy and the Christian Guido wilfully ignores; and, as will be seen, visual images have an especial importance in the central sections of the twenty-seventh canto. But another mode of synthesis is also at issue here: Dante is concerned with the extent to which true understanding depends not simply upon the ability to make progress, but also upon the capacity which the mind possesses to reflect, in judgement, upon its own developments and assess its own intentions – to the point of annihilating its own essential certainties – in acts of self-knowledge. Neither Ulysses nor Guido is capable of that. On the contrary, both press forward in single-minded pursuit of their ends. It is left to Dante to grasp and express the tensions that the sinners conceal, even if it means admitting how fallible and uncertain his own earlier pronouncements have been.

This is true, as it were, retrospectively in Dante's readjustment of the position he adopted in the *Convivio*. It is also true *prospectively* in the preparations which Dante lays here for the fifth canto of the *Purgatorio*, where the case of Guido will be deliberately contrasted with that of his son, Buonconte. The parallels between the two cases are themselves evidence of the extent to which the narrative design in the *Commedia* depends upon its author's capacity for broad and sustained imaginative synthesis. But we shall see equally that the judgements which emerge from that contrast demonstrate the value which Dante also places upon the mind's response to the intense and critical moment of understanding: at the point of death, the son achieves in an instant of repentance what the father could not achieve by determined and prolonged calculation; temporal precedence itself collapses, or is inverted, as the natural primacy of the father cedes to the primacy that the son attains in grace.

Canto XXVII stands, then, at the centre of an extensive network of cross-references, demonstrating the extent to which the *Commedia* is built upon a constant reassessment of cases and issues. We have now to consider the canto in relation to its immediate context and examine its internal structure.

In many respects, it will be seen that the structure of Canto XXVII stands, significantly, in contrast to the structure of Canto XXVI. After the ambiguities which Dante has aroused in the Ulysses episode, the aim of Canto XXVII is, in some sense, clarification and control; and in that respect Dante here repeats a pattern – familiar by now – in which sequences of 'difficulty' are followed by sequences of explicit analysis. (So, likewise, the case of Francesca was followed by that of Ciacco; and so too the tragic complexities of the violence cantos gave way to the well-known vocabulary of infernal punishments that Dante tends to draw upon in the Malebolge.) Yet clarity and control are themselves rendered problematical by Dante's present theme. From the beginning of the Malebolge, Dante has cast doubt upon the reliability of the rational means of signification. But in portraying Guido, he envisages the possibility that the apparently unambiguous signs of Christian revelation – as enshrined in the Church and its institutions – can themselves be misread and lead to damnation. In a word, lip-service to Christianity is not sufficient. The self must become a sign, down to the depths of its conscience. But Guido, who once seemed to be such a sign, now proves – as Dante inspects his own conscience – how the self may yield to mere arbitrariety. In the words which Guido is given to speak, terms and concepts of central importance to Dante himself deteriorate and slip into incoherence, even though the voice of Guido is – superficially at least – both magisterial and sophisticated. There are similarities in this regard between Guido and Ulysses. Yet the differences are more striking: for Guido lacks all capacity for coherent narrative; and, where Ulysses enforces his position through the glamorous excitements of the adventure story, Guido – particularly in the final speech – is concerned rather to exonerate himself by offering a factual record of the conversations which led him to his fate. But this itself leads to incoherence as Guido reports these conversations: within Guido's speech, there is the *verbatim* report of his damning dialogue with Pope Boniface (85–111); and this produces, in turn, the squabble over Guido's soul on the threshold of eternity (112–26), in which one hears both the arguments of the devils over Guido's soul and the voice of Minos (from *Inferno* III), and also becomes aware of the presence of St Francis (112), who arrives on the scene to claim his *soi-disant* follower.

In no other canto are there so many voices to contend with as one listens to the sinner, or such a background of accumulated and still-shifting significance to penetrate; and while the twenty-seventh canto may serve to clarify the issues of its predecessor, it also gains in density because of the silent presence of Ulysses – and, with him, of Aeneas and Virgil – in the parallels which Dante's structure invites one to construct.

But what of Dante himself? The extent to which the canto represents a test of his own command and clarity of judgement is demonstrated by the position of the protagonist. In Canto XXV the protagonist was silent; and in Canto XXVI, Virgil took the initiative in speaking to Ulysses, as though to shield the protagonist from the impact of the sinner's voice. But now – faced with a far more devious personality than Ulysses – the protagonist returns to the centre of the stage. His position is more authoritative than it has been since Canto XIX – where, as in the present canto, Dante involves himself in an oblique encounter with Pope Boniface VIII – and, as will be seen, the properties that Dante ascribes to his own speech are contrasted directly with the properties of Guido's tortuous reportage. Most significantly, visual clarity and firmness of viewpoint here replace the uncertainties or untrustworthiness of speech and argument.

The treatment of the protagonist points to more general characteristics on the level of structure and narrative form which distinguish Canto XXVII from the cantos that immediately precede it. In Canto XXV, the silence of the protagonist made way, so to speak, for the aggressive artistry of the poet himself in his attack upon the thieves. Canto XXVI began in the same way, with the ironic vigour of the authorial tirade against Florence; but Ulysses's voice was the last voice one heard in that canto, stimulating tones and suggestions which threatened to exceed the moral command of the author. In the present canto, there are no direct authorial interventions. Yet Guido is never allowed the freedom which Dante ascribes to Ulysses. Throughout, control is exercised in the silent pressures of irony: playing upon the web of cross-reference, irony becomes the agent of judgements in which author and protagonist are entirely at one, and so effective is this mechanism – so predictable in its operation – that the canto develops a comic tonality. Every sentence that the sinner speaks eludes his own control and serves as a judgement against himself, so that the canto ends with no authoritative voice, but with a farcical linguistic scuffle (which alone would make the sequence typical of the Malebolge).

Like Canto XXV and Canto XXVI, the present canto opens with a deferred judgement upon one of the damned – in this case, Ulysses – from the foregoing sequence. The canto-break is not used as violently as it was in the two earlier cases to stress authorial action. Even so, Ulysses – now silent, his flame now still – is brought firmly under control; the great sea-adventurer is allowed to depart only when Virgil permits: 'con la licenza del dolce poeta' (3); Rome – if temporarily defeated by the voice of Ulysses – here reasserts control.

    Control is also the characteristic of Dante's first description of Guido. As Ulysses departs, so another flame approaches: 'quand' un'altra che dietro a lei venìa, / ne fece volger li occhi ...' (4–5). For once, there is nothing sudden or surprising about the entry of the sinner. Indeed, certain comic qualities in the canto at once begin to reveal themselves with the realisation that there must be a mechanical succession of speaking flames in the bolgia: where one flame might be sublime, two are absurd. And this further underlines the judgements against Ulysses: so far from being the heroic exception, he has in effect a twin; the sign can be reapplied regardless of identity – one recalls how the forcible yoking of Farinata and Cavalcante reduced the former to moral size.

    This narrative detail leads to a simile which introduces the voice of Guido but simultaneously initiates the major ironies and moral judgements of the canto:

> Come 'l bue cicilian che mugghiò prima
> col pianto di colui, e ciò fu dritto,
> che l'avea temperato con sua lima,
>   mugghiava con la voce de l'afflitto,
> sì che, con tutto che fosse di rame,
> pur el pareva dal dolor trafitto.   (XXVII 7–12)

(Like the Sicilian bull who first roared / with the anguish of him – and this was just – / who had shaped him with his file, / roaring with the voice of the tortured victim, / so that, although it was all made of brass, / it still seemed to be pierced with pain.)

    The source of this simile is Ovid (*Tristia* III ii), who tells how the craftsman Perillus was commissioned by a tyrant to construct an instrument of torture in the form of a metal bull: the victims – placed in the stomach of the bull – would be roasted alive while their screams issued through its artificial vocal chords in the form of a realistic bellow. Perillus himself was made to test the efficacy of his handiwork by becoming its first victim.

In the simile, as in Guido's story, appearance and reality, surface and depth, are at odds, while skill and art are contrasted with a complex knot of perverse and warring intentions. The intentions of the artificer are, in both cases, inconsistent with those of his patron and generally with results. Incongruities arise between the bellowing of a bull or a flame and what is in fact a man confined within the punitive construct; the skilled craftsman who worked on the *surface* of the artefact is now reduced to pain and passivity *within* it; and finally there is the discrepancy – which, as will be seen, also has its bearing on Guido's case – between the inanimate mass of metal and the animation or appearance of life it receives, firstly from the art of the maker, and then from the force of his suffering voice.

In Canto xxv, the myths of Ovid were allowed to release a considerable imaginative charge, which the author had then to regulate and reapply; in Canto xxvi apparently incidental similes acted, on an imagistic level, to suggest the direction of Dante's thinking. Here the myth has none of the danger which surrounded the myth of metamorphosis; nor does it stimulate the wide range of suggestion that arose from the *villan* image. On the contrary, it possesses a specific and stated analytic purpose; and the confidence with which Dante translates image into moral emblem is first registered in the parenthetic phrase 'e ciò fu dritto', where voice intervenes to govern the application of the literary artifice.

Dante now concentrates upon the 'parole grame' of Guido. Visually, the flame of Guido – tormented and writhing – already has more in common with the flames that torment the feet of the simonists than with Ulysses, whose flame has been described in line 1 in terms of stillness or even dignity: 'Già era dritta in sù la fiamma e queta …'. Where Ulysses's speaking flame possessed a magical power, Guido's flame is characterised from the first by contortions which express the anxious and frustrated psychology of the sinner and also anticipate the essential incoherence that all his speeches in the canto will reveal.

The first words that Guido speaks contain curiously unsettling references both to Virgil and to the protagonist. First, addressing Virgil, he translates the solemn 'dolce licenza' which Virgil gave to Ulysses into harsh Lombard dialect: 'Istra ten va, più non t'adizzo'. Then, still speaking to Virgil, he seems to assume that these travellers through Hell are themselves dead, and prepares for the words he eventually addresses to the protagonist (61), in which – completely misapprehending Dante's position – he declares that he would be silent if he thought his words were ever to be reported on earth.

Unwittingly, Guido here threatens two of the main principles of signification in the *Inferno*, represented by the words of Virgil and the physical presence in eternity of the living protagonist. The authority of Virgil's voice is here diminished by being rendered in provincial dialect. And while, in part, this may be no more than a realistic grace-note characterising Guido's voice, the implications of such a reduction touch some of Dante's prevailing concerns. For, while Virgil may speak Dante's Italian throughout the *Commedia*, one knows from the *De Vulgari Eloquentia* the importance that Dante attached to Latin as the measure or grammatical model which all vernacular languages had to respect if they were to attain stability. Notably, when Dante returns to the image of flame in the *Purgatorio*, he *does* allow Arnaut Daniel the use of his own vernacular – on the implicit understanding that Arnaut understands what it means to follow the disciplines of a 'grammar'.

Considering the emphasis upon linguistic questions in Cantos XXV and XXVI, it is difficult to overlook Guido's opening lines. It is the first indication of a linguistic instability which Guido will consistently propagate that he should so convert to confusion the principle of linguistic authority. This conclusion is in harmony with the political positions that Dante attributes to Guido: where Virgil, by his presence, asserts the unity of Empire, Guido is obsessed with political faction and strife:

> dimmi se Romagnuoli han pace o guerra.   (28)

(tell me whether the Romagnuoli are at peace or war).

Parallel to the threat he offers to Virgil – though on a different semiotic level – is the threat which Guido presents to the human image of the protagonist. Other sinners have been amazed to see Dante in Hell; but Guido has no capacity for amazement at the sight, and speaks in unrelieved ignorance of its meaning.

By now we have seen that alongside, and even superior to, actual language, Dante has conceived a system of visual signs culminating in the visible miracle of the perfect human form. The *Messo da Ciel*, defending Dante's right to advance on his journey through Hell, was one such image; but, ironically enough, the historical Guido – as presented in the *Convivio* – has himself served a similar role as exemplar. Now the protagonist has taken his place; and Guido has no ability to read the significance either of Dante or – for that matter – of his own life. Evidently enough, Guido has failed to maintain the pattern of existence which he himself had exemplified, returning to active politics – which quickly became the politics of treachery – at the behest of Boniface. But a similar failing is expressed – in terms appropriate to the themes that Dante has developed since the *Convivio* – in perhaps the ugliest line of the canto:

> Mentre ch'io forma fui d'ossa e di polpe
> che la madre mi diè, l'opre mie
> non furon leonine, ma di volpe.   (73–5)

(While my soul was still in the form of the bone and pulp / my mother gave me, my actions / were those not of the lion, but of the fox.)

Here Guido attempts an act of self-knowledge; but his emphasis falls upon his own intellectual characteristics, and it cannot conceal the disparaging reference to his own bodily nature, which he reduces by his words to the level of bone and pulp. Where Ulysses showed a contempt for his home, Guido shows contempt for his own bodily origins, and in doing so he reveals how far he has alienated himself from the truths which can be perceived in the cycles of physical nature. In a similar way, the opening simile pictured physical mass at odds with intellect: the craftsman prides himself on mastering the mass of the bull he has created, only to suffer imprisonment in that mass. In the protagonist, on the other hand, intellect, spirit and bodily nature are reconciled in the destined journey through eternity. Salvation involves the salvation of the body as well as of the spirit, and allows the intellect to rediscover its own relationship to the physical form it inhabits. This is the truth that the protagonist tacitly declares by his progress through Hell. But Guido ignores that significance. The protagonist for him is nothing but a bearer of political information; Guido's one concern is to know how things stand in the Romagna. His urgent concern displays the fretfulness of spirit which destroyed the contemplative calm of his own last days; it also indicates the extent to which his mind is now enclosed in dead issues which no new revelation can penetrate.

The symptoms of Guido's malaise are displayed in the details of his speeches, and are brought into particular prominence by the contrasts between the linguistic properties of *his* utterances and the words of the protagonist.

Agitation of rhythm and sophistication of syntax are the two characteristics of Guido's language. From first to last, Guido is dominated by uncomprehending rancour as he contemplates his own fate; and this is expressed aurally as well as visually in the concluding lines of the episode:

> 'e sì vestito, andando, mi rancuro'.
> 　　Quand' elli ebbe 'l suo dir così compiuto,
> 　la fiamma dolorando si partio,
> 　torcendo e dibattendo 'l corno aguto.　　　　　　(129–32)

('and thus clothed, I go on my way in bitterness.' / When he had concluded his speech thus, / the grieving flame went off, / twisting and tossing its pointed horn.)

At the same time, Guido possesses the linguistic instruments for defining his position; his sophistication, though hollow, is reflected in long periodic sentences, twice introduced by conditional or subjunctive constructions:

> 　　Se tu pur mo in questo mondo cieco
> 　　caduto se' ...　　　　　　　　　　　　　　　(25–6)

(If you have just now [fallen] into this blind world...)

and

> 　　S'i' credesse che mia risposta fosse
> 　　a persona che mai tornasse al mondo,
> 　　questa fiamma staria sanza più scosse.　　　　　(61–3)

(If I thought my answer were / to someone who ever should return to the world, / this flame would stand without shaking more.)

Dante here creates a syntactic equivalent of the constructions that destroyed the artificer of the opening simile: intelligence attempts to exert control; but facts are totally misapprehended, and consequently the logic of Guido's conditions and hypotheses proves to be nothing but a fallacious and self-imprisoning tissue. At the same time, the reality of Guido's condition in Hell is unambiguously clear to his audience; irony controls the speech by emphasising Guido's obvious mistake, and also by an onomatopoeic insistence upon the physical features that even his words possess. Not only is the voice rancorous but the sound of the flame breaks through the syntax in 'fosse' and 'scosse'; the punishment and 'body' which Guido seeks to ignore or displace by his intellectual pretensions cannot be gainsaid: his language itself betrays, beneath its intellectual surface, a rooted physical reality.

Contrast this with the speech of the protagonist:

> E io, ch'avea già pronta la risposta,
> sanza indugio a parlare incominciai:
> 'O anima che se' là giù nascosta,
>   Romagna tua non è, e non fu mai,
> sanza guerra ne' cuor de' suoi tiranni;
> ma 'n palese nessuna or vi lasciai.
>   Ravenna sta come stata è molt' anni:
> l'aguglia da Polenta la si cova,
> sì che Cervia ricuopre co' suoi vanni.
>   La terra che fé già la lunga prova
> e di Franceschi sanguinoso mucchio,
> sotto le branche verdi si ritrova'.   (34–45)

(And I, who had my reply all ready, / began without delay to speak: / 'O soul hidden down there, / your Romagna is not and never was / without war in the heart of its tyrants; / but I have left no open war there now. / Ravenna stands as it has done for many years: / the Eagle of Polenta broods over it, / so that he covers Cervia with his wings. / The land that once made a long siege / – and a bloody heap of the French – / finds itself again beneath the green claws.')

One notes firstly the readiness with which Dante proceeds. Though Guido expects a response from Virgil, it is Dante who speaks, unleashing a reply which at once cuts through the convolutions of the sinner's voice; and here there is neither emotion nor syntactical complexity. In place of the subjunctive, Dante speaks with unfailing emphasis upon the indicative of the verb 'to be': things in Romagna are now as they always were.

Here too the visualness of Dante's speech begins to reveal itself: the very simplicity of word makes possible a confrontation between the eye and brute fact which the linguistic complexities of Guido's speech obscure. Guido draws nothing from the sphere of vision: he is 'hidden' in light (36) and recognises himself as an inhabitant of a 'blind world' (25). But the eye of the protagonist here conceives and enforces a moment of cruel revelation and synthesis; starkly portraying the brutality of the Romagna, Dante's words also span – in the tenses of the indicative – the past, present and future. Guido has spoken of the 'sweet land' of Italy (26); the protagonist penetrates the rhetoric of the phrase and reveals the inherent and inescapable divisiveness which characterises the political geography of that landscape. Dante draws here upon the visual idiom of heraldry to indicate the bestiality to which human nature has been reduced. Guido too speaks in emblematic terms of how his talents were 'vulpine rather than leonine'; but his phrase possesses no imagistic force – it is a neat linguistic tag, spoken with a certain complacency over the talents themselves and over the incisiveness of the distinction. In the mouth of the protagonist, the same image would have been viciously graphic; and, ironically enough, the heraldic signs which might to the world have seemed a source of family pride here express no dignity, but only degeneration, instability and aggression:

> E 'l mastin vecchio e 'l nuovo da Verrucchio,
> che fecer di Montagna il mal governo,
> là dove soglion fan d'i denti succhio.
> Le città di Lamone e di Santerno
> conduce il lïoncel dal nido bianco,
> che muta parte da la state al verno.   (46–51)

(And the old mastiff and the new from Verrucchio, / who made ill-management of Montagna, / still sink their fangs where they are used to do. / The cities of Lamone and Santerno / take as their ruler the young lion of the white lair, / who changes sides from summer to winter.)

In *Purgatorio* XIV – as we saw in Chapter 3 – Dante will ascribe to a penitent spirit from the Romagna a comparable vision of the violence in Tuscany. And that sequence reveals the value that Dante attaches to the power of, so to say, 'tragic seeing'. In penance, the mind – although assured of eventual order and security – cannot allow itself to enjoy that order; it must first train itself anew upon the contradictions and tensions it perceives in the natural world to which it once belonged. We have seen how Dante as protagonist is himself required throughout Hell to revive the pain of seeing and remembering sin – in spite of the confidence which Beatrice might have given him in his own salvation. And in the cantos which follow his meeting with Guido – especially in Canto XXVIII – the capacity for tragic seeing becomes a singularly important feature of the poet's own procedure. In Canto XXVII itself, however, there arises a direct opposition between true counsel which is based upon such seeing and the false counsel of Guido, where the sinner still attempts to assert control through his language and arguments over the facts and features of his temporal life. At first view, Guido's speech may seem to possess a tragic intensity of its own – of the kind one might associate with, say, Pier della Vigna. Yet even more clearly than in the Piero episode, Dante undermines the pretensions of the speaker by stressing the physical and visual features that the speaker attempts to keep at bay. So, for instance, one notes the almost patronising emphasis with which Dante introduces Guido's main speech: Guido's flame roars a little after its usual

fashion: 'Poscia che 'l foco alquanto ebbe rugghiato / al modo suo' (58–9). Against this background Guido's words prove to display all those features which make language itself a dangerous medium of counsel:
Consider the central section of the speech:

> Io fui uom d'arme, a poi fui cordigliero,
> credendomi, sì cinto, fare ammenda;
> e certo il creder mio vanìa intero,
>   se non fosse il gran prete, a cui mal prenda!,
> che mi rimise ne le prime colpe;
> e come e *quare*, voglio che m'intenda.   (67–72)

(I was a man of arms, and then I was a bearer of the Cord, / thinking that, so girded, I would make amends; / and certainly my hopes would have been fulfilled, / had it not been for the great priest. Let ill befall him! / He brought me back to the sins of before; / and how and why I wish you to hear from me.)

These lines begin with a certain heroic elevation; but on inspection the identity which Guido appears, self-knowingly, to claim begins to reveals its weaknesses and flaws. The repeated past-remote of the opening line relegates the dignity that Guido once possessed to the distant past: his military and religious roles are both discarded masks. Moreover, where Dante in the *Convivio* would have envisaged a steady progression from one stage of life to another, Guido, in the division of the line and the stress on 'poi', indicates discontinuity and contrast. Then, at the very point where Guido appears to have established order in his own heart by entering the ranks of the Franciscans – 'sì cinto' – a retrograde transformation begins. Linguistically, the origins of this process are marked by the use of the gerund 'credendomi', where the continuative undoes the finality of the first line; and from this Guido moves again into the conditional and subjunctive modes which characterise the introductions to both of his speeches: his life would have been complete and whole *had it not been* for the intervention of the 'great priest'. At this point, the control of the syntax is broken by a vocal gesture of malediction: 'a cui mal prenda'; and there follows the ironic (or mechanistically comic) conclusion that Guido ended exactly where he had begun: through the intervention of the Pope, the friar is led to exchange his pretensions to sanctity for the sins he had hoped to escape.

Already differences will be apparent between the narrative voices of Guido and Ulysses. Guido has none of the naive urgency that Dante attributes to the pagan. He attempts rather to exert a deliberate control over the events he is describing, and this is especially apparent when at line 72 he uses terms of philosophical analysis – 'e come e *quare*, voglio che m'intenda' – which would be quite alien to Ulysses. Equally, the sequence of events is dominated by Guido's initial anticipation of the conclusion: nothing that occurs is untouched by conscious interpretation; yet it was precisely such an interpretative power that Guido, in life, refused to bring to bear upon his conversations with Boniface.

Unlike the story of Ulysses – with its evocation of sea and wind – Guido's story concerns an interior scene. The corridors of power may never be mentioned, but the dialogue between Guido and Boniface depends upon diplomatic hints and suggestions; and within that dialogue Guido inserts references to his own inward and unspoken doubts about the implications of Boniface's words:

> io tacetti
> perché le sue parole parver ebbre.   (98–9)

(and I kept silent / because his words seemed drunken).

This is the moment of trial. From the opening simile onwards, the canto has been dominated by images of enclosure and restraint (lines 68, 81, 93, 103 and 124). Now the restraint of silence encloses Guido in the design that Boniface is constructing. The irony of this is that both Guido and Boniface are in their own ways seeking to penetrate an enclosure: Boniface requires advice as to how he might force a military entry into the city of Palestrina, while Guido – counselling outright treachery and broken promises – seeks to ensure his own entry into Heaven.

Artifice, innuendo, false arguments and lies divide Guido from all that he knows at heart to be true. And the contrast between Dante and Guido is here particularly strong. Dante has not been silent: Canto xxvii – like Canto xix – is simultaneously a re-examination of his own past judgements and a forthright attack upon Boniface VIII. But it is at this point too that the issues raised by Canto xxvii prepare most directly for *Purgatorio* Canto v: for Guido's son Buonconte is saved *without* the benefit of the Church, or of sophistical argument, in a sudden perception of the truth. Wounded in battle, Buonconte flees across open countryside, staining the ground with his blood (*Purg.* v 99). One notes here the contrast between the claustrophobia of Canto xxvii and the open, if tragic, landscape which is disclosed in Buonconte's story. One notes, too, Dante's emphasis upon the processes of nature in Buonconte's last moments: the agony of the dying man itself links him by blood with the earth, where Guido in the *Inferno* (though not in the *Convivio*) seeks to evade the natural movement and progress of life. But at the last moment Buonconte achieves a stability and certainty which in Hell as in life are wholly unavailable to his father – whom Dante last sees continuing to battle and twist in his fretful flame. Buonconte's last word and act are to utter the name 'Maria' and cross his arms over his breast:

> Quivi perdei la vista e la parola;
> nel nome di Maria fini', e quivi
> caddi, e rimase la mia carne sola.   (*Purg.* v 100–2)

(There I lost both sight and speech; / on the name of Maria I ended, and there / I fell, and my flesh alone remained.)

There is much here that can be taken to summarise the themes not only of Canto xxvii, but also of the sequence of cantos to which it belongs. So where, in portraying Guido, Dante has examined the weaknesses and lability of language at its most sophisticated, in Buonconte's dying breath he discerns an elemental language that is tainted by none of these weaknesses. It is the heartfelt language of prayer – and in the *Purgatorio* Dante will continually include prayer and hymns in the texture of his own verse; but it is also a language conceived in an instant of tragic intensity, where the same physical form which Guido affects to despise is itself shaped eloquently in the sign of the Cross. Buonconte, like the protagonist in *Inferno* XXVII, *suffers* the landscape of evil to the full and becomes, like the protagonist, an emblem of salvation. Linguistic signs here achieve stability through the sudden willingness with which the sinner yields to the pathos of order.

Here too one sees brought to a conclusion the themes of coherence and transition. Passing through death, Buonconte remains truly himself; this is emphasised by the line in which Buonconte introduces himself to Dante:

> Io fui di Montefeltro, io son Bonconte.   (*Purg.* v 88)

(I was of Montefeltro; I am Buonconte.)

This exactly parallels Guido's own introduction of himself. But Guido spoke of past attributes and discarded social roles; in Buonconte's words, the past tense of 'fui' points forward to the present tense of 'io son', while accidentals such as birthplace and family fall away to reveal the baptismal name which in Guido's case was hidden beneath periphrasis and circumlocution. Similarly, in poetic terms, Dante himself – looking into the mirror images of Vanni, Ulysses and Guido – has in imagination suffered change, and progressively tested the attributes of thought and literary procedure which concern him most nearly. To avoid creating a mind-constructed Babel, the craftsman, it seems, must pursue a course of continual re-examination and renewal.

But Canto XXVII also points forward to the final cantos of the *Inferno*, where, as we shall see, Dante realises what it means for his own words and imaginative constructions to die beneath his hand. For, if Dante has been clear in his analysis of Guido's case, then such clarity itself is finally subverted in Canto XXVII: the most lucid judgement upon Guido is spoken not by Dante or by Virgil but by the devil who claims the sinner's soul at the threshold of eternity:

> Francesco venne poi, com' io fu' morto,
> per me; ma un d'i neri cherubini
> li disse: 'Non portar; non mi far torto.
> ...
>   ch'assolver non si può chi non si pente,
> né pentere e volere insieme puossi
> per la contradizion che nol consente'.
>   Oh me dolente! come mi riscossi
> quando mi prese dicendomi: 'Forse
> tu non pensavi ch'io löico fossi!'.
>
> (*Inf.* XXVII 112–14; 118–23)

(Then Francis came when I died / for me; but one of the black Cherubim / said to him: 'Do not take him; do not do me wrong / ... for no one who does not repent can be absolved, / nor is it possible to repent and will a thing together; / the contradiction does not allow it.' / O wretched as I am! how I started / when he took me, saying: 'Perhaps / you did not think that I was a logician!')

The argumentative powers of Guido are here turned against himself; yet Dante, too, is incriminated by association with the analysis that the devil here offers. It is clearly an accurate assessment, but in the cantos we have now to consider Dante will call such accuracy into question, even though the validity of his own moral system appears to depend upon them. At the end of *Purgatorio* v in a scene exactly parallel to that which concludes the story of Guido, the absurd simplicity with which Buonconte secures his entry into Heaven is vindicated:

> Tu te ne porti di costui l'etterno
> per una lagrimetta che 'l mi toglie.   (*Purg.* v 106–7)

(You carry off the eternal part of him / for one little tear that takes him from me.)

In the *Purgatorio* Dante will again be free to admit such simplicity into the body of his own writing. The tragedy of the last cantos of the *Inferno* is that he is not yet free to do so: the logic of his own plan must still be carried to its conclusion.

6

Endings, tragic and comic:
Cantos XXVIII–XXXIII

I

How does Dante end the *Inferno*? This odd question arises for two reasons. In formal terms, while the *Inferno* is undoubtedly self-contained in subject and style, it is also the first phase of a three-part work. We need, therefore, to consider how Dante ends the *cantica* so as to link it with, at least, the *Purgatorio*. But the question has also a philosophical aspect. We have seen in Chapter 2 that the notion of an 'end' was great importance to Dante: he discussed it at length in his first essay in philosophy, the *Convivio*; and in the *Commedia* his concern with the end – or defining purpose – of human life is reinforced by a realisation that time, human history and human nature will all arrive at their true end on the Day of Judgement.

In its apocalyptic aspect, the Malebolge is a revelation of how strange the approach to that end must be: the way to the liberation of Purgatory runs through a region of unrelieved misery and increasing illusion; and certainly the conclusion – when it arrives in Purgatory – is one that contradicts the expectations of divine displeasure which the logic of Hell has aroused. We need not here investigate any further the principles of thought which underlie this development; they derive from that view of the Creator in his relation to the rational creature which our discussions of the *Paradiso*, in the introductory chapter, revealed to be central to Dante's thinking. Nor need we stress that the conception of narrative which Dante develops in the course of the *Inferno* derives from a recognition that, while there *is* a pattern in the life of the human being, the beginning and end of that pattern are located in eternity not time. However, all we have said so far suggests that, in technical and structural terms, the ending of the first *cantica* will present particular problems and is likely to prove, in that regard, especially representative of Dante's art.

Something of how Dante approaches his conclusion has already been suggested by the way in which Cantos XXIV to XXVII of the *Inferno* represent, so to say, a premature anticipation of Purgatory. But the final phases of the *Inferno* are designed to disappoint the expectations which the narrative itself

has just aroused, reimposing that sense of the inescapable reality of dam-
nation which the protagonist first experienced at the Gate of Hell. If imagery
and moral logic were the only considerations, there would be no difficulty in
speaking of the utter conclusiveness of the *Inferno*. The last four cantos insist
upon the absolute fixity of Hell, while images of enchainment and im-
prisonment dominate the portrayal of the giants in Canto XXXI. In Canto
XXXIII Ugolino tells of how he was incarcerated with his children in the
Tower of Hunger; and his earthly imprisonment prefigures his ultimate im-
prisonment in Hell. In the glaciers of Antenora and Caina, Ugolino and his
fellow-traitors are immobilised; and not only is all possibility of action
extinguished, but the faces of these supremely delusive sinners are revealed,
once and for all, to public scrutiny through the glaze of the ice in which they
are set.

In moral as well as imaginative terms, the consideration of treachery
constitutes a natural conclusion to the first *cantica*. Not every moral
commentator in the Middle Ages would have ranked treachery as low as
Dante does. But Dante's line of argument is clear. Treachery is the supreme
instance of fraud, where the mind in its subtlest and most sophisticated guise
plays to its own advantage upon the elemental bonds of community and trust.
The traitor only succeeds because he knows how to adopt a mask of
innocence and love; and, once we understand that human beings are capable
of treachery, no aspect of human life seems immune from perversion or
worthy of trust. Consequently, in Canto XXXIII 139–47 Dante can entertain the
fantastic suggestion that a man may be so consumed with evil that his soul
will descend to Hell while his body remains on earth, animated by an
indwelling devil. There could be no more potent image of the dominion
which evil may exert over a human being, nor any clearer expression of why,
in the end, humanity must rely upon a power beyond itself to order its
existence.

Yet any such general paraphrase underestimates the demands which the
poet continues to make upon himself, and upon his reader, in contemplating
this conclusion. For even when the mind acknowledges its own complete dis-
order and its absolute reliance upon God's judgement, it is still not released
from the responsibility to act towards its end, finding not only images but
also words and narrative forms in which to shape its experience. It is this
responsibility that inspires the peculiar virtuosity of moral and poetic
procedure which characterises the last three cantos of the *Inferno*. And even
before that, in the last three cantos of the Malebolge, Dante has already
begun to practise this virtuosity.

Cantos XXVIII to XXX show Dante still making his way over the last two
bolge, where the sowers of discord and various kinds of con-men and mad
scientists are severally confined; only in Canto XXXI are the two protagonists
lowered to the final circles of Hell by the Giant Nimrod. Yet the geographi-
cal boundaries of Hell do not always correspond to its imaginative or
thematic boundaries; and the reason for considering Cantos XXVIII–XXX along

with the last four cantos of the *Inferno* is that, in drawing to a conclusion the very long episode of the Malebolge, Dante practises in the three earlier cantos many of the techniques of conclusion which subsequently he will employ in the formal ending of the *cantica*.

The Apocalypse is never nearer than in the last two bolge, where the two most spectacular horsemen of the Apocalypse – War and Pestilence – are allowed free rein. So in Canto xxvIII the protagonist is overwhelmed, at the outset, by a vision of destruction and physical mutilation which, says the poet, could not have been greater if all the victims of war in Italy from the beginning of its history had been gathered together before his eyes (1–21); similarly, in the next bolgia the stench of the foul diseases from which the sinners suffer is said to be worse than if

> de li spedali
> di Valdichiana tra 'l luglio e 'l settembre
> e di Maremma e di Sardigna i mali
>   fossero in una fossa tutti 'nsembre ...   (xxIx 46–9)

([the diseases] of all the hospitals / of Valdichiana, of Maremma and of Sardinia [from July until September] / were gathered together in a single ditch).

Yet, because such images as these have a parallel in apocalyptic writing, they also demonstrate the capacity of the mind to receive and suffer divine revelation. It is this capacity that Dante now sets himself to exercise within the domain of his own poem, and the difficulties which this involves are considerable. We have seen how Ulysses and Guido fail to train intelligence upon its proper end; and the knowledge of their weaknesses must still haunt the poet. Beyond that, however, Dante has now to recognise that his end lies in the hands of a vengeful God; and in the coming sequence he will portray a God who exacts revenge with such subtlety that the precise equation between crime and punishment itself becomes a dreadful absurdity. So, it is in this sequence that Dante speaks for the first – and only – time of the 'contrappasso', when in Canto xxvIII the sower of discord Bertran de Born, carrying his severed head in his hand, cries out:

> Così s'osserva in me lo contrappasso.   (xxvIII 142)

(Thus retribution is observed in me.)

To tolerate – or create – an image such as this clearly places peculiar demands upon the spiritual eye of the visionary. But in Canto xxvII the protagonist has already begun to exercise a power, so to say, of tragic seeing in his contemplation of the violence of the Romagna. This power will constitute one essential feature of the technique which Dante employs in constructing his conclusions. At the same time, the realisation of the pre-eminence of vision is accompanied, as always, by a realisation of how limited speech must be in its ability to encompass or govern what the mind has seen. Thus, in spite of the linguistic achievements which Dante celebrates in the preceding sequence, the last phases of the *Inferno* are dominated by two passages which acknowledge the inadequacy of language in respect of experience. The first occurs at the opening of Canto XXVIII, where Dante writes:

> Chi poria mai pur con parole sciolte
> dicer del sangue e de le piaghe a pieno
> ch'i' ora vidi, per narrar più volte?   (XXVIII 1–3)

(Even with unloosed tongue [and telling it many times over,] who could / say to the full what blood and wounds I now saw there?)

Dante goes on to assert that even the tongue of Livy – 'which does not err' – would at this point have proved inadequate. Similarly, as he begins the cantos of treachery the poet writes:

> S'ïo avessi le rime aspre e chiocce,
> come si converrebbe al tristo buco
> sovra 'l qual pontan tutte l'altre rocce,
>   io premerei di mio concetto il suco
> più pienamente; ma perch' io non l'abbo,
> non sanza tema a dicer mi conduco;
>   ché non è impresa da pigliare a gabbo
> discriver fondo a tutto l'universo,
> né da lingua che chiami mamma o babbo.
>   Ma quelle donne aiutino il mio verso
> ch'aiutaro Anf&ïone a chiuder Tebe,
> sì che dal fatto il dir non sia diverso.   (XXXII 1–12)

(If I had rhymes that were harsh and hoarse, / as would befit that miserable hole / over which all other rocks bear down, / I would press out the juice of my conception / more fully. But since I do not, / it is not without fear that I bring myself to speak. / To describe the depth of all the universe is not a task to take as a jest, / nor for a tongue that cries 'mummy' or 'daddy'. / But may those ladies help me in my verse / who assisted Amphion to close the walls around Thebes, / so that the telling should not be unlike the fact.)

Dante, then, invokes the aid of the Muses who inspired Amphion in the building of Thebes. Here, the especial poignancy of his position reveals itself. It may indeed be that the depths of Hell are no subject for childish tongues, and the poet may indeed be required to exercise his linguistic virtuosity to the full in these cantos; but the tongues of children are at least innocent – and valued for being so elsewhere in the *Commedia*. Now Dante, in allying himself with Amphion, suggests the extent to which the virtuosity of his own dead poetry in these cantos may be considered a form of self-betrayal. For the Thebes of Amphion is, for Dante, the model of a corrupt city; and Dante is never further from his linguistic home in the sweet new style than in finding words to 'close' his own infernal Thebes.

In their different ways, both the eye and the tongue are under pressure in these concluding cantos. A part of the poet's final task here is to demonstrate how far the two faculties can co-operate in defining our human end. But it is also consistent with the art of difficulty – and Dante's conception of our proper end – that the poet should admit and demonstrate the failures, illusions and betrayals to which he, as a living being, is no less subject than the damned. It is this tension between clarity and confusion on both the linguistic and the imaginative plane that we must now begin to trace. In narrative terms, it will be found that the tension produces no single end, but broadly *two*, with distinct techniques of closure corresponding to the distinct activities of eye and speech. But even within the two forms of closure which these techniques yield, there is a high degree of fragmentation and subdivision. In Chapter 1, we began by noting how Dante defers the predictable opening of the *Inferno* until at least the third canto. Now a similar pattern emerges, in which the poet – while drawing together the main strands of thought and imagery – also acknowledges that his conclusion must be sought through wastelands of dead poetry. The true end of the *Inferno* is the new beginning of the *Purgatorio*.

II

Canto xxviii begins, as we have seen, with a confession of Dante's inability to express through words the full horror he has imagined in the ninth bolgia. Such protestations have a counterpart in classical literature, as when Virgil in *Aeneid* vi 625–7 writes: 'non mihi si linguae centum sint ... omnia poenorum percurrere nomina possim'; and to cite this instance is enough to suggest that Canto xxviii will be characterised by a high degree of rhetorical ornamentation and stylistic elevation. But Dante never uses the inexpressibility *topos* simply as a rhetorical figure: its appearance always identifies some moment of poetic self-consciousness in which the poet addresses a particular linguistic problem or recognises the logical limitations of discourse. In this case, Dante admits the particularly extreme possibility that the values hitherto associated with Virgil might be completely reversed. Virgil, as the epic historian of Rome, has demonstrated the ways in which both deeds and words can travel towards a providentially appointed end; but such an end seems here inconceivable. The history of Italy is shown – in the opening simile – to be a progressive and inexhaustible proliferation of violent events; and words not only appear inadequate to the truth, but actively contribute to the violence through lies (17) or else through that deliberate 'stirring-up of strife' for which all the sinners in the bolgia are condemned. Suddenly, history, discourse and violence seem all to be the same thing.

These initial suggestions are given especial emphasis by the presence in this canto of the Provençal poet Bertran de Born. Bertran himself appears, as will be seen, at the climax of the canto where (137) he admits the contribution he himself has made to the history of violence by stirring up discord between King Henry II of England and his son Prince Henry. In stylistic terms, however, Dante's own exordium – as well as containing classical allusions – may well have been influenced by poems in which, notoriously, Bertran glories in the experience of war and conflict.

In some sense Canto xxvIII is itself an example of war poetry; and in *De Vulgari Eloquentia* II ii, Dante expressed considerable admiration for the writings of Bertran de Born. At that point in his career, Dante saw war – along with love and moral rectitude – as a theme which the vernacular poet had an especial responsibility to tackle, and Bertran provided for such poetry a model which was lacking in the native Italian tradition. Dante, then, may be attempting now to remedy that lack – outdoing Bertran as he has outdone Ovid and Lucan in Canto xxv. Yet at the beginning and the end of the canto, the highest examples of the genre, in both the classical and vernacular traditions, are seen to be not only inadequate to Dante's vision, but also positively pernicious. In condemning Bertran to Hell, Dante must have distinguished his own present attempt from the examples offered by Bertran; his treatment of Bertran is as much a retraction – and as much a focus for self-criticism – as his treatment of Guido da Montefeltro in Canto xxvII.

How, then, is Dante to proceed? In moral terms the distinction between Bertran and Dante is not difficult to draw. In the *De Vulgari Eloquentia* Dante's interest in the poetry of arms arose from his concern with the ways in which the noblest form of poetic language should reflect the deepest interests of the soul, including the fundamental concern with survival which is expressed in acts of self-defence. 'War-poetry' in that sense reflects the desire for *salus*, safety or well-being. In the *Commedia*, however, *salus* is unambiguously identified with Christian salvation; and this advance must necessarily have involved a thorough revision of the poetry appropriate to the theme of *salus*.

We shall see in a moment how closely Dante distinguishes his own linguistic procedures in Canto xxvIII from the words he attributes to the damned. But the imagery of the canto is designed to identify the broad difference between, so to speak, a brute conception of safety and the Christian view.

The sinners here – defenceless against the sword of the single devil that tortures them – all suffer terrible mutilations. At the same time, in representing the protagonist Dante now returns to that emphasis upon his own physical presence in Hell which began with the episode of the centaurs; and he associates this with a further emphasis – which recalls his meeting with Brunetto – upon the comprehensiveness of his own journey through eternity. So Virgil introduces Dante thus:

> 'Né morte 'l giunse ancor, né colpa 'l mena',
> rispuose 'l mio maestro, 'a tormentarlo;
> ma per dar lui esperïenza piena,
>   a me, che morto son, convien menarlo
> per lo 'nferno qua giù di giro in giro;
> e quest' è ver così com' io ti parlo'.   (xxvIII 46–51)

('Death has not come to him yet, nor does guilt lead him,' / my master replied, 'to torment him; / but, to give him full experience, / it is fitting that I who am dead should lead him / through Hell down from circle to circle; / the truth is as I tell you.')

Here, the safety of Dante as he moves towards his appointed end is strongly stressed: the 'fullness of experience' which he seeks is implicitly contrasted with the divisiveness of spirit for which the sinners are condemned. The narrative, likewise, goes on to contrast the two effects of divine power, which punishes the sinners with the horror of physical division while miraculously ensuring the wholeness of the protagonist:

> Più fuor di cento che, quando l'udiro,
> s'arrestaron nel fosso a riguardarmi
> per maraviglia, oblïando il martiro.   (52–4)

(More than a hundred, hearing this, / halted in the ditch to gaze at me / in amazement, forgetting their torment.)

Ironically enough, while the bodies of the sinners are still tormented, their minds are momentarily unified and composed in contemplation of the protagonist. The importance of this will emerge as we proceed. However, one notes that the scene anticipates comparable reactions in the early *Purgatorio* (for instance at *Purg.* III 88–93). And this comparison serves to underline the moral distinction that appears, tragically, in *Inferno* XXVIII: for in Purgatory, Dante will understand to the full that salvation resides in no aggressive attachment to self but in a willingness to be 'unmade' by the divine law.

Consider, too, how mutilation is itself represented in the canto. There is no random violence here, but rather a dreadful precision (emphasised, in the passage below, by Dante's ironic use of the extremely precious verb *accismare*, to 'suit' or 'decorate', to denote the impact of the punishment). The damned progress in a continual circle around the rock which hides the demonic executioner, and as each sinner returns the wounds he has previously received have healed sufficiently to be reopened once more:

> Un diavolo è qua dietro che n'accisma
> sì crudelmente, al taglio de la spada
> rimettendo ciascun di questa risma,
>   quand' avem volta la dolente strada.   (37–40)

(Behind here is a devil who decorates us / so cruelly, putting [each of us in this party] to the cut of the sword again / when we have made our way around this painful road.)

This image is much more complicated than at first it appears. In part, it repeats the implications of the opening lines: the history of human violence is one of unending repetition and pointless renewal of injury. But, equally, Dante here reasserts the meaning of the contrast between the sinners and the protagonist: in emphasising both circularity and healing, the image represents the absolute order and conclusiveness of divine power which the sinners have disregarded in their lives and now experience as the violence of punishment. There is much here that recalls Canto XXV, in the simultaneous portrayal of wholeness and laceration, regeneration and destruction; but two further features of the punishment distinguish it from the metamorphosis of the thieves, and point to the special concerns of Canto XXVIII.

First, the punishment is designed to bring each sinner into momentary but intense prominence, as each in turn presents himself to the sword of the devil. Each circuit ends and begins in a moment of crisis which is also a moment of renewed judgement; the only 'end' that the sinners know is the renewal of division. Secondly, the pain itself is, as we shall see, usually concentrated in some precisely calculated mutilation of the organs of speech or hearing; and with the appearance of Dante and Virgil in the bolgia the crisis of physical pain becomes a crisis of speech, as the sinners – with torn tongues and lacerated chests – are required to offer the protagonist a clear account of their fate.

To speak, in Canto XXVIII, is to suffer to the full one's own insufficiencies. This is true of the poet himself, as the exordium suggests; but the pathos of language is explored most thoroughly in the speeches of the sinners, and it is a remarkable feature of these speeches that the sinners are allowed to speak, systematically and with the utmost clarity, about the mechanics of their own punishment. There is nothing here of that confusion over the nature of judgement that one saw in Guido da Montefeltro. On the contrary, no sinners in Hell show a clearer grasp of God's design than the sowers of discord. So, it is Bertran de Born, at line 142, who enunciates the law of the *contrappasso* which is regularly supposed to underlie Dante's whole conception of punishment in the *Inferno*; and other examples will emerge shortly.

What, then, are the implications of enunciating this notion of punishment through the mouth of a 'sower of strife'? Language – in expressing an understanding of divine law – is here at its highest pitch of intensity and clarity. Yet, tragically, it reveals only the pain and self-contradiction of the sinner. And now a suggestion begins to emerge which will grow stronger in the concluding cantos of the *Inferno*: that Dante's own language of judgement – here lent momentarily to the sinners – is itself a language which, while necessary, is also an inappropriate instrument for his ultimate purposes; the language of judgement can easily become a language of strife.

Against this, however, Canto XXVIII begins to develop another way in which ends can be realised and truths envisaged. As in the earliest cantos of the *Inferno*, so here, a distinction arises in Dante's text between what can be said and what can be seen. Structurally, this canto demands simultaneous concentration upon voice and image: as each sinner in turn is brought into prominence, his words are certainly submitted to close attention; at the same time the sinner is framed, in the singularity of his horrible punishment; and the eye, too, is required silently to read the intolerable significance of the image, as it contemplates the constitutional fragility of the human body. This twofold mode of attention will characterise all the subsequent cantos of the *Inferno*, with significant variations – most notably in the climactic Ugolino episode. In effect these two modes will correspond to two distinct ways of conceiving an 'end'. One will be linguistic – in which the resources of language strain, necessarily but painfully, to grasp the truth about a person or situation as clearly as possible. The other will be imagistic – in which, no less painfully, the eye is required to gaze without flinching upon the literally unspeakable contradictions that human nature suffers and creates in itself.

We shall return shortly to the structural characteristics of the canto; but consider firstly how Dante represents the sinners themselves, and the speeches they utter.

Mahomet is the first to speak; but to do so, he must drag open his thorax with his own hands:

> Mentre che tutto in lui veder m'attaco,
> guardommi e con le man s'aperse il petto,
> dicendo: 'Or vedi com' io mi dilacco!'.   (28–30)

(While I was wholly fixed upon the sight of him, / he gazed at me, and with his hands he opened up his chest / saying: 'Now see how I tear myself apart!')

One notes how the two figures, Mahomet and Dante, stare at each other; and it is from this gaze that the protagonist will gather his sense of the anatomy of physical pain and weakness. Mahomet, however, now proceeds to substitute words for that image:

> E tutti li altri che tu vedi qui,
> seminator di scandalo e di scisma
> fuor vivi, e però son fessi così.   (34–6)

(And all the others that you see here / were sowers of rancour and division / while they lived, and that is the reason why they are so cleft.)

One notes here that the logic of the *contrappasso* is already beginning to be traced in the 'però' or 'therefore' of line 36. One notes too the clarity of categorical definition which allows Mahomet to name the sinners of the bolgia. Evidently, however, there is an element of aggression and divisiveness in the very act of communicating these judgements.

It is appropriate enough that Mahomet – as the author of a creed in which truth was defended by the sword – should be the spokesman for the doctrine of divine vengeance. It is also clear that, in moral terms, Mahomet offers no more satisfactory an account of *salus* than Bertran can. In the *Paradiso*, after all, Dante will take as his example of Christian soldiership the crusader Cacciaguida, who died as a martyr on the field of battle. And the deeper lesson of the Cacciaguida sequence – in which Dante's forebear teaches the poet the practical value of poverty – stands in direct contrast to the conclusion of the Mahomet episode.

Mahomet's last words are addressed prophetically to Dante's contemporary Fra Dolcino, as a warning that he should make provision for a defensive siege against his enemies:

> Or dì a fra Dolcin dunque che s'armi,
> tu che forse vedra' il sole in breve,
> s'ello non vuol qui tosto seguitarmi ...   (55–7)

(Now say to Fra Dolcino, [you who perhaps will see the sun before long,] that if he does not wish to follow me quickly here, [he should prepare himself].)

The irony here is that Fra Dolcino – a heretic who was finally defeated in 1305 in a crusade preached by Pope Clement – defended, by force of arms, a position not unlike the position that Dante defended by *words* in *Inferno* XIX. Fra Dolcino's heresy consisted of a militant pauperism which set its face against the same manifestations of avarice and ecclesiastical corruption that Dante never tires of attacking. Thus the distinction in Dante's mind between himself and Fra Dolcino must have been a very fine one; yet Fra Dolcino remains firmly associated with Mahomet. The defence of Christian truth must be thought to depend upon suffering as much as action, and the poetic counterpart to that – which in Canto XIX involved Dante's own acceptance of absurd misrepresentation – becomes, in Canto XXVIII, the unassertive focus of the eye upon the tragic image. We need not stress that this amounts to a further emphasis upon the 'pathos of order'.

In the second encounter, the prophetic eye produces images which the tongue then translates into divisive words. A second speaker advances; and again his words are framed by an image that emphasises the tragedy of utterance. The sinner

> aprì la canna,
> ch'era di fuor d'ogne parte vermiglia ...   (68–9)

(opened his windpipe / which was all red on the outside).

But the voice which issues from the wound is one that delights in prophesying destruction:

> E fa sapere a' due miglior da Fano,
> a messer Guido e anco ad Angiolello,
> che, se l'antiveder qui non è vano,
>   gittati saran fuor di lor vasello
> e mazzerati presso a la Cattolica
> per tradimento d'un tiranno fello.   (76–81)

(And make it known to the two chief men of Fano, / to messer Guido and also to Angiolello, / that, if our foreseeing here is not vain, / they will be flung from their vessel / and done to death near to Cattolica / by the treachery of a dreadful tyrant.)

The speaker, Pier da Medicina, continues with the graphic image of a seascape, enhanced with mythological ornamentation:

> Tra l'isola di Cipri e di Maiolica
> non vide mai sì gran fallo Nettuno,
> non da pirate, non da gente argolica.   (82–4)

(Between the islands of Cyprus and Majorca / Neptune never saw so great a crime / at the hands either of pirates or of Greeks.)

We have seen how Vanni Fucci intended his prophecies to rob Dante of his peace of mind, and we shall see too that in Canto XXXIII the vivid account which Ugolino offers of the Tower of Hunger is inspired by a similar spirit of hatred and aggression. Here, Pier da Medicina cannot allow even the images of the natural world to remain unaffected by his divisive intentions. In a similar way, he will not tolerate that his fellow-sinner Curio (who coun-

selled Caesar to cross the Rubicon) should enjoy the comfort of silence. With
an action stressing to the full the crisis of utterance, he forces back the jaws
of his companion so that the tongue is seen, sliced in two:

> Allor puose la mano a la mascella
> d'un suo compagno e la bocca li aperse,
> gridando: 'Questi è desso, e non favella'.   (94–6)

(Then he laid his hand on the jaw / of one beside him and opened his mouth for him, /
crying: 'This is the one, and he does not speak.')

Pier has spoken vigorously to the point of loquaciousness. But Curio can
only go through the motions of speech. And his agonised silence is balanced
and contrasted with the silence of the protagonist. The poet too – so far from
pursuing the logic of the punishment – is reduced to an exclamation, as
though standing on the margins of speech and horrified silence:

> Oh quanto mi pareva sbigottito
> con la lingua tagliata ne la strozza
> Curïo, ch'a dir fu così ardito!   (100–2)

(Oh, how aghast he seemed to me, / his tongue sliced through in his gullet, / Curio who
was so daring in his speech!)

Dante now presents the two most important figures in the canto, Mosca dei
Lamberti and, finally, Bertran de Born – both of whom, in different ways,
raise issues of the utmost concern for the historical Dante and for Dante the
poet.

Mosca dei Lamberti – whose presence in Hell was first mentioned by
Ciacco in Canto VI – is a fellow-Florentine; and a direct comparison is drawn
between the two compatriots, recalling the comparisons which occurred in
the circles of violence between Dante – as the surviving hope and representa-
tive of a new order – and the failed leaders of an older generation. For
Mosca is the legendary originator of the strife in Florence which had des-
troyed the peace of the city for nearly a hundred years; and the encounter
ends with the protagonist speaking in terms of unresolved and uncompro-
mising antagonism, willing the extinction of all Mosca's tribe:

> E io li aggiunsi: 'E morte di tua schiatta'.   (109)

(And I replied: 'And death to your tribe.')

This acrimony however, is itself the product of speech and an indication of
the violence to which speech will reduce the most just of causes. No such
comment, however, accompanies the first appearance of Mosca. His figure is
drawn before the eye in an image which offers perhaps the most concentrated
and realistic image of suffering in the whole *Inferno*:

> E un ch'avea l'una e l'altra man mozza,
> levando i moncherin per l'aura fosca,
> sì che 'l sangue facea la faccia sozza.   (103–5)

(And one who had one and the other hand chopped off, / raising his stumps through the
dark air / so that the blood besmirched his face.)

Here, as throughout, the individual is singled out for attention: 'E un ...';
but the figure – as yet not even named – is robbed of any ability to make
signs or meanings of its own. The stumps of the hands make gestures only in
blood, the features are obscured by gore. Mosca is reduced to a suffering
anatomy. The stark image is there to be seen, and it is finally to such a con-
templation of the image that Dante returns, after the moment of aggressive
exchange. Mosca departs:

> per ch'elli, accumulando duol con duolo,
> sen gio come persona trista e matta. (110–11)

(And he went away adding misery to misery / like someone mad with grief.)

One notes here the continuative gerund, associated rather with the sterile
repetition of misery than with growth or process. In contrast, Dante remains
fixed and steadfast in contemplation of the scene, abandoning any attempt to
speak, excite or judge: 'Ma io rimasi a riguardar lo stuolo' (112) – And I
remained to gaze upon the troop.

It is as if sanity were itself brought to trial by the contemplation of such
images; and Dante's own words confirm this suggestion, as he insists that his
'conscience' was tested to the utmost by the sight that he now saw:

> Ma io rimasi a riguardar lo stuolo,
> e vidi cosa ch'io avrei paura,
> sanza più prova di contarla solo;
>   se non che cosci̇enza m'assicura,
> la buona compagnia che l'uom francheggia
> sotto l'asbergo del sentirsi pura.
>   Io vidi certo, e ancor par ch'io 'l veggia,
> un busto sanza capo andar sì come
> andavan li altri de la trista greggia. (112–20)

(But I remained to gaze upon the troop, / and saw there something I should fear [merely
to speak of] / without further proof, if conscience did not reassure me – / conscience,
that good companion which gives a man courage / under the breastplate of knowing
himself to be pure. I saw then – and it seems I see it still – / a trunk without a head
making its way, as were / the others of that miserable flock.)

The use of the military image – 'asbergo' – enforces the contrast between the
defence of selfhood through arms and the defence afforded by moral integ-
rity. At the same time, the passage is peculiarly rich in suggestions that touch
upon Dante's distinctively poetic activities. If Mosca tested the sanity of the
historical Dante, Bertran tests him as author of the *Commedia*; and where the
image of Mosca was all too realistic in its concentration upon the tortured
stumps of the sinner, the image of Bertran – carrying his own head in his
hand like a lantern – is the product of pure fantasy.

In its power to conceive an intolerable image, and then to impose order
upon it by the play of number, the Bertran episode recalls Canto xxv. So, in
the conceits of lines 124–5, 'two is one and one is two' in the divided figure
of Bertran:

Di sé facea a sé stesso lucerna,
ed eran due in uno e uno in due ...   (124–5)

(Of himself he made himself a lantern; / and they were two in one and one in two.)

Remarkably, Dante will ascribe to Bertran a far more lucid and well-controlled form of speech than his *own* text here lays claim to. Yet, where Bertran is divided from himself, Dante – in admitting the absurd image – claims a unity between past and present acts of seeing: I saw then and it seems I still do see. As in Canto XXV, Dante remains open to the impact of his own imaginings; his fiction tests him against himself.

The image of a body still capable of motion while separated from its head is dense with moral suggestions, pointing not only to the disruptive independence of physical powers, but also to the irresponsibility of the intellect in its control of the inarticulate brother-body. The dominant feature of the punishment is, however, an absurdity which subverts the logicality of Bertran's subsequent words.

Bertran's speech is cast in unambiguously factual language and traces – even more clearly than Mahomet's – the consequences of crime and punishment:

Io feci il padre e 'l figlio in sé ribelli;
Achitofèl non fé più d'Absalone
e di Davìd coi malvagi punzelli.
    Perch' io parti' così giunte persone,
partito porto il mio cerebro, lasso!,
dal suo principio ch'è in questo troncone.
    Così s'osserva in me lo contrappasso.   (136–42)

(Between father and son I caused mutual rebellion; / Achitophel did no worse to Absalom / and David with his vicious promptings. / And, because I divided those persons so closely joined, / so I carry my head, alas, divided / from its principle which is in this trunk. / Thus is retribution observed in me.)

There is no open violence here. Nor does Dante attempt – as he may have done in the exordium – to write a pastiche of Bertran's own style; but tragedy resides in the very clarity of the utterance. In communicating the judgement which Dante himself wishes to pass upon the sinner, the speech does violence to Bertran's own nature; as a master of language, he is alienated from his own sphere of speech, drawing upon references to the Scriptures (and even at times using phrases which reflect the style of Dante's own early poetry). But Dante himself – in transferring the language of judgement to the sinner – implicitly admits the danger and violence of such words. It is the voice of the sinner that ends the canto, and the tragedy is that speech must always strain to encompass such an end: to win by speaking last. But beyond the figure of Bertran, there is the figure of the protagonist:

Or vedi la pena molesta,
tu che, spirando, vai veggendo i morti:
vedi s'alcuna è grande come questa.   (130–2)

(Now see the dreadful penalty, / you who, breathing, go seeing the dead: / see whether any pain is as great as this.)

Here, the gerunds which expressed the sterile repetitions of punishment in Mosca are attached to an image of growth and true progress – Dante's own visionary journey. But, above all, the protagonist is one who 'goes seeing' the dead. The pathos of 'seeing' replaces the violence of speech.

In *The Principles of Literary Criticism*, I. A. Richards writes:

It is essential to recognise that in the full tragic experience there is no suppression. The mind does not shy away from anything, it does not protect itself with any illusion, it stands uncomforted, unintimidated, alone and self-reliant. The test of its success is whether it can face what is before it and respond to it without any of the innumerable subterfuges by which it ordinarily dodges the full development of experience ... The essence of Tragedy is that it forces us to live for a moment without them. When we succeed we find, as usual, that there is no difficulty; the difficulty came from the suppressions and sublimations.   (*The Principles of Literary Criticism*, p. 193)

In spite of the antagonism which, as we have seen, Richards expresses towards the *Commedia*, his comments correspond very closely to the implications of the twenty-eighth canto. Dante here does not allow himself the support of the system of judgement which the *Inferno* so readily offers: it is the sinners who enunciate the scheme of judgement. For Dante, sanity depends not upon the subterfuge of judgement, but upon a readiness to test, against the extreme and tragic images of Mosca and Bertran, the tolerance of his own imagination. Reason here does not resolve, but rather heightens the sense of contradiction and pain.

Thus, if we look back briefly over the canto, we shall find that it is organised in such a way as to allow persistently for an interruption of the logical progress of sense – that logic being entrusted to the sinners themselves – and to bring into relief the cruel contradictions of the images.

The canto is scanned by a sequence of pauses, as the succession of speakers passes before the sword of the devil and the eye of the protagonist, and associated with these pauses is the constantly repeated phrase 'I saw'. So, at the end of the long exordium, Dante makes a break to describe the first impact of the bolgia:

> Già veggia, per mezzul perdere o lulla,
> com' io vidi un, così non si pertugia,
> rotto dal mento infin dove si trulla.   (*Inf.* xxviii 22–4)

(Just as a cask, through losing a middle or endpiece / does not gape as much as one I saw / broken open from the chin down to where we fart.)

In a similar way, at the end of Mahomet's speech Dante writes:

> Poi che l'un piè per girsene sospese,
> Maömetto mi disse esta parola;
> indi a partirsi in terra lo distese.
> Un altro, che forata avea la gola

e tronco 'l naso infin sotto le ciglia,
e non avea mai ch'una orecchia sola,
    ristato a riguardar per maraviglia.   (62–8)

(Then, having raised one foot to go / Mahoment said this to me, / then set [his foot] on the ground to go. / Another, who had his throat pierced through / and his nose sliced off up to the eyebrow, / and had no more than a single ear, / stopped to gaze in astonishment.)

The interruption in the narrative is here especially clear; the second figure is introduced without any connection being drawn between him and the preceding figure, and again one notes that the break is accompanied, as in almost every other case, by an emphasis upon the word 'un'. By interrupting the line of narrative connection, the canto drives the mind to focus upon the static components of the image that the words present, and so here the pause brings into relief the precise, almost delicate, description of Mahomet's raised foot and deliberate forward pace.

The fragmented rhythm of the canto fully reveals its force in the presentation of Bertran de Born. The episode, as we have seen, is introduced by a parenthesis in which Dante speaks of his own security of conscience and then proceeds to focus upon Bertran with an emphasis both upon 'vidi' – I saw – and upon 'un':

Io vidi certo, e ancor par ch'io 'l veggia
  un busto sanza capo ...   (118–19)

This prepares for the play upon number – upon the paradox of two in one and one in two – which underlies the treatment of Bertran. Along with this, the picture of Bertran brings to a climax, for all its absurdity, the clinically precise observation of human anatomy which has characterised the descriptions in this canto from the first. Dante has envisaged bowels hanging from riven stomachs (25–7), dissected tongues and windpipes, and even now the fantasy of the picture of Bertran is enhanced by an emphasis upon how *suitable* the head is to being carried as a lantern: Bertran holds it by the handle of its hair.

So the eye is required silently to trace the outline, lineaments and physical vulnerability of the human form; and in doing so it witnesses, without any need of comment, *one* end to which humanity may come, a condition of utter self-division. The images of this canto express an irony which logic is powerless to explicate. It is indeed the very nature of the sowers of discord that they use the strengths of human intelligence and speech to exploit the physical weaknesses to which humanity is subject. It is nonetheless possible, as a way of meeting one's end, that, recognising the tragic limitations of speech, one should fix the mind upon the contradiction itself without flinching or resorting, in Richards's phrase, 'to subterfuge or self-delusion'. Dante, contriving to do this in the present canto, establishes a tragic technique which he will draw upon throughout the concluding cantos of the *Inferno*.

III

The tragic mode of Canto xxviii makes the canto an appropriate conclusion to a sequence in which heroic figures such as Ulysses and Guido demonstrate how words and thoughts may seek – or fail – to embrace the proper ends of human action. But the prevailing mode of the Malebolge has been comic, and the last two cantos of the series – which are linked, to form a single narrative episode – return to a comic idiom. These cantos present an alternative view of how Dante will eventually end the first *cantica*, displaying structural and features which recur in Canto xxxi and in the last canto of all.

In decided contrast to the previous canto, the sinners in this canto are viewed less as individuals than as members of a group: characteristically, the sequence concludes with the prolonged quarrel between Adam of Brescia and the Greek Sinon. Moreover, the punishment, which the sinners suffer also differentiates them from the sowers of discord. There is some connection between the two forms of punishment, in that Dante continues to investigate the weakness of the human body with clinical precision, as in his account of the dropsy from which Adam is suffering:

> La grave idropesì, che sì dispaia
> le membra con l'omor che mal converte,
> che 'l viso non risponde a la ventraia,
>   faceva lui tener le labbra aperte
> come l'etico fa, che per la sete
> l'un verso 'l mento e l'altro in sù rinverte.   (xxx 52–7)

(The weighty dropsy which makes [limbs] disproportionate / with an ill-disposal of humours / so that the face no longer corresponds to the belly, / made him hold his lips open / as the consumptive does [turning] – in thirst – / one lip towards the chin and the other upwards.)

Yet the emphasis in such passages does not fall upon the acute impact of pain, or upon subsequent healing. Attention is now concentrated upon process rather than crisis. The sinners are subject to natural diseases slowly working through the human organism, and the picture that Dante offers is one of progressive disintegration and deformation.

A further difference between the two bolge lies in the attitudes that Dante ascribes to the sinners in each: the sinners in the ninth bolgia are given a high degree of autonomy, speaking without any interruption either from Virgil, the protagonist or their fellows. Interruptions constantly occur in the tenth bolgia; nor do the damned here act as articulate spokesmen for their own punishments, but are rather physical agents, acting out the punishment in vicious deeds and violent words intended to malign or injure those around them. So, in the concluding quarrel, Adam and Sinon enact a drama of their own construction in which blows, not discourse, carry significance. The canto develops, so to say, a theatre of comic self-punishment, and the protagonist is so fascinated by the spectacle that he earns Virgil's reproof:

Or pur mira,
che per poco che teco non mi risso!   (XXX 131–2)

(Now just keep looking; / only a little more and I shall quarrel with you.)

These broad points of contrast between the two episodes are, as we shall
see, an indication of deeper differences in narrative dynamic and structure.
But on every level the specific features of the later sequence are all con-
nected to an alteration of thematic emphasis: where speech was at issue in
Canto XXVIII, it is the *eye* in these cantos that is brought into question.
Hitherto we have stressed the primacy that Dante persistently accords to
vision, but in the tenth bolgia even vision is fallible and subject to delusion.

As elsewhere in the *Inferno*, the central issue of the canto is presented in
two ways: firstly in the representation of the sinners, and secondly in the
procedures and reactions of Dante himself, both as protagonist and as poet.

At first view, the inhabitants of this bolgia are notable mainly for their
triviality. The protagonist here meets counterfeiters, alchemists and imperson-
ators, with false coining – represented by Adam of Brescia – being given
especial prominence. It may not be immediately apparent why such sinners
occupy the lowest position in the circles of fraud; but in large part it is their
triviality which qualifies them: in some way all of these sinners have
tampered for wholly fatuous reasons with the images of the natural world.
Intelligence in this case is still fraudulent, not because it perverts the human
institution of speech, but rather because it obfuscates the design of physical
objects which the eye is called upon to contemplate in its natural
environment.

Consider first the cases of Capocchio, from the conclusion of Canto XXIX,
and that of Gianni Schicchi, from Canto XXX.

sì vedrai ch'io son l'ombra di Capocchio,
che falsai li metalli con l'alchìmia;
e te dee ricordar, se ben t'adocchio,
com' io fui di natura buona scimia.   (XXIX 136–9)

(Thus you will see that I am the shade of Capocchio, / who made false metals by
alchemy; / and you must remember, if I see clearly who you are, / how good an ape of
nature I was.)

Capocchio is condemned as an alchemist; but to describe himself as an 'ape
of nature' exactly registers the extent to which his sin, in Dante's view,
involved an attempt to interfere with and trivialise the settled order of the
natural world. And this judgement is only strengthened by an anecdote –
recorded in early commentaries on the *Commedia* – which relates that
Capocchio was skilful enough in making 'false' images to portray the scene
of Christ's Passion on his own finger-nail. In such a case, art and intelligence
contrive to render ridiculous the very event which, for Dante, restored value
and meaning to the natural world.

A comparable case is that of Gianni Schicchi, who in Canto XXX rushes at
Capocchio like a wild boar and sinks his fangs into his neck:

> quant' io vidi in due ombre smorte e nude,
> che mordendo correvan di quel modo
> che 'l porco quando del porcil si schiude.
>   L'una giunse a Capocchio, e in sul nodo
> del collo l'assannò, sì che, tirando,
> grattar li fece il ventre al fondo sodo.   (xxx 25–30)

(So I saw two wan and naked shades / run biting as / a boar does, released from the sty. / The one came at Capocchio and [gored him] at the base of his neck, so that, as he dragged him along, / he made him scrape his belly on the hard floor.)

It is a sign of the deliberately comic level on which this sequence is written that the figures of Gianni, Capocchio and Adam should be drawn from the sphere of contemporary anecdote. As we shall see, there is also a strong vein of mock-heroic rhetoric and sustained mythological reference in these cantos. But Dante is never closer to the level of Boccaccian trickery than in his account of Gianni, who – as the story runs – having long coveted a mare in the stud of a certain Buoso Donati, took the opportunity of Buoso's death to dress himself as the dead man and then deliver a will in his own favour from Buoso's death-bed. The tale is told – to Gianni's discredit – by the ridiculous Capocchio in Canto xxx 43–5.

Yet Dante's judgement of Gianni remains unbendingly severe. Gianni is a falsifier of persons; and beneath the intrinsically comic possibilities of the story, there runs a sense – deriving from Dante's unfailing awareness of the dignity of human existence – of how seriously the actions of Gianni distort the patterns which physical nature traces in our lives. In the *Vita nuova* and the *Purgatorio* (xxiii 55–7) Dante speaks of how, at the death-beds of people he loved, he wept over their 'dead faces'. But Gianni's trickery deprives Buoso of that ultimate integrity and any dignified possession of his own physical identity, thus making a mockery of the natural arc of life which begins with birth and ends with death. Tears at the death-bed of 'Buoso' would have been illusory and ridiculous.

The question now arises as to how Dante himself is to cope with those insecurities of image and identity which are generated not only by degrading diseases, but also by the misapplication of human intelligence. The question is forcefully stated at the beginning of the sequence, where – as at the conclusion – Virgil rebukes the protagonist for his disproportionate attention to the sinners:

> La molta gente e le diverse piaghe
> avean le luci mie sì inebrïate,
> che de lo stare a piangere eran vaghe.
>   Ma Virgilio mi disse: 'Che pur guate?
> perché la vista tua pur si soffolge
> là giù tra l'ombre triste smozzicate?'   (xxix 1–6)

(The host of people and their many wounds / had so befuddled the light of my eyes / that they were longing to remain and weep. / But Virgil said to me: 'Why are you still staring? / Why do you plunge your eyes / down among the sad maimed shades?')

The remedy here is as important as the fault: to cure the protagonist of his bewilderment and paralysis, Virgil reminds Dante that a fixed term has been set for his visit to Hell, and he defines this term by referring to the scheme of natural movement in time which still exerts its hold over the protagonist:

> E già la luna è sotto i nostri piedi;
> lo tempo è poco omai che n'è concesso,
> e altro è da veder che tu non vedi.   (XXIX 10–12)

(And the moon already is beneath our feet. / Only a short time is allowed to us now; / there are other things to see than what you see here.)

The cold but constant patterns of lunar change stand in direct imagistic contrast to the description of the sinners, who slowly suffer physical degeneration as if confined in hospitals at the height of summer. But the protagonist is made to understand afresh what his own end is; the eye is released from the stasis of confusion, and – becoming once more a 'living' eye – is made to co-operate again with the forward movement of the journey, as it points towards the bottom of Hell:

> Noi discendemmo in su l'ultima riva
> del lungo scoglio, pur da man sinistra;
> e allor fu la mia vista più viva
>   giù ver' lo fondo, là 've la ministra
> de l'alto Sire infallibil giustizia
> punisce i falsador che qui registra.   (XXIX 52–7)

(We went down on to the final bank / from the long ridge, still bearing to the left, / and then my sight, [towards the depth,] was sharper and more lively, / seeing where the infallible justice of the High Lord / punishes the falsifiers whom it marks out there.)

The contrast between the protagonist and the sinners, in point of movement and well-directed attention, is further emphasised by Dante's account of the silent progress he makes among the heaps of heavy sinners:

> Passo passo andavam sanza sermone,
> guardando e ascoltando li ammalati,
> che non potean levar le lor persone.   (XXIX 70–2)

(Step by step we went on without speaking, / watching and listening to the sick, / who could not raise their bodies.)

But it will also be apparent that the poet – in conceiving the ways in which a mind such as Gianni's can distort the pattern of life – is also bringing into question the sense of comprehensible 'beginnings' and 'ends' which – as was seen in Chapter 3 – underlies his narrative procedure in the *Commedia* from the first line of the *Inferno*. In both the structure and the linguistic style of the sequence, Dante here creates – in tension with his overall design – a superbly parodic reflection of his own literary purposes.

This is seen most clearly in the story of Griffolino, told in *Inferno* XXIX:

> 'Io fui d'Arezzo, e Albero da Siena',
> rispuose l'un, 'mi fé mettere al foco;
> 'ma quel per ch'io mori' qui non mi mena.

Vero è ch'i' dissi lui, parlando a gioco:
"I' mi saprei levar per l'aere a volo";
e quei, ch'avea vaghezza e senno poco,
    volle ch'i' li mostrassi l'arte; e solo
perch' io nol feci Dedalo, mi fece
ardere a tal che l'avea per figliuolo.
    Ma ne l'ultima bolgia de le diece
me per l'alchìmia che nel mondo usai
dannò Minòs, a cui fallar non lece'.   (XXIX 109–20)

('I was from Arezzo; and Albero of Siena,' / the one replied, 'had me burned alive; / but that for which I died does not bring me here. / It is true that in jest I said to him; / "I know how I could rise through the air in flight"; / and he, being eager to see it and rather stupid, / wished me to demonstrate the art; and merely / because I did not do a Daedalus for him, he had me / burned by one who considered him to be his son. / But it was for alchemy which I practised in the world / that Minos, who is infallible, condemned me to the [last bolgia of the ten].')

Here, as the facetious suggestions of Griffolino are taken seriously by the stupid Albero, triviality reaches its climax. But Dante has just emphasised, through Virgil's mouth, his own 'magical' journey as a living man in Hell, a journey which precedes his eventual ascent of Purgatory and flight to Paradise:

I' son un che discendo
con questo vivo giù di balzo in balzo ...   (94–5)

(I am one who goes down with / this living man from crag to crag.)

In this context, the images of Griffolino's story cannot fail to look like a disconcerting parallel to Dante's own aspirations. This is true also on another level: we note that reference is made in Griffolino's speech to Minos the Judge; and momentarily we recall that one of Dante's own most serious narrative inventions is the categorisation of judgement which Minos administers in *Inferno* v. Yet this reference is wholly displaced in imaginative importance by the tonalities of Griffolino's 'funny story'. Judgement, which proved vicious in Canto XXVIII, is here on the point of degenerating into nonsense.

Linguistically too the canto – lacking all the clarity of the previous canto – vividly admits the same possibility of degeneration. As voice interrupts voice with renewed idiocy or bile, the protagonist and Virgil are drawn into the to-and-fro of backbiting comment:

E io dissi al poeta: 'Or fu già mai
gente sì vana come le sanese?
Certo non la francesca sì d'assai!'.   (121–3)

(And I said to the poet: 'Was there ever / a people as fatuous as the Sienese. / Not even the French, surely, by far.')

In many respects, the play of language between the poles of rhetorical or mythological elevation (note 'Dedalo' at 116) and banter, gossip and anecdote is characteristic of Dante's procedure throughout the Malebolge. So here – as, for instance, in Canto XXI – Virgil is in danger of being demeaned

when, at Canto XXIX 85, the high rhetoric of his opening apostrophe, 'O tu
che ... ', descends in the second half of the line to the comic 'con le dita ti
dismaglie'. But the special characteristics of the episode – in theme as well
as language – can be illustrated most powerfully by two similes from the
opening of Canto XXX:

> Atamante divenne tanto insano,
> che veggendo la moglie con due figli
> andar carcata da ciascuna mano,
>   gridò: 'Tendiam le reti, sì ch'io pigli
> la leonessa e ' leoncini al varco';
> e poi distese i dispietati artigli ...
>   Ecuba trista, misera e cattiva,
> poscia che vide Polissena morta,
> e del suo Polidoro in su la riva
>   del mar si fu la dolorosa accorta,
> forsennata latrò sì come cane
> tanto il dolor le fé la mente torta.   (XXX 4–9; 16–21)

(Athamas became so crazed / that, seeing his wife go laden in both hands with their two
children, / he cried: 'Let us spread out the nets so that I can take / the lioness and the
whelps at the pass'; / and then he stretched out his pitiless claws ... Hecuba, sad and
wretched and a captive, / when she saw Polyxena dead, / and [recognised] her
Polydorus on the shore / of the sea, was so overwhelmed by grief / that she barked like
a dog, / grief so twisted her mind.)

In the narrative, these lines prepare for the animal-like attack upon Capo-
cchio by Gianni Schicchi and the spirit of the legendary figure Myrrha. One
notes too that in thematic terms the mythic example of Myrrha restates the
theme of confusion over ends and beginnings which is also expressed in the
contemporary story of Gianni. As Ovid tells in *Metamorphoses* x 298–502,
Myrrha, the daughter of King Cinira of Cyprus, availed herself of disguise to
make incestuous love to her own father. Where Gianni's impersonation tra-
vesties the conclusion of life, Myrrha's perverse sexuality represents a
comparable distortion at its origins. These images, then, make important
connections in both thematic and narrative sequence with their context.

In structural terms, however, the opening similes not only are incongruous
– by virtue of their tragic and mythological reference – with the farcical
scene they describe, but also introduce into the main line of Dante's narrative
a set of parenthetic stories which arrest and fragment the advance of the
canto. In speaking of Athamas and Hecuba, Dante admits – as he rarely does
elsewhere – that delusion and disease can afflict the mind to the point of
madness. The poetic counterpart to this is the interwoven variety of vistas
and voices which occurs within the frame of the simile: space is found for
the direct speech of Athamas, and the story of Hecuba – evoking a complex
response of pity and revulsion – is firmly established against a visual back-
ground of sea and beach.

Nor does the confusion decrease when Dante returns to the burden of his
principal narrative. Lines 25–40 describe the frenetic attack of Gianni and

Myrrha, but the passage oscillates between comparison and literal descrip-
tion, so that, while the two aggressors are initially presented as 'ombre
smorte e nude' – wan and naked shades – the attack itself is indistinguishable
from an attack by enraged boars: Gianni 'gores' Capocchio in the nape of the
neck (29) and drags him off for some distance along the floor of the bolgia.

Thematically and stylistically, the issues of the tenth bolgia come to a climax
in Canto xxx, with Dante's encounter with Adam of Brescia. Though the
speeches Dante gives to this sinner are all characterised, in one respect, by a
high degree of rhetorical finish, Adam – when compared with Bertran de
Born – displays a distinct inability to trace a consistent line of cause and
effect. On the contrary, his rhetoric depends entirely upon affective emphases
and dislocations. Even before the final quarrel breaks out, Adam has, so to
speak, consistently interrupted himself with parenthetic expressions of incom-
prehension, exclamations and a pathetic stressing of key words:

> 'O voi che sanz' alcuna pena siete,
> e non so io perché, nel mondo gramo',
> diss' elli a noi, 'guardate e attendete
> a la miseria del maestro Adamo;
> io ebbi, vivo, assai di quel ch'i' volli,
> e ora, lasso!, un gocciol d'acqua bramo.'   (58–63)

('O you who are without any pain – / and I do not know why, in this fearful world,' /
he said to us, 'observe and attend / to the sad fate of Master Adam: / I had, living,
enough of all that I wished, / and now, alas! I crave a drop of water.')

At the same time, the image that Adam presents to the eye is equally
fragmented by incongruity. Thus the essence of his punishment is to
experience the disproportion between what he is (and was) and the single
drop of water which he now desires: the bulk of the parched, hydroptic body
is measured against the globule of refreshment that obsesses his imagination.

So, too, the text first represents Adam, his stomach swollen with disease,
in the fashion of a lute:

> Io vidi un, fatto a guisa di lëuto.   (49)

(I saw one shaped in the fashion of a lute.)

At the end of the episode, the musical comparison returns when, as Sinon
thumps Adam's belly, it resonates like a drum (103). Between empty volume
and weight, gross physicality and airy melody the incongruity here has an
evidently comic slant; but the musical reference also points to the central
feature of the episode, for Adam represents both a travesty of harmonious
sound and a travesty of harmony in a wider sense. Harmony implies the
orderly relation of one thing to another, each associated systematically with
some ultimate purpose or end. Adam – by his sin and by the image he pre-
sents in Hell – is an incarnate denial of any such congruence. So, as a
counterfeiter, the sinner is condemned for creating images of the coin which

bear no relation to the value they pretend to possess. This theme has a parallel in Dante's treatment of Adam: in spite of his corporeal bulk, Adam is mere emptiness and lack; and as we contemplate this image, an exceptionally wide range of correspondences is brought into disrepute. In Adam, images – and the meanings that images can and should convey – deteriorate into insignificance.

This is particularly evident in the correspondence which Dante admits between Adam and his own historical and poetic character. Notably, the opening lines of Adam's speech – 'O voi ... guardate e attendete' – exactly parallel a phrase of Dante's own from a poem included in the *Vita nuova*:

> O voi che per la via d'Amor passate,
> attendete e guardate
> s'elli è dolore alcun, quanto 'l mio grave.
>
> (Foster & Boyde, *Dante's Lyric Poetry* (1967), x 1–3)

(O you who pass by on Love's way, / attend and consider / whether there is any sorrow as heavy as mine.)

Beyond both lines there lies a biblical original in the Book of Jeremiah. But in the *Vita nuova* the use to which this scriptural original is put is, of course, quite different from the use which is made of it in the *Inferno*.

In the *Vita nuova*, the poem is one that Dante claims to have written for one of the 'screen-ladies' who enable him temporarily to conceal his love for Beatrice (*VN* vi). To that extent, the verses are a pure fiction, expressing sorrow for the absence of a lady other than Beatrice herself. But Dante claims that his love for Beatrice remains undimmed by the stratagem of concealment. In a word, the screen-ladies – and the poems written on their behalf – have an essential function in Dante's imaginative development: the ladies are part of a series or system of secondary images which will eventually lead Dante to a true understanding of Beatrice. Nor does the series end there; for in the *Paradiso* Beatrice herself will display to the full the value that a 'secondary image' may possess. It is Beatrice who leads Dante to the contemplation of the Virgin Mary, who is described as the 'termine fisso d'etterno consiglio' (*Par.* xxxiii 3) – the final goal of eternal counsel; and the Blessed Virgin in turn will make it possible for Dante to enjoy, finally, a direct vision of God. From the *Vita nuova* onwards, then, Dante does indeed recognise that the images the mind creates or perceives may point consistently towards a truth; the *Commedia* – as a 'journey to Beatrice' – is built around an ascending scale of these images.

In Adam's case, however, images are deprived of any such function, and beneath Dante's representation of the sinner one perceives a parodic inversion of his own procedures comparable to that which he performed in the Capocchio episode. Both Adam and Dante have the intelligence to create images; and both in a sense recognise a certain lack or distance which the mind must traverse in reaching the object of its desire. But where, for Dante, fiction is a means for filling and articulating the distance between himself and

God, Adam, motivated by simple greed, devoted his art and intelligence in life to the creating of images which were doubly delusive – in being false images of the inherently false good of the coin. We shall see how Dante further dramatises this mentality in the concluding lines of the episode. Here it is enough to note that, in allowing Adam to make meretricious use of words which are drawn both from the Scriptures and from the *Vita nuova*, Dante graphically illustrates the extent to which a tradition of words and images can itself degenerate: between the Book of Jeremiah and the *Vita nuova* Dante draws a coherent line, linking beginnings and ends, which will ultimately lead him towards the distant reality of God; in the Adam sequence the line is momentarily allowed to falter on the edge of absurdity.

In a similar, and still more remarkable, way the physical image of Adam in Canto xxx is presented as a parody of everything that a human being can be and should be if it uses the means which intelligence provides to encompass its own proper ends. In the *Vita nuova*, as we have suggested, the image of the human being itself may – if that human being is Beatrice – be taken as the means to return to God; but Adam of Brescia, as an image, is utterly gross, disappointing and repellent to the contemplative eye.

This becomes particularly clear if one draws the connection, which the name of the sinner alone would suggest, between Adam of Brescia and Adam of the Garden of Eden. For the Adam of Canto xxx is a manifestation of what humanity *would* have become if the sins of the original Adam had not been redeemed; he is, in that sense, the 'end' to which fallen humanity was doomed before Christ.

Consider, at this point, how Dante presents the true Adam in Canto xxvi of the *Paradiso*. There are striking similarities between this canto and *Inferno* xxx in point of structure and movement: where, at the beginning of the *Inferno* sequence, Dante's eyes are 'drunk' with the sights he sees, in the *Paradiso* he is initially blind – as he has been throughout the discourses on love in the previous canto. In both cases – as sight is restored – the narrative emphasises process and change; but where in the *Inferno* process is seen in terms of degeneration, in the *Paradiso* it is seen as growth and recuperation. Finally, where Dante's eye in the *Inferno* fixes upon the diseased rotundity of the counterfeiter, in the *Paradiso* it is brought to contemplate the 'ripe apple' (*Par.* xxvi 91) of the redeemed first father. So, in place of the tumultuous attack of Gianni and Myrrha upon Capocchio which precedes the Adam episode in the *Inferno*, Dante's eyes in the *Paradiso* slowly regather strength, until – having passed a sequence of intermediary 'veils' or screens – they are ready to look on Adam:

> E come a lume acuto si disonna
> per lo spirto visivo che ricorre
> a lo splendor che va di gonna in gonna,
>   e lo svegliato ciò che vede aborre,
> sì nescïa è la sùbita vigilia
> fin che la stimativa non soccorre;

così de li occhi miei ogne quisquilia
fugò Beatrice col raggio d'i suoi,
che rifulgea da più di mille milia.   (*Par.* XXVI 70–8)

(And just as someone awakes when a bright light suddenly shines, / because the spirit of sight runs / out to meet the splendour which penetrates from (skirt-like) membrane to membrane, / and just as someone, on waking, muddles what he sees / – knowing nothing in the first sudden moment of awakening / till aided by the power of estimation – / so [Beatrice] made every speck of impurity [flee] from my eyes / by the rays of eyes / which shine out more than a thousand miles.)

Adam in Paradise is a demonstration that beginnings and ends can be reconciled across the distance and emptiness which sin introduces into the human spirit; he is also, at one and the same time, the culmination of a hierarchy of human images representing God's intentions for human nature and an affirmation of the community that persists through time between all human beings. Above all, he is a reliable *sign* for the eye to rest upon. This is particularly important because in *Paradiso* XXVI – as in the last two bolge of the *Inferno* – Dante is much concerned with questions of language and signification, and Adam (at *Par.* XXVI 124–32) discusses the changes to which language is subject, allowing that language – like all other rational constructs – has always been prone to alteration. But, as we have emphasised in the previous chapter, the human figure may itself be a sign more potent than any linguistic sign. To be sure, in Paradise Dante is led to see this sign – in the form of Adam himself – through the blind discourse of the preceding cantos. *Seeing* is the fruit of that discourse. The dense but lucid image of Adam – wriggling like an animal in a bag of light (*Par.* XXVI 97–9) – is the complete opposite of Adam of Brescia, who is simultaneously impenetrable and empty; and it is not suprising that – inverting the pattern of the *Paradiso* – the profound disappointments of the image in the tenth bolgia should precede a return to the chaotic discourse of the final squabble.

In the last canto of the *Inferno* the issues and procedures of Canto XXX will return, as Dante, in presenting Satan, offers to view an image designed to resist and defeat the desire for meaning or contemplative focus. Just as Adam of Brescia is a delusive image of the true Adam, so Satan will be a delusive image of the Trinity itself.

Returning, however, to Canto XXX, one may finally consider how Dante depicts the mentality of Adam of Brescia. Here, inspecting the essential capacity that the mind possesses to conceive images and ends, Dante also dramatises the pain which arises when images prove incoherent and fail to act as means to an end.

Adam's first words expressed his burning desire for a single drop of water. He continues:

Li ruscelletti che d'i verdi colli
del Casentin discendon giuso in Arno,
faccendo i lor canali freddi e molli,
sempre mi stanno innanzi, e non indarno,

ché l'imagine lor vie più m'asciuga
che 'l male ond' io nel volto mi discarno.   (*Inf.* xxx 64–9)

(The brooks which run down from the green hills / of the Casentino, to the Arno, /
making their channels chill and moist, / are always there before me, and not in vain; /
for the image of them far more dries me up / than the sickness that takes the flesh from
my features.)

Throughout the sequence Dante has giving recurrent emphasis to the four
elements: earth, fire, water and air. Capocchio flies through the air, Adam
thirsts for water, and both are burned alive; as for earth, all the alchemists
and magicians are guilty of seeking to recast the base elements of the natural
world according to their own design. The full impact of that offence is now
realised in Adam's words: as a consequence of his sin, he suffers a divorce
from the natural order. It is nature itself in its simplest aspect that torments
him; and in the responsiveness of his words to the sensuous beauty of the
'ruscelletti', Adam reveals how eagerly the imagination desires to feed upon
the objects that constitute its physical ambience.

In effect, the true punishment that Adam suffers is to have his own origins
and nature turned against him; and, while he has no clear sense of the
contrappasso, the sinner all but acknowledges this when – speaking with
characteristically emotional suggestiveness of how he is not tormented 'in
vain' – he declares:

La rigida giustizia che mi fruga
tragge cagion del loco ov' io peccai
a metter più li miei sospiri in fuga.   (70–2)

(The unyielding justice that searches within me / finds a method – drawn from the place
where I sinned – / to drive sighs fleeing out of me the more.)

Having committed his sins in the Casentino, it is the memory of the Casen-
tino that torments him now, as surely as the memory of Eden torments any
descendant of the unredeemed Adam.

But if Adam of Brescia suffers a tantalising separation from the image of
his origins, so too he displays a power actively to pervert his own natural
end. Even stronger in his mind than the image of the 'ruscelletti' is the image
of the men who employed him in his counterfeiting, and the sinner venge-
fully proclaims that it would please him more to see these men in Hell than
to drink the purest water from the mountain streams:

Ma s'io vedessi qui l'anima trista
di Guido o d'Alessandro o di lor frate,
per Fonte Branda non darei la vista.   (76–8)

(But were I to see here the miserable soul / of Guido or Alessandro or their brother, / I
would not exchange Fonte Branda for the sight.)

Vengeance has become his only end; and it is this end which inspires him –
in a final parody of normal movement and intellectual aspiration – to ache for
power enough to shift his diseased bulk inch by inch, however long it might
take, over the whole course of the bolgia:

S'io fossi pur di tanto ancor leggero
ch'i' potessi in cent' anni andare un'oncia,
io sarei messo già per lo sentiero,
　　cercando lui tra questa gente sconcia,
con tutto ch'ella volge undici miglia,
e men d'un mezzo di traverso non ci ha.　　　　(82–7)

(If only I were light enough to travel / an inch in a hundred years, / I would already have set myself on that road, / seeking him out among these loathsome folk, / even if it is eleven miles around / and no less than a mile across.)

The major stylistic features of Canto XXX are all exemplified here: the disintegration of the mind into empty desire is captured in the subjunctives of lines 82 and 83, while the impossible journey of vengeance is a distorted image of Dante's journey to his true end in Beatrice. Comedy too is present in the incongruity between the physical facts of Adam's present situation and his most concerted mental aspirations.

It is, however, in the final phase of the canto that Dante displays the technique of comic closure to which he will return in the last canto of the *Inferno*. In keeping with the structure of the thirtieth canto at large – and in contrast to the synthesis which Dante attempted in Canto XXVIII – the sequence here offers no decisive conclusion. There is no equivalent to the single, strained voice of Bertran. On the contrary, Canto XXX possesses two simultaneous but incompatible endings, the one centred upon the quarrel between Adam and Sinon, the other on the potential quarrel between the protagonist and Virgil.

The first of these movements begins as Adam – incapable of revenge upon his patrons in the art of counterfeiting – treacherously divulges the names of two of his associates in the tenth bolgia, one of whom – Sinon, the Greek – takes the revelation amiss and strikes a blow at Adam's belly (100–2). If there were any doubt about Dante's concern in this canto with the theme of origins and ends, the introduction of Sinon alongside Adam would lay them to rest; for, if Adam can be interpreted as an epitome of fallen humanity, then Sinon, in the myths of Troy and Rome, is the originator of the disasters which fell upon the race of Rome: it was he whose pretence of desertion from the Greek camp persuaded the Trojans to admit the 'gift' of the wooden horse into their city. Moreover, the cause of the present quarrel is precisely that Sinon resents hearing himself reflected in Adam's words 'sì oscuro' (101) – so darkly. Neither of these can provide for the other a reliable or tolerable image – of the kind which Adam in Paradise will finally provide for Dante himself. The mirror here is fractured, and the signs it gives back are treacherously destructive.

Thus, in the process of the subsequent quarrel, Dante depicts a progressive erosion of meaning. One by one, the great myths of history and images of the natural world are rendered banal in the flux of insult: so, the tragedy of Troy is trivialised in Adam's gibe, while the word 'truth' itself becomes almost a term of abuse:

E l'idropico: 'Tu di' ver di questo:
ma tu non fosti sì ver testimonio
là 've del ver fosti a Troia richesto'.   (112–14)

(And the hydroptic: 'You speak the truth in this case; / but you were not so true a witness / when the truth was asked of you at Troy.')

Following from this, the exchange sets in motion a play upon the images of fire and water: these have been the constituents of Adam's earthly and eternal punishment, but they are now deprived both of moral force and of the lyrical suggestiveness which made them such a torment to the memory of the sinner. In the small change of insult, the elements become nothing more than agents of disease:

'E te sia rea la sete onde ti crepa',
disse 'l Greco, 'la lingua, e l'acqua marcia
che 'l ventre innanzi a li occhi sì t'assiepa!'
    Allora il monetier: 'Così si squarcia
la bocca tua per tuo mal come suole;
ché, s'i' ho sete e omor mi rinfarcia,
tu hai l'arsura e 'l capo che ti duole ...'.   (xxx 121–7)

('Then let the thirst which cracks [your tongue] / be cruel to you,' said the Greek, 'and also the foul water / which makes your belly a hedge around your eyes!' / In reply the coiner: 'So as usual your mouth is rent open to put you in the wrong; / for if I have a thirst and am stuffed with humours, / you are burning with fever and your head aches.')

Thus, in the end, even the account of punishment and judgement – which in the previous canto was articulated so clearly – is made the ammunition of contemptuous tit-for-tat. Nor does the poet himself enunciate any positive or final judgement. The canto leaves the two sinners in the midst of their quarrel. Indeed, just as the beginning of the episode was located in Canto xxix, so the description of the tenth bolgia continues into the opening lines of the thirty-first canto. Formal limits are blurred here; process, not conclusion, is Dante's prevailing concern.

Within the narrative, however, a balance to the continuing acrimony of the sinners is provided in the lengthy interchange between Virgil and the protagonist. Significantly enough, this exchange calls the protagonist back from the delusive realm of images to the realm of measured discourse. It remains true that Virgil's words will provide only a temporary and limited remedy: the truth must still be seen; and before the *Inferno* is over language will be tested, yet again, against the force of both the tragic and the comic images.

Yet for the moment Virgil's delicately modulated reproach not only restores the protagonist to sanity, but also revives a number of the words and images which, in the course of the canto, have been deprived of their force and implication.

Thus the protagonist stands speechless and in a daze:

Qual è colui che suo dannaggio sogna,
che sognando desidera sognare,

> sì che quel ch'è, come non fosse, agogna,
> tal mi fec' io, non possendo parlare ...   (136–9)

(Like one who dreams of his own harm, / and dreaming desires it to be a dream, / so that he yearns for that which is as if it were not, / so was I, unable to say a thing.)

In this final conceit of dreams within dreams, the language of the poet becomes as precious and conceited as his thought is complex. With Virgil, however, the canto returns to the language of common decency and good moral sense. The burden of Virgil's speech is that the shame which the protagonist has already shown washes away the fault he has committed and rids him of the weight of guilt:

> 'Maggior difetto men vergogna lava',
> disse 'l maestro, 'che 'l tuo non è stato;
> però d'ogne trestizia ti disgrava'.   (142–4)

('Less shame washes away a greater fault / than yours has been,' my master said, / 'so take from yourself the weight of all your misery.')

Here the 'waters' which, throughout the canto, have been the agents of disease and torment become the waters of moral purification; and the 'weight' which oppressed Adam of Brescia is now a moral weight lifted from Dante's shoulders. In this circle of distorting mirrors, Virgil may reveal to the protagonist the extent of his own excesses; but he also insists that Dante should not himself distort or exaggerate the extent of his guilt. Virgil may not be the true Adam; but he does give Dante back to himself. His speech allows the protagonist to proceed on a course which will eventually lead to the final washing away of guilt in the Earthly Paradise; and, as the cruel comedy of the tenth bolgia continues to run its course, so does the benign comedy of Dante's vision, under the regulating influence of Virgil's words.

IV

Cantos XXXI and XXXII are of a kind all too easily overlooked in a general survey of the *Inferno*, or discounted by critics who consider that Dante's art is best appreciated in a study of particular episodes. No one would deny that certain cantos of the *Inferno* have rightly come to occupy an especially eminent position in literary tradition – few more so than Canto XXXIII, which has been translated by at least four English poets, from Chaucer to Seamus Heaney. Nor can one doubt that Cantos XXXI and XXXII are ancillary to the last two cantos of the first *cantica*. Yet there is good reason not to move too rapidly to these last two cantos.

For one thing, the imaginative weight and moral sense of the Ugolino episode and the Satan canto can only be realised fully when these sequences are seen in the context of the whole of the last phase, and one function of Cantos XXXI and XXXII is to introduce the dominant images of this final phase. More specifically – as the argument of the present chapter suggests – it is contrary to the design of the *Commedia* to arrive swiftly at its conclusion.

The end is deferred, to the point at which it is scarcely possible to speak of an end in any save the most obvious sense, and the end to which Dante does come is dominated by a sense of tragic insufficiencies and illusion.

To take Cantos XXXI and XXXII as a pair illustrates broadly the two approaches which Dante adopts in reaching his conclusion, the thirty-first being 'comic' in type, the thirty-second possessing many of the characteristics of Canto XXVIII.

Canto XXXI is linked to the previous canto in tone and structure (thus yielding three consecutive cantos of comedy, against which the tragic episode of Ugolino, beginning in Canto XXXII, stands in particularly high relief). In fact, the conclusion to the momentary disagreement between the protagonist and Virgil is deferred until the first two *terzine* of Canto XXXI, where – speaking at disproportionate length of the shame which Virgil himself acknowledges to be disproportionate – Dante writes:

> Una medesma lingua pria mi morse,
> sì che mi tinse l'una e l'altra guancia,
> e poi la medicina mi riporse.   (XXXI 1–3)

(A single tongue first bit me, / so that it coloured both of my cheeks, / and then applied the remedy.)

But the opening passage also points forward to the coming sequence. Dante's emphasis now falls – as in, say, the opening lines of Cantos XXIII and XXIV – upon the delicacy of the relationship between himself and Virgil. Virgil acts as the custodian of the subtle shifts of feeling and conscience which give particularity and colour to the character of the protagonist; and Dante, drawing attention to the psychological and human comedy of the moment, describes the remedy that Virgil administers in a simile which (incongruously enough) was regularly applied in medieval romance to the effect which the smile of the courtly Lady had upon her servant:

> così od' io che solea far la lancia
> d' Achille e del suo padre esser cagione
> prima di trista e poi di buona mancia.   (4–6)

(Thus I have heard did the lance / of Achilles and his father work, being the cause, / first, of a painful then of a good gift.)

The refinement of feeling and behaviour registered here prepares, by contrast, for a sequence – opening with a depiction of the massive idiocy of the giants, and going on to examine the sin of treachery – in which delicacy of moral sentiment is deliberately extinguished.

For the moment, Virgil's words are sufficient to restore the protagonist to sanity, and one aspect of this sanity is that – in recognition of the ultimate insignificance of sin – the two travellers should be able to make a silent and perfunctory exit from the Malebolge:

> Noi demmo il dosso al misero vallone
> su per la ripa che 'l cinge dintorno,
> attraversando sanza alcun sermone.   (7–9)

(We turned our backs on the miserable gulf, / going up the bank which surrounds it, / and crossing it without saying a word.)

But now the comedy of illusion begins again; the two protagonists enter a region of swirling fogs and vapours in which the eye is in constant danger of deception. Moreover, sound and language also prove confusing and incapable, once more, of directing the mind to its goal:

> Quiv' era men che notte e men che giorno,
> sì che 'l viso m'andava innanzi poco;
> ma io senti' sonare un alto corno,
>   tanto ch'avrebbe ogne tuon fatto fioco,
> che, contra sé la sua via seguitando,
> dirizzò li occhi miei tutti ad un loco.
>   Dopo la dolorosa rotta, quando
> Carlo Magno perdé la santa gesta,
> non sonò sì terribilmente Orlando.   (10–18)

(Here it was less than night and less than day, / so that my sight went only a little forward. / But I heard the sound of a horn / so loud that it would have made any clap of thunder sound faint; / and this [directed my eyes,] tracing it back against its course, wholly to one place. / After the pitiful rout, when / Charlemagne lost his holy people, / Roland did not blow a blast so terrible.)

The trumpet blast which focuses Dante's attention cannot fail – after a sequence dominated by images of the Apocalypse – to call to mind the trumpet of the Last Judgement; indeed it *does* signal an end, announcing Dante's arrival at the lowest circles of Hell. But the end is bathetic and untrustworthy: the reference to the blast of Roland's horn reminds one of the treachery of Ganelon which led to Charlemagne's defeat – appropriately enough, where betrayal is to be Dante's theme – but also points to the defeat of the great culture of holiness and chivalry which defended virtues such as Dante and Virgil have just now displayed in their loyal and sensitive discourse. So far from proclaiming the final stability of God's Judgement, the sound threatens new confusion. And this threat is confirmed as Dante raises his eyes to see what, at first, appear to be the towers of a city – solid presences manifesting human constructiveness and civilisation:

> Poco portäi in là volta la testa,
> che me parve veder molte alte torri.   (19–20)

(I had not long turned my head in that direction / when I seemed to see many high towers.)

Yet these are not towers, and Virgil is immediately concerned that the eyes of the protagonist should not be deceived:

> Ed elli a me: 'Però che tu trascorri
> per le tenebre troppo da la lungi,
> avvien che poi nel maginare abborri'.   (22–4)

(And he to me: 'Because [your eyes] run / through the darkness from too far, / it happens that you are deceived in your imaginings.')

In outline, the scene recalls the episode before the Gates of Dis, where the signal-lights flash the warning of Dante's approach. But in detail Canto XXXI – though, like the Dis episode, a canto of transition – follows a different course. Dante does not have to wait here for the intervention of the *Messo da Ciel*, but rather, must make his own advance; nor does Virgil have to protect his follower by physical action from the danger ahead. Indeed, there is no danger: for the region is peopled by creatures who are utterly passive and inert. What Virgil *does* do is to prepare the protagonist to recognise the absurdity which lies at the centre of Hell and of sin. A comedy of false endings is about to begin, for the seeming towers of the city are in fact giants – images of once massive but now inane and disorderly power:

> Poi caramente mi prese per mano
> e disse: 'Pria che noi siam più avanti,
> acciò che 'l fatto men ti paia strano,
> sappi che non son torri, ma giganti ...'.   (28–30)

(Then tenderly he took me by the hand / and said: 'Before we go on any further, / – so that the fact should seem less strange to you – / know that these are not towers but giants'.)

This preliminary action points to the main structural characteristics of the thirty-first canto. Throughout, the canto is designed to disappoint our expectations of any such stable and impressive conclusion as was offered in the Dis episode by the *Messo da Ciel*. Here we have only the immobile giants, who, in theme as well as structure, reveal Dante's concern with the question of false ends.

Thus the giants are themselves a product or end which Nature itself has wisely discontinued:

> Natura certo, quando lasciò l'arte
> di sì fatti animali, assai fé bene
> per tòrre tali essecutori a Marte.   (49–51)

(Nature certainly [did well] when she abandoned the art / of making such creatures, / taking away from Mars his ministers.)

As in the *Messo* episode, so here, Dante appeals to his reader to examine the image with care: 'chi guarda sottilmente' (55). But in the giants all one discerns is the detritus – the fag-end – of nature and history. On the one hand, the processes of nature – here seen as 'just and discriminating' in its design – aim at order and harmony; on the other, the giants are emblems of disproportion, disruption and pride. So Ephialtes is the proud spirit who chose to try his strength against 'high Jove' (91), while Nimrod, the dominant figure in this episode, was, of course, the architect of the Tower of Babel. Nature extinguishes these creatures, in whom power and ill-will are dangerously united (56), and in Hell, likewise, their punishment ensures that they remain immobile and ineffectual – save to further Dante's own end by lowering him to the bottom of Hell. The giants were, and are, a mockery of what human nature is meant to be.

In conjunction with the giants, two other images – that of the tower and that of the pit or well – dominate this canto. As emblems, these images reinforce the moral significance that Dante attaches to the giants. The elevation of the tower is itself both a delusion and an expression of humanity's imprisonment in its own constructions; similarly, the well reveals only the emptiness that lies within the imposing heights – and stems not from running water but rather from the permanently frozen and sterile ice of the circles of treachery. Finally, like the giants, these images foreshadow the final cantos of the *Inferno*, where the giant Satan appears imprisoned at the centre of the earth, and where Ugolino tells the story of the Tower of Hunger. In this sense, the canto forms part of an orderly transition in which Dante brings together the moral and imaginative strands of the surrounding context; but, as in every other part of the *Inferno*, this orderliness is only one of the characteristics of Dante's procedure.

The structural qualities of the canto reveal themselves clearly in the central sequence, where Dante and Virgil encounter Nimrod. It is here that Dante concerns himself most intensely with the play of fact and fiction, experiencing a crisis both of langauge and of perception as he attempts to gauge the absurd non-entity of the giant by applying the normal measures of speech and seeing. Thus Dante claims that even three of the race of famously tall Frisians would have boasted in vain of reaching to the head of Nimrod: 's'averien dato mal vanto' (64). The question is: how does Dante avoid any similar 'mal vanto' – or, for that matter, avoid building a Babel of his own as he approaches Nimrod?

The answer lies in a certain submissiveness he shows both to process and to the limitations of human speech. Throughout the canto, the text displays an interest in details of motion and progression, while maintaining (in marked contrast to the strained virtuosity of the next canto) a certain austerity and almost child-like simplicity of diction.

Consider, for instance, the following lines:

> Come quando la nebbia si dissipa,
> lo sguardo a poco a poco raffigura
> ciò che cela 'l vapor che l'aere stipa,
>   così forando l'aura grossa e scura,
>   più e più appressando ver' la sponda,
>   fuggiemi errore e crescémi paura.   (34–9)

(As when mist grows thinner, / the gaze, little by little, begins again to piece together / whatever the vapour which thickens the air conceals, / so, as I pierced the thick and dark air / and came closer and still closer to the brink, / error fled from me and terror increased.)

Without emphasising – again – Dante's interest in the action of the eye, one notes the connections drawn in the gerunds 'forando' and 'appressando' between process, advance and perception. It is, however, the bare and balanced final phrase – 'fuggiemi errore e crescémi paura' – that now demands attention. For Dante offers here equation between truth and the most natural of emotions, fear at the stature of the giants. The natural flow of emotion, and the admission of fear itself, become guarantees of a truth that resides in the living protagonist.

In Canto XXXIII we shall see more fully the value that Dante places upon such simple emotional responses; but in Canto XXXI, this line establishes an important contrast between the giants – huge, immobile, apathetic – and the protagonist – tiny, advancing, terror-stricken; so does the following passage:

> E io scorgeva già d'alcun la faccia,
> le spalle e 'l petto e del ventre gran parte,
> e per le coste giù ambo le braccia.   (46–8)

(And now I was able to make out the face of one of them, / the shoulders, the breast, and a large part of the belly, / and both his arms by his sides.)

Here again one is invited to follow the movement of the eye, as it traverses the bulk of the giant, and again the language has an elemental simplicity in listing limbs and bodily features. But this simplicity itself reduces the giant to a human measure, representing him piecemeal (and, notably, substituting a cool neutrality of tone for the extravagant display of disgust which accompanied the descriptions of the body in Cantos XXVIII and XXX).

A final example occurs on a somewhat different level in the long and well-sustained syntactical period which precedes the ludicrous intervention of Nimrod:

> La faccia sua mi parea lunga e grossa
> come la pina di San Pietro a Roma,
> e a sua proporzione eran l'altre ossa;
> sì che la ripa, ch'era perizoma
> dal mezzo in giù, ne mostrava ben tanto
> di sovra, che di giugnere a la chioma
> tre Frison s'averien dato mal vanto;
> però ch'i' ne vedea trenta gran palmi
> dal loco in giù dov' omo affibbia 'l manto.   (58–67)

(His face appeared to me as long and bulky / as the pine-cone of St Peter's at Rome, / and his other bones were proportionate to it, / so that the bank which formed an apron for him / from the middle downwards still showed so much of him / above that three Frisians would have boasted [in vain of reaching to his hair]; / for I could see thirty palm-widths of him down / from the place where a man pins up his cloak.)

In the last line, the terms of Dante's estimate become simply domestic. But naivety is now combined with a skill in handling of syntax and the language of proportion and measure which makes virtuosity itself the servant of normality and everyday perception. This is particularly noticeable when the line which follows is Nimrod's incomprehensible cry:

> *Raphèl maì amècche zabì almi.*   (67)

Impressive as the *image* of Nimrod might have seemed, his *words* reveal his inherent absurdity; and Virgil proceeds to emphasise the comedy: the Giant, having dropped his horn so as to speak, is incapable of finding it again as it dangles around his neck. So Virgil commands:

> Cércati al collo, e troverai la soga
> che 'l tien legato, o anima confusa,
> e vedi lui che 'l gran petto ti doga.   (73–5)

(Search around your neck, and you will find the strap / that keeps it tied, O confused soul; / look how it is drawn across your great chest.)

Virgil, faced with the evidence of human pride and confusion, reasserts the role he adopted in the earliest cantos of the *Inferno* as custodian of clear speech and the guardian of Dante's purposes. Thus, just as he ordered the protagonist in Canto III not to speak of the sinners but 'to look and pass on', so here he commands:

> 'Lasciànlo stare e non parliamo a vòto;
> ché così è a lui ciascun linguaggio
> come 'l suo ad altrui, ch'a nullo è noto'.
> Facemmo adunque più lungo vïaggio,
> vòlti a sinistra ...   (79–83)

('Let us leave him be, and not speak pointlessly; / for to him every language is the same / as his to others, comprehensible to none.' / We then went further on in our journey, / turning to the left.)

The canto now resolves into a series of tableaux as the two travellers move from giant to giant until they arrive at Antaeus, who – being free from restraint – is able to lift the travellers down to the bottom of Hell.

The meeting with Antaeus defines clearly how the protagonist is to achieve his end, and the transition which Antaeus effects – in common with earlier instances of transition – displays the fundamental patterns which govern Dante's progress at every point. Like the whole journey through Hell, the next step is a descent into a void. The episode stresses both terror and absurdity, as Virgil cons Antaeus into giving assistance by promising that the protagonist will tell of his fame on his return to the world (128).

A further comedy, on the moral plane, lies in the play of parallels between the protagonist and Antaeus: so far from displaying pride, the protagonist only achieves his end by submitting to the grasp of the giant, and to the sheer terror which this grasp inspires. Again, suffering and simple emotion are graphically revealed to be the touchstones of truth.

The achievements of the protagonist in this canto point, finally, to the characteristics of the poet's own procedures in the sequence. We have seen how the diction, syntax and structure of the canto maintain a peculiarly modest and 'normal' tenor; one might, indeed, say that the canto is constructed around a form of the ineffability *topos*. As was seen in earlier chapters, the essential pattern for Dante's poetic procedure was first developed when the poet spoke of Beatrice in the *Vita nuova*; and in the *Paradiso*, where Beatrice is again of central importance, the *topos* likewise occupies a salient position. The procedure requires, in its usual form, that Dante should admit the superiority of a beatific object to any words or thoughts that he might apply to it. However, so far from straining language beyond its proper

Endings, tragic and comic

competence, Dante regularly admits and accepts the limits of his power, and we shall see in the concluding chapter how conscious Dante appears to be of this discipline as he ends the first *cantica*.

The present canto is built around an inversion of any such procedure: the object that Dante is describing is indeed great; but it is also empty and senseless. Here, the very admission of the size of the giants emphasises, as we have seen, not the limitations but the value of the normal categories of thought and speech.

In a similar way, the canto adopts and inverts those same procedures that, in the *Vita nuova* produce allegorical or typological prefiguration. Whenever Dante speaks of Beatrice as an angel he indicates how images – and supremely the human image – may act as messengers or signs of God's purposes, and in the *Messo* sequence of Canto IX we have already seen this notion introduced into the *Inferno*. But the giants – in common with Adam of Brescia – point in precisely the opposite direction: as emblems of pride and dissension they illustrate the *discontinuity* that can arise between human and divine purposes, rather than any possible reciprocation, and within the context of the *Inferno* their function is to 'prefigure' nothing save the ultimate emptiness and disappointment expressed in the figure of Satan.

The last lines of Canto XXXI provide a conclusion which, like the canto at large, is comic in its play upon normality and disproportion. Attention again falls upon the delusions of the eye: as the protagonist is lowered by Antaeus, the giant is compared to a high tower which seems to shift and bend as a cloud passes behind it. But the delusion expressed in this simile is benign, for it finally suggests the power which the imagination has to conceive the inconceivable in terms of ordinary experience and indeed to nourish or comfort itself by entering into the flow of such experience:

> Qual pare a riguardar la Carisenda
> sotto 'l chinato, quando un nuvol vada
> sovr' essa sì, ched ella incontro penda:
>   tal parve Antëo a me che stava a bada
> di vederlo chinare, e fu tal ora
> ch'i' avrei voluto ir per altra strada.
>   Ma lievamente al fondo che divora
> Lucifero con Giuda, ci sposò;
> né, sì chinato, lì fece dimora,
> e come albero in nave si levò.   (136–45)

(As the Garisenda appears when – seen / from the leaning side – a cloud passes / over it from the direction in which it leans, / thus Antaeus appeared to me as I stood watching / to see him bend; and it was at this moment / that I would gladly have gone by another road. / But he set us down lightly on the bottom which devours / Lucifer and Judas; and he did not delay, thus bent, / but rose up like the mast of a ship.)

The sequence began with the giants mistaken for towers. Now Antaeus is transformed, poetically, *back* into a tower – the leaning Garisenda at Bologna. The optical illusion which Dante describes reintroduces an image of process, where, however, the illusion is no longer produced by the murky unnatural fogs of Hell, but rather by a *cloud* moving across an open sky. Likewise, the image of the ship – keeling from side to side as it crosses the ocean – speaks of movements in the natural world which the mind can freely deal with. As the true 'end' for the protagonist in this canto is to continue his journey by whatever means might be provided, so too the poet concludes with a demonstration of how the imagination may move with the variations and illusions of the natural world, and, by yielding to them, maintain its freedom and balance.

                                              V

If Canto XXXI is dominated by illusion – and by the comedy which, for good or ill, is generated in the processes of perception – Canto XXXII returns to a tragic mode in which discourse strives painfully to achieve some clear and final statement of a moral truth. The child-like diction and imagery of the preceding canto are immediately displaced by the highly self-conscious rhetoric of the first four *terzine*, which were discussed at the opening of the present chapter: 'S'ïo avessi le rime aspre e chiocce ...' (1). One notes, however, that Dante here emphatically declares that it is no task for the voice of a child to describe the bottom of the universe:

> ché non è impresa da pigliare a gabbo
> discriver fondo a tutto l'universo,
> né da lingua che chiami mamma o babbo.   (XXXII 7–9)

(for it is no task to be taken as a joke, / to describe the bottom of the whole universe, / nor for a tongue that cries mummy and daddy).

The 'adult' poet, determined to deal fully – 'pienamente' (5) – with the last circles of Hell, puts aside childish things; and, aware of the virtuosity that his theme now requires him to exercise, he invokes the assistance of the Muses who helped Amphion to complete the building of Thebes: 'ch'aiutaro Anfïone a chiuder Tebe' (11). The damned, who are here the traitors, stand in a place where speech is hard: 'nel loco onde parlare è duro' (13); and, in response, the first half of the canto displays an exceptional degree of technically 'harsh' diction.

In *Inferno* III, when Dante described his entry into Hell, he spoke of how the 'hard sense' of Hell-Gate bewildered the protagonist, and then he proceeded in his own poetic text to display, for a first time, a conscious pride in his own artistry, matching – or even outdoing – Virgil in the depiction of Charon. Now, at the critical point where he must conclude the first *cantica*, Dante draws attention rather to the difficulties of the poet than to those of the protagonist: it is he – not Hell-Gate – who must now enunciate a judgement; speech is as 'hard' for him as it is for the damned. Thus we shall not find here the relatively uncomplicated virtuosity of the Charon episode, or, for that matter, the confidence in both tradition and the individual talent which emerged, more recently, in Canto XXV. To be sure, the adult poet has a

responsibility to be conclusive and clear; but already, in Canto XXXI, we have
begun to see the value that Dante attaches to the language of the child, and
we shall find that Dante's sense of this value grows stronger in the course of
the final cantos. In this light, the seriousness and single-mindedness of
Dante's endeavour come to be seen as a deviation from an elemental and
innocent grasp of truth. Virtuosity itself is here suspect; the reader of the
Commedia must wait for the *Purgatorio* before Dante recovers a style in
which fluency of emotion and artistic skill are reconciled.

With the opening of Canto XXXII, we enter the region of 'dead poetry', and
much of the interest of the canto lies in an appreciation of the pressures
under which signification of all kinds is seen to labour in Dante's own text.
Signs themselves are here as treacherous as the damned whom Dante
attempts to judge. In a word, Dante writes in the knowledge that he shares
his medium of discourse with the traitors themselves, so that eventually we
shall see that the language of judgement, and even the clarity which Dante
here achieves, are uncomfortable and unconvincing.

The issues of the canto are also dramatised in the second half of the canto
in Dante's encounter with the traitor Bocca degli Abati (79–123). The name
'Bocca' – 'the mouth' – has a particular importance, as we shall see, in the
context of the final cantos; but in Canto XXXII it focuses attention upon an
agony of utterance similar to that which we first observed in the sowers of
discord. Bocca, unlike Bertran or Mahomet, does not speak willingly. The
protagonist, however, cruelly wrenching back Bocca's head by its hair,
demands clear speech from him:

> Allor lo presi per la cuticagna
> e dissi: 'El converrà che tu ti nomi,
> o che capel qui sù non ti rimagna'.   (97–9)

(Then I took him by the hair on his nape / and said: 'It is better that you should name
yourself, / or not a hair will be left on you here.')

And, while Bocca does not respond to this physical torment, he does
eventually revenge himself – when a fellow-sinner names him – by betraying
the names of others who are condemned as traitors in the same circle as he
is:

> Se fossi domandato 'Altri chi v'era?',
> tu hai dallato quel di Beccheria
> di cui segò Fiorenza la gorgiera ...   (118–20)

(Should you be asked 'Who else was there?', / you have at your side him of the
Beccheria / whose gullet was slit by Florence ...)

Here, as in Canto XXVIII, the language of judgement becomes a language of
division and vindictive detestation. But the difference between this canto and
its predecessor is that the protagonist himself displays nothing of the
horrified detachment which marked his behaviour at the earlier point. On the
contrary, the physical violence with which he asserts his (apparently) justified
demand can only be matched in the *Inferno* by the vigour with which the

protagonist assails Filippo Argenti in Canto VIII. Here too there is a differ-
ence: for there is nothing in Canto XXXII that parallels the warm approbation
which Virgil bestows on Dante when he attacks Filippo. The protagonist acts
on his own initiative (82–4), and the reader is left to inspect the merits – or
otherwise – of his behaviour without any choric intervention to guide his
understanding of the scene. As we have seen, Dante in the Francesca episode
allows the sentiments of the protagonist to be judged by the reader; here
sentiment or fellow-feeling – which must surely suggest the perversity of
Dante's behaviour – is called to judge the judge.

We shall return shortly to the Bocca episode. But first we need to look
more generally at the way in which Dante pictures the sin of treachery, and
the images he uses in his portrayal. For, however difficult it may be for the
poet to carry through his plan of judgement, the outline and imaginative
vigour of the plan reside in Dante's powerful conception of what treachery
means, and in the scene by which he expresses that conception.

Dante judges treachery far more harshly than many of his contemporaries
would have done. One reason for this – which is apparent from his condem-
nation of Brutus and Cassius in Canto XXXIV – is that he sees in treachery a
destruction of the social bonds on which, in his view, the dignity and
happiness of human existence depend. But he is also concerned with the
ways in which treachery can offend the subtler and yet more deep-rooted
relationships which exist between friends, kinsmen and benefactors.
Treachery is not seen as a political crime alone. On the contrary, Dante
clearly understands – as will be apparent when one considers the images of
the canto – the existential significance of the sin. To be a traitor – in what-
ever specific sense – is also, in the deepest sense, to betray human nature.
This betrayal involves, as we have already suggested, a misapplication of the
human capacity for truthful signification. The traitor deliberately manipulates
all the principles which, for Dante, must have been characteristic of human
beings at their best, and knowingly misapplies the signs which express those
principles. The political traitor will wear a mask which promises devotion to
a common cause; the man who betrays his kinsmen or his guests will only
succeed if he makes a similar show of love and generosity. In this light, all
sin resolves itself into a form of betrayal, for certainly all the sinners in Hell
attempt to shroud themselves by their words in a show of human decency.
However, to appreciate the full force of this conclusion, one needs to consi-
der the two images which dominate the sequence, the image of the ice and
the image of the human countenance, which, as we shall see, is associated
with a number of subsidiary references to 'veiling' and 'mirrors'. Throughout
the sequence, the protagonist moves over the level surface of the ice at the
floor of Hell; the only features of note are human bodies, projecting from the
ice at various levels to demonstrate the degree of their guilt:

> Poscia vid' io mille visi cagnazzi
> fatti per freddo; onde mi via riprezzo,
> e verrà sempre, de' gelati guazzi.   (*Inf.* XXXII 70–2)

(Then I saw a thousand faces brutalised and purple / through the cold; at which a shivering comes over me, / and always will at the sight of frozen pools.)

This passage immediately suggests the dehumanisation that treachery represents in Dante's eyes, and it is worth noting the naive and spontaneous reaction which Dante attributes to himself as poet. The 'betraying' of emotion is momentarily contrasted with the icy betrayal of decency which the *contrappasso* diagnostically suggests is a part of treachery. But the implications of the ice image and the countenance image – severally and in conjunction – point to the very core of Dante's imaginative vocabulary. On that account it is worth pausing to examine these images – which are more complex than they first appear – in the light of antithetical references in the *Paradiso*.

Thus, in the first place, the ice is the most forceful portrayal in the *Inferno* of the condition of eternity. Eternity is changeless, and in the ice Dante imagines what unchangingness will be like in its effect upon those who, through a fixed determination to sin, are unready to enjoy eternity. For them, it will be a state of absolute fixity; and this can best be seen by comparing the scene in these circles with Dante's portrayal of the river of light in Canto xxx of the *Paradiso*.

> e vidi lume in forma di rivera
> fulvido di fulgore, intra due rive
> dipinte dimirabil primavera.
>   Di tal fiumana uscian faville vive,
> e d'ogni parte si mettien ne' fiori,
> quasi rubin che oro circunscrive.   (*Par.* xxx 61–6)

(and I saw light in the form of a river, / dazzling in brilliance, between two banks, / painted with wonderful spring. / Out of this river issued living sparks; / they dropped in the blossoms all around / as if they were rubies set within circles of gold.)

The images of the 'primavera sempiterna' and of a river in which light, fire, water and growth are all simultaneously present point to a condition – at once perfectly still and perfectly active – which is the exact reverse of the dead, wintry singleness of design that Dante associates with treachery. So in the *Inferno* we read:

> Non fece al corso suo sì grosso velo
> di verno la Danoia in Osterlicchi,
> né Tanaï là sotto 'l freddo cielo ...   (*Inf.* xxxii 25–7)

([The Danube of Austria] never made for its stream so thick a veil / in winter / nor the distant Don under a freezing sky).

Here ice is said to 'veil' the running stream, and this confirms the extent to which Dante is concerned in the canto with treachery on an existential level. For ice disguises – or betrays – the true nature of running water, and also of light. Light, as seen in Heaven, translates itself into the manifold forms of creation, playing freely and variously in the translucent matter of gems or water, so that each thing, constituted out of light, both is and is not itself. But the ice prohibits or mocks any such freedom. Thus in Canto XXXIV Dante depicts the worst of the traitors, who are frozen beneath the surface of the lake, fixed in apparently random attitudes which negate diversity, and each of these bodies is perforce transparent, like a vitrified straw rather than a gemstone:

> Già era, e con paura il metto in metro,
> là dove l'ombre tutte eran coperte,
> e trasparien come festuca in vetro.   (XXXIV 10–12)

(I was now – and with fear I put it into verse – / where the shades were wholly covered, / showing through like straws in glass.)

One notes here the oxymoron: the *shades* are transparent. Elsewhere in this region, the physical body is seen to be resistant to light, opaque, lurid in colour and alien to the medium in which it is set:

> livide, insin là dove appar vergogna
> eran l'ombre dolenti ne la ghiaccia,
> mettendo i denti in nota di cicogna.   (XXXII 34–6)

(livid, up to where the hue of shame appears / were the shades, grieving in the ice, / putting their teeth to the tune of the stork).

In Canto III, the judgement of God was spelled out with awful clarity and certainty in the words of Hell-Gate, while divine power drove the damned onwards with a force they are wholly unprepared to sustain. The ice is no less an expression of divine certainty; but God is not a presence here: he is known only through his total absence. Instead of words speaking – in however terrible a form – of divine power, wisdom, love and justice, the only signs which express the divine order are the isolated and static shapes of the damned. We see, then, in its final form, the complete infertility and passiveness of sin which Dante first depicted in the *ignavi* of Canto III. The sinners here have wholly deprived themselves of the possibility of new life, or of the 'vita *nuova*' which the '*nuova* gente' of Purgatory will enjoy. Moreover, there is no danger here – as there was as late as the Ulysses episode – that the human sign should be misread. That sign is either wholly vacant of meaning – as are the straw-like sinners of the last region here – or, like the 'visi cagnazzi', utterly unresponsive. Dante here pictures a relationship between what is, literally, the *in*significance of the human form and the overwhelming but distant significance of God, which is here expressed not in love or light but in absolute judgement.

In the specific case of the traitors, it is not difficult to see how appropriate the *contrappasso* is to their offence. Not only have they manipulated signs in pursuit of their treacherous aims, but they have treated their own persons as puppets dancing to some covert design: the traitor uses not only words to deceive, but actions, smiles and gestures. In Chaucer's phrase, he is the 'smiler with the knife under his cloak', and the *contrappasso* in the *Inferno* suggests that Dante would have understood him in a similar way. The whole physique of the traitor is now at last fixed and exposed to public view. Again, we need to recognise how deep a betrayal of human nature is represented in this aspect of treachery, and again to gauge this we must turn to the *Paradiso*. For it becomes increasingly clear in the course of the *Commedia* that Dante did attach quite exceptional value to acts of communication which are effected not by words but by spontaneous physical gestures.

Consider the importance of the smile in the *Paradiso*. In Canto xxvii the Universe itself is said to 'smile' upon Dante:

> Ciò ch'io vedeva mi sembiava un riso
> de l'universo ...   (*Par.* xxvii 4–5)

(And what I saw then seemed to me a smile / of the universe).

One notes that this occurs at the point where the protagonist arrives at the *primum mobile*, and the significance of this is not far to seek. For, as was seen in discussing the Ulysses episode, the First Mover – which itself is as much an antithesis to the frozen lake as is the River of Light – represents in Dante's scheme the very origin of the system which determines the movements of cause and effect in space and time. To arrive at the First Mover is to arrive at an absolutely certain knowledge of the physical world. The smile which Dante experiences at this point is an expression of the confidence that the human mind can enjoy in its reciprocal relationship with that world. There can be no betrayal in the *primum mobile*; the signs of the Universe are secure and make complete sense. Thus at every point in the *Paradiso* Beatrice has smiled to register the understanding which Dante shows for the truths which are progressively revealed to him. Again the implication must be that, beyond the actual meaning that Dante receives from his teacher, there lies a deeper and more subtle understanding which can only be expressed by the light in Beatrice's eye or the subtle movements of her lips.

The value that Dante attaches to the 'smile' is closely connected, throughout Dante's writing, with the view he takes of courtesy. I have suggested elsewhere – in a book on the *Paradiso* – the ways in which courtesy, for Dante, is an essential component in the philosophical life. Most notably, in the Heaven of Christian Philosophy, the understanding of truth is seen to depend as much upon a certain deference to the *person* of the philosopher as upon the acceptance of logical argumentation. In a similar way, a study of the *Purgatorio* might well begin with an examination of the courtesy which prevails between one penitent and another, and between the protagonist and all the figures he encounters in the second realm. The *Purgatorio* is certainly concerned with the many different ways in which meanings can be made and shared: music, sculpture, visions and dreams are, throughout, seen to be no less valid as instruments of communication than words. In this case I would take courtesy to imply the ability – which is common to any kind of closed circle, or 'court' – to create and use a private system of signs. Thus the subtlest signs which Dante has to read in Purgatory are those which appear fleetingly in the faces and gestures of the figures he meets. In earlier chapters, for instance, we have spoken of how Dante in *Purgatorio* XXIII responds to the sight of his old friend Forese Donati, whose features are marked, as a penance for gluttony, with the word *omo*. However, we need not pause to illustrate this at length, for already, in Canto II of the *Inferno*, we have seen what courtesy might mean for Dante, when he depicts the responses of the Ladies in the court of Heaven to the mute bewilderment of the sinful protagonist. There, the language of courtesy was able to produce an answer to the distresses of the individual which the language of Law – and Virgilian rationality – could not encompass. The play of eyes in that sequence – 'lucevan li occhi suoi ...' (*Inf.* II 55) – aroused pity and an understanding of what needed to be done if Dante himself were to be brought back to the court of Heaven. While the eyes of the Ladies do not yet there smile, but rather weep, it is nonetheless clear that the courtliness of the scene admits the value of a spontaneous language in which physical response possesses as much importance as mental design.

We arrive, then, at a view of signification in which the child-like language of tears and smiles – which Dante, as we have said, represses at the outset in Canto XXXII – is seen to be entirely at one with the highest sophistication of mutual understanding. (We shall have more to say about this in the concluding chapter.) We may for the moment recall that, since at least the canto of the hypocrites, Dante has been developing his interest in the language of physical reaction. The particular bearing of these considerations on the treachery cantos can be seen not only in the extreme distortions of face that the sinners suffer – from the sinner Bocca, to the blood-stained mouth of Ugolino, to the three ravening mouths of Satan – but also in the way in which Dante introduces the notion of 'courtesy' at the end of Canto XXXIII.

Here Dante depicts a scene which is no less discomfiting in its violence than the Bocca episode. The protagonist, having promised to clear the ice that freezes up the eyes of the sinner Frate Alberigo, refuses to do so, even though the sinner keeps his part of the bargain by revealing the names of his associates in Hell. Dante here might clearly be accused of a treacherous act; but instead he expresses his interpretation of the action in terms of courtesy:

> e cortesia fu lui esser villano.   (*Inf.* XXXIII 150)

(and it was courtesy to be base to him).

Here Dante acknowledges that there can be no reciprocity of the kind that courtesy fosters between himself and the sinner. The eyes of Alberigo remain dead, unweeping, evoking no pity from the protagonist; the sinner – who, as we shall see, uses gesture at a banquet to precipitate a treacherous murder – can claim no place at all in the circle of courtesy. He is left, like Bocca, in a state of unrelieved materiality.

As to the traitors themselves, then, one may now see that the rigid physicality of face and feature which their punishment imposes upon them expresses the absolute alienation in treachery between the traitor and his community and also between the traitor and *himself* as a sentient and, so to say, *significant* being. One need only emphasise that it is mind not body which has created this divorce. For the traitor, bodily form is merely a mask to adopt in pursuit of a perverse intention: he cannot allow its true responses to be known.

But how does this conclusion bear upon Dante himself, as protagonist and poet? Language itself, in the form of words, has here once again begun to look treacherous, and mind, too, has proved to be dangerously capable of alienating the human being from the sources of its strength. Moreover, witnessing the extreme viciousness of the protagonist, we are bound to ask what 'courtesy' the reader is expected to extend to him in this sequence. The bonds of common feeling seem no less threatened here than in the sin of treachery itself.

As to the protagonist, one must firstly note that his position in the circles of treachery is significantly different from what it has been in earlier regions of Hell. For instance, in the Malebolge Dante progressed, for the most part, over the bridges of the region, which allowed him to inspect the singularly loathsome condition of the fraudulent, while also maintaining a certain distance and a degree of moral superiority. But much of this is now changed, and with the change of scene – as in every other major division of Hell – there occurs an alteration in the dynamics of the narrative. Dante now progresses across the level surface of the ice and is freer than he has ever been before. (Ironically enough, the next time he enjoys any such freedom of movement will be when he enters the Earthly Paradise on the top of Mount Purgatory.) Thus it is he who initiates the first encounter in the episode, having taken stock of the situation: 'Quand' io m'ebbi dintorno alquanto visto, / volsimi a' piedi ...' (XXXII 40–1). Notably, he takes it upon himself to dictate to Virgil:

> E io: 'Maestro mio, or qui m'aspetta,
> sì ch'io esca d'un dubbio per costui;
> poi mi farai, quantunque vorrai, fretta'.   (82–4)

(And I: 'Master, now wait for me here, / so that I can get rid of a doubt about this person; / then you can make me hasten as much as you wish.')

In a similar way, the ice, as it were, sanitises the sinners, so that the protagonist need no longer fear contamination by his contact with them. It also serves to fix them passively for Dante to conduct his inspection. Thus the glaze of ice which forms on the features of the treacherous may indeed be referred to as a 'veil', as in Canto XXXIII where a sinner exclaims:

> levatemi dal viso i duri veli.   (*Inf.* XXXIII 112)

(take from my face the hard veil).

But the ice is not so much a veil as a lens. The traitors are caught in the insoluble contradiction of seeking to hide, while wishing, equally strongly, that the veil of ice should be lifted from their faces. For the protagonist, however, it is this veil that allows him to observe with the utmost clarity the true nature of treachery.

This much suggests that Dante has arrived at a conclusion: his mastery, even of the most devious of sins, seems now to be assured. Yet there are contra-indications, which invite us to ask whether the achievement of mastery is worth the price, in human decency, which the protagonist has to pay for it. For if Dante is independent, he is also a lonelier figure – and himself more exposed to view – than he has been since the opening lines of *Inferno* I. Not only is God silent, but Virgil is too. Dante is left to read meaning in the bodies of those who have demonstrated in their lives how completely the human being can erode or falsify meaning. He is required to judge in circumstances where the purpose of judgement – which elsewhere will preserve community or reconcile the individual to the love of God – seems to be wholly absent.

In these circumstances, where the defining purpose of judgement is hidden from view, the acts of justice which the protagonist performs – as well as his determination to achieve a clear and exhaustive account of Hell – come to seem indistinguishable from acts of demonic violence. And Dante as poet encourages this view: so far from allowing Virgil to stamp approval on the actions of the protagonist, Dante allows the damned themselves to interpret his own most brutal action:

> Io avea già i capelli in mano avvolti
> e tratti glien' avea più d'una ciocca,
> latrando lui con li occhi in giù raccolti,
>   quando un altro gridò: 'Che hai tu, Bocca?
> non ti basta sonar con le mascelle,
> se tu non latri? qual diavol ti tocca?'.   (*Inf.* XXXII 103–8)

(I had already twisted his hair in my hand, / and pulled out more than one tuft, / while he barked and kept his eyes close down, / when another cried out: 'What's wrong with you, Bocca? / Isn't it enough for you to make a noise with your jaws? / Have you got to bark as well? What devil has got to you?')

So, too, at line 54 the protagonist, staring at the damned, is asked why he should so 'mirror' himself in the sinners: 'Perché cotanto in noi ti specchi?'. Again, it is hard to repress the suggestion that there is indeed an identity here between the sinners and the protagonist. For once, the text requires us to blur rather than sharpen the distinction and, in doing so, to contemplate the collapse of all the principles which hitherto have been embodied in the protagonist. The reader too is reduced to the barren loneliness of using or judging the human sign in a place where nothing offers guidance or the promise of ulterior significance.

This conclusion will be supported if, looking for a last time beyond the *Inferno*, one considers the meaning of the 'mirror image' – which is no less important to Dante than to modern psychiatric theory – in the perspective of the whole *Commedia*. For, particularly in the *Paradiso*, the mirror image is taken to represent the essential nature of the relationship between creature

and Creator. Thus, at the conclusion of *Paradiso* XXIX, Dante compares the
angels to mirrors, reflecting God's light:

> Vedi l'eccelso omai e la larghezza
> de l'etterno valor, poscia che tanti
> speculi fatti s'ha in che si spezza,
> uno manendo in sé come davanti.   (*Par.* XXIX 142–5)

(Behold now the height and the breadth / of Eternal Goodness, when so many / mirrors
it has made in which it is broken / remaining in itself One, as before.)

The perfect creature is made so as to reflect, from beyond itself, the light of
its Creator. This too is the function of the angelic Lady, Beatrice. It is she in
the Earthly Paradise who reflects in her eyes the image of the Gryphon –
symbol of the twofold nature of Christ – so that Dante, too, can contemplate
that image: 'Come in lo specchio il sol, non altrimenti / la doppia fiera dentro
vi raggiava' (*Purg.* XXXI 121–2). In both these cases, the mirror reveals how a
creature is grounded in the 'otherness' of God and indicates that the true
function of the creature is to receive and communicate beyond itself the
divine light. In that sense, the image is consistent with the implications of the
River of Light, where likewise the objects of the natural world were seen to
exist – by virtue of their translucence – as bearers of Light. But there is a
further application of the mirror image which occurs at two points in the
Purgatorio: firstly, when the protagonist sees his own face reflected in
the polished step on the stairway to the Gate of Purgatory, and, secondly, in
the Earthly Paradise, when Dante, bowed down with shame in the presence
of Beatrice, catches sight of himself reflected in the waters of the river which
divides him from her and cannot bear the sight:

> Li occhi mi cadder già nel chiaro fonte;
> ma veggendomi in essa, i trassi a l'erba,
> tanta vergogna mi gravò la fronte.   (*Purg.* XXX 76–8)

(My eyes fell upon the clear stream; / but seeing myself in that, I drew them to the
grass, / so great a shame weighed down my brow.)

Both of these instances represent moments of self-knowledge, confession and
conversion. In both cases, Dante recognises his true self, seeing it – for good
or ill – as another might see it. His very conversion depends upon this
recognition of his own 'otherness'; through seeing clearly what he has been
and understanding what he might become, there lies the possibility of moral
change. The reciprocity which tears and smiles can express in courtesy
becomes, in the moment of repentance, an inward reciprocity.

But – as if, in some nightmare, the distance between subject and reflected
image could be collapsed – 'otherness' is annihilated in the mirrors of Hell,
leaving only the vision of a thousand faces all rendered identical by the
biting cold. There is certainly no God or source of being here; but there is no
reciprocity either, nor any play of difference; consequently there is no possi-
bility of meaning. Thus the 'why' in 'Perché cotanto in noi ti specchi?' is
repeated in Bocca's cry at line 79: 'Perché mi peste?' – Why do you trample

on me? There can be no answer to these questions, for there can be no appeal to a point beyond the violent impact of the moment. So, when Bocca finally uses the 'perché' in a concessive construction, he does so to assert that no meaning at all can be dragged from him; the violence is all that remains:

> Ond' elli a me: 'Perché tu mi dischiomi,
> né ti dirò ch'io sia, né mosterrolti
> se mille fiate in sul capo mi tomi'.   (*Inf.* 100–2)

(At which he said to me: 'Even if you strip all the hair from my head, / I will not tell you or show you who I am, / if you fall upon my head a thousand times.')

How, finally, does this reflect upon the logic of Dante's own plan in the *Inferno* and upon the virtuosity he displays in defending that plan?

In the first place, we should not now expect Dante's artistry to be the same as it was in, say, Canto XXV. Nor is the understanding of signification which emerges from the present canto the same as it was in the cantos devoted to false counsel. Earlier we saw that, in admitting the ambiguity and fluidity of language, Dante asserted his right to translate the idiom of Lucan and Ovid into a a form of poetry which possessed – among other things – a complex Christian resonance. Equally, we saw that the Ulysses episode revolves, as Canto XXXIII conspicuously does not, around an awareness of the 'altrui' or 'other': Ulysses and Dante, in their different ways and with different results, both seek meaning in deference to (or ignorance of) that 'other', and the reader of that canto is also required to enter into the play of distinctions which differentiate Dante and Ulysses. Yet to see how far Dante has now travelled from that position we have only to consider lines such as the following from Canto XXXII, where Dante describes two sinners who are frozen so tight together that the hairs on their heads seem to have fused:

> li occhi lor, ch'eran pria pur dentro molli,
> gocciar su per le labbra, e 'l gelo strinse
> le lagrime tra essi e riserrolli.
>   Con legno legno spranga mai non cinse
> forte così; ond' ei come due becchi
> cozzaro insieme, tanta ira li vinse.   (46–51)

(Their eyes, which before were moist only within, / dripped welling tears over their lips, and the frost bound / the tears between them, and locked them up together. / Wood to wood by clamp was never bound / so tight; and, like two goats / they butted together, such anger overcame them.)

Here the distinctions between body and body are violently extinguished; the sinners are not allowed to possess in privacy their own tears, which now solder them together: weeping itself becomes a cruel and unusual punishment. But Dante's language plays – as we shall see it also does in Canto XXXIII – upon the conceits rather than the pathos which the image of the *contrappasso* evokes. Nor is there any symbolic dimension to the references. We have of course seen that, in the full perspective of the *Commedia*, the ice does have a symbolic significance. But there is nothing in the local detail of the language to encourage us to look for it, or to indicate any order other than that presented in the scene before us. There are no allusions to 'divine art', or to the natural scheme, as there were in, say, the *ramarro* simile of Canto xxv. Even the internal logic of the description – passing in rapidly mixed metaphors from planks to goats – proves opaque and centripetal; and the dull repetition 'legno legno' expresses a perverse indulgence in the difficulty of advancing from one significant item to another.

Here, then, Dante all but imprisons himself – at the expense of meaning or descriptive clarity – in his own linguistic virtuosity. We shall stress in the concluding chapter how far the poet is in passages such as this from the spontaneous and measured style which he himself identifies in the *Vita nuova* as the source of his own poetic originality. Yet this is not the first time that Dante has written in such a vein, for a similar combination of virtuosity and frustration is to be found – before Dante begins the *Inferno* – in a series of poems addressed to a Lady quite different from Beatrice, the *Donna Petrosa*, the 'stony Lady'. In at least three ways in Canto xxxii Dante seems to recall the most important of these *rime petrose*, 'Così nel mio parlar voglio esser aspro ...'.

Thus the first line of the poem – which is quoted above – exactly corresponds to the opening invocation in Canto xxxii. In both cases the poet determines to find a diction harsh enough to suit the harshness of his subject. This, one might say, reflects the familiar desire of the rhetorician to write in a language which is adequate and 'convenient' to his theme. Yet it is a striking feature of the praise-style in the *Vita nuova* that Dante frees himself from this obligation, recognising that no words can be adequate when his subject is Beatrice. In that light, the opening sequences of both 'Così nel mio parlar ...' and Canto xxxii display a dangerous obsession on the author's part with his own artistry. In a similar way, Dante acknowledges in 'Così nel mio parlar ...' how far his fascination with the Lady who will not yield to his advances diverts him from the true principles of courtesy. Here – as in *Inferno* xxxiii – he seeks to repress the promptings of any such virtue:

> e non sarei pietoso né cortese.
>
> ('Così nel mio parlar ...' 70)

(and I would show no pity or courtesy).

Then, finally, this leads Dante to a violence exactly comparable to that which he displays towards the traitor, Bocca. For, where the courtly lover is prepared to love from a distance, allowing distance itself to purify and refine his sentiments, Dante here longs to assail the Lady who torments him and vent his frustration in hauling her by the hair:

> S'io avessi le belle trecce prese,
> che fatte son per me scudiscio e ferza,
> pigliandole anzi terza,
>   con esse passerei vespero e squille.   (66–9)

(Once I had taken in my hand the fair tresses / which have become for me a scourge and lash, / seizing them before terce, / I would pass through vespers with them, and the evening bell.)

Now it would be surely impossible to deny that the frustrations reflected in 'Così nel mio parlar ...' are sexual in character: Dante is plainly unable to provide any 'other', or sublimated, meaning for the stony Lady – as he does for Beatrice whenever he views her as the bearer of Christian truth, or even for the *Donna Gentile* of the *Convivio* when he insists that she is Lady Philosophy. But precisely that resistance to interpretation suggests the way in which the *rime petrose* may contribute to an understanding of the intellectual and linguistic issues which have concerned us in Canto XXXII. In fact, the experience of a certain 'hardness' or stoniness is one that recurs at regular intervals throughout Dante's poetic career; most notably, there comes a point in the *Convivio* where Dante's enthusiastic exposition of philosophical issues is brought to a halt by questions which are beyond his competence to solve (*CNV* IV 1), so that Lady Philosophy herself approaches him with a hard and proud bearing, with 'atti disdegnosi e feri' ('Le dolci rime d'amor ch'i solia ...' 5). We have also seen how harsh Beatrice can be to Dante in the Earthly Paradise. In brief, there are moments in every project which Dante under-takes where clarity of purpose, technical skill and enthusiasm prove insuffi-cient to ensure his progress. Problems arise – on the philosophical and poetic plane – which refuse, like the stony Lady, to yield a meaning, and the signs which Dante has hitherto employed with the utmost confidence become un-readable, acting merely to fixate the mind. So, for instance, the images of eyes and fire which, in poems addressed to Beatrice, invariably express illu-mination, guidance and the possibility of purification, become, in 'Così nel mio parlar ...', expressions of sheer torment which Dante reflects in unchar-acteristically tense and even paradoxical phrases:

> Ancor ne li occhi, ond'escon le faville
> che m'infiammano il cor, ch'io porto anciso,
> guarderei presso e fiso,
> per vendicar lo fuggir che mi face.   (74–7)

(Still more, into those eyes, from which come the sparks / that inflame my heart which I carry slain within me, / I would gaze close and fixedly, / to revenge myself on her for fleeing me as she does.)

It is not difficult to see in these lines a stylistic anticipation of the *legno* passage from *Inferno* XXXII: 'eyes' in both passages are the focus of an almost witty anxiety, which prevents any clear view of the relationship between victim and avenger. But, more generally, one might well argue – on the understanding I have pursued throughout this book – that the *Inferno* at large is Dante's most sustained account of the difficulties he first dramatised in the *rime petrose*. Certainly, the Gate of Hell, with its 'hard sense', represents an initial experience of that intellectual stoniness, and the ice of the lowest circles is another form of that 'stone'. However, it is not only the linguistic texture of the canto that verges – at a point where judgement seems most secure – on the annihilation of significance. So, too, in a number of respects, do the central images of the narrative. To be sure, one function of the canto is to establish diagnostic images of ice and countenance – and thus to summarise the whole nature of Hell; but another function is to erode and incriminate some of the central tenets of the judgements on which the now-almost-finished enterprise has depended. And this can be seen, firstly, in Dante's treatment here of the image of the journey, secondly, in his treatment of the image of his own corporeal presence in Hell and, finally, in the use he proposes to make of the text he is at this point writing.

As always, the image of the journey is especially indicative of Dante's moral position; but, as we have suggested, the progress of the journey, without the active guidance of Virgil, becomes far more vague and undetermined than it has ever been before:

> E mentre ch'andvam inver' lo mezzo
> al quale ogne gravezza si rauna,
> e io tremava ne l'etterno rezzo;
>   se voler fu o destino o fortuna,
> non so; ma, passeggiando, tra le teste,
> forte percossi 'l piè nel viso ad una.   (*Inf.* XXXII 73–8)

(And as we went on towards the centre / at which all heaviness is drawn together – / I trembling in the eternal shade – / and whether by will, by destiny or chance / I do not know; but, passing among the heads, / I struck my foot heavily in the face of one of them.)

Here especially one realises the difference between this canto and the Filippo Argenti episode, which in respect of its physical brutality appeared to be so similar. In Canto VIII Dante was just beginning to establish the validity and moral significance of his journey, and the *Messo da Ciel* entered to emphasise its ultimate purpose. Now, however, Dante limits the horizon of his journey to the dead centre of the Universe, where 'all heaviness is gathered'; and he is unable to give any definite name at all to the agency which guided his foot in its vicious action. Providence is not mentioned here, only destiny and chance. Moreover, where the journey has hitherto been one of witness and contemplation – allowing a distance between Dante and the damned – it is now the essential mechanism of the journey itself, one foot being placed before another, that leads the protagonist into collision with the sinners: reduced to their level, his trek becomes an actual instrument of vengeance.

In a similar way, the physical presence of Dante, which was once a source of astonishment to the damned, now actively contributes to their torment. As before in, say, Cantos XXIII and Canto XXVIII, the protagonist draws attention to his possession of a true, rather than a 'ghost', body: 'Vivo son io' (91) – I am alive. But the great myth of the Resurrection has no place here. On the contrary, the sanctified body is at once put to trivial and cruel use, the tearing out of Bocca's hair; the farce with which the episode ends is possible only because Dante *is* still in the flesh.

Then, at last, in promising to record Bocca's name among the 'altre note' of his poem (93), Dante's reveals that even the narrative he is writing may serve a vengeful and even equivocal end, since a name recorded in this context can win no praise at all. A point has already has been reached at which clarity of utterance and certainty of design have themselves become treacherous, and where, equally, words of judgement have become incapable of leading Dante to his true intellectual goal. This is the tragic conclusion that was foreshadowed in Canto XXVIII.

VI

The images and procedures that Dante develops in Cantos XXXI and XXXII prepare us for the last two cantos of the *Inferno*, yet the conclusion of the *cantica* is anything but a *simple* climax. Indeed, the nominal ending – the vision of Satan – is more anti-climactic than conclusive. Only the first half of Canto XXXIV is concerned with Satan, while the second describes how Virgil and Dante climb to Purgatory over his passive body. Moreover, in terms of style and imagery, the representation of Satan is itself far less impressive than one might have expected. It is true that the protagonist expresses his horror at what he sees (XXXIV 25–7). Yet there is no corresponding sense that the poet has any difficulty in arriving at an imaginative conception of the fallen angel. The figure is first described disparagingly as a 'contraption' – 'dificio' (7) – and throughout he remains all but motionless, acting only as a machine designed to cool the ice in the last circle of Hell, to torment the three traitors Judas, Brutus and Cassius, or, finally, to convey Virgil and the protagonist to Purgatory:

> Non avean penne, ma di vispistrello
> era lor modo; e quelle svolazzava,
> sì che tre venti si movean da ello:
>   quindi Cocito tutto s'aggelava.
> Con sei occhi piangëa, e per tre menti
> gocciava 'l pianto e sanguinosa bava.
>   Da ogne bocca dirompea co' denti
> un peccatore, a guisa di maciulla,
> sì che tre ne facea così dolenti.   (*Inf.* XXXIV 49–57)

([His wings] had no feathers; they were like a bat's. / And he wafted these / so that three winds went out from him: / and all Cocytus was frozen by them. / He was weeping with six eyes; and over his three chins / the tears and bloody foam dripped down. / In each of his mouths he crushed [a sinner] with his teeth / like a combing machine, / and thus made three of them suffer.)

To I. A. Richards, the passivity which Dante ascribes to Satan is particularly offensive, as an indication of the ease with which Dante was able to judge – and even dismiss – the problem of evil. Nor can one doubt that, in itself, the thirty-fourth canto is indeed designed to celebrate Dante's mastery over the forces of evil. In theological terms, the reader is brought to see that evil possesses no independent existence. As Aquinas would define it, it is mere absence and lack of true activity; and Dante's portrayal of Satan corresponds closely with that definition. Likewise, in terms of the development of theme in the *Inferno*, it becomes clear in the thirty-fourth canto that one reason for Dante's journey through Hell has been, as it were, to demythologise evil. The protagonist now realises not only that evil is a *non*-entity, but also that it may become an instrument in his spiritual progress. Similarly the poet or reader will be invited, in the course of the canto, to see – behind the myth or delusive veil of Satan – a manifestation of the purposes and nature of God. Here, as always, Dante's intention is to 'treat of the good that he found in Hell'.

It follows from all this that the final canto should be predominantly comic in tenor. One need think only of medieval mystery plays to realise that Satan could regularly be a comic subject to the medieval mind. But in the *Inferno*, Canto XXXIV stands as the culmination of a comic sequence that began with the last cantos of the Malebolge and the representation of the giants in Canto XXXI. Now, as in Canto XXXI, the eye of the protagonist is at the outset confused by Satan, as if assailed by a delusive mist – 'Come quando una grossa nebbia spira ...' (XXXIV 4); and, as we shall see, the canto has other properties which align it with these earlier instances.

Yet Canto XXXIV stands as only one of the endings that Dante provides for the *Inferno*. And if the Satan episode is anti-climactic, this, in part, is because the representation of Ugolino in the preceding canto has already displayed many of the properties of a true climax. This is appropriate enough in the moral as well as the imaginative scheme of the *Inferno*. Evil, in the figure of Satan, may be revealed as illusion, but sin remains a reality with which human beings have to cope as long as they live in the temporal world. Sin finally is a betrayal of the best that humanity is capable of in earthly existence, and the possibility of such a betrayal is ever-present. Dante has already begun to express this through the prevailing images of ice and countenance. In the Ugolino episode the same point is made in dramatic form, through a study of the mentality of a particular sinner. Ugolino is a traitor specifically in that he betrayed certain Pisan castles into enemy hands; but he is also a traitor even in the Tower of Hunger when – although he himself is the *victim* of treachery – he persistently refuses to respond to the demands for fellow-feeling that his children make upon him.

The crisis of Canto XXXIII is one that bears not only upon Ugolino, but also upon the author of the *Inferno*. In taking treachery as his subject, Dante acknowledges the extent to which all words, gestures and motives can be shifting or uncertain if devoted to a perverse end. He writes the canto in the knowledge of that uncertainty; and in its second half he enacts the problem in a sequence that represents his own treacherous dealings, as protagonist, with the sinner Frate Alberigo. Here, for a last time, Dante develops a contrast between his own narrative procedures – displayed in the canto at large – and the narrative and linguistic procedures he has attributed to Ugolino.

In view of the painfulness and historical reality of Ugolino's story, it may seem artificial to suggest that Dante judges the sinner on the grounds, as it were, of his narrative ability. Yet by now such a judgement should not come as a surprise. In Chapter 3 we saw the extent to which the poet could make narrative competence a test of moral competence – as in the portrayal, say, of Pier della Vigna; and the story that Ugolino relates is an appropriate conclusion to the *Inferno* not least insofar as it exemplifies many of the linguistic and narrative devices which have already been observed in Francesca, Piero and Ulysses. But the issues raised in the story go much deeper than any other in the *Inferno*. Hitherto, each story in turn has concentrated upon some quite specific moral or intellectual problem. In Francesca, Dante examined the potential incompatibility between language and sentiment. In the case of Pier della Vigna, he looked at the way in which the human being deals with the gap between itself and external events or facts – a gap which tests the faith of the human mind on every level. That same gap, in Ulysses's case, is momentarily seen to be unbridgeable: the 'folle volo' leads Ulysses to a collision with the reality of Mount Purgatory; and, in a world where the nature of goodness has still to be revealed, the sum of courage and intellectual aspiration in Ulysses's case comes to nothing.

But the story of Ugolino raises questions more primitive and more comprehensive than any of these: the questions are those which anyone who lives, eats and feels must confront at every moment of existence – and those from which the human mind most naturally shies away, protecting itself with sophisticated veils of illusion. Dante here concerns himself with the physical and emotional needs of 'unaccommodated man' – with our human dependence upon food and family, and with the suffering that arises when any interruption occurs in the fragile links of dependency. Nor – since treachery and deliberate cruelty are themselves part of the story – does Dante ignore the fact that human beings can themselves precipitate the circumstances that lead to the tragic question: why do we suffer?

Canto XXXIII offers a view of the tragic end to which human nature is bound; but the questions raised by that theme cannot be separated from the consideration of how we are to formulate our responses and shape ourselves towards that end. It is an essential test of the mind that, recognising its own capacity for illusion and violence, it should also find a way in which to face the truth of the suffering it can cause or experience. Thus, as well as creating a scene of the utmost horror and pathos, Dante here investigates the action of mind and word in the perspectives that are opened by that scene.

Throughout, the events in the Tower of Hunger need to be understood simultaneously as Ugolino's story and as a part of Dante's own narrative. Ugolino's story will represent a model of perversion and concealment; in a manner consistent with his psychology as a traitor, Ugolino displays the extent to which intellect and language can conspire with the frailty of physical nature so as to aggravate even the most extreme disasters. Yet, when seen as a part of Dante's own story, the same tragic account reveals the one resource that we possess in confronting our end. There will be no answer in terms of general consequence or dogma to the problem of suffering; any such answer would be likely to evade the impact and implication of the particular case. Here, as in Canto xxvIII, the pretensions of language and judgement give way, and the eye is called upon to witness an image of humanity in all its contradictions, weaknesses and violence.

This is the case from the first lines of the canto:

> La bocca sollevò dal fiero pasto
> quel peccator, forbendola a' capelli
> del capo ch'elli avea di retro guasto.   (xxxIII 1–3)

(His mouth he lifted from the savage food, / that sinner, wiping it on the hair / of the head he had ravaged behind.)

On any account this is a powerful opening; it is the more so in context. In the first place, the *terzina* marks a complete change of linguistic direction from the line which introduced Ugolino at the conclusion of Canto xxxII. Horrific as the first sight of the sinner had been, Dante's language initially registered only a dead factuality, overlaid with a high degree of rhetorical polish. The horror of the scene was expressed through a classical analogue, as if Dante were either vying – once again – with a Latin exemplar or framing and distancing the lurid spectacle by means of sophisticated allusion:

> non altrimenti Tidëo si rose
> le tempie a Menalippo per disdegno ...   (xxxII 130–1)

(in just this way Tydeus gnawed / the temples of Menalippus in his anger...)

Likewise, when the protagonist speaks, his words, though attentive to detail are cast in commandingly rhetorical tones and contain – for all the dreadful absurdity of the scene – a demand that Ugolino should offer a rational explanation of how he came to be where he is:

> 'O tu che mostri per sì bestial segno
> odio sovra colui che tu ti mangi,
> dimmi 'l perché', diss' io ...   (xxxII 133–5)

('O thou who declarest by such a beast-like showing / thy hatred towards the man that you eat, / tell me the cause,' I said).

When Ugolino begins to speak his words will not at first be very different in register from those of the protagonist in these earlier lines; and, in requesting an account of the 'perché', Dante is simply displaying the same trust in narrative, as a register of moral consequence, which he showed in his earliest encounters in Hell.

Yet, with the opening of Canto xxxIII, there occurs a radical interruption of linguistic and narrative procedure. Not for the first time, classical allusion evaporates before a single and brutally disconcerting detail. Indeed, even syntax and logical emphasis are now displaced; for, while 'bocca' is the grammatical object of the sentence, the word is strong enough in its visual impact to outweigh the true subject of the sentence – 'quel peccator' – and to distract attention from the explicit judgement expressed in that designation.

Similarly, the simple line of description is broken by a verbal stroke demanding that the imagination should work upon the implications of 'bocca', regardless of narrative logic. In his use of the canto-break, Dante has invariably shown how far his narrative is from pursuing plain sequence. Here, the canto-break stimulates, so to speak, a dreadful lyric fascination at the way in which the image of the mouth rhymes and resonates with comparable images in its vicinity. In the ghastly etiquette which leads Ugolino to wipe the slaver of blood and brains from his lips with the hair of his victim, one sees the extent to which the 'bocca' image in the cantos of treachery inverts or parodies courtesy and refinement: where courtesy, at its best, is respect, freely given, for the identity of another person, treachery aims at possession and is figured forth in this more-than-bestial preying of one man on another. At the same time, the word 'bocca' here prepares for the subsequent developments in the canto, where the 'mouth' will emphasise both the tragic reliance of the human being upon food and also our tragic inability to govern or control the words which mark us off from the beasts. In the Tower of Hunger, suffering is caused not only by the pangs of starvation, but also by the uncomforted cry in which suffering itself is voiced.

In his opening verse, then, Dante has established already an understanding of the contradictions in the human being, from the heights of sophistication, through natural appetite to the utmost depravity. And, so far from inviting analysis or explanation, the same image points – as surely as do the tortured tongues of Canto xxviii – to the inadequacies and inherent treacheries of speech. For this same blood-stained mouth will speak throughout the first half of the canto, attempting to consume its victim, Ruggieri, as much by expressions of judgement and condemnation as by physical force. Here, certainly, the sinner is cast as judge. It is as painful for Ugolino to speak as it was for Bocca degli Abati. He nonetheless insists upon speaking; he is determined, quite single-mindedly that his words will bring notoriety upon Ruggieri, who is now as much the speaker's victim as, once, the speaker was his.

Already a distinction is apparent between Ugolino and Dante as narrators. Dante's pursuit of judgement – if not wholly suspended – is at least transferred to Ugolino, and, in conceiving the first image of the canto, the poet has laid himself, and his reader, open to the extreme perversities of human behaviour. Likewise, in Dante's own text the subsequent story of incarceration, darkness, starvation and death will be offered as an increasingly complex emblem of the human condition at large. Ugolino, on the contrary, has a particular and unswervingly malicious end in view. For him, every word he speaks is intended to defame Ruggieri, and, as we shall see, he seeks – unsuccessfully – to keep at bay the complexities of emotion and thought which the images of his own predicament generate. Like Ulysses, Ugolino aims to master his audience, imposing upon them a palpable design – as he does upon his victim – and never pausing to admit the insufficiencies of that design. In this respect, the attitude he adopts towards the protagonist is significant. Unlike the sowers of discord, he shows no interest at all in the miraculous fact of Dante's presence in Hell: his only concern is that his interlocutor is a Florentine and a contemporary, who – knowing the details of Pisan history – will be able to supply essential background to his tale of hatred:

> Io no so chi tu se' né per che modo
> venuto se' qua giù; ma fiorentino
> mi sembri veramente quand' io t'odo.   (XXXIII 10–12)

(I do not know who you are, nor by what means / you have come down here. / But when I hear you speak, you seem to me truly [a Florentine].)

Both the protagonist and Ruggieri are then, *possessed* by Ugolino and made a part of his plan. But the same may be said of Ugolino himself. Unlike most of the figures whom Dante meets in the lower circles of Hell, Ugolino is fully prepared to identify himself without being asked:

> Tu dei saer ch'i' fui conte Ugolino.   (13)

(You need to know that I was Count Ugolino.)

There is no pride in this: Ugolino declares himself only to initiate revenge for the wrong that has been done to him. His own name and dignity – subordinated to his overmastering purpose – are themselves instruments of his hatred.

The story of the Tower of Hunger does not begin until line 21 of the canto, but the preceding six *terzine* are important in illustrating the principal characteristics of Ugolino's voice and – so to say – of his narrative technique. Three main features emerge: elevation of style (to begin with, at least), intensity of phrase and fragmentation of rhythm. Each of these features in turn can be viewed ironically in the perspective of Dante's own story; and the fragmentation of rhythm, which is especially evident in the concluding parts of the whole speech, serves to indicate how Ugolino will ultimately fail in his attempt to control the action which his story sets in motion.

Consider his opening *terzina*:

> Poi cominciò: 'Tu vuo' ch'io rinovelli
> disperato dolor che 'l cor mi preme
> già pur pensando, pria ch'io ne favelli'.   (4–6)

(Then he began: 'You wish me to renew / the desperate grief that [even as I think about it,] presses at my heart / before I begin to speak.')

These lines are not only as elevated as those of the protagonist in Canto XXXII, but also allude to the high style of the *Aeneid*, where, in Book II 3, Aeneas declares: 'infandum, regina, iubes renovare dolorem'. Yet, for all the strength of Ugolino's rhetoric, his words are penetrated by ironic suggestions beyond his control and alien to his intent. In the context of the eternal ice, where nothing can ever be 'renewed', the verb 'rinovellare' carries implications which reveal the sterility of the sinner's purpose; and a similar perversity or emptiness is apparent in his use of the images of seed and fruit:

Ma se le mie parole esser dien seme
che frutti infamia al traditor ch'i' rodo,
parlare e lagrimar vedrai insieme.   (7–9)

(But if my words are to be the seed / which bears as fruit the infamy of the traitor whom I gnaw, / you will see me weep and speak together.)

The irony here reveals the moral charge against Ugolino; and if one appreciates this at all, it is because the words that Ugolino speaks are not – as he supposes them to be – merely his own possession, but rather belong to, and proceed from, the unspeaking pattern of imagery that Dante himself has instituted in his text.

Similar pressures are brought to bear upon the affective or emotional aspects of Ugolino's speech. It is typical of him that he should seek to invest every part of his utterance with an intense emotional energy. Indeed, when he proclaims that he will weep and speak 'together' – 'insieme' – he employs a rhetorical figure which is regularly associated with effects of pathos. Likewise, at the height of his narrative, he appeals directly to the emotions of his audience in an oratorical bid for pity:

Ben se' crudel, se tu già non ti duoli
pensando ciò che 'l mio cor s'annunziava.   (40–1)

(You are truly cruel if you do not already grieve, / thinking of that which my heart then foretold.)

One need not *deny* the pathos of this moment; yet there is an unmistakable contradiction in the fact that Ugolino should appeal for pity at all. Here he voices the assumption that a capacity for pity is a mark of humanity, as if his own intensely pathetic words might test or revive a bond of essential sympathy between one person and another. Dante himself, as we shall see, would agree with such an assumption. Yet it rings false in the mouth of Ugolino, not only because his speech is directed by voracious hatred, but also because, in the Tower of Hunger, his own silence, when faced with the distresses of his children, firmly resisted any such claim.

The emotional intensity of the speech is closely akin to a certain intellectual intensity: Ugolino persistently attempts to annihilate the distinction between past, present and future, collapsing all time into a single point of imprisonment and death. Francesca was overcome by the 'sol punto' in the text she was reading; Ugolino is subject to a process of increasing constriction, focusing at last upon his own lonely death. But from the outset his words reflect and mimic that constriction. He will speak and weep *insieme*; and even before he speaks of the Tower of Hunger, a desperate grief 'already' presses down upon his heart: 'che 'l cor mi preme / già pur pensando, pria ch'io ne favelli' (5–6).

Were it not for the background of eternal ice against which he speaks, this characteristic might seem to be a strong psychological motive, expressing the obsessions of Ugolino's imagination. Yet the image of the ice calls to mind that eternity is a condition in which time has indeed been compressed into fixity: only in the infinite mind of God can the 'sol punto' that Ugolino seeks be found. Dante will eventually see that point in Canto XXVIII of the *Paradiso*. But for Ugolino it is one of the final conditions of damnation – foreshadowed in the 'split' vision of Farinata – that the mind should be condemned to spell out its experiences in constant repetition of the temporal sequence in which it had first imprisoned itself.

Ugolino seeks to omit from his story all references which do not bear upon the single case of his hatred for Ruggieri. But the passage in which he attempts his elimination begins to display the third major feature of his speech, its fragmentation and dislocation of rhythm:

> Che per l'effetto de' suo' mai pensieri,
> fidandomi di lui, io fossi preso
> e poscia morto, dir non è mestieri;
>   però quel che non puoi avere inteso,
> cioè come la morte mia fu cruda,
> udirai, e saprai s'e' m'ha offeso. (16–21)

(That as a result of his evil designs, / trusting him, I was taken / and then killed, there is no need to say; / however, that which you cannot have heard – / that is, how cruel was my death – / you will hear now and know whether he has offended me or done me wrong.)

One notes the tortured inversion of syntax, most significantly in the emotional intrusion of the parenthesis: 'cioè come la morte mia fu cruda'; one notes too that here, as throughout the speech, the tenses of the verbs range in confusion over all points on the temporal scale, from the continuative 'fidandomi di lui' to the past absolute 'io fossi preso', and into the future – 'udirai', 'saprai'.

In his attempt to find clear words in which to judge Ruggieri, Ugolino is comparable to Bertran de Born; in his search for the eternally present moment, he is as self-defeating and frustrated as Adam of Brescia in *his* desire for the waters of the Casentino.

Dante himself, however, by this stage of the *Inferno* has developed a way of dealing with the problem that Ugolino faces. On the one hand, the narrative is gradual, resisting any premature attempt to grasp the point of synthesis; on the other, Dante constantly allows the revelatory impact of the *image* to interrupt the steady progress of his tale. Now, as Ugolino attempts to command in words the full horror of the scene in the Tower, the images that this story produces constitute – for the eye that can bear to look at them – a silent chorus to the tragic and ultimately futile attempts of language. The sequence begins:

> Breve pertugio dentro da la Muda,
> la qual per me ha 'l titol de la fame,
> e che conviene ancor ch'altrui si chiuda
>   m'avea mostrato per lo suo forame
> più lune già quand' io feci 'l mal sonno . . .   (22–6)

(A little hole in the wall of the Mew, / which has taken from me the title of hunger / – and which must still close others in – / had shown through its slit / many moons to me already, when I had the bad dream.)

Three features here express Ugolino's attempts at mastery. First, one notes the parenthesis in which he urgently associates his own case with the title of the Tower; earlier he names himself so as to defame Ruggieri; now he does not hesitate to identify himself with the source of his own miseries – the be-all and end-all of his existence, temporal and eternal. In the second place – characteristically projecting his thoughts into the future – Ugolino insinuates the menacing suggestion that others, too, will suffer the fate he suffered; future time is, for Ugolino, composed – and discomposed – in the shadow of 'his' Tower. Thirdly, the syntax itself here describes a sustained – if tremulous – arc of parentheses and subordinate clauses: commandingly, Ugolino's voice presses forward over the details of the scene to arrive at the precise moment when – in line 26 – he can speak of the dream that prophesied his death.

It is, however, these same details that arrest the eye, establishing in imagination a cross-rhythm against Ugolino's voice. Imagistically, the lines are no less reverberant than the opening *terzina*. So, 'breve pertugio dentro' – insisting upon notions of constriction and concentration – is directly linked with the 'forame' of line 25. Light is admitted into the scene only to emphasise the absence and unattainability of light. And if the 'mouth' of line 1 points to the fundamental needs of the human being, the chink of light in the wall also indicates the way in which those needs, when denied, can themselves become a form of imprisonment. The human being is confined not only by his enemies, but also by his own reliance upon bread, upon light, or even upon the simple scheme of time – which is registered in the Tower only by the sinister light of the moon shining through a little crack. The mind may seek to concentrate upon the single moment, but, frozen into that moment, it will remain imprisoned in its own constructions and alienated from its proper nature.

These implications are consolidated by the word 'Muda'. The Tower – before Ugolino stamped it with his own tragedy – was named the 'Mew', a stable for hunting-birds. In the *Purgatorio*, Dante will repeatedly refer to the image of the falcon as an emblem for the highest aspirations of the spirit (for instance at *Purg.* XIX 64–9); the human being can be trained, by sufferings, to return to its divine Master. Here the emphasis falls upon the interruption of any such aspiration. Movement, in time or eternity, is as much the natural end of man as flight is the 'end' of the falcon; but it is just as common, though not *natural*, that human beings should turn their own 'training-ground' into a prison in which that end is betrayed.

From the perspective of the *Purgatorio*, it is clear how Ugolino, like Pier della Vigna before him (but unlike that other prisoner, Boethius, or any of the penitents), betrays himself, by refusing to translate the concentration of view that his prison imposes upon him into a moment of insight. In place

of revelation, there is only nightmare; and, though Ugolino's account of his
dream is the first climax of his narrative, this climax – like the subsequent
account of his death – is one in which finality and certitude are themselves
the source of yet more intense anxiety. The urgent rhythms of the preparatory
terzine dissolve at the point of crisis into dream, 'seeming' and unspeakable
suggestion:

> quand' io feci 'l mal sonno
> che del futuro mi squarciò 'l velame.
> Questi pareva a me maestro e donno,
> cacciando il lupo e ' lupicini al monte
> per che i Pisan veder Lucca non ponno.
> Con cagne magre, studïose e conte
> Gualandi con Sismondi e con Lanfranchi
> s'avea messi dinanzi da la fronte.
> In picciol corso mi parieno stanchi
> lo padre e ' figli, e con l'agute scane
> mi parea lor veder fender li fianchi.   (26–36)

(... when I had the bad dream / which ripped the veil of the future open to me. / This
man (Ruggieri) appeared to me as a master and lord, / hunting the wolf and his whelps
on that mountain / which makes it impossible for the Pisans to see Lucca. / With lean
bitches, eager and sharp, / [he had sent ahead] the Gualandi with the Sismondi and
Lanfranchi. / After a short run, the father and the children seemed to me to tire, / and it
seemed that I saw their flanks torn open [by the sharp fangs].)

Here, even the structure of Ugolino's own subconscious imprisons him.
For a moment, he displays that same mental capacity to leap beyond the con-
fines of the present which, in Dante's case, produces the vision – or 'high
dream' – of the *Commedia*. Here too Ugolino does reach a moment of syn-
thesis. Anticipating the conclusions of latter-day dream psychology, the pas-
sage is governed by effects of condensation, transference and substitution:
Ugolino is the victim of the hunt, yet confesses to his own ferocity in pictur-
ing himself as a wolf at all; likewise, his own pangs of hunger are translated
into the sharp fangs of the hunting-dogs. But this inward concentration is as
cruel and destructive for Ugolino as it was for Adam of Brescia.

The same passage, however, is also a contribution to Dante's own tragic
dream of violence – comparable to the violent inner landscape that was
evoked, in Canto xxvii, with the vision of the Romagna, and similar also to
the vision that Dante will attribute to Guido del Duca in *Purgatorio* xiv.
Here, the images offer a particularly acute sense of contradiction. The only
image of an open landscape and free movement that the canto contains is
equally an image of fixity and enclosure: for the action – following the
sudden tearing of the veil, expressed in a past historic (27) – is itself one of
stasis or indirection designated by imperfects and gerunds. Even the hills
provide no simple or natural perspective, but are said to *obstruct* the view
from Pisa to Lucca in a suggestion of confinement, enmity and division.
Moreover, Dante here begins a play upon the polar oppositions of internal
and external which will now continue until the end of the canto. In the

second half, indeed he will suggest that a human being can, so to speak, be imprisoned from the *inside*, by the indwelling presence of a demon. Not only does the dream prove to be no release; it is also part of an internal prison which immures Ugolino in the cold certainty that his food will fail.

The certainties that the dream communicates precipitate a crisis; the mind is tested against the intense perception of its own inevitable fate; but neither in the Tower nor in Hell does Ugolino have the resources to deal with this perception. Waking from his dream, he is now faced with the dreadful conformity between the dream itself and the reality of his imprisonment. But in Hell – so far from allowing the impact of this synthesis to make its own effect – Ugolino summons up words to make his most overt and eloquent pitch for the sympathy of his audience – 'Ben se' crudel ...' (40). In the Tower, on the other hand – at precisely the same point – Ugolino begins the long silence which lasts until all his children are dead. Both discourse and silence in Ugolino's case are treacherous: it is only in Hell that he acknowledges the demands of feeling; and, ironically enough, when he speaks of silence, he does so either with a rhetorical flourish or with pretensions to stoic dignity:

> Queta'mi allor per non farli più tristi;
> lo dì e l'altro stemmo tutti muti;
> ahi dura terra, perché non t'apristi?   (64–6)

(Then I made myself silent so as not to make them the sadder. / That day and the next we all stayed silent; / ah stony earth, why do you not open?)

As Ugolino awakes, he hears his own presentiments echoed in the sleeping cries of his children. Here too there is a 'synthesis', as dream reciprocates dream. But the synthesis is one which conceivably *could* be spelled out in terms of human community and mutual comfort, and the same is true at the next crisis, which occurs with the final locking of the gate. That act emphasises the utter dependence of one being on another, for sustenance and freedom; but it also emphasises the primal kinship of hunger and fear, and it is this kinship that Ugolino betrays, locking himself into final and absolute silence:

> e io senti' chiavar l'uscio di sotto
> a l'orribile torre; ond' io guardai
> nel viso a' mie' figliuoi sanza far motto.   (46–8)

(I heard below the locking / of the dreaful tower; and so I gazed / in the faces of my children and uttered no word.)

From this point on, as inwardly Ugolino petrifies, his language in Hell loses all its earlier pretension to command:

> Io non piangëa, sì dentro impetrai:
> piangevan elli; e Anselmuccio mio
> disse: 'Tu guardi sì, padre! che hai?'   (49–51)

(I did not weep, I grew so stony within; / they wept; and my little Anselm / said: 'You look so, father; what is wrong with you?')

Ugolino's speech now becomes increasingly marked by the fragmentation of rhythm already evident in this *terzina*. Moreover, voices other than Ugolino's own are allowed to interrupt and punctuate the final phases of the action. And in two ways these voices – no less than Dante's own – contrast with the voice of the sinner that records them. First, in response to the crisis of imprisonment, the children offer an alternative to the monumental heroism of Ugolino. Linguistically too, where Ugolino evokes the voices of the children only to serve his own single and vengeful purpose, their words possess an independence and a freedom of suggestion which together reveal the emptiness of that purpose.

So it is left to the children to express not only the natural emotion that the events in the Tower call forth, but also a sublimely *un*natural spirit of self-sacrifice in offering their own bodies for Ugolino to eat:

> e disser: 'Padre, assai ci fia men doglia
> se tu mangi di noi: tu ne vestisti
> queste misere carni, e tu le spoglia'. (61–3)

(and they said: 'Father it would pain us less / if you were to eat of our [bodies]: you clothed us / in this wretched flesh, you may dispoil us of it'.)

The heroism of Ugolino is here contrasted with an instinct for martyrdom which foreshadows the ethic of the *Purgatorio*. At the same time, it is notable that the response of the children arises not from clear understanding but from a *mis*reading of Ugolino's actions: where Ugolino bites his hands in melodramatic grief or fortitude, the children translate this into the elemental language of appetite. Ambiguity itself has here a value of its own, against the domination of clear – or cruelly sophisticated – purpose, and this is increasingly evident. Approaching the climax of the story, Ugolino's own language breaks down into bare and starkly factual utterances in which his initial intentions are wholly defeated or forgotten. The words of the children, however, are surrounded by an aura of liturgical or religious implication as irrelevant to Ugolino's aim as were the imagistic suggestions of his opening verses. So the first report of how the children asked, simply, for bread (39) echoes the words of the Lord's Prayer; while similarly, when Gaddo cries out at the point of death

> Padre mio, ché non m'aiuti? (69)

(Father, why do you not help me?)

it is impossible for the reader – though not for Ugolino – to ignore the echo of Christ's words on the Cross: 'My God, my God, why hast thou forsaken me?'

In Gaddo's words lie the possibility of salvation, and of unity with the lonely sufferings of Christ, and, in Christ the community of suffering does have its significance. But Ugolino is deaf to such suggestion, and the last phase of his speech – governed by rhythms which bring him close to inarticulacy – concentrates upon the cold mathematics of death in which no salva-

tion or ultimate resonance of meaning is admitted. As one by one his chil-
dren die, Ugolino, at last, does speak their names into the vacancy; and
nothing could illustrate more forcefully the futility or belatedness of words
than that:

> Quivi morì; e come tu mi vedi,
> vid' io cascar li tre ad uno ad uno
> tra 'l quinto dì e 'l sesto; ond' io mi diedi,
>   già cieco, a brancolar sovra ciascuno,
> e due dì li chiamai, poi che fur morti.
> Poscia, più che 'l dolor, poté 'l digiuno.   (70–5)

(At this he died; and as you see me now, / I saw the three of them, one by one, fall /
between the fifth day and the sixth; at which I began, / already blind, to crawl over each
of them; / and for two days, now that they were dead, I called out their names. / Then
fasting had more power than grief.)

It would be one conclusion to say that Ugolino has refused to pray. The
words of the Lord's Prayer lie beneath the text of the canto, insisting
positively – as Canto XXXIII does *ex negativo* – that all creatures should
recognise their dependence on the being that gave them life, and demanding
that even those who have sinned should be forgiven by those who are them-
selves sinners. When Dante eventually does introduce his own version of the
Lord's Prayer, he ascribes it (in *Purgatorio* XII) to the penitent proud, who
are the first sinners he meets 'locked in' to salvation beyond the Gate of
Purgatory. It is pride to assume that the human mind can encompass its own
ends in purely rational or discursive terms, and the language of prayer –
which is a language of need, community and dependence upon God – is one
which admits and reflects these limitations.

Since at least the appearance of Farinata, Dante has contrasted the illusory
heroism of human beings with their dependence upon the Creator; and in
moral terms, it would be appropriate enough if Dante ended the *cantica* with
an emphasis upon this contrast. Yet it would be out of keeping with the
poetic strategy of Canto XXXIII – and much of the *Inferno* at large – to admit
such an explicit and clear-cut solution. The *Inferno* is a test of what can be
said and done in the absence of explicitly Christian remedies. In pursuit of
this almost agnostic theme, Dante, in the opening cantos of the *cantica*, has
explored the extent to which reason alone can deal with sin, while in the
Malebolge he has painfully recognised the inadequacy of that resource and,
increasingly in the last cantos of the work, has seen the extent to which
human beings can be trapped and imprisoned in their own constructions.
Canto XXXIII is a canto of total loneliness. Even the words of Christ which are
remembered most directly here are those which express his despair on the
Cross. In *Purgatorio* XXIII, of course, Dante will speak of how 'gladly' Christ
utters his cry of desperation, and by that time, he will be ready to envisage
suffering as part of a paradoxical and miraculous answer to the tragedies of
existence. But such an answer would be premature in *Inferno* Canto XXXIII,
where the reader, no less than Ugolino, has to fix the eye upon the stark

evidence of suffering, without any support from religious or even rational solutions.

So the episode ends with an emblem of mortality in its most pitiable and degraded state, as Ugolino, imprisoned and blind, crawls over the bodies of his children, belatedly breaking his own silence in voicing their names. But the episode also ends on an ambiguity:

Poscia, più che 'l dolor, poté 'l digiuno.   (75)

(And then fasting had more power than grief.)

Either this means that Ugolino's hunger led him to eat the bodies of his children or that, until hunger at last killed him, he had been kept alive by the sharpness of his suffering. We do not, however, need to resolve this ambiguity; the whole episode demands that we should be able to face its warring and insoluble implications. Indeed, it is an indication of how limited Ugolino's mastery is that he should conclude on a line which – so far from incriminating Ruggieri – may point to an horrendous act of which he himself was guilty. As for Dante, the ambiguity is nurtured by everything that has preceded it. We have seen enough to suggest that suffering is the very nerve of life: the animation of Ugolino's children is itself a result of their pangs of hunger, and, in that sense, Ugolino may have been kept alive by grief. Equally, it is impossible to ignore the suggestion of *post-mortem* cannibalism in a context where Ugolino is gnawing the head of Ruggieri, where his children actually offer their bodies as food, and where Satan is shortly seen eating the bodies of three traitors.

The time, however, for adding a further charge to the case against Ugolino is past. With the ambiguity of the final line we are now concerned again with the subversion of judgement. From the first, the canto has operated at the very limits of what is tolerable or can be reduced to a scheme of judgement: the blood-stained mouth with which it begins is a parody of all human decency, the scene in the Tower a parody of a domestic interior. But, at last, Dante goes further than that, and enters a realm where there is no comfort, and where even the Christian associations which are so richly evoked by the words of the children have no competence to assuage or pacify. The possibility that Ugolino *did* eat his children touches a chord that lies in the area of taboo, not of morality. Judgement is powerless here; the only response will be one of shame and pain at the potentialities which are here acknowledged to be a part of human nature; and if morality lives at all in such a region it will draw its energy from outrage not from judgement – from the agony of the offended nerve.

So, for a moment the voice of the poet does indeed break through the fiction both of Ugolino's story and of his own narrative, in tones where savage indignation and pity are inextricably mixed:

Ahi Pisa, vituperio de le genti
del bel paese là dove 'l sì suona,
poi che i vicini a te punir son lenti,

muovasi la Capraia e la Gorgona,
e faccian siepe ad Arno in su la foce,
sì ch'elli annieghi in te ogne persona!
   Che se 'l conte Ugolino aveva voce
d'aver tradita te de le castella,
non dovei tu i figliuoi porre a tal croce.
   Innocenti facea l'età novella,
novella Tebe, Uguiccione e 'l Brigata
e li altri due che 'l canto suso appella.   (79–90)

(Ah, Pisa, shame of the people / of the lovely land where the 'si' sounds, / since your neighbours are so slow to punish you, / let the Caprara and Gorgona move, / and make a bar across the Arno at its mouth, / so that every one of your people be drowned. / For even if Count Ugolino has been said / to have betrayed your castles, / you ought not to have put his sons to such a torment. / Their youth made them innocent, / new Thebes – Uguiccione, Brigata / and the other two whom my song names above.)

In these lines Dante wholly eludes the grip that Ugolino has sought to exert over the protagonist, saying nothing that contributes to the infamy of Ruggieri. Nor does he reassert the law of the *contrappasso*, or underline any aspect of his own judgement upon Ruggieri. Ugolino is last seen, almost in caricature, setting his strong teeth into the skull of Ruggieri like a dog (76–8); but the voice of the poet's natural indignation breaks through the perversity of that fictional image, calling upon the enemies of Pisa to harness nature itself against the corruption which is rife in that city. There is, certainly, a wild and extravagant cruelty in Dante's desire to see the whole population of Pisa drowned for its crimes against humanity, but it is an extravagance of voice, tone and emotion, not of cold ingenuity. After the imprisonment of emotion which Dante has hitherto been depicting, the very spontaneity of this passage is cathartic.

The same catharsis produces the moral poise of the second set of *terzine*. Here the judgement against Ugolino is relegated to a subordinate clause – as if, finally, it were an irrelevance whether he were guilty of treachery or not. The voice now responds immediately to the case of the children – even to the extent of lightly repeating the Christian suggestions that their voices have carried: 'porre a tal *croce*'. Truth at this point appears to reside in pity, not in judgement; and here Dante begins to admit – as he will throughout the *Purgatorio* – the primacy of that simple concern of one person for another which he was obliged to treat so tentatively in his first meeting with Francesca.

In his meeting with the simoniac popes, Dante allowed the authority of his own text to be broken by the urgent simplicity of scriptural voices, in order to arrive at judgements more compelling than the text itself could encompass. So, too, in the present case – though the source from which Dante draws his vocabulary is that of natural emotion rather than Scripture.

At the same time, as Dante returned to the plan of his text in Canto xx after the indignant excursus of Canto XIX, he expressed weariness at the task of finding 'new material for the twentieth canto of the first *cantica*'; subsequently the pressure of achieving such novelty led him to the barrators sequence and the 'nuovo ludo' of his own burlesque virtuosity. A similar pattern can be observed in the second half of Canto XXXIII as Dante returns to his fiction to finish his journey and fill out the appointed space: 'Noi passammo oltre' (91) – We passed beyond. Ends, strictly, may be unreachable, yet Dante cannot literally leave the *cantica* unfinished. (He is, after all, not Spenser; nor is he Michelangelo, who could make a virtue of the unfinished.) So, in the *Inferno* judgement – and artifice – return, but cast now in the same mode of cruel farce as characterised the barrators sequence, and also the conclusion of Canto XXXII.

The result is a masterpiece of 'dead poetry', in which the inadequacies of language are fully revealed, and where the narrative itself breaks into at least four separate movements, each as distinct from the other in tone as they are, taken together, from the first half of the canto.

One cannot ignore this sequence – which is a major instance of Dante's encounter with the difficulties of his own enterprise. The protagonist, certainly, is subjected again to cold observation, and proves himself to be as treacherous in his treatment of Frate Alberigo as he was vicious towards Bocca degli Abati. The poet too, writing in a style which he will never again adopt in the *Commedia*, introduces a sequence which not only erodes the tragic achievements of the Ugolino episode, but also casts a light of lurid comedy over much that has characterised the thought and procedure of the whole *Inferno*.

This is most evident in the final episode of the canto. Here, in his last direct encounter with any human sinner in Hell, Dante entertains the fantastic – and heretical – notion that the human soul may be taken to Hell even before the day of its death, leaving the body apparently alive but in fact inhabited by a devil. The protagonist is astonished to learn from Frate Alberigo that a certain Branca Doria is already in Hell, although historically his death was not recorded until after 1325:

> 'Io credo', diss' io lui, 'che tu m'inganni;
> ché Branca Doria non morì unquanche,
> e mangia e bee e dorme e veste panni'.
> 'Nel fosso sù', diss' el, 'de' Malebranche,
> là dove bolle la tenace pece,
> non era ancora giunto Michel Zanche,
> che questi lasciò il diavolo in sua vece
> nel corpo suo, ed un suo prossimano
> che 'l tradimento insieme con lui fece.'   (139–47)

('I think,' I said to him, 'that you are fooling me; / for Branca Doria never died; / he eats and drinks and sleeps and puts on clothes.' / '[Michel Zanche had not yet arrived] in the ditch of the Malebranche,' he said, / 'where the clinging pitch boils / when that man left a devil instead of himself / in his own body, as occurred also to one of his kinsmen / who did the treacherous deed along with him.')

There can be no doubt about the narrative impact of this conception; and, out of context, it might well be taken as an adequate summary of Dante's theme: human beings can fall totally into the power of the devil; and no one can trust another, for fear that he might be a devil in disguise. Yet in thought and style the passage is perverse, and quite out of keeping with the expectations that the *Inferno*, and in particular Canto XXXIII, has raised. In terms of thought, the passage is not only heretical, but also trivialises the two most essential principles of Dante's Christianity: first, his understanding of the union of body and soul as both a sacred and a logical necessity; and, secondly, his belief in the absolute responsibility of the human will, acting within the sphere that temporal and physical nature defines for it. The sanctified figure of Beatrice embodies the first of these truths; the second is driven home in every judgement that Dante passes upon the sinners in Hell, not least upon Ugolino, who, even *in extremis*, is judged by the failure of his responsibility towards his children. Yet neither of these principles could stand if the Devil had power to usurp the sovereignty of will and expel the soul from occupation of its allotted time and place.

In the Gianni Schicchi episode, Dante considered with moral horror the possibility that the temporal pattern of life – being denied a properly solemn end – might dwindle into absurdity and delusion. Yet in the last moments of the *cantica*, the poet who began so gravely 'nel mezzo del cammin' is prepared to invent a story in which the austere image of a pilgrimage is replaced by a comic invention – shot through with elements of fairy-tale and primitive superstition: 'ends' – both literary and moral – are here in a state of thorough confusion.

A similar reversal occurs in the imagery of the concluding passage, which pointedly negates and debases the moral emblems of the Ugolino episode. As we have seen, the first half of the canto places considerable emphasis upon the polarities of internal and external in its portrayal of both actual and psychological imprisonment. These contrasts are now treated almost wittily, as the subject for conceited verbal play. Branca's body continues to live according to the rhythms of temporal life, but his soul is imprisoned in Hell: the inner self is absent, yet it shackles Branca to his destiny more surely than any earthly prison. Likewise, where the Ugolino episode sees tragedy in the day-to-day activities of eating and sleeping, the Branca passage casts a light of surreal comedy over these same activities, in the almost dead-pan phrase which records how the body of the sinner still 'eats, drinks, sleeps and clothes itself'.

The Branca sequence is, then, a desperate imaginative squib – as Dante all but admits when the protagonist declares 'I think you are fooling me' (139). A similar spirit of anarchic equivocation also runs through the exchange between Dante and Frate Alberigo. Earlier, ambiguity was part of the test which Dante set in seeking to avoid the destructive clarity of Ugolino's purpose; in the second half of the canto, language veers constantly towards pun or total misapplication.

This conversation begins with a misapprehension, as Alberigo mistakes Dante and Virgil for two souls so heinous as to be destined for a place alongside Judas, Cassius and Brutus:

> gridò a noi: 'O anime crudeli
> tanto che data v'è l'ultima posta,
>   levatemi dal viso i duri veli,
> sì ch'ïo sfoghi 'l duol che 'l cor m'impregna,
> un poco, pria che 'l pianto si raggeli'.   (110–14)

(he cried out to us: 'O souls so cruel / that the last place of all is allotted to you, / lift these hard veils from my face, / so that I might give vent to the sorrow growing to fullness at my heart / – a little at least before weeping again freezes over.')

This same passage contains two further instances of word-play which implicate poetic phraseology itself in the charge of banality. Out of context the phrase 'duri veli' is rich in its complex suggestion of contrasting tactile effects. Yet the 'veli' are not veils at all, but rather windows revealing to view the nature of the sinner; and to speak of them as veils is to conceal, with a verbal flourish, the moral function of the punishment that Alberigo suffers. Likewise, when Alberigo speaks of his heart being 'pregnant with pain' he repeats the imagery of seed and fruition which stamped the opening of Ugolino's speech; yet he avoids the moral horror of treachery in which, as Ugolino so openly declares, hatred itself can mimic the processes of cultivation and fruition. Finally, Alberigo's very identity and past history fragment into punning references as the sinner recounts the act which brought him to Hell. Under the guise of hospitality he betrayed his guest to death. His name carries suggestions both of tree, 'albero' and safe resting-place, 'albergo'; and both senses have a place in his canting references to orchards, fruit and yield:

> Rispuose adunque: 'I' son frate Alberigo;
> i' son quel da le frutta del mal orto,
> che qui riprendo dattero per figo'.   (118–20)

(Then he replied: 'I am Frate Alberigo: / I am he of the fruit of the evil orchard. / And here I am repaid with date for fig.' [*that is*: *I got more than I bargained for*].')

Beneath its flippancy, this speech recalls how, as a signal for an assassination, Alberigo called for fruit at a banquet where his victims were assembled. The disproportion between the enormity of the deed and the frivolity both of the gesture and of Alberigo's account of it is paralleled at line 124 by the weak irony – or simple laxity – of the phrase which suggests that the circles of treachery have the 'advantage' of receiving sinners still alive from earth:

> Cotal vantaggio ha questa Tolomea,
> che spesse volte l'anima ci cade
> innanzi ch'Atropòs mossa le dea.   (124–6)

(Tolomea has this advantage, / that often souls fall into it / before Atropos has caused them to move.)

But the protagonist is not himself immune to comparable triviality. It is he indeed who – in preparation for the act of betrayal with which the episode ends – equivocates on the very nature of his journey, vowing that he will go down to the very core of the ice rather than fail in his promise to Alberigo:

> dimmi chi se', e s'io non ti disbrigo,
> al fondo de la ghiaccia ir mi convegna.   (116–17)

(Tell me who you are, and if I do not disencumber you, / let me rightly go down to the depths of the ice.)

Dante, as protagonist, is living proof that it *is* possible to descend into Hell before death and still escape. (He is both a parallel to Branca d'Oria and a contradiction of the heresy implied in the story of Branca.) But now he plays upon the central features of that myth as cruelly and irresponsibly as he did in *Inferno* XXXII. The moral journey itself is becoming a 'nuovo ludo'.

Dante's own narrative structure provides, then, material for barren witticism. But, in conclusion, it is the language of this part of the canto that reveals how far Dante now is from his true imaginative home.

Consider his description of the icy tears that form on the face of the sinners:

> Lo pianto stesso lì pianger non lascia,
> e 'l duol che truova in su li occhi rintoppo,
> si volge in entro a far crescer l'ambascia;
>   ché le lagrime prime fanno groppo,
> e sì come visiere di cristallo,
> rïempion sotto 'l ciglio tutto il coppo.   (94–9)

(Weeping itself does not let them weep there, / and the grief which finds a stopper at the eyes / turns itself inward to increase the anguish; / for the tears first form a cluster, / and then, like a visor of crystal / fill up the whole receptacle beneath the eyebrow.)

This passage has aptly been described as baroque in its willed artificiality, but it also carries to a high degree Dante's erosive play upon the conceptual bases of the present canto. The wit of the passage thus derives from the depiction of a process in which the process itself produces interruption: imprisonment increases in relation to the free expression of grief; grief breeds tears, but tears produce only an obstacle to grief. The themes of freedom, spontaneity and sincerity which Dante first raised in the moral discussion of treachery are here lost – as also in the phrases 'duri veli' and 'cor s'impregna' – beneath the brilliance of rhetorical artifice.

In the Ugolino episode, one saw how urgently Dante recognised the need for words which could express emotion simply and directly. A comparable need is portrayed in this final punishment: the weeping of the sinners is as natural and – to them – as destructive as Ugolino's need for food. In our conclusion we shall see the extent of Dante's own concern with such simplicity of expression; but Canto XXXIII ends with an illustration of how difficult it is to achieve or maintain this spontaneity. Here, momentarily, Dante appears to break through his own artifice in a repetition of his outburst against the Pisans:

> Ahi Genovesi, uomini diversi
> d'ogne costume e pien d'ogne magagna,
> perché non siete voi del mondo spersi?
>   Ché col peggiore spirto di Romagna
> trovai di voi un tal, che per sua opra
> in anima in Cocito già si bagna,
>   e in corpo par vivo ancor di sopra.   (151–7)

(Ah you Genoese, men set apart / from all good behaviour and full of all kinds of corruption, / why are you not driven out from the world. / For, along with the worst spirit of Romagna, / I found one of your number, who by his deeds / already bathes as a soul in Cocytus / and in body appears still to live above.)

Yet indignation is here contaminated by the narrative conceit of demonic possession. In the concluding line, the pathos of history degenerates once more into fantasy, and it is on this lurid but uncertain note that the canto ends. This is not to suggest that the conceits which Dante has here produced are in themselves poor poetry. Nonetheless, there is reason to think that Dante – in the light of his own poetic aspirations – might have been ashamed of having written them. As we have suggested, a poet who writes a palinode admits at least the possibility of regret over his own literary achievements. And, moving now to a conclusion, we shall see that Dante himself would not have excluded such sentiments. The desire for free and simple utterance was the heartfelt motive of his earlier poetry; in writing a narrative as many-voiced as the *Inferno*, the poet has put in jeopardy, or even risked betraying, the origin and end of that authentic aspiration.

7

Conclusion: dead poetry:
Inferno XXXIII and the *Vita nuova*

This book ends as it began some distance beyond the confines of the *Inferno*. In the introductory chapter, I examined certain cantos of the *Paradiso*, to show how Dante's thinking on questions of justice and love gave us reason to emphasise the instability of the intellectual system that he constructs in the *Inferno*. We also saw in the same chapter, on the evidence of *Purgatorio* XXX, how the difficulty or surprise associated with love and justice, seeing and discourse, could be reflected in the narrative and linguistic structures of the *Commedia*. In conclusion, we might have moved forward once again into the *Purgatorio*, as Dante does at the end of the *Inferno*, to see how the 'living' poetry of that *cantica* depends upon a continual openness to surprise on both a moral and an imaginative plane. Yet the patterns and poetic structures which Dante develops in the *Purgatorio* are already present in his earliest work, the *Vita nuova*, and this work makes it clear that, even before Dante had elaborated the philosophical system which he relies upon in the *Commedia*, certain forms of linguistic and narrative procedure which were to characterise his poetry throughout his life had already established themselves. The *Vita nuova* is not a philosophical work; it is a preliminary to philosophy, and retains that character in all aspects of its structure. Thought hovers here, on the margins of conscious analysis, in the realm of dreams, visions and images. For that reason we may turn to the *Vita nuova* to see in their purest and simplest state the formulae and thematic motifs that underlay the poetry of the *Commedia*. The *Vita nuova* is, poetically, the origin that Dante seeks in the *Purgatorio* and *Paradiso*, as he draws closer to Beatrice. It is also the origin which in the *Inferno* he increasingly betrays; and nowhere is this more apparent than in the dead poetry of the final cantos.

Thus we have already spoken of how treachery may be seen as an extreme perversion of courtesy; and it is, of course, in the *Vita nuova* that Dante first begins to deepen and refine the notions of courtesy that he had received from his forebears, in the tradition of vernacular love-poetry. Already in the *Vita nuova*, the codes of language and behaviour which were embodied in the love-poetry of the troubadours and their Italian imitators had begun to yield a vocabulary in which Dante could speak of the spiritual or existential value of

love. It is clear too that, on Dante's understanding of that code, any moment
of departure from the single-minded love of perfection could be construed as
an act of betrayal. Certainly, Dante is prepared to accuse himself of such a
betrayal, and does so most strikingly in the Earthly Paradise, when Beatrice –
denying the protagonist her smile – records how he deviated at the time of
her death from the love he had originally professed in the *Vita nuova*:

> Quando di carne a spirto era salita,
> e bellezza e virtù cresciuta m'era,
> fu' io a lui men cara e men gradita;
> e volse i passi suoi per via non vera.   (*Purg.* xxx 127–30)

(When I had risen from the flesh to the spirit, / and beauty and virtue had increased in
me, / I was to him less dear and less pleasing; / and he turned his footsteps into untrue
paths.)

In a similar way, we have seen – in examining the significance of mirror
images in the *Commedia* – that all sin is treachery, betraying the nature of
the relationship between Creator and creature. Dante needed no formal the-
ology to teach him this. In the *Vita nuova* an understanding of what that
relationship should truly be is expressed whenever Dante speaks of Beatrice
as a 'miracle' or an 'angel', carrying meaning from beyond her own person:

> Ella si va, sentendosi laudare
> benignamente d'umiltà vestuta;
> e par che sia una cosa venuta
> da cielo in terra a miracol mostrare.
>   ('Tanto gentile ...', *VN* xxvi 5–8)

(She goes on her way, hearing herself praised, / graciously clothed with humility; / and
she seems a creature come down / from heaven to earth to make the miracle known.)

In the final moments of the *Inferno*, the fallen angel Lucifer is the very re-
verse of this. Where pride is the source of Satan's sin, humility in the human
Beatrice is itself the source of legitimate pride and a reason why Dante
should praise her. So, too, where the beauty of Beatrice mirrors the orderli-
ness of God's creation, the brute ugliness of Satan evinces his rejection of
that order. Like every other traitor, Satan absorbs and consumes significance;
his three faces, mechanically gnawing the bodies of Judas, Brutus and
Cassius, still reflect the structure of the Trinity, but they deny all meaning to
that structure.

These issues can be taken to summarise many of the ethical issues which
were raised in the first half of the *Inferno*. Where in the *Vita nuova* – and
also in the *Convivio* – Dante had written so as to celebrate the possibility of
human perfection, in the *Inferno* he realises for a first time the utter imper-
fection of which human beings are capable. But the shock of that realisation,
so far from producing despair, leads him to look at sin as a failure of that
same inherent rationality and spiritual finesse as he had first seen displayed in
Beatrice and will seek to reaffirm in the last two *cantiche* of the *Commedia*.

In conclusion, however, defining the nature of dead poetry, our concern must be not with the ethical principles of the *Commedia*, but with the ethical act of writing. And here the *Vita nuova* enables us to assess the extent to which the *Inferno* develops and disturbs the equilibrium that Dante had achieved in the linguistic and structural features of his earlier writing.

On the question of language, we have seen particularly in Canto ii and in the Capaneus episode of Canto xiv the importance which Dante attaches to praise as an essential function of human speech. But 'praise' is the supreme purpose of Dante's poetry in the *Vita nuova*; and it remains to take seriously the suggestion that Dante himself makes in the *Vita nuova* and in *Purgatorio* xxiv that the key to his own poetic achievement lies in his discovery of the 'praise-style' of 'Donne ch'avete intelletto d'amore ...' (*VN* xix):

> Donne ch'avete intelletto d'amore,
> i' vo' con voi de la mia donna dire,
> non perch'io creda sua laude finire
> ma ragionar per isfogar la mente.

(Ladies who have intelligence of love, / I wish to speak of my Lady with you, / not because I think I shall ever end her praises, / but rather to speak out and express my own mind.)

Here – and in the surrounding chapters of the *Vita nuova* – Dante declares his new-found intention to seek nothing in his love of Beatrice: he will not hope to gain by his devotion to her but, as a poet, will praise her virtues as fully as he knows how. In one respect, this decision represents a considerable ethical achievement, for Dante here disinterestedly admits the distance that must always prevail between himself and the object of his devotion. To realise the importance of that distance, one has only to recall the *rime petrose*, where Dante's violent desire to obliterate the distance between himself and the Lady issues in an assault upon her 'otherness' or distinctive integrity. In that same desire lies the source of the literally consuming hatred which the sinners of lower Hell display towards their victims. At the same time, the opening lines of 'Donne ch'avete ...' mark a technical as well as a moral advance; for, as Dante confirms in the *Purgatorio*, the merit of these lines is to combine art and spontaneity. Dante writes to 'express' his mind, but also recognises that spontaneity is the product not of confused vehemence, but rather of linguistic measure and control whereby a form is created in which the natural and authentic character of the voice can display its full complexity. Thus at lines 6 and 7 Dante – achieving, in response to the humility of Beatrice, his own artistic moderation – asserts that he will not fall into abject ignobility by attempting to write in a style too high for his competence. The result is a fluency of rhythm and refinement of word, remote alike from rhapsody and frustration.

We have seen in Capaneus how far the sinners of the *Inferno* are from any such moderation of word, but Alberigo in *Inferno* xxxiii is given phrases which parody every aspect of 'Donne ch'avete ...' and the praise-style when he demands:

> levatemi dal viso i duri veli,
> sì ch'ïo sfoghi 'l duol che 'l cor m'impregna.
>
> (*Inf.* xxxiii 112–13)

(Take from my face the hard veils, / so that I might give vent to the grief that grows so big at my heart.)

Like Ugolino, the traitor Alberigo is motivated by a determination to possess and destroy, annihilating all distance between himself and others; and the cruellest part of his punishment is that he should be wholly alienated from the springs of spontaneous utterance. To give vent to grief is as much a natural necessity as praise was found to be in the *Vita nuova*; and, in the *Vita nuova*, the style which Dante first conceives in 'Donne ch'avete ...' proves flexible enough to express – in the later *canzoni* 'Donna pietosa ...' and 'Li occhi dolenti ...' – the extent of Dante's grief over Beatrice's death. But writing for Alberigo in the *Inferno* – as Dante's project of judgement demands that he should – the idiom of the praise-style produces only a frustrated and frentic wittiness, as much on Dante's part – in conceiving the punishment of the 'duri veli' – as on the sinner's part.

The crucial feature of the praise-style is the inexpressibility *topos*, which admits at one and the same time the logical limitations of language and the moral distance between the speaker and the object of his contemplation. And it is easy to see from all we have said in the last chapter that the language of praise will at a certain point come to seem wholly at odds with the language of judgement, where the speaker must attempt to affirm his final assessment of others. To speak of dead poetry is to speak, in one sense, of how far Dante has travelled from the praise-style.

But, in a similar way, the *Vita nuova* also provides a gauge, on the level of narrative structure, by which to assess the character of the *Inferno*. For this is a text which from first to last admits and draws strength from its own openness. Thus in the opening chapter of the *Vita nuova* Dante declares that the origins of the work lie beyond its immediate confines in the 'book of memory', and he concludes likewise with an admission that he cannot yet command the words that will be appropriate to his vision of Beatrice:

Appresso questo sonnetto apparve a me una mirabile visione, ne la quale io vidi cose che mi fecero proporre di non dire più di questa benedetta infino a tanto che io potesse più degnamente trattare di lei.   (*VN* xliii)

(After this sonnet, there appeared to me a wonderful vision, in which I saw things that made me determine to say no more of that blessed one until I could treat more worthily of her.)

There is a certain paradox here, for – unlike the *Convivio*, which also precedes the *Commedia* – the *Vita nuova* is, by its own logic, a finished work. Yet the *Convivio* aimed to be a comprehensive – and conclusive – encyclopaedia of knowledge. There could be few clearer indications of the dangers involved in any attempt at intellectual mastery, or, conversely, of the sanity which arises from the recognition of limit. The complexity of Dante's project in the *Inferno* depends upon the interplay between a desire such as Dante conceived in the *Convivio* to be exhaustive and a renewed awareness that a finished work must, like the *Vita nuova*, admit its own proper limits and consequent openness.

The whole organisation of the *Vita nuova* must have revealed to Dante how far from restrictive any such admission would be. For it is precisely this that allows all the features which are collected within the frame of the text to accumulate and generate significance. For instance, the number nine occurs at first almost accidentally in the narrative of the *Vita nuova*, until a point is reached where the poet can recognise the pattern which has gradually established itself beneath the apparent chaos and misdirection of his emotion. Order here is not enforced, but rather discovered:

Tuttavia, però che molte volte lo numero del nove ha preso luogo tra le parole dinanzi, onde pare che sia non sanza ragione, e ne la sua partita cotale numero pare che avesse molto luogo, convenesi di dire quindi alcuna cosa, acciò che pare al proposito convenirsi. (*VN* xxviii 3)

(However, because the number nine has often found a place in the foregoing words, it would appear that this is not without reason that the number had an important place in her passing, and it is right and entirely to the purpose to say something about it.)

One need hardly emphasise the differences between the treatment of number here and the use made of it in the *Inferno*: where the 'miraculous' number nine shines through the death of Beatrice, making even *that* significant, the transmutation of the thieves in *Inferno* xxv is governed by a sterile play upon the factors one and two which never achieves the integrity of the number three, while, similarly, the death of Ugolino and his children manifests a distintegration of the same number as, between the fifth day and the sixth, Ugolino sees his sons fall senselessly into oblivion: 'vid'io cascar li tre ad uno ad uno' (*Inf.* xxxiii 71).

But this is the fruitless conclusion to which all attempts at mastery must come; and, though the *Purgatorio* will explore fully the abdication of any such control, the *Vita nuova* has already revealed what alternatives there are to such a course.

This is seen firstly in the continual willingness that Dante displays there to admit that his own poetry may be superseded or 'die'. This is most strikingly revealed in a later chapter of the work, which speaks of the comfort that Dante receives on Beatrice's death from the *Donna Gentile*. This is no negligible figure: in the *Convivio*, the poet will explain allegorically that the comforts which the *Donna Gentile* offered him were the comforts of philosophy, and in that sense the *Donna Gentile* may well be said to represent a principle of order and control comparable to the principle which Virgil embodies in the *Commedia*. But, just as the influence of Virgil has to be abandoned in the Earthly Paradise, so in the *Vita nuova* Dante has realised, by the final poems of the collection, that the composure which the *Donna Gentile* instils in him must be swept aside to allow for a new and passionate sense of the significance of Beatrice.

In a comparable way, Dante is prepared throughout the *Vita nuova* to adopt and then discard the secondary images or 'screens' that allow him to approach Beatrice. In discussing the episode of Adam da Brescia in *Inferno* XXX, we have seen how important to Dante was the hierarchy of screens and images which led him from the first confused comprehension of love, through his contemplation of Beatrice, to the unmediated vision of God. Now we must stress that Dante will never allow the mind to cultivate an absolute attachment to any one of these images. Beatrice's death teaches him this, and even in the *Paradiso* the protagonist has finally to lift his eyes from his Lady if he is to look directly at God (*Par.* XXXI). The pattern for such a moment is first established in the twelfth chapter of the *Vita nuova*, where Dante is told by Amore that the time has come to put aside all 'simulacra' or secondary images of love and to approach Beatrice without any of the 'screens' which have hitherto shielded him from her influence: 'Fili mi, tempus est preter-mictantur simulacra nostra.' To attach the mind to any one of these constructions is to risk that same idolatry for which the counterfeiter, Adam of Brescia, is condemned – the devotion to the image of the coin.

In this light, it becomes a matter of positive value – whether in the spiritual or the poetic life – to acknowledge the moment of death. For that is the way to new significance. So, at the end of the *Vita nuova*, the very absence of Beatrice leads Dante to write a sonnet, 'Oltre la spera ...', which, already advancing beyond the *canzoni* of the praise-style, anticipates the universal perspective which the poet will eventually traverse in the *Commedia*. The journey which Dante envisages in this poem will certainly require him at every point to seek philosophical conclusions; but the impulse which sets him on his way – the source of originality – is the spontaneous impulse of the tear and sigh which the lack of Beatrice inspires in him:

> Oltre la spera che più larga gira
> passa 'l sospiro ch'esce del mio core:
> intelligenza nova, che l'Amore
> piangendo mette in lui, pur su lo tira.
>
> Quand'elli è giunto là dove disira,
> vede una donna, che riceve onore,
> e luce sì, che per lo suo splendore
> lo peregrino spirito la mira.
>
> Vedela tal, che quando 'l mi ridice,
> io non lo intendo, sì parla sottile
> al cor dolente, che lo fa parlare.
>
> So io che parla di quella gentile,
> però che spesso ricorda Beatrice,
> sì ch'io lo 'ntendo ben, donne mie care.

(Beyond the sphere that circles the widest / passes the sigh that comes from my heart: / a new understanding that Love, / weeping, imparts to him, draws him always upwards. / When he arrives where his desires have led, / he sees a lady who receives honour, / and who shines so that because of her splendour / the pilgrim spirit gazes in contemplation upon her. / He sees her such that when he repeats this to me / I do not understand, he speaks so subtly / to the sorrowing heart that makes him speak. / I know he speaks of that noble one, / because he often recalls Beatrice, / so that I understand him well, my dear ladies.)

When at line 68 of *Inferno* xxxiv Virgil declares

> Ma la notte risurge, e oramai
> è da partir, ché tutto avem veduto

(Night is rising, and now already / it is time to leave, for we have seen everything)

the poetry of the *Inferno* is at last dead. As surely as in the twelfth chapter of the *Vita nuova*, Dante must now put aside *simulacra*, even those constructions of judgement which he himself has created. By their very perfunctoriness, Virgil's words reveal both the emptiness of Hell and the insignificance of a vision which can be terminated so casually; but they are also a reaffirmation of the need to continue the pilgrimage that Dante began in the *Vita nuova*. What follows is a sequence which is transitional – in the manner of, say, *Inferno* xxiv – and comic in direct parallel to Canto xxxi, as Dante and Virgil encounter Satan, the gigantic 'screen' of evil. A comedy of images begins as soon as the protagonist, peering through the fog, begins to discern the figure of Satan:

> Come quando una grossa nebbia spira,
> o quando l'emisperio nostro annotta,
> par di lungi un molin che 'l vento gira,
> veder mi parve un tal dificio allotta.   (xxxiv 4–7)

(As – when a thick mist breathes, / or when the night draws in on our hemisphere – / a mill appears at a distance moved by the wind, / such a contraption did I now seem to see.)

This comedy will lead Dante for a last time into realms of self-parody, but so do the linguistic procedures of the canto. Throughout, Virgil asserts a degree of control over the progress of the journey which he has not enjoyed for several cantos. This control, however, is wry, even ironic, in execution. As if to acknowledge that language has no true competence in this sphere, Virgil possesses himself of the wittiness which in the previous canto was displayed by the desperate equivocations of Frate Alberigo. So the canto opens with the only words of Latin which Virgil speaks in the *Commedia*; but these words are a tight-lipped parody of the sixth-century hymn, *Vexilla regis*:

> '*Vexilla regis prodeunt inferni*
> verso di noi; però dinanzi mira',
> disse 'l maestro mio, 'se tu 'l discerni'.   (1–3)

('*Vexilla regis prodeunt inferni* / towards us; therefore look forward ahead of you,' / my Master said, 'if you can make him out.')

Here, as we should expect, the eye is granted primacy, but there is nothing of any value to see. And Virgil exerts precisely that control in his language which he – almost – failed to exert in the last canto of the Malebolge sequence, where the protagonist was left gazing at the scuffle between Adam and Sinon. So, with a casualness which anticipates his final 'tutto avem veduto', Virgil is allowed to decide the moment in the progress of the journey when the protagonist can properly look upon Satan:

> Quando noi fummo fatti tanto avante,
> ch'al mio maestro piacque di mostrarmi
> la creatura ch'ebbe il bel sembiante,
> d'innanzi mi si tolse e fé restarmi. (16–19)

(When we had advanced so far / that it pleased my Master to show me / the creature who had the lovely visage once, / he took himself from before me and made me stop.)

As the screen which Virgil has formed shifts from its place in front of Dante, the eye is exposed to the ultimate object in Hell, and attention turns from Virgil's words to Dante's own text, as he begins to construct and manipulate this object.

The first move is an address to the reader in the form of a confession of inexpressibility:

> Com' io divenni allor gelato e fioco,
> nol dimandar, lettor, ch'i' non lo scrivo,
> però ch'ogne parlar sarebbe poco.
> Io non mori', e non rimasi vivo;
> pensa oggimai per te, s'hai fior d'ingegno,
> qual io divenni, d'uno e d'altro privo. (22–7)

(How chill I became and how hoarse, / O reader, do not ask; for I write it not, / since all speech would fail to tell it. / I did not die, nor did I remain alive; / now think for yourself, if you have any wit at all, / what I then became, deprived of both the one and the other, death and life.)

The ineffability *topos* dominates the portrayal of Satan; yet this is far from being a passage of the type we have seen in the *Vita nuova*. It is not the size of Satan, but – as in Canto XXXI – the magnitude of Dante's natural emotion that exceeds the scope of language, and that emotion is to be located *beyond* the present text, not in any such fluency of word as appears in the poem 'Donne ch'avete': 'i' non lo scrivo'. Dante, then, directly reverses the idiom of the praise-style; and well he might. There is no object to praise here, nor any possibility of the composure that praise fostered in the earlier work. Instead, the poet must pursue to the bitter end the fantastic logic of the scheme he has contrived in writing the *Inferno*, building the picture of Satan out of the bits and pieces of imagery which have fallen to the floor of his poem. So, there is no marvel here, in spite of Dante's exclamation at line 37:

> Oh quanto parve a me gran maraviglia!

(Oh how great a marvel it seemed to me.)

There is at best a witty play upon the language and logic of Dante's own poem. So, for instance, Satan is seen as the 'Emperor' of the infernal region:

'lo 'mperador del doloroso regno' (28). Dante here assumes the parodic language that Virgil introduced with his opening line: *Vexilla regis*. This is followed, firstly, by a recourse to the giant motif which has already been rendered comic by its appearance in Canto xxxi, then, secondly, to a calculated play upon conceits of proportion and incongruity which also appeared in that sequence:

> Lo 'mperador del doloroso regno
> da mezzo 'l petto uscia fuor de la ghiaccia;
> e più con un gigante io mi convegno,
>   che i giganti non fan con le sue braccia:
> vedi oggimai quant' esser dee quel tutto
> ch'a così fatta parte si confaccia.
>   S'el fu sì bel com' elli è ora brutto,
> e contra 'l suo fattore alzò le ciglia,
> ben dee da lui procedere ogne lutto.   (28–36)

(The Emperor of the sorrowful realm, / stood out of the ice from half-way up his chest; / and I am more like a giant in size / than giants are to his arms; / now see how great the whole must be / to correspond to such a part. / If he was once as beautiful as now he is ugly, / and raised his eyebrow against his Maker, / well may all misery proceed from him.)

One notes here the ingenuous introduction of Dante's own body as a standard of measure, the equally ingenuous repetition of the hypothetical 'dee', and the play upon the simple proportion of present loathsomeness to past beauty. In turn, these calculations lead to the precise visualisation of the countenance of Satan. But, as we should expect, the very colours and numbers which in another context might be filled – as was the number nine in the *Vita nuova* – with secret eloquence, here have none. Satan absorbs the search for significance as surely as he absorbs the sinners in his three cold mouths. Even the drama of the Ugolino episode here seeps away: we have seen this image of eating before; Satan is mere repetition.

The last view which Dante has of Satan assimilates him to the simoniac popes of Canto xix:

> Io levai li occhi e credetti vedere
> Lucifero com' io l'avea lasciato,
> e vidili le gambe in sù tenere.   (88–90)

(I raised my eyes, and expected to see / Lucifer as I had left him; / and I saw him holding his legs aloft.)

The absurdity of the image at once deprives Lucifer of all possible dignity and – in repeating perhaps the most ludicrous punishment in the *Inferno* – seals the first *cantica* in its own grotesque logicality.

But the second *cantica* has in spirit already begun. After this final moment of mastery, Dante characteristically turns the comedy against himself. As Virgil climbs 'panting like a tired man' (83), and Dante – showing quite as much bewilderment as he did at the sight of Satan – wonders why he can no longer see the ice of Caina (103), normality of form and humility of mind are both brought back into play. The laws of the natural world too reassert themselves against the fixity of Hell: 'Ma la notte risurge' (69); and the ascent – corresponding to the *descent* which Dante has taken thirty-four cantos to describe – is accomplished in the space of fifty lines, as Virgil explains the science that governs the structure of the terrestrial globe. From now onwards, the difficulty which the protagonist must face is that of realising how simple salvation should always have been. For the poet, the difficulty of *Purgatorio* will likewise be to realise anew how rich the resources of his imagination have always been, how ready his language to express experience. The *Purgatorio*, like the *Inferno*, will be an unfinished work. But where the end of the *Inferno* reflects the fragmentation that tragically attends any attempt at a merely rational control, the *Purgatorio* concludes with an acknowledgement of the abundance of word and image which is available to those who can both dispense with the past in the waters of Lethe and recover it in the marvellous remembrance of Eunoe:

> S' io avessi, lettor, più lungo spazio
> da scrivere, i' pur cantere'n parte
> lo dolce ber che mai non m'avria sazio.   (*Purg.* xxxiii 136–8)

(Reader if I had more space / to write, I would sing in part / of the sweet drink of which I would never be sated.)

Beyond the difficult order that reason can – and must – create, there is always the surprise of one's own free nature, constantly awaiting recovery.

Suggestions for further reading

Almansi, Guido. *L'estetica dell'osceno* (Turin, 1974)
Anderson, William. *Dante the Maker* (London, 1980)
Auerbach, Erich. *Dante, Poet of the Secular World*, trans. R. Manheim (Chicago, 1961)
  'Farinata and Cavalcanti', in *Mimesis: The Representation of Reality in Western Literature*, trans. Willard R. Trask (Princeton, 1953)
  'Figura', in *Scenes from the Drama of European Literature*, trans. R. Manheim (Gloucester, Mass., 1959)
  Literary Language and its Public in Late Latin Antiquity, trans. R. Manheim (London, 1965)
Avalle, D'Arco Silvio. *Modelli Semiologici nella Commedia di Dante* (Milan, 1975)
Bárberi Squarroti, G. *L'artificio dell'etternità* (Verona, 1972)
Barbi, Michele. 'Razionalism e misticismo in Dante', *Studi danteschi*, XVII (1933), 5–44, and XXI (1937), 5–91
Barolini, Teodolinda. *Dante's Poets: Textuality and Truth in the 'Comedy'* (Princeton, 1984)
Batard, Y. *Dante, Minerve et Apollon: Les images de la 'Divine Comédie'* (Paris, 1952)
Boccaccio, Giovanni. *Esposizioni sopra la Comedia* a cura di G. Padoan *(Milan, 1964)*
Bonora, E. Gli ipocriti di Malebolge (Milan–Naples, 1953)
Boyde, Patrick. Dante Philomythes and Philosopher: Man and the Cosmos (Cambridge, 1981)
Brandeis, I. The Ladder of Vision (London, 1960)
Cambon, G. Dante's Craft (Minneapolis, 1969)
Chiampi, James T. Shadowy Prefaces: Conversion and Writing in the Divina Commedia (Ravenna, 1981)
Chiavacci-Leonardi, A. M. La guerra e la pietate: saggio per una interpretazione dell' 'Inferno' di Dante (Naples, 1979)
Colish, Marcia. The mirror of language, rev. edn (Lincoln, Nebr.–London, 1983)
Comparetti, D. Virgilio nel medioevo (Livorno, 1872)
Contini, G. Varianti ed altra linguistica: una reccolta di saggi (Florence, 1970)
Corti, Maria. La felicità mentale: nuove prospettive per Dante e Cavalcanti (Turin, 1983)
Costanza, L. Il linguaggio di Dante nella Divina Commedia (Naples, 1968)
Croce, B. La poesia di Dante (Bari, 1921)
Curtius, E. R. European Literature and the Latin Middle Ages, trans. Willard R. Trask (Princeton, 1967)
Daiches, David, and Antony Thorlby, The Medieval World (London, 1973)
Davies, C. T. Dante and the Idea of Rome (Oxford, 1957)
De Sanctis, F. Storia della letteratura italiana, rev. edn L. Russo (Milan, 1950)
Di Pino, G. Studi di lingua poetica (Florence, 1961)
Di Salvo, T. Lettura critica della Divina Commedia, 3 vols. (Florence, 1969)

Dragonetti, R. *Aux frontières du langage poétique (Études sur Dante, Mallarmé, Valéry) (Ghent, 1961)*

Dronke, P. *Dante and Medieval Latin Traditions (Cambridge, 1986)*

Eliot, T. S. *Dante (London, 1929)*

Enciclopedia dantesca, ed. U. Bosco, G. Petrocchi et al. *(Rome, 1970–6)*

Fergusson, Francis. *Dante (1966)*

Foster, Kenelm. *God's Tree (London, 1957)*
   The Two Dantes (London, 1977)
   'The Mind in Love: Dante's Philosophy', in *Dante*, ed. J. Freccero *(Englewood Cliffs, NJ, 1965)*, pp. 43–60
   and Boyde, P., eds. *Dante's Lyric Poetry (Oxford, 1967)*

Fowlie, Wallace. *A Reading of the Inferno (Chicago, 1981)*

Freccero, John. 'Dante's Ulysses: from epic to novel', in *Concepts of the Hero in the Middle Ages and the Renaissance*, ed. Norman T. Burns and Christopher Reagan *(Albany, NY, 1975)*, pp. 101–19
   ed. *Dante: A Collection of Critical Essays (Englewood Cliffs, NJ, 1965)*

Getto, Giovanni. *Aspetti della poesia di Dante*, 2nd edn *(Florence, 1966)*
   ed. *Letture dantesche (Florence, 1964)*

Giacalone, Giuseppe. *La Divina Commedia (with commentary and critical notes)*, 3 vols. *(Rome, 1968–9)*

Gilbert, Allan H. *Dante's Conception of Justice (Durham, NC, 1925)*

Gilson, Etienne. *Dante and Philosophy*, trans. David Moore *(rpt London, 1948)*
   The Spirit of Mediaeval Philosophy, trans. A. H. C. Downs *(London, 1936)*

Girardi, E. N. 'Dante personaggio', *Cultura e Scuola*, IV (1965), 332–42

Guidubaldi, E., ed. *Lectura Dantis Mystica (Florence, 1969)*

Hardison, O. B. Jr. *The Enduring Moment: A Study of the Ideas of Praise in Renaissance Literary Theory and Practice (rpt Hamden, Conn., 1973)*

Jacomuzzi, A. *Il palinsesto della retorica e altri saggi danteschi (Florence, 1972)*

Kirkpatrick, Robin. *Dante's Paradiso and the Limitations of Modern Criticism (Cambridge, 1978)*
   'Courtesy and Imagination in Purgatorio XIV', *Modern Language Review*, LXXVI (1981), 68–80
   The Divine Comedy (Cambridge, 1987)

Leo, Ulrich. 'The Unfinished *Convivio* and Dante's Re-Reading of the *Aeneid*', *Mediaeval Studies*, XIII (1951), 41–64

Lewis, C. S. *Studies in Medieval and Renaissance Literature* (Cambridge, 1966)

Limentani, U., ed. *The Mind of Dante* (Cambridge, 1965)

McIntyre, A. *After Virtue* (London, 1981)

Malagoli, L. *Linguaggio e poesia nella Divina Commedia* (Genoa, 1949)

Marti, M. *Realismo dantesco e altri studi* (Milan–Naples, 1961)
   Storia dello stil novo (Lecce, 1973)

Marcazzan, M., ed. *Lectura Dantis Scaligera* (Florence, 1968)

Mazzotta, Giuseppe. *Dante, Poet of the Desert* (Princeton, 1979)

Mengaldo, P. V. *Linguistica e retorica di Dante* (Pisa, 1978)
   ed. *De Vulgari Eloquentia* (Padua, 1968)

Mineo, N. *Dante* (Bari, 1970)
   Profetismo e appocalittica in Dante (Catania, 1968)

Moleta, V. *Guinizzelli in Dante* (Rome, 1980)

Nardi, B. *Dante e la filosofia medievale* (Bari, 1940)
   Dal 'Convivio' alla 'Commedia' (Rome, 1960)

Nolan, D., ed. *Dante Soundings* (Dublin, 1977)

Padoan, G. *Introduzione a Dante* (Florence, 1975)

Pagliaro, A. *Altri saggi di critica semantica* (Messina–Florence, 1961)
    La parola e l'immagine (Naples, 1957)
    Ulisse: ricerche semantiche sulla 'Divina Commedia', 2 vols. (Milan–Florence, 1967)
Paratore, E. *Tradizione e struttura in Dante* (Florence, 1968)
Pasquazi, S. *All'eterno dal tempo* (Florence, 1966)
Pautasso, S. *Le frontiere della critica* (Milan, 1972)
Pazzaglia, M. *Il verso e l'arte della canzone nel 'De Vulgari Eloquentia'* (Florence, 1967)
Petrocchi, G., ed. *La Commedia secondo l'antica vulgata*, 4 vols. (Milan, 1966–7)
Pézard, A. *Dante sous la pluie de feu* (Paris, 1950)
Philips, T. *The Inferno* (London, 1985)
Pirandello, L. 'Il Canto xxii dell'*Inferno*', in *Letture dantesche*, ed. G. Getto (Florence, 1964)
Renucci, P. *Dante, disciple et juge du monde grec–latin* (Paris, 1954)
Richards, I. A. *Beyond.* (London, 1973)
    Principles of Literary Criticism (rpt of 2nd edn, London, 1970)
Righter, William. *Myth* (London, 1975)
Sanguinetti, E. *Il realismo di Dante* (Florence, 1966)
    Interpretazione di Malebolge (Florence, 1961)
Sarolli, G. R. *Prolegomena alla Divina Commedia* (Florence, 1971)
Scott, John A. *Dante magnanimo: studi sulla 'Commedia'* (Florence, 1977)
Segre, C. *Lingua, stile e società* (Milan, 1963)
Singleton, C. S. 'Dante and myth', *Journal of the History of Ideas*, X (1949), 482–502
Sollers, P. 'Dante et la traversée de l'écriture', *Tel Quel* (Autumn, 1965), 12–33
Spitzer, L. 'Il canto xiii dell'*Inferno*', in *Letture dantesche*, ed. G. Getto (Florence, 1964)
Terracini, B. *Analisi stilistica: teoria, storia, problemi* (Milan, 1966)
Terza, Dante della. 'An Unbridgeable Gap? Medieval Poetics and the Contemporary Dante Reader', *Medievalia et humanistica*, new series, VII (1976), 65–76
Ungaretti, G. 'Il Canto i dell'*Inferno*', in *Letture dantesche*, ed. G. Getto (Florence, 1964)
Vallone, A. *Dante* (Milan, 1971)
Vessey, David. *Statius and the Thebaid* (Cambridge, 1973)
Williams, Bernard. *Moral Luck* (Cambridge, 1981)